# Texts and Monographs in Computer Science

Editor
## David Gries

Advisory Board
F.L. Bauer
S.D. Brookes
C.E. Leiserson
F.B. Schneider
M. Sipser

# Texts and Monographs in Computer Science

Suad Alagić
**Object-Oriented Database Programming**
1989. XV, 320 pages, 84 illus.

Suad Alagić
**Relational Database Technology**
1986. XI, 259 pages, 114 illus.

Suad Alagić and Michael A. Arbib
**The Design of Well-Structured and Correct Programs**
1978. X, 292 pages, 68 illus.

S. Thomas Alexander
**Adaptive Signal Processing: Theory and Applications**
1986. IX, 179 pages, 42 illus.

Michael A. Arbib, A.J. Kfoury, and Robert N. Moll
**A Basis for Theoretical Computer Science**
1981. VIII, 220 pages, 49 illus.

Friedrich L. Bauer and Hans Wössner
**Algorithmic Language and Program Development**
1982. XVI, 497 pages, 109 illus.

Kaare Christian
**A Guide to Modula-2**
1986. XIX, 436 pages, 46 illus.

Edsger W. Dijkstra
**Selected Writings on Computing: A Personal Perspective**
1982. XVII, 362 pages, 13 illus.

Edsger W. Dijkstra and Carel S. Scholten
**Predicate Calculus and Program Semantics**
1990. XII, 220 pages

W.H.J. Feijen, A.J.M. van Gasteren, D. Gries, and J. Misra, Eds.
**Beauty Is Our Business: A Birthday Salute to Edsger W. Dijkstra**
1990. XX, 453 pages, 21 illus.

Melvin Fitting
**First-Order Logic and Automated Theorem Proving**
1990. XIV, 242 pages, 26 illus.

Nissim Francez
**Fairness**
1986. XIII, 295 pages, 147 illus.

*continued after index*

# Beauty Is Our Business

## A Birthday Salute to Edsger W. Dijkstra

Edited by
**W.H.J. Feijen**
**A.J.M. van Gasteren**
**D. Gries**
**J. Misra**

Springer-Verlag New York Berlin Heidelberg
London Paris Tokyo Hong Kong

W.H.J. Feijen
Mathematics and Computer Science Department
Eindhoven University of Technology
5600 MB Eindhoven
The Netherlands

D. Gries
Department of Computer Science
Cornell University
Ithaca, NY 14853
U.S.A.

A.J.M. van Gasteren
Department of Computer Science
University of Utrecht
3508 TB Utrecht
The Netherlands

J. Misra
Department of Computer Science
The University of Texas
Austin, TX 78712-1188
U.S.A.

*Series Editor*

David Gries
Department of Computer Science
Cornell University
Ithaca, NY 14853
U.S.A.

**Library of Congress Cataloging-in-Publication Data**
**Beauty is our business: a birthday salute to Edsger W. Dijkstra/**
 W.H.J. Feijen . . . [et al.], editors.
  p. cm. — (Texts and monographs in computer science)
  ISBN 0-387-97299-4 (alk. paper)
  1. Computer science. 2. Dijkstra, Edsger W. I. Feijen, W.H.J.
 II. Series.
 QA76.B326 1990
 004—dc20                                        90-33578

Printed on acid-free paper.

Typeset with LaTeX by Hilary Backhouse, The Netherlands.
Index prepared by Jim Farned of the Information Bank, Summerland, California.
Printed and bound by R.R. Donnelley & Sons, Harrisonburg, Virginia.
Printed in the United States of America.

9 8 7 6 5 4 3 2 1

ISBN 0-387-97299-4 Springer-Verlag New York Berlin Heidelberg
ISBN 3-540-97299-4 Springer-Verlag Berlin Heidelberg New York

Dedicated to Edsger W. Dijkstra

on the occasion of his 60th birthday

Edsger W. Dijkstra

The working vocabulary of programmers everywhere is studded with words originated or forcefully promulgated by E.W. Dijkstra — display, deadly embrace, semaphore, go-to-less programming, structured programming. But his influence on programming is more pervasive than any glossary can possibly indicate. The precious gift that this Turing Award acknowledges is Dijkstra's *style* ... We have come to value good programs in much the same way as we value good literature. And at the center of this movement, creating and reflecting patterns no less beautiful than useful, stands E.W. Dijkstra.

Doug McIlroy

[Extract from the Turing Award Citation by Doug McIlroy, chairman of the ACM Turing Award Committee, at the presentation of this lecture on August 14, 1972, at the ACM Annual Conference in Boston.]

This extract was published in the *CACM* 15:10 (October 1972), page 859 and is reprinted here by permission of the Association for Computing Machinery.

# Foreword

Edsger W. Dijkstra is one of a very small number of people who, through their research and teaching, have provided computing with an intellectual foundation that can justifiably be termed a science. His seminal contributions to such fields as language and compiler design, operating systems, and programming methodology have led to his receiving numerous honours and awards, including the 1972 ACM Turing Award, recognized by all as the highest award in computing.

This book is another such expression of the debt that our subject owes to Edsger. It has been prepared, as a surprise present for him on the occasion of his sixtieth birthday, by some of the many people whose own contributions to our field have been inspired or assisted by him. In view of the galaxy of talent represented here by this book's collective authorship, and the great personal debt that I owe to Edsger, I feel doubly privileged to have been invited to write a foreword.

I have had the pleasure of knowing Edsger for almost thirty years. I first met him when he lectured in Brighton, UK, on the ALGOL 60 compiler that he and his colleague J.A. Zonneveld had just produced for the Electrologica X-1 computer. Their compiler, it should be noted, had been completed in August 1960, just seven months after they had received a copy of the ALGOL-60 Report. This was long before anyone else had learnt how to cope with all the problems and opportunities that the new language provided.

A year or so later, in 1963, I asked his opinion on the suggestion that my colleague Lawford Russell and I write a book about the ALGOL 60 compiler that we had produced. This compiler, for the English Electric KDF9 computer, was based in no small measure on the design of his original X-1 compiler. Edsger was very supportive, but gave us some very valuable, albeit uncomfortable, advice: instead of just describing our compiler, we should try to describe all the alternatives we had considered for each design choice and the basis on which we had chosen amongst these alternatives. Moreover, he advised that we should make a point of admitting it when our choice had been arbitrary and/or had in retrospect proved to be wrong. I have always been extremely grateful for this advice — and have taken care to pass it on to all my graduate students.

One final personal note about my interactions with Edsger concerns the 1968 NATO Software Engineering Conference. We have both since gone on record as to how the discussions at this conference on the "software crisis", and on the potential for software-induced catastrophes, strongly influenced our thinking and our subsequent research activities. In Edsger's case it led him into an immensely fruitful long-term study of the problems of producing high quality programs. In my own case, it led me to consider the then very novel, and still somewhat controversial, idea of design fault tolerance. Suffice it to say that our respective choices of research problem suitably reflect our respective skills at program design and verification.

Edsger's 1963 advice to me is of course in line with the fact that he has always himself set and followed very high standards for clarity and presentation of writing and lecturing. Although the lecturing style that he has developed has its critics (some of whom mistakenly interpret his reflective pauses as mere theatricality), my own regret is that I cannot match either his clarity or his skill in inventing or choosing suitable examples.

The problems he chooses to concentrate on are always very skillfully selected (e.g. the dining philosophers problem, on-the-fly garbage collection), and many have become famous standards by which subsequent research is judged. The vivid and effective visual metaphors he still uses serve as a reminder of the effectiveness of the excellent actual pictures he invented many years ago to describe, for example, the process of translating arithmetic expressions to post-fix form, and the problem of deadlocks amongst processes competing for shared resources.

Edsger is, with all that the word implies, a perfectionist. His programming and his mathematics are strongly guided by his concern for clarity of notation and exposition, and indeed for what he quite justifiably terms *beauty*. Thus his descriptions of problems and solutions, both in his lectures and published papers, and in his EWD series of documents,[1] distributed via a network of friends and colleagues in a fashion reminiscent of Russian "samizdat" literature, are often vivid and compelling.

Although over the years much of his work has had a very immediate and beneficial impact, on debate if not always on practice, some of his more recent diagnoses and prescriptions concerning the current state of computing science and mathematics have not been so widely accepted.

---

[1] A superb collection of these EWD documents, which includes several characteristically acerbic and entertaining trip reports on his experiences at Newcastle's Annual International Seminar on the Teaching of Computing Science, and a number of equally amusing and pointed memoranda written in his purported role as Chairman of Mathematics Inc., is to be found in "Selected Writings on Computing: A Personal Perspective", by E.W. Dijkstra. Springer-Verlag, New York, 1982.

This is in part because he is sometimes concerned more with the truth of his arguments than with whether they are expressed in terms that will help to ensure that they have the intended effect on his audience. Nevertheless, careful study of all his writings is highly recommended to all who care for the future health of computing science.

His most recent work, as represented by his continuing series of EWD documents, is mainly on the effective structure of logical arguments, applied to mathematics as much as programming — a distinction whose validity he would deny, since to him programming *is* mathematics. This work sets standards that many cannot even recognise, let alone aspire to. However I am confident that it will eventually have deep and long-lasting effects, much of it indirect, through the inspiration that it is providing to close colleagues.

The present book is, in effect, part of this dissemination process, since it contains many examples of the inspiration he has provided to his numerous "disciples". Thus they, and I, hope that this book will not just serve as an affirmation of the debt computing scientists already owe to Edsger's work and teaching. Rather, we hope that it will also help to explain to readers who do not have close personal contact with Edsger the continuing impact of his current work.

Let me end with a quotation from George Bernard Shaw:

> The reasonable man adapts himself to the world: the unreasonable one persists in trying to adapt the world to himself. Therefore all progress depends on the unreasonable man.

Edsger W. Dijkstra is, in many ways, just such a man. Needless to say, the world of computing science could well do with many more "unreasonable" men, and women, of his calibre!

Brian Randell,
Newcastle upon Tyne,
25 September 1989

# Preface

More than anything else, this book is a tribute to Edsger W. Dijkstra, on the occasion of his sixtieth birthday, by just a few of those fortunate enough to be influenced by him and his work and to be called his friend or relation, his master, colleague, or pupil.

The decision to pay our respects to him was easy to make: his scientific achievements, service, and friendship had earned it. But we did have difficulty deciding on the form of the tribute. Opening it up to the entire computing community would most likely have evoked hundreds of responses, far too many for us to manage. Limiting it to a chosen few whose scientific view was closest to Dijkstra's would have barred too many who call him their friend but whose views and areas of expertise differ radically.

In the end, on Dijkstra's fifty-ninth birthday, we asked fifty-odd friends and colleagues of his to contribute to this birthday salute. We requested mainly technical contributions, and we asked that they be relatively short. Fifty-odd authors responded, and we are proud to place their contributions before Edsger Dijkstra.

A number of people declined to participate, citing lack of time or suitable material. (Nevertheless, all were enthusiastic about the tribute.) There are others who might be expected to take part in this tribute but were overlooked by us. To them, and to Edsger, we offer our apologies, and we hope that all will overlook our mistakes at this time of celebration.

Essentially all the papers were critiqued by the editors (or their colleagues) and then revised by the authors. We thank the authors for their very quick responses. We also thank typist Anneke Johnson-Hoekzema and Hilary Backhouse, who was in complete charge of typesetting this tribute. Together, they have done an excellent job. We are grateful to Rein Smedinga and Harm Paas for producing the figures, and to the Department of Computing Science of the University of Groningen, The Netherlands, for allowing the typesetter to use their computing facilities. Our gratitude also goes to Gerhard Rossbach of Springer-Verlag for his necessary and timely support in this venture.

While many know of Dijkstra's technical contributions, they may not be aware of his ultimate goal, the mastery of complexity in mathematics and computing science, and of his belief that beauty and elegance are essential to this mastery. Even in the early EWD32 he wrote "... the greatest virtues a program can show [are] Elegance and Beauty.". And later, in 1978, in conveying some beautiful arguments using mathematical induction in EWD697, he wrote the following:

> ... when we recognize the battle against chaos, mess, and unmastered complexity as one of computing science's major callings, we must admit that "Beauty is our Business",

which gave us the title for this book.

Wim Feijen,
Netty van Gasteren,
David Gries,
Jayadev Misra.

# Table of Contents

# 0

# Proving Termination of Parallel Programs

**Krzysztof R. Apt**
**Frank S. de Boer**
**Ernst-Rüdiger Olderog**

## Abstract

In Owicki and Gries [2] a well known proof method for verifying parallel programs based on the interference freedom test was introduced. We show that their extension of the method to deal with termination is incorrect and suggest two ways of repairing it.

## 1   Introduction

The Owicki-Gries method [2] for verifying partial correctness of parallel programs calls for finding interference free proof outlines for partial correctness of component programs. A proof outline for a partial correctness proof of $\{p\}$ $S$ $\{q\}$, where $p$ and $q$ are assertions and $S$ is a program, is a construct of the form $\{p\}$ $S^*$ $\{q\}$, where $S^*$ is the program $S$ annotated with the assertions used in the proof of $\{p\}$ $S$ $\{q\}$. For example, consider the two component programs

$$S_1 \equiv \textbf{while } x > 0 \textbf{ do}$$
$$y := 0;$$
$$\textbf{if } y = 0 \textbf{ then } x := x - 1 \textbf{ else } y := 0 \textbf{ fi}$$
$$\textbf{od}$$

and

$$S_2 \equiv \textbf{while } x > 0 \textbf{ do}$$
$$y := 1;$$
$$\textbf{if } y = 1 \textbf{ then } x := x - 1 \textbf{ else } y := 1 \textbf{ fi}$$
$$\textbf{od}.$$

Here is a proof outline for $\{\textbf{true}\}\,S_1\,\{\textbf{true}\}$ (the one for $\{\textbf{true}\}\,S_2\,\{\textbf{true}\}$ is similar):

```
{true}
while x > 0 do
      {true}
      y := 0;
      {true}
      if y = 0  then  {true}
                      x := x − 1
                      {true}
                else  {true}
                      y := 0
                      {true}
      fi
od
{true}.
```

Proof outlines for component programs are *interference free* if the component programs do not invalidate the assertions in each others' proof outlines. In this case, the proof outlines remain valid annotations when the component programs are executed in parallel. In the above example, showing that $S_2$ does not invalidate the assertions of the above proof outline for $S_1$ requires proving the following. Let $r$ be any assertion in the proof outline for $S_1$, let $R$ be any assignment in $S_2$, and let $pre(R)$ be the precondition for $R$ in the proof outline for $S_2$. Then the following must be proved:

$$\{r \,\wedge\, pre(R)\}\ R\ \{r\}.$$

Showing interference freedom for the proof outlines for $S_1$ and $S_2$ above is trivial, since all assertions in the proof outlines equal **true**. Hence, the proof outlines for $S_1$ and $S_2$ are interference free.

To extend the method to total correctness, Owicki and Gries proposed two steps. First, in the usual fashion, associate a bound function with each loop of each component program. A bound function is an integer expression that decreases with each loop iteration and remains non-negative. Clearly, the existence of a bound function ensures that the loop terminates when considered in isolation.

Second, to ensure termination of the parallel execution of the component programs, add the following interference freedom requirement: no component program increases a bound function of a loop of another component program.

Now consider the component programs $S_1$ and $S_2$ above. Using $x$ as the bound function for both loops, it is clear that the additional interference freedom requirement is satisfied. And yet, it is also clear that $S_1$ and $S_2$ when executed in parallel need not terminate, for they may synchronize in such a fashion that $x$ is never decreased. Hence, the additional interference freedom requirement proposed by Owicki and Gries is not correct.

## 2  A solution

The proof of total correctness of a loop requires showing that the bound function is decreased with each iteration. Formally, we can use the following proof rule motivated by Dijkstra [1] (EWD 573):

**WHILE**-RULE

$$\frac{\begin{array}{c} \{p \wedge B\} \, S \, \{p\}, \\ \{p \wedge B \wedge t = z\} \, S \, \{t < z\}, \\ p \wedge B \rightarrow t > 0 \end{array}}{\{p\} \text{ while } B \text{ do } S \text{ od } \{p \wedge \neg B\}}$$

where $t$ is an integer expression and $z$ is an integer variable that does not appear in $p, t, B$ or $S$.

The first premise states that $p$ is a loop invariant, the second that the bound function $t$ is decreased with each iteration, and the third that if another iteration can be performed then $t$ is positive.

If such a loop apppears in a component process, then interference freedom should require that the proof of the loop's correctness, using the above rule is not invalidated. The partial correctness proof outline already includes the necessary assertions concerning the first premise $\{p \wedge B\} \, S \, \{p\}$. However, it does not include the assertions concerning the second premise $\{p \wedge B \wedge t = z\} \, S \, \{t < z\}$. Returning to our example, it is readily seen that it is this part of the proof of the loop of component $S_1$ that is falsified by execution of component $S_2$. If the assertions from this second assumption are included in the proof outline, then the original interference freedom requirement of Owicki and Gries will suffice.

One way to achieve this is by starting from a modification of this proof rule where the first two premises are replaced with

$$\{p \wedge B \wedge t = z\} \, S \, \{p \wedge t < z\}$$

and by introducing the following formation rule for a proof outline for total correctness of **while**-loops.

**Definition (Proof Outline I: while-loops)**

$$\frac{\{p \,\wedge\, B \,\wedge\, t = z\} \; S^* \; \{p \,\wedge\, t < z\}, \quad p \,\wedge\, B \to t > 0}{\{\textbf{inv} : p\} \; \textbf{while} \; B \; \textbf{do} \; \{p \,\wedge\, B \,\wedge\, t = z\} \; S^* \; \{p \,\wedge\, t < z\} \; \textbf{od} \; \{p \,\wedge\, \neg B\}}$$

where $t$ is an integer expression, $z$ is an integer variable not occurring in $p, t, B$ or $S$ and $\{p \,\wedge\, B \,\wedge\, t = z\} \; S^* \; \{p \,\wedge\, t < z\}$ is a proof outline for total correctness.
□

The annotation $\{\textbf{inv} : p\}$ represents the invariant of the loop **while** $B$ **do** $S$ **od**. Since the bound functions are now absorbed into the assertions, we can drop the condition for interference freedom of the bound functions and simply use the original definition of interference freedom for partial correctness.

With these changes the Owicki-Gries method for verifying total correctness of parallel programs is correct.

A drawback of the above method is that it forces us to mix the proofs of the invariance of $p$ and of the decrease of $t$. The resulting proof outlines therefore become quite heavy. On the other hand this method provides a close relationship between program annotation and program execution. Since

$$\{p \,\wedge\, B\} \; z := t \; \{p \,\wedge\, B \,\wedge\, t = z\},$$

we can expand the conclusion of the above formation rule so that every **while**-loop starts with an assignment $z := t$:

> $\{\textbf{inv} : p\}$
> **while** $B$ **do**
> $\{p \,\wedge\, B\} \; z := t \; \{p \,\wedge\, B \,\wedge\, t = z\} \; S^* \; \{p \,\wedge\, t < z\}$
> **od**
> $\{p \,\wedge\, \neg B\}$.

With this expansion, the following pleasing property of proof outlines for partial correctness holds again:

**Claim**    Let $\{p_i\} \; S_i^* \; \{q_i\}$, $i \in \{1, \dots, n\}$, be interference-free expanded proof outlines for total correctness and let $S_i'$ for $i \in \{1, \dots, n\}$ be the program resulting from $S_i^*$ by deleting all assertions but keeping the new assignments of the form $z := t$. Consider an execution of the parallel program $[S_1' \| \dots \| S_n']$ starting in a state satisfying $p_1 \,\wedge\, \dots \,\wedge\, p_n$. Whenever the control in one of the component programs reaches a point annotated by an assertion, this assertion is true.

# 3   Another solution

Another possibility is to assume that the proof of decrease of $t$ is of a particularly simple form, namely that for a loop body $S$

(i) all assignments inside $S$ decrease $t$ or leave it unchanged,

(ii) on each syntactically possible path through $S$ at least one assignment decreases $t$.

By a *path* we mean here a possibly empty finite sequence of assignments. Sequential composition $\pi_1$; $\pi_2$ of paths $\pi_1$ and $\pi_2$ is lifted to sets $\Pi_1$ and $\Pi_2$ of paths by putting

$$\Pi_1;\ \Pi_2 = \{\pi_1;\ \pi_2 \mid \pi_1 \in \Pi_1 \text{ and } \pi_2 \in \Pi_2\}.$$

By $\varepsilon$ we denote the empty sequence. For any path $\pi$ we have $\pi$; $\varepsilon = \varepsilon$; $\pi = \pi$.

**Definition**   Let $S$ be a **while**-program. We define the path set of $S$, denoted by $path(S)$, by induction on the structure of $S$:

- $path(skip) = \{\varepsilon\}$,
- $path(u := t) = \{u := t\}$,
- $path(S_1;\ S_2) = path(S_1);\ path(S_2)$,
- $path(\textbf{if } B \textbf{ then } S_1 \textbf{ else } S_2 \textbf{ fi}) = path(S_1) \cup path(S_2)$,
- $path(\textbf{while } B \textbf{ do } S_1 \textbf{ od}) = \{\varepsilon\}$.

$\square$

Thus, each path through $S$ is identified with the sequence of assignments lying on it. Note that in the last clause we take into account only the case when the loop is terminated immediately. This is sufficient for establishing condition (ii) above.

We define the notion of a *proof outline for total correctness* as for partial correctness, except for the case of **while**-loops for which we use the following formation rule.

**Definition (Proof Outline II: while-loops)**

(1)     $\{p \wedge B\}\ S^*\ \{p\}$,

(2)     $\{pre(R) \wedge t = z\}\ R\ \{t \leq z\}$ for every assignment $R$ within $S$,

(3)     for each path $\pi \in path(S)$ there exists an assignment $R$ in $\pi$ such that $\{pre(R) \wedge t = z\}\ R\ \{t < z\}$,

(4)     $p \wedge B \rightarrow t > 0$

$\{\textbf{inv} : p\}\{\textbf{bd} : t\}\ \textbf{while } B \textbf{ do } \{p \wedge B\}\ S^*\ \{p\}\ \textbf{od}\ \{p \wedge \neg B\}$

where $t$ is an integer expression and $z$ is an integer variable not occurring in $p, t, B$ or $S^*$. Here $\{p \wedge B\}\ S^*\ \{p\}$ is a proof outline for total correctness and $pre(R)$ stands for the assertion preceding $R$ in this proof outline.
□

The annotation $\{\mathbf{bd} : t\}$ represents the bound function of the loop **while** $B$ **do** $S$ **od**. With this new definition of a proof outline for total correctness, the Owicki-Gries method for verifying total correctness of parallel programs is correct.

With this definition we can no longer justify the proof outlines for the component programs used in Section 1. Indeed, along the path $y := 0;\ y := 0$ of the first loop body the proposed bound function $x$ does not decrease.

Observe that when the empty path $\varepsilon$ is an element of $path(S)$, we cannot verify premise (3) of the above rule. Thus it may happen that we can prove total correctness of a **while**-program using the **while**-rule but are unable to record this proof as a proof outline for total correctness. An example is the program

$b := \mathbf{true};$
**while** $b$ **do**
    **if** $b$ **then** $b := \mathbf{false}$ **else** $skip$ **fi**
**od**

whose termination can be easily established. This shows some limitations of the above approach to recording proofs of total correctness.

However, various parallel programs can be successfully handled in this way. For example, the bound function given in the proof of termination of program *Findpos* in Owicki and Gries [2] satisfies the more stringent conditions (2)–(4) given above. This provides a justification for their proof.

**Note**    We discovered, when attempting to prove its soundness, that the original version of the Owicki-Gries method for proving total correctness is incorrect.
□

*Acknowledgements*: Detailed comments from David Gries enabled us to improve the presentation.

## References

[1] E. W. Dijkstra. *Selected Writings on Computing*. Springer-Verlag, New York, 1982.

[2] S. Owicki and D. Gries. An axiomatic proof technique for parallel programs. *Acta Informatica*, 6:319–340, 1976.

Krzysztof R. Apt,
Centre for Mathematics and Computer Science,
Kruislaan 413,
1098 SJ Amsterdam,
The Netherlands,
and
Department of Computer Sciences,
The University of Texas at Austin,
Taylor Hall 2.124,
Austin, Texas 78712–1188,
U.S.A.

Frank S. de Boer,
Department of Mathematics and Computing Science,
Eindhoven University of Technology,
P.O. Box 513,
5600 MB Eindhoven,
The Netherlands.

Ernst-Rüdiger Olderog,
Department of Computer Science,
University of Oldenburg,
2900 Oldenburg,
Federal Republic of Germany.

# 1

# On a Relation on Functions

## Roland C. Backhouse

## 1  Introduction

It is rare that one has the opportunity to study a new operator undistracted
and unfettered by previously published work. It is an opportunity to be
relished not only because of the chance to be innovative but also because
one can indulge one's own taste for elegance in formal calculation.

This paper is devoted to a preliminary study of a binary operator that,
applied to two relations, constructs a relation on functions. The operator
was, to my knowledge, first introduced by Reynolds [3] but independently
rediscovered by de Bruin [1] who stimulated my interest in it. Reynolds'
purpose in introducing the operator appears to have been to *describe* certain so-called "representation independence" properties of polymorphic
functions; my purpose here is to explore the possibilities for *calculation*
with the operator.

The paper is concluded with a theorem on a class of relations proved by
structural induction over the elements of the class. Cognoscenti of "natural
polymorphism" (see [4,1]) will find it a straightforward step to show that
all naturally-polymorphic functions are "dinatural" [2]; for other readers
of this article we hope that the theorem's statement and proof will be a
delight for their own sake.

It is intended that the paper be entirely self-contained in the sense that
any reader familiar with the predicate calculus will be able to check directly
all our proof steps as well as filling in, without difficulty, those proofs that
have not been supplied.

Our goal is to build up a catalogue of laws in such a way that the pro-
gression to the next law is relatively obvious and involves no tricks; the
goal will have been achieved if the reader's reaction to the final theorem is
"oh, but of course!"

## 2 Relations and functions

This section contains standard definitions of the basic operations on relations — membership, equality, superset, composition and reverse. It also
defines (total) functions as a subclass of relations. For the most part it may
be safely skimmed and referred to later as the need arises. However, the
reader's attention is drawn to the possibly less-familiar inequalities (13) and
(14) expressing the single-valuedness and totality of functions, respectively.

Let $A$ and $B$ denote types. A *relation on $A$ and $B$* is a subset of the
cartesian product $A \times B$. The set of all relations on $A$ and $B$ is denoted
by $A \sim B$ and we write $R \in A \sim B$ to mean that $R$ is a relation on $A$ and
$B$. If the pair $(a, b)$, where $a \in A$ and $b \in B$, is an element of $R$ we write
$a \langle R \rangle b$.

The equality and superset operations on two relations $R, S \in A \sim B$ are
defined in the usual way. That is,

$$(1) \qquad R = S \quad \equiv \quad \forall(x, y :: \ x\langle R \rangle y \ \equiv \ x\langle S \rangle y)$$

and

$$(2) \qquad R \supseteq S \quad \equiv \quad \forall(x, y : \ x\langle S \rangle y : \ x\langle R \rangle y)$$

Given relation $R \in A \sim B$ we denote by $R^{\cup}$ the *reverse* of $R$, that is the
relation in $B \sim A$ with defining property,

$$(3) \qquad x\langle R^{\cup} \rangle y \quad \equiv \quad y\langle R \rangle x$$

Obviously we have

$$(4) \qquad R^{\cup\cup} \ = \ R$$

Given relations $R \in A \sim B$ and $S \in B \sim C$ the *composition* of $R$ and $S$
is denoted by $R \circ S$ and is that relation in $A \sim C$ with defining property

$$(5) \qquad x\langle R \circ S \rangle z \quad \equiv \quad \exists(y :: \ x\langle R \rangle y \ \wedge \ y\langle S \rangle z)$$

A well-known property relating composition and reverse is the following.

$$(6) \qquad (R \circ S)^{\cup} \ = \ (S^{\cup}) \circ (R^{\cup})$$

The monotonicity properties of composition and reverse are equally well
known:

$$(7) \qquad R \supseteq S \quad \equiv \quad R^{\cup} \supseteq S^{\cup}$$
$$(8) \qquad R \supseteq S \quad \Rightarrow \quad R \circ T \supseteq S \circ T$$
$$(9) \qquad R \supseteq S \quad \Rightarrow \quad T \circ R \supseteq T \circ S$$

For each type $A$ the identity relation on $A$ is denoted by $I$. By definition:

$$(10) \qquad x\langle I \rangle y \quad \equiv \quad x = y$$

(Some would argue for writing $I_A$, thus distinguishing the type of the relation; we assume, however, that the reader has sufficient mathematical maturity to be able to fill in the type information for themself.)

That $I$ is a unit of composition, and its own reverse, will be used without mention.

A function $f$ of type $A \longleftarrow B$ [1] defines a relation in $A \sim B$ given by the set of pairs $(u, v)$ such that $v \in B$ and $u = f.v$. We make no notational distinction between a function and the relation defined by that function. Thus we have the defining property:

$$(11) \qquad u\langle f \rangle v \;\equiv\; u = f.v$$

Note that for functions $f$ and $g$

$$(12) \qquad x\langle f \circ g \rangle z \;\equiv\; x = f.(g.z)$$

Thus $f \circ g$ is the usual composition of functions $f$ and $g$.

That functions are single-valued can be expressed very succinctly. For all functions $f$ we have:

$$(13) \qquad I \;\supseteq\; f \circ f^{\cup}$$

We work exclusively with total functions. That is, we assume for all functions $f$:

$$(14) \qquad f^{\cup} \circ f \;\supseteq\; I$$

We shall be systematic in our choice of symbols throughout. Thus we use capital letters $A, B, C, \ldots$ at the beginning of the alphabet to denote types, capital letters $R, S, T, \ldots$ at the end of the alphabet to denote relations, and small letters $f, g, h, \ldots$ to denote functions. We also use the Greek letter $\alpha$ to denote an implicitly quantified type variable. Thus to say that the identity function $I$ has type $\alpha \longleftarrow \alpha$ means that $I$ has type $A \longleftarrow A$ for all types $A$. Finally we use small letters $u, v, x, \ldots$ at the end of the alphabet to denote objects of types. (Thus in some cases $u, v, x, \ldots$ denote functions, in others not.)

## 3    The arrow constructor

For relations $R \in A \sim B$ and $S \in C \sim D$ the relation $R \longleftarrow S \in (A \longleftarrow C) \sim (B \longleftarrow D)$ is defined by:

---

[1] $A \longleftarrow B$ denotes the set of total functions with range $A$ and domain $B$. Having chosen to denote function application in the form $f.x$ we find it desirable to write function composition in reverse order of application —i.e. $f \circ g$ instead of $g \,;\, f$— and to write the function type constructor in the form $A \longleftarrow B$ and not $B \longrightarrow A$.

$$(15) \qquad f\langle R\!\leftarrow\!\!-S\rangle g \;\; \equiv \;\; \forall(u,v: \;\; u\langle S\rangle v: \;\; f.u\langle R\rangle g.v)$$

The operator "$\leftarrow\!\!-$" just introduced is the object of study in this paper.

Experience has shown that dummies should be avoided like the plague, at least if compact calculation is one's goal. We begin our analysis, therefore, by seeking alternative definitions of the operator. One such definition is the following.

$$(16) \qquad f\langle R\!\leftarrow\!\!-S\rangle g \;\; \equiv \;\; f^{\cup} \circ R \circ g \;\supseteq\; S$$

**Proof**

$$f\langle R\!\leftarrow\!\!-S\rangle g$$

$\equiv \qquad$ {definition (15)}

$$\forall(u,v: \;\; u\langle S\rangle v: \;\; f.u\langle R\rangle g.v)$$

$\equiv \qquad$ {one-point rule — twice}

$$\forall(u,v: \;\; u\langle S\rangle v: \;\; \exists(x,y: \;\; x=f.u \,\wedge\, y=g.v: \;\; x\langle R\rangle y))$$

$\equiv \qquad$ {(11), reverses (3)}

$$\forall(u,v: \;\; u\langle S\rangle v: \;\; \exists(x,y: \;\; u\langle f^{\cup}\rangle x \,\wedge\, y\langle g\rangle v: \;\; x\langle R\rangle y))$$

$\equiv \qquad$ {composition (5)}

$$\forall(u,v: \;\; u\langle S\rangle v: \;\; u\langle f^{\cup} \circ R \circ g\rangle v)$$

$\equiv \qquad$ {extensionality (2)}

$$f^{\cup} \circ R \circ g \;\supseteq\; S$$

$\square$

Equation (16) has the desired dummy-free form and one may be forgiven for discontinuing any search for alternative definitions. However, that would be short-sighted. There are indeed four different dummy-free definitions of the operator. Specifically, the following are all equivalent:

$$(17) \qquad f\langle R\!\leftarrow\!\!-S\rangle g$$
$$(18) \qquad f^{\cup} \circ R \circ g \;\supseteq\; S$$
$$(19) \qquad R \circ g \;\supseteq\; f \circ S$$
$$(20) \qquad R^{\cup} \circ f \;\supseteq\; g \circ S^{\cup}$$
$$(21) \qquad R \;\supseteq\; f \circ S \circ g^{\cup}$$

**Proof**

We know already that (17) and (18) are equivalent. It remains therefore to prove that the remaining three expressions are all equivalent to (18). We do this by showing that $(18) \Rightarrow (19) \Rightarrow (20) \Rightarrow (21) \Rightarrow (18)$.

$$f^{\cup} \circ R \circ g \;\supseteq\; S$$

$\Rightarrow$   {monotonicity (9)}

$$f \circ f^{\cup} \circ R \circ g \;\supseteq\; f \circ S$$

$\Rightarrow$   {$f$ is single-valued (13)}

$$R \circ g \;\supseteq\; f \circ S$$

$\Rightarrow$   {monotonicity (8)}

$$R \circ g \circ g^{\cup} \;\supseteq\; f \circ S \circ g^{\cup}$$

$\Rightarrow$   {$g$ is single-valued (13)}

$$R \;\supseteq\; f \circ S \circ g^{\cup}$$

$\equiv$   {reverses (7), (4), (6)}

$$R^{\cup} \;\supseteq\; g \circ S^{\cup} \circ f^{\cup}$$

$\Rightarrow$   {monotonicity (8)}

$$R^{\cup} \circ f \;\supseteq\; g \circ S^{\cup} \circ f^{\cup} \circ f$$

$\Rightarrow$   {$f$ is total (14)}

$$R^{\cup} \circ f \;\supseteq\; g \circ S^{\cup}$$

$\Rightarrow$   {monotonicity (8)}

$$g^{\cup} \circ R^{\cup} \circ f \;\supseteq\; g^{\cup} \circ g \circ S^{\cup}$$

$\Rightarrow$   {$g$ is total (14)}

$$g^{\cup} \circ R^{\cup} \circ f \;\supseteq\; S^{\cup}$$

$\equiv$   {reverses (7), (4), (6)}

$$f^{\cup} \circ R \circ g \;\supseteq\; S$$

$\square$

Of these four expressions we prefer the form (19) (since it involves no reverses) and we shall use it as the definition of the $\longleftarrow$ operator from now on. The equivalence between it and (20) is worth highlighting since it will prove to be central to a number of our calculations.

(22)    $R \circ g \;\supseteq\; f \circ S \;\;\equiv\;\; R^{\cup} \circ f \;\supseteq\; g \circ S^{\cup}$

The importance of (22) can already be partly recognised in that it sub-sumes equations (14) (by instantiating $R$ to $g^{\cup}$, and $f$ and $S$ to $I$) and (13) (by instantiating $R$ and $f$ to $I$, and $S$ to $g$). It also predicts that equality of two functions can be proved by showing that one contains the other:

(23)    $g = f \;\;\equiv\;\; g \supseteq f$

**Proof**

From equation (22) with the instantiations $R := I$ and $S := I$ we obtain:

$$g \supseteq f \;\equiv\; f \supseteq g$$

The equation follows immediately from the definition of equality as the conjunction of two inequalities.

□


# 4  Algebraic properties

In this section we begin by asking some obvious questions about the algebraic properties of the operator. Much to our disappointment (perhaps, delight?) positive answers to such questions appear to be rather quickly exhausted causing us to digress in the next section to a deeper study of functions.

The most obvious question to ask is what happens when we instantiate $R$ and/or $S$ to $I$ in equation (19). We quickly discover:

(24)     $I \longleftarrow I \;=\; I$

**Proof**

$$f \langle I \longleftarrow I \rangle g$$

$\equiv$     {definition (19)}

$$g \supseteq f$$

$\equiv$     {(23)}

$$f = g$$

□

However neither the form $R \longleftarrow I$ nor the form $I \longleftarrow S$ seem to be of particular interest.

Inspection of (22) leads, more or less instantaneously, to the observation that $\cup$ distributes over $\longleftarrow$; equally obvious from the definition (19) is that $\longleftarrow$ is monotonic in its first argument and anti-monotonic in its second argument:

(25)     $(R \longleftarrow S)\cup \;=\; (R\cup) \longleftarrow (S\cup)$

(26)     $R \supseteq S \;\Rightarrow\; R \longleftarrow T \supseteq S \longleftarrow T$

(27)     $R \subseteq S \;\Rightarrow\; T \longleftarrow R \supseteq T \longleftarrow S$

The next obvious question to ask is what the operator's distributivity properties are with respect to composition. A partial answer is the following.

(28)    $(R \circ P) {\longleftarrow} (S \circ T) \;\; \supseteq \;\; (R {\longleftarrow} S) \circ (P {\longleftarrow} T)$

**Proof**

$$f \langle (R {\longleftarrow} S) \circ (P {\longleftarrow} T) \rangle h$$

$\equiv$      {composition (5)}

$$\exists (g :: \;\; f \langle R {\longleftarrow} S \rangle g \;\wedge\; g \langle P {\longleftarrow} T \rangle h)$$

$\equiv$      {definition (19)}

$$\exists (g :: \;\; R \circ g \supseteq f \circ S \;\wedge\; P \circ h \supseteq g \circ T)$$

$\Rightarrow$      {monotonicity (9)}

$$\exists (g :: \;\; R \circ g \supseteq f \circ S \;\wedge\; R \circ P \circ h \supseteq R \circ g \circ T)$$

$\Rightarrow$      {monotonicity (8), transitivity of $\supseteq$}

$$R \circ P \circ h \supseteq f \circ S \circ T$$

$\equiv$      {definition (19)}

$$f \langle (R \circ P) {\longleftarrow} (S \circ T) \rangle h$$

□

The fact that (28) is an inequality rather than an equality is very disappointing, so much so that one can be forgiven for immediately abandoning a pursuit of the operator's algebraic properties. Consideration of special cases yields some, but not much, solace. It is indeed the case that

(29)    $(R \circ S) {\longleftarrow} I \;\; = \;\; (R {\longleftarrow} I) \circ (S {\longleftarrow} I)$

but the inequality in

(30)    $I {\longleftarrow} (R \circ S) \;\; \supseteq \;\; (I {\longleftarrow} R) \circ (I {\longleftarrow} S)$

cannot, in general, be strengthened to an equality. Moreover, whereas from (28) we obtain

(31)    $R {\longleftarrow} S \;\; \supseteq \;\; (R {\longleftarrow} I) \circ (I {\longleftarrow} S)$

and

(32)    $R {\longleftarrow} S \;\; \supseteq \;\; (I {\longleftarrow} S) \circ (R {\longleftarrow} I)$

the relations $(R {\longleftarrow} I) \circ (I {\longleftarrow} S)$ and $(I {\longleftarrow} S) \circ (R {\longleftarrow} I)$ are, in general, incomparable. (These claims are left as non-trivial exercises for the reader.)

Had (28) been an equality then any relation built from some class of primitive relations by means of the operator would be decomposable into a composition of relations of the forms $R {\longleftarrow} I$ and $I {\longleftarrow} S$ where $R$ and $S$

are primitive. In spite of (28), our goal in this paper is to discover some such decomposition property; for reasons that we do not wish to go into, we seek further progress by limiting the primitive relations to functions.

## 5  Functions as primitives

Contrary to our initial experience, substituting a function, $f$, for $R$ and $I$ for $S$ in the definition of $R \longleftarrow S$ does yield something of interest.

(33)     $g\langle f \longleftarrow I\rangle h \;\equiv\; f \circ h = g$

**Proof**

$\quad g\langle f \longleftarrow I\rangle h$

$\equiv \quad$ {definition (19)}

$\quad f \circ h \;\supseteq\; g$

$\equiv \quad$ {(23)}

$\quad f \circ h \;=\; g$

□

Equation (33) says that $f \longleftarrow I$ is a function (whenever $f$ is a function) and it encourages us to introduce special notation; specifically, for function $f \in A \longleftarrow B$ we define $(f\circ) \in (A \longleftarrow \alpha) \longleftarrow (B \longleftarrow \alpha)$ by

(34)     $(f\circ).h \;=\; f \circ h$

With the aid of this new notation, equation (33) can be rewritten as follows:

(35)     $f \longleftarrow I \;=\; (f\circ)$

A similar investigation of the form $I \longleftarrow g$ reveals that

(36)     $I \longleftarrow g \;=\; (g\tilde{\circ})\cup$

where, for function $g \in A \longleftarrow B$, we define $(g\tilde{\circ}) \in (\alpha \longleftarrow B) \longleftarrow (\alpha \longleftarrow A)$ by

(37)     $(g\tilde{\circ}).h \;=\; h \circ g$

Exploiting properties (4) and (25) of reverses, we prefer to rewrite equation (36) as follows:

(38)     $I \longleftarrow (g\cup) \;=\; (g\tilde{\circ})$

Some readers will be unfamiliar with "curried" function compositions, i.e. functions of the form $(f\circ)$ or $(g\tilde{\circ})$. For me, however, they are old friends that call to mind many properties. In particular, I know several ways in which associativity of function composition can be expressed. Here are three of them:

$$(39) \quad ((f \circ g)\circ) \;=\; (f\circ) \circ (g\circ)$$
$$(40) \quad ((f \circ g)\tilde{\circ}) \;=\; (g\tilde{\circ}) \circ (f\tilde{\circ})$$
$$(41) \quad (f\circ) \circ (g\tilde{\circ}) \;=\; (g\tilde{\circ}) \circ (f\circ)$$

What is the relevance of (39)–(41)? Well, recall the discussion immediately following the proof of (28). Using the property (35) to rewrite (39) we recognise it as just an instance of (29); using (38) to rewrite (40) we recognise (30), but now we do have the desired equality; finally, using both (35) and (38) to rewrite the left and right sides of (41) we recognise the right sides of (31) and (32), respectively — but now we have equality rather than incomparability! We are, thus, encouraged to check the following identity:

$$(42) \quad (f\circ) \circ (g\tilde{\circ}) \;=\; f \longleftarrow g^\cup \;=\; (g\tilde{\circ}) \circ (f\circ)$$

(The check is easily carried out. But we shall not include it here since (42) is subsumed by equations (45) and (46) proved shortly.)

This is indeed progress, giving confidence that the consideration of functions as primitive relations is a useful avenue to explore.

By instantiating the right side of (28) using either (35) or (38) we obtain four inequalities. Two of these, expressing *left* distributivity properties of functions over the "⟵" operator, cannot be strengthened to equalities. These are:

$$(43) \quad (f \circ P)\longleftarrow T \;\supseteq\; (f\circ) \circ (P\longleftarrow T)$$
$$(44) \quad P\longleftarrow((g^\cup) \circ T) \;\supseteq\; (g\tilde{\circ}) \circ (P\longleftarrow T)$$

The *right* distributivity properties are, however, equalities.

$$(45) \quad (R \circ f)\longleftarrow S \;=\; (R\longleftarrow S) \circ (f\circ)$$
$$(46) \quad R\longleftarrow(S \circ (g^\cup)) \;=\; (R\longleftarrow S) \circ (g\tilde{\circ})$$

We prove just one as an example.

**Proof of (45)**

$$g\langle(R\longleftarrow S) \circ (f\circ)\rangle h$$
$$\equiv \quad \{(34), \text{composition } (5)\}$$
$$g\langle R\longleftarrow S\rangle(f \circ h)$$
$$\equiv \quad \{\text{definition } (19)\}$$
$$R \circ f \circ h \;\supseteq\; g \circ S$$

$\equiv \quad \{\text{definition (19)}\}$

$g\langle (R \circ f) {\longleftarrow} S\rangle h$

□

(The reader is invited to return now to (42) in order to check its validity.)

# 6 The theorem

We consider a language of relations restricted to those formed from functions via the arrow constructor and/or reverse, that is, relations with the following syntax.

$\langle relation\rangle ::= \langle function\rangle \mid \langle relation\rangle \text{``}\cup\text{''} \mid \langle relation\rangle \text{``}{\longleftarrow}\text{''} \langle relation\rangle$

For this language we assert the following:

**Theorem** Given $R \in \langle relation\rangle$ it is possible to construct functions $f$ and $g$ such that

$$R \circ f \;\supseteq\; g \;\supseteq\; f \circ R$$

The proof is by induction on the structure of elements of $\langle relation\rangle$. For a function $h$ we have

$$h \circ I \;\supseteq\; h \;\supseteq\; I \circ h$$

Thus the assignments $f := I, g := h$ establish the basis of the induction.

For relations of the form $R^\cup$ the adjunction (22) supplies the key insight. By making, first, the assignments $f, g, R, S := g, f, R, I$ and, second, the assignments $f, g, R, S := f, g, I, R$ we obtain:

(47) $\qquad R \circ f \;\supseteq\; g \;\supseteq\; f \circ R \;\equiv\; R^\cup \circ g \;\supseteq\; f \;\supseteq\; g \circ R^\cup$

For the case of a relation of the form $R{\longleftarrow}S$ we make the inductive assumptions:

(48) $\qquad R \circ h \;\supseteq\; k \;\supseteq\; h \circ R$

(49) $\qquad S \circ i \;\supseteq\; j \;\supseteq\; i \circ S$

Equivalently, rewriting (49) using the adjunction (47) we have the alternative form:

(50) $\qquad S^\cup \circ j \;\supseteq\; i \;\supseteq\; j \circ S^\cup$

We verify that the assignments

(51) $\qquad f := (h\circ) \circ (j\tilde{\circ})$

(52) $\qquad g := (i\tilde{\circ}) \circ (k\circ)$

establish the induction hypothesis.

The verification is straightforward. For the record here it is

$$(R\longleftarrow S) \circ (h\circ) \circ (j\tilde{\circ})$$

= {right distributivity (45)}

$$(R \circ h)\longleftarrow S \circ (j\tilde{\circ})$$

⊒ {assumption (48)} {monotonicity (26),(8)}

$$k\longleftarrow S \circ (j\tilde{\circ})$$

= {right distributivity (46)}

$$k\longleftarrow (S \circ j\cup)$$

= {reverse (4),(6)}

$$k\longleftarrow (j \circ S\cup)\cup$$

⊒ {assumption (50)} {monotonicity (7), (27)}

$$k\longleftarrow i\cup$$

⊒ {assumption (50)} {monotonicity (7), (27)}

$$k\longleftarrow (S\cup \circ j)\cup$$

= {reverse (6),(4)}

$$k\longleftarrow (j\cup \circ S)$$

⊒ {left distributivity (44)}

$$(j\tilde{\circ}) \circ k\longleftarrow S$$

⊒ {assumption (48)} {monotonicity (26),(9)}

$$(j\tilde{\circ}) \circ (h \circ R)\longleftarrow S$$

⊒ {left distributivity (43)}

$$(j\tilde{\circ}) \circ (h\circ) \circ R\longleftarrow S$$

We have proved that

$$(R\longleftarrow S) \circ (h\circ) \circ (j\tilde{\circ}) \sqsupseteq k\longleftarrow i\cup \sqsupseteq (j\tilde{\circ}) \circ (h\circ) \circ (R\longleftarrow S)$$

Since by (42), $k\longleftarrow i\cup = (i\tilde{\circ}) \circ (k\circ)$, and by (41), $(h\circ) \circ (j\tilde{\circ}) = (j\tilde{\circ}) \circ (h\circ)$ the proof is complete.

□

*Acknowledgements*: Thanks go to Peter de Bruin, Paul Chisholm and Grant Malcolm for critical comments and careful proof-reading of the several versions of this note. Thanks also to the editors for rejecting the first submitted version and for their careful reading of the final version.

## REFERENCES

[1] P. J. de Bruin. *Naturalness of Polymorphism*. Technical Report CS8916, Department of Mathematics and Computing Science, University of Groningen, 1989.

[2] S. MacLane. *Categories for the Working Mathematician*. Volume 5 of Graduate Texts in Mathematics, Springer-Verlag, 1971.

[3] J. C. Reynolds. Towards a theory of type structure. In *Programming Symposium*, pages 408–425, Springer-Verlag, 1974. Proceedings, Colloque sur la Programmation, Paris, April 9–11 1974.

[4] J. C. Reynolds. Types, abstraction and parametric polymorphism. In R.E. Mason, editor, *IFIP '83*, pages 513–523, Elsevier Science Publishers, 1983.

Roland C. Backhouse,
Department of Computing Science,
Rijksuniversiteit Groningen,
P.O. Box 800,
9700 AV  Groningen,
The Netherlands.

# 2

# Efficient Solution of a Non-Monotonic Inverse Problem

## F. L. Bauer

"'Beauty is truth, truth beauty,'—that is all
Ye know on earth, and all ye need to know."
Keats, Ode on a Grecian Urn

## Abstract

The Divine Proportion and, in connection with it, Fibonacci numbers have for centuries evoked aesthetic enthusiasm. We use Fibonacci numbers in a problem aimed at modern coding theory; we demonstrate in this context modern algorithmic methods of program development in the line of the Munich school.

## 1 Introduction

The Fibonacci numbers (Leonardo Pisano, 1202), defined as usual by the recurrence

(0) $\qquad F_0 = 0, \qquad F_1 = 1, \qquad F_{i+2} = F_{i+1} + F_i, \qquad i$ a natural number,

can be reduced modulo $n$ for $n > 0$:

(1) $\qquad F_i^{(n)} =_{def} F_i \bmod n.$

Since $0 \le F_i^{(n)} < n$, it is expected that for any $n$ the sequence $F_i^{(n)}$ is periodic. Indeed, among the $(n+1)^2$ pairs $(F_i^{(n)}, F_{i+1}^{(n)})$ for $i$ in the range $0 \le i \le n$, there are at most $n^2$ different ones, so that there is a period of at most $n^2$. The purpose of this paper is to derive an algorithm to determine a period of the sequence $F_i^{(n)}$, and, since a multiple of a period is a period, to determine the smallest period.

Integer $k > 0$ is a period iff $F_k \overset{n}{=} F_0 = 0$ and $F_{k+1} \overset{n}{=} F_1 = 1$, i.e.

(2)    $n \mid F_k$  and  $n \mid (F_{k+1} - 1)$,   i.e.  $n \mid gcd(F_k, F_{k+1} - 1)$.

The condition is clearly sufficient, and it is necessary since $F_{i-1}^{(n)}$ is uniquely determined from $F_i^{(n)}$ and $F_{i+1}^{(n)}$. Since there is a period that is at most $n^2$, we can define our desired result $s(n)$ as the smallest solution $k$ of the predicate

(3)    $\Phi(k, n) =_{def} 0 < k \le n^2 \ \wedge \ n \mid f(k)$

where

(4)    $f(k) =_{def} gcd(F_k, F_{k+1} - 1)$.

Finding the smallest solution can be performed by a linear search beginning with the smallest natural number, but we would hope to do better than that. Bisection over some interval would be quicker, but it can be applied only if $f(k)$ is monotonic in $k$, and a glance at Table 1 shows that it isn't. Hence, we try to make progress by investigating properties of the Fibonacci numbers. First, we mention a simplification. It is easily seen that $f(1) = 1$ and $f(2) = 3$. The rest of this paper restricts attention to the case $3 \le n$.

# 2   Investigating Fibonacci numbers

Consider the companion matrix $F =_{def} \begin{pmatrix} 0 & 1 \\ 1 & 1 \end{pmatrix}$. The Fibonacci numbers satisfy the equation

(5)    $F^i = \begin{pmatrix} F_{i-1} & F_i \\ F_i & F_{i+1} \end{pmatrix}$        for $1 \le i$.

Obviously, $k$ is a period iff $(F^k) \bmod n = I$, the unit matrix. Since the determinants of $I$, $F$, and $F^k$ are 1, $-1$, and $(-1)^k$ respectively, $k$ is a period implies $(-1)^k \overset{n}{=} 1$. For $3 \le n$, this means that the period is even. Therefore, we can redefine $\Phi(k, n)$ as follows:

(6)    $\Phi(k, n) =_{def} 0 < k \le n^2 \ \wedge \ 2 \mid k \ \wedge \ n \mid f(k)$.

This cuts the search space in half. To make further progress, we investigate function $f(k)$ defined in (4). From a closer look at Table 1, we could guess that

(7) **Theorem**

   If $2 \mid k \ \wedge \ 4 \mid k$, then $f(k) = F_{k/2}$,
   If $2 \mid k \ \wedge \ 4 \nmid k$, then $f(k) = F_{(k-2)/2} + F_{(k+2)/2}$.

**Proof**   We introduce the Lucas numbers (8). A straightforward induction shows that consecutive Lucas numbers, like consecutive Fibonacci numbers, are relatively prime.

(8)       $E_i =_{def} F_{i-1} + F_{i+1}$

The definition of $f_k$ involves the values $F_k$ and $F_{k+1} - 1$. Since we are assuming that $k$ is even, let us write $k = 2i$ and investigate these values. We have

(9)   $F_{2i}$

=       {Identity due to (Lucas 1876), derived from $F^{2i} = F^i * F^i$}

$F_i * (F_{i-1} + F_{i+1})$

=       {Definition (8) of the Lucas numbers}

$F_i * E_i$

(10)   $F_{2i+1} + (-1)^i$

=       {Identity due to (Lucas 1876), derived from $F^{2i} = F^i * F^i$}

$F_i^2 + F_{i+1}^2 + (-1)^i$

=       {Replace $F_i^2 + (-1)^i$ using (5) and the fact that the
          determinant of $F^i$ is $(-1)^i$}

$F_{i+1}F_{i-1} + F_{i+1}^2$

=       {Factor out $F_{i+1}$ and use definition (8)}

$F_{i+1} * E_i$

In the same manner, but substituting for $F_{i+1}^2 + (-1)^{i+1}$, we can prove

(11)       $F_{2i+1} + (-1)^{i+1} = F_i * E_{i+1}.$

Now let us return to the proof of (7). We investigate $gcd(F_k, F_{k+1} - 1)$. Assume $k = 2i$ and $i = 2j$. From (9) and (11) we have

$$F_k = F_{4j} = F_{2j} * E_{2j},$$
$$F_{k+1} - 1 = F_{4j+1} - 1 = F_{2j} * E_{2j+1}.$$

Thus, $F_{2j}$ is a common factor and, since $E_{2j}$ and $E_{2j+1}$ are relatively prime, $F_{2j} = F_{k/2}$ is the gcd of $F_k$ and $F_{k+1} - 1$. Thus, we have proved the first half of (7). Assuming $i = 2j+1$, the second half follows in a similar manner, using (9) and (10).
□

Substituting the values of $f(k)$ as given in (7) into definition (6) of $\Phi(k, n)$ yields

(12)       $\Phi(k, n) = 0 < k \leq n^2 \wedge 2 \mid k \wedge$
              $(even(k/2) \Rightarrow n \mid F_{k/2}) \wedge (odd(k/2) \Rightarrow n \mid E_{k/2}).$

Since we are looking for the smallest integer that satisfies (12), we can write our solution as

(13)     $s(n) = 2* \min\{i : 0 < 2i \le n^2 \wedge$
$(even(i) \Rightarrow n \mid F_i) \wedge (odd(i) \Rightarrow n \mid E_i)\}.$

This can be viewed as finding the first sequence index for which $n$ is a divisor in the sequence

(14)     $(F_0 + F_2, \; F_2, \; F_2 + F_4, \; F_4, \; F_4 + F_6, \; F_6, \; \cdots)$

and then doubling the index to obtain a solution. The two-step recurrence $F_{i+4} = 3F_{i+2} - F_i$ can be used to calculate the even-subscripted $F_i$. For the interlaced sequence (14), we could use the following tandem recurrence, in which the number 5, so deeply connected with the Fibonacci sequence, nicely turns up.

$$F_{i+2} = E_{i+1} - F_i \quad \text{and} \quad E_{i+3} = 5F_{i+2} - E_{i+1}.$$

# 3   Investigating the case that $n$ is prime

As with any number-theoretic function, it may be useful to analyze $\Phi(k, p)$ for prime $p$. The patterns in the prime decomposition of the $F_k$ in Table 1 urge us to investigate the following facts, which happen to be well-known.

(15)  **Theorem**   For odd prime $p, p \ne 5$,

If $p \bmod 10 \in \{1, 9\}$, then $p \mid F_{p-1}$,
If $p \bmod 10 \in \{3, 7\}$, then $p \mid F_{p+1}$.

**Proof**   From $2^i \sqrt{5} F_i = (1 + \sqrt{5})^i - (1 - \sqrt{5})^i$ (Binet 1843) follows result (16), which is due to (Catalan 1857):

(16)     $2^{i-1} F_i = \Sigma(k : 0 \le k \wedge 2k + 1 \le i : 5^k \binom{i}{2k+1}).$

Consider $i = p$, $p$ an odd prime. Since $\binom{p}{k}$ is divisible by $p$ for $0 < k < p$ and since $\binom{p}{p} = 1$, all but the last of the terms in the sum of (16) are divisible by $p$, so (16) leads directly to

(17)     $F_p \overset{p}{=} 5^{(p-1)/2}.$

In a similar manner, choosing $i = p - 1$ in (16) for $p$ an odd prime and using the fact that Fermat's theorem yields $2^{p-1} \overset{p}{=} 1$, we obtain

(18)     $F_{p-1} \overset{p}{=} \dfrac{1 - 5^{(p-1)/2}}{2}.$

Note the appearance of $5^{(p-1)/2}$ in (17) and (18). Since $(5^{(p-1)/2})^2 = 5^{p-1} \overset{p}{=} 1$, we have

$$5^{(p-1)/2} \overset{p}{=} 1 \quad \text{or} \quad 5^{(p-1)/2} \overset{p}{=} -1.$$

The theory of quadratic residues then leads to the following for any odd prime, $p \neq 5$:

$$\text{If } p \bmod 10 \in \{1,9\}, \text{ then } 5^{(p-1)/2} \overset{p}{=} 1,$$
$$\text{If } p \bmod 10 \in \{3,7\}, \text{ then } 5^{(p-1)/2} \overset{p}{=} -1.$$

Together with (17) and (18), this yields

(19)  $\text{If } p \bmod 10 \in \{1,9\}, \text{ then } F_{p-1} \overset{p}{=} 0, F_p = 1,$
$$\text{so } F_{p+1} \overset{p}{=} 1,$$
$\text{If } p \bmod 10 \in \{3,7\}, \text{ then } F_{p-1} \overset{p}{=} 1, F_p = -1,$
$$\text{so } F_{p+1} \overset{p}{=} 0, F_{p+2} \overset{p}{=} -1.$$

This ends the proof of theorem (15).
□

Theorem (15), together with the fact that any period of $F_i^{(n)}$ is a multiple of its minimum period, leads to the following as a direct consequence of formulas (12) and (13):

(20)  $\text{If } p \bmod 10 \in \{1,9\}, \text{ then } \Phi(2(p-1),p) \text{ and } s(p) \,|\, 2(p-1),$
$\text{If } p \bmod 10 \in \{3,7\}, \text{ then } \Phi(2(p+1),p) \text{ and } s(p) \,|\, 2(p+1).$

But we can do better than that. In proving Theorem (15), we have actually shown that for $p \bmod 10 \in \{1,9\}$, $p \,|\, F_{p-1}$ and $p \,|\, F_{p-1}$ hold. Therefore, $p \,|\, f(p-1)$ (see (4)), and we can change (20) to

(21)  $\text{If } p \bmod 10 \in \{1,9\}, \text{ then } \Phi(p-1,p) \quad \text{and } s(p) \,|\, p-1,$
$\text{If } p \bmod 10 \in \{3,7\}, \text{ then } \Phi(2(p+1),p) \text{ and } s(p) \,|\, 2(p+1).$

Result (21) was obtained by D. D. Wall in 1960, using less elementary tools.

We have gained other insight as well. Since $F_{p\pm1}$ has an even subscript, $p \,|\, F_{p\pm1}$ means that either $p \,|\, F_{(p\pm1)/2}$ or $p \,|\, E_{(p\pm1)/2}$. Again, observing the patterns in Table 1 suggests some conjectures:

(22) **Theorem**  For any odd prime, $p \neq 5$,

$$\text{If } p \bmod 20 \in \{\ 1,\ 9\}, \text{ then } p \,|\, F_{(p-1)/2},$$
$$\text{If } p \bmod 20 \in \{11,19\}, \text{ then } p \,|\, E_{(p-1)/2},$$
$$\text{If } p \bmod 20 \in \{\ 3,\ 7\}, \text{ then } p \,|\, E_{(p+1)/2},$$
$$\text{If } p \bmod 20 \in \{13,17\}, \text{ then } p \,|\, F_{(p+1)/2}.$$

**Proof**  These follow directly from the following Lemma (23), with $i = (p-1)/2$ and $F_{2i+1} = F_p \overset{p}{=} 1$ in the first two cases and with $i = (p+1)/2$ and $F_{2i+1} = F_{p+2} \overset{p}{=} -1$ in the second two cases.
□

**(23) Lemma**

Suppose $F_{2i+1} \overset{p}{=} (-1)^i$. Then either $p \mid F_{2i+2}$ or $p \mid F_i$.

Suppose $F_{2i+1} \overset{p}{=} -(-1)^i$. Then either $p \mid F_{2i+2}$ or $p \mid E_i$.

**Proof** Consider the first claim, and assume $p \nmid F_i$. We have

$$p \nmid F_i$$

$$\Rightarrow \quad \{(11) \text{ and hypothesis}\}$$

$$p \mid E_{i+1}$$

$$\Rightarrow \quad \{\text{proof (9), with } i := i + 1\}$$

$$p \mid F_{2i+2}$$

The second claim follows in a similar manner using (10) and (9). □

It is now a simple matter to rewrite formula (13), which is

$$s(n) \;=\; 2* \min\{i : 0 < 2i \le n^2 \;\wedge$$
$$(even(i) \Rightarrow n \mid F_i) \;\wedge\; (odd(i) \Rightarrow n \mid E_i)\},$$

for the case that $n$ is a prime, taking into account our result (21). First, assume that $p$ is a prime and insert a case analysis, taking into account the results for $p = 2$ and $p = 5$:

$$s(p) \;=\; \textbf{if } p = 2 \textbf{ then } 3$$
$$\textbf{if } p = 5 \textbf{ then } 20$$
$$\textbf{if } p \textbf{ mod } 10 \in \{1, 9\} \textbf{ then}$$
$$2* \min\{i : 0 < 2i \le p^2 \;\wedge$$
$$(even(i) \Rightarrow p \mid F_i) \;\wedge\; (odd(i) \Rightarrow p \mid E_i)\}$$
$$\textbf{if } p \textbf{ mod } 10 \in \{3, 7\} \textbf{ then}$$
$$2* \min\{i : 0 < 2i \le p^2 \;\wedge$$
$$(even(i) \Rightarrow p \mid F_i) \;\wedge\; (odd(i) \Rightarrow p \mid E_i)\}.$$

Next, use (21) to replace the ranges on the min quantifications:

(24) $$s(p) \;=\; \textbf{if } p = 2 \textbf{ then } 3$$
$$\textbf{if } p = 5 \textbf{ then } 20$$
$$\textbf{if } p \textbf{ mod } 10 \in \{1, 9\} \textbf{ then}$$
$$2* \min\{i : 0 < i \;\wedge\; 2i \mid p - 1 \;\wedge$$
$$(even(i) \Rightarrow p \mid F_i) \;\wedge\; (odd(i) \Rightarrow p \mid E_i)\}$$
$$\textbf{if } p \textbf{ mod } 10 \in \{3, 7\} \textbf{ then}$$
$$2* \min\{i : 0 < i \;\wedge\; i \mid p + 1 \;\wedge$$
$$(even(i) \Rightarrow p \mid F_i) \;\wedge\; (odd(i) \Rightarrow p \mid E_i)\}$$

Now replace the min quantifications of (24) by recursion equations:

$$
\begin{aligned}
(25) \qquad s(p) \;=\; & \textbf{if } p = 2 \textbf{ then } 3 \\
& \textbf{if } p = 5 \textbf{ then } 20 \\
& \textbf{if } p \bmod 10 \in \{1,9\} \textbf{ then } h_{1,9}(p,1) \\
& \textbf{if } p \bmod 10 \in \{3,7\} \textbf{ then } h_{3,7}(p,1) \\
h_{1,9}(p,i) \;=\; & \textbf{if } 2i \,|\, p-1 \;\wedge\; (even(i) \Rightarrow p \,|\, F_i) \;\wedge\; (odd(i) \Rightarrow p \,|\, E_i) \\
& \textbf{then } 2i \\
& \textbf{else } h_{1,9}(p, i+1) \\
h_{3,7}(p,i) \;=\; & \textbf{if } i \,|\, p+1 \;\wedge\; (even(i) \Rightarrow p \,|\, F_i) \;\wedge\; (odd(i) \Rightarrow p \,|\, E_i) \\
& \textbf{then } 2i \\
& \textbf{else } h_{3,7}(p, i+1)
\end{aligned}
$$

# 4  Dealing with composite numbers

For composite numbers $n$, $s(n)$ may be computed using the trivial result

$$s(a*b) = s(a)*s(b) \quad \text{provided} \quad gcd(a,b) = 1.$$

Thus, apart from $s(p)$, we still need $s(p^e)$, where $p$ is prime and $e \geq 1$. Wall showed in 1960 that if $s(p^2) \neq s(p)$, then $s(p^e) = p^{e-1}s(p)$. So far, no example with $s(p^2) = s(p)$ has been found. Nevertheless, if we distrust the conjecture, algorithm (25) still works for $s(p^2)$ if only the conditions $2i \,|\, p-1$ and $i \,|\, p+1$ are replaced by $2i \,|\, p(p-1)$ and $i \,|\, p(p+1)$, respectively.

# 5  Conclusions

Clearly, a search from below as we have done is superior to a search from above. Nevertheless, the search uses the relation $\leq$ in the linear intervals $2 \leq 2i \leq p-1$ and $1 \leq i \leq p+1$ while in this (as in many other number-theoretic problems) the lattice intervals $2i \,|\, p - 1$, $i \,|\, p + 1$ respectively would be more appropriate. Linear interval search is supported by classical machines. Special hardware could be devised, however, to support search on lattice intervals — for example, by representing a natural number by the bag of its prime factors, giving essentially a Gödel representation. Both linear and lattice interval exhaustion can be done on parallel machines, too.

F. L. Bauer,
Villenstrasse 19,
D–8081 Kottgeisering,
West Germany.

| $k$ | $F_k$ | $F_{k+1}-1$ | $f(k) = gcd(F_k, F_{k+1}-1)$ | $F_{k/2}$ | $E_{k/2}$ |
|---|---|---|---|---|---|
| 0 | 0 | 0 | 0 | | |
| 1 | 1 | 0 | 1 | | |
| 2 | 1 | 1 | 1 | | 1 |
| 3 | 2 | 2 | 2 | | |
| 4 | 3 | 4 | 1 | 1 | |
| 5 | 5 | 7 | 1 | | |
| 6 | 8 | 12 | 4 | | 4 |
| 7 | 13 | 20 | 1 | | |
| 8 | 21 | 33 | 3 | 3 | |
| 9 | 34 | 54 | 2 | | |
| 10 | 55 | 88 | 11 | | 11 |
| 11 | 89 | 143 | 1 | | |
| 12 | 144 | 232 | 8 | 8 | |
| 13 | 233 | 376 | 1 | | |
| 14 | 377 | 609 | 29 | | 29 |
| 15 | 610 | 986 | 2 | | |
| 16 | 987 | 1596 | 21 | 21 | |
| 17 | 1597 | 2583 | 1 | | |
| 18 | 2584 | 4180 | 76 | | 76 |
| 19 | 4181 | 6764 | 1 | | |
| 20 | 6765 | 10945 | 55 | 55 | |
| 21 | 10946 | 17710 | 2 | | |
| 22 | 17711 | 28656 | 199 | | 199 |
| 23 | 28657 | 46367 | 1 | | |
| 24 | 46368 | 75024 | 144 | 144 | |

TABLE 1. Values of $gcd(F_k, F_{k+1}-1)$ for $1 \le k \le 24$.

| $n$ | $s(n)$ | $n$ | $s(n)$ |
|---|---|---|---|
| 1 | 1 | 6 | 24 |
| 2 | 3 | 7 | 16 |
| 3 | 8 | 8 | 12 |
| 4 | 6 | 9 | 24 |
| 5 | 20 | | |

TABLE 2. Periods of the Fibonacci sequence modulo $n$ for $1 \le n \le 9$.

# 3

# Semantics of Quasi-Boolean Expressions

## A. Bijlsma

## Introduction

In deriving programs, it is often useful to consider certain expressions as well-defined although they contain subexpressions to which no value can reasonably be attributed. For instance, one wishes to consider the expression

$$0 \leq i < n \quad \textbf{and} \quad a[i] = 0$$

as false when $i = n$, without worrying whether or not $n$ is in the subscript range of array $a$. Expressions like these are called *quasi-boolean* in [3]. Traditionally, they are treated by introducing the conditional connectives **cand** and **cor** [2, chapter 4] [4, §4.1].

However, **cand** and **cor** do not satisfy pleasant algebraic laws: they are not commutative and do not in general distribute over each other. This makes calculations involving these connectives exceedingly burdensome; for this reason their introduction was termed "a strategic mistake" in [3]. It is the purpose of this note to suggest a possible alternative.

Let it be clear from the outset that the semantics of quasi-boolean expressions defined below is not intended for implementation in a programming language. Its aim is merely to facilitate the calculational derivation of programs. That these derivations are most easily expressed in a richer language than the programs themselves, one that need not be implementable, is a well-known observation.

On the other hand, in order to be suited for its purpose, any proposed semantics of quasi-boolean expressions should satisfy the following criteria:

(i) if all atomic subexpressions of a certain expression are well-defined, the value attached to that expression should be the one that would follow from ordinary logic;

(ii) no expression should be left undefined if it can be given a meaning by the introduction of conditional connectives;

(iii) the relation "having the same value" between expressions should satisfy simple calculational laws.

The option of considering an expression undefined when any of its subexpressions is, satisfies (i) and (iii) but not (ii). The use of conditional connectives satisfies (i) and (ii) but not (iii). It is possible to do a bit better by considering two-sided conditional connectives [5] [1, §A0.3.2]. This restores commutativity, but, as we shall see in the next section, there remain important laws that fail to hold. The semantics defined in this note has the property that *all* laws of propositional calculus carry through.

## Conventions and notations

We suppose a set $At$ of logical *atoms* and a *valuation* $av \in At \to \{F, U, T\}$ given: this is meant to model the fact that formulae without logical connectives can be false, undefined or true respectively. For convenience's sake it is assumed that $F$ and $T$ do not themselves belong to $At$. The problem dealt with here is how to extend the given valuation $av$ if logical connectives are introduced. Let $Ex$ be the set of all finite expressions that can be formed with the elements of $At \cup \{F, T\}$, the unary operator **non** and the binary operators **and** and **or** . As yet, no meaning is attached to the elements of $Ex$; in fact, discovering how to define such a meaning in a sensible way is precisely our purpose. (The formal operators **non** , **and** , **or** must not be confused with those of the ordinary logic in which our proofs will be expressed. These will be denoted by the symbols $\neg, \wedge, \vee$.)

We introduce a linear ordering $\sqsubseteq$ on the set $\{F, U, T\}$ such that $F \sqsubseteq U \sqsubseteq T$. For $p$ and $q$ in $\{F, U, T\}$, denote by $p \sqcap q$ the minimum and by $p \sqcup q$ the maximum of $p$ and $q$ with respect to the ordering $\sqsubseteq$. Furthermore, the prefix operator $\sim$ is defined by $\sim F = T$, $\sim U = U$, $\sim T = F$.

For $v \in At \to \{F, U, T\}$, we define $c.v \in Ex \to \{F, U, T\}$ by

$$
\begin{array}{llll}
(0) & E \in \{F, T\} & \Rightarrow & c.v.E = E \ , \\
(1) & E \in At & \Rightarrow & c.v.E = v.E \ , \\
(2) & c.v.(\textbf{non } E) & = & \sim(c.v.E) \ , \\
(3) & c.v.(E0 \textbf{ and } E1) & = & c.v.E0 \sqcap c.v.E1 \ , \\
(4) & c.v.(E0 \textbf{ or } E1) & = & c.v.E0 \sqcup c.v.E1
\end{array}
$$

for all $E, E0, E1 \in Ex$.

What we are looking for is a mapping $ev \in Ex \to \{F, U, T\}$ with

$ev \mid At = av$ that satisfies criteria (i)–(iii). An obvious candidate for $ev$ would be $c.av$; in fact, this is precisely what is meant in the introduction by "two-sided conditional connectives". However, as

$$U \sqcap (\sim U \sqcup F) = U \ ,$$
$$U \sqcap F = F \ ,$$

the complement rule

$$ev.(E0 \textbf{ and } (\textbf{non } E0 \textbf{ or } E1)) = ev.(E0 \textbf{ and } E1)$$

would fail to hold with $ev$ chosen as $c.av$. Therefore this choice is not considered satisfactory.

In fact, there is a simple way to ensure that $ev$ attaches the same value to expressions that are equivalent in propositional calculus. Note that for $w \in At \to \{F,T\}$, rules (0)–(4) define $c.w \in Ex \to \{F,T\}$. Now the restrictions of $\sim$, $\sqcap$, $\sqcup$ to $\{F,T\}$ model ordinary logic. Hence, if $E0$ and $E1$ can be transformed into one another by the rules of propositional calculus, then for any $w \in At \to \{F,T\}$ we have $c.w.E0 = c.w.E1$. If for $ev \in Ex \to \{F,U,T\}$ the implication

(5)    $(\textbf{A} w : w \in At \to \{F,T\} : c.w.E0 = c.w.E1) \ \Rightarrow \ ev.E0 = ev.E1$

holds, criterion (iii) is satisfied in the sense that all rules of propositional calculus apply. The rest of this note is concerned with the construction of such an $ev$.

## The construction of $ev$

For $w \in At \to \{F,T\}$ we define

(6)    $f.w \ \equiv \ (\textbf{A} x : x \in At \ \wedge \ av.x \neq U : w.x = av.x) \ .$

(Actually, the $\wedge$ in (6) should strictly speaking be a conditional and, since $av.x$ is undefined when $x \in At$ is false. However, at the end of this note we shall have succeeded in showing that such scruples are unnecessary.)

For $E0, E1 \in Ex$ we define

(7)    $E0 == E1 \ \equiv \ (\textbf{A} w : w \in At \to \{F,T\} \wedge f.w : c.w.E0 = c.w.E1).$

For later use we note that $==$ is an equivalence relation on $Ex$,

Now we are ready to define the mapping $ev \in Ex \to \{F,U,T\}$ we have been looking for. For any $E \in Ex$,

(8)    $ev.E = \textbf{if } E == F \to F$
$\quad\quad\quad [] \ E == T \to T$
$\quad\quad\quad [] \ \neg(E == F) \wedge \neg(E == T) \to U$
$\quad\quad \textbf{fi} \ .$

The rest of this note is organised as follows. First we show that (8) is a proper definition in the sense that the quards are mutually exclusive (Theorem 0). Then we show that $ev$ as defined by (8) indeed satisfies $ev \mid At = av$ (Theorem 1). Finally, we deal with criteria (i)–(iii) (Theorems 2–4).

**Theorem 0**    For $E \in Ex$,
$$\neg(E == F) \ \lor \ \neg(E == T) \ .$$

**Proof**

$$\neg(E == F) \ \lor \ \neg(E == T)$$

$\Leftarrow \qquad \{\ == \text{ is an equivalence relation}\}$

$\qquad \neg(F == T)$

$= \qquad \{(7)\}$

$\qquad (\mathbf{E}\, w : \ w \in At \rightarrow \{F, T\} \ \land \ f.w : \ c.w.F \neq c.w.T)$

$= \qquad \{(0)\}$

$\qquad (\mathbf{E}\, w : \ w \in At \rightarrow \{F, T\} \ \land \ f.w : \ F \neq T)$

$= \qquad \{\text{nonempty domain}\}$

$\qquad F \neq T \ .$

$\square$

**Theorem 1**    For $x \in At$,
$$ev.x = av.x.$$

**Proof**    For $q \in \{F, T\}$,

$\qquad ev.x = q$

$= \qquad \{(8)\}$

$\qquad x == q$

$= \qquad \{(7)\}$

$\qquad (\mathbf{A}\, w : \ w \in At \rightarrow \{F, T\} \ \land \ f.w : \ c.w.x = c.w.q)$

$= \qquad \{(1), (0)\}$

$\qquad (\mathbf{A}\, w : \ w \in At \rightarrow \{F, T\} \ \land \ f.w : \ w.x = q)$

$= \qquad \{(6), \text{nonempty domain}\}$

$\qquad av.x = q \ .$

$\square$

We have now reached the point where it has been established that (8) really does define a mapping $ev \in Ex \rightarrow \{F, U, T\}$ with $ev \,|\, At = av$. Next we turn to criterion (iii).

As observed in a previous section, in order to show that $ev$ attaches the same value to expressions that are equivalent in propositional calculus, it is sufficient to show that $ev$ satisfies (5). This will be a corollary of the next theorem.

**Theorem 2**    For $E0, E1 \in Ex$,
$$E0 == E1 \;\Rightarrow\; ev.E0 = ev.E1.$$

**Proof**

$\quad E0 == E1$

$\Rightarrow \quad \{== \text{ is an equivalence relation}\}$

$\quad (E0 == F \;\equiv\; E1 == F) \;\wedge\; (E0 == T \;\equiv\; E1 == T)$

$\Rightarrow \quad \{(8)\}$

$\quad ev.E0 = ev.E1 \;\;.$

$\square$

**Remark**    The implication in the theorem is not an equivalence. If $x$ and $y$ are distinct elements of $At$ such that $av.x = av.y = U$, then $ev.x = ev.y$ but not $x == y$.
$\square$

**Corollary**    $ev$ satisfies (5).

**Proof**

$\quad (5)$

$= \quad \{\}$

$\quad (\mathbf{A}\, w : w \in At \rightarrow \{F, T\} : c.w.E0 = c.w.E1) \;\Rightarrow\; ev.E0 = ev.E1$

$\Leftarrow \quad \{\text{strengthening the domain}\}$

$\quad (\mathbf{A}\, w : w \in At \rightarrow \{F, T\} \;\wedge\; f.w : c.w.E0 = c.w.E1) \;\Rightarrow$

$\qquad ev.E0 = ev.E1$

$= \quad \{(7)\}$

$\quad E0 == E1 \;\Rightarrow\; ev.E0 = ev.E1$

$= \quad \{\text{Theorem 2}\}$

$\quad \text{true} \;\;.$

$\square$

There is still more to be said about criterion (iii), since not all steps in a derivation consist in the application of a rule from propositional calculus. The remaining ones consist in replacement of a logical atom that has a defined value by that value. That expressions linked by such a step have the same value under $ev$ is not trivial, since $ev$ is not defined by induction on the structure of its argument. Nevertheless it is correct, as is shown by the following theorem.

**Theorem 3**   For $E \in Ex$, $x \in At$ with $av.x \neq U$,

$$ev.E \;=\; ev.((x := av.x).E) \;\;.$$

**Proof**   It is clear from (0)–(4) that, for any $v \in At \to \{F, U, T\}$,

$$(9) \qquad c.v.E \;=\; c.v.((x := v.x).E) \;\;.$$

Now for $q \in \{F, T\}$,

$$ev.E = q$$
$$= \qquad \{(8)\}$$
$$E == q$$
$$= \qquad \{(7)\}$$
$$(\mathbf{A}\, w : w \in At \to \{F, T\} \;\wedge\; f.w : c.w.E = c.w.q)$$
$$= \qquad \{(9)\}$$
$$(\mathbf{A}\, w : w \in At \to \{F, T\} \;\wedge\; f.w : c.w.((x := w.x).E) = c.w.q)$$
$$= \qquad \{(6),\, av.x \neq U\}$$
$$(\mathbf{A}\, w : w \in At \to \{F, T\} \;\wedge\; f.w : c.w.((x := av.x).E) = c.w.q)$$
$$= \qquad \{(7),\, (8)\}$$
$$ev.((x := av.x).E) \;=\; q \;\;.$$

$\square$

Finally, we deal with criteria (i) and (ii) simultaneously by showing that $ev.E$ equals $c.av.E$ except perhaps when the latter value is $U$. This disposes of (i) since it follows from the definition of $c$ that the exceptional case does not arise if all atoms $x$ occurring in $E$ satisfy $av.x \neq U$. It also disposes of (ii) since the definition of $c$ shows that $c.av.E \neq U$ whenever $E$ can be given a meaning by the introduction of conditional connectives.

**Theorem 4**   For $E \in Ex$,

$$ev.E = c.av.E \;\vee\; c.av.E = U \;\;.$$

**Proof**    For $E \in Ex$ with $c.av.E \neq U$,

$$ev.E = c.av.E$$
$$= \quad \{(8)\}$$
$$E == c.av.E$$
$$= \quad \{(7), (0)\}$$
$$(\mathbf{A}\, w:\ w \in At \to \{F,T\} \ \wedge\ f.w:\ c.w.E = c.av.E) \ .$$

Assume $w \in At \to \{F,T\}$ with $f.w$ fixed. We shall prove
(10)    $c.w.E = c.av.E \ \vee\ c.av.E = U$
by induction on the structure of $E$.

**Case 0**    $E \in \{F,T\}$.    Then

$$c.w.E = c.av.E \ \vee\ c.av.E = U$$
$$= \quad \{(0)\}$$
$$E = E \ \vee\ E = U$$
$$= \quad \{\}$$
$$\text{true} \quad .$$

**Case 1**    $E \in At$.    Then

$$c.w.E = c.av.E \ \vee\ c.av.E = U$$
$$= \quad \{(1)\}$$
$$w.E = av.E \ \vee\ av.E = U$$
$$= \quad \{f.w, (6)\}$$
$$\text{true} \quad .$$

**Case 2**    $E = \mathbf{non}\ E0$, with $(E := E0).(10)$.    Then

$$c.w.E = c.av.E \ \vee\ c.av.E = U$$
$$= \quad \{(2)\}$$
$$\sim c.w.E0 = \sim c.av.E0 \ \vee\ \sim c.av.E0 = U$$
$$= \quad \{\text{definition of } \sim\}$$
$$\sim c.w.E0 = \sim c.av.E0 \ \vee\ c.av.E0 = U$$
$$= \quad \{(E := E0).(10)\}$$
$$\text{true} \quad .$$

**Case 3** $E = E0$ **and** $E1$, with $(E := E0).(10)$ and $(E := E1).(10)$. Then

$$c.w.E = c.av.E \ \lor \ c.av.E = U$$

$= \quad \{(3)\}$

$$c.w.E0 \sqcap c.w.E1 \ = \ c.av.E0 \sqcap c.av.E1 \ \lor \ c.av.E0 \sqcap c.av.E1 \ = \ U$$

$= \quad \{\text{definition of } \sqcap, \text{ distribution}\}$

$(c.w.E0 \ \sqcap \ c.w.E1 \ = \ c.av.E0 \ \sqcap \ c.av.E1 \ \lor$
$\quad c.av.E0 \ = \ U \ \lor \ c.av.E1 \ = \ U)$
$\land \quad (c.w.E0 \ \sqcap \ c.w.E1 \ = \ c.av.E0 \ \sqcap \ c.av.E1 \ \lor \ U \ \sqsubseteq \ c.av.E0)$
$\land \quad (c.w.E0 \ \sqcap \ c.w.E1 \ = \ c.av.E0 \ \sqcap \ c.av.E1 \ \lor \ U \ \sqsubseteq \ c.av.E1)$

$= \quad \{(E := E0).(10), (E := E1).(10), \text{ complement rule}\}$

$(F \ \sqcap \ c.w.E1 \ = \ F \ \sqcap \ c.av.E1 \ \lor \ U \ \sqsubseteq \ c.av.E0)$
$\land \quad (c.w.E0 \ \sqcap \ F \ = \ c.av.E0 \ \sqcap \ F \ \lor \ U \ \sqsubseteq \ c.av.E1)$

$= \quad \{F \sqcap q = F \text{ for all } q\}$

true .

**Case 4** $E = E0$ **or** $E1$, with $(E := E0).(10)$ and $(E := E1).(10)$.
Consider $E' = \textbf{non} \ (\textbf{non} \ E0 \ \textbf{and} \ \textbf{non} \ E1)\}$.
As, for any $p, q$ in $\{F, U, T\}$,

$$p \sqcup q \ = \ \sim(\sim p \sqcap \sim q) \ ,$$

it follows from the definition of $c$ that for any $v \in At \to \{F, U, T\}$ we have $c.v.E = c.v.E'$, in particular for $v = w$ and for $v = av$. Hence this case reduces to a combination of cases 2 and 3.

$\square$

*Acknowledgement*: The introduction of the ordering $\sqsubseteq$ was suggested to me by Jaap van der Woude.

## References

[1] R. L. Barber. *The Spine of Software*. John Wiley & Sons, Chichester, 1987.

[2] E. W. Dijkstra. *A Discipline of Programming*. Prentice-Hall, Englewood Cliffs, 1976.

[3] E. W. Dijkstra and W. H. J. Feijen. The linear search revisited. *Struct. Prog.*, 10:5–9, 1989.

[4] D. Gries. *The Science of Programming.* Springer-Verlag, New-York, 1981.

[5] E. C. R. Hehner, L. E. Gupta, and A. J. Malton. Predicative methodology. *Acta Informatica*, 23:487–505, 1986.

A. Bijlsma,
Department of Mathematics and Computing Science,
Eindhoven University of Technology,
P.O. Box 513,
5600 MB  Eindhoven,
The Netherlands.

# 4

# Small Specification Exercises

## Richard S. Bird

## Introduction

Sometimes it seems easier to construct a program for a problem than a suitable specification of the problem. Consider for instance the following exercise, expressed as it might occur in an introductory text on programming:

> In the sequence
>
> $$[\underline{5}, 7, 5, \underline{3}, 4, \underline{1}, 7]$$
>
> the underlined numbers are defined by the rule that each number, apart from the first, is the next element of the original sequence strictly smaller than the last underlined number. The first underlined number is the first element of the sequence. Call these numbers the *drops* of the sequence. Write a program to produce the drops of a given sequence.

The solution consists of a simple loop and can be written down immediately. Using a left-reduction (see [1] and [2] for the notation used in this paper), we have

$$drops \;=\; \oplus\!\!\not\!\rightarrow_{[]}$$

where

$$x \oplus a \;=\; (last\; x > a \rightarrow x + [a], x)$$

Here, $last\; x$ returns the last element of $x$ if $x$ is a non-empty sequence, and $\infty$ otherwise.

Some would argue that this definition of *drops* is a perfectly adequate specification since it corresponds closely to the operational description given above. Others would demand a more abstract specification. We shall give no fewer than four alternative specifications. Two of them make use of the function *parts* which returns the set of partitions of a sequence. A little of the theory of *parts* is then presented.

# First specification

Three people to whom I posed the problem thought that what was wanted was the longest decreasing subsequence beginning with the first element. However, consideration of the sequence $[4, 1, 3, 2]$ quickly convinced them otherwise.

One straightforward specification, using just the predicate calculus, can be given in the following way. Let $x(0 \leq i < N)$ be the given sequence. Required is the subsequence of $x$ with indices $\phi(0 \leq i < n)$, where $\phi$ : $int \rightarrow int$ satisfies the conditions:

(i) (boundary conditions)

$$\phi(0) = 0 \quad \text{and} \quad \phi(n) = N$$

(ii) (solution is a subsequence)

$$(\forall i, j : 0 \leq i < j < n : 0 \leq \phi(i) < \phi(j) < N)$$

(iii) (solution is decreasing)

$$(\forall i, j : 0 \leq i < j < n : x(\phi(i)) > x(\phi(j)))$$

(iv) (solution is left-minimal)

$$(\forall j : 0 \leq j < n : (\forall k : \phi(j) \leq k < \phi(j+1) : x(\phi(j)) \leq x(k)))$$

The first two conditions say that what is wanted is a subsequence of $x$ beginning with the first element of $x$. The third condition says that this should be a decreasing sequence, and the fourth says that there is no "earlier" sequence and, in conjunction with the second boundary condition, that all drops are included.

The specification can be criticised on a number of grounds. It is long, somewhat clumsy, and a perfect example of the disease that David Gries and others have called "indexitis". Furthermore, conditions (iii) and (iv) are closely related and perhaps could be combined in some way.

# Second specification

Two quite different specifications arise depending on whether we focus on the decreasing or the left-minimal property of the solution. Suppose we keep the left-minimal property and ask for the *shortest* sequence of indices satisfying (i), (ii), and (iv). Then (iii) can be derived as a consequence. Moreover, with this approach it turns out we can avoid all mention of indices.

Say that a sequence $x$ of numbers is *left-minimal* if all elements of $x$ are at least as large as the first:

$$leftmin\ x\ =\ all\ (head\ x \leq)\ x$$

Here, *head x* returns the first element of *x* if *x* is a non-empty sequence, and $-\infty$ otherwise. The condition *all p x* holds if *p a* holds for every element *a* of *x*.

Suppose we partition the given sequence into left-minimal segments, choosing the shortest such partition. Then the drops will be the sequence of first elements of the segments in the partition:

$$drops\ =\ head* \cdot \sqcap_\#/ \cdot all\ leftmin\triangleleft \cdot parts$$

In this definition the binary operator $\sqcap_\#$ is parameterised by a linear ordering $<_\#$ which respects the length function $\#$:

$$\#x < \#y \Rightarrow x <_\# y$$

The value of $x \sqcap_\# y$ is the lesser of $x$ and $y$ according to $<_\#$. The important point is that there are many such orderings and, if it is not specified which, then the reduction $\sqcap_\#/xs$ is only guaranteed to return *some* shortest sequence in *xs*.

The second specification is shorter than the first but uses more machinery. However, it has the advantage that sufficient theory is known about partitions for a solution as a left reduction to be deduced immediately. This is gone into below.

# Third specification

In the third specification, suggested to me by Carroll Morgan, we formalise the idea that the required sequence is the "earliest" decreasing subsequence. For this we need a suitable ordering on sequences of indices. The usual lexicographic ordering is almost what is wanted, except that we must reverse the standard convention that initial segments of a sequence precede the sequence itself. Let $\sqcap_L$ be a binary operator that selects the lesser, under this modified lexicographic ordering, of its two arguments. Then we have

$$drops\ x\ =\ index\ x * \sqcap_L/ down\ x \triangleleft subs\ [0 \ldots \#x - 1]$$

where *subs z* returns the set of subsequences of $z$, the predicate *down x z* determines whether the $x$-values of the sequence of indices $z$ is strictly decreasing, and *index x i* returns the $i$-th element of $x$.

This style of specification has some attractions. First of all, one can argue as a general principle that if the "customer" has expressed his informal requirements in terms of indices, a specification that makes use of the customer's terms and concepts is to be preferred whenever possible. Second, the idea of the modified lexicographic ordering finds application in a number of other problems. For example, suppose we want to remove duplicate elements from a sequence, under the restriction that elements should be retained in order of first occurrence. We can define

$$remdup\ x\ =\ index\ x\ *\ \sqcap_L/\ nodups\ x \triangleleft\ subs\ [0 \ldots \#x - 1]$$

using exactly the same idiom as before.

## Fourth specification

Finally we mention one other specification of the problem, although whether one should call it a specification or a high-level algorithm is a matter of taste. The idea is to compute the running minimums of the sequence and remove duplicates. For example, the running minimums of the sequence $[5, 7, 5, 3, 4, 1, 7]$ are $[5, 5, 5, 3, 3, 1, 1]$ and removing duplicates yields $[5, 3, 1]$. The idea leads to

$$drops\ =\ remdup\ \cdot\ \sqcap/ * \cdot\ inits^+$$

where $inits^+\ x$ returns the sequence of non-empty initial segments of $x$ in order of increasing length.

To define $remdup$ we can use the specification given above. Alternatively, since duplicate elements always occur together in our problem, we can define a modified version

$$remdup'\ =\ head* \cdot \sqcap_\#/ \cdot\ all\ dup \triangleleft \cdot\ parts,$$

where

$$dup\ x\ =\ all\ (head\ x =)\ x$$

This reads: take the first elements of members of the shortest partition in which all components are sequences of the same element. Thus $remdup'$ removes *adjacent* duplicates only.

We give this fourth specification mainly to demonstrate that a surprising number of problems about sequences can be formulated in terms of partitions. It would be difficult to specify the operation of removing adjacent duplicates without recourse to partitions. Standard theory can be invoked to express $remdup'$ as a homomorphism:

$$remdup'\ =\ \oplus/ \cdot [\cdot]*$$

where

$$
\begin{aligned}
(x +\!\!+ [a]) \oplus ([b] +\!\!+ y)\ &=\ x +\!\!+ [a] +\!\!+ y, && \text{if } a = b \\
&=\ x +\!\!+ [a, b] +\!\!+ y, && \text{otherwise}
\end{aligned}
$$

The advantage of homomorphic characterisations such as this resides in the fact that they can be implemented by parallel computations in logarithmic time (in the number of $\oplus$ operations). In fact, $drops$ itself is a homomorphism on lists:

$$drops\ =\ \oplus/ \cdot [\cdot]*$$

where

$$x \oplus y \;=\; x + (< last\ x) \triangleleft y$$

We omit the proof that $\oplus$ is associative.

# Standard theory

There is some interesting theory behind the specifications given above. Consider again the two functions

$$
\begin{aligned}
drops &= head* \cdot \sqcap_\#/ \cdot all\ leftmin\triangleleft \cdot parts \\
remdup' &= head* \cdot \sqcap_\#/ \cdot all\ dup\triangleleft \cdot parts
\end{aligned}
$$

where

$$
\begin{aligned}
leftmin\ x &= all\ (head\ x \le)\ x \\
dup\ x &= all\ (head\ x =)\ x
\end{aligned}
$$

The two predicates *leftmin* and *dup* are clearly very similar. Both are prefix-closed, and *dup* is also suffix-closed. (Recall that a predicate $p$ is prefix-closed if $p\,[\,]$ holds and

$$p(x + y) \;\Rightarrow\; p\,x$$

for all $x, y$. Similarly, $p$ is suffix-closed if $p\,[\,]$ holds and

$$p(x + y) \;\Rightarrow\; p\,y$$

for all $x, y$. A predicate that is both prefix- and suffix-closed is said to be segment-closed.)

They also share another property. Say that a predicate $p$ is *robust* if

$$p(x + y) \;\wedge\; p(y + z) \;\Rightarrow\; p(x + y + z)$$

for all $x, y, z$ with $y \ne [\,]$. Both *leftmin* and *dup* are robust predicates. Another example of a robust predicate is *down*, the condition that a sequence is in descending order. On the other hand, the predicate *nodups*, which says that a sequence has no duplicated elements, is segment-closed but not robust.

The importance of robustness comes from the following observation: if $p$ is robust, then $all\,p \triangleleft\ parts\ x$ contains a *unique* shortest partition of $x$, all of whose components satisfy $p$. In fact, more is true. Say $ys$ is a *refinement* of $xs = [x_1, x_2, \ldots, x_n]$ if $ys = ys_1 + ys_2 + \cdots + ys_n$, where $ys_i$ is a partition of $x_i$ for $1 \le i \le n$.

**Lemma 1**    Suppose $p$ is robust. Then for all $x$, the set $P = all\,p \triangleleft\ parts\ x$ has a unique shortest member $xs$ and every element of $P$ is a refinement of $xs$.

**Proof**    Let $xs = [x_1, x_2, \ldots, x_n]$ be some shortest member of $P$ and $ys = [y_1, y_2, \ldots, y_m]$ another member of $P$. It is sufficient to show that $ys$

is a refinement of $xs$. It then follows that if $ys$ is another shortest member of $P$, then each of $xs$ and $ys$ is a refinement of the other, and so $xs = ys$.

If $ys$ is not a refinement of $xs$, then some element $y_i$ of $ys$ "spans" some segment $x_j, x_{j+1}, \ldots, x_k$, where $j < k$, of $xs$ in the sense that $x_j = u + v$, $x_k = w + t$, where $v, w \neq [\,]$, and $y_i = v + x_{j+1} + \cdots + x_{k-1} + w$. Using the robustness condition on $p$, we now obtain that $p(x_j + \cdots + x_k)$ holds, contradicting the assumption that $xs$ is a shortest element of $P$.
□

**Theorem 2**    Suppose $p$ is a robust prefix-closed predicate that holds for all singletons. Then

$$\sqcap_{\#}/ \cdot \ all\, p \triangleleft \cdot parts \ = \ \oplus \!\not\!\!\rightarrow_{[\,]}$$

where

$$
\begin{aligned}
[\,] \oplus a &= [[a]] \\
(xs + [x]) \oplus a &= xs + [x + [a]], \quad \text{if } p\,(x + [a]) \\
&= xs + [x] + [[a]], \quad \text{otherwise}
\end{aligned}
$$

**Proof**    We use the following recursive characterisation of *parts*:

$$
\begin{aligned}
parts\,[\,] &= \{[\,]\} \\
parts\,(x + [a]) &= \cup/ \ add\, a * \ parts\, x
\end{aligned}
$$

where

$$
\begin{aligned}
add\, a\,[\,] &= \{[[a]]\} \\
add\, a\,(xs + [x]) &= \{xs + [x + [a]],\ xs + [x] + [[a]]\}
\end{aligned}
$$

Let $f = \sqcap_{\#}/ \cdot \ all\, p \triangleleft \cdot \ parts$. We omit the proof that $f[\,] = [\,]$ (it uses the fact that $p[\,]$ holds). For the general case we argue:

$$f(x + [a])$$

=    {definition of $f$}

$$\sqcap_{\#}/ \ all\, p \triangleleft \ parts\,(x + [a])$$

=    {characterisation of *parts*}

$$\sqcap_{\#}/ \ all\, p \triangleleft \ \cup/ \ add\, a * \ parts\, x$$

=    {filter and reduce promotion}

$$\sqcap_{\#}/ \ (\sqcap_{\#}/ \cdot \ all\, p \triangleleft \cdot \ add\, a) * \ parts\, x$$

=    {claim (1); see below}

$$\sqcap_{\#}/ \ (\oplus a) * \ all\, p \triangleleft \ parts\, x$$

=    {claim (2); see below}

$$(\sqcap_{\#}/ \ all\, p \triangleleft \ parts\, x) \oplus a$$

$$= \quad \{\text{definition of } f\}$$

$$f \, x \oplus a$$

completing the proof.

The first claim invoked above is:

(1) $\qquad (\sqcap_\# / \cdot all \, p \triangleleft \cdot add \, a)* \;=\; (\oplus a)* \cdot all \, p \triangleleft$

Equation (1) can be proved from the fact that $p$ is prefix-closed and holds for all singletons. We omit details.

Abbreviating $all \, p \triangleleft parts \, x$ by $P$, the second claim is:

(2) $\qquad \sqcap_\# / \, (\oplus a) * P \;=\; (\sqcap_\# / P) \oplus a$

Restated, (2) is equivalent to the assertion that

(3) $\qquad (ys \sqcap_\# zs) \oplus a \;=\; (ys \oplus a) \sqcap_\# (zs \oplus a)$

for all $ys$ and $zs$ in $P$.

If we let $ys = \sqcap_\# / P$ and $zs$ be any element of $P$ with $zs \neq ys$ (and so $\#ys < \#zs$, by Lemma 1), then (3) follows from the inequality

(4) $\qquad \#(ys \oplus a) < \#(zs \oplus a)$

To establish (4) note, by Lemma 1, that $zs$ is a refinement of $ys$. In particular, the last element $z$ of $zs$ is a (non-empty) tail segment of the last element $y$ of $ys$. Since $p \, y$ holds, the robustness of $p$ gives

$$p(z \mathbin{+\mkern-8mu+} [a]) \;\Rightarrow\; p(y \mathbin{+\mkern-8mu+} [a])$$

Using the definition of $\oplus$, we can now establish (4). We omit further details.
□

A virtually identical theorem can be given for the case of a segment-closed predicate. The proof, which is omitted, follows the same lines except that the justification of (3) is trickier.

**Theorem 3** Suppose $p$ is a segment-closed predicate that holds for all singletons. Then there exists an ordering $<_\#$ such that

$$\sqcap_\# / \cdot all \, p \triangleleft \cdot parts \;=\; \oplus \mathbin{\not{\mkern-2mu\leftarrow}}_{[\,]}$$

where $\oplus$ is as defined in Theorem 2.

It is worth giving an example to show that the above results do not hold if the robustness or suffix-closure conditions are not met. Let $p$ be the predicate on sequences of positive integers which says that no element of the sequence is equal to its position in the sequence (counting from 0). We have that $p$ is prefix-closed, since

$$p(x \mathbin{+\mkern-8mu+} [a]) \;=\; p \, x \,\wedge\, a \neq \#x$$

and $p$ holds for all singletons, since no positive integer is zero. However, $p$ is neither robust nor suffix-closed. Theorems 2 and 3 fail for $p$ since, for example,

$$(\sqcap_\# /\ all\ p \lhd\ parts)[2,2,2,1]\ =\ [[2],[2,2,1]]$$

whereas

$$\oplus \not\!\!\to_{[\,]}[2,2,2,1]\ =\ [[2,2],[2],[1]]$$

as one can easily check.

Finally, we put the robustness and segment-closed conditions together to get a third theorem.

**Theorem 4**    Suppose $p$ is a robust and segment-closed predicate that holds for all singletons. Then

$$\sqcap_\# /\ \cdot\ all\ p \lhd\ \cdot\ parts\ =\ \oplus/\ \cdot\ [\cdot]*$$

where

$$
\begin{aligned}
(xs +\!\!+ [x]) \oplus ([y] +\!\!+ ys)\ &=\ xs +\!\!+ [x +\!\!+ y] +\!\!+ ys, && \text{if } p(x +\!\!+ y)\\
&=\ xs +\!\!+ [x] +\!\!+ [y] +\!\!+ ys, && \text{otherwise}
\end{aligned}
$$

and $[\,]$ is the identity element of $\oplus$.

The conditions on $p$ are needed to ensure that $\oplus$ is an associative operator.

## REFERENCES

[1] R. S. Bird. An introduction to the theory of lists. In M. Broy, editor, *Logic of Programming and Calculi of Discrete Design*, pages 3–42, Springer-Verlag, 1987. NATO ASI Series F, Vol. 36.

[2] R. S. Bird. Lectures on constructive functional programming. In M. Broy, editor, *Constructive Methods in Computing Science*, Springer-Verlag, 1989. NATO ASI Series F, Vol. 55.

Richard S. Bird,
Oxford University Computing Laboratory,
Programming Research Group,
8–11, Keble Road,
Oxford   OX1 3QD,
England.

# 5

# Architecture of Real-Time Systems

## Maarten Boasson

## Introduction

Large computer-assisted systems generally have shortcomings of one or more kinds: their functionality may differ from their specification, performance can be less than desirable, system flexibility is often unacceptably low, fault tolerance is all but absent, etc. Particularly worrying is the almost total lack of confidence in a system's correctness.

Such problems are generally attributed to a variety of reasons (some technical, many related to project management), but are in fact often related to insufficient separation between functional units. Although several design strategies exist to prevent excessive coupling between units at higher levels of abstraction, implementation of these units introduces dependencies that can hardly be avoided in classical architectures. More often than not, these implementation issues inadvertently (mis)guide the design of a system.

It is this influence of a system's architecture on its design that prompted the research described in this paper. Rather than inventing complex tools to allow greater independence from implementation issues, an architecture is developed that both significantly simplifies system implementation and greatly enhances system flexibility [2,3].

In this paper, only real-time, embedded systems will be considered. Typically, these systems build models of their environment by processing information obtained through a variety of sensing devices. Some systems also influence their environment by initiating actions in it. Examples are systems for chemical plant control, air traffic control, and factory automation.

The continuous nature of the environment at the same time demands high performance (decisions must be taken in real-time, i.e. in relation to the dynamics of the environment) and permits a slightly relaxed attitude towards synchronization and consistency (as opposed to e.g. banking systems ).

## Solution outline

Dependence of one program module on another is a direct result of the use of knowledge about that other module during its design. In order to minimize such dependencies it is therefore necessary to avoid the need for global knowledge as much as possible.

The obviously dangerous ways of using knowledge about other modules have long been recognized, and various design strategies for preventing them have been widely adopted [7,8]. However, the results of all these efforts have not been convincing.

This suggests that improvements in productivity, software re-use or system quality are hindered by other, less obvious ways of using global knowledge.

In classical architectures data communication between processes is meaningful only if data is communicated at precise moments between specific processes. This is a consequence of the predominant attention for processes, resulting in the loss of vital semantic information through data abstraction. Thus, organizing systems in such a way that correct interpretation of data is guaranteed requires extensive knowledge about all the processes involved as well as mechanisms to control process activity. Addressing, which is needed to achieve communication, and complex synchronization mechanisms, which are necessary to ensure correct timing, create strong dependencies between modules. The fact that the existing strategies for software development advocate rather than reduce this kind of dependence suggests that addressing and synchronization are at the root of the problem, given the meagre results obtained.

It is proposed to focus on data instead, and to hide details of how and where it is produced or consumed. This implies that data must have meaning independent of where and when it is used, that processes must control their own activity, and that no process can address another. For communication between processes to be possible, processes must explicitly state which data must be communicated rather than which other process is their partner in communication.

Other research has recently taken similar directions, although details are quite different from the approach taken here [6,9,11].

The benefits of this approach are many:

- a module designer no longer needs knowledge about other modules; only the commonly used data must be known. This clearly is very desirable for separate development of large systems, where design teams are often geographically dispersed;
- great improvements are expected in the area of correctness demonstration;

- modules, containing no references to any other module, are likely to be applicable in a large variety of configurations; apart from making re-use possible, this will simplify modifying and extending systems;
- by the same token, dynamic reconfiguration and graceful degradation in the presence of hardware failures become feasible.

Within the scope of real-time systems, there are but few disadvantages, most of which can be characterized in terms of necessary extra machinery. Some effort on the part of systems' designers will be required, however, to take full advantage of the architecture; there may be no trivial evolution from classical systems to the proposed architecture.

## The architecture

First, the essence of the architecture is described; then successive refinements and extensions are introduced, each dealing with a particular problem.

A system is composed of the following components:

**Applications**
These are independent, autonomous processes each of which implements part of the total system function. Applications are totally isolated one from another and their only interaction with the rest of the system occurs through a well-defined, rather narrow interface with so-called agents.

**Agents**
Each application interacts with exactly one agent. An agent embodies both storage capacity and processing facilities for handling all communication needs of the application it serves. All agents are identical and need no a priori information about either the applications or their communication requirements.

Communication between agents is possible through a message passing mechanism.

**Network**
Messages between agents are handled by the network connecting them. The network must support broadcasting, but should preferably also support addressing of agents. It is assumed to be of sufficient bandwidth to deal with all traffic situations.

It is immaterial whether applications, agents and the network share resources of the processing system or are distributed over a possibly wide variety of devices. We will assume that agents and applications are distributed, since this is the more interesting case. The non-distributed implementation is a trivial simplification.

All data that has relevance outside of an application must be labeled, so that there exists a one-to-one correspondence between a label and the interpretation of the data. Only the collection of labels used in a particular (sub)system and the details of the data structures associated with those labels must be known to application designers.

The communication needs of the applications are established by distributed action of their agents upon requests for, and delivery of data by the various consuming and producing applications, respectively. Thus, all communication decisions, which are normally taken during system design, are deferred until execution time. As a result, no application relies on the presence of any particular other application; the only requirement is that the necessary data is produced somewhere in the system.

The use of a unique label for data by both producing and consuming applications is enough for the agents to determine their communication obligations. Note that careful design of labeled data structures is essential for this mechanism to be practical. Neither of the extreme cases seems very useful: neither one label for the union of all data nor a separate label for each instance of data is desirable. More research in this area will be necessary before well founded guidelines can be formulated. However, in practical systems studied thus far, no serious problems were encountered.

Applications in the real-time domain deal mostly with data instances that represent continuous quantities: they are either observations sampled from the system's environment or derived from such samples. This allows us to slightly relax the consistency requirements normally associated with distributed systems: there is no need to synchronize applications in their processing of newly produced data, nor is it necessary to guarantee that all instances are processed.

Within bounds depending on the dynamic properties of the physical quantities represented, it is acceptable if at the same moment in time two applications process different samples from a single object, provided it is known at which moment the samples were valid.

Neither is it harmful if an application occasionally misses a sample: the continuity of the physical phenomena will permit the missing data to be synthesized, based on built-in models and accumulated information [4].

*For example, consider a system designed to support an air traffic controller. Typically, such a system will handle a number of so-called tracks, i.e. data structures representing the aircraft being controlled. One application will be responsible for maintaining these tracks while another will make the aircraft's position visible on a display. There is no need to ensure that both applications are synchronized in their processing of the data, within limits imposed by the speed and distance of the aircraft.*

This observation leads to the notion of subscription: application requests for data with a particular label (a "sort") are interpreted by the agents as requests for the currently available instance of that sort and for all future instances. The pair of agents involved in the communication between two applications therefore undertake to make newly produced data available at the consumer's agent as fast as possible, regardless of whether the consuming application actually requested a new instance. The agent serving the producer guarantees that data delivered to it is sent to all established consumer agents. On the other hand, of data for which no consumer is known, only the last instance is kept by the agent (a refinement to this scheme will be developed shortly).

The delay between a request for data and the actual delivery by the agent is thus minimized, except for the very first time the application issues such a request. In that case the agent broadcasts the request to all other agents and, during an application-specified period, awaits arrival of the requested data.

The delay between production and consumption of an instance is a function of the network and the agents and their activity as well as the relative timing of producer and consumer. No hard figures can be given for these delays, but, in general, sufficiently strong statistical estimates can be derived. Careful design of a system will permit dealing with so-called hard real-time constraints locally within a single application.

The architecture described thus far is sufficiently powerful for building simple systems. However, extra features are needed for designing complex systems. In the sequel these features will be introduced.

# Refinements

It is assumed that a new instance of a given sort invalidates the previous instance and that therefore buffering of more than one instance in the agents is unnecessary. For this assumption to always hold, the storage scheme in the agent needs to be refined, since otherwise a potentially unbounded number of sorts may be required.

An application may specify fields in the data structure associated with a given sort as so-called key-fields. An instance that differs in any of its key-fields from already stored instances will be stored separately. Only those new instances that are identical in all key-fields with already stored instances will replace the old ones. Obviously, this mechanism can lead to unbounded storage requirements; however, in all systems studied, limitations in the capacity to handle physical quantities induce acceptable upperbounds on the amount of storage needed.

This data-dependent storage mechanism is available to both producing and consuming applications. Although the data structures are common to producer and consumer, the definition of key-fields is strictly local and may be different for both.

A consumer may use the facility, for example, for traditional buffering in order to average out differences in processing time for different instances of the data.

A more elaborate use of this data-value induced storage structure is the possibility for a consumer to specify a hyperplane from which to extract data. The hyperplane is specified by constraints placed on the values of some (or all) of the key-fields when requesting data. Subsequent requests for data from the same hyperplane will produce successive instances of the sort with respect to a fixed order.

The need for such a mechanism at the producer's site is slightly more involved. Since no assumption can be made about the order in which applications become active, a consuming application must be able to obtain the currently valid instances of the collection of sorts consumed before beginning execution. Therefore, a producer may instruct its agent to store all instances that differ in the key-fields separately, so that at any time a complete set of relevant instances of the sort is available within the agent. Whenever an application becomes interested in the sort, the producer's agent will first send all stored instances and then send new instances as before.

*Consider again the air traffic control system introduced earlier. If for some reason a process becomes active (as a consumer of tracks) long after the rest of the system, it may have to obtain the complete set of all track data. If the agent serving the producer of tracks (assuming for simplicity's sake that there is only one producer) stores only the latest instance, the new consumer would somehow have to request the producing application to produce all old track data once again. This, although not necessarily against the principle of total isolation between applications, is highly undesirable. Thus, the producer may e.g. instruct its agent to use the aircraft-identity-field as a key.*

Not all data in a real-time system represents continuous quantities, however. The assumption that an instance invalidates a previous instance of the same sort is generally false in this case, and thus provisions are necessary to prevent overwriting. The key-field induced storage structure as described above is sufficiently general to achieve the desired properties, possibly through some extra effort by the designers.

Typically, with event-like data, i.e. data not representing a continuous quantity, the response time of the intended receiving application is important. Latency between the arrival of data from the network and reaction by the application depends on the behaviour of the application; one way of achieving fast response is for the consumer to frequently issue requests for data to its agent. This is attractive in its simplicity and effectiveness, but unpractical when more applications share a processor. Therefore, two primitives are available for requesting data from the agent: one that immediately returns (possibly stale) data, if available, and status information about the sort, and another that only terminates when fresh data is available (or an error is detected).

As a further extension to the basic primitives for requesting data, a consuming application may refine its interest in a sort through a boolean expression over certain fields of the sort. The agent will evaluate this so-called filter for each arriving instance and discard all those failing.

This facility is practical in that it allows applications' programmers to state declaratively which is the relevant subspace (of the space spanned by the sorts operated on by the application) in any given state of the application. Although such selections could also be handled by the application itself, a filter is preferable, since the agents can use the information for optimizing message traffic.

A more powerful use of the mechanism is to split too large a data stream over two or more identical applications, provided the application is such that this kind of parallelization is possible.

*Consider sensor-data processing as an example. Again in the case of air traffic control, a surveillance radar will generate massive amounts of raw data (depending on the situation in the environment, obviously). A tracking process will need to obtain all data belonging to the tracks it handles, but has no use for data relevant to other tracks. Filter expressions that permit data to be classified accordingly provide an elegant way of configuring a system in terms of number of tracks it can handle.*

# Extensions

A major problem in the design of systems of the kind considered here is the need to provide for upgrades and other modifications, preferably to be implemented without stopping the existing system. There are two distinct cases to be considered:

- either the addition uses only data already available in the existing system (e.g. a new display unit),

- or the addition can be effective only if existing applications are modified to either react to data produced by the new application or produce hitherto non-existent data, or both.

It is obvious that this architecture can deal with the first case without further refinements. Simply installing and starting the new application will be enough.

The second case, clearly, is more difficult. One special, but important, category of additions can be handled by the agents in an elegant way.

Consider the problem of upgrading a system by replacing an existing application with one that implements the same function, but with better performance. In many systems it is not possible to physically replace the old application with the new one, since this would require the system to be stopped. Simply adding the new application to the system does not solve the problem either, because the consumers will receive data from one of the producers, more or less at random. Moreover, if data from both producers were received (e.g. through very fast polling), the consuming applications would have to be designed for potentially more than one producer, which is unrealistic since improvements can not generally be foreseen.

A related problem is the need for redundancy in safety-critical systems, such as aircraft flight control systems. There, too, several applications performing the same function will be present while consumers of multiply-produced sorts should not need to be aware of this multiplicity. If one producer fails, the others will continue to produce the necessary data, and the consuming applications should be able to continue without interruption.

As will be shown, it is possible to hide from a consuming application the selection from instances of multiple producers performed by the agent serving the consumer.

A producer must associate an absolute quality indication with every produced instance of every sort (for each sort there must be a universal norm, used by all producing applications). A request for data from an application results in delivery of the best instance (with respect to the indicated quality), selected among the locally available instances from all producers of the sort.

In certain cases, it can be very useful to retain instances in the agent after delivery to the application, since this permits very high-quality, but old, data to be preferred over low-quality new data. Consumer applications therefore have control over the persistence of data stored in the agents through modifiers of the request primitives. Essential for this usage is that producers not only qualify the data, but also indicate how fast that quality deteriorates with age, since otherwise one very high-quality data instance could block all further data.

However, some applications need to receive instances from all producers, and therefore cannot rely on the selection mechanism of the agents (an example of such an application is one that correlates measurements from different sensors). This can simply be achieved by declaring the producer's agent identity (which is always inserted in the data by the producer's agent) to be a key-field. Note that the consumer need not know what the identities are.

Finally, each agent, upon detection of a failure in either the network, the other agents or the application, will generate both an instance of a predefined error sort and indicate the problem in the status associated with each application-agent interaction.

Only errors are indicated, since it is perceived useless to report correct functioning: reception of an acknowledgement of the arrival of a message by an addressed agent results in no action and is therefore a waste of both communication bandwith and processing capacity. On the other hand, upon failure to receive such an acknowledgement nothing useful can be done. If at the level of the applications handshake protocols are desired, it is the responsibility of the application designers to implement them.

## Status and further work

The architecture described has been formally specified [5] and implemented on a transputer [1] network, where one agent is mapped onto one transputer. Applications execute either in transputers, directly connected to their agents through transputerlinks (links, for short), or on traditional machines, connected to their agents through appropriate interfaces.

A routing algorithm, which makes communication between agents possible, uses the links connecting the agents. Characteristic of the algorithm is its totally dynamic nature, without any need for a priori information about the network topology [10]. The algorithm elegantly uses the broadcast, which is necessary for establishing communication needs, for building its internal routing tables. All changes in the network are automatically detected and incorporated in routing tables.

Appropriate error messages are generated and delivered to the agents as predefined data sorts, which may then be handled by applications as required.

Experience in developing applications for this architecture is very promising and appears to confirm the claim that problems with current systems are due largely to insufficient isolation between application processes.

The influence of the architecture on the application design strategy needs to be further investigated. Of particular interest is the relation between granularity, the number of data sorts needed and design complexity.

It is hoped that, based on a formal specification of the architecture and complete specifications of all the applications (which should be feasible, given the total isolation between applications), it will be possible to prove properties about the total system.

REFERENCES

[1] *The Transputer Databook.* Inmos, November 1988.

[2] M. Boasson. 1986. Patent applications in numerous countries.

[3] M. Boasson. Software design and system architecture. NATO AC/243 Panel 11, RSG01 Workshop "On Distributed System Design Methodology", Brussels 1987.

[4] M. Boasson. Modeling in real-time systems. *Computer Standards & Interfaces*, 6:107–114, 1987.

[5] J. A. Droppert, H. B. M. Jonkers, and H. M. H Loomans. *A COLD-1 Specification of SPLICE.* Technical Report, Natuurkundig Laboratorium Philips, August 1989.

[6] D. H. Gelernter. Generative communication in Linda. *ACM Transactions on Programming Languages and Systems*, 80–112, January 1985.

[7] D. Gries. *Programming Methodology. A Collection of Articles by Members of IFIP WG2.3.* Springer-Verlag, New York, 1978.

[8] C. Henry and M. Lott. La methode de conception MACH2. In *Proc. International Workshop Software Engineering & its Applications*, pages 301–320, Toulouse, December 1988.

[9] G.-C. Roman, H. C. Cunningham, and M. E. Ehlers. *A Shared Dataspace Language Supporting Large-scale Concurrency.* Technical Report WUCS-88-9, Washington University, March 1988.

[10] R. vd Land. *SPLICE Routing.* Technical Report, University of Leiden, Dept of Computer Science, July 1989.

[11] G. Wiederhold. *Data Engineering.* Stanford University, February 1988.

Maarten Boasson,
Hollandse Signaalapparaten BV,
P.O. Box 42,
7550 GD  Hengelo,
The Netherlands.

# 6

# The Use of a Formal Simulator to Verify a Simple Real Time Control Program

## Robert S. Boyer
## Milton W. Green
## J Strother Moore[1]

## Abstract

We present an initial and elementary investigation of the formal specification and mechanical verification of programs that interact with environments. We describe a formal, mechanically produced proof that a simple, real time control program keeps a vehicle on a straightline course in a variable crosswind. To formalize the specification we define a mathematical function which models the interaction of the program and its environment. We then state and prove two theorems about this function: the simulated vehicle never gets farther than three units away from the intended course and homes to the course if the wind ever remains steady for at least four sampling intervals.

Key Phrases: autopilot, formal specification, real time control, mechanical theorem-proving, modeling, program verification, simulation.

## 1 Background

Formal computer program verification is a research area in computer science aimed at aiding the production of reliable hardware and software. Formal verification is based on the observation that the properties of a computer program are subject to mathematical proof.

---

[1]The work reported here was performed while the authors were in the Computer Science Laboratory, SRI International, Menlo Park, California 94025.

This research was supported in part by NASA Contract NAS1-15528, NSF Grant MCS-7904081, and ONR Contract N00014-75-C-0816.

## 1.1   Program verification

Consider, for example, the following FORTRAN program for computing integer square roots using a special case of Newton's method[2]

```
          INTEGER FUNCTION ISQRT(I)
          IF ((I .LT. 0)) STOP
          IF ((I .GT. 1)) GOTO 100
          ISQRT = I
          RETURN
100       ISQRT = (I / 2)
200       IF (((I / ISQRT) .GE. ISQRT)) RETURN
          ISQRT = ((ISQRT + (I / ISQRT)) / 2)
          GOTO 200
          END
```

It is possible to prove, mathematically, that the program satisfies the following (informally stated) specification:

> If the program is executed on a machine implementing ANSI FORTRAN 66 or 77 [13,1], and the input to the program is a nonnegative integer representable on the host machine, then the program terminates, causes no arithmetic overflow or other run time error, and the output is the largest integer whose square is less than or equal to the input.

Such program proofs are generally constructed in two steps. In the first step, the code and its mathematical specifications are transformed into a set of formulas to be proved. In the second step the formulas are proved using the usual laws of logic, algebra, number theory, etc. For an introduction to program verification, see [9,10,11,2].

Because the mathematics involved in program verification is often tedious and elementary, mechanical program verification systems have been developed. One such system is described in [8]. That system handles a subset of ANSI FORTRAN 66 and 77 and has verified the above mentioned square root program [6], among others.

To admit mechanical proof, the specifications must be written in a completely formal notation. For example, in the square root example the specification of the program's output is:

$$j^2 \leq i < (j+1)^2 \quad \& \quad 0 \leq j,$$

---

[2]V. Kahan, of U.C. Berkeley, reports that the algorithm was in fact advocated by Heron of Alexandria before 400 A.D.

where it is understood that $i$ refers to the value of the FORTRAN variable I on input to ISQRT and $j$ refers to the value returned by ISQRT.

## 1.2 Boebert's challenge

The square root program is a good example of a programming task in which the specification "obviously" captures the intent of the designer. At issue is whether some algorithm satisfies the specification. However, for some programming tasks it is difficult to find mathematical specifications that obviously capture the designer's intention. Real time control programs are an especially important example of such tasks.

To spur the interest of the program verification research community to consider such specification problems, a version of the following problem was proposed by Earl Boebert.[3] Consider the task of steering a vehicle down a straightline course in a crosswind that varies with time. Let the desired course be down the $x$-axis of a Cartesian plane (i.e, towards increasing values of $x$). Suppose the vehicle carries a sensor that, in each sampling interval of time, reads either $+1$, $0$, or $-1$, according to whether the vehicle is to the left of the course ($y > 0$), on the course ($y = 0$), or to the right of the course ($y < 0$). Suppose also that the vehicle has some actuator that can be used to change the $y$-component of its velocity under the control of some program reading the sensor. Problem: state *formally* what it means to keep the vehicle on course and, for some particular control program, prove *mechanically* that the program satisfies its high level specification.

Observe that the problem necessarily involves a specification of the environment with which the program interacts. Furthermore, unlike the square root example, what is desired is not merely a description of a single input/output interchange between the environment and the program but rather the effects of repeated interchanges over time.

In this paper we describe one solution to Boebert's challenge. Our method involves writing a simulator for the system in formal logic. We present our formal simulator after explaining informally the model and control program we will use.

# 2 The informal model

The mechanized logic into which we cast the model provides the integers and other discrete mathematical objects but does not provide the ratio-

---

[3]Honeywell Systems and Research Center, 2600 Ridgway Parkway, Minneapolis, Minnesota 55413.

nals or reals.[4] Thus, we will measure all quantities, e.g., time, wind speed, vehicle position, etc., in unspecified integral units.

We ignore the $x$-axis and concentrate entirely on the $y$-axis. For example, we do not consider the $x$-component of the vehicle's velocity and we ignore any $x$-component of the wind velocity. Thus, our model more accurately represents a one-dimensional control problem, such as maintaining constant temperature in an environment where the outside temperature varies, or maintaining constant speed, as in an automobile's "cruise control."

We measure the wind speed, $w$, in terms of the number of units in the $y$-direction the wind would blow a passive vehicle in one sampling interval. We assume that from one sampling interval to the next $w$ can change by at most one unit. Some such assumption is required since no control mechanism can compensate for an external agent capable of exerting arbitrarily large instantaneous forces. Thus, we assume that the wind speed at time $t+1$ is the speed at time $t$ plus some increment, $dw$, that is either $-1$, $0$, or $1$.

$$w(t+1)  =  w(t) + dw(t+1)$$

where

$$dw(t+1)  =  -1, 0, \text{ or } 1.$$

We permit the wind to build up to arbitrarily high velocities.

At each sampling interval the control program may increment or decrement the $y$-component of its velocity (e.g., by turning a rudder or firing a thruster). We let $v$ be the accumulated speed in the $y$-direction measured as the number of units the vehicle would move in one sampling interval if there were no wind. We make no assumption limiting how fast $v$ may be changed by the control program; our illustrative program changes $v$ by at most $\pm 5$ each sampling interval. We permit $v$ to become arbitrarily large.

The $y$-coordinate of the vehicle at time $t+1$ time is thus its $y$-coordinate at time $t$, plus the accumulated $v$ at time $t$, plus the displacement due to the wind at time $t+1$:

$$y(t+1)  =  y(t) + v(t) + w(t+1).$$

The sensor reading at any time is the sign of $y$, $sgn(y)$. The control program changes $v$ at each sampling interval as a function of the current sensor reading (and perhaps previous readings). Our illustrative control program is a function of the current reading and the previously obtained reading:

$$v(t+1)  =  v(t) + deltav(sen1, sen2)$$

---

[4]This is not a limitation of mechanized logic in general. Several existing mechanical theorem-provers, e.g., those of Bledsoe's school [4,3], and the MAXSYMA symbolic manipulation system [12], provide analytic capability.

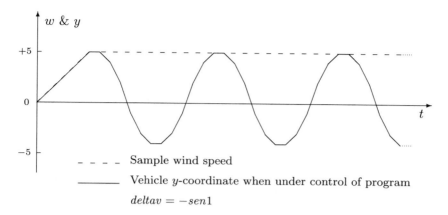

FIGURE 1.

where

$$sen1 = sgn(y(t+1))$$
$$sen2 = sgn(y(t)),$$

and *deltav* is the mathematical function specifying the output of the control program.

## 3 The control program

It is instructive to consider first the control program with the following specification:

$$deltav(sen1, sen2) = -sen1$$

A steadily increasing wind can blow the vehicle arbitrarily far away from the $x$-axis. Furthermore, should the wind ever become constant, the vehicle begins to oscillate around the $x$-axis. See Figure 1.

The control program we consider includes a damping term that also causes the vehicle to resist more strongly any initial push away from the $x$-axis.

$$deltav(sen1, sen2) = -sen1 + 2(sen2 - sen1).$$

See Figure 2 for an illustration of the behavior of the vehicle under this program.

The following trivial FORTRAN program implements this specification in the following sense. If SEN1 is the current sensor reading, *sen1*, and the

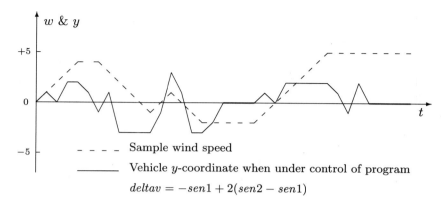

FIGURE 2.

value of the global variable SEN2 is the previous sensor reading, $sen2$, and $sen1$ and $sen2$ are both legal sensor readings, then at the conclusion of the subroutine, the global ANS is set to $deltav(sen1, sen2)$ and the global SEN2 is set to $sen1$.

```
SUBROUTINE DELTAV(SEN1)
INTEGER SEN1, SEN2, ANS
COMMON /DVBLK/SEN2, ANS
ANS = ((2 * SEN2) - (3 * SEN1))
SEN2 = SEN1
RETURN
END
```

Proving that the program satisfies its specification is, of course, trivial. At issue is whether the vehicle stays on course.

By observing the behavior of the simulated vehicle under several arbitrarily chosen wind histories we made two conjectures about the behavior of the vehicle:

1. No matter how the wind behaves (within the constraints of the model), the vehicle never strays farther than 3 units away from the $x$-axis.

2. If the wind ever becomes constant for at least 4 sampling intervals, the vehicle returns to the $x$-axis and stays there as long as the wind remains constant.

How can we state such specifications in a form that makes them amenable to mechanical proof?

# 4 Formalizing the model

To state the conjectures formally we must formalize the model of the control program and its environment. We will define this model as a function in the same mechanized mathematical logic used by the FORTRAN verification system [8]. The logic and a mechanical theorem-prover for it are completely described in [5].

The syntax of the logic is akin to that of Church's lambda-calculus. If $f$ is a function in the logic and $e1$ and $e2$ are two expressions in the logic, then we write $(f\ e1\ e2)$ to denote the value of $f$ on the two arguments $e1$ and $e2$.[5] The more traditional equivalent notation is $f(e1, e2)$. For example, suppose ZPLUS is defined as the usual integer addition function. Then (ZPLUS X Y) is how we write X+Y. Thus, (ZPLUS 3 $-10$) $= -7$.

Our formal model is expressed as a recursive function that takes two arguments, a description of the behavior of the wind over some time period and the initial state of the system. The value of the function is the final state of the system after the vehicle has traveled through the given wind under the direction of the control program. Thus, the recursive function may be thought of as a simulation of the model.

Formally, we let states be triples, $<w, y, v>$, containing the current wind speed, $y$-position of the vehicle, and accumulated $v$. The function STATE, of three arguments, is axiomatically defined to return such a triple, and the functions W, Y, and V are defined to return the respective components of such a triple. Thus, the expression (STATE 63 $-2$ $-61$) denotes a state in which the wind speed is 63, the $y$-position of the vehicle is $-2$, and the accumulated $v$ is $-61$.

```
(W (STATE 63 -2 -61)) = 63
(Y (STATE 63 -2 -61)) = -2
(V (STATE 63 -2 -61)) = -61
```

The function NEXT.STATE is defined to return as its value the next state, given the change in the wind and the current state. The formal definition of NEXT.STATE is:

```
Definition.
(NEXT.STATE DW STATE)
    =
```

[5]This choice of notation is convenient because most symbols used in program specification are user-defined and do not have commonly accepted names or symbols. Furthermore, the uniformity of the syntax makes mechanical manipulation easier.

```
(STATE (ZPLUS (W STATE) DW)
       (ZPLUS (Y STATE) (V STATE) (W STATE) DW)
       (ZPLUS (V STATE)
              (DELTAV (SGN (ZPLUS (Y STATE)
                                  (V STATE)
                                  (W STATE)
                                  DW))
                      (SGN (Y STATE)))))).
```

The definition of next state follows immediately from our equations for $w(t+1)$, $y(t+1)$ and $v(t+1)$. The function DELTAV is formally defined as was *deltav* in our informal model.

The behavior of the wind over $n$ sampling intervals is represented as a sequence of length $n$. Each element of the sequence is either $-1$, $0$, or $1$ and indicates how the wind changes between sampling intervals. Formally, a sequence is either the empty sequence, NIL, or is an ordered pair $<hd, tl>$, where $hd$ is the first element of the sequence and $tl$ is a sequence containing the remaining elements. Such pairs are returned by the function CONS of two arguments. The functions HD and TL return the respective components of a nonempty sequence, and the function EMPTYP returns true or false according to whether its argument is an empty sequence.

In general we are not interested in wind behaviors other than those permitted by our model. Thus, we define a function that recognizes when an arbitrary sequence consists entirely of $-1$'s, $0$'s, and $1$'s.

```
Definition.
(ARBITRARY.WIND LST)
  =
(IF (EMPTY LST)
    T
    (AND (OR (EQUAL (HD LST) -1)
             (EQUAL (HD LST) 0)
             (EQUAL (HD LST) 1))
         (ARBITRARY.WIND (TL LST))))).
```

(ARBITRARY.WIND LST) returns true or false according to whether every element of LST is either $-1$, $0$, or $1$. The definition is recursive. The empty sequence has the property. A nonempty sequence has the property provided that (a) the HD of the sequence is $-1$, $0$, or $1$, and (b) the TL of the sequence (recursively) has the property.

The recursive function FINAL.STATE takes a description of the wind and an initial state and returns the final state:

```
Definition.
(FINAL.STATE L STATE)
   =
(IF (EMPTY L)
    STATE
    (FINAL.STATE (TL L)
                 (NEXT.STATE (HD L) STATE))).
```

Note that FINAL.STATE is recursively defined and may be thought of as simulating the state changes induced by each change in the wind.

We can now state formally the two properties conjectured earlier.

```
Theorem. VEHICLE.STAYS.WITHIN.3.OF.COURSE:
(IMPLIES (AND (ARBITRARY.WIND LST)
              (EQUAL STATE
                     (FINAL.STATE LST
                                  (STATE 0 0 0))))
         (AND (ZLESSEQP -3 (Y STATE))
              (ZLESSEQP (Y STATE) 3)))
```

This formula may be read as follows. If LST is an arbitrary wind history and STATE is the state of the system after the vehicle has traveled through that wind starting from the initial state $<0,0,0>$, then the $y$-coordinate of STATE is between $-3$ and 3. Put another way, regardless of how the wind behaves, the vehicle is never farther than 3 from the $x$-axis.

A formal statement of the second conjecture is:

```
Theorem. VEHICLE.GETS.ON.COURSE.IN.STEADY.WIND:
(IMPLIES (AND (ARBITRARY.WIND LST1)
              (STEADY.WIND LST2)
              (ZGREATEREQP (LENGTH LST2) 4)
              (EQUAL STATE
                     (FINAL.STATE (APPEND LST1 LST2)
                                  (STATE 0 0 0))))
         (EQUAL (Y STATE) 0))
```

The function STEADY.WIND recognizes sequences of 0's. The function APPEND is defined to concatenate two sequences. The formula may be read as follows. Suppose LST1 is an arbitrary wind history. Suppose LST2 is a history of 0's at least 4 sampling intervals long. Note that the concatenation of the two histories describes an arbitrary initial wind that eventually becomes constant for at least 4 sampling intervals. Let STATE be the state of the system after the vehicle has traveled through the concatenation of those two wind histories. Then the $y$-position of the vehicle in that final STATE is 0.

# 5   Proving the conjectures

The foregoing conjectures can be proved mathematically. Indeed, they have been proved by the mechanical theorem-prover described in [5]. The key to the proof is that the state space of the vehicle can be partitioned into a small finite number of classes. In particular, any state $<w, y, v>$ reachable under the model starting from $<0, 0, 0>$ can be put into one of the following classes according to $y$ and $w + v$:

| $y$ | $w + v$ |
|:---:|:---:|
| $-3$ | 1 |
| $-2$ | 1 or 2 |
| $-1$ | 2 or 3 |
| 0 | $-1$, 0 or 1 |
| 1 | $-2$ or $-3$ |
| 2 | $-1$ or $-2$ |
| 3 | $-1$ |

The automatic theorem-prover is incapable of discovering this fact for itself. Instead, the human user of the theorem-prover may suggest it by defining the function (GOOD.STATEP STATE) to return true or false according to whether STATE is in one of the 13 classes above, and then commanding the theorem-prover to prove the following key lemma:

```
(IMPLIES (AND (GOOD.STATEP STATE)
              (OR (EQUAL DW -1)
                  (EQUAL DW 0)
                  (EQUAL DW +1)))
         (GOOD.STATEP (NEXT.STATE DW STATE))).
```

This theorem establishes that if the current state of the vehicle is one of the "good states" and the wind changes in an acceptable fashion then the next state is a good state. After proving this lemma (by considering the cases and using algebraic simplification) the theorem-prover can establish by induction on the number of sampling intervals that the final state of the vehicle is a good state. From that conclusion it is immediate that the $y$-position of the vehicle is within $\pm 3$ of the $x$-axis.

The proof of the second theorem is similar. The vehicle is in a good state after LST1 has been processed. But if the vehicle is in a good state and the wind remains steady for four sampling intervals, it is easy to show by cases and algebraic simplification that the vehicle returns to the $x$-axis with $w + v = 0$. But in this case, it stays on the $x$-axis as long as $w$ stays constant.

# 6    Comments on the model

We have proved that the simulated vehicle stays on course under each of the infinite number of different wind histories to which it might be subjected under the model.

Just as the user of a square root or sorting subroutine must look at the specifications to determine whether the subroutine is suitable for his application, so too should the user of this control program. In particular, it is up to the user to determine whether the restrictions on the wind behavior and the model of the environment are sufficiently realistic for his application.

Here are a few of the more obvious oversimplifications:

- Real sensors sometimes give spurious readings due to vibration or other forms of disturbance. The program makes no allowance for such noise.

- No consideration is given to motion or forces in the $x$- or $z$-directions. Furthermore, no consideration is given to the orientation of the vehicle with respect to its preferred direction of travel.

- The model of the physics of the vehicle is too simple. The use of discrete measurement is unsatisfying but perhaps justifiable under suitable assumptions about scale. But many physical aspects of real control situations have been ignored: inertia, reaction times of the actuators, response time of the vehicle, maximum permitted $g$-forces.

Allowance for noise in the sensors can be handled by existing program verification technology. For example, if one provides redundant sensors and employs a signal select algorithm based on software majority voting, DELTAV can be rewritten to use an algorithm such as that verified in [7] to compute the majority sensor reading (if any). The proof that the vehicle stays on course can then be carried over directly if one is willing to assume that at each sampling interval a majority of the sensors agree.

However, the other two unrealistic aspects of our problem are more difficult to handle. While it is easy to define more sophisticated formal simulators it may well be practically impossible to prove interesting properties mechanically. Certainly the proof paradigm used here, depending as it did on the existence of a small partitioning of the state space, will not suffice for more sophisticated models.

# 7    Conclusion

We have illustrated how a formal simulator can be used to specify in a machine readable form the high level intention of a simple real time control program. We have also shown how such a program has been mechanically proved to satisfy its specifications.

Simulation programs are used today to test a variety of applications programs. Among the applications that come to mind are real time control, scheduling, and page fault handling in operating systems. Such simulators suffer the inaccuracy introduced by finite precision arithmetic and resources and in addition offer only the testing of the applications program on a finite number of situations.

Formal simulators are mathematical functions. They need not be realizable on machines and thus need not suffer resource limitations. In addition, formal simulators theoretically permit mechanical analysis of the behavior of the system in an infinite number of possible situations.

**Note added in proof.**
For references to the subsequent development and use of the mechanized logic and theorem prover described here see *A Computational Logic Handbook*, by Robert S. Boyer and J Strother Moore, Academic Press, 1988.

## REFERENCES

[1] American National Standards Institute Inc. *American National Standard Programming Language FORTRAN.* Technical Report ANSI X3.9-1978, American National Standards Institute Inc., 1430 Broadway, N.Y. 10018, April 1978.

[2] R. B. Anderson. *Proving Programs Correct.* John Wiley & Sons, New York, 1979.

[3] A. M. Ballantyne and W. W. Bledsoe. *Automatic Proofs of Theorems in Analysis using Non-standard Techniques.* Technical Report ATP-23, Department of Mathematics, University of Texas at Austin, July 1975.

[4] W. Bledsoe, R. Boyer, and W. Henneman. Computer proofs of limit theorems. *Artificial Intelligence*, 3:27–60, 1972.

[5] R. S. Boyer and J. S. Moore. *A Computational Logic.* Academic Press, New York, 1979.

[6] R. S. Boyer and J. S. Moore. *The Mechanical Verification of a FORTRAN Square Root Program.* SRI International, 1981.

[7] R. S. Boyer and J. S. Moore. *MJRTY — A Fast Majority Vote Algorithm.* Technical Report ICSCA-CMP-32, Institute for Computing Science and Computer Applications, University of Texas at Austin, 1982. Also available through Computational Logic, Inc., Suite 290, 1717 West Sixth Street, Austin, TX 78703.

[8] R. S. Boyer and J. S. Moore. A verification condition generator for FORTRAN. In R. S. Boyer and J. S. Moore, editors, *The Correctness Problem in Computer Science*, Academic Press, London, 1981.

[9] R. Floyd. Assigning meaning to programs. In *Mathematical Aspects of Computer Science, Proceedings of Symposia in Applied Mathematics*, pages 19–32, American Mathematical Society, Providence, Rhode Island, 1967.

[10] J. C. King. *A Program Verifier*. Ph.D. thesis, Carnegie-Mellon University, 1969.

[11] Z. Manna. *Mathematical Theory of Computation*. McGraw-Hill Book Company, New York, 1974.

[12] J. Moses. Algebraic simplification: a guide for the perplexed. *ACM*, 1971. 2nd Symposium on Symbolic and Algebraic Manipulations.

[13] United States of America Standards Institute. *USA Standard FORTRAN*. Technical Report USAS X3.9-1966, United States of America Standards Institute, 10 East 40th Street, New York 10016, 1966.

Robert S. Boyer,
Department of Computer Sciences,
The University of Texas at Austin,
Taylor Hall 2.124,
Austin, Texas 78712–1188,
U.S.A.


Milton W. Green,
440 Sherwood Way,
Menlo Park, California 94025,
U.S.A.


J Strother Moore,
Computational Logic, Incorporated,
1717 West Sixth Street, Suite 290,
Austin, Texas 78703–4776,
U.S.A.

# 7

# Exploring the Future: Trends and Discontinuities

## Donald W. Braben

## Preamble

I first met Professor Dr. Edsger W. Dijkstra on 7 November 1980 on a cold day in Eindhoven. He met me at my hotel and we drove to his home in Nuenen where he introduced his wife Ria. We had coffee and began to talk about mathematics. As our conversation developed, it became clear that although I had had a formal training in physics and in the sort of mathematics physicists use, there was so much of mathematics I did not understand. Over the years, Edsger Dijkstra has illuminated a world of beauty and elegance whose existence I had not suspected. Thanks to his patience and skill, I have seen some of the light, but it is still a mystery why his critics seem to believe that additional lighting in general is not required.

The perfection of mathematical beauty is not only an aesthetic duty. The potential value of mathematics to computing science is immense. One of the most important concerns in computing is the derivation of means by which computers and other electronic machines may be programmed to execute tasks precisely as required. At present, the complete behaviour of a significant computer program cannot be predicted before it is used in practice. The traditional approach to this problem is to accept the situation, to debug the program when it is assembled, and to take a statistical approach to its completion. Thus, the program is tested until most of the errors or bugs have been identified and a point of diminishing returns has been reached in the search for the rest. At that stage, the prospective failure of the system in normal operation is accepted as a reasonable risk even though there can be no indication whether the failure will be of minor or major importance.

Edsger Dijkstra and his colleagues have shown that a sequence of steps in a streamlined mathematical proof can be likened to moving on a logical staircase of even pitch with each step following inevitably from the last. These techniques have already been applied to the production of computer programs on a modest scale, and the programs are themselves a proof that their specification has been achieved. The disadvantages of some traditional approaches to mathematics which include imaginative creations produced like rabbits out of a hat would seem to be immediately obvious in the context of computing science.

At present, the techniques by which new discoveries in mathematics are assessed and scaled up for significant application in the computing market place are still in the early stages of their evolution. But progress is being made, and eventually it seems that these techniques will be as well developed as they are now in the natural sciences.

My meeting with Edsger Dijkstra arose as part of my Venture Research interests. Venture Research is a crusade to show that intellectual pursuits can have tangible value if free rein is given to creativity. In effect, Venture Research is an attempt to identify the science and technology that will be important in the future. We do not use crystal balls, but instead try to build up close associations with some of those people who are challenging received wisdom and whose own ideas may help to shape the future.

The following piece is a guide to exploring the future in general. It is dedicated, with gratitude, to my friend and colleague Edsger W. Dijkstra on the occasion of his 60th birthday.

# Exploring the future: trends and discontinuities

Somerset Maugham once said that it was bad enough to know the past: it would be intolerable to know the future. I would agree. Life would be very boring if the future rolled towards us on a pre-ordained scroll. Fortunately however, we neither have that problem nor one remotely like it.

My purpose is to explore the future. But before embarking on their travels explorers need to know something of the terrain they might encounter even though they should be ready for anything. Someone prepared for the arctic would have little success in the tropics. The future is, of course, a concept which has no existence outside our imaginations. Our experience is limited to the present, that is the set of events taking place around each one of us, an experience that is strongly influenced both by our perception of what has gone before, and by the objectives we wish to achieve at some later time. The prediction game would seem therefore to be an ideal intellectual playground. If we look long enough into the future, we're unlikely to be remembered if we're wrong, whereas if we turn out to be right, and around, we can always remind people of our amazing prescience. What I would like to do is to outline some of the rules of the game as I see it, and how they may be used to hedge one's bets on the future no matter what it may throw at us.

For short timescales our expectations can be very high and bordering on certainty. Typically, we may set out by car to arrive at a destination at some later time. However, we might be delayed unexpectedly by a parade that had been planned for months, to find the police dealing with the traffic jam they had expected and of which we were a part. With sufficient information, this type of disruption to future expectations can be avoided. But there are some events whose effects are not necessarily predictable even though we may know everything there is to know about the factors which eventually give rise to them.

One of these is the weather. As late as the 1960's, it was widely believed that if we had enough information on temperatures, currents, pressures, etc. over a wide enough area, and had computers adequate to the task of compiling the information, we could predict the main features of weather with reasonable accuracy over long periods — weeks or months ahead. We now know that this is not the case, not because of limitations to our technology or to our lack of commitment, but because of the intrinsic properties of complex systems.

There are many aspects of complex systems we do not understand, but we do know that they have a broad spectrum of types of behaviour. At one extreme, there are systems like the sun and its planets whose future motions can be predicted with high accuracy over timescales of decades. We can say with confidence for example that there will be a total eclipse of the sun visible in the South West tip of England (weather permitting!) at 10.12 Universal Time on 11th August 1999. Tide tables for any port in the world are available over long periods. At the other extreme, there is the chaotic and unpredictable behaviour that would be shown by say feathers in a wind, or indeed even one.

Until a few decades ago, it was thought that the smooth, continuous predictable behaviour of systems like the planets was quite ubiquitous. The ideas behind the evolution of the species are a classical example of this way of thinking. Today's animals and plants are thought to be the result of a continual adjustment over a very long time "to numerous, successive, slight and favourable variations" in Darwin's language. Many scientists believe that the diversity of species we see today can be smoothly traced back to a small number of common roots. But serious cracks are appearing in this neat structure. The extinction of the dinosaurs 60 million years ago is a well known source of problems, as is the sudden appearance in the plant world of flowering species. Our present understanding of evolution is strongly influenced by genetic factors, and it would seem that the genotype (the genetic information stored in the chromosomes) might indeed change very slowly and perhaps even continuously. However, dramatic and abrupt changes to the phenotype (the physical structure and physiological make-up of the individual) can be caused by quite small changes to the mechanisms regulating gene expression or interaction. On Nature's timescales therefore, evolution would seem to be no more predictable than the weather.

Far from being ubiquitous, it would seem therefore that predictably varying systems are the exception rather than the rule. Predictable variation seems to be a consequence of behaviour dominated by one overwhelming factor — like the sun for the motion of the planets, or the earth's gravity for the motion of a shell through the air. For such systems the contributions of all other factors can be treated as small perturbations and hence behaviour can be predicted reasonably accurately. These ideas are not restricted to the natural sciences. On the social scene too, the behaviour of a powerful or dominant individual or cartel can often be reasonably well predicted, and in economics, it is easier to predict the price of commodities for which there are no substitutes —drinking water for example— than those for which substitutes abound.

But, the world is rarely as simple as this. In general, a more accurate view would be of a complex network of interacting systems of comparable importance. For non-linear systems like these we know that they are anything but simple. Although there may be timescales over which their behaviour will be approximately linear, there will be others where relatively unimportant events can conspire to produce big changes. For the latter, it will usually be possible to predict limits on the behaviour we will see, but within those limits behaviour will generally be totally unpredictable, no matter how much information we may have.

The pendulum is a simple example. Set gently swinging, its motion is predictable and hence it can be used as an accurate clock. But if the pendulum bob is made of iron say, and we place a simple system of magnets underneath the bob, then the motion becomes unpredictable and the system ceases to have value as a clock — although it may be a good executive toy. This will be true even if we know the precise strength of the magnets and the strength of the earth's gravitational field.

On a much wider canvas, East-West relations have been so institutionalised as to be relatively stable and therefore mainly predictable. But how many times in history have apparently stable relationships between major powers been reduced to turmoil (or non-linearity) by some small and localised disturbance?

This non-linear picture should be familiar. For the sake of a nail a shoe was lost, for the sake of a shoe a horse was lost, for the sake of a horse the battle was lost etc. A football team may have won ten matches in succession and then succumb to the weakest opposition. Stock exchange prices may go through periods of stability only to be followed by erratic behaviour. The weather next week in Britain might be almost anything from glorious sunshine to freezing fog. Indeed, in the light of all this it is remarkable that the linear view of the world has survived for so long.

Those who would explore the future need to understand these things. For the technological, and also for the economic and other social matters, we should know that even if we understand the basic determinants of behaviour with respect to gravity say, or to inflation, and even barring major catastrophes like war, we should know that the next few decades will contain discontinuous events ranging in importance from the minor to the dominating, and there is no way of knowing in advance what they will be or how they might affect our lives.

The last quarter of a century has been rocked by many upheavals. The electronic revolution, the two oil shocks, glasnost and perestroika are just some of the major discontinuities we could not see in the 1960's. Each has led, or is leading, to radical changes in our lives, and to the destruction of the careful and rational assessments of the long term planners. But eventually we adjust, and that which was once radical becomes so commonplace as to establish a new trend, whence the planners set to work again with apparently undiminished enthusiasm. They will, of course, be determined not to repeat their previous errors in failing to anticipate the last upheaval. And their confidence will be increased by the seemingly endless analyses following in the wake of major change which often conclude that if we had been more careful and read the various writings on the walls we should not have been taken by surprise. The logic of this sort of hindsight can be difficult to resist especially as there is usually a latter day Nostradamus somewhere who can claim to have predicted the momentous event (Black Monday for example), but no one would listen. There is indeed a vast literature, and it is not surprising that some of it might turn out to have been accurate. Consider the following prediction made by Bouladon in 1967[2]:

> "The last buses (electric, of course, because of the antipollution laws of about 1980) will have disappeared about 1990. Labour costs will have come to represent 90% of the operating cost of buses, which will still be plagued by strikes of the dissatisfied drivers. Buses will finally become too heavy and cumbersome to be able to be integrated into the centrally and electronically-guided traffic flow...."

Many of us in London in 1989 suffered a plague of strikes by dissatisfied bus drivers and others, but there is nothing new in that, and what of the rest of those predictions, each one of which would have been quite plausible in 1967? And staying for the moment with motor transport, who would have predicted, say in the 1920's, that the development of cheap mass-produced cars which readily provided self-contained, private and mobile environments, would lead especially among the young to radical changes in acceptable sexual behaviour?

It is extraordinary how often the view is expressed that the future is unpredictable, and how often that statement is followed by the words — but..., either literally or metaphorically. I believe this is because it is deeply engrained in us all to rebel against the idea that some types of knowledge are forbidden to us, particularly as we can plausibly argue from hindsight how a particular set of events came to pass.

There is also the idea that things change very slowly. There is the French proverb "The more things change the more they are the same". We know that some trends in modern life can be very resistant to change. The motor car came into general use at the turn of the century, but even in what was then the developed world, horse drawn transport was still widely used 4 or 5 decades later, and today animal traction is widespread elsewhere. The characteristics of the internal combustion engine with its exhilarating acceleration, high speed and long range are such that it is unlikely to be replaced by electrical power for many decades even in the highly unlikely event that the recent claims for cold fusion turn out to be reality, or for any other reason cheap and portable sources of electric power become available. But the dangers of extrapolation are there for all to see. Cavalry regiments were still operating in early stages of the second World War. War is always tragic, but although today we would all regard any comparisons between the relative military capabilities of horses and tanks as grotesque, there were some generals who thought otherwise. More recently, the second oil shock and the succeeding rapid increases in petrol prices led to predictions of a decline in the use of the motor car. However, the opposite has occurred. One of the legacies of that prediction was a decision to reduce the London orbital motorway —the notorious M25— from 8 to 6 lanes, a decision which will now cost a billion dollars to rectify.

In the light of all this, is there a future for long term planning? Strictly speaking, I would argue that there is not. But what is to be done, because the implementation of so many policies of industry and government in areas such as motorways, power stations, oil fields and new production lines have lead times of a decade or so? For matters of population or of the global environment even longer lead times are indicated. Nevertheless, to attempt to plan, in the sense of arranging our procedures or actions beforehand, when we can be virtually certain over such time-scales that some unforeseen factor could blow us off course, would seem to be futile. Instead, it would seem to be more appropriate to prepare for the future, rather than to plan for it.

To return again to the second World War, Winston Churchill visited Paris on 16 May 1940 to discuss what could be done to prevent the imminent fall of France. General Gamelin described the deteriorating situation, and as Churchill related[1]:

"he spoke for perhaps 5 minutes without anyone saying a word. When he stopped there was a considerable silence. I then asked: "Where is the strategic reserve?" and, breaking into French which I used indifferently (in every sense): "Ou est la masse de manoeuvre?" General Gamelin turned to me and, with a shake of the head and a shrug, said "Aucune" —there is none . . . . Past experience carries with its advantages the drawback that things never happen the same way again. Otherwise, I suppose life would be too easy . . . . I was dumbfounded. I admit that this is one of the greatest surprises I have had in my life."

Notwithstanding the subtle differences in the meanings of these two words —planning and preparation— policies based on planning for the future will be significantly different from those based on preparation. For technology, companies whose research policies are based on planning might be expected to concentrate on research commissioned in support of specific business development. Inevitably, research of this type will be seen as a cost or an overhead to be reduced as much as possible, rather than an investment. On the other hand, those companies who would wish to be prepared would in addition to these specific research programmes invest in research aimed at increasing flexibility of response. The proportion of the total technological effort that should be committed to providing this strategic reserve for the corporation as a whole will of course be a difficult question to resolve. Planners are familiar with discounted cash flow techniques for assessing the value of future investments, techniques which can be readily modified to take technological factors into account. In the electronics sector say, there is rapid change and technological discount rates are high. In sectors like construction say, they will be relatively low. However, in general these questions will be no more difficult in principle than questions on exchange rates, inflation, fluidity, debt-equity ratios and the like which determine the financial health and flexibility of an organisation. Technological strategic reserves are no less important than the financial, not only for companies, but for governments too, but how often are these two issues given equal priority at the highest levels of decision-making?

How can we provide for flexibility? My response would be that since we cannot be confident about anything in the future, we should concentrate on understanding the present. In science, as in other areas, our experience should tell us that even those fields generally supposed to be well understood can reveal new and important structure to those who challenge conventional wisdom. And in addition there are so many things that are not understood at all. In these circumstances, it seems astonishing that so much of our academic research is being steered towards refining the known as if 1989 were some special year in the history of scientific discovery. Little of our present understanding will survive intact to 2039, and new understanding usually provides new options, and hence increased flexibility.

Every advanced country commits considerable resources to the support of basic research. Levels of support vary, but policies governing the ways research is selected are much the same everywhere. Increasingly, scientists are required to demonstrate the relevance of their proposed work to the development of a field, and to exploitable outcome. These policies work well in those fields whose importance is reasonably well established. The great majority of scientists, perhaps more than 90%, are content with current policies although at times they may be critical of the levels of support available in their field. However, when scientists realise that understanding is seriously flawed or incomplete, or they become aware of research opportunities which do not fit easily into an established field, or when they otherwise wish to do something unconventional, they often have considerable difficulty in getting support, particularly if resources are generally in short supply.

There will be new discoveries like monoclonal antibodies, and warm superconductivity if we provide total intellectual freedom to those people who can reasonably demonstrate that they need it: for example, to scientists who are both seriously dissatisfied with the status quo and who can credibly outline a viable alternative, or to scientists who have noticed something significant we have all ignored. Unfortunately, these rare endeavours require equally imaginative approaches to the support of research, but the trend today is in the opposite direction, towards a uniformity both of funding policies, the research programmes being supported, and the fostering of productivity rather than creativity. As heretical endeavours are rare, the cost of providing support for them will always be inexpensive — so inexpensive indeed that any nation can afford to support them all. They will yield a return in terms of flexibility and new options which cannot be achieved by targeted investments alone, and so help to achieve competitive advantage even from a relatively weak economic position.

*Acknowledgements*: I would like to acknowledge helpful discussions with Herbert Huppert at Cambridge, Harry Swinney at Texas, and my colleagues at Venture Research in London.

# REFERENCES

[1] Winston Churchill. *The Second World War.* Volume II, The Reprint Society, 1951. Page 52.

[2] C. H. Waddington. *Tools for Thought.* Palladin, 1977. Page 205.

Donald W. Braben,
Venture Research,
BP International Limited,
Britannic House,
Moor Lane,
London,   EC2Y  9BU,
U.K.

# 8

# On a Renewed Visit to the Banker and a Remarkable Analogy

## Coen Bron

In the mid-1960's I was in the fortunate circumstances to exchange my ill-chosen future in chemistry for an apprenticeship in Computing Science by joining Edsger Dijkstra's group which was —at that time— deeply involved with the design and implementation of the T.H.E. Operating System. I deliberately put in the dots where Edsger may have just as deliberately left them out in his original publication[4], to suggest that the E. stands for Eindhoven and there was no attempt to suggest that this system was to be the final word in this area (a position that now seems to be claimed by Unix, whether we like it or not).

The main impact on my personal career was the recognition that —in spite of the T.H.E. System's beautiful structure— the tools that we had used in its implementation were far from adequate. Operating systems are (also) just programs, and so any higher level approach to writing programs may be applied to the construction of systems programs as well. Knowledge of assembly language should be necessary only for those responsible for the code generating part of a compiler, and high level languages should provide the loop-holes to escape from the (sometimes too) strictly enforced rules to enable the writing of those parts of an Operating System that otherwise would necessitate an overall escape to assembly language.

$$\star \quad \star \quad \star$$

Before I digress any further from my intended visit to the Banker, let me return to those memorable years of the T.H.E. System. These were the years of the invention of concepts and paradigms that have already immortalized Edsger Dijkstra: Co-operating Sequential Processes, Semaphores with $P-$ and $V-$operations[2] (they are the only concept for which a one letter mnemonic to me seems acceptable[5]), the Banker's Algorithm[6], the Dining (quintuple of) Philosophers[3].

The Banker's Algorithm models the decision by an Operating System when a process requests non-preemptable resources, whether allocating the request can be done without the risk of an ensuing deadlock. If more than one resource type is involved, the problem is modelled by a banker who can lend his customers units of several non-exchangeable currencies. The Banker must decide if, when granting a loan, he can be sure to get all of his money back eventually. The customers are well behaved in the sense that they are accepted as such when they can give an upper limit for the number of units of different currencies they will want to borrow at any moment, and they will —given their maximal loan— return everything in due time.

For several years, teaching a course in Operating Systems at the University of Twente, I have presented the algorithm in the following form:

```
TYPE process = 1..??;
     units   = ...; {Say: some vector, each element
                          denoting the number of units of
                          one particular currency}

VAR claim, loan:  ARRAY [process] OF units;
    {claim[i] "+" loan[i] = max[i]}

FUNCTION safe({if} p: process
               ;{given} sop: SET OF process
                {having loan > 0}
               ;{wanting} request: units
               ;{while available} cash: units
               );
{Determines if, given that the initial state of the
 Banker is safe, a safe state would result if the
 request were granted
}
   VAR otherp: process;

BEGIN {assert: request "<=" claim[p]}
      DO ( NOT claim[p] "<=" cash) AND
         exists( otherp, {in} sop
                 , {satisfying}
                   claim[otherp] "<=" cash - request
               )
      -> cash :+ loan[otherp]; sop :- [otherp]
      OD
   ;  safe := claim[p] "<=" cash
END;
```

This algorithm provides a slight speed-up, compared to the way it is commonly presented in text books on Operating Systems, because it judges the situation safe (with respect to the request) if a termination order of processes can be found that leads to an amount of cash sufficient to grant the remaining claim of the requesting process. The rationale being that, if — starting from a safe state— the requesting process can terminate, the state —after termination— will certainly be safe. Nevertheless, the algorithm is $O(n^2)$, if $n$ is the number of processes involved.

Recently I attended a seminar on Real-Time Systems, where I had a chance to deliver a lecture closely related to the subjects I learned during my stay in Eindhoven[1]. At this seminar, one of the other speakers discussed a scheduling algorithm with the self-explanatory name *Earliest Deadline First*. The way in which this problem was (or rather: could have been) tackled reminded me so much of the Banker's Algorithm that I decided to see if there was indeed an analogy. The remainder of this contribution is devoted to this question.

Let me first step into the loan office and suggest an improvement in the performance of the algorithm for the single currency case. The Banker will maintain a list of its clients in order of increasing claim. (The fact that this is a total ordering when only a single currency is involved is crucial to what is to follow.) Any index occurring in any of the subsequent formulae will be an index in that list. The safety condition for any client $i$ in the list is:

$$s_i \geq c_i$$

with

$$. \quad s_i \;=\; cash + (\mathbf{S}\,j : 0 \leq j < i : l_j)$$

This obviously represents a safe situation, because the order of the list is a termination sequence for the Banker's clients. If we have a list of clients, ordered by increasing claim in which a client violates the safety condition, the state of the Banker is, equally obvious, unsafe because the violating client can not get its claim granted under the assumption that loans monotonically increase before they are fully returned.

Finally, *any* safe state for the Banker can be described by a sequence of clients satisfying the safety condition, not necessarily arranged in order of increasing claim. From such a sequence, we can (conceptually by interchanging neighbouring pairs) derive an *ordered* sequence which does not violate the safety condition, since the swap has no effect on the sequence following the pair, nor on that part of the sequence preceding the pair (because only the sum of the loans is involved). And it will be clear (even without calculation) that the swap does not violate the safety condition of either of the swapped clients.

We may conclude that the Banker's ordered list satisfying the safety condition is a necessary and sufficient condition for a safe state. Any request by a client for an increased loan, thereby reducing its claim, can be handled by moving the requesting client closer to the front of the list and checking that the new list still satisfies the safety condition. This must be an $O(n)$ algorithm.

What are the effects of granting a request on the sequence of clients maintained by the Banker?

- because the claim of the requesting client decreases, the sequence must be rearranged. Conceptually, this is again done by interchanging the requesting client with its left neighbour repeatedly.
- Granting the request does not affect the clients following the requesting client (r.c.), because the decrease of cash is compensated by the increased loan of the r.c.
- Granting does not affect the safety condition of any of the clients with which the r.c. is swapped, because the decrease in cash is (more than) compensated by the *additional* term in the sum due to the r.c.
- However, the argument that two neighbouring clients may be swapped leading from a safe state to a safe state is no longer valid since, with a decreased amount of cash, clients preceding the r.c. in the sequence may not fulfill the safety condition. This means that clients preceding the r.c. after it has been inserted in its new position must satisfy the safety condition with $(cash - r)$ substituted for $cash$.

Combining the above observations, we may conclude that the state after granting a request $r$ by a r.c. is safe if we can find an insertion position $i$ in the remaining sequence of clients, being the largest value of $i$ satisfying:

$$(\mathbf{A}\, j : 0 \le j < i : (s_j - r) \ge c_j \ \wedge \ c_j < cr)$$

where $cr$ is the remaining claim of the r.c. (i.e. $c_p - r$ if the r.c. originally occupies position $p$ in the sequence).

The algorithm to determine this value of $i$ is straightforward because the above invariant is trivially established for $i = 0$:

```
i,    cr,        sum    :=
0,    cp - r,    cash - r
;DO (sum >= c[i]) AND (c[i] < cr)
    -> sum :+ l[i]; i :+ 1
 OD
;safe := (c[i] >= cr) AND (sum >= cr)
```

The first term in the result is due to the ordering requirement on the sequence of clients, and the second one is necessary to ensure the safety condition of the r.c. itself. Note that the term $c_i \le c_p$ provides a natural bound for the search since the r.c. appears in the list at position $p$ and here we have $\neg(c_p < cr)$ (since $cr = c_p - r$).

$$\star \qquad \star \qquad \star$$

Now let me return to my original motive to reconsider the Banker's algorithm: the scheduling of real-time tasks, for which a deadline $(d)$ and an amount of computation time $(t)$ is known. It takes little imagination to see that time-multiplexing of these tasks won't do any good to the termination times of tasks, so the only problem left is to schedule the order in which the tasks are completed, all meeting their deadlines. A *schedule* will be defined as an order in which tasks are performed (this may be viewed as a sequence of tasks). A *feasible schedule* is a schedule in which each task is completed before its deadline. A schedule is therefore feasible if all tasks in the schedule satisfy:

$$s_i \leq d_i$$

with

$$s_i \;=\; (\mathbf{S}j : 0 \leq j \leq i : t_j)$$

As in the Banker's algorithm, any feasible schedule can be transformed into a feasible schedule ordered by increasing deadline (conceptually by swapping neighbouring tasks in the schedule, for which $d_i > d_{i+1}$). It is easily verified that this swap maintains feasibility, because:

(a)      $s_i \;\;\leq\; d_i$
(b)      $s_{i+1} \leq d_{i+1}$
(c)      $d_i \;\;> \; d_{i+1}$

After the swap, it suffices to show for the two swapped tasks:

$$s_{i+1} \leq d_i, \qquad \text{which follows from (a) and (c)}$$
$$s_i - t_i + t_{i+1} \leq d_{i+1}, \quad \text{which follows from (b) and } t_i > 0.$$

So any feasible schedule can be realized by treating tasks in the order of increasing deadline. This also demonstrates that, if a schedule arranged by increasing deadline is not feasible, there exists no feasible schedule for this set of tasks, for if there was, it could be rearranged into an ordered schedule, which is unique, but *not* feasible.

For the sake of completeness we should consider (sub)sets of tasks sharing the same deadline. In this case the ordered schedule is not unique. But it is easily seen that its feasibility is not influenced by the internal order of tasks with the same deadline. There is an analogy with the Banker's ordered list of clients: the safety condition of the list is not affected by the internal order of clients with equal claims.

So far, the analogy with the Banker is complete: the test on a safe state, or the feasibility of a schedule is reduced to a test on a unique, ordered sequence of clients or tasks respectively. What analogy is there for the real-time scheduling problem with the Banker's case of a resource request? This must be due to an attempt to rearrange the schedule, and the only incentive to do so would be for a deadline to be moved to an earlier point in time. In other words, if we have a feasible schedule, any task is allowed to make a request for an earlier deadline, which will be granted if the resulting schedule (in its canonic form) is still feasible.

The algorithm is, again, straight forward: the requesting task can (again conceptually) be swapped with its neighbours until its deadline has reached its insertion position. Note that the swap now only affects the feasibility of the swapped neighbours, and not that of any of the tasks following the requesting task in the sequence. For a feasible schedule, the insertion position $i$ is characterized by the largest possible set of tasks that can be swapped with the requesting task, i.e. by the smallest value of $i$ satisfying:

$$(\mathbf{A}\, j:\ 0 \le i < j < p:\ s_j + t_p \le d_j\ \wedge\ d_j > d_p - r)$$

which together with $(sum = s_i + t_p)$ forms the invariant of the following algorithm:

```
i,         dr,          sum :=
p - 1,     d[p] - r,    "s[p]"
;DO (sum <= d[i]) AND (d[i] > dr)
       -> sum :- t[i]; i :- 1
OD
;feasible := (d[i] <= dr) AND (sum <= dr)
```

As in the safety result of the Banker, the first term ensures that the insertion of the new deadline dr maintains the ordering, and the second term ensures that the deadline of the requesting task will be met.

**Note 1:**    We have written "s[p]" to suggest that if the value of this sum is not stored for every task, it may have to be recalculated.

**Note 2:**    It may be desirable to have a "sentinel" task with $t_0 = 0$ and $d_0 = 0$, or to add an additional term (ensuring $i \ge 0$) to the boolean expressions, to ensure proper termination of the above algorithm. This was not necessary for the Banker.

REFERENCES

[1] C. Bron. *Controlling Real-Time Systems with Parallel Processes.* University of Newcastle upon Tyne / ICL Joint International Seminar on the Teaching of Computing Science: "Real-Time Systems", 5-8 Sept. 1989.

[2] E. W. Dijkstra. Co-operating sequential processes. In F. Genuys, editor, *Programming Languages*, Academic Press, 1968.

[3] E. W. Dijkstra. Hierarchical ordering of sequential processes. *Acta Informatica*, 1:115–138, 1971.

[4] E. W. Dijkstra. The structure of the "THE"–multiprogramming system. *Comm. ACM*, 11(5):341–346, 1968.

[5] E. W. Dijkstra. To hell with "meaningful identifiers". 1989. Technical Note EWD 1044, University of Texas, Austin.

[6] A. N. Habermann. *Harmonious co-operation of abstract machines.* Ph.D. thesis, Technical University, Eindhoven, 1967.

Coen Bron,
Department of Computing Science,
Rijksuniversiteit Groningen,
P.O. Box 800,
9700 AV Groningen,
The Netherlands.

# 9

# On Bounded Buffers: Modularity, Robustness, and Reliability in Reactive Systems

## Manfred Broy

## Abstract

Several specifications of bounded buffers are given. The specifications are discussed with respect to the question of robustness and reliability. It is shown that under certain conditions bounded buffers can be composed such that we obtain bounded buffers again. Thus a functional, composition-oriented treatment of communicating systems is demonstrated by a simple example.

## 1 Introduction

A reactive system is a component of a distributed system that reacts or interacts with its environment. The purpose of this paper is

(a) to analyse the behavior of systems and components in exceptional cases, where certain requirements expected by the components with respect to the environment are not fulfilled,

(b) to search for a simple concept of composition such that specifications of systems and system components can be composed from smaller parts.

Buffers are certainly among the most fundamental modules in communicating systems. They are a simple test case for specification and design techniques suggested for distributed systems. In the following we give functional specifications of bounded buffers. We prove simple lemmas showing that the sequential composition of bounded buffers yields bounded buffers again.

## 2 Specifying simple bounded buffers: buffers as stream processing functions

We define the set $M^\omega$ of streams over a given (finite or infinite) set $M$ by

$$M^\omega = M^* \cup M^\infty$$

Here $M^*$ denotes the finite sequences and $M^\infty$ denotes the infinite sequences (total mappings from the set of natural numbers to $M$).

On streams we use the following functions (here $\bot$ is used as a pseudo element for expressing divergences; we write $M^\bot$ for $M \cup \{\bot\}$):

$$\mathit{ft} : M^\omega \to M^\bot, \quad \mathit{rt} : M^\omega \to M^\omega, \quad .\&. : M^\bot \times M^\omega \to M^\omega.$$

Here $\mathit{ft}$ stands for first and $\mathit{rt}$ stands for rest. Note that $m \& x$ denotes the stream obtained by putting $m$ in front of $x$. We denote the totally undefined ("empty") stream by $\varepsilon$ and the stream consisting of just the element $x \in M$ by $<x>$. We assume the following axioms for streams (for $d \in M$):

$$\bot \& c = \varepsilon, \quad \mathit{ft}.\varepsilon = \bot, \quad \mathit{ft}(d \& c) = d, \quad \mathit{rt}.\varepsilon = \varepsilon, \quad \mathit{rt}(d \& c) = c.$$

To avoid too many brackets we often write $f.x$ instead of $f(x)$ for function application. By $s\,\hat{}\,r$ we denote the concatenation of streams $s$ and $r$.

The set $M^\omega$ is partially ordered by the prefix ordering $\sqsubseteq$. For two streams $s, r$ we write $s \sqsubseteq r$, if $s$ is a prefix of $r$. Formally we have

$$s \sqsubseteq r \quad \text{iff} \quad \exists u \in M^\omega : s\,\hat{}\,u = r$$

The set $M^\omega$ is complete with respect to the prefix ordering $\sqsubseteq$, i.e. every directed set $S \subseteq M^\omega$ has a least upper bound $\sup S$ in $M^\omega$. A function

$$f : M^\omega \to M^\omega$$

that is monotonic with respect to the prefix ordering is called *prefix continuous* if for every directed set $S$ we have:

$$f.\sup S = \sup \{f.x : x \in S\}$$

Clearly then, the empty stream $\varepsilon$ is the least element with respect to the prefix ordering. We use two further auxiliary functions on streams. The function

$$.\copyright. : \mathcal{P}(M) \times M^\omega \to M^\omega$$

filters out the elements from a given set in a given stream (let $m \in M$, $S \in \mathcal{P}(M)$):

$$\begin{aligned}
S \copyright \varepsilon &= \varepsilon, \\
m \in S \Rightarrow S \copyright (m \& x) &= m \& (S \copyright x), \\
\neg(m \in S) \Rightarrow S \copyright (m \& x) &= S \copyright x.
\end{aligned}$$

The expression $\#s$ gives the number of elements in stream $s$. Formally we have

$$\# : M^\omega \to \mathbb{N} \cup \{\infty\}.$$

This function can be specified by the following simple equations (let $m \in M$):

$$\#\varepsilon = 0, \quad \#(m\,\&\,x) = 1 + \#x.$$

Note that $\#x$ may be infinite.

A bounded buffer can be understood as a module to which we send data to be placed in the buffer (if the buffer is not full) and to which we send requests to take some data back from the buffer (if the buffer is not empty). As long as we send data only if the buffer is not full and requests only if the buffer is not empty, then the required behavior of a buffer seems obvious. If we try to place data on a buffer that is full or try to take data from a buffer that is empty, the behavior of a buffer is less obvious. We speak of the buffer's behavior in *exceptional* cases.

We assume a given set $D$ of data elements. For buffers we just consider two classes of actions:

- $p.d$ denotes the action of putting the data element $d$ in the buffer,
- $t.d$ denotes the action of taking the data element $d$ from the buffer.

By $T$ we denote the set $\{t.d : d \in D\}$ and by $P$ we denote the set $\{p.d : d \in D\}$.

According to an input/output-oriented view, a bounded buffer can be modelled by a stream-processing function which takes streams of data and requests as input and produces a stream of data labeled by $t$. Requests are represented by "?". We consider prefix-continuous functions of the form

$$f : (P \cup \{?\})^\omega \to T^\omega$$

The predicate $buf(f,n)$ specifies, whether the stream processing function $f$ models the behavior of a buffer which is bounded by $n$ and which is initially empty. For specifying $buf$ we make use of the predicate $rely$ specified by

$$
\begin{aligned}
rely(x,n) \quad &\equiv_{df} \\
\forall z : z \sqsubseteq x \;&\Rightarrow\; \#(\{?\}\copyright z) \leq \#(P\copyright z) \leq n + \#(\{?\}\copyright z).
\end{aligned}
$$

$rely(x,n)$ specifies whether the input stream $x$ fulfils the restrictions assumed by a bounded buffer: data is only put in the buffer if it is not full and data is only requested from the buffer, if the buffer is not empty.

$$
\begin{aligned}
buf(f,n) \quad &\equiv_{df} \\
\forall x : rely(x,n) \;&\Rightarrow\; strip.f.x \sqsubseteq strip.x \,\wedge\, \#f.x = \#(\{?\}\copyright x).
\end{aligned}
$$

The function

$$strip : (T \cup P \cup \{?\})^\omega \to M^\omega$$

transforms a stream $x$ of actions and "?" into the stream of data elements contained in it. It is specified by the following equations:

$$\begin{aligned}
strip.\varepsilon &= \varepsilon, \\
strip(?\,\&\,s) &= strip.s, \\
strip(t.d\,\&\,s) &= strip(p.d\,\&\,s) = d\,\&\,strip.s
\end{aligned}$$

Note that trivially we have for $m \leq n$:

$$rely(x, m) \;\Rightarrow\; rely(x, n).$$

The predicate *rely* defines a (safety) condition for the input given to the buffer. Only if the input $x$ fulfils the condition $rely(x, n)$, does the function $f$ with $buf(f, n)$ produce output following the rules of a buffer. The proposition $rely(x, n)$ asserts that in the input stream $x$ data output is never requested (by "?") in a state where the buffer is empty nor is data input given to the buffer in a state where the buffer is full. The monotonicity of $f$ guarantees in addition that, if a prefix $z$ of $x$ fulfils $rely(z, n)$, then $f$ behaves like a buffer for $z$, i.e. $f.z$ is prefix of $f.x$ and fulfils the buffer specification (independent of the question of whether $rely(x, n)$ is valid). As soon as the condition is not fulfilled nothing is specified about the further output of the buffer.

Note the similarity to the rely/guarantee concept in [5]. The predicate *rely* defines the rely-condition. Only as far as the rely condition is fulfilled for the input, is the required buffer condition guaranteed for the output.

We may formalize the notion of a buffer being full or being empty by predicates on finite input streams $x$:

$$\begin{aligned}
rely(x, n) &\;\Rightarrow\; full(x, n) &\equiv\; (\#(P\copyright x) = \#(\{?\}\copyright x) + n), \\
rely(x, n) &\;\Rightarrow\; empty(x, n) &\equiv\; (\#(P\copyright x) = \#(\{?\}\copyright x)).
\end{aligned}$$

We may even extend the predicates *full* and *empty* to exceptional cases by assuming that input in conflict with the rely conditions is ignored.

$$\begin{aligned}
rely(x, n) \;&\wedge\; \neg rely(x\char`^{<}a{>}, n) \;\Rightarrow\; \\
full(x\char`^{<}a{>}\char`^ y, n) &= full(x\char`^ y, n) \qquad \wedge \\
empty(x\char`^{<}a{>}\char`^ y, n) &= empty(x\char`^ y, n).
\end{aligned}$$

With these axioms for *full* and *empty* we can prove:

$$rely(x, n) = \forall z \in (P \cup \{?\})^* : \begin{aligned}(z\char`^{<}?{>} \sqsubseteq x &\;\Rightarrow\; \neg empty(z, n)) \;\wedge \\ (z\char`^{<}p.d{>} \sqsubseteq x &\;\Rightarrow\; \neg full(z, n))\end{aligned}$$

The proof proceeds as follows: We have $\neg rely(x, n)$, iff there exists some $z$ where $z\char`^{<}a{>} \sqsubseteq x$ with $rely(z, n)$, but $\neg rely(z\char`^{<}a{>}, n)$. We have to consider two cases: if $a = ?$ then according to the definition of *rely* we have $\#(\{?\}\copyright z\char`^{<}?{>}) > \#(P\copyright z)$ and thus $\#(\{?\}\copyright z) = \#(P\copyright z)$ which is by definition $empty(z, n)$. The proof for $a = p.d$ is carried out by analogy.

We may also compare buffers with different capacity.

**Lemma**    For finite streams $x$ we have

$$n \geq m \; \wedge \; full(x, n) \; \Rightarrow \; full(x, m),$$
$$n \geq m \; \wedge \; empty(x, n) \; \Rightarrow \; empty(x, m).$$

**Proof**    Induction on the length of $x$.
The specification $buf(f, n)$ is equivalent to the following equation:

$$\forall x, y : \; P©x = x \; \wedge \; \#x < n \; \Rightarrow$$
$$f(<p.d>^\wedge x^\wedge <?>^\wedge y) = t.d \,\&\, f(x^\wedge y) \; \wedge \; f(<p.d>^\wedge x) = \varepsilon$$

This equivalence can be proved by first showing that *rely* is characterized by the following equations:

$$\neg rely(? \,\&\, y, n),$$
$$P©x = x \; \wedge \; \#x < n \; \Rightarrow$$
$$rely(<p.d>^\wedge x^\wedge <?>^\wedge y, n) = rely(x^\wedge y, n) \; \wedge \; rely(<p.d>^\wedge x, n),$$
$$P©x = x \; \wedge \; \#x \geq n \; \Rightarrow \; \neg rely(<p.d>^\wedge x^\wedge y, n),$$

Based on this we may prove the equivalence of the specification above to $buf(f, n)$ by induction on the length of $<p.d>^\wedge x^\wedge <?>^\wedge y$.

The question of what a bounded buffer should do if used in an incorrect way seems crucial. If a bounded buffer obtains some data when it is already full (and similarly if data is requested when it is empty), it may show reactions according to the following policies:

(1) it may collapse (diverge) or show any behavior (chaos),

(2) it may ignore the input or issue some message that the input cannot be accepted due to the current state of the buffer and just delete the incorrect input,

(3) it may save the input and react to it as soon as it gets into a state where it is ready for that.

Possibility (1) is specified above. Possibility (2) is considered in the following by the predicate *robust_buffer*

$$robust\_buffer(f, n) \; \equiv_{df} \; buf(f, n) \; \wedge$$
$$\forall x : \; rely(x, n) \; \wedge \; \neg rely(x^\wedge <a>, n) \; \Rightarrow \; f(x^\wedge <a>^\wedge y) = f(x^\wedge y).$$

Possibility (3) is chosen in [9]. It is somewhat artificial since it means that a bounded buffer would be able to store an unbounded number of open requests.

**A Note on Compositionality**
A simple additional requirement that we may wish to have for buffers might be that if we compose two bounded buffers with capacities $n$ and $m$ resp., then we obtain a bounded buffer with capacity $n + m$. A simple form

of composition is functional composition. Functional composition between bounded buffers represented by stream processing functions is not possible, since domain and range do not coincide. Thus we may extend our considerations to functions of the form

$$f : (T \cup P \cup \{?\})^\omega \to (T \cup P \cup \{?\})^\omega$$

With the specification above unfortunately the property formalized by $(*)$ does not hold.

$(*) \qquad buf(f, n) \ \wedge \ buf(g, m) \ \Rightarrow \ buf(g \circ f, \ n + m)$

The reason is simple. To obtain the property $(*)$ we have to develop a specification that specifies the behavior of $f$ (and $g$) also in cases where input is from $T$. Moreover, exceptional cases for the first buffer have to be signalled to the second one and properly treated. Accordingly, we now try to give a more sophisticated description of bounded buffers that meet these requirements.

# 3 Buffers with better compositional properties

We strengthen the specification for a bounded buffer represented by stream processing functions to the following specification. We consider functions of the form

$$f : (T \cup P \cup \{?\})^\omega \to (T \cup P \cup \{?\})^\omega$$

that fulfil the specification for buffers as formulated above:

$P©x = x \ \wedge \ \#x < n \ \Rightarrow$
$\quad f(<p.d>\hat{\ }x\hat{\ }<?>\hat{\ }y) = t.d \& f(x\hat{\ }y) \ \wedge \ f(<p.d>\hat{\ }x) = \varepsilon$

and in addition show the compositional property described above. For obtaining compositionality we require for $f$ and $g$, where we assume $buf(f, n)$ and $buf(g, m)$, that $g \circ f$ behaves like a buffer of capacity $n + m$:

$P©x = x \ \wedge \ \#x < n + m \ \Rightarrow$
$\quad (g \circ f)(<p.d>\hat{\ }x\hat{\ }<?>\hat{\ }y) = t.d \& (g \circ f)(x\hat{\ }y) \ \wedge \ (g \circ f)(<p.d>\hat{\ }x) = \varepsilon$

We distinguish two cases:

(1) $\quad P©x = x \ \wedge \ \#x < m$: then by the properties of g we obtain
$$(g \circ f)(<p.d>\hat{\ }x\hat{\ }<?>\hat{\ }y) \ = \ f(t.d \& g(x\hat{\ }y))$$
and by the requirement for $g \circ f$:
$$f(t.d \& g(x\hat{\ }y)) \ = \ t.d \& f.g(x\hat{\ }y)$$
This suggests the equation for bounded buffers $f$:
$$f(t.d \& x) \ = \ t.d \& f.x$$

(2)   $P©x = x \;\land\; m \leq \#x < n + m$:   then by the properties of *rely* we
obtain for the input $<p.d>^\wedge x$ an exceptional situation for $g$. We assume that $g$ reacts to the exceptional situation for $x = r^\wedge <p.e>^\wedge z$
with $\#z = m - 1$ by some error messages $c \,\&\, r'$ and reduces the input
$<p.d>^\wedge x$ according to

$$(g \circ f)(<p.d>^\wedge r^\wedge <p.e>^\wedge z^\wedge <?>^\wedge y) \;=$$
$$f(c \,\&\, r'^\wedge g(<p.e>^\wedge z^\wedge <?>^\wedge y)) \qquad =$$
$$f(c \,\&\, r'^\wedge <t.e>^\wedge g(z^\wedge y)).$$

This suggests the choice $c = p.d$ and $r' = r$:

$$(g \circ f)(<p.d>^\wedge r^\wedge <p.e>^\wedge z^\wedge <?>^\wedge y) \;=$$
$$f(<p.d>^\wedge r^\wedge g(<p.e>^\wedge z^\wedge <?>^\wedge y)) \qquad =$$
$$f(<p.d>^\wedge r^\wedge <t.e>^\wedge g(z^\wedge y)).$$

This suggests the equation (for $P©r = r$, $\#r < n$):

$$f(<p.d>^\wedge r^\wedge <t.e>^\wedge x) \;=\; t.d \,\&\, f(r^\wedge <p.e>^\wedge x)$$

Finally we have to decide the result for $f(? \,\&\, x)$. An inspection of the
equations suggests:

$$f(? \,\&\, x) \;=\; ? \,\&\, f.x$$

This allows us to indicate exceptional cases by producing "?" and elements
from $P$ as output. The output of an element from $P$ may occur as a reaction
to an input of an element from $P$ and indicates that the buffer is full and
this way indicates an overflow. The output of "?" may occur as a reaction
to an input of "?" and indicates that the buffer is empty and therefore
cannot fulfil a request.

The input of an element from $T$ is understood as a combination of a
put and take request and is always answered by a take answer. According
to these considerations a buffer is specified based on the following predicates.

$$buffer\_guarantee(f, x) \;\equiv_{df}$$
$$strip.f.x \sqsubseteq strip.x \;\land\; \#f.x = \#((T \cup \{?\})©x).$$

We specify additional requirements for exceptional cases. In these exceptional cases where a buffer receives a request by input message "?" although
it is empty or where it receives a data element $e$ indicated by the input
message $p.e$ although the buffer is full a well-specified behavior is required.
In these cases input messages "?" and $p.e$ are reproduced as output. However, in the case of the input message $p.e$, the output $p.d$ is produced, where
$d$ is the first element in the buffer.

$exceptional\_guarantee(f, n) \quad \equiv_{df} \quad \forall x, y, d, e: \quad rely(x, n) \Rightarrow$
$(n = 0 \Rightarrow f(p.d \& y) = p.d \& f.y) \wedge$
$(f(x\,\hat{}\,y) = f.x\,\hat{}\,r \wedge \neg rely(x\,\hat{}\,{<}?{>}, n) \Rightarrow f(x\,\hat{}\,{<}?{>}\,\hat{}\,y) = f.x\,\hat{}\,{<}?{>}\,\hat{}\,r) \wedge$
$(f(x\,\hat{}\,{<}?{>}\,\hat{}\,{<}p.e{>}\,\hat{}\,y) = f.x\,\hat{}\,{<}t.d{>}\,\hat{}\,r \wedge \neg rely(x\,\hat{}\,{<}p.e{>}, n) \Rightarrow$
$\quad f(x\,\hat{}\,{<}p.e{>}\,\hat{}\,y) = f.x\,\hat{}\,{<}p.d{>}\,\hat{}\,r).$

With these requirements we can give a specification of a compositional, bounded buffer as follows:

$buffer(f, n) \quad \equiv_{df} \quad (\forall x: \quad rely(x, n) \Rightarrow buffer\_guarantee(f, x)) \wedge$
$\qquad\qquad\qquad\qquad exceptional\_guarantee(f, n)$

By this specification, we require a controlled behavior of the buffer even in cases where the initial specification above did not require anything. If the buffer gets data when it is full, then the datum in the buffer that was sent first is produced as output in order to provide free space for the incoming datum. If it gets output requests when it is empty, these requests simply are reproduced as output.

From the specification $buffer(f, n)$ we may derive a number of equations:

(a) $f(t.d \& x) = t.d \& f.x,$

(b) $P\copyright x = x \wedge \#x < n \Rightarrow f({<}p.d{>}\,\hat{}\,x\,\hat{}\,{<}?{>}\,\hat{}\,y) = t.d \& f(x\,\hat{}\,y) \wedge$
$\qquad\qquad\qquad\qquad\qquad\qquad f({<}p.d{>}\,\hat{}\,x\,\hat{}\,{<}t.e{>}\,\hat{}\,y) = t.d \& f(x\,\hat{}\,{<}p.e{>}\,\hat{}\,y),$

(c) $P\copyright x = x \wedge \#x \leq n \Rightarrow f.x = \varepsilon,$

(d) $P\copyright x = x \wedge \#x = n \Rightarrow f({<}p.d{>}\,\hat{}\,x\,\hat{}\,y) = p.d \& f(x\,\hat{}\,y),$

(e) $f(? \& x) = ? \& f.x.$

These equations determine $f$ uniquely. They can be derived as follows:

(a) follows from $rely(t.d \& x, n) = rely(x, n)$ and $buffer(f, n)$ and the monotonicity of $f$, since we have $rely({<}t.d{>}, n)$;

(b) follows by $rely({<}p.d{>}\,\hat{}\,x\,\hat{}\,{<}?{>}, n)$ and $rely({<}p.d{>}\,\hat{}\,x\,\hat{}\,{<}t.e{>}, n)$ and by $buffer\_guarantee$;

(c) follows by $P\copyright x = x \wedge \#x \leq n \Rightarrow rely(x, n)$ and by $buffer\_guarantee(f, x)$, since $\#((T \cup \{?\})\copyright x) = 0$;

(d) follows by (c) and $exceptional\_guarantee(f, n)$;

(e) follows by $exceptional\_guarantee(f, n)$.

We have for $buffer(f, n)$:

$$full(x, n + m) = full(f.x, m)$$
$$empty(x, n + m) = empty(f.x, m)$$

From this we can conclude

$$rely(x, n + m) = rely(f.x, m).$$

Now we can prove the intended property $(*)$.

**Lemma**    Compositionality

$$buffer(f,n) \; \land \; buffer(g,m) \;\; \Rightarrow \;\; buffer(f \circ g, n+m)$$

We see basically two possibilities for the proof. We may prove the properties (a)–(e) for $f \circ g$. The other possibility is that the proof is carried out by induction on $m$. We first prove some special cases.

**Lemma**    The buffer with capacity 0 is the identity.

$$buffer(f,0) \;\; \Rightarrow \;\; \forall x : \; f.x = x$$

**Proof**    We have for $x \in T^{\omega}$

$$buffer(f,n) \;\; \Rightarrow \;\; f.x = x$$

and for all $x$ with $\neg(x \in T^{\omega})$:

$$\neg rely(x,0)$$

We obtain from $exceptional\_guarantee(f,0)$ for $x \in T^{\omega}$:

$$\forall y,d : \; f(x\hat{\;}<?>\hat{\;}y) = x\hat{\;}<?>\hat{\;}f(y) \;\; \land \;\; f(x\hat{\;}<p.d>\hat{\;}y) = x\hat{\;}<p.d>\hat{\;}f(y).$$

From this we may conclude for all $x$ that $f.x = x$.
□

Next we prove some properties of bounded buffers with capacity 1.

**Lemma**    Characterisation of buffer with capacity 1. Assume $buffer(f,1)$; there we have

(a) $f(t.d \,\&\, x) \,=\, t.d \,\&\, f.x \;\; \land$

(b) $f(p.d \,\&\, ? \,\&\, x) \,=\, t.d \,\&\, f.x \;\; \land \;\; f(p.d \,\&\, t.e \,\&\, x) \,=\, t.d \,\&\, f(p.e \,\&\, x) \;\; \land$

(c) $f.\varepsilon \,=\, \varepsilon \;\; \land \;\; f(p.d \,\&\, \varepsilon) \,=\, \varepsilon \;\; \land$

(d) $f(p.d \,\&\, p.e \,\&\, x) \,=\, p.d \,\&\, f(p.e \,\&\, x) \;\; \land$

(e) $f(? \,\&\, x) \,=\, ? \,\&\, f.x$

**Proof**    (a)–(e) are just special cases of the general ones given above.
□

Next we prove a lemma that allows us to apply induction techniques.

**Lemma**    Stepwise construction of buffers

$$buffer(f,n) \; \land \; buffer(g,1) \;\; \Rightarrow \;\; buffer(g \circ f, n+1)$$

**Sketch of proof**    Assume $buffer(g,1)$ and $buffer(f,n)$. First observe that we have

$$rely(x, n+1) \;\; = \;\; rely(g.x, n)$$

The proof is done straightforward by case analysis. To complete the proof we distinguish two cases

(1) $rely(x, n+1)$:    case analysis for $g$ shows $buffer\_guarantee(g \circ f, x)$

(2) $\neg rely(x, n+1)$:    induction on the length of $n$ shows
$$exceptional\_guarantee(g \circ f, x)$$

$\square$

We define an algorithmic version for a buffer represented by the function $f$ with $buffer(f, n)$ for $n > 0$ by the auxiliary function
$$h : \ (T \cup P \cup \{?\})^\omega \times D^* \to (T \cup P \cup \{?\})^\omega$$

where:

$$f.x \ = \ h(x, \varepsilon)$$

and

$$
\begin{aligned}
h(? \, \& \, x, <d>\hat{\ }q) \ &= \ t.d \, \& \, h(x, q), \\
\#q < n \ &\Rightarrow \ h(p.d \, \& \, x, q) \ = \ h(x, q\hat{\ }<d>), \\
\#q = n - 1 \ &\Rightarrow \ h(p.d \, \& \, x, <e>\hat{\ }q) \ = \ p.e \, \& \, h(x, q\hat{\ }<d>), \\
h(? \, \& \, x, \varepsilon) \ &= \ ? \, \& \, h(x, \varepsilon), \\
h(t.d \, \& \, x, <e>\hat{\ }q) \ &= \ t.e \, \& \, h(x, q\hat{\ }<d>), \\
h(t.d \, \& \, x, \varepsilon) \ &= \ t.d \, \& \, h(x, \varepsilon).
\end{aligned}
$$

The correctness of this version can easily be proved by proving

$$n = 1 \ \Rightarrow \ buffer(\lambda x : \ h(x, \varepsilon), 1),$$
$$n > 1 \ \wedge \ buffer(j, n-1) \ \wedge \ buffer(g, 1) \ \Rightarrow \ \lambda x : \ h(x, \varepsilon) \ = \ j \circ g.$$

# 4   Concluding remarks

The specifications of a communicating system should not only be governed by simple input/output considerations, but also by the question how a version can be obtained that can conveniently and systematically be composed with other communicating entities.

REFERENCES

[1] J. A. Bergstra and J. V. Tucker. Top-down design and the algebra of communicating processes. *Science of Computer Programming*, 5:171–199, 1985.

[2] M. Broy. Algebraic methods for program construction: the project CIP. In P. Pepper, editor, *Program Transformation and Programming Environments*, pages 199–222, Springer-Verlag, Berlin-Heidelberg-New York-Tokyo, 1984. NATO ASI Series, Series F: 8.

[3] M. Broy. Specification and top down design of distributed programs. In H. Ehrig et al., editors, *TAPSOFT 85*, pages 4–28, Springer-Verlag, Berlin-Heidelberg-New York-Tokyo, 1985. Lecture Notes in Computer Science, Vol. 185.

[4] M. Broy. Views of queues. *Science of Computer Programming*, 11:65–86, 1988.

[5] C. B. Jones. Specification and design of (parallel) programs. *Information Processing*, 83:321–392, 1983. (Editor R. E. A. Mason).

[6] S. Kaplan and A. Pnueli. Specification and implementation of concurrently accessed data structures: an abstract data type approach. In F. J. Brandenburg, G. Vidal-Naquet, and M. Wirsing, editors, *STACS 87*, pages 220–244, Springer-Verlag, 1987. Lecture Notes in Computer Science, Vol. 247.

[7] L. Lamport. A simple approach to specifying concurrent systems. DIGITAL Systems Research Report 15, December 1986. (See also: *CACM* 32:1).

[8] M. L. Minsky. *Computation: Finite and Infinite Machines*. Prentice Hall, 1967.

[9] J. Misra. Specifications of concurrently accessed data. In Jan L. A. van de Snepscheut, editor, *Mathematics of Program Construction*, pages 91–114, Springer-Verlag, 1989. Lecture Notes in Computer Science, Vol. 375.

[10] S. Owicki. Specifications and proofs for abstract data types in concurrent programs. In F. L. Bauer and M. Broy, editors, *Program Construction*, pages 174–197, Springer-Verlag, 1979. Lecture Notes in Computer Science, Vol. 69.

Manfred Broy,
Institut für Informatik,
Technische Universität,
Arcisstr. 21,
D-8000 München 2,
Germany.

# 10

# Examples in Program Composition

## K. Mani Chandy
## Stephen Taylor[1]

## 1  The notation

This paper describes a few examples in Program Composition Notation (PCN), a notation for composing programs. PCN runs on a variety of machines including sequential machines, message-passing multicomputers and shared-memory machines. PCN uses four primitive composition operators: sequential, parallel, choice and fair composition with the symbols ';', '∥', '?', and '[]', respectively. PCN uses (*mutable*) *variables* as in imperative programming —variables whose value can change— and definition names (*defnames*, for short), which can be assigned at most once. The value of a definition name is either the special symbol *undefined* or an expression that does not refer to (mutable) variables. For example, the value of a definition name can be $x$, or $x+5$, or $\{x, \{y\}, 5\}$, where $x$ and $y$ are definition names. (Note that a tuple is a form of expression.)

Initially, all defnames are undefined. An undefined defname becomes defined by executing a define-statement in which it appears on the left-hand side. Once defined, a defname never changes.

**Proof Obligation for Definitions**   Programmers must prove that a defname is defined at most once and that definitions are not circular:

1. At most one define-statement is executed for each defname, and
2. At each point in the computation, there exists an ordering of definitions such that if $x$ is defined as $e$, $y$ is defined as $f$, and $f$ refers to $x$, then the definition for $x$ appears before the definition for $y$ in the ordering.

**Reduction**   A defname $y$ reduces to an expression or tuple $e$ at a point $t$ in the computation if $y$ is defined as $e$ at $t$, or if $y$ reduces to $e'$ at $t$ and $e$ can be obtained from $e'$ by substituting the definition for a defname in

---
[1]Supported by ONR and AFOSR,N00014-89-J-3201

$e'$, or if $e$ can be obtained from $e'$ by simplifying terms that reference only constants (e.g. replace 2+3 in $e'$ by 5 in $e$).

**Values of Expressions**    The value of an expression is a special symbol, *unknown*, if the expression refers to a defname that does not reduce to a constant; otherwise the value is obtained by replacing each defname by the constant to which it reduces, replacing each variable by its value, and evaluating.

The value of an expression is said to be known if its value is not *unknown*. Once the value of an expression is known, it remains known forever after.

## 1.1  PROGRAMS

A program consists of a *heading*, a *declaration section*, and a *block*. The heading is the program name and a list of arguments, as in other notations. The heading and the declaration section are not discussed here.

Parameters are passed by reference. The scope of a variable is limited to the program in which it appears.

The syntax of a block is given below in BNF. All nonterminal symbols are in italics, and all terminal symbols are in plain type. The notation $\prec su \succ$, where $su$ is a syntactic unit represents a list of zero or more instances $su$, separated by commas.

$$
\begin{aligned}
block ::=\ &define\text{-}statement\mid \\
&assignment\mid \\
&program\text{-}call\mid \\
&\{\ control\text{-}composition\text{-}operator\ \prec block \succ\ \}\mid \\
&\{\ selection\text{-}composition\text{-}operator\ \prec guard \rightarrow block \succ\ \}\mid \\
&\{\ user\text{-}defined\text{-}composition\text{-}operator\ \prec argument \succ\ \}
\end{aligned}
$$

**Define Statement**    A define-statement has the form $v \leftarrow rhs$ for $v$ a defname and $rhs$ an expression. Execution of the statement causes $v$ to become defined as $e$, where $e$ is obtained from $rhs$ by replacing all variables in $rhs$ by their current values.

**Assignment**    An assignment has the form $v := rhs$ for $v$ a mutable variable and $rhs$ an expression. The assignment is executed by waiting until $rhs$ becomes known and then assigning its value to $v$:

> **while** $rhs$ is *unknown* **do** skip;
>
> assign the value of $rhs$ to $v$.

**Program Call**    A program call is like a procedure call in Pascal; the invoked program is initiated with its parameters replaced by the arguments; parameter passing is by reference.

## 1.2  CONTROL-COMPOSITION OPERATORS

The control-composition operators are ';' (for sequential composition) and
'||' (parallel composition). They are associative, so we describe the operators
in terms of composition of *two* blocks. (For both operators, execution of an
empty list of blocks is equivalent to skip, and execution of a composition
of a single block $b$ is an execution of $b$.)

**Sequential Composition**   Let $d$ be the block $\{;\ h, g\}$. Execution of
$d$ consists of executing $h$ and, when it terminates, executing $g$. Block $d$
terminates (if and) when $g$ terminates. The usual axiom of sequential composition applies:

Given $\{p\}\ h\ \{q\}$ and $\{q\}\ g\ \{r\}$ we conclude $\{p\}\ d\ \{r\}$.

**Parallel Composition**   Let $d$ be the block $\{||\ h, g\}$. Since operator '||'
is associative and commutative, the following discussion is symmetric in $h$
and $g$. Execution of $d$ consists of executing both $h$ and $g$; $d$ terminates when
both $h$ and $g$ terminate. An interleaving semantics is used to represent concurrent execution of $h$ and $g$. Execution is fair in the sense that eventually
a statement in $h$ will be executed if $h$ has not terminated, and similarly, for
$g$. Operator '||' is the only composition operator in which an interleaving
semantics is used; the other three operators are inherently sequential.

**Proof Obligations for Parallel Composition**   Assignment and definition are atomic actions. Programmers have certain proof obligations with
regard to parallel composition; they must prove that in an execution of $d$:
*all mutable variables that are accessed by both h and g remain unchanged.*

We give the semantics of $d$ only in the case that $h$ does not modify
a variable that is read or modified in $g$ (and vice versa). Provided this
restriction is met, the value of a known expression that occurs in $h$ remains
unchanged until $h$ changes it; this is because all variables referenced in
$h$ can be changed only by $h$, and the only change to a defname is from
undefined to defined. Therefore, the only possible change in an expression
referenced in $h$, while $h$ does not take a step, is from unknown to known.
While an expression is unknown, $h$ does nothing with it, so atomicity is
not an issue in proving safety properties.

If $g$ does not modify variables that are named in $h$ or its proof, then the
proof of $h$ is independent of $g$: The proof of $h$ in isolation is also a proof
of $h$ when it is composed in parallel with $g$. In PCN, however, $g$ can define
defnames that are employed in $h$ and its proof. Therefore, to demonstrate
that $h$ and $g$ do not interfere, it should be shown that the proof of $h$

1. does not name a mutable variable that is modified in $g$, and
2. does not employ the assertion '$x$ is undefined' if defname $x$ is defined
   in $g$.

(By symmetry, the same proof obligation holds for $g$.)

**Note Composition of Definitions**    The blocks $\{; \ v \leftarrow e, \ v' \leftarrow e'\}$, $\{; \ v' \leftarrow e', \ v \leftarrow e\}$, and $\{\| \ v \leftarrow e, \ v' \leftarrow e'\}$ are equivalent provided that they terminate. Control-composition operators play a role only if mutable variables are modified in the blocks that are composed.


## 1.3    GUARDS AND CHOICE COMPOSITION

The selection-composition operators are '?' (for choice) and '[]' (for fair, or UNITY, composition).

**Guards**    The syntax of a guard is

$$\begin{aligned} guard \qquad &::= \prec pattern \Leftarrow defname \succ : boolean\_expression \ | \\ &\quad \prec pattern \Leftarrow defname \succ \ | \\ &\quad boolean\_expression \\ pattern \qquad &::= \{ \ \prec pattern\_element \succ \ \} \\ pattern\_element &::= constant \ | \\ &\quad variable \ | \\ &\quad pattern \end{aligned}$$

Within a guard, a variable can appear at most once in a pattern.

**Examples of Pattern Matches**
$$\{\} \Leftarrow z, \ \{hd, tl\} \Leftarrow z, \ \{x, \{y\}, 2\} \Leftarrow z.$$

A pattern is merely a syntactic convenience. A pattern_element on the left side of a pattern-match serves as a place-holder for elements within the tuple on the right side of the match.

A guarded block with pattern $pat \Leftarrow z$ is transformed into an equivalent one in which $pat \Leftarrow z$ is removed, as follows:

1. Add the conjunct $sizeof(z) = k$, where $k$ is the number of pattern_elements in $pat$, and $sizeof(z)$ is the number of elements in $z$.

2. If the $i$-th pattern_element in $pat$ is a constant $j$, add the conjunct, $(z[i] = j)$, where $z[i]$ is an alias for the $i$-th element of tuple $z$.

3. If the $i$-th pattern_element in $pat$ is a variable $v$, replace all instances of $v$ in the guarded block by $z[i]$.

4. If the $i$-th pattern_element in $pat$ is a pattern $q$, add the pattern-match $q \Leftarrow z[i]$.

The execution of a choice block $d$: $\{? \ \ g_0 \rightarrow b_0, \ldots, g_n \rightarrow b_n \ \}$ where $n \geq 0$ is as follows where the value of $(\exists i :: g_i)$ is *unknown* means at least one of the guards in the quantification is *unknown* and no guard has value *true*.

> **while** $(\exists i :: g_i)$ is *unknown* **do** skip;
> **if** $(\exists i :: g_i)$ **then** nondeterministically select any one $i$
> for which $(g_i = true)$ and execute $b_i$
> **else** skip.

We can conclude $\{p\} \ d \ \{q\}$ if

1. $(p \ \Rightarrow \ (\exists i :: g_i) \text{ is known}) \ \wedge$
2. $(\forall i :: \{p \wedge g_i\} \ b_i \ \{q\}) \ \wedge \ (p \wedge \neg(\exists i :: g_i)) \Rightarrow q$ .

**Fair Composition**   Fair composition is as in UNITY. Execution of a fair composition block $\{ \ [] \ \ g_0 \to b_0, \ldots, g_n \to b_n \ \}$ where $n \geq 0$ is given next. The guards are treated as 3-valued with values *unknown*, *true* and *false*.

> **while** $(\exists i :: \ (g_i = unknown) \vee (g_i = true))$ **do**
> select an $i$ fairly and **if** $g_i = true$ **then** execute $b_i$ **else** skip.

The fairness constraint is that either the 'block terminates in a finite number of guard evaluations or each guard is evaluated infinitely often. We shall not discuss this composition operator further because a similar operator has been treated extensively in UNITY.

**Quantification**   The notation uses quantification as in UNITY: $\ll i$ in $0 \ .. \ n :: \ b_i \gg$ is the same as the ordered list $b_0, \ldots, b_n$. A difference with UNITY is that here the list $b_0, \ldots, b_n$ is ordered, whereas in UNITY the quantification represents a set.

# 2   Examples

In this section a few programs are developed to illustrate the composition operators. In these examples, defnames are not declared but variables are. (As in C, the size of one-dimensional arrays need not be declared.) The first few examples deal only with variables, and the later examples deal only with defnames.

We begin with a simple program *flip* with two integer arguments, which interchanges the values of its arguments. The body of the program is a sequential composition block.

> $flip(u, v)$
> integer $u, v, w$
> $\{; \ w := u, \ u := v, \ v := w \ \}$

Next consider a program $f$ with two arguments: a one-dimensional array $x$ and an index $j$. The program flips $x[j-1]$ and $x[j]$ if they are not in ascending order.

$$f(j,x)$$
integer $j$, $x[\,]$
$$\{?\ \ x[j-1] > x[j]\ \ \rightarrow\ \ \textit{flip}(x[j-1],x[j])\ \}$$

Next we write programs, each with the two arguments, $n$ and $x$, that sort $x[0..n-1]$ into ascending order.

**Fair Composition**    The simplest sorting routine is to repeatedly flip *any* pair of elements of $x$ that are out of order until all pairs are in order.

$$fc(n,x)$$
integer $n$, $x[\,]$
$$\{[]\ \ll i \text{ in } 1 .. n-1 ::\ x[i-1] > x[i]\ \ \rightarrow\ \ \textit{flip}(x[i-1],x[i]) \gg\ \}$$

**Choice Composition**    Fair selection is not necessary in the last example, so we can use choice composition as shown next. This program flips an arbitrary pair of elements of $x$ that are out of order and then calls itself.

$$s0(n,x)$$
integer $n$, $x[\,]$
$$\{?\ \ll i \text{ in } 1 .. n-1 ::$$
$$x[i-1] > x[i]\ \ \rightarrow\ \ \{;\ \textit{flip}(x[i-1],x[i]), s0(n,x)\ \}$$
$$\gg$$
$$\}$$

**Sequential Composition**    Bubble sort is defined in the obvious way using sequential composition.

$$s1(n,x)$$
integer $n$, $x[\,]$
$$\{;\ \ll t \text{ in } 1 .. n-1 ::\ \ \ll i \text{ in } 1 .. n-t ::\ f(i,x) \gg \gg\ \}$$

**Parallel Composition**    Odd-even transposition sort is defined using sequential and parallel composition. On every odd step, for all odd $i$, $x[i-1]$ and $x[i]$ are flipped if they are out of order, and on even steps the same is done for even $i$. Thus, on step number $t$, program $f(i,x)$ is called for all $i$ such that $(t-i) \bmod 2 = 0$.

$s2(n, x)$
integer $n,x[\ ]$
$\{;\ \ll t$ in $0\ ..\ n-1 ::$
    $\{\|\ \ll i$ in $1\ ..\ n-1 ::\ \{?\ ((t-i)\bmod 2\ =\ 0)\ \rightarrow\ f(i,x)\ \}\gg\ \}$
    $\gg$
$\}$

The next few programs are developed for Hamming's problem. These programs use only definitions.

**m2**    Program $m2$ has three defname arguments: two input tuples $u$ and $v$ and and output tuple $w$. All three represent lists. The program is symmetric in $u$ and $v$. The specification is:

$$((u = \{\})\ \Rightarrow\ w = \{\})\ \wedge\ ((v = \{\})\ \Rightarrow\ w = \{\})\ \wedge$$
$$\forall\ hu,\ tu,\ hv,\ tv ::\ (\{hu, tu\} = u)\ \wedge\ (\{hv, tv\} = v)\ \Rightarrow$$
$$hu < hv\ \Rightarrow\ w = \{hu, tw\}\ \text{where } tw \text{ is defined by } m2(tu, v, tw)\ \wedge$$
$$hu > hv\ \Rightarrow\ w = \{hv, tw\}\ \text{where } tw \text{ is defined by } m2(u, tv, tw)\ \wedge$$
$$hu = hv\ \Rightarrow\ w = \{hu, tw\}\ \text{where } tw \text{ is defined by } m2(tu, tv, tw).$$

$m2(u, v, w)$
$\{?$
    $(\{\}\ \Leftarrow\ u)\ \rightarrow\ w \leftarrow \{\},$
    $(\{\}\ \Leftarrow\ v)\ \rightarrow\ w \leftarrow \{\},$
    $(\{hu,\ tu\}\ \Leftarrow\ u)\ ,(\{hv, tv\}\ \Leftarrow\ v)\ \rightarrow$
        $\{?$
            $hu < hv\ \rightarrow\ \{\|\ w \leftarrow \{hu, tw\},\ m2(tu, v, tw)\ \},$
            $hu > hv\ \rightarrow\ \{\|\ w \leftarrow \{hv, tw\},\ m2(u, tv, tw)\ \},$
            $hu = hv\ \rightarrow\ \{\|\ w \leftarrow \{hu, tw\},\ m2(tu, tv, tw)\ \}$
        $\}$
$\}$

**mult**    All three arguments of *mult* are defnames; the first is input list $z$, the second is input integer $q$, and the third is output list $v$, which is obtained by multiplying each element of $z$ by $q$.

$mult(z, q, v)$
$\{?\ \{\}\ \Leftarrow\ z\ \ \ \ \ \ \ \ \rightarrow\ v \leftarrow \{\},$
   $\{hz, tz\}\ \Leftarrow\ z\ \ \rightarrow\ \{\|\ v \leftarrow \{w, tv\},\ w \leftarrow hz * q,\ mult(tz, q, tv)\ \}$
$\}$

**Hamming**    The program is required to produce an output $z$ that is an infinite increasing sequence of integers of the form $2^i * 3^j * 5^k$ for all natural numbers $i, j, k$. (We leave it to the reader to modify this program so that it terminates with $z$ having $n$ values.) After a few refinement steps we obtain the following specification. Define $z$ as $\{1, y\}$ where $y$ is defined by $m2(w, x, y)$, $x$ by $m2(u, v, x)$, $w$ by $mult(z, 2, w)$, $u$ by $mult(z, 3, u)$, and $v$ by $mult(z, 5, v)$. The proof that this specification is a refinement of that given earlier is carried out by induction on the length of prefixes of $z$. The progam derived from the specification is:

$$hamming(z)$$
$$\{\| \ z \leftarrow \{1, y\}, \ m2(w, x, y), \ m2(u, v, x),$$
$$mult(z, 2, w), \ mult(z, 3, u), \ mult(z, 5, v)$$
$$\}.$$

K. Mani Chandy,
Department of Computer Science,
California Institute of Technology,
Pasadena, CA 91125,
U.S.A.


Stephen Taylor,
Department of Computer Science,
California Institute of Technology,
Pasadena, CA 91125,
U.S.A.

# 11

# On the Mechanism of the Hydrogenation of Edible Oils

## Albert J. Dijkstra

Beauty is fortunately not limited to mathematics. Science, and in particular chemistry, can also provide those engaged in these fields with a sense of beauty and although others, e.g. mathematicians, may well somewhat condescendingly remark that "beauty is in the eye of the beholder", I will nevertheless try to illustrate that chemistry has a beauty of its own.

However, most readers of this Birthday Salute to Edsger W. Dijkstra will not be familiar with chemistry, let alone the chemistry of edible oils and fats. Therefore, I will try to explain whatever knowledge of chemistry is required to understand my illustration of its beauty. In this respect, I am somewhat privileged because of the many teachers in our family. In addition, I have chosen my illustration from the field of physical chemistry and, after all, Edsger started his academic career as a physicist.

Chemically speaking, the edible oils and fats encountered in daily life in cooking oils, margarine, butter, mayonnaise (and adipose tissue) are triglycerides, that is to say molecules made up of one molecule of glycerol (1, 2, 3-propanetriol) and three fatty acids that have been esterified to the alcohol groups of the glycerol. These fatty acids denote a group of compounds characterized by a carboxylic acid group linked to the end of a chain of carbon atoms. Because of the biosynthetical route of fatty acids in plants, the total number of carbon atoms in fatty acids of vegetable origin is always even. It is only by bacterial degradation, for instance in the rumen of cows, that fatty acids with odd-number chain lengths are formed.

Fatty acids can be fully saturated or can have one or more double bonds in the carbon chain. In fat chemistry, it is customary to denote a fatty acid by the symbol "C", the number of carbon atoms in the fatty acid chain, a colon, and the number of double bonds in this chain. Thus, palmitic acid, a saturated fatty acid with a chain length of sixteen carbon atoms, is denoted by C16:0. Other commonly occurring fatty acids are for example:

C18:0 = stearic acid
C18:1 = oleic acid
C18:2 = linoleic acid
C18:3 = linolenic acid

Tropical oils like palm oil and coconut oil, which are subject to a lot of negative publicity in the USA (but not elsewhere), are relatively rich in saturated fatty acids, whereas oils from seeds grown in the USA (soybean oil, cottonseed oil, corn oil) contain triglycerides with more unsaturated fatty acids.

Fatty acid compositions have only been studied in depth since an analytical technique (gas liquid chromatography, GLC) became available in the early 60's. Before that time, it was only possible to determine some fatty acids by a complicated and hardly accurate technique of fractional crystallization and weighing of fractions of the fatty acids formed by saponification (= hydrolysis) of the triglycerides, often in combination with titrimetric methods. At an even earlier time, titrimetric methods were the only analytical techniques available, and fat properties like saponification value and iodine value stem from those days. The saponification value is nowadays hardly used to characterize an oil or fat but the iodine value, indicating the "degree of unsaturation" of an oil, can still be of use, especially when studying the hydrogenation of edible oils. The determination of the iodine value involves adding iodine to the double bonds and measuring how much iodine is left after this reaction.

The hydrogenation or hardening process of triglyceride oils was invented early this century, when demand for solid fats started to outstrip supply (tallow, lard). In this process, hydrogen is added catalytically to the double bonds in the fatty acid chains and, simultaneously, double bonds originally in the cis-configuration are isomerized to a trans-configuration. Both reactions lead to triglycerides with higher melting points and thus cause an oil to be converted into a solid fat suitable for e.g. margarine or shortening production.

The mechanism of the hydrogenation reaction has intrigued many scientists, including myself. A reaction mechanism in this context means a breakdown of an overall reaction into its elementary steps, the rate of which can be expressed mathematically as a function of the concentrations of the reagents and (reaction rate) constants. Kinetic studies, being the measurement of compositional changes as a function of time and purposely induced reaction conditions, therefore play an important role in unravelling reaction mechanisms.

Whereas a mathematical theorem can be proven, a reaction mechanism can only be proposed as being in accordance with (kinetic) observations and established chemical theory. As soon as observations are made that cannot be explained by the proposed reaction mechanism or are contrary to its predictions, the mechanism has be to amended to take the new observations into account or scrapped altogether.

In this contribution to Edsger's Birthday Salute, I intend to do the latter and to propose a novel reaction mechanism for the part of the hydrogenation process that concerns the relative rates of hydrogenation of linoleic acid (C18:2) and oleic acid (C18:1), the so-called linoleic acid selectivity ratio.

This linoleic acid selectivity ratio was introduced a long time ago. I suspect it was introduced to distinguish between products that, although hydrogenated to the same extent (same iodine value), nevertheless exhibited different properties like melting point etc. Analysis of such products may well have revealed that the higher melting product had a higher C18:0 content, implying that more C18:1 had been hydrogenated than in the lower melting product where (same iodine value) therefore more C18:2 had been hydrogenated than in the higher melting product. Apparently, things can vary, and since they did so for no apparent reason, this required investigation.

Such investigations soon revealed that polyunsaturated fatty acids are more "reactive" than monounsaturated ones, and this difference in reactivity was quantified by the introduction of the selectivity ratio after a number of assumptions was made.

a) The hydrogenation reaction is consecutive, i.e. C18:3 reacts to form C18:2 only and does not form C18:1 or C18:0 in a single step. Similarly, C18:2 only forms C18:1 and does not form C18:0 in a single step.

b) The fatty acids form a kind of "common pool", i.e. the rate of reaction of a certain fatty acid does not depend upon the chemical nature of the two other fatty acids present in the triglyceride molecule. This assumption allows a mathematical treatment of the hydrogenation process by greatly reducing the number of potential rate constants, there being far fewer fatty acid species than triglyceride species. In a lecture given in Budapest and subsequently published in "Fat Science 1983", I demonstrated this assumption to be incorrect, but in practice, the effect of this "triglyceride selectivity" is only marginal.

c) All unsaturated fatty acids display the same hydrogenation kinetics, the only difference between C18:3, C18:2 and C18:1 being the numerical values of their reaction rate constants. In fact it is assumed that the rate of reaction is proportional to the concentration of the fatty acid concerned, the proportionality constant being the pseudo-rate constant, which includes the catalytic activity and the hydrogen concentration. Since these latter two factors are the same for a given hydrogenation experiment during which C18:3, C18:2 and C18:1 are hydrogenated simultaneously, pseudo-rate constants can be used when calculating selectivity ratios. In symbols, where square brackets indicate the concentration of the compound between these brackets and $k_a$, $k_b$ and $k_c$ represent the pseudo first-order rate constants of C18:3, C18:2 and C18:1 respectively:

$$\frac{d[\text{C18:3}]}{dt} = -k_a[\text{C18:3}]$$

$$\frac{d[\text{C18:2}]}{dt} = k_a[\text{C18:3}] - k_b[\text{C18:2}]$$

$$\frac{d[\text{C18:1}]}{dt} = k_b[\text{C18:2}] - k_c[\text{C18:1}]$$

$$\frac{d[\text{C18:0}]}{dt} = k_c[\text{C18:1}]$$

with the linolenic acid selectivity being defined as

$$S_{\text{Ln}} = \frac{k_a}{k_b}$$

and the linoleic acid selectivity as

$$S_{\text{L}} = \frac{k_b}{k_c}$$

Calculating selectivity ratios in pre-computer days was not easy but could be achieved by using a nomogram worked out for this purpose. By using the fatty acid compositions of both starting material and hydrogenation product, the selectivity ratio is read from a graph.

However, before describing the experiment that enabled me to refute the last assumption underlying the definition of the linoleic acid selectivity ratio, I will provide some background information on how such experiments can be carried out. In the laboratory, hydrogenation reactions are carried out as batch reactions. Oil is fed into the reaction vessel (a closed reactor with a hydrogen inlet, a vent and an agitator), a certain amount of catalyst (metallic nickel on an inorganic carrier) is added and the temperature is raised to the desired level (e.g. 180°C) and kept there. When this temperature is reached, the hydrogenation reaction is started by bubbling hydrogen through the oil. If then a constant rate of hydrogenation is to be achieved, so that all hydrogen supplied is consumed by the hydrogenation reaction, the hydrogen supply rate is kept constant and supply and demand are matched by controlling the rate of agitation.

This is achieved in a very simple manner indeed. One end of a tube is attached to the vent of the reaction vessel, the other end to a wash bottle, an open-ended tube dipping into a liquid. If more hydrogen is supplied than is consumed in the reaction, the excess hydrogen bubbles out of the open-ended tube through the liquid. If the rate of agitation is then increased slightly, this increases the rate of dissolution of the hydrogen in the oil so that its concentration increases, as a result of which the reaction rate is found to increase. If on the other hand liquid is sucked up into the open-ended tube, this indicates that consumption exceeds supply, and a slight reduction in the rate of agitation is required.

Whereas most (sponsored) work on the hydrogenation of edible oils has been devoted to the study of soybean oil, a commercially important oil containing C18:3, C18:2 and C18:1 as unsaturated fatty acids, I decided to simplify matters by studying sunflower oil, which contains only C18:2 (about 70%) and C18:1 (about 18%) as unsaturates.

In practice, this control method works quite well. Once the right rate of agitation has been found, it requires little adjustment for quite some time, but when the C18:2 content of the sunflower oil has decreased to about 15%, the rate of agitation must be increased continuously in order to maintain a constant rate of hydrogenation. The experiment was stopped when the rate of agitation had reached the maximum the agitator drive could manage.

Samples were taken at regular intervals and analyzed for fatty acid composition. On the basis of these fatty acid compositions, linoleic acid selectivity ratios were calculated (this time using a computer) for consecutive intervals. Calculating selectivity ratios for consecutive intervals is not normal practice, because this ratio, being the ratio of two reaction rate constants, is assumed to be constant as well, and calculating the selectivity ratio of the overall reaction (starting product to final product) is far more accurate. But why stick to normal practice?

Why indeed, because calculating the linoleic acid selectivity ratio for consecutive intervals showed this ratio to be far from constant. In the early stages of the experiment, the ratio was high, with the calculated value fluctuating around 60. These fluctuations are an artefact, because when calculating a selectivity ratio, the difference calculated between the successive C18:0 values is very sensitive to analytical errors if the C18:0 content increases very little, as during the beginning of the reaction. As and when the rate of agitation had to be increased, the selectivity ratio gradually dropped to about 5. Again, these calculated values fluctuated somewhat, this time because of the large effect of analytical errors in the determination of the C18:2 content.

Factors quoted in the literature as affecting the selectivity ratio (temperature, catalyst type, amount of catalyst) were kept constant during this experiment, so that the conclusion must be that the assumption underlying the definition of the selectivity ratio, viz. that "both C18:2 and C18:1 display the same reaction kinetics", is wrong.

In fact, the literature quotes more factors than listed above as "affecting the selectivity ratio". Pressure and rate of agitation are also listed and a review article even mentions a common characteristic in that all factors leading to an increased selectivity ratio also involve a reduced hydrogen concentration. However, the logical conclusion from this observation, i.e. that C18:2 and C18:1 apparently exhibit different kinetics and that the hydrogen concentration is the key to this difference, was not drawn. Selectivity ratios had apparently become established facts, and the fact that they were based upon mere assumptions had been quietly forgotten.

However, more lessons can be drawn from the above experiment. At the beginning of the experiment, when almost only C18:2 was being hydrogenated, an increased rate of agitation led to an increased rate of reaction (hydrogen consumption). Agitation is a driving force for the dissolution of hydrogen, so an increased rate of agitation leads to an increased rate of dissolution and thus to an increased concentration of dissolved hydrogen. If an increased concentration of dissolved hydrogen leads to an increased rate of reaction, the rate of hydrogenation may well be proportional to this concentration. Kineticists are fond of such proportionalities and therefore like to demonstrate their presence. However, to fulfil this wish, it must be possible to measure the hydrogen concentration, and no measurement system exists for this at present; nor can the rate of dissolution be worked out from the rate of agitation.

The rate of agitation was mentioned as a driving force for the dissolution of hydrogen into the oil, but there is a second driving force: the difference between the hydrogen solubility at the prevailing temperature and pressure and the actual hydrogen concentration in the oil. (This is where the physical chemistry referred to earlier comes in.)

Thus a second experiment, almost identical to the first one, was carried out: same oil, same temperature, same (amount of) catalyst, same rate of hydrogen supply, same initial rate of agitation, same sampling rate, the only difference being that instead of maintaining a constant rate of hydrogenation by controlling the agitator speed, the rate of hydrogenation was maintained (at constant agitator speed) by closing the vent on the reaction vessel. No hydrogen can then escape from the reaction vessel and thus all hydrogen supplied (at constant rate) is consumed in the hydrogenation reaction, apart from the small amount that builds up the pressure inside the vessel. This pressure increase was registered as a function of time.

Analysis of the samples from the second experiment revealed that they were practically indistinguishable from those from the first one. This means that the concentration of the hydrogen dissolved in the oil, now known to affect the rate of hydrogenation, must also have followed the same profile in both experiments. In the second experiment, the pressure started at atmospheric (just as in the first experiment) but started to increase at about that degree of hydrogenation at which (in the first experiment) the agitator speed had to be increased, rising to reach a value that was close to 2 atm absolute.

During the second experiment, the speed of agitation was kept constant. Since the rate of dissolution was also kept constant, it can therefore be concluded that the other driving force, i.e. the difference between solubility and concentration, was also constant. Since the hydrogen solubility is proportional to the absolute pressure and this pressure almost doubled during the second experiment, it can therefore be concluded that the actual concentration during the early parts of both experiments was almost negligible, perhaps only a few percent of the solubility at atmospheric pressure. During both experiments, it rose gradually but in absolute terms so little as to hardly affect the difference between the solubility and its actual value, so that no agitator speed adjustment was necessary and no pressure increase was noted, until the "reactivity" of the oil, being fairly depleted of C18:2, fell to such a low level that a substantial increase in hydrogen concentration was required to maintain hydrogenation rate. At the end of the first experiment, when the agitator speed was maximum, the oil must have been very close to saturation, and supersaturation, required to further compensate for the reduced "reactivity" of the oil, could not be achieved by agitating more rapidly.

Apparently, the hydrogen concentration is quite low at the beginning of each experiment, then increases slowly in absolute terms and then increases substantially at the same point at which the ill-fated linoleic acid selectivity ratio as previously defined also starts to change. This observation, which is only qualitative, is of the kind that kineticists like to use as a clue when studying a reaction mechanism.

How to explain the thought process that finally led to the proposal of a novel reaction mechanism? I think I started with the observation that the linoleic acid selectivity ratio was far from constant. This ratio is high during the early stages of both experiments and drops to much lower values as and when the hydrogen concentration increases. In fact, the product of the selectivity ratio and the hydrogen concentration looks more like being constant throughout the whole reaction. (I realize that to a mathematician this must all sound rather frightful.)

Assuming the product $S_L[H_2]$ to be constant, this means that

$$\frac{k_b}{k'_c}[H_2]$$

is also constant and that now the rate constant $k_b$ and $k'_c$ are also true reaction rate constants. Kinetically, this means that the hydrogen concentration must be included in the rate equation describing the hydrogenation of C18:1 to C18:0.

$$\frac{d[\text{C18:0}]}{dt} = k'_c[\text{H}_2][\text{C18:1}]$$

However, this would imply that the rate equation of the hydrogenation of C18:2 does not contain the hydrogen concentration, and this is not in accordance with the observations: increasing the rate of agitation during the first experiment led to an increase in hydrogen concentration and to an increased rate of hydrogen consumption. I therefore have to use a rate equation for the reaction of C18:2 that includes the hydrogen concentration:

$$\frac{d[\text{C18:2}]}{dt} = -k'_b[\text{H}_2][\text{C18:2}]$$

and therefore I have to include an additional hydrogen concentration in the rate equation of the reaction of C18:1 :

$$\frac{d[\text{C18:0}]}{dt} = k''_c[\text{H}_2]^2[\text{C18:1}]$$

in order to keep this concentration in the ratio of these new rate constants $k'_b$ and $k''_c$. That leaves me with the question of how to explain this chemically. Termolecular reactions are very rare, but a rate equation containing the product of three concentrations can also be explained in a different way: by the "vorgelagertes Gleichgewicht", a concept most concisely expressed in German and which I will now try to explain in English.

"Gleichgewicht" means "equilibrium" and my German-English dictionary translates "vorlagern" as "to extend in front of". In kinetic terms, it means that two reagents are in equilibrium with their reaction product and that both forward and backward reaction rates are very fast in comparison with a subsequent reaction of the equilibrium reaction product. In that case, the concentration of the equilibrium reaction product is always equal to the product of the concentrations of the reagents times the equilibrium constant, the latter being defined as the ratio of the rate constants of the forward and the backward reactions. Consequently, the rate of the subsequent, slow reaction is proportional to the concentration of the equilibrium product and the concentration of the compound it reacts with, and thus proportional to three concentrations.

If, on the other hand, the forward and backward rates are slow in comparison with the rate of the subsequent reaction, the rate of the latter reaction is dominated by the slowest element in the chain, the forward reaction involved in the equilibrium; then the rate of this subsequent reaction is proportional to the concentrations of the reagents involved in the equilibrium only. This latter case may apply to the hydrogenation of C18:2. In symbols, where L stands for C18:2 (Linoleic acid), O for C18:1 (oleic acid) and S for C18:0 (stearic acid):

| | | | |
|---|---|---|---|
| (1) | $L + H_2 \longrightarrow$ "LH" | | rate determining |
| (2) | "LH" $\longrightarrow L + H_2$ | | reverse of (1) |
| (3) | "LH" $+ H_2 \longrightarrow O + ?$ | | fast compared to (1) |
| (4) | $O + H_2 \longrightarrow$ "OH" | $\Big\}$ | vorgelagertes |
| (5) | "OH" $\longrightarrow O + H_2$ | | Gleichgewicht |
| (6) | "OH" $+ H_2 \longrightarrow S + ?$ | | rate determining |

In the above reaction mechanism, the breakdown of a complex system into elementary steps, reactions (1) and (2) are an equilibrium involving C18:2 and constitute the first step in the reaction leading to an intermediate product "LH", the chemical nature of which I leave undefined. This intermediate product reacts with hydrogen (3) to form C18:1 and perhaps a co-product of an unknown nature, which is therefore denoted as a question mark. To comply with the observations, it is assumed that reaction (1) determines the rate of the overall reaction, which means that reaction (2) in practice hardly ever occurs: all "LH" formed is snapped up almost immediately after it is formed.

When hydrogenating C18:1, the situation is both similar and different in that the same reaction steps form part of the reaction mechanism but their relative importance is quite different. Reactions (4) and (5) are the "vorgelagertes Gleichgewicht" and reaction (6) is rate-determining. Thus, because the concentration of "OH" at equilibrium is proportional to both [O] and [$H_2$] and the rate of formation of S is proportional to ["OH"] and [$H_2$], the overall rate is in fact proportional to [O] and that of [$H_2$]$^2$.

Both C18:2 and C18:1 behave similarly in that they follow the same pattern of reaction but differ in the magnitude of the rate constants involved, which is in accordance with the observations. In a chemical sense, this constitutes an attractive proposition. I ask all molecules to walk along the same path but accept that some steps are more difficult for some of them.

Having proposed the above reaction mechanism, I would now like to provide it with additional support, for instance by calculating rate constants for different experimental conditions and observing that they are equal despite the different experimental conditions. This would not prove it to be a true representation of what actually happens, but it would make it less speculative.

I have therefore designed a series of experiments that should allow the rate constants of the individual steps outlined above to be calculated. These experiments take into account that, sadly enough, I have no means of measuring the actual concentration of the dissolved hydrogen but compensate this lack (of equations) by incorporating experiments at different external parameters. Accordingly, I hope to provide the additional support and at the same time to be able to compare catalysts on a quantitative basis, but that is another (beautiful) story.

Albert J. Dijkstra,
Albijn Van den Abeelelaan 2,
B–8500 Kortrijk,
Belgium.

# 12

# The Problem of the Majority Network

## The Eindhoven Tuesday Afternoon Club[1]

We consider a connected undirected graph. Its node set $S$ is finite and contains at least two elements; its edge set is finite. There are no further restrictions on the topology of the graph; in particular it may contain multiple edges and autoloops.

We said that the graph is undirected, although each edge will carry precisely one arrow. The point is that the direction of these arrows is not fixed, since with each node we will associate a machine that may flip incoming arrows on edges incident with that machine.

For the description of the game to be played on the graph we need the excess $e.V$ of incoming arrows of $V$; it is defined by

$$e.V = \text{(the number of arrows from } \overline{V} \text{ to } V)$$
$$- \text{(the number of arrows from } V \text{ to } \overline{V}) \ ,$$

for all subsets $V$ of $S$, where $\overline{V}$ denotes $V$'s complement with respect to $S$, and where

"the number of arrows from $\overline{V}$ to $V$"

is short for

"the number of arrows pointing from
some node in $\overline{V}$ to some node in $V$".

Without proof we mention

(0)     $e.S = 0$;

(1)     $e.V = (\mathbf{S}\, x : x \in V : e.x)$, for all $V$, where $e.x$ is short for $e.\{x\}$.

⋆   ⋆   ⋆

[1]A. Bijlsma, R. W. Bulterman, W. H. J. Feijen, C. S. Scholten and J. C. S. P. van der Woude.

The rules of the game to be played are as follows. Each machine is in one of two distinct states, to wit black or white.

By postulate, white machines adhere to

**Rule 0**    (for white machines)

A white machine $x$ blackens itself when and only when $e.x > 0$.

(**End** of Rule 0.)

Since this will be the only rule to be imposed on white machines, flipping of incoming arrows will have to be carried out by black machines.

When machine $x$ becomes black, $e.x > 0$ holds, implying that $x$ has at least one incoming arrow. Therefore, we can safely adopt the postulate that black machines adhere to

**Rule 1**    (for black machines)

A machine that becomes black flips one incoming arrow, and a black machine repeatedly
>    either flips an incoming arrow
>    or becomes white.

(**End** of Rule 1.)

So much for the rules imposed on the machines.

⋆    ⋆    ⋆

Our purpose is to design additional rules for the machines so that each computation of the network will satisfy

(2)        No machine is eventually white.

**Intermezzo**    (on "eventually"-calculus)

The notion "eventually" has the following operational interpretation. For predicate $P$, a computation satisfies "eventually $P$" if $P$'s value changes only finitely often and ends up with the value *true*. Our demands on the notion are, however, calculational, and therefore we will postulate a number of its algebraic properties. With $\langle P \rangle$ short for "eventually $P$", we will rely on

(3)        $\langle \rangle$ is conjunctive, i.e. $\langle P \wedge Q \rangle \equiv \langle P \rangle \wedge \langle Q \rangle$    for all $P, Q$;

(4)        $\langle \rangle$ is monotonic, i.e. $\langle P \rangle \Rightarrow \langle P \vee Q \rangle$    for all $P, Q$;

(5)        $\langle P \rangle \equiv P$    for any predicate $P$ that is not affected by the computation;

(6)        $\neg \langle \neg P \rangle \Leftarrow (P$ is an invariant$)$,    for all $P$ .

It goes without saying that the above properties are not independent; they are the ones we need.

(**End** of Intermezzo.)

For later use, we mention two relations involving "eventually" that are implied by the Rules 0 and 1 for our machines:

(7)        $(\mathbf{A}\, x :: \langle white.x \rangle \equiv \langle white.x \wedge e.x \leq 0 \rangle)$
(8)        $(\mathbf{A}\, x :: (x \text{ flips incoming arrows infinitely often}) \vee \langle white.x \rangle)$ .

Note that (8) is based on the fact that a black machine can —and will— always move, i.e. flip an incoming arrow or become white.

$$\star \quad \star \quad \star$$

Now the time has come to tackle target relation (2). With our notation for "eventually" it can be rendered more formally as

$$\neg(\mathbf{E}\, x :: \langle white.x \rangle) \ .$$

Unfortunately, none of our calculational rules for "eventually" can be used to manipulate it, so that we will have to look for a different formulation of the target relation.

To that end, we should bear in mind that in demonstrating the absence of "eventually white" machines we will have to take into account that machines interact with each other via the edges of the given network. Therefore we cannot expect to discuss the set of "eventually white" machines without dragging the other machines into the picture as well. With this in mind, the following detour towards reformulating the target relation (2) will not be too big a surprise.

For any computation of the network, we will consider set $V$ of machines, defined by

(9)        $x \in V \equiv \langle white.x \rangle$ .

We then have

    (2)

=        {with definition of $V$}

    $V = \emptyset$

=        {by the graph's connectivity, and
          by the set of nodes being nonempty}

    $\overline{V} \neq \emptyset \ \wedge \ (\text{the number of edges between } V \text{ and } \overline{V}) = 0$ .

With this expression for the target relation, we have attained a promising disentanglement: while the first conjunct mainly addresses machines and their colours, the second conjunct mainly mentions edges of the connecting network. We will therefore tackle the two conjuncts separately.

**First Conjunct**    We observe

$$\overline{V} \neq \emptyset$$

= {definition of complement}

$$\neg(\mathbf{A}\, x :: \ x \in V)$$

= {(9)}

$$\neg(\mathbf{A}\, x :: \ \langle white.x \rangle)$$

= {(7)}

$$\neg(\mathbf{A}\, x :: \ \langle white.x \ \wedge \ e.x \leq 0 \rangle)$$

= {(3), using that the range of $x$ is finite}

$$\neg\langle \ (\mathbf{A}\, x :: \ white.x \ \wedge \ e.x \leq 0) \ \rangle$$

= {de Morgan, using $\neg white \ \equiv \ black$}

$$\neg\langle \ \neg(\mathbf{E}\, x :: \ black.x \ \vee \ e.x > 0) \ \rangle$$

$\Leftarrow$ {(6), to eliminate "eventually"}

$(\mathbf{E}\, x :: \ black.x \ \vee \ e.x > 0)$ is an invariant ,

and we therefore propose to equip the machines with additional rules so that they maintain the invariance of

(10)    $(\mathbf{E}\, x :: \ black.x \ \vee \ e.x > 0)$ .

The initialization of (10) can be done in a variety of ways. They need not concern us here.

For falsifying (10) there are at most two possibilities, viz. a decrement of an $e$-value and a transition of a black machine to the white state.

As for a decrement of an $e$-value, we observe that this is the result of some flipping action, but these actions are carried out by black machines only, thus ensuring that (10) is not falsified.

As for a transition of a black machine to the white state, the required invariance of (10) almost dictates that such a transition can only take place safely in a state satisfying

(11)    $(\mathbf{E}\, x :: \ e.x > 0)$ .

We could now adopt the rule that a black machine $x$ can become white only when $e.x > 0$, but this guard is unnecessarily strong, thereby unnecessarily constraining the degree of parallelism. By (0) and (1), (11) is equivalent to

$$(\mathbf{E}\, x :: \ e.x < 0) \ ,$$

and, therefore, equivalent to

$$(\mathbf{E}\,x :: \ e.x \neq 0)\ ,$$

so that we can now adopt

**Rule 2**    (for black machines)

A black machine $x$ becomes white only when $e.x \neq 0$.

(**End** of Rule 2.)

With the incorporation of Rule 2, black machines have been constrained in their moves, viz. in becoming white. We therefore reconsider the validity of (8), which is based on the fact that black machines can always move.

A black machine that cannot flip an arrow has outgoing arrows only. Because the network is connected and contains at least two nodes, there is at least one such outgoing arrow. Therefore, the machine's $e$-value $< 0$, so that the machine can move to the white state.

With the incorporation of Rule 2, we may also wish to investigate the danger of deadlock. Since —by the above— black machines can always move, we consider a state in which all machines are white. From the invariance of (10), we then conclude the existence of a white machine with an $e$-value $> 0$, so that this machine can move to the black state. Hence, there is no danger of deadlock.

(**End** of First Conjunct.)

**Second Conjunct**

In demonstrating the absence of edges between $V$ and $\overline{V}$ we will have to take into account that the computation interacts with edges by flipping their arrows. Therefore, we cannot expect to discuss edges between $V$ and $\overline{V}$ without dragging their arrows into the picture as well. With $p$ and $q$ defined by

$$
\begin{aligned}
p &=\ \text{the number of arrows from } \overline{V} \text{ to } V. \\
q &=\ \text{the number of arrows from } V \text{ to } \overline{V},
\end{aligned}
$$

we may observe for the Second Conjunct,

(the number of edges between $V$ and $\overline{V}$) $= 0$

$=$      {(5), using that set $V$ as defined in (9)
         is a constant of the computation}

$\langle$ (the number of edges between $V$ and $\overline{V}$) $= 0$ $\rangle$

$=$      {each edge carries precisely one arrow; definitions of $p$ and $q$}

$\langle p + q = 0 \rangle$

$=$      {$p$ and $q$ are natural-valued}

$$\langle p \leq q \ \wedge \ q = 0 \rangle$$

$=$      {(3), i.e. $\langle\rangle$ is conjunctive}

$$\langle p \leq q \rangle \ \wedge \ \langle q = 0 \rangle$$

$=$      {definitions of $p$, $q$, and $e.V$}

$$\langle e.V \leq 0 \rangle \ \wedge \ \langle q = 0 \rangle \ .$$

Now we take care of the Second Conjunct by taking care of $\langle e.V \leq 0 \rangle$ and $\langle q = 0 \rangle$ separately.

As for $\langle e.V \leq 0 \rangle$, we observe

$$\langle e.V \leq 0 \rangle$$

$=$      {(1)}

$$\langle\, (\mathbf{S}\, x : \ x \in V : \ e.x) \leq 0 \,\rangle$$

$\Leftarrow$      {(4), i.e. $\langle\rangle$ is monotonic}

$$\langle\, (\mathbf{A}\, x : \ x \in V : \ e.x \leq 0) \,\rangle$$

$=$      {(9), i.e. definition of $V$}

$$\langle\, (\mathbf{A}\, x : \ \langle white.x \rangle : \ e.x \leq 0) \,\rangle$$

$=$      {(3), i.e. $\langle\rangle$ is conjunctive}

$$(\mathbf{A}\, x : \ \langle white.x \rangle : \ \langle e.x \leq 0 \rangle)$$

$=$      {(7)}

$$(\mathbf{A}\, x : \ \langle white.x \ \wedge \ e.x \leq 0 \rangle : \ \langle e.x \leq 0 \rangle)$$

$=$      {(4), i.e. $\langle\rangle$ is monotonic}

$$true \ ,$$

so that $\langle e.V \leq 0 \rangle$ is for free.

As for $\langle q = 0 \rangle$, nothing else can be done than to use the definition of $q$ and to require

(12)      $\langle$(the number of arrows from $V$ to $\overline{V}$) $\ = \ 0 \rangle \ .$

When the computation has reached a state in which all machines of $V$ are white and will remain white, the only machines that can flip arrows are those of $\overline{V}$. Requirement (12) expresses that in such a state *all* arrows from $V$ to $\overline{V}$ are to be flipped by the machines of $\overline{V}$. By the definition of $V$, a machine $x$ of $\overline{V}$ satisfies $\neg\langle white.x \rangle$. By (8), $x$ therefore flips incoming arrows infinitely often. Thus requirement (12) can be met by requiring that the arrows from $V$ to $x$ should not be "forgotten" indefinitely. This we will realize by adopting

**Rule 3**   (for black machines)

For any incoming arrow $i$ of a black machine $x$ the flipping of arrows takes place subject to the condition:

   ($x$ flips incoming arrows infinitely often)

$\Rightarrow$

   ($x$ will flip $i$).

(**End** of Rule 3.)

The implementation of Rule 3 can be done in a variety of ways. They need not concern us here.

(**End** of Second Conjunct.)


This completes the derivation of the algorithm.




ETAC,
Department of Mathematics and Computing Science,
Eindhoven University of Technology,
P.O. Box 513,
5600 MB  Eindhoven,
The Netherlands.

# 13

# A Little Exercise in Deriving Multiprograms

## W. H. J. Feijen

In this note we record an experiment in deriving multiprograms from their functional specifications, with the predicate calculus and the theory of Owicki and Gries as our only tools for reasoning. For the benefit of the experiment we have selected an example problem that is so simple that it need not divert our attention from the subject matter, which is the process of derivation.

Someone who is familiar with the theory of Owicki and Gries may, right at the outset, be amazed by our choice to use that theory for the purpose of deriving multiprograms. Since, after all,

(i) isn't that theory too simple to deal with something as complicated as parallel programs?

(ii) and isn't it the case that that theory addresses partial correctness only, thus completely ignoring the important issues of deadlock and individual starvation?

(iii) and hasn't that theory been designed just for a posteriori verification of multiprograms?

We think that these questions are legitimate, and we therefore wish to spend a few words on them.

As for (iii), we have to bear in mind that the theory of Owicki and Gries emerged in a period when computing scientists had just begun to explore the possibility of deriving —sequential— programs. In those days the formal derivation of multiprograms was not within the scope of immediate interest, and definitely beyond the then technical competence. We mention the latter so explicitly because in the meantime we have learnt that the possibility to derive programs formally cannot come without the willingness to abandon interpretative reasoning. In the mid-70's, operational understanding of programs and interpretation of mathematical formulae still were the predominant options. In particular, computing scientists still had to develop the predicate calculus and by now we know that without its mastery, program derivation can hardly be done. With this in mind, it is quite understandable why the theory of Owicki and Gries has received the stigma of having been *designed* just for a posteriori verification: it has always been *used* for that.

As for (ii), the only thing we can do for the moment is to refer the reader to our forthcoming example. It gives us the opportunity to derive a whole spectrum of solutions to the programming problem, with at the one end of the spectrum a solution that displays a wealth of potential parallelism and doesn't suffer from the danger of starvation, and with at the other end of the spectrum a solution that displays deadlock and, hence, no parallelism at all. Drawing from limited experience we can say that the spectrum is always there and that the "good" half of it remains within reach, provided one adheres to a design discipline in which one doesn't commit oneself too easily to premature decisions.

As for (i), what else can we say than that the most effective weapon against lurking mathematical complexity is a simple formalism to begin with. And as yet, we have no indication that the theory of Owicki and Gries could be too naive.

$$\star \qquad \star \qquad \star$$

The theory of Owicki and Gries can be briefly explained as follows. A multiprogram is a set of sequential programs, that may be annotated with assertions. The theory tells us that we can then rely on the correctness of the annotation whenever for each assertion we can show

- that it is established by the program in which it occurs, the so-called local correctness of the assertion,
- and that it is maintained by the atomic statements of the other programs, the so-called global correctness of the assertion.

In principle this is it. Note that in using the theory, we will always have to be very explicit about which are the atomic statements.

In dealing with multiprograms we use weakest liberal preconditions for the characterization of statements. The most noticeable difference with weakest preconditions is that we now have for the alternative construct (with one guard)

$$wlp.(\textbf{if } B \rightarrow S \textbf{ fi}).R \quad \equiv \quad \neg B \ \lor \ wlp.S.R.$$

It entitles us to conclude the local correctness of assertion $B$ in the program fragment

$$\textbf{if } B \rightarrow skip \textbf{ fi } \{B\}.$$

and this, in fact, is the most important thing we need to know for what follows.

Near the very end of our example derivation we will also use a program transformation, the validity of which is captured by the following lemma that we mention without proof. The purpose of the transformation is to reduce the grain of atomicity, thus enhancing the degree of potential parallelism, but without impairing the program's correctness.

**Lemma**    We consider replacing an atomic alternative construct

> **if** $B \wedge C \to skip$ **fi**

in one of the component programs with the sequence

> **if** $B \to skip$ **fi**
> ; **if** $C \to skip$ **fi**

of two atomic alternative constructs. The lemma is, that the replacement is harmless to the correctness of the annotation, provided $B$ is not falsified by any atomic statement of any other component program. Moreover, the replacement does not introduce the danger of deadlock.
(**End** of Lemma)

And after these preliminaries, we are ready for our example derivation.

$$\star \quad \star \quad \star$$

We consider a terminating multiprogram in which, at the outset, each component program consists of a single assignment to a local boolean variable:

> *Program i*:    $|[\, y.i :\, bool;\ y.i := B.i \,]|$ ,

for some boolean expression $B.i$ still to be determined. The problem is to synchronize the components in such a way that the final state of the multiprogram satisfies

(0)        $(\mathbf{N}\, i :: y.i)\ =\ 1,$

i.e., precisely one of the booleans $y$ has the value *true*. The synchronization has to be realized by means of atomic statements of the traditional type "at most one access to at most one shared variable". Furthermore the synchronization has to be carried out so as to meet the following "fairness" requirement.

Relation (0), viewed as an equation in $y$, has as many solutions as there are component programs, and the fairness requirement is that our ultimate multiprogram can generate each solution of (0). Since we do not allow this requirement to penetrate our discussion, we immediately satisfy it by deciding that our design be symmetric in the component programs.

So much for the problem statement.

Our design process —and this is typical— comprises two stages. In the first stage we design a program annotation so that its assumed correctness implies the synchronization condition —(0) in our case— . In the second stage we use the theory of Owicki and Gries to realize the correctness of the annotation. We begin with the first stage.

$$\star \qquad \star \qquad \star$$

Given the assignment $y.i := B.i$, we cannot assert much more than that *Program i* establishes postcondition $y.i \equiv B.i$, and we cannot hope for much more than that the other programs will maintain it. So we decide that

$$y.i \;\equiv\; B.i \quad \text{is a correct postcondition in } \textit{Program i}$$

with expression $B$ still to be determined.

Expression $B$ has to follow from what we now know, viz. that the multiprogram establishes postcondition

$$(\mathbf{A}\, i :: \; y.i \;\equiv\; B.i),$$

and from what we have to guarantee, viz. that it establishes postcondition (0). We can now satisfy (0), provided we can design $B$ such that the postcondition satisfies

$$(\mathbf{N}\, i :: B.i) \;=\; 1,$$

or —equivalently—

(1)     $(\mathbf{E}\, i :: B.i)$     and
(2)     $(\mathbf{A}\, i, j :: \; B.i \wedge B.j \;\Rightarrow\; i = j)$

And this is precisely what we shall do.

Choice *false* for $B$ evidently meets (2), and it is the only choice that does so without taking the implication's consequent into account. But the choice is no good for (1), so that we had better consider that consequent. It mentions an equality sign, and here we have to remember that the only way to conclude the equality of two arbitrary expressions is by using that equality is transitive. Thus we arrive at our next (and last) choice for $B$, viz.

$$B.i \;\equiv\; v = i,$$

for some $v$. Having satisfied (2), we are left with the obligation to ensure that the postcondition of the multiprogram satisfies (1).

With our choice for $B$, *Program i* can establish (1) by an assignment $v := i$ to a fresh shared variable $v$. In view of the desired symmetry between the component programs there is hardly any other possibility!

And here we have reached the end of the first stage. Summarizing, we have achieved that the multiprogram with shared variable $v$ and with components given by

*Program i:*  $\|[$  ...
$;$  $v := i$
$\ldots$
$;$  $y.i := v = i$
$\{y.i \equiv v = i\}$
$]\|$ ,

meets target relation (0), provided the assertion $y.i \equiv v = i$ in *Program i* is correct. It is this proviso which we shall realize in the second stage of our design.

$\star$    $\star$    $\star$

**Intermezzo**    In showing the global correctness of an assertion $P$ in one of the programs, we have to show that for each atomic statement $S$, with precondition $Q$, in a different program,

$$P \wedge Q \;\Rightarrow\; wlp.S.P$$

is a theorem. But what if it isn't? The answer is that in that case the annotation of the programs is not strong enough. It is standard practice then to strengthen the annotation by adding a new assertion $C$, say, as a conjunct to $P$, and by adding a new assertion $D$, say, as a conjunct to $Q$, and to design the newly-introduced assertions in such a way that they are correct and satisfy

$$C \wedge D \;\Rightarrow\; (P \wedge Q \Rightarrow wlp.S.P)$$

Note that for given $P$, $Q$ and $S$ this implication yields an equation in the unknown predicates $C$ and $D$, and that it has at least one solution, viz. for $C \wedge D \equiv false$.

(**End** of Intermezzo)

Now we address the required correctness of assertion $y.i \equiv v = i$ in *Program i*. Its local correctness is obvious. For its global correctness we observe that the only statements from other programs that may falsify it are the assignments to $v$, for which we have to guarantee that they don't. I.e. we have to ensure that for any $j$, $j \neq i$,

$$(y.i \equiv v = i) \;\Rightarrow\; wlp.(v := j).(y.i \equiv v = i),$$

or —equivalently, using the axiom of assignment and $j \neq i$—

$$(y.i \equiv v = i) \;\Rightarrow\; \neg y.i,$$

or —equivalently, using predicate calculus—

(3)    $\neg y.i \;\vee\; v \neq i.$

This, however is hardly a theorem and we therefore strengthen the annotation as indicated in the above Intermezzo:

$$
\begin{array}{l}
Program\ i:\quad \|[\quad \ldots \\
\qquad\qquad\ \{D.i\} \\
\qquad\quad ;\quad v := i \\
\qquad\qquad\ \ldots \\
\qquad\quad ;\quad y.i := v = i \\
\qquad\qquad\ \{C.i\}\ \{y.i\ \equiv\ v = i\} \\
\qquad\ \|]\ .
\end{array}
$$

(Juxtaposition of assertions denotes their conjunction.) Now the global correctness of assertion $y.i \equiv v = i$ is guaranteed, provided we can design $C$ and $D$ in such a way that

(4a)   Assertions $C.i$ and $D.i$ are correct;
(4b)   $(\mathbf{A} j : j \neq i : C.i \wedge D.j \Rightarrow (3))$.

And this is precisely what we shall do.

As yet we cannot do much with requirement (4a), but (4b) enables us to eliminate $C.i$; by (3) and predicate calculus, (4b) is equivalent to

$$C.i \Rightarrow (\mathbf{A} j : j \neq i : \neg D.j \vee \neg y.i \vee v \neq i) .$$

We "strengthen" this requirement on $C.i$ a little bit by removing the disjunct $\neg y.i$, yielding

$$C.i \Rightarrow (\mathbf{A} j : j \neq i : \neg D.j \vee v \neq i) .$$

(This "strengthening" is done in view of the fact that $C.i$ is a postassertion of an assignment to $y.i$; anticipating that we still have to ensure $C.i$'s local correctness, it is attractive to have $C.i$'s solution space as independent of $y.i$ as possible. Moreover the "strengthening" is no real strengthening, since assertion $C.i$ occurs in conjunction with the already established assertion $y.i \equiv v = i$.) We now have an abundance of choices for $C.i$, for instance

(a)   $false$
(b)   $(\mathbf{A} j : j \neq i : v \neq i)$
(c)   $(\mathbf{A} j : j \neq i : \neg D.j)$
(d)   $(\mathbf{A} j : j \neq i : \neg D.j \vee v \neq i),$

but we will select the weakest one, i.e. we choose

$$C.i : \ (\mathbf{A} j : j \neq i : \neg D.j \vee v \neq i) .$$

The more pragmatic reason for this choice is that the weaker we choose our assertions the less we constrain the potential parallelism of our ultimate solution. The more fundamental reason is that we can always strengthen an assertion later on, should the need arise.

Having settled (4b), we are left with the task of ensuring (4a). Assertion $C.i$ is so wildly different from any other assertion in *Program i* that there is hardly any other way of ensuring its local correctness than by "testing" it. Thus we obtain

$$
\begin{aligned}
\textit{Program i:} \quad &[\![ \quad \dots \\
&\quad \{D.i\} \\
&; \quad v := i \\
&\quad \dots \\
&; \quad \textbf{if } C.i \rightarrow \textit{skip } \textbf{fi} \\
&\quad \dots \\
&; \quad y.i := (v = i) \\
&\quad \{C.i\} \{y.i \equiv v = i\} \\
&]\!] \; .
\end{aligned}
$$

By incorporating the $D$'s in the guard, we have more or less committed ourselves to a representation of the predicates $D$ by, say, a fresh bunch of shared boolean variables, one per program. In view of assertion $D.i$, their initial values had better be *true*.

The global correctness of $C.i$ offers no problem at all. The assignments $v := j$, for $j \neq i$, just make $C.i$ more true. In this respect, we could also easily accommodate assignments $D.j := \textit{false}$, which are absent now . . . .

The latter remark is of course related to the observation that the multiprogram as we have it now, is a pretty naive one. Without assignments $D := \textit{false}$, we can simplify $C.i$ into the rejected alternative (b), and we can eliminate the $D$'s altogether. The resulting program suffers from the danger of starvation, and that is not what we are after. So let us accommodate assignments $D := \textit{false}$.

By the place of occurrence of assertion $D.i$ in *Program i*, the assignment $D.i := \textit{false}$ has to succeed $v := i$, and as far as the correctness of the annotations $D$ is concerned there are no other constraints on where to plug it in. For reasons of "maximal progress", however, we plug it in so that the guards become true "as soon as possible", i.e. immediately following $v := i$. Thus we arrive at what, apart from a final transformation, will be our ultimate program. Fully encoded and completely annotated, it is

$$
\begin{aligned}
\textit{Initially:} \quad &(\textbf{A} \, i :: D.i) \\
\textit{Program i:} \quad &[\![ \quad \{D.i\} \\
&\quad v := i \\
&; \quad D.i := \textit{false} \\
&; \quad \textbf{if } (\textbf{A} \, j : j \neq i : \neg D.j \lor v \neq i) \rightarrow \textit{skip } \textbf{fi} \\
&; \quad y.i := v = i
\end{aligned}
$$

$$\{(\mathbf{A}\,j\,:\,j\neq i\,:\,\neg D.j\,\lor\,v\neq i)\}\,\{y.i\ \equiv\ v=i\}$$
$$]|$$
$$\{(\mathbf{N}\,i\,::\,y.i)\ =\ 1\}\ .$$

We omit the proof that there is no danger of deadlock or starvation.

The final transformation concerns the breaking up of the rather coarse-grained alternative construct into a sequence of fine-grained ones. Here we can use the Lemma mentioned in the beginning of this note. Since the guard is a finite conjunction and since none of the conjuncts $\neg D.j\,\lor\,v\neq i$ is falsified outside *Program i*, the evaluation of the conjunction can be carried out conjunct-wise, even in any order. Finally, each atomic statement **if** $\neg D.j\,\lor\,v\neq i\rightarrow skip$ **fi** is of a type that can be implemented by "at most one access to at most one shared variable".

And this concludes the derivation of the algorithm.

$$\star\quad\star\quad\star$$

One may wonder how the potential parallelism would have been constrained had we chosen a stronger $C.i$. With e.g. choice (c), we would have obtained all but the same multiprogram, except that the alternative construct would have been **if** $(\mathbf{A}\,j\,:\,j\neq i\,:\,\neg D.j)\rightarrow skip$ **fi**. The resulting algorithm would have been a "two-phase algorithm", in which first all component programs perform their assignment to $v$ and then when they have all done so, their assignments to $y$. In our current algorithm no such "system-wide synchronization point" exists: the two phases are sweetly interleaved. With the still stronger choice (a) for $C.i$, we would have derived programs containing **if** $false\rightarrow skip$ **fi**. This would further cut down the potential parallelism, even dramatically so, because the multiprogram would be guaranteed to come to a premature halt.

W. H. J. Feijen,
Department of Mathematics and Computing Science,
Eindhoven University of Technology,
P.O. Box 513,
5600 MB  Eindhoven,
The Netherlands.

# 14

# Experimenting with a Refinement Calculus

## A. J. M. van Gasteren

Meeting Carroll Morgan, some time ago, started me doing what I had wanted to do for a long time, viz. investigating to what extent refinement calculus is a helpful vehicle in presenting the development of an imperative algorithm in such a way that

- reasoning is as calculational as possible;
- the design decisions stand out clearly and
- can be described concisely; and
- the structure of the development is highly visible in the presentation.

Here I show refinement calculus in action in an example programming problem. The example has been chosen because it illustrates a variety of properties of the calculus, and because of the way the solution developed avoids indexitis. My main goal is to give an introduction to the *use* of the calculus. The reader is assumed to be familiar with program development.

## Preliminaries : refinement

A considerable amount of work has gone into laying the mathematical foundations of a refinement calculus for sequential, imperative programs. R. J. R. Back [1] did pioneering work; more recently, Carroll Morgan [2] at Oxford and Joseph M. Morris [3] at Glasgow joined in, partly redoing, partly extending Back's work, and continuing a development that was also inspired by others — such as Dijkstra, Hoare, and Jones. Here I shall only mention what is actually needed in the development of the example problem. The program notation used is Dijkstra's Guarded Command notation, except that we use a fat dot to delimit variable declarations; other notations and the calculational rules, to be presented next, have largely been adopted from [2].

Firstly, in order that a program development be a calculation, specifications and programs need to be expressions of the same kind. Here we choose a specification to be a program. The introduction of a special statement, the *specification statement*, enables us to do so:

$v : [P, Q]$ is a program establishing postcondition $Q$ from precondition $P$, by changing variables of list $v$ of program variables.

Formally, for all points in the state space and for all $R$,

$$wp.(v : [P, Q]).R \equiv P \wedge (\mathbf{A}\, v :: Q \Rightarrow R) .$$

Sometimes we omit the precondition $P$, writing $v : [Q]$ ; we only do so if the precondition is valid and takes the form "viewed as an equation in $v$, postcondition $Q$ has a solution".

Secondly, we need a notion of calculation. It is provided by "$\sqsubseteq$", pronounced "refines to":

for programs $S$ and $T$, $S \sqsubseteq T$ means
($\mathbf{A}\, R ::$ for all points in state space $wp.S.R \Rightarrow wp.T.R$) .

Program development amounts to refining a specification (statement) into a program that is free of specification statements. The refinement relation $\sqsubseteq$ is reflexive and transitive, and the program constructors are monotonic with respect to it; therefore, expressions can be refined by refining their subexpressions.

Specification statements can be refined in all the familiar ways, such as

$$x : [P, Q] \quad \sqsubseteq \quad \text{skip} \qquad \text{if for all states } P \Rightarrow Q$$
$$x : [P, Q] \quad \sqsubseteq \quad x := E \qquad \text{if for all states } P \Rightarrow Q(x := E) .$$

Finally, it will prove to be convenient to use the construct $v : |[ \mathbf{inv}\ Q \bullet S ]|$, for list $v$ of program variables, predicate $Q$, and statement $S$, to stand for an "extension" of program $S$ that —by assigning to variables of $v$— maintains $Q$ over $S$, i.e. if $Q$ holds as a precondition of $S$ it will hold as a postcondition of the construct as well. (That is why such a $Q$ is called an invariant.) It typically appears where we generalize a pre- and a post-condition.

The most important property is that $v : |[ \mathbf{inv}\ Q \bullet \dots ]|$ distributes over the program constructors; for instance,

$$v : |[\, \mathbf{inv}\ Q \bullet S\, ;\, T\, ]| \quad \sqsubseteq \quad v : |[\, \mathbf{inv}\ Q \bullet S\, ]|\, ;\, v : |[\, \mathbf{inv}\ Q \bullet T\, ]| .$$

In this paper, only two elimination rules for such constructs are needed, viz. elimination rules (0) and (1):

(0)    $v : |[\ \textbf{inv}\ Q \bullet w : [P, R]\ ]| \quad \sqsubseteq \quad w : [P \wedge Q, R]$
if the variables of $w$ do not occur in $Q$;

(1)    $v : |[\ \textbf{inv}\ Q \bullet x := E\ ]| \quad \sqsubseteq \quad v : [Q, Q(x := E)]\ ;\ x := E\ .$

# Preliminaries : the programming problem

The problem is to refine $p := p^{-1}$, where $p$ is (an array representing) a cyclic permutation, to be defined shortly; the solution has to be in situ, i.e. it can only use a fixed amount of extra space.

In order to postpone reasoning in terms of array elements —a common source of indexitis— we need an "intermediate" representation :

**Definition0**    (Ring definition.) For a finite sequence $S$ of distinct elements, $(\!(S)\!)$ , pronounced "ring $S$", denotes the bijective function on $S$'s elements defined for each element $c$ of $S$ by

$$(\!(S)\!).c \ = \ c\text{'s right neighbour in } S \ \ ,$$

where, by convention, the right neighbour of $S$'s rightmost element is $S$'s leftmost element.
**End** Definition0.

Given this definition, we can now express "function $p$ is a cyclic permutation" as $(\,\mathbf{E}\,S : S$ a sequence (of distinct elements) $: p = (\!(S)\!)\,)$  .

In the above and in what follows, sequences are indicated by capitals, elements by lower case letters, and concatenation by juxtaposition; elements and singleton sequences are identified; the empty sequence is indicated by $\phi$.

As a consequence of Definition0, we have two calculationally pleasant properties, given here without proof:

**Property0**    (The rule of rotation.) For $XY$ a sequence of distinct elements,

$$(\!(XY)\!) = (\!(YX)\!)\ \ .$$

**Property1**    $(\!(X)\!)^{-1} = (\!(r.X)\!)$, where $r.X$ is the reverse of sequence $X$, i.e. for all $c$, $X$, and $Y$ :

$$\begin{aligned} r.\phi &= \phi \\ r.c &= c \\ r.(XY) &= (r.Y)(r.X)\ \ . \end{aligned}$$

Note that $(\!(\phi)\!)^{-1} = (\!(\phi)\!)$ and $(\!(c)\!)^{-1} = (\!(c)\!)$ ; therefore, we confine our attention to cyclic permutations of at least two elements.

# The derivation

$$p := p^{-1}$$

⊑    {using $p$ is a cyclic permutation with at least two elements}

  |[ **var** $a, b, T$ •

(i)      $a, b, T : [\, p = (\!(Tab)\!) \,]$

(ii)    ; $p : [\, p = (\!(Tab)\!) \,,\, p = (\!(Tab)\!)^{-1} \,]$

  ]|  .

———————————————— where (i) and (ii) ————————————————

   (i)

⊑    {Definition0: ring definition}

     $a :=$ any element of $p$ ; $b := p.a$

   ; $T : [\, p = (\!(Tab)\!) \,]$

——————————— and

   (ii)

=    {rewriting the postcondition using Property1, $r$'s
       definition, and the rule of rotation (Property0)}

   $p : [\, p = (\!(Tab)\!) \,,\, p = (\!(a(r.T)b)\!) \,]$

⊑    {generalizing pre- and post-condition: introduction
       of local variables —$X, Y$— and invariant —$Q$—}

  |[ **var** $X, Y$ •

     $X, Y := T, \phi \; \{Q : p = (\!(XaYb)\!)\}$

(iii)    ; $p : |[$ **inv** $Q$ •

(iv)       $X, Y : [\, X = T \wedge Y = \phi \,,\, X = \phi \wedge Y = r.T \,]$

     ]|

  ]|  .

——————————————————— where (iii) ———————————————————

**Remark**    For the time being, there are only two tasks left: we must refine (iv), which is shown later in the Lemma, and then we can refine the surrounding program (iii) by distributing $p : |[$ **inv** $Q$ • ... ]| over (iv)'s refinement.

**End** Remark.

(iii)

$\sqsubseteq$      {replacing (iv) by a refinement —see Lemma—}

$p : |[$ **inv** $Q \bullet$

    **do** $X \neq \phi \rightarrow$

       $|[$ **var** $c, Z \bullet c, Z : [\,cZ = X\,]$

       $; X, Y := Z, cY$

       $]|$

    **od**

   $]|$

$\sqsubseteq$      {distributing $p : |[$ **inv** $Q \bullet \ldots ]|$ over the repetition,
replacing the guard using $Q \Rightarrow (X \neq \phi \equiv p.b \neq a)$ ; then
distribution over ";" in the body}

   **do** $p.b \neq a \rightarrow$

     $|[$ **var** $c, Z \bullet$

(v)        $p : |[$ **inv** $Q \bullet c, Z : [\,cZ = X\,] ]| \; \{cZ = X\}$

(vi)       $; p : |[$ **inv** $Q \bullet X, Y := Z, cY ]|$

     $]|$

   **od** .

———————————— where (v) and $\{cZ = X\}$ (vi) ————————————

(v)

$\sqsubseteq$      {$c$ and $Z$ do not occur in $Q$ : using **inv**-elimination (0)}

$c, Z : [\,Q\,,\, cZ = X\,]$

$\sqsubseteq$      {ring definition and definition of $Q$}

$c, Z := p.b, tail.X$

——————— and

$\{cZ = X\}$ (vi)

$\sqsubseteq$      {using **inv**-elimination (1)}

(vii)    $p : [\,Q \wedge cZ = X\,,\, Q(X, Y := Z, cY)\,]$

     $; X, Y := Z, cY$ .

——————————————— where (vii) ———————————————

(vii)

$\sqsubseteq$      {weakening the precondition, calculating the postcondition}

$$p : [\ p = (\!|cZaYb|\!)\ ,\ p = (\!|ZacYb|\!)\ ]$$

$\sqsubseteq$ {ring definition, using that for elements of $Z$ and $Y$ the right neighbour remains unchanged}

$$p.a,\ p.b,\ p.c : [\ p.a = hd.(Yb)\ \wedge\ p.b = c\ \wedge\ p.c = hd.(Za)$$
$$,\ p.c = hd.(Yb)\ \wedge\ p.a = c\ \wedge\ p.b = hd.(Za)$$
$$]$$

$\sqsubseteq$ {assignment}

$$p.a,\ p.b,\ p.c := p.b,\ p.c,\ p.a\ \ .$$

This is the end of the main derivation. What remains to be done — besides proving the correctness of (iv)'s refinement— is the removal of sequence variables, so as to arrive at an in-situ program. To that end we first assemble the refinements. We find that all sequence variables are auxiliary and, hence, can be omitted :

$$p := p^{-1}$$

$\sqsubseteq$

```
|[ var a, b, T • a := any element of p ; b := p.a
; T : [ p = (|Tab|) ]
; |[ var X, Y • X, Y := T, φ
   ; do p.b ≠ a →
           |[ var c, Z • c, Z := p.b, tail.X
           ; p.a, p.b, p.c := p.b, p.c, p.a
           ; X, Y := Z, cY
           ]|
      od
   ]|
]|
```

$\sqsubseteq$ {$X$, $Y$, $Z$, and $T$ only occur in assignments to $X$, $Y$, and $Z$ and, hence, can be removed}

```
|[ var a, b • a := any element of p ; b := p.a
; do p.b ≠ a →
        |[ var c • c := p.b
        ; p.a, p.b, p.c := p.b, p.c, p.a
        ]|
   od
]|  .
```

# The refinement of (iv)

**Lemma**

$$X,Y : [\, X = T \wedge Y = \phi \,,\, X = \phi \wedge Y = r.T \,]$$

$\sqsubseteq$

$$\textbf{do}\ \ X \neq \phi \rightarrow \|[\ \textbf{var}\ c, Z \bullet c, Z : [\, cZ = X \,]\ ;\ X, Y := Z, cY\ ]\|\ \textbf{od}.$$

**Proof**

$$X,Y : [\, X = T \wedge Y = \phi \,,\, X = \phi \wedge Y = r.T \,]$$

$\sqsubseteq$    {generalizing pre- and post-condition: introducing
invariant $Q0$ defined by $Q0$: $(r.X)Y = r.T$ }

$$Y : \|[\ \textbf{inv}\ Q0 \bullet X : [\, X = T \,,\, X = \phi \,]\ ]\|$$

$\sqsubseteq$    {refining the inner specification by a repetition and
distributing $Y : \|[\ \textbf{inv}\ Q0 \bullet \dots\ ]\|$ over the latter}

$$\textbf{do}\ \ X \neq \phi \rightarrow\ (\text{viii})\ Y : \|[\ \textbf{inv}\ Q0 \bullet X := tail.X\ ]\|\ \textbf{od}\ \ .$$

———————————————— where (viii) ————————————————

(viii)

$\sqsubseteq$    {**inv**-elimination (1)}

$$Y : [\, Q0\,,\, Q0(X := tail.X) \,]\ ;\ X := tail.X$$

$=$    {substitution}

$$Y : [\, (r.X)Y = r.T \,,\, (r.(tail.X))Y = r.T \,]\ ;\ X := tail.X$$

$\sqsubseteq$    { $r.X = (r.(tail.X))\,hd.X$ }

$$Y := (hd.X)Y\ ;\ X := tail.X$$

$\sqsubseteq$    {introduction of variables and properties of assignment}

$$\|[\ \textbf{var}\ c, Z \bullet c, Z : [\, cZ = X \,]\ ;\ X, Y := Z, cY\ ]\|\ \ .$$

**End** Proof.

# Epilogue

In the above derivation, have we achieved what I hoped the refinement
calculus would help us achieve? Certainly the derivation is as calculational

as possible; in fact there is nothing but calculation. This is due to the use of the specification statement.

The example derivation shows that the expressions quickly become too long to be carried along through all the refinements. Therefore, it is unavoidable to refine subexpressions in isolation. To make the structure of the derivation as visible as possible, it is then useful to have some conspicuous separator between an expression and the refinements of its subexpressions. Here, a horizontal line serves that purpose.

As for the design decisions, note that the calculational format invites the explicit formulation of rules such as (0) and (1), distribution rules for $v : |[ \text{ inv } Q \bullet \ldots ]|$, etc. .

## REFERENCES

[1] R. J. R. Back. A calculus of refinements for program derivations. *Acta Informatica*, 25:593–624, 1988.

[2] C. C. Morgan, K. A. Robinson, and P. H. B. Gardiner. On the refinement calculus. Technical Monograph PRG–70, Oxford University Computing Laboratory, 1988.

[3] Joseph M. Morris. A theoretical basis for stepwise refinement and the programming calculus. *Science of Computer Programming*, 9(3):298–306, 1987.

*Acknowledgements*: Carroll Morgan deserves many thanks for providing the inspiration, the notation, and the rules, and for commenting promptly on the first version of this development. The Eindhoven Tuesday Afternoon Club has studied and improved both versions. Lincoln A. Wallen's suggestion to treat $( S )$ as a function —rather than merely the representation of a function— is greatfully acknowledged: it enabled the use of compact expressions like $( S ).c$ and $P = ( S )$ .

A. J. M. van Gasteren,
Department of Computer Science,
University of Utrecht,
P.O. Box 80.089,
3508 TB Utrecht,
The Netherlands.

Department of Computing Science,
Rijksuniversiteit Groningen,
P.O. Box 800,
9700 AV Groningen,
The Netherlands.

# 15

# Serializable Programs, Parallelizable Assertions: A Basis for Interleaving

## Mohamed G. Gouda

## 1 Introduction

Many formal models of concurrent programs are based on the notion of *interleaving*: in executing a concurrent program, only one enabled action is executed at each step. This notion has both its advantages and disadvantages.

The main advantage of interleaving is that it tends to simplify the verification of concurrent programs. For instance, to verify that a given predicate is an invariant of some program requires showing that each action of the program preserves the invariant when executed in isolation. Were it possible for actions to be executed in parallel, checking the same invariant would require showing that each set of actions preserves the invariant when executed in parallel. In other words, the number of cases needed to verify an invariant would have increased from $n$ to $2^n - 1$, where $n$ is the number of actions in the program.

The main disadvantage of interleaving is that it does not reflect our understanding that multiple actions of a concurrent program may in fact be executed at the same time. The discrepancy between our assumption of how concurrent programs are executed (interleaving) and how they are "actually" executed can lead to programs that, although provably correct under interleaving, do not perform as expected when executed. This point is made clearer by the next two examples.

Consider the following program with two boolean variables *left* and *right* and two actions:

$$left \neq right \quad \rightarrow \quad left := right$$
$$left \neq right \quad \rightarrow \quad right := left$$

If this program starts in a state satisfying *left* $\neq$ *right*, its next state, under interleaving, satisfies *left* = *right*. On the other hand, if the two actions are allowed to execute in parallel, then the program may remain within the states satisfying $left \neq right$ indefinitely. This discrepancy is caused by the fact that the program can make a transition from $left \neq right$ to $left \neq right$ by executing its two actions in parallel, but cannot make a similar transition by executing the two actions in some sequence.

In order to avoid such a discrepancy, concurrent programs should be designed so that any state that can be reached by executing some actions in parallel can still be reached by executing the same actions in some sequence. We refer to such programs as serializable. (A more formal definition of serializable programs is given in Section 4.)

Consider the following serializable program with three boolean variables and two actions.

$$left \neq middle \quad \rightarrow \quad left := middle$$
$$right \neq middle \quad \rightarrow \quad right := middle$$

This program satisfies the assertion

$$(left \neq middle \ \wedge \ right \neq middle) \quad leads\text{-}to \quad left \neq right$$

under interleaving; this is because if the program starts at a state where $left \neq middle$ and $right \neq middle$, which implies $left = right$, then after executing exactly one action the next state satisfies $left \neq right$. On the other hand the program does not satisfy the assertion if the two actions are allowed to execute in parallel. Thus, the correctness of this program should not be based on this or similar assertions. Rather, it should be based on what we call parallelizable assertions, i.e. assertions that if satisfied under interleaving are also satisfied when actions are executed in parallel. (A more formal definition of parallelizable assertions is given in Section 3.)

In summary, as long as verification of concurrent programs is based on interleaving (and as mentioned earlier, there are good reasons for continuing this practice), one should design only serializable programs and base their correctness only on parallelizable assertions.

In the remainder of this note, we define the notions of parallelizable assertions and serializable programs and identify a reasonable set of parallelizable assertions for the family of serializable programs.

# 2   Concurrent programs

Consider a *program* that consists of a set of *variables* and a set of *actions*; both sets are finite and nonempty. Each action is of the form

$$G \rightarrow x.1, \ldots, x.n := F.1, \ldots, F.n$$

where $G$ is a predicate called the *guard* of the action, the $x.i$'s are distinct variables, and the $F.i$'s are total functions of the program variables.

The set of actions is partitioned into one or more (mutually exclusive) subsets such that each variable is written by the actions of at most one subset. We call these subsets *processes*.

A *state* is defined by one value for each variable.

A *transition* is a nonempty set of actions with at most one action from each process. A transition that has exactly one action is called a *serial transition*.

A state $q$ *follows* a state $p$ *over* a transition $t$ iff the guard of each action in $t$ is true at $p$, and $q$ can be computed starting from $p$ by parallel execution of all the actions in $t$.

This notion of "follows-over" can be extended to finite sequences of transitions. A state $q$ *follows* a state $p$ *over* $(t.1, \ldots, t.r)$ iff there are states $p.1, \ldots, p.(r+1)$ such that $p = p.1$, $q = p.(r+1)$, and for each $i$, $p.(i+1)$ follows $p.i$ over $t.i$.

A *(serial) computation* is a maximal sequence

$$p.1, t.1, p.2, t.2, \ldots, p.r, t.r, p.(r+1)$$

where each $p.i$ is a state, each $t.i$ is a (serial) transition, and for each $i$, $p.(i+1)$ follows $p.i$ over $t.i$. The maximality condition means that either the sequence is infinite or it is finite and the guard of every action in the program is false in the last state of the computation.

# 3  Parallelizable assertions

Logical properties of programs are expressed as assertions. An assertion *holds* for a program iff program states, transitions, and computations satisfy some condition called the *holding condition* for the assertion. Each assertion has a "serial version", which is also an assertion. The holding condition for the serial version of an assertion is the same as that for the assertion except that all occurrences of "transition", "computation", and any other assertion are respectively replaced by "serial transition", "serial computation", and the serial version of that assertion. In this note, we identify three classes of assertions: closure, activity, and convergence. The holding conditions for the assertions in these classes are defined next.

**Closure under execution:**    A closure assertion has the form ($P$ is closed); it holds for a program iff $P$ is a set of program states and for every $p$ in $P$ and every program transition $t$, if $q$ follows $p$ over $t$, then $q$ is in $P$. The serial version of this assertion is ($P$ is serially closed); it has the same holding condition as that of its assertion except that "transition" is replaced by "serial transition".

**Activity within a closure:** An activity assertion has the form $(u$ is active in $P)$; it holds for a program iff $u$ is a set of program actions, $P$ is a closed set of program states, and for every program computation that starts in a state in $P$ there is at least one action in $u$ that occurs infinitely many times in the transitions of the computation. The serial version of this assertion is $(u$ is serially active in $P)$; it has the same holding condition as that of its assertion except that "closed" and "computation" are replaced by "serially closed" and "serial computation", respectively.

**Convergence to a Closure:** A convergence assertion has the form $(P$ is convergent to $Q)$; it holds for a program iff both $P$ and $Q$ are closed sets of program states and every program computation that starts in a state in $P$ has a state in $Q$. The serial version of this assertion is $(P$ is serially convergent to $Q)$; it has the same holding condition as that of its assertion except that "closed" and "computation" are replaced by "serially closed" and "serial computation", respectively.

One program property that can be expressed as a closure assertion is "mutual exclusion". A property that can be expressed as an activity assertion is "freedom from starvation". Examples of properties that can be expressed as convergence assertions are "termination" and "stabilization".

A class of assertions is called *parallelizable* for a program iff for each assertion in the class, if the serial version of the assertion holds for the program, then the assertion holds for the program. For example, closure is parallelizable for a program iff for each $P$, if $(P$ is serially closed) holds for the program, then $(P$ is closed) holds for the program.

We mentioned in the introduction that program correctness should be based on parallelizable assertions. We can now be more explicit about the reason for making this statement. The serial version of an assertion is what we prove, under interleaving, about program execution; the assertion itself is what actually is maintained during program execution. Thus, basing program correctness on parallelizable assertions guarantees that what we prove is what actually is maintained (or occurs) during execution.

It is straightforward to show that none of our assertion classes —closure, activity, or convergence— is parallelizable for arbitrary programs. In the next section, we identify a large family of programs for which these three classes of assertions are parallelizable.

# 4 Parallelizable assertions for serializable programs

A program is called *P-serializable* iff $P$ is a serially closed set of program states, and for every $p$ in $P$ and every program transition $t$, if $q$ follows $p$

over $t$, then $t$ can be partitioned into serial transitions $t.1, \ldots, t.r$ such that $q$ follows $p$ over $(t.1, \ldots, t.r)$.

The family of serializable programs is reasonably large. For example, if program variables are partitioned into shared and private, where a shared variable is one that is read or written by the actions of two or more processes, then any program in which no action both reads and writes shared variables is $P$-serializable, where $P$ is the (closed) set of all program states. This shows that serial programs, i.e. those programs that consist of single processes, are serializable.

The next theorem, whose proof follows from the above definitions, states that the assertion classes, closure, activity and convergence, are parallelizable for serializable programs.

**Theorem 1**    If a program is $P$-serializable, then the following three statements are satisfied for every subset $Q$ of $P$ and every set $u$ of program actions.

   **a.**    If ($Q$ is serially closed) holds for the program,
        then ($Q$ is closed) holds for the program.

   **b.**    If ($u$ is serially active in $Q$) holds for the program,
        then ($u$ is active in $Q$) holds for the program.

   **c.**    If ($P$ is serially convergent to $Q$) holds for the program,
        then ($P$ is convergent to $Q$) holds for the program.

□

As a result of Theorem 1, verification of serializable programs can be carried out under interleaving, provided that all derivations are based solely on the assertion classes: closure, activity, and convergence.

So far, serializable programs is the largest family of programs for which rich classes of assertions are known to be parallelizable. This should explain our earlier recommendations: as long as verification of concurrent programs is based on interleaving, one should design only serializable programs and base their correctness only on parallelizable assertions.

The main result in this note (Theorem 1) is based on the assumption that any pair of program actions, belonging to different processes, are executed either in sequence or in exact parallel. The validity of this assumption hinges on the actions being "small", with each of them accessing the shared variables in a "minimal" way. This requirement can be achieved by resorting to the well-known autamicity condition of Gries and Owicki, namely that each action has at most one reference to a shared variable. (A recent result of my student Jim Anderson shows this restriction can be relaxed somewhat.)

*Acknowledgements*: I would like to thank Anish Arora and James Burns for helpful discussions concerning this work. The comments of James Anderson, David Gries and Jayadev Misra on earlier drafts of this note are greatly appreciated.

Mohamed G. Gouda,
Department of Computer Sciences,
The University of Texas at Austin,
Taylor Hall 2.124,
Austin, Texas 78712–1188,
U.S.A.

# 16

# Binary to Decimal, One More Time

## David Gries

## Introduction

In [1] Knuth presents an algorithm for converting a binary fraction to a decimal fraction that satisfies certain conditions. Knuth found the algorithm interesting not only because it was short and useful but because he could "see no way to demonstrate its correctness by conventional methods". He hoped that "others with more experience in formal methods will agree that the algorithm is interesting and will help me figure out what I should have done.".

The problem *is* interesting, and I am indebted to Knuth for bringing it to our attention. In this note, I attempt to present the algorithm in terms of an ideal development, using techniques first proposed by Edsger W. Dijkstra and so ably expounded upon and used by him for well over a decade.

## The problem

Knuth's problem is to convert an integer $n$, $0 \leq n < 2^{16}$, representing the fraction $n/2^{16}$ into a sequence $d$ of digits representing the decimal fraction $.d$ that satisfies certain properties. (Actually, Knuth required $0 < n$; we extend the problem to cover the case $n = 0$, in which case $d$ will be the empty sequence $\varepsilon$.) First, of course, the $d_i$ are really digits:

(0)     $R0$:  $\forall(j: 0 \leq j < \#d: 0 \leq d.j < 10)$.

Next, letting $S.d$ denote the value of the fraction,

(1)     $S.d = \Sigma(j: 0 \leq j < \#d: d.j/10^{j+1})$,

we indicate that the fraction approximates $n/2^{16}$ closely enough:

(2)     $R1$:  $n - 1/2 \leq 2^{16}*S.d < n + 1/2$.

Third, sequence $d$ is as short as possible, i.e. no shorter solution exists:

(3)     $R2$:  $\forall(D: seq: R0_D^d \land R1_D^d: \#d \leq \#D)$.

Fourth and finally, several fractions might satisfy $R1$; we want the closest one to $n/2^{16}$ (we leave this informal):

(4)     $.d$ is the closest fraction of shortest length to $n/2^{16}$ — and largest if two closest ones exist.

A few properties of fractions that satisfy $R0$ and $R1$ will prove useful. First, there is at most one solution of length at most 4 (barring adding zeroes to the right). This is because the left and right values of $R1$ differ by 1, but any two different fractions of length at most 4 differ by at least $10^{-4}$ and $2^{16}*10^{-4} = 6.5536 > 1$. Second, at most two different fractions of length 5 satisfy $R1$, because the maximum distance among three such fractions is at least $2*10^{-5}$ and $2^{16}*2*10^{-5} = 1.31072 > 1$.

Finally, the shortest solution has at most length 5. This we prove by exhibiting a solution of length 5. Consider

$$D = floor(10^5*n/2^{16} + 1/2).$$

Since $0 \le n < 2^{16}$, we have $0 \le D < 10^5$, so $D$ has at most 5 digits and $D/10^5$ can be written as a fraction $d'$ (say) of at most 5 digits. We show that $d'$, with $S.d' = D/10^5$, is a solution of $R1$:

| | |
|---|---|
| $2^{16}*D/10^5$ | $2^{16}*D/10^5$ |
| $>$    {$floor(x) > x - 1$} | $\le$    {$floor(x) \le x$} |
| $(2^{16}/10^5)*(10^5*n/2^{16} + 1/2 - 1)$ | $(2^{16}/10^5)*(10^5*n/2^{16} + 1/2)$ |
| $=$    {Arithmetic} | $=$    {Arithmetic} |
| $n - 2^{15}/10^5$ | $n + 2^{15}/10^5$ |
| $>$    {Arithmetic} | $<$    {Arithmetic} |
| $n - 1/2$ | $n + 1/2$ |

## Development of the loop of the algorithm

Since a shortest sequence $d$ is desired, we look for an algorithm that begins with $d = \varepsilon$ and iteratively catenates a new digit to it until a solution is found. Note that $R0_\varepsilon^d$ holds. The first relation of $R1_\varepsilon^d$ is false if $n \ne 0$ (since $S.\varepsilon = 0$), but the second relation is true. Also, $R2_\varepsilon^d$ holds. Hence, we can obtain a loop invariant by deleting the single false part of $R0 \wedge R1 \wedge R2$. Introducing

(5)     $P1$:  $2^{16}*S.d < n + 1/2$,   i.e.  $0 < n + 1/2 - 2^{16}*S.d$,

we have the loop invariant

(6)     $R0 \wedge P1 \wedge R2$.

143     David Gries

The chance of establishing the first relation of $R1$ is greatest when $S.d$ is as large as possible, i.e. when $.d$ is the largest fraction of its length that satisfies $P1$. Therefore, we are inclined to introduce an invariant indicating that the next highest fraction of the same length is too large (in order to shorten the story a bit, in $P3$, we use the stronger $<$ instead of $\leq$ because it is needed later on):

(7)      $P3$: $n + 1/2 < 2^{16}*(S.d + 10^{-\#d})$.

Hence, our loop will produce the largest possible fraction, and some code after the loop will have to change it to the closest.

Our loop should terminate when the first relation of $R1$ holds, and to test this we need to maintain in some fashion the value $S.d$. We do this using a new variable $s$ with definition

(8)      $P4$: $s = 10^{\#d+1}*(n + 1/2 - 2^{16}*S.d)$.

This choice is motivated by the second form of $P1$ in (5), with the scaling $10^{\#d+1}$ motivated by the definition of $S.d$ in (1) and the desire to have $s$ be an integer. A more important motivation is that Knuth [1] used a similar variable; and we admit that we have pulled this rabbit out of a (Knuthian) hat.

As mentioned earlier, our result is established when the first relation of $R1$ is true, and thus the loop guard is the complement of this relation. We manipulate the first relation of $R1$ as follows:

$n - 1/2 \leq 2^{16}*S.d$

$=$      {Use $P4$ to substitute for $2^{16}*S.d$}

$n - 1/2 \leq n + 1/2 - s/10^{\#d+1}$

$=$      {Arithmetic}

$s \leq 10^{\#d+1}$.

So that $10^{\#d+1}$ need not be calculated again and again, we introduce a variable $t$ defined by

(9)      $P5$: $t = 10^{\#d+1}$.

Hence, termination of the loop can occur when $s \leq t$, and the loop guard is $s > t$.

We now introduce an additional invariant, prematurely, simply to speed up the presentation. The need for it arises later on, when attempting to prove that one of the other invariants is maintained by the body of the loop.

$P6$: $s$ is an odd multiple of $2^{\#d}$.

In (10) we collect the components of the invariant in a single place for later reference. At the same time, we have rewritten $P1$ and $P3$ using the definition of $s$ in $P4$.

(10)     $R0$:  $\forall(j : 0 \le j < \#d : 0 \le d.j < 10)$

          $P1$:  $0 < s$

          $R2$:  there is no solution of length less than $\#d$ digits

          $P3$:  $s < 10*2^{16}$

          $P4$:  $s = 10^{\#d+1}*(n + 1/2 - 2^{16}*S.d)$

          $P5$:  $t = 10^{\#d+1}$

          $P6$:  $s$ is an odd multiple of $2^{\#d}$

All the invariants can be established with $d, s, t := \varepsilon, 10*n + 5, 10$, and we can write the following algorithm.

> $d, s, t := \varepsilon, 10*n + 5, 10;$
> {invariant: $R0 \wedge P1 \wedge R2 \wedge P3 \wedge P4 \wedge P5 \wedge P6$}
> **do** $s > t \rightarrow$  Extend $d$ while maintaining $P$ **od**

We now develop the body of the loop, which should contain a statement like $d := d\char`^v$ for some digit $v$ ( $\char`^$ denotes catenation). We focus our attention on $P4^d_{d\char`^v}$, because it should aid us in determining $v$ as well as the assignment to $s$. Establishing $P4^d_{d\char`^v}$ calls for assigning to $s$ the value

$$10^{\#(d\char`^v)+1}*(n + 1/2 - 2^{16}*S.(d\char`^v)).$$

We manipulate this expression, trying to receive guidance on $v$ and the assignment to $s$ :

$\qquad 10^{\#(d\char`^v)+1}*(n + 1/2 - 2^{16}*S.(d\char`^v))$

$=\qquad$ {Definition of $\#$ and $S$}

$\qquad 10^{\#d+2}*(n + 1/2 - 2^{16}*(S.d + v/10^{\#d+1}))$

$=\qquad$ {Arithmetic}

$\qquad 10*(10^{\#d+1}*(n + 1/2 - 2^{16}*S.d) - 2^{16}*v)$

$=\qquad$ {P4}

$\qquad 10*(s - 2^{16}*v)$

$=\qquad$ {We are looking for a value for $v$. The form of the
          expression urges us to rewrite $s$ as shown.}

$\qquad 10*(s \bmod 2^{16} + 2^{16}*(s \div 2^{16}) - 2^{16}*v)$

$=$        {Choosing $v = s \div 2^{16}$ makes $s$ easy to update}

$10*(s \bmod 2^{16})$.

Hence, we may use $v = s \div 2^{16}$ and the assignment $s := 10*(s \bmod 2^{16})$.

$P5^d_{d\,\widehat{}\,v}$ is established using $t := t*10$, and we therefore have the algorithm

(11)    $d, s, t := \varepsilon, 10*n + 5, 10;$
        {invariant $P$:  $R0 \wedge P1 \wedge R2 \wedge P3 \wedge P4 \wedge P5 \wedge P6$}
        **do** $s > t \rightarrow d, s, t := d\,\widehat{}\,(s \div 2^{16}), 10*(s \bmod 2^{16}), t*10$ **od**
        $\{R0 \wedge R1 \wedge R2 \wedge P3\}$

## Verifying the invariance of $P$

We remark that the next digit $v$ and the assignment to $s$ were suggested by the calculations. However, we still have to be sure that all the invariants are maintained by the body of the loop. For each one, we show that its weakest precondition with respect to the loop body is implied by the invariant and the truth of the loop guard.

**$R0$ (see (10)) is maintained.**    We have:

$wp(body, R0)$

$=$        {Definition of $wp$}

$\forall(j: 0 \le j < \#(d\,\widehat{}\,(s \div 2^{16})): 0 \le d.j < 10)$

$=$        {range split, one-point rule}

$\forall(j: 0 \le j < \#d: 0 \le d.j < 10) \wedge 0 \le s \div 2^{16} < 10$

$\Leftarrow$        {$P1$ yields the lower and $P3$ the upper bound on $s$}

$R0 \wedge P1 \wedge P3$

**$P1$ (see (10)) is maintained** (this required the introduction of $P6$). We have:

$wp(body, P1)$

$=$        {Definition of $P1$ and $wp$}

$0 < 10*(s \bmod 2^{16})$

$=$        {Arithmetic}

$0 < s \bmod 2^{16}$

$\Leftarrow$     {$P1$ yields $0 < s$. By $P6$, since $\#d \leq 5 < 16$,
                $s$ is not a multiple of $2^{16}$}

$P1 \wedge P6$

**$R2$ (see (10)) is maintained.**   We have (informally):

$wp(body,\ R2)$

$=$       {Definition of $wp$}

There is no solution of length $\#d$ or less

$R2$ yields the absence of a solution of length less than $\#d$, and the guard of the loop together with $P1$ and $P3$ yields the absence of a solution of length $\#d$.

**$P3$ (see (10)) is maintained.**   We have:

$wp(body,\ s < 10*2^{16})$

$=$       {Definition of $wp$}

$10*(s \bmod 2^{16}) < 10*2^{16}$

$\Leftarrow$       {Arithmetic}

$true$

**$P4$ and $P5$ (see (10)) are maintained.**   The assignments to $d$, $s$, and $t$ were developed precisely to maintain these.

**$P6$ (see (10)) is maintained.**   We have:

$wp(body,\ s$ is an odd multiple of $2^{\#d})$

$=$        {Definition of $wp$ and property of sequences}

$10*(s \bmod 2^{16})$ is an odd multiple of $2^{\#d+1}$

$=$        {Write $s = q*2^{16} + r,\ 0 \leq r < 2^{16}$, and $0 \leq \#d < 5$}

$10*r$ is an odd multiple of $2^{\#d+1}$

$=$        {Arithmetic}

$r$ is an odd multiple of $2^{\#d}$

$=$        {By $P6$, $s = q*2^{16} + r$, and $k \leq 5$,
            $r$ is an odd multiple of $2^{\#d}$}

$true$

# Finding the shortest solution that is closest

Algorithm (11) finds the largest shortest solution; we want the closest shortest solution to $n/2^{16}$. By the analysis given just after the problem statement, if $S.d$ is the largest shortest solution, then the only other possible solution is $S.d - 10^{-\#d}$, i.e. $d$, but with the last digit one less. Note that this fraction actually exists, because the last digit of $d$ is not a 0 for if it were, then it could be deleted to yield a shorter solution.

The following relation is true iff the latter is closest:

$$2^{16}*S.d - n \; > \; n - 2^{16}*(S.d - 10^{-\#d})$$

$=$ {Arithmetic}

$$0 \; > \; 2*(n - 2^{16}*S.d) + 2^{16}/10^{\#d}$$

$=$ {Definition $P4$ gives $n - 2^{16}*S.d = s/10^{\#d+1} - 1/2$}

$$0 \; > \; 2*(s/10^{\#d+1} - 1/2) + 2^{16}/10^{\#d}$$

$=$ {Arithmetic}

$$10^{\#d+1} \; > \; 2*s + 10*2^{16}$$

$=$ {Definition $P5$ of $t$}

(12)  $t \; > \; 2*s + 10*2^{16}$

If $\#d \le 4$, i.e. $t \le 10^5$, (12) is false since $10^4 < 2^{16}$, which is expected since there is at most one solution of shortest length in this case. If $\#d = 5$, the truth of this relation implies $t > s + 10*2^{16}$, which means that $S.d - 10^{-\#d}$ is indeed a solution.

We give the final algorithm, which is (11) followed by a conditional statement that changes the largest solution to the closest. Before writing (12) as the guard of the conditional statement, we divided both sides of it by 10 in order to keep computed values as small as possible.

$d, s, t := \varepsilon, 10*n + 5, 10;$
**do** $s > t \;\rightarrow\; d, s, t := d\hat{\ }(s \div 2^{16}), 10*(s \bmod 2^{16}), t*10$ **od**;
**if** $t/10 > s/5 + 2^{16} \;\rightarrow\; d.(\#d - 1) := d.(\#d - 1) - 1$
$[] \; t/10 \le s/5 + 2^{16} \;\rightarrow\; skip$
**fi**

*Acknowledgements*: I thank Geoffrey Smith, Wim Feijen, Earlin Lutz, Jay Misra and Fred Schneider for a careful reading of an earlier draft. Geoffrey Smith is responsible for cleaning up my version of $P6$.

REFERENCES

[1] Donald E. Knuth. A simple program whose proof isn't. In *Beauty is our Business*, chapter 27, Springer-Verlag, New York, 1990.

David Gries,
Department of Computer Science,
Cornell University,
Upson Hall,
Ithaca, New York 14853,
U.S.A.

# 17

# Rotate and Double

## A. N. Habermann[1]

## Abstract

The program developed in this paper solves the problem of finding numbers $X$ such that $2X = Y$, where $Y$ is derived from $X$ by right-rotating $X$ one digit position so that the rightmost digit becomes the leftmost digit. The problem is particularly interesting because it has vastly different solutions for number systems other than the decimal system. The developed program has the characteristic that, while it is not difficult to design, it requires a non-trivial proof of termination. This makes the development a nice candidate for demonstrating the merit of Dijkstra's "separation of concerns." Once termination is proven, we gain so much insight into the program that it can be substantially improved. Finally, analysis of the "useful" solutions leads to another version and an even more significant improvement in performance.

## 1   Introduction

More than thirty years ago I solved a numeric puzzle published in "Het Algemeen Handelsblad," the Dutch equivalent of the Wall Street Journal and won the first prize of Hfl 10,– , the equivalent of $5. The problem was to find a number $X$ such that $2X = Y$, where $Y$ is derived from $X$ by taking the least significant digit on the right and placing it all the way on the left, making it the most significant digit. Some examples where this derivation rule fails:

---

[1]Copyright © A. N. Habermann
This work was supported in part by the ZTE division of Siemens Corporation, Munich, Germany and by a grant from Westinghouse Corporation, Pittsburgh, Pennsylvania.

$$
\begin{array}{llllll}
X = & 33445 & X = & 675432 & X = & 222227 \\
Y = & 53344 & Y = & 267543 & Y = & 722222 \\
2X = & 66890 & 2X = & 1350864 & 2X = & 444454
\end{array}
$$

It is clear that these numbers $Y$, although derived from $X$ by moving the rightmost digit all the way to the left, do not satisfy the first requirement $2X = Y$. A number $X$ that generates a number $Y$ that satisfies both requirements is:

$$
\begin{array}{rl}
X = & 421052631578947368 \\
 & \underline{421052631578947368} \quad + \\
Y = & 842105263157894736
\end{array}
$$

For someone not familiar with this problem, it may come as a surprise to know that the last example is the shortest solution (in terms of the number of digits) in the decimal system. There is no number $X$ with fewer than eighteen digits in the decimal system that solves the problem.

Such shortest solutions are of particular interest, but we also want to know how many solutions there are and to enumerate them if possible. Moreover, we want to generalize the problem to numerals in *any* base $p$ $(p > 1)$, and not restrict it to the decimal system (for which $p = 10$).

In subsequent sections we first present a more precise statement of the problem and then develop a program for its solution. Then we prove that the program terminates for any base $p > 1$ and for any choice of rightmost digit in range $(1..p-1)$. From this discussion we derive an improved program that has the advantage over the first program of printing the digits of the solution in the usual left-to-right order. Finally, we change the $O(p^2)$ algorithm into an $O(p)$ algorithm that produces all interesting solutions.

## 2  Problem statement and program

The generalized problem is stated more precisely as follows:

let $X$ be a numeral in base $p$ $(p > 1)$, and let $RightRotate(X)$ be the numeral that is derived from $X$ by rotating $X$ one digit position to the right, e.g.,

$$RightRotate(X = x_n \ldots x_1 y) = y x_n \ldots x_1;$$

find all numerals $X$ in base $p$ such that

$$value(RightRotate(X)) = 2 value(X),$$

while no proper subsequence $X'$ of $X$ also satisfies

$$value(RightRotate(X')) = 2 value(X').$$

Stated in another way, find all numerals $X$ in base $p$ such that

$$X = x_n x_{n-1} \ldots x_2 x_1 y$$

$$\frac{x_n x_{n-1} \ldots x_2 x_1 y}{y\, x_n x_{n-1} \ \ldots \ x_2 x_1} \quad +$$

while no proper subsequence of $X$ has the same property.

My interest in the problem was renewed when Dick Garwin, IBM fellow, brought it up in the coffee break of one of our Science Advisory Committee meetings. On our way back to the airport Len Kleinrock (UCLA), Michael Rabin (Harvard) and I thought about the problem a little more and made the following observations:

1. $2x_n < p$, because the last digit of $X$ may not produce a carry.
2. $y = 0$ implies $x_1 = 0$, which by induction implies all $x_i = 0$. We wish to exclude such a trivial solution; Thus, $y \neq 0$.
3. We do allow $x_n = 0$, but no more than one leading zero. If $x_n = x_{n-1} = 0$, we can show then also $x_{n-2} = 0$ and all $x_i = 0$.
4. If $X = x_n \ldots x_1 y$ is a solution then $XX = x_n \ldots x_1 y x_n \ldots x_1 y$ also satisfies the relationship $value(RightRotate(XX)) = 2value(XX)$. This type of solution and longer sequences such as $XXX, \ldots$ are now ruled out, because they violate the stipulation that no proper subsequence may also satisfy the requirements.
5. All successive digits of $X$ can be computed from the rightmost digit $y$; Hence, there is at most one solution for each $y$ in $(1..p-1)$.

The last observation can be expressed more precisely by introducing the carry $c_i$ and by writing out the relationship between the pairs $(c_i, x_i)$ and $(c_{i+1}, x_{i+1})$ for $i = 0, 1, \ldots$, where $c_0 = 0$ and $x_0 = y$ :

$$x_{i+1} = (2x_i + c_i)\%p, \quad \text{where } \% \text{ is the remainder function}$$
$$c_{i+1} = (2x_i + c_i)/p, \quad \text{where } / \text{ is integer division.}$$

The first relation states that the next digit is twice the preceding digit incremented by the carry, modulo base $p$. The second relation states that a carry is produced when the preceding addition resulted in a sum $\geq p$. The two relations basically express the well-known integer addition algorithm. (One can easily prove by induction that all $c_i$ are either 0 or 1.)

These two relations can serve as the basis for a program that computes the successive digits of $X$ for given $p > 1$ and for each rightmost digit $y$ in $(1..p-1)$. The inner loop of this program starts with $(digit, carry) = (y, 0)$ and finds a solution for this particular initial value of $y$ when its computation of $(digit, carry)$ reproduces the initial value pair $(y, 0)$. This is so when

$$x_{i+1} = (2x_i + c_i)\%p = 2x_i + c_i = y,$$
$$c_{i+1} = (2x_i + c_i)/p = 0.$$

The termination condition is discussed in detail in the next section.

> **program** $Xdigits(p : Nat)$ **is**
>> $c, x, y, sum : Nat$
>
> **begin**
>> **for** $y := 1$ **to** $p - 1$ **do**
>>> $x := y; c := 0$
>>>
>>> **repeat**
>>>> $printdigit(x); sum := 2*x + c$
>>>>
>>>> **if** $sum < p$ **then** $x := sum; c := 0$
>>>>> **else** $x := sum - p; c := 1$
>>>>
>>>> **fi**
>>>
>>> **until** $x = y$ **and** $c = 0$
>>>
>>> $newline$
>
>> **od**
>
> **end**

The program produces for given $p > 1$ all solutions for all possible right-most digits $y$ in $(1..p-1)$. It produces a solution for every pair $(rightmost\text{-}digit, initial\ carry) = (y, 0)$. Procedure "$printdigit$" converts the numeric value of $x$ into a string and prints it as next digit. The sequence of digits is printed from right to left. Since the number of digits in $X$ is not known in advance, we test the next digit and compare it to the initial digit $y$. If it is equal to $y$ and at the same time $carry = 0$, the initial state has been reproduced. The computation must be terminated at this point or else it will produce a cyclic number of the type $XX\ldots$.

The relationship between $(x_{i+1}, c_{i+1})$ and $(x_i, c_i)$ is expressed by the assignment to variable $sum$[†] and the conditional statement in the inner loop. If $sum = 2x + c$, then

$$
\begin{aligned}
x_{i+1} &= (2x_i + c_i)\%p &= sum_i\%p \\
c_{i+1} &= (2x_i + c_i)/p &= sum_i/p.
\end{aligned}
$$

The **if**-statement distinguishes two cases:

$$
\begin{aligned}
sum_i < p &\Rightarrow & x_{i+1} &= sum_i\%p &= sum_i \\
& & c_{i+1} &= sum_i/p &= 0 \\
sum_i \geq p &\Rightarrow & x_{i+1} &= sum_i\%p &= sum_i - p \\
& & c_{i+1} &= sum_i/p &= 1.
\end{aligned}
$$

---

[†]The program can be slightly optimized by eliminating variable $sum$ and using variable $x$ for storing the sum result. Variable $sum$ was introduced for clarity.

It is indeed true that $sum\%p = sum - p$ and $sum/p = 1$ when $sum \geq p$, because

$$p \leq sum = 2x + c \leq 2(p-1) + 1 = 2p - 1,$$

since all $x_i \leq p-1$ and all $c_i \leq 1$. This shows that the conditional statement correctly computes the next pair $(x_{i+1}, c_{i+1})$ from the current pair $(x_i, c_i)$.

## 3    Proof of Termination

Although the program generates a sequence of digits that satisfy the relationship between $(x_{i+1}, c_{i+1})$ and $(x_i, c_i)$, it is questionable whether or not the program terminates for given $p > 1$ for all $y$ in $(1..p - 1)$. It is for instance conceivable that the program produces a sequence of digits of the form

$$\ldots x_n \ldots x_k x_{k-1} \ldots x_1 y$$

in which, after an initial sequence $x_k x_{k-1} \ldots x_1 y$, the subsequence $x_n \ldots x_k$ is repeated indefinitely. In this type of sequence, it may happen that digit $y$ does not occur a second time at all. If the program were to produce this type of sequence, it will never meet its termination condition, which tests for the recurrence of $y$. In such a case the program will not find a valid solution.

Fortunately, we can show that the program will not produce such unsatisfactory sequences and that it will meet its termination condition for given $p > 1$ for all $y$ in $(1..p - 1)$. To do this, we introduce the sequence $(sum_0, sum_1, \ldots)$, where

$$sum_i = 2x_i + c_i \text{ for } i \geq 0 \quad \text{and} \quad (x_0, c_0) = (y, 0).$$

Since all $c_i$ are either 0 or 1, we note that

$$\begin{aligned}
even(sum_i) &\equiv c_i = 0, \\
odd(sum_i) &\equiv c_i = 1, \\
x_i &= sum_i/2, \\
0 &\leq sum_i \leq 2p - 1,
\end{aligned}$$

because $sum = 2x + c \leq 2(p-1) + 1 = 2p - 1$.

We can go one step further and base the computation entirely on sums, eliminating the computation of $x_i$ and $c_i$ altogether. This is accomplished by showing that $sum_{i+1}$ can be expressed in terms of its predecessor, $sum_i$.

$$\begin{aligned}
sum_{i+1} &= 2x_{i+1} + c_{i+1} \\
&= 2((2x_i + c_i)\%p) + (2x_i + c_i)/p \\
&= 2(sum_i\%p) + sum_i/p.
\end{aligned}$$

Working with sequence $(sum_0, sum_1, \ldots, sum_n)$, we can uniquely derive the sequence $(x_0, x_1, \ldots, x_n)$ by the rule $x_i = sum_i/2$. Observe that

- by deriving $sum_{i+1}$ from $sum_i$ the computation of carry $c_i$ is no longer needed
- $sum_i < p \equiv even(sum_{i+1})$ and $sum_i \geq p \equiv odd(sum_{i+1})$
- substitution shows that the termination condition $(x_{n+1}, c_{n+1}) = (y, 0)$ is equivalent to $sum_{n+1} = 2y$, which in turn is equivalent to $sum_n = y$.

Instead of working with pairs $(x_i, c_i)$, the program can now start with initializing variable $sum$ to $y$, compute $sum = sum_0 = 2y$ and then compute the sequence $sum_1, sum_2, \ldots$ until it encounters $sum_n = y$. In this form the program reads

```
program Xdigits(p : Nat) is
    sum, q, y : Nat
begin q := 2*p - 1
    for y := 1 to p - 1 do
        sum := y
        repeat
            if sum < p then sum := 2*sum
                       else sum := 2*sum - q
            fi
            printdigit(sum/2)
        until sum = y
        newline
    od
end
```

In order to prove that this program terminates, we will show that the sequence $(sum_0, sum_1, \ldots)$ has an element $sum_n = y$, $n > 0$, for all initial values of $y$ in $(1..p-1)$. Leading up to the proof, we define $q = 2p - 1$ and show

**Lemma**    $sum_i$ is in range $(1..q-1)$ for all $i \geq 0$.
(This means that no $sum_i = 0$ and particularly no $sum_i = q$.)

**Proof**    The statement is true for $sum_0$, because
$$1 \leq y \leq p - 1 \quad \Rightarrow \quad 2 \leq sum_0 = 2y \leq 2(p-1) = q - 1$$
Assume the statement is true for some $k > 0$.
$$1 \leq sum_k \leq p - 1 \quad \Rightarrow \quad \begin{aligned} 2 \leq\ & sum_{k+1} = 2sum_k \\ & \leq 2(p-1) = q - 1. \end{aligned}$$

$$p \le sum_k \le q-1 \quad \Rightarrow \quad 1 = 2p - q \le sum_{k+1} = 2sum_k - q$$
$$\le 2(q-1) - q = q - 2.$$

The statement follows by induction.
**End** of Proof

**Corollary 1**    The two equations determining the relationship between $sum_{i+1}$ and $sum_i$ can be succinctly expressed by a single equation

$$sum_{i+1} = 2sum_i\%q.$$

**Corollary 2**

$$sum_0 = 2y, \ sum_{i+1} = 2sum_i\%q \ \Rightarrow \ sum_i = (2^{i+1}y)\%q,$$
$$S(y) = (y, sum_0, sum_1, \ldots) = (y, 2y, 2^2y, \ldots)\%q.$$

**Main Theorem**    The elements of sequence $S(1) = (1, 2, 2^2, \ldots)\%q$ form a cyclic group under multiplication modulo $q$.

**Proof**    Prefix $S' = (1, 2, 2^2, \ldots, 2^{q-1})\%q$ is a finite subsequence of $S(1)$ with $q$ elements. The lemma implies that all elements in $S(1)$ and $S'$ have values in the range $(1..q-1)$. This means there is one more element in $S'$ than there are possible values for its elements. Hence, there must be at least one pair of elements in $S'$ with the same value. Let $u$ be the smallest exponent for which $2^u\%q$ is equal to one of its predecessors (i.e., all elements preceding element $2^u\%q$ have different values and $2^u\%q = 2^v\%q$ for some $v < u$). We show that $v = 0$ and $2^u\%q = 1$. Assume $2^u\%q = 2^v\%q$ and $v > 0$. Since $q$ is odd, $(2^v, q)$ are relatively prime. In that case we can apply the reduction theorem [2, page 17] and find $2^{u-v}\%q = 1$. Since $0 < u - v < u$, we find an exponent $w = u - v \ne 0$ smaller than $u$ for which a value recurs. But that contradicts the assumption that $u$ is the smallest exponent for which a value recurs. Thus, $v$ must be zero and

$$2^u\%q = 1,$$
$$2^{u+i}\%q = 2^u\%q.2^i\%q = 2^i\%q.$$

The last equation shows that $S(1)$ is periodic and that all different numbers in $S(1)$ form the set $G = \{1, 2, 2^2\%q, \ldots, 2^{u-1}\%q\}$. One can easily check that $G$ is a cyclic multiplicative group generated by 2 with unit element $= 1$, while the inverse of element $2^a\%q$ is element $2^b\%q$, where $b$ is the solution of the equation $a + x = 0 \ mod \ u$.

**End** of Proof

The smallest exponent $u$ for which $2^u\%q = 1$ is called the *order* of $2 \ mod \ q$ [2, page 86]. This number $u$ is also the *period* of sequence $S(1) = (1, 2, 2^2, \ldots)\%q$. One can easily see that the sequence

$$S(y) = (y, 2y, 2^2y, \ldots)\%q = (y, sum_0, sum_1, \ldots)\%q$$

is also periodic for all $y$ in $(1..p-1)$, because for all $i \geq 0$

$$sum_{u+i}\%q = (2^{u+i}y)\%q = (2^{i}y)\%q = sum_{i}.$$

It follows that $period(S(y)) \leq period(S(1))$. The termination of our program that tests for $sum_{n} = y, n > 0$ is thus assured for every initial value $y$ in $(1..p-1)$.

## 4 A left-to-right algorithm

The programs so far have the drawback that the solutions are produced from right-to-left, starting with the least significant digit. This order runs counter to our customary representation of numbers from left-to-right, starting with the most significant digit. This flaw can be corrected in several ways. One way of improving the algorithm is to introduce intermediate storage in which all generated digits are kept and then printed in reverse order. The proper structure for such intermediate storage is a stack. This solution has the drawback that the program now needs $O(p)$ storage, whereas up to this point the programs need only constant storage.

There is really no need to introduce $O(p)$ intermediate storage for printing the digits from left-to-right. The program can be rewritten so that it directly produces the digits from left-to-right. This is accomplished by observing that we can reverse the order of computing the sequence of sums. Instead of calculating $sum_{i+1}$ from $sum_{i}$, we can start with $sum_{n}$ and compute $sum_{i}$ from $sum_{i+1}$ as follows:

$$
\begin{aligned}
sum_{i} < p &\Rightarrow & sum_{i+1} &= 2sum_{i} \\
&\Rightarrow & even(sum_{i+1}) &\Rightarrow & sum_{i} &= sum_{i+1}/2 \\
sum_{i} \geq p &\Rightarrow & sum_{i+1} &= 2sum_{i} - q \\
&\Rightarrow & odd(sum_{i+1}) &\Rightarrow & sum_{i} &= (sum_{i+1} + q)/2.
\end{aligned}
$$

Since we proved that the algorithm terminates with $sum_{n} = y$, we can use the last two equations, start the program with the leftmost sum, $sum_{n}$, and compute the sequence $sum_{n}, sum_{n-1}, \ldots, sum_{0}$ where $sum_{0} = 2y$ and $successor(sum_{0}) = y$. The modified program using the latter equation as termination condition reads as follows:

**program** $Xdigits(p : Nat)$ **is**
    $sum, q, y : Nat$
**begin**
    $q := 2*p - 1$
    **for** $y := 1$ **to** $p - 1$ **do**
        $sum := y$

```
                    repeat printdigit(sum/2)
                        if even(sum) then sum := sum/2
                                     else sum := (sum + q)/2
                        fi
                    until sum = y
                    newline
            od
    end
```

It is interesting to note that the two equations relating $sum_i$ to $sum_{i+1}$ can also be expressed by a single equation of the form

$$sum_{n-k} = (p^k y)\%q \qquad \text{for all } k \text{ in } (0..n).$$

**Proof**   Since $sum_n = y2^{n+1}\%q = y$ and $q = 2p - 1$, we have

$$
\begin{aligned}
(yp^k)\%q &= (y(2p)^k 2^{n+1-k})\%q \\
          &= (y(q+1)^k 2^{n+1-k})\%q \\
          &= (y2^{n+1-k})\%q \\
          &= sum_{n-k}
\end{aligned}
$$

**End** of Proof

Termination of the left-to-right version of the program could have been proved with this last relationship instead of with the result of the main theorem. A proof to that effect is based on the fact that, similar to $S(1)$, the elements of sequence $T = (1, p, p^2, \ldots)\%q$ form a cyclic group under multiplication modulo $q$ and $period(T) \leq q - 1$. Base $p$ is a generator of this cyclic group, because $(p, q)$ are relatively prime. Further development of this approach is left to the reader.

# 5   A linear space/time algorithm

The set of residues $R = \{0, 1, \ldots, q-1\}$ is a semi-group under multiplication modulo $q$. Let $G = \{g | g \in S(1)\}$ be the set of numbers that occur in sequence $S(1) = (1, 2, 2^2, \ldots)\%q$. $G$ is a proper subset of $R$ and also a subgroup of $R$ under multiplication modulo $q$ (cf. Main Theorem). We are interested in the cosets $yG$ of $G$ in $R$ for $y$ in $(1..q-1)$, because the different numbers in sequence $S(y) = (y, 2y, 2^2 y, \ldots)\%q$ form precisely coset $yG$.

The theorem that two cosets either have all elements in common or are disjoint [2, page 89] holds not only for subgroups of a group, but also for subgroups of a semi-group. Applied to our problem, this means that two solutions generated starting with different values of $sum_n = y$ either consists of the same collection of sums (in different order) or have no element in common. For example, for $p = 9$, $q = 17$

$$
\begin{aligned}
y = 1 &\Rightarrow \{1\ 9\ 13\ 15\ 16\ 8\ 4\ 2\} &\Rightarrow X = 04678421 \\
y = 2 &\Rightarrow \{2\ 1\ 9\ 13\ 15\ 16\ 8\ 4\} &\Rightarrow X = 10467842 \\
y = 3 &\Rightarrow \{3\ 10\ 5\ 11\ 14\ 7\ 12\ 6\} &\Rightarrow X = 15257363 \\
y = 4 &\Rightarrow \{4\ 2\ 1\ 9\ 13\ 15\ 16\ 8\} &\Rightarrow X = 21046784 \\
y = 5 &\Rightarrow \{5\ 11\ 14\ 7\ 12\ 6\ 3\ 10\} &\Rightarrow X = 25736315 \\
y = 6 &\Rightarrow \{6\ 3\ 10\ 5\ 11\ 14\ 7\ 12\} &\Rightarrow X = 31525736 \\
y = 7 &\Rightarrow \{7\ 12\ 6\ 3\ 10\ 5\ 11\ 14\} &\Rightarrow X = 36315257 \\
y = 8 &\Rightarrow \{8\ 4\ 2\ 1\ 9\ 13\ 15\ 16\} &\Rightarrow X = 42104678
\end{aligned}
$$

The sum sequences for $y = 1, 2, 4$ and $8$ have all elements in common and so have those for $y = 3, 5, 6$ and $7$. But the former have no element in common with any of the latter.

The example shows that solutions derived from sequences that have sum elements in common can be derived from each other by rotation. Such solutions are called *congruent*. We can easily see that congruent solutions are derived from sum sequences that form one and the same coset. It is also true that all sum sequences that form the same coset generate congruent solutions. This is so, because the computation of $sum_i$ for given $p$ depends solely on its predecessor $sum_{i+1}$ (where $sum_0$ is the predecessor of $sum_n$), and not on its position in the sequence. Thus, a particular value $v$ has for given $p$ a unique successor value in every sequence in which value $v$ occurs. (Note that for even value $v$ the successor value is not even dependent on $p$!)

So far, the programs generate all congruent solutions separately, because they generate sequences for all $y$ in $(1..p-1)$. The algorithm they use is clearly $O(p^2)$, because the range of $y$ is $O(p)$ and the length of each solution produced is $O(p)^\ddagger$. Since there is little point in separately generating all solutions of a congruent collection, we could do less work and generate only "base" solutions, one for each coset. We take as the base solution of a set of congruent solutions the one that generates the number with the smallest numeric value. This solution is of course generated by the sequence that starts with the smallest $sum_n = y$. For example, the base solutions for $(p, q) = (8, 15)$ are

$$
\begin{aligned}
y = 1 &\Rightarrow \{1\ 8\ 4\ 2\} &\Rightarrow X = 0421 \\
y = 3 &\Rightarrow \{3\ 9\ 12\ 6\} &\Rightarrow X = 1463 \\
y = 5 &\Rightarrow \{5\ 10\} &\Rightarrow X = 25 \\
y = 7 &\Rightarrow \{7\ 11\ 13\ 14\} &\Rightarrow X = 3567,
\end{aligned}
$$

---

$\ddagger$To be precise, we can show that 1: $period(S(1))$ is $O(p)$, 2: $period(S(y)) = period(S(1))$ for all $y$ in $(1..q-1)$ coprime with $q$, and 3: $\#coprimes(q)$ is $O(p)$.

while the base solutions of the preceding example for $(p, q) = (9, 17)$ are

$$y = 1 \;\Rightarrow\; \{1 \; 9 \; 13 \; 15 \; 16 \; 8 \; 4 \; 2\} \quad \Rightarrow X = 04678421$$
$$y = 3 \;\Rightarrow\; \{3 \; 10 \; 5 \; 11 \; 14 \; 7 \; 12 \; 6\} \;\Rightarrow X = 15257363.$$

The program is modified to generate only base solutions in the following way: In addition to assigning values to variable sum, we let the inner loop also record all values assigned to *sum*. When the inner loop is executed again, the starting value $sum_n = y$ skips all values already assigned in previous iterations, because we know that, if two sequences have a single value in common, they have all values in common and generate congruent solutions. But if the outerloop sets $y$ to a value not used in a previous iteration, we know that the new sequence cannot have any value in common with the previously generated sequences. To make sure that the algorithm generates base solutions, the next value assigned to $y$ should be the smallest unused value so far.

Since all sequences start with $y < p$, it is actually not necessary to remember all values that were assigned to *sum* in previous iterations. It is sufficient to remember the previously assigned values $< p$. We therefore introduce an array "$unused[1..p-1]$", initialized to all *true*, in which the used and unused values are recorded. The modified version of the program is

```
program Xdigits(p : Nat) is
    sum, q, y : Nat; unused[1..p − 1] : *Bool
begin
    q := 2*p − 1
    for y := 1 to p − 1 do unused[y] := true od
    for y := 1 to p − 1 do
    if unused[y] then
        sum := y
        repeat printdigit(sum/2)
            if odd(sum) then sum := (sum + q)/2
            else sum := sum/2; unused[sum] := false
            fi
        until sum = y
        newline
    fi
    od
end
```

Array *unused* is initialized to a sequence of $p-1$ Boolean elements, all set to *true*. The inner loop is executed only for starting values $y$ that have not been previously used. There is no need to operate on array *unused* when $odd(sum)$, because the new value of *sum* is in that case $\geq p$, whereas array *unused* has only $p-1$ elements. It suffices to operate on array *unused* when $even(sum)$, because only then is the new $sum \leq (2p-2)/2 < p$.

The new version does worse in requiring $O(p)$ intermediate storage space compared to the earlier version requiring only constant intermediate storage space. But the execution time of the new version is $O(p)$ versus $O(p^2)$ for the old version. That the execution time of the new version is $O(p)$ can easily be derived from the fact that only base solutions are generated, which implies that every possible sum value is assigned only once, because successively generated sequences have no sum values in common. The assignment to $y$ in the outer loop adds no more than $O(p)$ work to generating the base solutions.

The length of a solution $X(p, y)$ in terms of the number of digits of $X$ is determined by the period of sequence $S(y)$. For all $p > 1$ and all $y$ in $(1..p-1)$

$$length(X) = period(S(y)) \leq q - 1.$$

For example,

$$
\begin{aligned}
(p, q) &= (10, 19): &\quad length(X) &= period(S(1)) = 18 = q - 1 \\
(p, q) &= (9, 17): &\quad length(X) &= period(S(1)) = \phantom{0}8 < q - 1.
\end{aligned}
$$

Working respectively from right-to-left and from left-to-right, we found

$$sum_i = 2^{i+1}y\%q = sum_{n-(n-i)} = p^{n-i}y.$$

Replacing $i$ by $i - 1$, $length(X) = n + 1$ can be derived from the formula

$$2^i\%q = p^{n+1-i}\%q.$$

Some examples.

$$length(X)$$

| | | | | | |
|---|---|---|---|---|---|
| $(p, q) = (7, 13)$ | $2^{12}\%q = 1$ | | $\Rightarrow (n+1) - 12 = 0$ | | 12 |
| $(p, q) = (8, 15)$ | $2^3\%q = p$ | | $\Rightarrow (n+1) - 3 = 1$ | | 4 |
| $(p, q) = (9, 17)$ | $2^4\%q = -1$ | | $\Rightarrow (n+1) - 8 = 0$ | | 8 |
| $(p, q) = (10, 19)$ | $2^6\%q = 7$ | $\Rightarrow 2^9\%q = -1 \Rightarrow$ | $(n+1) - 18 = 0$ | | 18 |
| $(p, q) = (11, 21)$ | $2^5\%q = p$ | | $\Rightarrow (n+1) - 5 = 1$ | | 6 |
| $(p, q) = (18, 35)$ | $2^6\%q = -6$ | $\Rightarrow 2^{12}\%q = 1$ | $\Rightarrow (n+1) - 12 = 0$ | | 12 |
| $(p, q) = (60, 119)$ $p\%q = 60$ | $2^7\%q = 9$ $p^3\%q = 15$ | $\Rightarrow 2^{15}\%q = 43\}$ $\Rightarrow p^9 \phantom{\%q} = 43\}$ | $\Rightarrow (n+1) - 15 = 9$ | | 24. |

# 6  Conclusion

Working with digits and a carry had the drawback that the very first algorithm writes out solutions starting with the least significant digit, counter to the customary convention of writing numbers from left to right starting with the most significant digit. If the first algorithm were to print the solutions in the conventional way, it must store the generated digits in a stack and at the end print out the digits in reverse order by repeatedly popping the stack. With this modification, the space requirement of the first algorithm is $O(p)$. Programs based on computing successive *sums* are able to generate the digits in the preferred order by starting with $sum_n = y$ and working backwards. These versions do not need a stack for intermediate storage. However, introducing $O(p)$ intermediate storage can have the beneficial effect of reducing the runtime complexity from $O(p^2)$ to $O(p)$.

This paper is a clear demonstration of the point that Edsger Dijkstra has made so frequently that the design of an algorithm is a scientific enterprise [1]. It also supports Dijkstra's view that a program cannot be understood without a description of its design that proves its correctness. The third version of the program looks deceivingly simple, but could not have been constructed without a careful design process based on Dijkstra's idea of "separation of concerns". The design was successful because of considering four separate aspects one by one: the design of an algorithm, a program representation for that algorithm, analysis of the termination condition and improving the performance.

*Acknowledgements*: I am grateful for the useful comments I received from colleagues and students. I am particularly indebted to Steve Brookes who provided extensive comment on the presentation. He showed me an elegant proof of the $O(p^2)$ property of the algorithm used in the first three programs based on Euler's indicator $\phi(q) = \#coprimes(q)$ which is $O(p)$ [2, page 14]. He also pointed out that the problem can be generalized in the following sense: Let $k \in (2..p - 1)$; Find all numerals $X$ such that $value(RightRotate(X)) = value(kX)$. Steve showed in a personal note to me that the reasoning and the programs are still valid with proper substitution of $k$ for the specific number 2 used in the paper. He showed that the expression of sum in terms of digit and carry

$$s_i = kx_i + c_i$$

leads to the generalized right-to-left and left-to-right relationships between sums

$$s_{i+1} = (ks_i)\%q \qquad \text{where } q = kp - 1.$$
$$s_i = s_{i+1}/k + p(s_{i+1}\%k).$$

Termination is assured, because the generalized version of the main theorem is valid since $(k, q)$ are relatively prime. The length of solution $X(p, k, y)$ can be derived from the generalized formula

$$(k^i y)\%q = (p^{n+1-i} y)\%q.$$

An example for $k = 3$ and $(p, q) = (7, 20)$:

$$
\begin{aligned}
y = 1 &\Rightarrow \{1\ 7\ 9\ 3\} &\Rightarrow X = 0231 \\
y = 2 &\Rightarrow \{2\ 14\ 18\ 6\} &\Rightarrow X = 0462 \\
y = 4 &\Rightarrow \{4\ 8\ 16\ 12\} &\Rightarrow X = 1254 \\
y = 5 &\Rightarrow \{5\ 15\} &\Rightarrow X = 15
\end{aligned}
$$

## REFERENCES

[1] E. W. Dijkstra. On the role of scientific thought. In *Selected Writings on Computing: A Personal Perspective*, page 60, Springer-Verlag, New York, 1982.

[2] H. Loonstra. *Inleiding tot de Algebra*. P. Noordhof, Groningen, 1968.

A. N. Habermann,
School of Computer Science,
Carnegie Mellon University,
Pittsburgh, Pennsylvania   15213–3890,
U.S.A.

# 18

# Beautifying Gödel

## Eric C. R. Hehner

## Introduction

The incompleteness theorems of Kurt Gödel [1931] are considered to be among the most important results of mathematics. They are regarded as "deep", and they strongly influenced the course of modern mathematics. They are popularly thought to prove the limitations (or even futility!) of mathematical formalism. At any rate, they deserve to be presented as simply, as elegantly, as beautifully as possible. Gödel's own presentation was careful and clear, but not nearly as simple as it could be.

Our beautification is made in stages. It is tempting to skip the stages and present just the final form: a three line proof. Unfortunately the stages are necessary to convince the reader that the essence of Gödel's theorems has not been lost. And there are some lessons to learn along the way. The theorems belong to the branch of mathematics known as metamathematics, so we start there.

## Metamathematics: the study of formalisms

To study the stars, it is helpful to design a mathematical formalism for the purpose. Mathematics is not limited, however, to the study of nature. It also helps us to study the artificial worlds of bridges, economics, music, and even thought processes. And if we want to make mathematical formalisms objects of study, it is helpful to design a mathematical formalism for the purpose.

We design a formalism (synonymously, a theory) so that its sentences represent statements about the objects of study. Some of these statements are true, and others are false; we design the theory so that its theorems (provable sentences) represent true statements and its antitheorems (disprovable sentences) represent false statements. Suppose, for example, that the object of study is a version of number theory; let us call it $\mathcal{NT}$. Here are eight examples of true statements about (not in) $\mathcal{NT}$.

(a)     $1 + 1 = 2$ is a theorem of $\mathcal{NT}$.
(b)     $1 + 1 = 3$ is an antitheorem of $\mathcal{NT}$.
(c)     $0 \div 0 = 4$ is neither a theorem nor an antitheorem of $\mathcal{NT}$.
(d)     $(0 \div 0 = 4) \ \lor \ \neg(0 \div 0 = 4)$ is a theorem of $\mathcal{NT}$.
(e)     A sentence is an antitheorem of $\mathcal{NT}$ if and only if
       its negation is a theorem of $\mathcal{NT}$.
(f)     A sentence is a theorem of $\mathcal{NT}$ if and only if
       its negation is an antitheorem of $\mathcal{NT}$.
(g)     No sentence is both a theorem and an antitheorem of $\mathcal{NT}$.
(h)     Every sentence of the form $s \ \lor \ \neg s$ is a theorem of $\mathcal{NT}$.

Here are six false statements about $\mathcal{NT}$.

(i)     $1 + 1 = 2$ is an antitheorem of $\mathcal{NT}$.
(j)     $1 + 1 = 3$ is a theorem of $\mathcal{NT}$.
(k)     $0 \div 0 = 4$ is either a theorem or an antitheorem of $\mathcal{NT}$.
(l)     A sentence is an antitheorem if and only if
       it is not a theorem of $\mathcal{NT}$.
(m)     A sentence is either a theorem or an antitheorem of $\mathcal{NT}$.
(n)     Either a sentence or its negation is a theorem of $\mathcal{NT}$.

Statement (a) shows us a simple theorem. In mathematics texts, it saves space to write a sentence such as $1 + 1 = 2$ without saying anything about it, thereby meaning that it is a theorem. But in this paper we shall not do so. Statement (g) says that $\mathcal{NT}$ is consistent. The false statement (m) says that $\mathcal{NT}$ is complete. We included division in $\mathcal{NT}$ to give a simple sentence that is neither a theorem nor an antitheorem; Gödel's surprise result was that, even without division, with only addition and multiplication, there are sentences that are neither theorems nor antitheorems.

Let us call our theory to study theories $\mathcal{TT}$. For any theory $\mathcal{T}$ and sentence $s$ of $\mathcal{T}$ we introduce the sentence (of $\mathcal{TT}$)

$$\mathcal{T} \vdash s$$

to represent the (true or false) statement that $s$ is a theorem of $\mathcal{T}$. And we introduce

$$\mathcal{T} \dashv s$$

to represent the statement that $s$ is an antitheorem of $\mathcal{T}$. When it is clear which theory is under study, we may omit its name and write simply $\vdash s$ and $\dashv s$. Because of statement (e) we may be tempted to dispense with the symbol for "antitheorem", and to speak instead of the negation of a theorem. However, it is not necessary for all theories to include negation, and it may be interesting to study some that do not. Because of (c) we certainly cannot take "is an antitheorem" to mean "is not a theorem". We need a symbol for "antitheorem" for the same reason that boolean algebra needs symbols for both "true" and "false", and indeed "true" and "false" are a primitive theorem and antitheorem respectively. We also need symbols for "or", "and", "not", "if and only if", and quantifiers, as seen by our example statements. To avoid confusion, we might insist (as did Kleene) that the symbols of theory $\mathcal{TT}$ differ from those of the theories under study. But we may want to use $\mathcal{TT}$ to study $\mathcal{TT}$ as well, and as we see in the next paragraph, there is a better way to avoid confusion. We therefore reuse $\vee$, $\wedge$, $\neg$, $=$, $\forall$, and $\exists$ in $\mathcal{TT}$.

The way to avoid confusion was known to Gödel and is well-known to programmers: it is to distinguish program from data. A compiler writer knows the difference between her program and her data, even though her data is someone else's program, even if it is in the same language. To her, the incoming data is a character string, and her program examines its characters. Similarly in metamathematics one theory can describe another without confusion, even if that other theory is itself, by realising that, to the describing theory, expressions of the described theory are data of type character string.

In modern logic, the distinction between program and data is not always made, and $\vdash$ is applied directly to sentences. To partially compensate, logicians distinguish between "extensional" and "intensional" operators, and make rules stating when something cannot be substituted for its equal. For the sake of simplicity and clarity, let us maintain the programmer's distinction: we apply $\vdash$ to a character string representing a sentence. Thus

$$\mathcal{NT} \vdash \text{``}1 + 1 = 2\text{''}$$

is the sentence of $\mathcal{TT}$ representing statement (a).

Omitting the name $\mathcal{NT}$, the statements (a) to (n) are represented (formalized) in $\mathcal{TT}$ as follows. (Juxtaposition of character strings indicates (con)catenation; quantification is over character strings.)

(aa)  $\vdash \text{``}1 + 1 = 2\text{''}$

(bb)  $\dashv \text{``}1 + 1 = 3\text{''}$

(cc)  $\neg \vdash \text{``}0 \div 0 = 4\text{''} \;\wedge\; \neg \dashv \text{``}0 \div 0 = 4\text{''}$

(dd)  $\vdash \text{``}(0 \div 0 = 4) \;\vee\; \neg(0 \div 0 = 4)\text{''}$

(ee)  $\forall s \cdot \dashv s \;=\; \vdash (\text{``}\neg\text{''}s)$

(ff)  $\forall s \cdot \vdash s \;=\; \dashv (\text{``}\neg\text{''}s)$

(gg)  $\neg \exists s \cdot \vdash s \;\wedge\; \dashv s$

(hh)  $\forall s \cdot \vdash (s\text{``}\vee \neg\text{''}s)$


(ii)  $\dashv \text{``}1 + 1 = 2\text{''}$

(jj)  $\vdash \text{``}1 + 1 = 3\text{''}$

(kk)  $\vdash \text{``}0 \div 0 = 4\text{''} \;\vee\; \dashv \text{``}0 \div 0 = 4\text{''}$

(ll)    $\forall s\cdot \dashv s \ = \ \neg \vdash s$
(mm)   $\forall s\cdot \vdash s \ \vee \ \dashv s$
(nn)    $\forall s\cdot \vdash s \ \vee \ \vdash (\text{``}\neg\text{''} s)$

We try to design $\mathcal{TT}$ so that (aa) to (hh) are theorems, and (ii) to (nn) are antitheorems. When we design a theory to study the stars, we should always retain some doubt about how well our theory matches the facts. The same goes for a theory to study theories.

## Classical and constructive mathematics

In the previous section, statements (h) and (n) are very similar, but (h) is true and (n) false. Which of them is the Law of the Excluded Middle? The truth of this "law" was hotly disputed for a while by mathematicians who conducted their mathematics informally; perhaps the informality was necessary to the dispute. For a formal theory like $\mathcal{NT}$, we can distinguish (h), which is the "law", from (n), which (given (e)) is a statement of completeness.

There are interesting theories for which the Law of the Excluded Middle does not hold; instead a proof of a disjunction requires a proof of one of the disjuncts. We may represent this in $\mathcal{TT}$ as follows.

$$\forall s\cdot \forall t\cdot \vdash (s\text{``}\vee\text{''}t) \ = \ \vdash s \ \vee \ \vdash t$$

These theories are called "constructive". Similarly a proof of $\exists x\cdot p\,x$ requires a term $t$ such that $p\,t$ is a theorem. A proof of $\forall x\cdot \exists y\cdot p\,x\,y$ is a program for constructing from input $x$ a satisfactory output $y$.

Theories in which the Law of the Excluded Middle holds are called "classical". Most people are willing to agree that "either God exists or God does not exist" without a proof of either disjunct. These people prefer a classical theory in which

$$(0 \div 0 = 4) \ \vee \ \neg(0 \div 0 = 4)$$

is a theorem even though neither disjunct is a theorem. In the next section we prove the equality of two sentences even though neither is a theorem nor an antitheorem.

The preceding discussion conceals a subtle point. We have said that in a classical theory, a disjunction may be a theorem even though neither of its disjuncts is. If our metatheory $\mathcal{TT}$ is classical, then perhaps $\vdash s \ \vee \ \vdash t$ can be a theorem (for some choice of $s$ and $t$) even though neither of its disjuncts is. If so, then the $\mathcal{TT}$ sentence

$$\forall s\cdot \forall t\cdot \vdash (s\text{ ``}\vee\text{'' }t) \ = \ \vdash s \ \vee \ \vdash t$$

does not represent our intention to describe a constructive theory. For this reason, we may prefer our metatheory to be constructive. Unfortunately, if the metatheory is used to describe itself, it cannot tell us whether it has this constructive property.

# Gödel's first incompleteness theorem

Very roughly, Gödel's argument goes as follows. He first created an elaborate scheme to encode sentences as numbers. He then created a sentence which, on the surface, concerns natural numbers, but which may be viewed as code for "I am not a theorem". The "I" in that sentence is the number that encodes that very sentence. It is the Liar's Paradox in a new suit. If this sentence is a theorem, then it is saying something false, so the logic is inconsistent. Assuming, as is reasonable, that his logic (Russell and Whitehead's *Principia Mathematica*) is consistent, he concludes that the sentence is true and unprovable.

Gödel shows how to construct his true but unprovable sentence, but he does not construct it. It involves immense numbers, and the encoding is so opaque that we would not be enlightened by it. In order to examine Gödel's sentence, we shall use the transparent encoding of the previous sections: character strings.

Gödel defined the "is a theorem" predicate (he called it *Bew*) on numbers (a predicate is a function with a boolean range). We shall instead define $\vdash$ on strings so that $\vdash s$ is a theorem if and only if $s$ represents a theorem. This may be done either by adding the symbol $\vdash$ to the formalism and giving the rules for its use, or by defining a function using the symbols already in the formalism. Either way, it amounts to writing a theorem-proving program. The important point is that we have a single theory serving both as the object of study and as the formalism in which to do the study.

Next, Gödel defined an embedding relation $Q$, again on numbers; we shall define $Q$ as a function from strings to strings. When applied to a string that represents a predicate, it produces another string that represents a sentence by replacing all occurrences of substrings that represent free variables with the entire quoted string. For example, the string

$$\text{``}\exists u\cdot t = u\ u\text{''}$$

represents a predicate in free variable $t$. Applying $Q$ to that string, we obtain the theorem

$$Q\text{``}\exists u\cdot t = u\ u\text{''}\quad =\quad \text{``}\exists u\cdot \underline{\text{``}}\exists u\cdot t = u\ u\underline{\text{''}} = u\ u\text{''}$$

The inner quotes are underlined to indicate that they are just characters in the string. (Every programming language has some special convention to allow quotes within strings.) Again, this function may be defined either by adding the symbol $Q$ to the formalism and giving the rules for its use, or by defining a function using the symbols already in the formalism. Either way, it amounts to writing a program.

All the pieces are now in place. In particular, we have the theorem

$$Q\text{``}\neg \vdash Qs\text{''} \quad = \quad \text{``}\neg \vdash Q\underline{\text{``}}\neg \vdash Qs\underline{\text{''}}\text{''}$$

Applying $\neg \vdash$ to both sides of the above equation, we obtain the theorem

$$\neg \vdash Q\text{``}\neg \vdash Qs\text{''} \quad = \quad \neg \vdash \text{``}\neg \vdash Q\underline{\text{``}}\neg \vdash Qs\underline{\text{''}}\text{''}$$

Taking a liberty with substitution inside quotes, we can say that this theorem has the form

$$G \quad = \quad \neg \vdash \text{``}G\text{''}$$

with each occurrence of $G$ standing for

$$\neg \vdash Q\text{``}\neg \vdash Qs\text{''}$$

This is the famous Gödel sentence but using a string encoding. If $G$ were a theorem, then $\vdash \text{``}G\text{''}$ would be a theorem and $\neg \vdash \text{``}G\text{''}$ an antitheorem. Thus we would prove a theorem equal to an antitheorem, and the theory would be inconsistent. But we believe the theory is consistent. So we conclude that $G$ is not a theorem. If $G$ were an antitheorem, then $\neg \vdash \text{``}G\text{''}$ would be an antitheorem because they are proven equal, hence $\vdash \text{``}G\text{''}$ would be a theorem. Since $\vdash \text{``}G\text{''}$ is a theorem if and only if $G$ is a theorem, $G$ would be a theorem, which is inconsistent. Therefore $G$ is not an antitheorem either. The theory is incomplete.

How shall we interpret $G$? For it to represent a true statement, it must at least be a formal sentence. Is it? To establish that the Gödel utterance

$$\neg \vdash Q\text{``}\neg \vdash Qs\text{''}$$

is a sentence, we must show that

$$\vdash Q\text{``}\neg \vdash Qs\text{''}$$

is a sentence. If $\vdash$ applies only to strings that represent sentences, then we must show that

$$Q\text{``}\neg \vdash Qs\text{''}$$

represents a sentence. Since we can prove

$$Q\text{``}\neg \vdash Qs\text{''} \quad = \quad \text{``}\neg \vdash Q\underline{\text{``}}\neg \vdash Qs\underline{\text{''}}\text{''}$$

we can ask instead if the string

$$\text{``}\neg \vdash Q\underline{\text{``}}\neg \vdash Qs\underline{\text{''}}\text{''}$$

represents a sentence. It does if and only if

$$\neg \vdash Q\text{``}\neg \vdash Qs\text{''}$$

is a sentence, but that is the original question. The only way out is to allow that $Qs$ is a sentence for any string $s$, and/or that $\vdash s$ is a sentence for any string $s$, whether or not $s$ represents a sentence. We must, at least temporarily, suspend our desire to interpret; we must consider only the formal manipulation of symbols in order to arrive at Gödel's result.

Given the reflexive axiom of equality, a formalist is willing to accept $0 \div 0 = 0 \div 0$ as a theorem of $\mathcal{NT}$. He is not concerned with what mathematical object is referred to by $0 \div 0$. He is likewise willing to accept $\vdash$ ") $+ x =$ (" as a sentence of $\mathcal{TT}$, though it is not a theorem. We defined $\vdash$ as a predicate on strings, so that $\vdash s$ is a sentence no matter what string $s$ may be. Similarly Gödel, in his formal presentation, uses an encoding that assigns a distinct natural number to every sequence of symbols, whether it is an expression or not, and defines his predicate $Bew$ on all natural numbers. Prior to the formal presentation of his result, Gödel gives an informal presentation for motivation, in which he proposes to encode only predicates onto the natural numbers: "We think of the class-signs [predicates] as being somehow arranged in a series, and denote the $n$-th one by $R(n)$". This is possible because predicatehood is defined by a program; the program can print a list of all and only the predicates, assigning each the next natural number. This encoding has the attraction that metamathematical sentences and predicates can always be interpreted, through the code, as talking about sentences and predicates. But it is a fatal attraction. Indeed, in the introduction to the English translation of Gödel's paper, R. B. Braithwaite considered it a flaw of the formal presentation that Gödel encoded all sequences of symbols. Far from being a flaw, it was essential! Later we shall be in a position to make this point more simply and clearly.

# Gödel's second incompleteness theorem

Gödel's First Incompleteness Theorem says that a particular theory, if consistent, is incomplete. Its interest comes from the effort that was spent trying to make that theory complete. When a sentence is discovered that is neither a theorem nor an antitheorem, it can be made either one of those, at our choice, by adding an axiom. Gödel's Second Incompleteness Theorem says that this process of adding axioms can never make the theory complete (and still consistent).

When we add an axiom to a theory, we obtain a different theory. For the second theorem we must put back the theory name in front of $\vdash$ and $\dashv$. The first theorem says that the sentence

$$\neg \mathcal{TT} \vdash Q \text{``} \neg \mathcal{TT} \vdash Qs\text{''}$$

is unclassified in theory $\mathcal{TT}$. We can create theory $\mathcal{TTT}$ from theory $\mathcal{TT}$ by adding the previous sentence as an axiom. But the second theorem says that the sentence

$$\neg \boldsymbol{T}\boldsymbol{T}\boldsymbol{T} \vdash Q\text{``}\neg \boldsymbol{T}\boldsymbol{T}\boldsymbol{T} \vdash Qs\text{''}$$

will be unclassified. Speaking informally, the second theorem is the same as the first theorem but letting the theory name be variable. Henceforth we shall not distinguish between them.

## Semantics and interpreters

As we have seen, some sentences are theorems, some are antitheorems, and some are neither. It is tempting to say that the sentences which are neither are in a third class, and to invent a third symbol $\perp$ to go with $\vdash$ and $\dashv$. In some circles, three-valued logic is popular. Unfortunately, any attempt to formalize the third class will run into the same problem: there will be a gap, and a temptation to invent a fourth class, and so on. I prefer to say that those sentences that are neither theorem nor antitheorem are "unclassified".

In this section we present a simpler and less expressive metatheory than in the previous sections, using only one symbol. For any theory $\boldsymbol{T}$ and string $s$ we introduce the sentence

$$\boldsymbol{T}\mathbf{I}\,s$$

Predicate $\mathbf{I}$ is said to interpret string $s$ in theory $\boldsymbol{T}$. When it is clear which theory is meant, we may omit its name. For each theory, we want $\mathbf{I}\,s$ to be a theorem if and only if $s$ represents a theorem, and an antitheorem if and only if $s$ represents an antitheorem. It is related to $\vdash$ and $\dashv$ by the two implications

$$\vdash s \;\Rightarrow\; \mathbf{I}\,s \;\Rightarrow\; \neg \dashv s$$

In fact, if we have defined $\vdash$ and $\dashv$, those implications define $\mathbf{I}$. But we want $\mathbf{I}$ to replace $\vdash$ and $\dashv$ so we shall instead define it by showing how it applies to every form of sentence. Here is the beginning of its definition.

$$\begin{aligned}
\mathbf{I}\,\text{``}true\text{''} &= true \\
\mathbf{I}\,\text{``}false\text{''} &= false \\
\forall s\cdot \mathbf{I}\,(\text{``}\neg\text{''}s) &= \neg\mathbf{I}\,s \\
\forall s\cdot \forall t\cdot \mathbf{I}\,(s\text{``}\wedge\text{''}t) &= \mathbf{I}\,s \;\wedge\; \mathbf{I}\,t \\
\forall s\cdot \forall t\cdot \mathbf{I}\,(s\text{``}\vee\text{''}t) &= \mathbf{I}\,s \;\vee\; \mathbf{I}\,t
\end{aligned}$$

And so on. Notice that $\mathbf{I}$ acts as the inverse of quotation marks; it "unquotes" its operand. That is what an interpreter does: it turns passive data into active program. It is a familiar fact to programmers that we can write an interpreter for a language in that same language, and that is just what we are doing here.

To finish defining $\mathbf{I}$ we must decide the details of an entire theory. We shall not do so here, but we give one more case of special interest. $\mathbf{I}$ is defined on strings beginning with $\mathbf{I}$ as

$$\forall s\cdot \mathbf{I}\left(\text{``}\mathbf{I}\text{\_``''}s\text{``''\_''}\right) \;=\; \mathbf{I}\,s$$

Thus the interpreter becomes part of the interpreted logic.

# Gödel simplified

Our presentation of Gödel's argument was parallel to his, but using strings instead of numbers. The argument would be essentially unchanged if we had used $\mathbf{I}$ in place of $\vdash$. The heart of the argument is a transformation from one level of quotes to two levels, and back down to one, with a "$\neg$" appearing in the process. We can simplify the argument without loss of content by going from zero to one and back. We don't take $Q$ to be a function from strings to strings, but simply a string. It is defined as

$$Q \;=\; \text{``}\neg \mathbf{I}\,Q\text{''}$$

By its addition we do not make a theory incomplete: $Q$ equals a completely known 3-character string. Now let us suppose that we can construct (or define) an unquoting function $\mathbf{I}$ (it does not matter how). Then we have the theorem

$\mathbf{I}\,Q$

$=$ {replacing $Q$ with its equal}

$\mathbf{I}\,\text{``}\neg\mathbf{I}\,Q\text{''}$

$=$ {because $\mathbf{I}$ unquotes}

$\neg\mathbf{I}\,Q$

and the inconsistency is apparent. So are the properties necessary to make the argument: a theory must allow us to replace something with its equal, and it must include or allow us to define its own interpreter. To save such a theory from inconsistency, we could suspend the ability to replace something with its equal under certain circumstances, but that is a distasteful option. Instead we leave the interpreter incomplete. In particular, if

$$\mathbf{I}\,\text{``}\neg\mathbf{I}\,Q\text{''} \;=\; \neg\mathbf{I}\,Q$$

is a theorem then we have inconsistency, and if it is an antitheorem then $\mathbf{I}$ is not an interpreter, so we leave it unclassified.

As before, we must consider $\mathbf{I}\,s$ to be a sentence for all strings $s$, even those that do not represent sentences. Otherwise we cannot show that $\mathbf{I}\,Q$ is a sentence. It is tempting to interpret $Q$ as representing a sentence saying that it ($Q$) is not interpretable. But in a very real sense, we must refrain from interpreting $Q$: in programming terms, applying interpreter

**I** to string $Q$ will cause an infinite execution loop, and yield no result. Gödel's argument is a version of the halting problem.

## Conclusion

After the pioneering work of Frege, Russell, and other logicians at the beginning of this century, David Hilbert hoped it would be possible to formalize all of mathematics. But in 1931, Kurt Gödel arrived at a result which is commonly interpreted as saying that any formalism that includes arithmetic allows us to express truths of mathematics that cannot be proven in the formalism. And with that, Hilbert's hope died. The important point of Gödel's result is not the existence of true but unprovable sentences; it is easy to design an incomplete theory in which some of the unprovable sentences were intended to represent truths. Gödel's result says that no one formalism completely describes all formalisms (including itself). But it is equally true that every formalism is completely describable by another formalism, and in that more modest sense Hilbert's hope is achievable.

We believe that our presentation of Gödel's Incompleteness Theorem(s) nicely illustrates E. W. Dijkstra's contention that computing science can now repay with interest its debt to mathematics. Specifically, the distinction between program and data, the use of the character string data type, the use of an interpreter, and counting from zero, reduced the proof to three lines.

*Acknowledgement*: I thank Bill McKeeman for suggesting that I rescue this presentation of Gödel's theorem from a longer, philosophically inclined paper.

## REFERENCES

[1] K. Gödel. Über formal unentscheidbare Sätze der Principia Mathematica und verwandter Systeme I. *Monatshefte für Mathematik und Physik*, 38:173–198, Leipzig, 1931.

[2] K. Gödel. *On Formally Undecidable Propositions of Principia Mathematica and Related Systems*. Oliver & Boyd, Edinburgh, 1962. Translated into English by B. Meltzer, with Introduction by R. B. Braithwaite.

Eric C. R. Hehner,
Department of Computer Science, University of Toronto,
Toronto,Canada, M5S 1A4.

# 19

# A Striptease of Entropy

## G. Helmberg

Let $(p,q)$ be a point in the truncated unit square $]0,1[ \times [0,1]$. The two straight lines connecting $(p,q)$ with $(0,0)$ resp. $(1,0)$ may be considered as the graph of a piecewise linear, unimodal function on the unit interval $[0,1]$ given by

$$(1) \qquad f(x) = \begin{cases} \frac{q}{p}x & \text{for } 0 \le x \le p \\ \frac{q}{1-p}(1-x) & \text{for } p \le x \le 1. \end{cases}$$

Let $f^{(1)} = f$ and $f^{(n+1)} = f^{(n)} \circ f$ for $n \ge 1$. Depending on the position of $(p,q)$, the function $f^{(n)}$ will have a number of maximal monotonicity intervals on which the graph of $f^{(n)}$ is again given by a line segment. This number will be denoted by $c(f^{(n)})$. It is easy to check that e.g. for $0 < q \le p$ one has $c(f^{(n)}) = 2$ for all $n \ge 1$, and for $q = 1$ one has $c(f^{(n)}) = 2^n$ for all $n \ge 1$. The total variation of $f^{(n)}$ on $[0,1]$ will be denoted by $var(f^{(n)})$. Again it may easily be checked that e.g. for $p = \frac{1}{2}$ one has $var(f^{(n)}) = (2q)^n$ for all $n \ge 1$.

Considered as a continuous transformation of the compact space $[0,1]$, $f$ has a topological entropy $h(f)$. Its definition may be looked up e.g. in [1], but in the present situation we may use two formulas due to Misiurewicz and Szlenk [3]:

$$(2) \qquad h(f) = \lim_{n \to \infty} \frac{\log c(f^{(n)})}{n} = \lim_{n \to \infty} \frac{\log var(f^{(n)})}{n}.$$

Especially the first formula reflects that $h(f)$ measures roughly the mean uncertainty per action of $f$ about where in $[0,1]$ one comes from after having been transported by a large number of actions of $f$.

The formulas (2) together with some additional properties of entropy imply that

$$(3) \qquad h(f) = \begin{cases} \log 2 & \text{if } q = 1, \quad 0 < p < 1 \\ \log 2q & \text{if } p = \frac{1}{2}, \quad \frac{1}{2} < q \le 1 \\ 0 & \text{if } q \le p \text{ or } q \le 1-p. \end{cases}$$

If we consider the entropy $h(f)$ as a function $h(p,q)$ of the point $(p,q) \in$

$]0, 1[ \times [0, 1]$ defining $f$ as in (1), the numerical evidence (3) suggests a nice symmetric behaviour of $h$ with respect to the middle line $x = \frac{1}{2}$ of the unit square, although it may be disturbing to note an evident discontinuity of $h$ in the forbidden points $(0, 1)$ and $(1, 1)$. In fact, when taking a mock ballot even in an audience familiar with ergodic theory, inevitably a strong majority feels this way. On second thoughts, however, one realizes that the behaviour of $f$ in the neighbourhood of the fixed point 0 is significantly different from that in the point 1 which is also mapped into 0. A more elaborate study [2] reveals that for fixed $\bar{h} \in ]\frac{1}{2} \log 2, \log 2]$ the points $(x, y)$ satisfying $h(x, y) = \bar{h}$ fill a continuous curve joining $(0, 1)$ with a point on the diagonal $y = x$ (both points excluded, but with a horizontal tangent in $(0, 1)$). The set of points $(x, y)$ satisfying $\frac{1}{2} \log 2 \le h(x, y) \le \log 2$ fills the area between the straight line $y = 1$ $(\bar{h} = \log 2)$, the parabola $y^2 = (1 - x)$ $(\bar{h} = \frac{1}{2} \log 2)$ and the diagonal $y = x$ $(\bar{h} = 0$; the point $(0, 1)$ and the diagonal are excluded).

In what follows we shall concentrate on a second somewhat surprising fact. Consider that part $A$ of the equilateral triangle

$$(4) \qquad \max(x, 1 - x) < y \le 1$$

which lies to the right of the hyperbola

$$(5) \qquad x^2 - xy - 2x + 1 = 0$$

(This hyperbola passes through the point $(\frac{1}{2}, \frac{1}{2})$ and has its centre at $(0, -2)$; it has the $y$-axis as an asymptote and the $x$-axis as a tangent in $(1, 0)$.) The transformation $T$ given on $[0, 1] \times [0, 1]$ by

$$(6) \qquad T(x, y) = (1 - x, \sqrt{xy})$$

maps $A$ onto that part of the equilateral triangle (4) which lies below the parabola $y^2 = 1 - x$ [2]. The significance of $T$ lies in the fact that for $(x, y) \in A$ one has

$$h(1 - x, \sqrt{xy}) = \frac{1}{2} h(x, y).$$

(Note that $T$ maps the line $y = 1$ onto the parabola $y^2 = 1 - x$ and recall that $h(x, 1) = \log 2$, $h(x, \sqrt{1 - x}) = \frac{1}{2} \log 2$, note also that $T$ maps the points $(x, y)$ on the hyperbola (5) into the diagonal points $(1 - x, 1 - x)$.) The transformation $T$ "halves the entropy". The reason for this is that passing from the function $f$ defined by the point $(1 - p, \sqrt{pq})$ to that defined by the point $(p, q)$ the total variation of $f$ and of its iterates $f^{(n)}$ is roughly squared.

Let us now repeat the process of passing from a "line of constant entropy $\bar{h}$" to the "line of constant entropy $\bar{h}/2$", starting with $\bar{h} = \log 2$ $(y = 1)$ and applying every time the transformation $T$. For the time being we disregard the fact that we should only care about the region $A$. By induction on $n$ we find that the lines of constant entropy $\bar{h} = (\log 2)/2^n$ are given by the points

$$T(x, (1-x)^{E_1/2} \cdot x^{E_1/4}) = (1-x, x^{E_2/2} \cdot (1-x)^{E_1/4}) \qquad (n = 2m+1)$$
$$T(x, (1-x)^{E_2/2} \cdot x^{E_1/4}) = (1-x, x^{E_2/2} \cdot (1-x)^{E_2/4}) \qquad (n = 2m+2)$$

where $E_1 = \sum_{k=0}^{m-1} 4^{-k}$ and $E_2 = \sum_{k=0}^{m} 4^{-k}$.

For $n \to \infty$ these curves converge uniformly on $[0, 1]$ to the limit curve

(7) $\qquad y = x^{1/3}(1-x)^{2/3}$

which again passes through $(\frac{1}{2}, \frac{1}{2})$ and which is a "fixed curve" for $T$. For anybody who may care let us note that $T$ is on $]0, 1[ \times ]0, 1]$ the restriction of a purely dissipative, invertible transformation given by the same formula (6) on the strip $]0, 1[ \times ]0, \infty[$ on which $T$ commutes with an "inversion" $S$ defined by

$$S(x, y) = (x, \frac{x^{2/3}(1-x)^{4/3}}{y}).$$

As a conclusion we obtain the following information about the behaviour of the entropy $h(x, y)$ in the neighbourhood of the point $(\frac{1}{2}, \frac{1}{2})$: for large $n$ the points $(x, y)$ satisfying

$$\frac{\log 2}{2^n} \leq h(x, y) \leq \frac{\log 2}{2^{n-1}}$$

fill a small strip above $(\frac{1}{2}, \frac{1}{2})$ inclined with slope approximately $-\frac{1}{3}$, the derivative of (7) at $(\frac{1}{2}, \frac{1}{2})$.

## References

[1] M. Denker, C. Grillenberger, and K. Sigmund. *Ergodic Theory on Compact Spaces*. Volume 527 of Lecture Notes in Mathematics, Springer-Verlag, Berlin – New York, 1976.

[2] G. Helmberg. Die Entropie einer linear gebrochenen Funktion. *Mh. Math.*, 94:213–248, 1982.

[3] M. Misiurewicz and W. Szlenk. Entropy of piecewise monotone mappings. *Studia Math.*, 67:45–63, 1980.

G. Helmberg,
Institut für Mathematik und Geometrie,
Universität Innsbruck,
Technikerstrasse 13,
A-6020  Innsbruck,
Austria.

# 20

# On a Theorem of Jacobson

## Ted Herman

Sometimes, even a simple algebra problem can be the source of a design exercise. In this note we consider the design of a proof of the commutativity of an algebraic ring, provided that $x^3 = x$ for every element $x$ in the ring.

Recall that in an algebraic ring there are two operations defined on its elements, addition ( + ) and multiplication ( × ). Addition associates, is symmetric, and has an identity element 0; negation of elements is also defined. Multiplication associates and distributes over addition. Thus, axioms for the ring are

$$
\begin{array}{rrcl}
(1) & -0 &=& 0 \\
(2) & 0 + x &=& x \\
(3) & (-x) + x &=& 0 \\
(4) & -(-x) &=& x \\
(5) & (x + y) + z &=& x + (y + z) \\
(6) & -(x + y) &=& (-x) + (-y) \\
(7) & x + y &=& y + x \\
(8) & (x \times y) \times z &=& x \times (y \times z) \\
(9) & x \times (y + z) &=& (x \times y) + (x \times z) \\
(10) & (x + y) \times z &=& (x \times z) + (y \times z).
\end{array}
$$

The following properties of multiplication are provable from from axioms (1)–(10), but we shall call them axioms as well:

$$
\begin{array}{rrcl}
(11) & x \times 0 &=& 0 \\
(12) & 0 \times x &=& 0 \\
(13) & x \times (-y) &=& -(x \times y) \\
(14) & (-x) \times y &=& -(x \times y).
\end{array}
$$

Note that multiplication is not necessarily symmetric, nor does there necessarily exist an identity element for multiplication.

To streamline the presentation, we use notational conventions typical to algebra: subtraction is defined in terms of addition and negation, multiplication is denoted by juxtaposition, multiplication has a higher binding power than addition, and exponents (restricted to positive integers) abbreviate multiplication. Free variables in an equation are implicitly universally quantified — the scope of quantification is a single line of text in all cases.

Our task is to prove the theorem $(\forall x :: x^3 = x) \Rightarrow (\forall x, y :: xy = yx)$. To that end, we give the theorem's antecedent the status of an axiom, namely

$$(15) \qquad x^3 = x$$

and propose to derive the symmetry of multiplication from axioms (1)–(15).

The basis of our proof design is pattern matching. The simplest proof would consist of a sequence of steps, based on known identities, that transform the term $xy$ into the term $yx$. Unfortunately, the term $xy$ does not match the axioms in any promising way, so we shall look to progress on some other path. Observe that our pattern matching can be liberalized if we find equivalent forms of $xy = yx$ or stronger equations that imply the symmetry of multiplication. For example,

$$(16) \qquad xy - yx = 0 \Rightarrow xy = yx$$

can be proved from the ring axioms, so we can consider proving $xy - yx = 0$. In fact, this is already a promising development: four of the axioms have zero for their right-hand sides and the antecedent of (16) has zero for its right-hand side. However, at this stage there does not appear to be any obvious way to progress without appeal to some new equations; in view of the peculiar axiom (15), there is reason to suspect that new identities await discovery.

Before embarking on a search for new equations and lemmas, it is wise to aim the search by appropriate heuristics. For instance, it is natural to try to exploit axiom (15). In view of the previous paragraph, it also makes sense to look for results with right-hand sides equal to zero or $yx$. The strengthening heuristic that motivated (16) also directs the search. For example, a lemma of the form "$Z \Rightarrow xy - yx = 0$" will add "$Z$" to the list of forms advantageous for pattern matching. Given these search heuristics, the following lemma is not too hard to find.

**Lemma 1**    $x^2 = 0 \Rightarrow x = 0$.

**Proof**

$$x^2 = 0$$
$$= \qquad \{\text{pre-multiply each side by } x\}$$
$$x^3 = x0$$

$=$ {apply (15) on the left, (11) on the right}

$x = 0$.

This result finds immediate application to the antecedent of (16) if we instantiate "$x := xy - yx$" in Lemma 1. To prove multiplication's symmetry it suffices to prove

$(xy - yx)^2 = 0$

$=$ {(9)}

$(xy - yx)xy + (xy - yx)(-yx) = 0$

$=$ {(13), (14), (6), (4), (7)}

$(xy - yx)xy + (yx - xy)yx = 0$

There is a striking symmetry in the two summands of this equation. One summand can be obtained from the other by interchanging the rôles of $x$ and $y$. This observation, cast in terms of the strengthening heuristic, is

(17)     $(\forall x, y :: (xy - yx)xy = 0) \Rightarrow (\forall x, y :: (xy - yx)^2 = 0)$.

Unfortunately, the antecedent of (17) does not provide any immediate insight. We therefore return to the search for new results, this time with an eye toward equations containing "$xy$" terms. The following lemma proves one of the simplest conjectures that satisfy our search heuristics.

**Lemma 2**   $xy = 0 \Rightarrow yx = 0$.

**Proof**

$xy = 0$

$=$ {pre-multiply each side by $y$, post-multiply each side by $x$}

$yxyx = y0x$

$=$ {(11), (12)}

$(yx)^2 = 0$

$\Rightarrow$ {Lemma 1}

$yx = 0$.

Lemma 2 has an encouraging structure; it shows that multiplication is symmetric in one special case. Lemma 2 can be applied to the antecendent of (17), but doing so doesn't seem to advance the cause, so we continue in the search for new equations.

A reasonable way to synthesize an equation is to take an appropriate axiom, instantiate it with some "$xy$" terms, and then apply axiom (15).

We propose to do this starting from axiom (3), since it is one of the four axioms having zero as a right-hand side. Therefore we shall investigate

$$xy - xy = 0.$$

There are several ways one might apply the identity (15) to this equation. The following two lemmas are separate paths in this investigation.

**Lemma 3**    $xy = y^2xy.$

**Proof**

    *true*

$=$       $\{(3)$ with $x := yx$, then $(7)$ with $x, y := -yx, yx\}$

    $yx - yx = 0$

$=$       $\{(15)\}$

    $yx - yx^3 = 0$

$=$       $\{(10)\}$

    $(y - yx^2)x = 0$

$=$       $\{(15)\}$

    $(y^3 - yx^2)x = 0$

$=$       $\{(9)\}$

    $y(y^2 - x^2)x = 0$

$\Rightarrow$     $\{$Lemma 2 with $x, y := y, (y^2 - x^2)x\}$

    $(y^2 - x^2)xy = 0$

$=$       $\{(10)\}$

    $y^2xy - x^3y = 0$

$=$       $\{(15)\}$

    $y^2xy - xy = 0$

$=$       $\{$add $xy$ to both sides$\}$

    $y^2xy = xy.$

**Lemma 4**    $(xy - yx)yx = 0.$

**Proof**

    *true*

$=$       $\{(3), (7)\}$

$$xy - xy = 0$$
$$= \quad \{(15)\}$$
$$x^3y - (xy)^3 = 0$$
$$= \quad \{(8)\}$$
$$x^3y - x(yx)^2y = 0$$
$$= \quad \{x^3y = x^2(xy); \text{ then apply Lemma 3 to } (xy)\}$$
$$x^2y^2xy - x(yx)^2y = 0$$
$$= \quad \{(9) \text{ factors } x \text{ to the left}, (10) \text{ factors } y \text{ to the right}\}$$
$$x(xy^2x - (yx)^2)y = 0$$
$$\Rightarrow \quad \{\text{Lemma 2 with } x, y := x, (xy^2x - (yx)^2)y \}$$
$$(xy^2x - (yx)^2)yx = 0$$
$$= \quad \{(10)\}$$
$$(xy - yx)(yx)^2 = 0$$
$$= \quad \{\text{post-multiply each side by } yx\}$$
$$(xy - yx)(yx)^3 = 0yx$$
$$= \quad \{(15), (12)\}$$
$$(xy - yx)yx = 0.$$

By happy accident, Lemma 4 precisely matches the antecedent of (17). The symmetry of multiplication is thereby established.

$$\star \quad \star \quad \star$$

The "$x^3 = x$" problem was brought to the attention of the Austin Tuesday Afternoon Club by a note from David Gries [3]. His interest in the problem was motivated by Zohar Manna's report that an automated theorem prover solved the problem in about 200 steps. Gries's interest and our interest is to produce a proof oriented toward human comprehension; as one might expect, Gries's proof is considerably shorter than 200 steps. The diversity and complexity in published proofs to the "$x^3 = x$" problem is surprising [2,5,1].

A related exercise is given in most texts on abstract algebra: prove that a ring is commutative provided $x^2 = x$ for every element $x$ in the ring. This exercise is taken from a theorem in Stone's foundational work on boolean algebra. Subsequently, Jacobson proved that $x^k = x$, for any integer $k > 1$, is a sufficient condition to establish commutativity. In a very beautiful theorem, Jacobson strengthened this result: if for every element $x$ of the ring there is an integer $n$, $n > 1$, such that $x^n = x$, then the ring is commutative (for a proof of this theorem, see [1,4]).

*Acknowledgements*: Without Austin Tuesday Afternoon Club, this note could not be.

## REFERENCES

[1] Raymond Ayoub and Christine Ayoub. On the commutativity of rings. *American Mathematical Monthly*, 71:267–271, 1964.

[2] N. Bourbaki. *Elements of Mathematics Algebra I*. Springer-Verlag, London, 1989. Chapters 1-3, second printing.

[3] David Gries. *A Proof Concerning Rings*. Technical Report, Computer Science Department, Cornell University, September 1987.

[4] I. N. Herstein. Wedderburn's theorem and a theorem of Jacobson. *American Mathematical Monthly*, 68:249–251, 1961.

[5] Jiang Luh. An elementary proof of a theorem of Herstein. *Mathematical Magazine*, 38:105–106, 1965.

Ted Herman,
Department of Computer Sciences,
The University of Texas at Austin,
Taylor Hall 2.124,
Austin, Texas  78712–1188,
U.S.A.

# Modalities of Nondeterminacy

## Wim H. Hesselink

## 0  Introduction

The purpose of this note is to clarify and relate various aspects of nondeterminacy in programming. We concentrate on the relationship between relational semantics and predicate transformer semantics. Up till recently, these two approaches were carefully kept consistent, in the sense that the predicate transformers can be defined in terms of the relations, and vice versa. In recent proposals, cf. [2,11] and [14], however, predicate transformer semantics has been allowed to deviate from the narrow path of relational semantics. The new semantics can be seen operationally as a game between an angel that strives to establish the postcondition and an opposing demon. We formalise this point of view by proving that every monotone predicate transformer can be written as a composition of a "demonic" predicate transformer and an "angelic" one, and also as a composition of an "angelic" predicate transformer and a "demonic" one . The relevant definitions will be given below.

## 1  Nondeterminacy in relational semantics

Relational semantics is the most primitive way of specifying the input–output behaviour of a computational mechanism. From the point of view of programming methodology, Hoare triples or weakest preconditions are usually more convenient, but in a discussion of nondeterminacy relational semantics is a natural starting point.

Let $X$ be the set of the possible input–values of the mechanism and let $Y$ be the set of the possible output–values. As we also want to specify whether or not a computation must or may terminate, a formal symbol "$\infty$", with $\infty \notin Y$, is introduced to stand for the output–value in the case of a non–terminating computation. We write $Y^+$ to denote the union $Y \cup \{\infty\}$. Now the input–output behaviour can be specified by a binary relation $R$ between $X$ and $Y^+$. The interpretation is

(0)    $\langle x, y \rangle \in R \;\equiv\;$ a computation with input $x$ may yield output $y$,
         $\langle x, \infty \rangle \in R \;\equiv\;$ a computation with input $x$ need not terminate.

The specification is called *determinate* if and only if relation $R$ is a function, i.e. for every $x \in X$ there is precisely one $z \in Y^+$ with $\langle x, z \rangle \in R$. Thus, at this level, *nondeterminacy* is the phenomenon that relation $R$ need not be a total function.

If $R$ is not a function there are two (not exclusive) possibilities. First, it may be that there exist $x \in X$ and $y, z \in Y^+$ such that $\langle x, y \rangle \in R$ and $\langle x, z \rangle \in R$ and $y \neq z$. In the *strict* interpretation of nondeterminacy, one requires that both $y$ and $z$ are possible output–values of the mechanism in case of an input $x$. In the *loose* interpretation, cf. [13, page 514], however, relation $R$ is only regarded as a specification: the mechanism itself might well be deterministic (e.g. it may always choose $y$). In programming methodology, the loose interpretation is to be preferred.

The second possibility of nondeterminacy is the existence of a value $x \in X$ such that $\langle x, z \rangle \notin R$ for all $z \in Y^+$. This could be called *overdeterminacy*. In [6], I did not admit this possibility. Since [8], however, I follow De Bakker's book [3] in admitting overdeterminacy, as advocated strongly in [12] and [10]. We do not claim that overdeterminacy is implementable.

For ease of reference, we propose four definitions. Let a set $X$ be called *strict* if and only if $\infty \notin X$. For strict sets $X$ and $Y$, let a binary relation between $X$ and $Y^+$ be called an *operation* from $X$ to $Y$. We write $Op(X, Y)$ to denote the set of the operations from $X$ to $Y$. An operation $R \in Op(X, Y)$ is called *terminating* if and only if $\langle x, \infty \rangle \notin R$ for all $x \in X$.

We will need composition of operations. For strict sets $X$, $Y$ and $Z$, and operations $R \in Op(X, Y)$ and $S \in Op(Y, Z)$ the *composition* $R \,;\, S \in Op(X, Z)$ is defined by

(1)    $\langle x, z \rangle \in R \,;\, S \;\equiv$
         $(z = \infty \;\wedge\; \langle x, \infty \rangle \in R) \;\vee\; \exists (y \in Y :: \langle x, y \rangle \in R \;\wedge\; \langle y, z \rangle \in S)$

for all $x \in X$ and $z \in Z^+$. It is well known that composition is associative:

(2)    $(R \,;\, S) \,;\, T \;=\; R \,;\, (S \,;\, T)$

for all $R \in Op(X, Y)$, $S \in Op(Y, Z)$ and $T \in Op(Z, W)$. The proof is straightforward but not illuminating.

## 2    Angelic and demonic nondeterminacy

Let a mechanism be specified by some operation $R$ between strict sets $X$ and $Y$. If someone wants the mechanism to establish a certain postcondition (i.e. a result in a given subset of $Y$), he may be satisfied by the mere existence of a computation that establishes the postcondition. In this case, he is optimistic and seems to expect his guardian angel to guide the computation in the right direction. Alternatively, he may want all admitted computations to establish the postcondition. Now, the user is pessimistic and is prepared against all demons that might lead the computation astray.

Therefore, the operation $R$ has two different aspects: an *angelic* aspect *ang.R* and a *demonic* aspect *dem.R*. These aspects are associated with predicate transformers in the following way. Let $\mathbb{B}$ denote the set of the two boolean values *true* and *false*. Let $\mathbb{B}^X$ and $\mathbb{B}^Y$ denote the sets of the boolean functions on $X$ and $Y$, respectively. By an abuse of language, the elements of $\mathbb{B}^X$ and $\mathbb{B}^Y$ are called *predicates*. Notice, however, that we do not impose any syntax. Now, functions $\mathbb{B}^Y \to \mathbb{B}^X$ can be called *predicate transformers*. We define the predicate transformers *ang.R*, *dem.R* $\in \mathbb{B}^Y \to \mathbb{B}^X$ by

(3)     $\quad ang.R.f.x \quad \equiv \quad \exists(y \in Y : \langle x,y \rangle \in R : f.y),$
        $\quad dem.R.f.x \quad \equiv \quad \forall(y \in Y^+ : \langle x,y \rangle \in R : y \neq \infty \wedge f.y),$

for arbitrary $x \in X$ and $f \in \mathbb{B}^Y$. Notice that we use the infix operator "." to denote function application. It binds to the left, so that currying is allowed. The reader may recognise Dijkstra's weakest precondition, cf. [4], in the predicate transformer *dem.R*. We come back to that later.

Since both operations and predicate transformers can be composed, one may hope for some relationship. Well, for operations $R \in Op(X,Y)$ and $S \in Op(Y,Z)$ we have

(4)     $\quad ang.(R\,;S) \;=\; ang.R \circ ang.S \quad (\in \mathbb{B}^Z \to \mathbb{B}^X),$
        $\quad dem.(R\,;S) \;=\; dem.R \circ dem.S \quad (\in \mathbb{B}^Z \to \mathbb{B}^X).$

Here, we use the convention that the composition operator "$\circ$" has lower priority than ".". The first formula of (4) is proved by observing that for any $f \in \mathbb{B}^Z$ and any $x \in X$

$\quad (ang.R \circ ang.S).f.x$

$\equiv \qquad \{\text{composition of functions}\}$

$\quad ang.R.(ang.S.f).x$

$\equiv \qquad \{(3)\}$

$\quad \exists(y \in Y : \langle x,y \rangle \in R : ang.S.f.y)$

$\equiv \qquad \{(3)\}$

$\quad \exists(y \in Y : \langle x,y \rangle \in R : \exists(z \in Z : \langle y,z \rangle \in S : f.z))$

$\equiv \qquad \{\text{interchange and trading}\}$

$\quad \exists(z \in Z : \exists(y \in Y :: \langle x,y \rangle \in R \wedge \langle y,z \rangle \in S) : f.z))$

$\equiv \qquad \{z \in Z \text{ implies } z \neq \infty, \text{ and } (1)\}$

$$\exists(z \in Z : \langle x, z \rangle \in R \,; S : f.z)$$

$\equiv \quad \{(3)\}$

$\mathrm{ang}.(R\,; S).f.x.$

The second formula of (4) is proved by observing that for any $f \in \mathbb{B}^Z$ and any $x \in X$

$(\mathrm{dem}.R \circ \mathrm{dem}.S).f.x$

$\equiv \quad \{\text{like first 3 steps above}\}$

$\forall(y \in Y^+ : \langle x, y \rangle \in R$
$\qquad\qquad : y \neq \infty \ \wedge \ \forall(z \in Z^+ : \langle y, z \rangle \in S : z \neq \infty \ \wedge \ f.z)$
$\quad )$

$\equiv \quad \{\text{splitting } y \in Y^+ : \text{either } y = \infty \text{ or } y \in Y\}$

$\langle x, \infty \rangle \notin R$
$\wedge \quad \forall(y \in Y : \langle x, y \rangle \in R : \forall(z \in Z^+ : \langle y, z \rangle \in S : z \neq \infty \ \wedge \ f.z))$

$\equiv \quad \{\text{calculus: interchange, trading and De Morgan}\}$

$\langle x, \infty \rangle \notin R$
$\wedge \quad \forall(z \in Z^+ : \exists(y \in Y :: \langle x, y \rangle \in R \ \wedge \ \langle y, z \rangle \in S) : z \neq \infty \ \wedge \ f.z)$

$\equiv \quad \{\text{range splitting}\}$

$\forall(z \in Z^+$
$\quad : (z = \infty \ \wedge \ \langle x, \infty \rangle \in R) \ \vee \ \exists(y \in Y :: \langle x, y \rangle \in R \ \wedge \ \langle y, z \rangle \in S)$
$\quad : z \neq \infty \ \wedge \ f.z$
$\quad )$

$\equiv \quad \{(1)\}$

$\forall(z \in Z^+ : \langle x, z \rangle \in R\,; S : z \neq \infty \ \wedge \ f.z)$

$\equiv \quad \{(3)\}$

$\mathrm{dem}.(R\,; S).f.x.$

These proofs are not nice, because of the case distinctions induced by the symbol "$\infty$".

# 3   Formal languages as an aside

Angelic nondeterminacy was first introduced in the theory of automata and formal languages. As an example we describe the language accepted by a nondeterministic automaton. For simplicity of presentation, we assume that the automaton has no silent transitions and that it is permitted to have non–terminating transitions. So, it is a quintuple $\langle A, X, D, s, f \rangle$ where $A$ is the alphabet of symbols, $X$ is the state space of the automaton, $D \in A \to Op(X,X)$ is the transition function, $s \in X$ is the initial state, and $f \in \mathbb{B}^X$ is the acceptance function. We write $A^*$ to denote the set of the finite strings of elements of $A$. Since composition of operations is associative, cf. (2), function $D$ has a unique extension $D^* \in A^* \to Op(X,X)$ with

$$D^*.\varepsilon = id,$$
$$D^*.(p\,;q) = (D^*.p)\,;(D^*.q) \quad \text{for all strings } p \text{ and } q.$$

Here, $\varepsilon$ stands for the empty string, $id \in Op(X,X)$ is the identity relation, and $p\,;q$ is the catenation of the strings $p$ and $q$. The language accepted by the automaton is defined to be the subset $L$ of $A^*$ given by

(5) $\qquad p \in L \quad \equiv \quad \exists(x \in X : \langle s,x \rangle \in D^*.p : f.x)$

This is a form of angelic nondeterminacy, for, by (3), formula (5) is equivalent to

$$p \in L \quad \equiv \quad ang.(D^*.p).f.s$$

# 4  Conjugate predicate transformers

For any predicate transformer $h \in \mathbb{B}^Y \to \mathbb{B}^X$, the *conjugate* is defined to be the predicate transformer $h^c \in \mathbb{B}^Y \to \mathbb{B}^X$ given by (cf. [5, chapter 6])

(6) $\qquad h^c.f \quad \equiv \quad \neg(h.\neg f),$

where $\neg f \in \mathbb{B}^Y$ is the predicate given by $(\neg f).y = \neg(f.y)$. No information is lost by conjugation, because of the easily verified formula

(7) $\qquad (h^c)^c = h.$

Conjugation behaves functorially: for $h \in \mathbb{B}^Y \to \mathbb{B}^X$ and $m \in \mathbb{B}^Z \to \mathbb{B}^Y$

(8) $\qquad h^c \circ m^c \quad = \quad (h \circ m)^c \qquad (\in \mathbb{B}^Z \to \mathbb{B}^X).$

For an operation $R \in Op(X,Y)$, the predicate transformers $dem.R$ and $ang.R$ are almost conjugates. In fact, for $f \in \mathbb{B}^Y$, one can obtain from (3), (6) and De Morgan's law

(9) $\qquad (dem.R)^c.f.x \quad \equiv \quad \exists(z \in Y^+ : \langle x,z \rangle \in R : z = \infty \vee f.z).$

Therefore, we have

(10) $\qquad (dem.R)^c = ang.R \quad \equiv \quad R$ is terminating.

# 5  Programming language

As we want to compare various semantical interpretations, we distinguish between a command and its semantics. As before, we start with the relational semantics.

In this section, we assume that every command $C$ has a relational meaning $[\![C]\!] \in Op(X, X)$ for some fixed state space $X$. Now, Dijkstra's weakest precondition $wp.C$, cf. [4], can be defined as the predicate transformer

$$(11) \qquad wp.C \;=\; dem.[\![C]\!] \qquad (\in \mathbb{B}^X \to \mathbb{B}^X).$$

In [7], we introduced a *weakest angelic precondition*

$$(12) \qquad wap.C \;=\; ang.[\![C]\!] \qquad (\in \mathbb{B}^X \to \mathbb{B}^X).$$

This predicate transformer contains the same information as Dijkstra's weakest liberal precondition $wlp.C$, cf. [4]. In fact, they are conjugates: $wlp.C = (wap.C)^c$.

In relational semantics the *composition* of commands is defined by

$$(13) \qquad [\![C \,;D]\!] \;=\; [\![C]\!] \,; [\![D]\!].$$

Now it follows from (11), (12), (13) and (4) that

$$(14) \qquad \begin{aligned} wp.(C \,;D) &\;=\; wp.C \circ wp.D, \\ wap.(C \,;D) &\;=\; wap.C \circ wap.D. \end{aligned}$$

In Dijkstra's axiomatic semantics, the composition of commands is defined by the formulae (14). The success of axiomatic semantics in programming is related to the fact that formula (14) is much more useful than (13).

The *nondeterminate choice* $C \,[\!]\, D$ between commands $C$ and $D$ is defined in relational semantics by means of a union

$$(15) \qquad [\![C \,[\!]\, D]\!] \;=\; [\![C]\!] \cup [\![D]\!].$$

Using (3), (11), (12) and (15), one can easily derive the formulae for the axiomatic semantics

$$(16) \qquad \begin{aligned} wp.(C \,[\!]\, D) &\;=\; wp.C \wedge wp.D, \\ wap.(C \,[\!]\, D) &\;=\; wap.C \vee wap.D, \end{aligned}$$

where the conjunction and disjunction of predicate transformers are defined through the usual lifting of the corresponding operators on predicates.

For a predicate $b \in \mathbb{B}^X$, the *guard* $?b$ is defined as the command with the relational meaning $[\![?b]\!]$ given by

$$(17) \qquad \langle x, y \rangle \in [\![?b]\!] \;\equiv\; b.x \,\wedge\, (x = y)$$

for all $x \in X$ and $y \in X^+$. Clearly, the operation $[\![?b]\!]$ may be overdeterminate. Guards are extremely useful commands, however, for they allow the construction of conditional commands by the definition (cf. [3, page 271])

$$\textbf{if } b \textbf{ then } C \textbf{ else } D \textbf{ fi} \;=\; (?b \,;C \,[\!]\, ?\neg b \,;D).$$

For the axiomatic semantics, one can derive

$$(18) \qquad \begin{aligned} wp.(?b).f &\;=\; \neg b \vee f, \\ wap.(?b).f &\;=\; b \wedge f. \end{aligned}$$

One can say that, due to the overdeterminacy of $[\![?b]\!]$, the predicate transformer $wp.(?b)$ behaves rather angelically, whereas $wap.(?b)$ has demonic features.

# 6    Commands without relational meaning

The introduction of the predicate transformers $wp$ and $wlp$ in [4] was accompanied by the postulation of so–called healthiness conditions. These conditions are equivalent to the existence of consistent relational semantics, together with the prohibition of overdeterminacy and of unbounded nondeterminacy. In the meantime, overdeterminacy and unbounded nondeterminacy have become acceptable. The acceptance of overdeterminacy is due to [9,3,12,10]. Unbounded nondeterminacy was prohibited in [4] because of problems with the interpretation of loops and recursion. These problems have been solved in [1,5,6,8].

Recently, several authors have proposed language constructs with $wp$–semantics that cannot be based on relational semantics, cf. [2,11,14]. Usually, the new construct has a $wp$ that requires more or less angelic behaviour of the executing mechanism. The easiest example is the *angelic choice* $C \Diamond D$ of commands $C$ and $D$, the semantics of which is given by

(19)      $wp.(C \Diamond D)  =  wp.C \vee wp.D.$

For example the command $E = (x := 0 \Diamond x := 1)$ satisfies

$$wp.E.(x = 0)  =  true,$$
$$wp.E.(x = 1)  =  true,$$
$$wp.E.false  =  false.$$

So, the agent that executes $E$ is supposed to know the postcondition, and to choose an adequate computation if one exists. Therefore, we propose to use the term *teleological* for such commands. The predicate transformer $wp.E$ is not conjunctive. Therefore, if we admit operator $\Diamond$, function $wp$ loses its classical interpretation. From this example, it can also be seen that command $C \Diamond D$ has nothing to do with the intersection $[\![C]\!] \cap [\![D]\!]$.

If we compare definition (19) with formula (16), we see that the choice between angelic and demonic nondeterminacy has been taken from the semantic level and incorporated in the programming language (which at this point is usually called a specification language). In view of the above example, this incorporation is called *teleology*. An advantage of teleology is that there is no longer a special rôle for the $wap$ (or its equivalent form $wlp$). A more serious point is that teleology is needed in a calculus of program refinement, cf [11]. In program derivation, however, it may be that the combination of $wp$ and $wap$ is sometimes more useful. For example, in [7], we used $wp$ and $wap$ to specify and derive a language acceptor.

# 7   A factorisation theorem

Commands without a relational interpretation may be a bit difficult to swallow. For this reason, Back and Von Wright ([2]) suggested a game–theoretic interpretation in which $wp.C.p$ holds if and only if, in the game according to $C$ between angel and demon, the angel has a winning strategy to establish postcondition $p$. The rules of the game between angel and demon seem to depend on the syntactic structure of command $C$ and not only on the predicate transformer $wp.C$. In our opinion, the way through syntax and game theory is a diversion. On the other hand, the construction in theorem 2 of [2] suggests that every monotone predicate transformer is a composition of predicate transformers as introduced in (3). This turns out to be true.

We start by introducing monotonicity. The order for predicates on a strict set $X$ is defined by

(20)    $[f \Rightarrow g] \equiv \forall(x \in X : f.x : g.x).$

A predicate transformer $h \in \mathbb{B}^Y \to \mathbb{B}^X$ is called *monotone* if and only if

(21)    $\forall(f, g \in \mathbb{B}^Y : [f \Rightarrow g] : [h.f \Rightarrow h.g]).$

It is well known and easy to prove that for any operation $R \in Op(X, Y)$ the predicate transformers $ang.R$ and $dem.R$ are both monotone. Now the idea is

**Conjecture**    Let $X$ and $Y$ be strict sets and let $m \in \mathbb{B}^Y \to \mathbb{B}^X$ be a monotone predicate transformer. Then there is a strict set $Z$ and operations $R \in Op(X, Z)$ and $S \in Op(Z, Y)$ such that

(22)    $m = dem.R \circ ang.S$ , or perhaps
(23)    $m = ang.R \circ dem.S.$

After an initial investigation of (22), I tried (23) and obtained the following proof. We start with the righthand side of (23). We first observe that for any $f \in \mathbb{B}^Y$ and $x \in X$

(24)   $(ang.R \circ dem.S).f.x$

$\equiv$        {function composition}

$ang.R.(dem.S.f).x$

$\equiv$        $\{(3)\}$

$\exists(z \in Z : \langle x, z \rangle \in R : dem.S.f.z)$

$\equiv$        $\{(3)\}$

$\exists(z \in Z : \langle x, z \rangle \in R : \forall(y \in Y^+ : \langle z, y \rangle \in S : y \neq \infty \wedge f.y)).$

At this point we have to propose a set $Z$ and two operations $R$ and $S$. These objects must be independent of $f$ and $x$, and may depend on the predicate transformer $m$. In view of (23), the aim is to reduce the expression to $m.f.x$. We have to use that $m$ is monotone. There are two ways to use monotonicity of $m$ in relation to the term $m.f.x$. In fact, we have

(25)     $m.f.x \equiv \forall(g \in \mathbb{B}^Y : [f \Rightarrow g] : m.g.x)$ , and

$\phantom{(25)}$     $m.f.x \equiv \exists(g \in \mathbb{B}^Y : [g \Rightarrow f] : m.g.x).$

Both equivalences can be proved by mutual implication, where one implication follows from monotonicity of $m$, cf. (21), and the other from the substitution $g := f$. Since the final expression of (24) starts with "$\exists$", we use the second line of (25) and take $Z = \mathbb{B}^Y$, with typical elements $g$. This heuristical argument was given by J.C.S.P. van der Woude. Now, in view of the types, the simplest meaningful choice for $R$ and $S$ is

(26)     $\langle x, g \rangle \in R \equiv g \neq \infty \wedge m.g.x,$

$\phantom{(26)}$     $\langle g, y \rangle \in S \equiv y \neq \infty \wedge g.y.$

Lo and behold! For any $f \in \mathbb{B}^Y$ and $x \in X$ we observe

$\quad (ang.R \circ dem.S).f.x$

$\equiv \quad \{(24), (26)\}$

$\quad \exists(g \in \mathbb{B}^Y : g \neq \infty \wedge m.g.x$
$\qquad\qquad : \forall(y \in Y^+ : y \neq \infty \wedge g.y : y \neq \infty \wedge f.y))$

$\equiv \quad \{\text{calculus}\}$

$\quad \exists(g \in \mathbb{B}^Y : m.g.x : \forall(y \in Y : g.y : f.y))$

$\equiv \quad \{(20), \text{trading, second line of } (25)\}$

$\quad m.f.x.$

This proves (23). Actually, the result is slightly stronger than the conjecture. For, the set $Z$ and the operation $S$ are independent of $m$ and $X$, and the operations $R$ and $S$ are terminating, cf. (26):

(27) **Theorem**  Let $Y$ be a strict set. There is a strict set $Z$ and a terminating operation $S \in Op(Z, Y)$ such that for every strict set $X$ and every monotone predicate transformer $m \in \mathbb{B}^Y \to \mathbb{B}^X$ there is a terminating operation $R \in Op(X, Z)$ with

$\quad m = ang.R \circ dem.S.$

For conjecture (22), the heuristics that yielded (23) do work, but we can also prove (22) by means of conjugation. More precisely, we have

(28) **Corollary** Let $Y$ be a strict set. The set $Z$ and the operation $S$ of theorem (27) are such that there is also a terminating operation $T \in Op(X, Z)$ with

$$m = dem.T \circ ang.S.$$

**Proof**    We observe that for terminating $T$

$$m = dem.T \circ ang.S$$

$\equiv \quad \{(7), (8)\}$

$$m^c = (dem.T)^c \circ (ang.S)^c$$

$\equiv \quad \{(10), (7),\ S \text{ and } T \text{ are terminating}\}$

$$m^c = ang.T \circ dem.S.$$

Since $m^c$ is easily seen to be monotone, the existence of $T$ follows from (27) applied to $m^c$.
(**End** of proof)

*Remarks.* The theorem and its corollary are independent of a syntactic description of function $m$. Two game theoretic interpretations are suggested. In both cases, we get a game that lasts only two moves. According to the theorem, function $m$ is interpreted as a game between a universal demon $S$ and a particular angel $R$ (specific for $m$). The demon starts and the angel answers. The scene might remind us of Goethe's Faust. In the corollary, however, $S$ has the rôle of a universal angel and there is a particular demon $T$ that has the last word. The scene, although equivalent, looks more gloomy.

In the proof of the theorem, some rabbits may have been pulled out of the magician's hat. The main rabbit, however, was introduced at the beginning of the paper, where we distinguished between input–values and output–values. This distinction led us to formulate the conjecture with a free intermediate state space $Z$. In this way, the index set used in theorem 2 of [2] could acquire the status of a state space $Z = \mathbb{B}^Y$.

## References

[1] K. R. Apt and G. D.Plotkin. Countable nondeterminism and random assignment. *J. ACM*, 33:724–767, 1986.

[2] R. J. R. Back and J. von Wright. A lattice-theoretical basis for a specification language. In J. L. A. van de Snepscheut, editor, *Mathematics of Program Construction*, pages 139–156, Springer-Verlag, Berlin, 1989. Lecture Notes in Computer Science, Vol. 375.

[3] J. W. de Bakker. *Mathematical Theory of Program Correctness.* Prentice-Hall, 1980.

[4] E. W. Dijkstra. *A Discipline of Programming.* Prentice-Hall, Englewood Cliffs, 1976.

[5] E. W. Dijkstra and C. S. Scholten. *Predicate Calculus and Program Semantics.* Springer-Verlag, New York, 1990.

[6] W. H. Hesselink. Interpretations of recursion under unbounded nondeterminacy. *Theoretical Computer Science,* 59:211–234, 1988.

[7] W. H. Hesselink. *LR-Parsing Derived* (WHH 56). Technical Report CS 8906, Department of Mathematics and Computing Science, University of Groningen, May 1989.

[8] W. H. Hesselink. Predicate transformer semantics of general recursion (WHH 8). *Acta Informatica,* 26:309–332, 1989.

[9] C. A. R. Hoare. Some properties of predicate transformers. *J. ACM,* 25:461–480, 1978.

[10] C. C. Morgan. Data refinement by miracles. *Information Processing Letters,* 26:243–246, 1987/88.

[11] C. C. Morgan and P. Gardiner. Data refinement by calculation. In C. C. Morgan, K. Robinson and P. Gardiner, *On the Refinement Calculus,* Techical Monograph PRG–70, pages 103–134, Oxford 1988.

[12] G. Nelson. *A Generalization of Dijkstra's Calculus.* Technical Report 16, Digital Systems Research Center, April 1987.

[13] D. Park. On the semanics of fair parallelism. In *Abstract Software Specifications,* pages 504–526, Springer-Verlag, Berlin, 1980. Lecture Notes in Computer Science, Vol. 86.

[14] J. Zwiers and W. -P. de Roever. *Predicates are Predicate Transformers: a Unified Compositional Theory for Concurrency.* June 1989. (Preliminary version).

Wim H. Hesselink,
Department of Computing Science,
Rijksuniversiteit Groningen,
P.O. Box 800,
9700 AV Groningen,
The Netherlands

# 22

# A Theory for the Derivation of C-mos Circuit Designs

## C. A. R. Hoare

## Summary

This paper shows how propositional logic may be used to reason about synchronous sequential switching circuits implemented in C-mos. It develops a simple formalism and theory for describing and predicting their behaviour. On this it builds a calculus of design which is driven by proof obligations. The design philosophy for software introduced in [1] is thereby extended to a certain kind of hardware design.

No prior knowledge of hardware is assumed of the reader; but useful background, motivation, examples and pictures may be found in [2]. Many of the problems described in that paper have been solved in this one.

## 1 Operation of C-mos circuits.

A C-mos circuit is a collection of transistors connected to each other by wires. A *transistor* acts like an electrical switch, which may be in one or two states, either *on* or *off* —for our purposes any intermediate states are transient, and can be ignored. When it is on, the transistor makes a conducting path between two wires attached to its *source* and its *drain*. When it is off, these two wires are disconnected. Note that connection between source and drain is the same as connection between drain and source. Connection and disconnection are therefore symmetric relations. It is a valuable property of our theory that it preserves and takes advantage of this naturally occurring symmetry.

Each *wire* of a circuit also may be in one of two states, either at *high* voltage (1 or power or VDD) or at *low* voltage (0 or ground or GND); for our purposes, any intermediate voltages are transient and can be ignored. If two wires with different voltages are connected through a transistor which is switched on, a current will flow between them; and this will tend to reduce the difference between their voltages. If one of the two wires is permanently connected to the power supply and the other is permanently connected to ground, then the current will flow forever. This counts as failure of a C-mos circuit; our theory shows how to avoid such failures, and so does not need to describe their effects in detail. In correct operation, all currents rapidly subside, with equalisation of voltages at the source and the drain of all the transistors that are in the on state.

In contrast to the familiar manual domestic switch, the state of a transistor is controlled electronically by the voltage on a third wire attached to its *gate*. There are two kinds of C-mos transistor, the N-transistor and P-transistor. In the case of an N-transistor, a high voltage at the gate causes it to switch on, and a low voltage switches it off. In the case of a P-transistor, it is a low voltage that switches it on, and a high voltage switches it off.

The state of a complete circuit is determined by the state of each of its wires. Since each wire may take either of two states (high or low), the total number of states is therefore two raised to the power of the number of wires of the circuit (excluding the power wire and the ground wire, which have only one state each). But a great many of these states are impossible, because they ascribe different voltages to wires connected to the source and the drain of a transistor which happens to be in the on state. We therefore define a state as *consistent* if

1. The power wire is high and the ground wire is low.
2. Wherever the wire attached to the gate of an N-transistor is high, then the two wires attached to its source and drain have the same voltage; and similarly for a P-transistor, if its gate is low.

At the beginning of each cycle of operation of the circuit, a voltage (high or low) is applied from outside to each of a certain subset of wires, the chosen *input* wires for this cycle. As a result certain of the transistors switch on, thereby creating connections between power or ground and certain other wires. These wires then acquire a high or low voltage, thereby causing further transistors to switch on or off. The signals thus propagate rapidly through the circuit. In a *synchronous* circuit, enough time is allowed for the propagation to complete; and finally, the voltages on the set of wires chosen for *output* on this cycle are read by the environment of the circuit. The next cycle of operation is now ready to begin.

It is usual for the selection of input and output wires to remain the same on all cycles of operation. When this is not so, the circuit is called *multi-directional*. Wires that are never used for input or output are called *local*. They will not be physically connected to the environment of the circuit. It is a primary goal of any circuit theory to ensure that the behaviour of a circuit can be specified and understood without any reference to the voltages or even the existence of such local wires.

As a result of the propagation described above, the state reached by the circuit at the end of each cycle should certainly be consistent; for otherwise the circuit would fail by perpetual conduction of current. If there is only one final state consistent with the input state, the voltages on all the output wires at the end of the cycle cannot differ from those ascribed in this unique consistent state. If there is more than one consistent extension, any wire that takes differing voltages in differing extensions is said to *float*, because at the end of the current cycle it is connected neither to power nor to ground. In a real circuit, such a wire retains as electrical *charge* the same voltage which it had at the end of the previous cycle. A charge at the gate of a transistor will keep it switched on or off at least for the duration of a single cycle (unless the cycle is specially extended). Our theory states that *all* floating gate wires retain their charge to the end of the cycle. We make this a condition of consistency of the circuit, so it is the responsibility of the *environment* of the circuit to ensure that it is met. This also avoids some of the dangers of *charge sharing*, which leads to weakening or cancellation of opposite charges on floating wires that become connected to each other on the current cycle.

The description given above has ignored a vital property of a switch (either manual or electronic) that it is incapable of changing its state as a result of voltages applied to its source and drain. Consider for example an N-transistor with its source connected to power and its drain connected to ground. The only consistent voltage for its gate is low. However the wire connected to its gate will not automatically assume this voltage at the end of the cycle. In practice, it is likely to take some intermediate voltage, which allows current to flow perpetually between the source and drain; and this leads to failure of the circuit.

To avoid the risk of this kind of failure, we need to distinguish between two states of each wire, either *driven* or not. At the beginning of each cycle of operation, the chosen input wires are assumed to be driven. If a transistor is in the on state and its gate is driven, then any drive on its source will propagate to its drain and vice-versa. At the end of the cycle, a wire will be driven if and only if it acquires drive as a result of the propagation rules described above; they never specify that drive should be propagated from source or drain to the gate of the same transistor.

To avoid the danger of perpetual flow of current, it is necessary to ensure that the gates of certain transistors are driven. A circuit state is said to be *adequate* if the gate of every transistor is driven, with the possible exception of transistors whose source and drain are equal anyway. It is the responsibility of the environment of the circuit to drive a sufficient set of input wires to ensure that, after the internal propagation described above, the circuit state will be adequate; and furthermore that all output wires will be driven.

There is one further complexity that we cannot ignore. A switch which is on should continue to conduct current until the voltages at its source and drain are equal. Unfortunately, an N-transistor will stop conducting when its source (or drain) is high and its drain (or source) is still at a somewhat lower voltage. Such lower voltages can be further weakened by passage through other transistors. Similarly, a P-transistor will stop conducting when its source is low and its drain is at a somewhat higher voltage. We need to adapt our theory to avoid the circuit failure that could result from use of these weakened signals at the gates of its transistors.

The problem could be tackled by introducing a further distinction between wires carrying strong or weak signals. A simpler solution to equate all weakened signals with the undriven state of a wire. This is achieved by making propagation of drive conditional on the voltage of the source and the drain: in the case of an N-transistor these must be low; and for a P-transistor they must be high. Now the adequacy condition ensures that weakened signals will not be used in circumstances in which they could lead to failure.

# 2   Formalisation of the theory.

The previous section has given an informal description of the operational behaviour of a synchronous sequential switching circuit as implemented by C-mos transistors. It has explained some of the simplifications which can reasonably be made in a theory which explains this behaviour: they are justified because they err on the side of pessimism, and will not predict correct operation of a circuit that is subject to risk of failure. The present section gives a formal treatment of the theory: its formulae may be used to calculate the behaviour of circuits in a way that abstracts from operational detail. The only mathematics required comes from propositional logic.

In order to describe the behaviour of a physical system by a formula, it is necessary to establish a convention whereby free variables of the formula stand for values that can be observed at certain points in the system at certain instants during its evolution. In the case of a C-mos circuit, we give an alphanumeric name (typically $w, s, d, g, \ldots$) to each wire; and we use the same name in a formula to denote the voltage observed at the end of a typical cycle of operation. In the case of input wires, this will be the same as the value at the beginning of the cycle. A high voltage is represented by a "true" value for the name, and a low voltage by a "false" value.

Our first task is to describe the consistent states of a circuit by a propositional formula containing wirenames as free variables: the formula will be true for just those combinations of voltages of the wires that are consistent, and false for the inconsistent ones. Consider first a single N-transistor with gate wire named $g$, source wire named $s$, and drain wire named $d$. The inconsistent states of this simple circuit are just those in which it is on (i.e., $g$ is true) but the voltages of the source and drain differ. These are the states described by the propositional formula

$$(g \wedge s \wedge \neg d) \vee (g \wedge \neg s \wedge d).$$

The *consistent* states are therefore defined as the negation of this, which by propositional logic may be rewritten to

$$g \Rightarrow (s \equiv d).$$

Similar reasoning applies to a P-transistor, except that it is on when its gate wire is low. Its consistent states are described by the formula

$$\neg g \Rightarrow (s \equiv d).$$

A complete circuit is in a consistent state in just those cases when *all* its component transistors are consistent. The formula defining these states is just the conjunction of the formulae for all its individual component transistors. This very simple way of computing the behaviour of a complex system from that of its components is characteristic of many kinds of parallel composition.

The formula defining the consistent states of a circuit serves as a specification of the externally visible states of the input and output wires. It also mentions the values of all the local wires in the circuit, even though these wires are not connected externally, and their values can never be observed. The formula would be much more useful as a specification if we could abstract away from these wires, removing all mention of their names.

Let $C(w)$ be the consistency formula for a circuit with a local wire $w$ not connected to its external environment. The easiest way to remove this name from the formula is by quantification $\exists w.C(w)$. Since $w$ can take only two values true or false, this is equivalent to $C(\text{true}) \vee C(\text{false})$. After simplification by partial evaluation, this is usually rather simpler and so more useful than the original $C(w)$. The use of existential quantification rather than universal to hide a local wire is justified by the fact that consistency is achieved merely by the *existence* of a consistent voltage for all the wires in the circuit. Convergence of the local wire to a consistent value will be assured by methods described in the next section.

Now suppose the wire $w$ is intended on some cycles to retain as charge the voltage which it had at the end of the previous cycle. We need to introduce a new propositional variable $w^-$ to refer to this voltage. Let $C(w)$ be the consistency condition for a circuit containing the wire name $w$. Suppose that the values of all the other wires of the circuit are such that it is consistent for $w$ to take the same value that it did on the previous cycle; then in fact it does so. This fact is expressed

$$C(w^-) \;\Rightarrow\; (w \equiv w^-).$$

This must be conjoined to the original statement of the combinational behaviour. We therefore define a sequentialisation operator S:

$$Sw.\, C(w) \;\;\widehat{=}\;\; C(w) \wedge C(w^-) \wedge (C(w^-) \;\Rightarrow\; (w \equiv w^-))$$

This operator converts a combinational formula (without -) into a sequential formula; and so it is invalid to apply it more than once. We therefore need a more complicated definition to sequentialise on two or more wires simultaneously:

$$\begin{aligned}
Sv, w \ldots C(v, w, \ldots) \;\;\widehat{=}\;\;\; & C(v, w, \ldots) \wedge C(v^-, w^-, \ldots) \\
& \wedge\, (C(v^-, w, \ldots) \Rightarrow (v \equiv v^-)) \\
& \wedge\, (C(v, w^-, \ldots) \Rightarrow (w \equiv w^-)) \;\wedge \ldots
\end{aligned}$$

Our next task is to describe by formula the way in which drive is propagated through the circuit. For this we need to introduce for each wire $w$ a new free variable $Dw$, which is true just if the wire $w$ is driven at the end of the cycle. Consider first an N-transistor with gate wire $g$, source $s$ and drain $d$. If the transistor is on and the gate is driven, and either the source or drain wire is driven, then the other one is too. This fact is expressed by the propositional formula

$$g \wedge Dg \;\Rightarrow\; (Ds \equiv Dd).$$

The corresponding formula for a P-transistor is

$$\neg g \wedge Dg \;\Rightarrow\; (Ds \equiv Dd).$$

Unfortunately this is too simple. For C-mos transistors one must use a formula that specifies propagation of drive only when the propagated signal is at the right level, i.e., low for an N-transistor, high for a P-transistor. Thus the formulae given above should be weakened to

$$\begin{aligned}
g \wedge Dg \wedge (\neg s \vee \neg d) \;&\Rightarrow\; (Ds \equiv Dd) \\
\neg g \wedge Dg \wedge (s \vee d) \;&\Rightarrow\; (Ds \equiv Dd)
\end{aligned}$$

for an N-transistor and a P-transistor respectively.

The propagation of drive through a whole circuit is achieved by the propagation through each of its component transistors. The formula describing this is nothing but the conjunction of the formulae for all its individual component transistors.

In order to deal with retention of drive from a previous cycle, we need to introduce for each gate wire $w$ yet another variable $Dw^-$, which stores the previous value of $Dw$. The condition $Dg$ for drive propagation between source and drain of a transistor can now be weakened to

$$Dg \vee (Dg^- \wedge (g \equiv g^-));$$

this reflects the fact that when the wire retains its previous value ($g \equiv g^-$) a drive at the previous cycle ($Dg$-) is sufficient to cause propagation between source and drain. For example, the drive condition for an N-transistor now reads

$$g \wedge (Dg \vee (Dg\text{-} \wedge (g \equiv g\text{-}))) \wedge (\neg s \vee \neg d) \ \Rightarrow \ (Ds \equiv Dd).$$

The extra complexity can be avoided in cases where correct operation does not depend on state retention by the wire $g$; or the complexity could be increased by further clauses added to describe retention of drive for more than one cycle.

Finally, we need to define the adequacy condition for a circuit. As before, this is just the conjunction of the adequacy conditions for all the transistors of the circuit. A transistor is adequate if its source equals its drain, because then the status of its gate does not matter. Otherwise, the gate must be driven either on the current cycle, or (in the case of a retained charge) on the previous cycle. For both kinds of transistor the adequacy condition is defined as

$$(s \equiv d) \vee Dg \vee (Dg\text{-} \wedge (g \equiv g\text{-})).$$

# 3    Some simplifications

The arguments in the previous section suggest that the behaviour of any circuit can be characterised by three propositions $(C, D, A)$, where $C$ is the consistency condition and $D$ is the drive condition and $A$ is the adequacy condition.

For example, a circuit consisting of a single N-transistor is the triple

$$((g \ \Rightarrow \ (s \equiv d)),$$
$$g \wedge (\neg s \vee \neg d) \wedge (Dg \vee (Dg\text{-} \wedge (g \equiv g\text{-}))) \ \Rightarrow \ (Ds \equiv Dd),$$
$$(s \equiv d) \vee Dg \vee (Dg\text{-} \wedge (g \equiv g\text{-})))$$

where $g$ is the name of the gate wire, $s$ the source, and $d$ the drain. The formula for a P-transistor is similar, except that $\neg g$ is substituted for $g$, $\neg s$ for $s$ and $\neg d$ for $d$.

A more complex circuit is built up as a collection of P-transistors and N-transistors, connected to each other by named wires. When two circuits are connected to each other in this way, the behaviour of the resulting circuit is described by the componentwise conjunction of the three conditions describing the components. We can define this as a parallel composition operator on the triples

$$(C, D, A) \parallel (C', D', A') \ \ \widehat{=} \ \ (C \wedge C', D \wedge D', A \wedge A').$$

This operator obviously shares all properties of conjunction, for example associativity, commutivity and even idempotence. These are exactly the properties one would expect when putting circuits together in practice.

The three formulae describing each individual transistor are already quite complicated; and when these formulae are joined by parallel composition, they will get very long as well. Of course, considerable simplifications can be made by the laws of Boolean algebra; in this section we shall introduce some even more powerful laws, specific to the design of C-mos switching circuits.

Our main simplifications are justified, like earlier simplifications, by the fact that we are not interested in making distinctions between circuits that are not functioning correctly. A similar simplification is introduced into Dijkstra's calculus of sequential programming by its identification of all incorrect programs with "abort". In our case we choose not to make any distinctions between inconsistent states of a circuit; for example, it is wholly irrelevant whether an inconsistent state satisfies the drive condition or not. Similarly, assuming consistency of the state, operation of the circuit will guarantee the truth of the drive condition. Of the states that do not satisfy the drive condition, it is wholly irrelevant whether they satisfy the adequacy condition or not.

We therefore define two circuits be *equivalent* if they differ only on states which we have decided to regard as irrelevant. They must have exactly the same consistent states; their states which are both consistent and driven must be the same; and states which are consistent, driven and adequate must be the same. This implicitly allows a circuit to satisfy some of its own adequacy condition. So we define

$$(C, D, A) \equiv (C', D', A')$$

to mean $[C \equiv C']$ and $[C \wedge D \equiv C' \wedge D']$ and $[C \wedge D \wedge A \equiv C' \wedge D' \wedge A']$, where the square brackets indicate that the enclosed propositional formula is a tautology (notation due to Dijkstra).

Clearly, this defines an equivalence relation among circuits. The most important consequence of this is

$$(C, D, A) \equiv (C,\ C \wedge D,\ C \wedge D \Rightarrow A)$$

The right hand side of this equivalence will be taken as a canonical form of the description of a process. Two processes are equivalent if and only if they have the same canonical forms.

Take two equivalent circuit descriptions and combine each of them in parallel with a third description. You would certainly hope that the resulting pair of descriptions are also equivalent —otherwise the definition of equivalence could not be used to simplify component subcircuits of a large circuit. So the parallel composition operator should respect equivalence, as guaranteed by the following congruence theorem:

$$\text{If} \quad (C, D, A) \equiv (C', D', A')$$
$$\text{then} \quad (C, D, A) \| (P, Q, R) \equiv (C', D', A') \| (P, Q, R).$$

The main purpose of an accurate description of the behaviour of a circuit is to serve as its specification, for the benefit of a designer who will incorporate the circuit into some larger environment. For this purpose, it is important that the specification be simple; to achieve this we can even allow it to be inaccurate! The inaccuracy will be harmless, provided that the specification describes a circuit that is systematically *worse* than the actual one, worse in all ways and in all environments. It is the responsibility of the designer of the environment to ensure correct operation in spite of the apparently reduced quality of the component; our theory will ensure that it continues to do so when the actual quality of the component is superior to that specified. The only disadvantage of weakening the specification of a circuit is that it reduces the apparent range of environments in which it may be used. But a specification that is too complicated can make a circuit even more useless.

It is a fact of circuit design that a driven wire is always more useful than an undriven one. Given two circuits with the *same* consistent states, the better one is the one that in each consistent state has more driven wires, or at least as many. The drive condition of the better circuit will therefore be *stronger* than the drive condition of the other. In this way, the drive condition of a circuit acts like the post-condition of a sequential program: to weaken it makes the program appear worse than it actually is; but no errors can result.

Similarly, the adequacy condition of a circuit is like the precondition of a sequential program. It describes an obligation that must be met by the environment within which the component is embedded. The designer of the component may assume that this has been done, and correct operation of the component may depend upon it. Given two circuits with the same consistent states and the same drive condition, the better circuit is the one with the *weaker* adequacy condition, since this places less restriction upon the environment in which it may be used.

According to this reasoning, the canonical form of a process description is the one that paints the process in the most favourable light: the charge condition is as strong as possible, and the adequacy condition as weak as possible. Let us formalise the definition of our merit ordering:

$$(C, D, A) \sqsubseteq (C', D', A')$$

means $[C \equiv C']$ and $[D' \Rightarrow D]$ and $[A \Rightarrow A']$ where both sides of the inequation are taken to be in canonical form. This relation is clearly a preorder (reflexive and transitive). Furthermore, it induces the already familiar equivalence relation by the usual definition

$$P \sqsubseteq P' \quad \text{and} \quad P' \sqsubseteq P \quad \text{iff} \quad P \equiv P'.$$

Take two circuit descriptions, one better than the other, and combine each of them in parallel with a third description. You would certainly hope that the system with the better component would behave better than the other, or at least no worse —otherwise replacement of a component by a better one would be invalid, and so would the whole design philosophy based on our ordering relation. In other words, the parallel composition operator should respect the ordering relation $\sqsubseteq$, as guaranteed by the following monotonicity theorem

$$\text{If} \quad (C, D, A) \ \sqsubseteq \ (C', D', A')$$
$$\text{then} \quad (C, D, A) \parallel (P, Q, R) \ \sqsubseteq \ (C', D', A') \parallel (P, Q, R).$$

One of the most important simplifications in a specification is that which conceals the voltage, the name, and even the existence of a local wire $w$. The result is allowed to be worse than the original, i.e., the drive condition can be weakened by existential quantification, and the adequacy condition can be strengthened by universal quantification, as justified by the theorem

$$(C, (\exists w, Dw.D), (\forall w, Dw.A)) \ \sqsubseteq \ (C, D, A).$$

As explained before, the wire name $w$ is concealed from the consistency condition (which does not contain $Dw$) by existential quantification on $w$. We therefore define a concealment operator $\mathsf{H}$ by the equation

$$\mathsf{H}w.(C, D, A) \ = \ ((\exists w.C), (\exists w, Dw.D), (\forall w, Dw.A)),$$

where the argument is assumed to be in canonical form.

This definition enjoys algebraic properties similar to those of other quantifiers; they are the same properties that one would expect of the actual hardware of a circuit:

(a) $\quad (\mathsf{H}w.Q) \quad \equiv \quad Q$, if $w$ and $Dw$ are not free in $Q$.

(b) $\quad (\mathsf{H}w.Qw) \quad \equiv \quad (\mathsf{H}v.Qv)$, where $Qw$ contains $w$ and $Dw$ in just those positions where $Qv$ contains $v$ and $Dv$.

(c) $\quad$ If $P \sqsubseteq Q$ then $(\mathsf{H}w.P) \sqsubseteq (\mathsf{H}w.Q)$.

(d) $\quad (\mathsf{H}w.P) \parallel Q \equiv (\mathsf{H}w.(P \parallel Q))$, if $w$ and $Dw$ are not free in $Q$.

(e) $\quad \mathsf{H}v.(\mathsf{H}w.P) \equiv \mathsf{H}w.(\mathsf{H}v.P).$

There are some complex interactions between hiding and sequentialisation; we leave these unexplored.

# 4 A calculus of design

The previous section has shown how a C-mos circuit design can be built up from individual P-transistors and N-transistors by means of parallel composition ($\parallel$) and hiding of local wires ($\mathsf{H}$). With each design, it associates a triple of propositional formulae, which can be used to predict the behaviour of a given circuit, and in particular to analyse and avoid the risk of failure. Like other scientific theories, it is purely descriptive, and could be supported or refuted by experiment on actual C-mos circuits (provided that these satisfy the design rules of the fabrication line on which they are produced).

In this section we shall develop the theory into a design calculus for deriving the design of a circuit directly from its specification. By following the rules step by step, a design engineer will be prevented from introducing logical errors into the design. Since each step is small and uses only propositional logic, its correctness can be easily checked, even by computer. The fact that correctness of each step guarantees correctness of the whole design is established by mathematical reasoning, based on theorems like those of the previous section.

A formal design calculus must start with a formal specification of the product to be designed. The specification should be expressed in the clearest possible fashion, to reduce the terrible risk that it fails to describe what is really required. Thus it should be free to use concepts and notations which are more abstract and more general than those in which the design is described. The restriction in the design notation is needed only to permit direct and efficient implementation, for example as a C-mos circuit etched onto silicon; such restrictions can have only a deleterious effect on a specification.

In the case of a C-mos circuit, we will start with a specification containing three propositional formulae $(C, D, A)$, with the same free variables $(w, w^-, Dw, Dw^-)$ as the eventual behavioural description of the circuit; however they may be combined freely by arbitrary propositional connectives, not just parallel composition and hiding. It is the task of the designer to invent a circuit, expressed solely in terms of transistors, parallel composition and hiding, whose behaviour is as good as or better than that specified.

In a correct design, the consistency condition $C$ for the specification must be equivalent to the consistency condition $C'$ of the design. In the absence of hiding, the latter is just the conjunction of the consistency conditions for the individual transistors of the circuit. Each of these must therefore be a logical consequence of $C$. This fact can be checked separately for each individual transistor, before it is added to the circuit. In this way, the correctness of the whole circuit is assured by proofs conducted piecemeal during its design.

The decision to introduce a local wire $w$ into a circuit, like the introduction of a local variable into a sequential program, requires the good judgement of a designer. The designer presumably knows the intended properties of the local variable, and should express this as a proposition $I(w)$. The consistency of this needs to be checked by proof (from $C$) of $\exists w.I(w)$. $I(w)$ may then be added as an assumption to the condition $C$, and used to derive the individual transistors of the circuit. The role of the "invariant" is like that in a proof-oriented development of a loop in a sequential program: it has no effect on the actual behaviour of the circuit; however, it is essential to the progress and documentation of the design.

Treatment of drive and adequacy is a little more complicated. The goal of the design is to prove the drive condition of the specification, which plays the role of the postcondition of a sequential program. At the beginning, the designer may assume the adequacy condition of the specification, which is a sort of precondition, ensured by the environment of the circuit. During the design, the set of assumptions and the set of proof obligations will change. As each transistor is added to the circuit, its drive condition is added to the assumptions, and its adequacy condition is added to the proof obligations. Further transistors are added until the accumulated proof obligations can all be proved from the accumulated assumptions. At this point, the design is complete, and the accumulated set of transistors is better than required by the specification. In theory, one should then check that the consistency condition of the specification can be proved from the consistency conditions of all the transistors; but in practice this seems to be unnecessary.

In the design of a large system, it would be intolerable to add just one transistor at a time. Instead, the designer wants to call up and insert a complete subcircuit which has been previously designed to meet some generally useful specification. A similar facility is offered by the call of a procedure in a sequential programming language. The method of inserting a complete subcircuit is identical to that of inserting a single transistor. The consistency condition of the subcircuit must first be proved; then its drive condition is added to the assumptions and its adequacy condition is added to the proof obligations. The validity of this method of composing subcircuits is guaranteed by the fact that parallel composition and hiding are both monotonic operators, so replacement of a subcircuit specification by its actual transistors can only improve the entire product.

The overall effect of this design methodology is that the design emerges as a byproduct of the proof, and it is not possible that it contains an error. In principle, each line of the proof can be checked by computer. The research reported in this paper therefore is a contribution to the modern engineering philosophy "design right first time". However, no claim is made that it will be useful in hardware circuit design.

*Acknowledgements*: For inspiration, encouragement, and helpful comments to Jonathan Bowen, Geoff Brown, Mani Chandy, Paul Gardiner, Mike Gordon, Mohamed Gouda, Jifeng He, Roy Jenevein, Geraint Jones, Chris

Lengauer, Quentin Miller, Jay Misra, Ian Page, Jeff Sanders, Juzer Shaik-hali, David Shepherd, André Stern, David Wheeler. The research was supported in 1986/87 by the Admiral B.R. Inman Centennial Chair of Computing Theory at the University of Texas at Austin.

## REFERENCES

[1] E. W. Dijkstra. Guarded commands, non-determinacy, and the formal derivation of programs. *Comm. ACM*, 18(8):453–457, August 1975.

[2] C. A. R. Hoare and M. J. C. Gordon. Partial correctness of C-mos switching circuits: an exercise in applied logic. In *Proceedings of the third annual symposium on logic in computer science, Edinburgh*, pages 28–36, July 1988.

C. A. R. Hoare,
Oxford University Computing Laboratory,
Programming Research Group,
8–11, Keble Road,
Oxford   OX1  3QD,
England.

# 23

# On Mathematical Induction and the Invariance Theorem

## Rob Hoogerwoord

## Introduction

Roughly speaking, two kinds of mathematical theorem exist. Theorems of the first kind serve to record the results of mathematical labour. Such theorems may represent deep insights and their proofs may be difficult. They are the theorems theories are made of. Theorems of the second kind are used as building blocks in proofs of other theorems or in derivations of programs. They need not be deep nor need their proofs be difficult. What counts is whether they embody a meaningful separation of concerns: in order to be useful they must contribute to the disentanglement of the mathematical reasoning in which they are used.

In this paper we present a theorem of the second kind, a generalisation of the principle of Mathematical Induction. It is not deep and it is probably not new either. The idea behind it is used implicity in many designs of proofs and programs. We believe that this theorem indeed embodies a meaningful separation of concerns and that its explicit formulation contributes to a better disentanglement of the designs in which it is used. To provide some support for this opinion we show an application of the theorem. In addition, this paper is an exercise in proof construction.

## Mathematical induction

$V$ and $C$ are sets. Dummies $u$ and $v$ range over $V$, whereas $x$ and $y$ range over $C$. Predicates on $V$ are denoted by $P$, and $Q$ and $R$ denote predicates on $C$. Furthermore, $<$ is a binary relation on $C$.

**Theorem**     $(0) \land (1) \Rightarrow (2)$, with:

(0)      $t : V \to C$

(1)      $(\mathbf{A}\, R :: (\mathbf{A}\, x :: R{\cdot}x) \;\Leftarrow\; (\mathbf{A}\, x :: R{\cdot}x \;\Leftarrow\; (\mathbf{A}\, y : y < x : R{\cdot}y)))$

$$(2) \qquad (\mathbf{A}\, P :: (\mathbf{A}\, u :: P{\cdot}u) \;\Leftarrow\; (\mathbf{A}\, u :: P{\cdot}u \Leftarrow (\mathbf{A}\, v : t{\cdot}v < t{\cdot}u : P{\cdot}v)))$$
□

Formula (1) expresses that (the universal truth of) predicates on $C$ may be proved by mathematical induction; this is a property of $C$ together with $<$. In most applications $<$ is (the non-reflexive part of) a partial order; partially ordered sets $(C,<)$ satisfying (1) are also called *well-founded* sets. The theorem states that, for well-founded sets $C$, predicates on $V$ may be proved by *mathematical induction on (the values of)* $t$, so to speak, for any function $t$ of type $V \to C$.

**Proof of theorem**    Assuming $(0) \wedge (1)$, we prove, for predicate $P$ (on $V$), the term of (2) by transforming it into an instance of (1). For this purpose, we need a predicate $R$ (on $C$) coupled to $P$ in such a way that this transformation is possible; postponing the choice of $R$, we derive:

$$(\mathbf{A}\, u :: P{\cdot}u)$$

$=$ {lemma about $P$ and $R$ (see below), with $Q{\cdot}x \leftarrow true$}

$$(\mathbf{A}\, x :: R{\cdot}x)$$

$\Leftarrow$ {(1)}

$$(\mathbf{A}\, x :: R{\cdot}x \;\Leftarrow\; (\mathbf{A}\, y : y < x : R{\cdot}y))$$

$=$ {the same lemma, with $Q{\cdot}x \leftarrow (\mathbf{A}\, y : y < x : R{\cdot}y)$}

$$(\mathbf{A}\, u :: P{\cdot}u \;\Leftarrow\; (\mathbf{A}\, y : y < t{\cdot}u : R{\cdot}y))$$

$=$ {trading (preparing for application of the lemma to $R{\cdot}y$)}

$$(\mathbf{A}\, u :: P{\cdot}u \;\Leftarrow\; (\mathbf{A}\, y :: R{\cdot}y \Leftarrow y < t{\cdot}u))$$

$=$ {again the lemma, with $Q{\cdot}y \leftarrow y < t{\cdot}u$
and dummy renaming $u \leftarrow v$}

$$(\mathbf{A}\, u :: P{\cdot}u \;\Leftarrow\; (\mathbf{A}\, v :: P{\cdot}v \Leftarrow t{\cdot}v < t{\cdot}u))$$

$=$ {trading}

$$(\mathbf{A}\, u :: P{\cdot}u \;\Leftarrow\; (\mathbf{A}\, v : t{\cdot}v < t{\cdot}u : P{\cdot}v))$$

This concludes the proof of (2). The lemma is a generalisation of the first step of this derivation. The lemma represents the coupling of $P$ and $R$ as we need it above. By proving the lemma we construct a suitable $R$.

**Lemma**    For all predicates $Q$ (on $C$):

$$(\mathbf{A}\, x :: R{\cdot}x \Leftarrow Q{\cdot}x) \;\equiv\; (\mathbf{A}\, u :: P{\cdot}u \Leftarrow Q{\cdot}(t{\cdot}u))$$

**Proof**    The lemma must hold for all predicates $Q$. For the special case that $Q$ is the point-predicate $(=y)$, we derive:

$$(\mathbf{A}\,x :: \; R\cdot x \; \Leftarrow \; x = y) \;\; \equiv \;\; (\mathbf{A}\,u :: \; P\cdot u \; \Leftarrow \; t\cdot u = y)$$

$=$     {trading}

$$(\mathbf{A}\,x : x = y : R\cdot x) \;\; \equiv \;\; (\mathbf{A}\,u : t\cdot u = y : P\cdot u)$$

$=$     {one-point rule}

$$R\cdot y \;\; \equiv \;\; (\mathbf{A}\,u : t\cdot u = y : P\cdot u)$$

Using this as definition of $R$ we now prove the lemma for arbitrary $Q$:

$$(\mathbf{A}\,x :: \; R\cdot x \; \Leftarrow \; Q\cdot x)$$

$=$     {definition of $R$}

$$(\mathbf{A}\,x :: \; (\mathbf{A}\,u : t\cdot u = x : P\cdot u) \; \Leftarrow \; Q\cdot x)$$

$=$     { $(\Leftarrow Q\cdot x)$ distributes over $\mathbf{A}$ }

$$(\mathbf{A}\,x :: \; (\mathbf{A}\,u : t\cdot u = x : \; P\cdot u \; \Leftarrow \; Q\cdot x))$$

$=$     {shuffling dummies}

$$(\mathbf{A}\,u :: \; (\mathbf{A}\,x : t\cdot u = x : \; P\cdot u \; \Leftarrow \; Q\cdot x))$$

$=$     {(0) : one-point rule}

$$(\mathbf{A}\,u :: \; P\cdot u \; \Leftarrow \; Q\cdot(t\cdot u))$$

□

□

The main calculation in the proof of the theorem consists of four steps (plus two trading steps); one step is a (necessary) appeal to (1), the other three steps are applications of the lemma, needed to replace $P$ by $R$ or vice versa. Because (2) contains three occurrences of $P$, three applications of the lemma are not surprising. The lemma itself captures what these three replacements have in common. It is the interface between the definition of $R$ and its use in the proof of the theorem. So, the lemma is a theorem of the second kind too: it is introduced for the modularisation of the proof. Finally, we note that the theorem is independent of the properties of $<$ .

## The invariance theorem

In her Ph.D. thesis [1], A.J.M. van Gasteren presents a formal derivation of a proof of (an abstract version of) the invariance theorem. After a minor simplification, the theorem is, in the nomenclature of [1]:

**Theorem**    For

$P, Q$     : predicates on a set $V$,

$t$        : a function of type $V \to C$, where $(C, <)$ is partially ordered,

$f$        : a predicate transformer (for predicates on $V$),

we have that $[P \Rightarrow Q]$ follows from the conjunction of

(0)      $(C, <)$ is well-founded

(2)      $(\mathbf{A}\, x :: [P \wedge t = x \;\Rightarrow\; f \cdot (P \wedge t < x)])$

(3)      $[f \cdot Q \Rightarrow Q]$

(4)      $f$ is monotonic, i.e. for all predicates $X, Y$ on $V$ :

         $[X \Rightarrow Y] \;\Rightarrow\; [f \cdot X \Rightarrow f \cdot Y]$

$\square$

In this theorem square brackets denote universal quantification over $V$. In (2) and in what follows dummies $u$ and $v$ range over $V$, and $x$ ranges over $C$.

The presence of function $t$ and premiss (0) are indications that we could try to prove this theorem by mathematical induction on $t$. This even seems to be the only way to exploit (0). Before doing so, however, we simplify premiss (2) —the most complicated one— :

$$(\mathbf{A}\, x :: [P \wedge t = x \;\Rightarrow\; f \cdot (P \wedge t < x)])$$

$=$      {definition of $[\ldots]$}

$$(\mathbf{A}\, x :: (\mathbf{A}\, u :: P \cdot u \wedge t \cdot u = x \;\Rightarrow\; f \cdot (P \wedge t < x) \cdot u))$$

$=$      {shuffling dummies}

$$(\mathbf{A}\, u :: (\mathbf{A}\, x :: P \cdot u \wedge t \cdot u = x \;\Rightarrow\; f \cdot (P \wedge t < x) \cdot u))$$

$=$      {trading}

$$(\mathbf{A}\, u :: (\mathbf{A}\, x : t \cdot u = x : P \cdot u \;\Rightarrow\; f \cdot (P \wedge t < x) \cdot u))$$

$=$      {one-point rule}

$$(\mathbf{A}\, u :: P \cdot u \Rightarrow f \cdot (P \wedge t < t \cdot u) \cdot u)$$

$=$      {introduction of predicate $R_u$, see below}

$$(\mathbf{A}\, u :: P \cdot u \Rightarrow f \cdot R_u \cdot u)$$

The formula thus obtained is simpler than (2): it contains quantifications over $V$ only, whereas (2) contains quantifications over *different* ranges ($C$ and $V$). Instead of (2), we therefore use (2a) and (2b) with:

(2a)      $(\mathbf{A}\, u :: P \cdot u \Rightarrow f \cdot R_u \cdot u)$

(2b)      $(\mathbf{A}\, v :: R_u \cdot v \;\equiv\; P \cdot v \wedge t \cdot v < t \cdot u)$

**Aside on notation**

The definition of $R_u$ contains global variable $u$. As an aide-mémoire, we have used subscription to indicate this: on the one hand we do not want to leave the dependence on $u$ implicit, on the other hand $u$ occurs as a constant in the following calculations. Omission of the subscript is not without danger: it might seduce us to rewrite (2a) to $[P \Rightarrow f \cdot R]$, which is incorrect. If so desired, name $R_u$ can be avoided by means of $\lambda$-notation: $R_u = (\lambda v :: P \cdot v \wedge t \cdot v < t \cdot u)$.

To some extent, the notation used in formula (2) is misleading: the occurrence of $t = x$ in the antecedent of the implication could inspire us to eliminate $x$ by replacing —equals for equals— its occurrence in the consequent by $t$, which is certainly wrong. This can be discovered by looking at the types of the variables occurring in the formula: $t$ has type $V \to C$ whereas $x$ has type $C$. Apparently, $t = x$ does not mean "$t$ equals $x$" but it denotes the predicate $(\lambda u :: t \cdot u = x)$. Similarly, $\wedge$ does not denote the boolean operator but the predicate connective $\wedge$ defined by $(\mathbf{A}\, u :: (P \wedge Q) \cdot u \equiv P \cdot u \wedge Q \cdot u)$. Overloading $\wedge$ with the meaning of $\wedge$ is harmless, but overloading $=$ is not: then, what does, for functions $f$ and $g$ of the same type, $f = g$ mean? By assigning to $=$ a meaning that differs from equality we deny ourselves the possibility to use Leibniz's rule of substitution of equals for equals; according to [1, page 155] "such substitution is the simplest type of manipulation one can imagine". (In view of this, we might consider to extend the use of $\equiv$ and define $f \equiv g$ by $(\mathbf{A}\, x :: (f \equiv g) \cdot x \equiv (f \cdot x = g \cdot x))$, for all functions $f$ and $g$ of the same type, predicates or not; then, we have $(f = g) \equiv [f \equiv g]$.)

Formula (2) can be rewritten in two ways: by use of an explicit dummy for the quantification implied by $[\ldots]$, as we did above, or by use of dummy-free notation designed for the purpose; for example:
$$(\mathbf{A}\, x :: [P \wedge (=x) \circ t \Rightarrow f \cdot (P \wedge (<x) \circ t)])$$

□

**Proof of theorem**  Having decided to use mathematical induction, we derive:

$$[P \Rightarrow Q]$$
= \qquad {definition of $[\ldots]$}
$$(\mathbf{A}\, u :: P \cdot u \Rightarrow Q \cdot u)$$
⇐ \qquad {mathematical induction on $t$ (using (0))}
$$(\mathbf{A}\, u :: (P \cdot u \Rightarrow Q \cdot u) \Leftarrow (\mathbf{A}\, v : t \cdot v < t \cdot u : P \cdot v \Rightarrow Q \cdot v))$$

We prove this as follows:

$$(\mathbf{A}\,v : t{\cdot}v < t{\cdot}u : P{\cdot}v \Rightarrow Q{\cdot}v)$$

$$= \quad \{\text{trading (preparing for (2b))}\}$$

$$(\mathbf{A}\,v :: P{\cdot}v \wedge t{\cdot}v < t{\cdot}u \Rightarrow Q{\cdot}v)$$

$$= \quad \{(2b) \text{ (definition of } R_u)\}$$

$$(\mathbf{A}\,v :: R_u{\cdot}v \Rightarrow Q{\cdot}v)$$

$$\Rightarrow \quad \{(4) \text{ (to introduce } f\text{'s)}\}$$

$$(\mathbf{A}\,v :: f{\cdot}R_u{\cdot}v \Rightarrow f{\cdot}Q{\cdot}v)$$

$$\Rightarrow \quad \{\text{instantiation (to eliminate the quantification)}\}$$

$$f{\cdot}R_u{\cdot}u \Rightarrow f{\cdot}Q{\cdot}u$$

$$\Rightarrow \quad \{(2a), (3) \text{ (to get rid of the } f\text{'s)}\}$$

$$P{\cdot}u \Rightarrow Q{\cdot}u$$

□

The above proof is shorter and simpler than A.J.M. van Gasteren's proof. It may very well be that formula (2) is the culprit: it is the only formula in the theorem in which (elements of) both $V$ and $C$ occur. By rewriting it into (2a) $\wedge$ (2b) we have uncoupled $V$ and $C$ : now the whole proof can be carried out in terms of $V$. The principle of generalised mathematical induction takes care of the coupling, via $t$, of $V$ and $C$. Thus, it contributes to a better modularisation of the proof.

## REFERENCES

[1] A. J. M. van Gasteren. *On the Shape of Mathematical Arguments.* Ph.D. thesis, Eindhoven University of Technology, 1988.

Rob Hoogerwoord,
Department of Mathematics and Computing Science,
Eindhoven University of Technology,
P.O. Box 513,
5600 MB  Eindhoven,
The Netherlands.

# 24

# Formalizing Some Classic Synchronization Primitives

## J. J. Horning

## Introduction

*Semaphores*, introduced by Dijkstra in 1968, and *condition variables*, introduced by Hoare in 1974, are still useful in structuring concurrent systems. It is important that programmers using them understand their precise properties. Concurrent programming is difficult enough without uncertainty about the details of the synchronization primitives. This note documents the version provided by the Threads interface of the Modula-2+ programming system [7].

The Threads package supplies an interface for creating and controlling a virtually unlimited number of threads ("lightweight processes"), which may or may not share memory. Its simple and familiar synchronization facilities are based on three data types: *Mutex*, *Semaphore*, and *Condition*, and enable threads to cooperate in the use of shared resources. It also provides a facility enabling threads to "alert" other threads, which I will not discuss here. For details, see [1].

SRC has two implementations of the Threads package. One runs within any single process on a normal Unix system and is implemented using a co-routine mechanism for blocking one thread and resuming another. The other implementation runs on a symmetric multiprocessor and uses multiple processors to provide true concurrency. Programmers need not be concerned about which processors a thread executes on, and the scheduler is free to move them from processor to processor. The way it assigns threads to processors can affect performance but has no effect on the semantics of the synchronization primitives.

The specifications that follow are abstracted from the actual specifications of the threads synchronization primitives. They are intended to give complete and precise descriptions of the properties that programmers can rely on when using these facilities — provided they are not using alerts. These specifications should answer any questions about whether and how these primitives differ from those with which you are familiar. They represent one of our first attempts to use a Larch interface language [3] to specify concurrent behavior.

# Informal descriptions of the synchronization primitives

This is how Dijkstra described P and V in his paper on the "THE" operating system:

> A process, "$Q$" say, that performs the operation "P(sem)" decreases the value of the semaphore called "sem" by 1. If the resulting value of the semaphore concerned is nonnegative, process $Q$ can continue with the execution of its next statement; if, however, the resulting value is negative, process $Q$ is stopped and booked on a waiting list associated with the semaphore concerned. Until further notice (i.e., a V-operation on this very same semaphore), dynamic progress of process $Q$ is not logically permissible and no processor will be allocated to it . . . .
>
> A process, "$R$" say, that performs the operation "V(sem)" increases the value of the semaphore called "sem" by 1. If the resulting value of the semaphore concerned is positive, the V-operation in question has no further effect; if however, the resulting value of the semaphore concerned is nonpositive, one of the processes booked on its waiting list is removed from this waiting list, i.e., its dynamic progress is again logically permissible and in due time a processor will be allocated to it . . . .
>
> During system conception it transpired that we used the semaphores in two completely different ways. The difference is so marked that, looking back, one wonders whether it was really fair to present the two ways as uses of the very same primitives. On the one hand, we have the semaphores used for mutual exclusion, on the other hand, the private semaphores. [2]

The Threads package provides binary semaphores with their traditional P and V operations, for synchronization with interrupt routines in low-level system code. However, most programmers are discouraged from using semaphores directly, since the disciplined use of mutexes and condition variables provides more useful structure.

Mutexes are the basic objects enabling threads to cooperate on access to shared resources. A mutex $m$ is used to ensure that a *critical section*, a set of related actions on a group of resources, can be made *atomic* relative to any other thread's actions on these resources, by bracketing it with the procedure calls Acquire($m$) and Release($m$). The LOCK statement of Modula-2+ makes it easy to ensure that textual bracketing is reflected by temporal bracketing — in particular, that Release($m$) is called regardless of how control leaves the critical section.

This is how Hoare described condition variables in his paper on monitors:

> Any dynamic resource allocator will sometimes need to delay a program wishing to acquire a resource which is not currently available, and to resume that program after some other program has released the resource required. We therefore need: a "wait" operation, issued from inside a procedure of the monitor, which causes the calling program to be delayed; and a "signal" operation, also issued from inside a procedure of the same monitor, which causes exactly one of the waiting programs to be resumed immediately. If there are no waiting programs, the signal has no effect. In order to enable other programs to release resources during a wait, a wait operation must relinquish the exclusion which would otherwise prevent entry to the releasing procedure....
>
> In many cases, there may be more than one reason for waiting, and these need to be distinguished by both the waiting and the signalling operation. We therefore introduce a new type of "variable" known as a "condition"; and the writer of a monitor should declare a variable of type condition for each reason why a program might have to wait .... Note that a condition "variable" is neither true nor false; indeed it does not have any stored value accessible to the program. In practice, a condition variable will be represented by an (initially empty) queue of processes which are currently waiting on the condition. [4]

A Modula-2+ condition variable $c$ should be associated with a predicate $Q$ based on some shared variables $v$ protected by a mutex $m$. A thread acquires $m$ and evaluates $Q$ to see whether it can proceed; if not, it suspends its execution by calling Wait($m$, $c$). This atomically releases $m$ and suspends execution of the thread. A thread that changes $v$ so that $Q$ might be satisfied should call Signal($c$) or Broadcast($c$) to notify blocked threads to resume execution. When a thread returns from Wait it should re-evaluate $Q$ to determine whether to proceed or to call Wait again.

There are several subtleties in the semantics of these synchronization procedures that are difficult to express adequately in an informal description. Some of these are mentioned by Hoare [4] and others are discussed by Birrell, *et al.* [1].

# The Larch specification approach

The specifications are written in the Larch/Modula-2+ interface language. The logical basis for its treatment of concurrency is very similar to one developed by Lamport [5,6]. Any behavior of a concurrent system is viewed as the execution of a sequence of *atomic actions*, each of which appears indivisible, both to the thread invoking it and to all other threads. Each concurrent execution of a group of atomic actions has the same observable effects as some sequential execution of the same actions. This *serializability* makes it possible to ignore concurrency in reasoning about the effects of any atomic action.

Larch specifications of concurrent programs are similar to those for sequential programs. A procedure specification describes its observable effects without saying how these effects are achieved. In a sequential program a procedure is specified by a predicate relating the state when it is called and the state when it returns. Similarly, in a concurrent program an atomic action is specified by a predicate relating the states that immediately precede and follow the action. The specification of an atomic action does not specify how the appearance of atomicity is to be achieved, only that it must be; atomic actions may proceed concurrently as long as this concurrency isn't observable.

An *atomic procedure* executes just one atomic action per call and is specified like a sequential procedure, plus an additional pre-condition restricting when it can execute the atomic action. A *non-atomic procedure* has observable effects that may span more than two states, with actions of other threads interleaved. For example, the specification of `Wait` requires that each call of the procedure be equivalent to executing the atomic action `Enqueue` and later the atomic action `Resume`.

A Larch/Modula-2+ specification of a sequential procedure has three clauses:

- The `REQUIRES` clause states a precondition that the implementation can rely on; it is the responsibility of the caller to ensure that the condition holds when the procedure is called. The specification does not constrain the implementation to any particular behavior if the precondition is not satisfied. An omitted `REQUIRES` clause is equivalent to `REQUIRES TRUE`.
- The `MODIFIES AT MOST` clause identifies the variables that the procedure is allowed to change.
- The `ENSURES` clause states a postcondition that the procedure must establish if its precondition was initially true.

Larch/Modula-2+ has the following extensions to deal with concurrency:

- **ATOMIC** preceding **PROCEDURE** or **ACTION** indicates that any execution of the procedure or action must be atomic relative to the other actions of the interface.

- A **WHEN** clause states a condition that must be satisfied for the atomic action to take place. This may impose a delay until actions of other threads make the predicate true. An omitted **WHEN** clause is equivalent to **WHEN TRUE**.

- A **COMPOSITION OF** clause indicates that any execution of the procedure must be equivalent to execution of the named actions in the given order, possibly interleaved with actions of other threads.

- An **ATOMIC ACTION** clause specifies a named action in much the same way as an **ATOMIC PROCEDURE** specification does. It is within the scope of the procedure header and can refer to its formal parameters.

- The keyword **SELF** stands for the identity of the thread executing the action.

An unsubscripted program variable in a predicate stands for its value in the pre-state. A program variable subscripted by *post* stands for its value in the post-state.

# Formal specifications of the synchronization primitives

The formal specifications are intended to be definitive; the informal descriptions of Threads primitives are not necessary (and should not be trusted) to determine their precise semantics. However, the formal specifications were written for use in conjunction with informal material that provides intuition and guidance on how to use them effectively.

> TYPE Mutex = Thread INITIALLY NIL
>
> ATOMIC PROCEDURE Acquire(VAR $m$: Mutex)
>   MODIFIES AT MOST $[\, m \,]$
>   WHEN $m =$ NIL ENSURES $m_{post} =$ SELF
>
> ATOMIC PROCEDURE Release(VAR $m$: Mutex)
>   REQUIRES $m =$ SELF
>   MODIFIES AT MOST $[\, m \,]$
>   ENSURES $m_{post} =$ NIL
>
> TYPE Semaphore = (available, unavailable) INITIALLY available
>
> ATOMIC PROCEDURE P(VAR $s$: Semaphore)
>   MODIFIES AT MOST $[\, s \,]$
>   WHEN $s =$ available ENSURES $s_{post} =$ unavailable

```
ATOMIC PROCEDURE V(VAR s: Semaphore)
    MODIFIES AT MOST [ s ]
    ENSURES s_post = available
```

TYPE Condition = SET OF Thread INITIALLY {}

```
PROCEDURE Wait(VAR m: Mutex; VAR c: Condition)
    = COMPOSITION OF Enqueue; Resume END
    REQUIRES m = SELF
    MODIFIES AT MOST [ m, c ]
    ATOMIC ACTION Enqueue
        ENSURES (m_post = NIL) & (c_post = (c ∪ {SELF}))
    ATOMIC ACTION Resume
        WHEN (m = NIL) & (SELF ∉ c)
        ENSURES (m_post = SELF) & (c_post = c)
```

```
ATOMIC PROCEDURE Signal(VAR c: Condition)
    MODIFIES AT MOST [ c ]
    ENSURES (c_post = {}) | (c_post ⊂ c)
```

```
ATOMIC PROCEDURE Broadcast(VAR c: Condition)
    MODIFIES AT MOST [ c ]
    ENSURES c_post = {}
```

# Discussion

The specifications above appear almost trivial. Doubtless one of the reasons for the continued popularity of these synchronization primitives is that they *are* simple. The most challenging part of writing the formal specifications was choosing abstractions for the three data types that would make the procedure specifications simple (e.g., taking as the "value" of a mutex the identity of the thread holding it). I encourage you to choose your own abstractions and your own favorite specification method and compare the results. You may find the exercise as instructive as we did.

It should be clear from the specifications that critical sections temporally bracketed by Acquire(m) and Release(m) are mutually exclusive; once Acquire has set m, only the acquiring thread can change m (using Release or Wait). If Release(m) is executed when there are several threads waiting to perform Acquire(m), the WHEN clause of each of them will be satisfied. Only one thread will hold m next, because —by atomicity of Acquire— it must appear that one of the Acquires is executed first; its ENSURES clause falsifies the WHEN clauses of all the others. The specification does not say which of the blocked threads will be unblocked first, nor when this will happen.

Although mutexes and semaphores happen to have identical implementations (P is the same as `Acquire` and V is the same as `Release`), the interface provides distinct types with different specifications. `Mutexes` have holders and semaphores don't; `Release` has a `REQUIRES` clause and V doesn't. The choice to have two types for the two different ways of using the underlying mechanism was made by the designers, not the specifiers. Client programs that rely only on the specified properties of these types would continue to work even if their implementations were different.

Any implementation that satisfies `Broadcast`'s specification also satisfies `Signal`'s. The multiprocessor implementation of `Signal` usually unblocks just one waiting thread, but may unblock more when certain race conditions occur. The designers consciously chose not to strengthen `Signal`'s postcondition, in order to allow a more efficient implementation. This is one of many non-trivial (i.e., debatable) design decisions in the interface. Because the design and implementation were completed before the specifications were started, we can at least be certain that the design was not warped by considerations of what would be easy to specify.

*Acknowledgments*:    A prose description of the Threads synchronization primitives was written when the interface was first designed [7]. While it gave an indication of how the primitives were intended to be used, it left too many questions about the details of the interface unanswered. To provide more precise information for programmers, Andrew Birrell wrote operational specifications. They were both precise and (for the most part) accurate. The main problems were that they were too subtle and that important information was rather widely distributed. Andrew challenged John Guttag and me to produce a clearer specification using Larch. Leslie Lamport and Jeannette Wing helped us to understand the issues involved and to develop the specifications. Roy Levin provided an implementation perspective.

These specifications were included in a paper presented at the ACM Symposium on Operating System Principles [1].

# REFERENCES

[1] A. D. Birrell, J. V. Guttag, J. J. Horning, and R. Levin. Synchronization primitives for a multiprocessor: a formal specification. *Operating Systems Review*, 21(5):94–102, Nov. 1987. Proceedings of the Eleventh ACM Symposium on Operating Systems Principles.

[2] E. W. Dijkstra. The structure of the "THE"–multiprogramming system. *Comm. ACM*, 11(5):341–346, 1968.

[3] John V. Guttag, James J. Horning, and Jeannette M. Wing. The Larch family of specification languages. *IEEE Software*, 2(5):24–36, 1985.

[4] C. A. R. Hoare. Monitors: an operating system structuring concept. *Comm. ACM*, 17(10):549–557, 1974.

[5] Leslie Lamport. A simple approach to specifying concurrent systems. *Comm. ACM*, 32(1):32–45, 1989.

[6] Leslie Lamport. Specifying concurrent program modules. *ACM TOPLAS*, 5(2):190–222, 1983.

[7] Paul Rovner. Extending Modula-2 to build large, integrated systems. *IEEE Software*, 3(6):46–57, 1986.

J. J. Horning,
Digital Equipment Corporation,
Systems Research Center,
130 Lytton Avenue,
Palo Alto, CA  94301–1044,
U.S.A.

# 25

# Consequences

## Cliff B. Jones

## Abstract

A proof is a chain of reasoning in which each step is mediated by a consequence relation. A variety of consequence notions exist. This paper explores the extent to which congruences between consequence notions can be used to yield congruent proofs in different theories.

## Introduction

Edsger Dijkstra has spent much effort in expounding ideas about the structure, presentation and beauty of proofs. In particular the "calculational" style suggested by Wim Feijen (cf. [2,3]) can be used to link steps in a proof with "equivales" ($\Leftrightarrow$) as a consequence notion where many logical texts use the deducibility ($\vdash$) concept. There is nothing mysterious about using different links in chains of deduction: mathematicians are happy to employ chains of $\leq, \sqsubseteq$ etc. as required.

Work at Manchester University on providing computer support to the (human) task of constructing proofs is reported in [5,6,8,1]. Not surprisingly, some of the issues that have arisen are orthogonal to those that Edsger Dijkstra might consider interesting. One area of our endeavours that should be of interest —no matter how proofs are constructed— is ensuring the widest applicability of theorems. The organisation of a body of mathematics into theories presents one possibility to widen applicability: relationships between theories can be exploited so that, for example, the associativity of set union and sequence concatenation can be covered by a single proof. (See [4] for example; see [9] for a description of the "theory morphisms" used in our system.)

This short paper discusses the extent to which a similarity between two consequence notions can be exploited to create congruent proofs. The slightly negative results are offered to Edsger Dijkstra in the hope that resolving (or circumventing) the problem might provide pleasure.

Cliff B. Jones

# Natural deduction proofs

One part of the fact that "or distributes over and"[1] can be stated as:

$$E_1 \vee E_2 \wedge E_3 \;\vdash\; (E_1 \vee E_2) \wedge (E_1 \vee E_3)$$

A natural deduction proof (see [10]) of this is given in Figure 1; the inference rules used are listed in the left column of Figure 2. The detail of the chosen proof style is not the central issue; the presentation happens to follow [7]. In that textbook, the proof that set union distributes over intersection is proved by induction over the generators for finite sets. Although of pedagogic value, the symmetry between the pairs of operators ($\vee, \cup$; $\wedge, \cap$; and $\vdash, \subseteq$) is totally missed.[2] In this case, at least, the missing link can be provided —as is shown below— but in general, the symmetry cannot be fully utilized.

| | from | $E_1 \vee E_2 \wedge E_3$ | |
|---|---|---|---|
| 1 | | from $E_1$ | |
| 1.1 | | $E_1 \vee E_2$ | $\vee\text{-}I(h1)$ |
| 1.2 | | $E_1 \vee E_3$ | $\vee\text{-}I(h1)$ |
| | | infer $(E_1 \vee E_2) \wedge (E_1 \vee E_3)$ | $\wedge\text{-}I(1.1, 1.2)$ |
| 2 | | from $E_2 \wedge E_3$ | |
| 2.1 | | $E_2$ | $\wedge\text{-}E(h2)$ |
| 2.2 | | $E_3$ | $\wedge\text{-}E(h2)$ |
| 2.3 | | $E_1 \vee E_2$ | $\vee\text{-}I(2.1)$ |
| 2.4 | | $E_1 \vee E_3$ | $\vee\text{-}I(2.2)$ |
| | | infer $(E_1 \vee E_2) \wedge (E_1 \vee E_3)$ | $\wedge\text{-}I(2.3, 2.4)$ |
| | infer | $(E_1 \vee E_2) \wedge (E_1 \vee E_3)$ | $\vee\text{-}E(h, 1, 2)$ |

FIGURE 1. Natural deduction proof

The first step towards a proof structure that is similar for both theorems is to convert Figure 1 into a full sequent form; this is done in Figure 3, where the numbering of the steps has been chosen to clarify the link to Figure 1. If symmetry is to be investigated, it is necessary to be meticulous about the use of inference rules, and those given in Figure 2 are actually not general enough for the steps of the proof in Figure 3. For example, the rule that justifies the introduction of a disjunction in line 2.3 should be:

---

[1]It is assumed that $\wedge$ binds more strongly than $\vee$.

[2]One way of linking $\vee, \cup$ and $\wedge, \cap$ is to use the logical result in a set proof by expanding out the set definitions by comprehension. This does not solve the problem here.

$$\boxed{\vee\text{-}I}\ \frac{E_i}{E_1 \vee \cdots \vee E_n}\ 1 \leq i \leq n \qquad \boxed{\cup\text{-}I}\ \frac{}{s_i \subseteq s_1 \cup \cdots \cup s_n}$$

$$\boxed{\wedge\text{-}E}\ \frac{E_1 \wedge \cdots \wedge E_n}{E_i}\ 1 \leq i \leq n \qquad \boxed{\cap\text{-}E}\ \frac{}{s_1 \cap \cdots \cap s_n \subseteq s_i}$$

$$\boxed{\wedge\text{-}I}\ \frac{E_1;\ \cdots;\ E_n}{E_1 \wedge \cdots \wedge E_n} \qquad \boxed{\cap\text{-}I}\ \frac{s \subseteq s_1;\ \cdots;\ s \subseteq s_n}{s \subseteq s_1 \cap \cdots \cap s_n}$$

$$\boxed{\vee\text{-}E}\ \frac{E_1 \vdash E;\ \cdots;\ E_n \vdash E}{E_1 \vee \cdots \vee E_n \vdash E} \qquad \boxed{\cup\text{-}E}\ \frac{s_1 \subseteq s;\ \cdots;\ s_n \subseteq s}{s_1 \cup \cdots \cup s_n \subseteq s}$$

FIGURE 2. Proof rules

| 1.1 | $E_1$ | $\vdash E_1 \vee E_2$ | $\vee\text{-}I$ |
|---|---|---|---|
| 1.2 | $E_1$ | $\vdash E_1 \vee E_3$ | $\vee\text{-}I$ |
| 1 | $E_1$ | $\vdash (E_1 \vee E_2) \wedge (E_1 \vee E_3)$ | $\wedge\text{-}I(1.1, 1.2)$ |
| 2.1 | $E_2 \wedge E_3$ | $\vdash E_2$ | $\wedge\text{-}E$ |
| 2.2 | $E_2 \wedge E_3$ | $\vdash E_3$ | $\wedge\text{-}E$ |
| 2.3 | $E_2 \wedge E_3$ | $\vdash E_1 \vee E_2$ | $\vee\text{-}I(2.1)$ |
| 2.4 | $E_2 \wedge E_3$ | $\vdash E_1 \vee E_3$ | $\vee\text{-}I(2.2)$ |
| 2 | $E_2 \wedge E_3$ | $\vdash (E_1 \vee E_2) \wedge (E_1 \vee E_3)$ | $\wedge\text{-}I(2.3, 2.4)$ |
| | $E_1 \vee E_2 \wedge E_3$ | $\vdash (E_1 \vee E_2) \wedge (E_1 \vee E_3)$ | $\vee\text{-}E(1, 2)$ |

FIGURE 3. Sequent proof

| 1.1 | $s_1$ | $\subseteq s_1 \cup s_2$ | $\cup\text{-}I$ |
|---|---|---|---|
| 1.2 | $s_1$ | $\subseteq s_1 \cup s_3$ | $\cup\text{-}I$ |
| 1 | $s_1$ | $\subseteq (s_1 \cup s_2) \cap (s_1 \cup s_3)$ | $\cap\text{-}I(1.1, 1.2)$ |
| 2.1 | $s_2 \cap s_3$ | $\subseteq s_2$ | $\cap\text{-}E$ |
| 2.2 | $s_2 \cap s_3$ | $\subseteq s_3$ | $\cap\text{-}E$ |
| 2.3 | $s_2 \cap s_3$ | $\subseteq s_1 \cup s_2$ | $\cup\text{-}I(2.1)$ |
| 2.4 | $s_2 \cap s_3$ | $\subseteq s_1 \cup s_3$ | $\cup\text{-}I(2.2)$ |
| 2 | $s_2 \cap s_3$ | $\subseteq (s_1 \cup s_2) \cap (s_1 \cup s_3)$ | $\cap\text{-}I(2.3, 2.4)$ |
| | $s_1 \cup s_2 \cap s_3$ | $\subseteq (s_1 \cup s_2) \cap (s_1 \cup s_3)$ | $\cup\text{-}E(1, 2)$ |

FIGURE 4. Set proof

$$\boxed{\vee\text{-}I}\frac{E \;\vdash\; E_i}{E \;\vdash\; E_1 \vee \cdots \vee E_n}\; 1 \leq i \leq n$$

If this (and corresponding changes to other rules) are made, the sequent form needs extra steps like $E_1 \vdash E_1$ before 1.1. One of the advantages of the style used in Figure 1 is that the simpler rules suffice.

## A corresponding proof about sets

A proof of

$$s_1 \cup s_2 \cap s_3 \;\subseteq\; (s_1 \cup s_2) \cap (s_1 \cup s_3)$$

is presented in Figure 4. The congruence between this and Figure 3 is very pleasing. It has, of course, been achieved by basing the proof on inference rules about the set operators that ape the lattice-theoretic properties of the logical operators. This relationship can be seen by comparing the two columns of Figure 2. As one would wish, there is in a real sense a single proof which can be presented with either of two sets of symbols.

The proof of

$$s_1 \cap s_2 \cup s_1 \cap s_3 \;\subseteq\; s_1 \cap (s_2 \cup s_3)$$

also mimics that of

$$E_1 \wedge E_2 \vee E_1 \wedge E_3 \;\vdash\; E_1 \wedge (E_2 \vee E_3)$$

## A problem with the congruence

Unfortunately, the process of finding analogous proofs fails on

$$s_1 \cap (s_2 \cup s_3) \;\subseteq\; s_1 \cap s_2 \cup s_1 \cap s_3$$

which is the set version of the other part of "and distributes over or" (see proof in Figure 5). The source of the difficulty can be seen in Figure 6. Here, the ability to write sequents with more than one logical expression on the left of the turnstile is used. (Once again, slight infelicities of the translation from Figure 5 have been tolerated to simplify the search for a set proof; these do not affect the main argument.) The link between pairing of hypotheses and conjunction is clear from the $\wedge$-$I$ rule. But in set notation there is no obvious equivalent. In order to mimic line 3.1 of Figure 6 it is necessary to observe that $s_2 \subseteq s_1 \cap s_2$ is true "in a context" where only $s_1$ is considered. Superficially, one might try to reduce the question to the problem of finding an analogous way of setting contexts. (For particular examples, it is also likely that the difficulty can be circumvented by presenting a different proof.) For our work, the interest is in what light can be shed —by both the congruence and its limits— on the nature of links

$$
\begin{array}{lll}
& \text{from} \quad E_1 \wedge (E_2 \vee E_3) & \\
1 & \quad E_1 & \wedge\text{-}E(h) \\
2 & \quad E_2 \vee E_3 & \wedge\text{-}E(h) \\
3 & \quad \text{from} \quad E_2 & \\
3.1 & \qquad E_1 \wedge E_2 & \wedge\text{-}I(1, h3) \\
& \quad \text{infer} \quad E_1 \wedge E_2 \vee E_1 \wedge E_3 & \vee\text{-}I(3.1) \\
4 & \quad \text{from} \quad E_3 & \\
4.1 & \qquad E_1 \wedge E_3 & \wedge\text{-}I(1, h4) \\
& \quad \text{infer} \quad E_1 \wedge E_2 \vee E_1 \wedge E_3 & \vee\text{-}I(4.1) \\
& \text{infer} \quad E_1 \wedge E_2 \vee E_1 \wedge E_3 & \vee\text{-}E(2, 3, 4)
\end{array}
$$

FIGURE 5. Another natural deduction proof

$$
\begin{array}{llll}
1 & E_1 \wedge (E_2 \vee E_3) & \vdash E_1 & \wedge\text{-}E \\
2 & E_1 \wedge (E_2 \vee E_3) & \vdash E_2 \vee E_3 & \wedge\text{-}E \\
3.1 & E_1, E_2 & \vdash E_1 \wedge E_2 & \wedge\text{-}I \\
3 & E_1, E_2 & \vdash E_1 \wedge E_2 \vee E_1 \wedge E_3 & \vee\text{-}I(3.1) \\
4.1 & E_1, E_3 & \vdash E_1 \wedge E_3 & \wedge\text{-}I \\
4 & E_1, E_3 & \vdash E_1 \wedge E_2 \vee E_1 \wedge E_3 & \vee\text{-}I(4.1) \\
5 & E_1, E_2 \vee E_3 & \vdash E_1 \wedge E_2 \vee E_1 \wedge E_3 & \vee\text{-}E(3, 4) \\
& E_1 \wedge (E_2 \vee E_3) & \vdash E_1 \wedge E_2 \vee E_1 \wedge E_3 & cut(1, 2, 5)
\end{array}
$$

FIGURE 6. Another sequent proof

between formulae. An extreme view has led us to contemplate storing (in our support system) massive numbers of these links. There are practical difficulties with the implementation of this idea. There are also aesthetic objections. Mathematics has not developed by recording all possible facts in a uniform notation. Structure has been found by observing that some properties are important in the sense that they both act as a basis for non-trivial results and admit specialisation to many areas that differ only in detail. This note suggests that further consideration of the consequence notion itself could be valuable.

*Acknowledgements*: This is a beautiful opportunity to express thanks to Edsger Dijkstra for the inspiration that he has provided to so many computing scientists. For stimulation in the work related to this paper Kevin Jones, Peter Lindsay, Richard Moore, Lockwood Morris, Michel Sintzoff and Alan Wills deserve thanks. Peter Lindsay and David Gries also kindly commented on drafts of this paper. My research is currently supported by grants from the SERC and the Wolfson foundation as well as a Senior Fellowship from SERC.

## REFERENCES

[1] J. C. Bicarregui and B. Ritchie. Providing support for the formal development of software. In *Proceedings of the 1st International Conference on System Development Environments and Factories*, 1989. Berlin.

[2] E. W. Dijkstra. *Our Proof Format*. 26 January 1987. EWD999.

[3] A. J. M. van Gasteren. *On the Shape of Mathematical Arguments*. Ph.D. thesis, Eindhoven University of Technology, 1988.

[4] J. V. Guttag, J. J. Horning, and J. M. Wing. *Larch in Five Easy Pieces*. Technical Report 5, DEC, SRC, 1985.

[5] C. B. Jones and P. A. Lindsay. A support system for formal reasoning: requirements and status. In R. Bloomfield, L. Marshall, and R. Jones, editors, *VDM'88: VDM—The Way Ahead*, pages 139–152, Springer-Verlag, 1988. Lecture Notes in Computer Science, Vol. 328.

[6] C. B. Jones and R. Moore. Muffin: a user interface design experiment for a theorem proving assistant. In R. Bloomfield, L. Marshall, and R. Jones, editors, *VDM'88: VDM—The Way Ahead*, pages 337–375, Springer-Verlag, 1988. Lecture Notes in Computer Science, Vol. 328.

[7] Cliff B. Jones. *Systematic Software Development using VDM*. Prentice Hall International, second edition, 1990.

[8] P. A. Lindsay. Formal reasoning in an IPSE. In K. H. Bennet, editor, *Software Engineering Environments: Research and Practice*, pages 235–253, Ellis Harwood Ltd, 1989.

[9] P. A. Lindsay. A formal system with inclusion polymorphism. IPSE Document 060/pal014/2.3, December 1987. Manchester University.

[10] D. Prawitz. *Natural Deduction*. Almquist and Wiksell, 1965.

Cliff B. Jones,
Department of Computer Science,
The University,
Manchester   M13 9PL,
England.

# 26

# Shortest and Longest Segments

## Anne Kaldewaij

## 1 Introduction

In this paper we present program schemes for so-called segment problems. Segment problems were originally invented at the Eindhoven University to serve as exercises and exams in programming courses (cf.[1, Part 1]). Nowadays, they are more widely used as test cases for programming methodologies, for instance in functional programming. There are two types of segment problems: shortest segment problems and longest segment problems. In our experience, people find the shortest segment problems the more difficult ones. We show that both types can be solved in the same way.

A segment is a consecutive subset of the set of integers. The segment consisting of all $i$ for which $p \leq i < q$ is denoted by $[p..q)$. We will only consider segments $[p..q)$ for which $p \leq q$. Segment $[p..q)$ has length $q-p$. Longest segment problems are of the form

$$\begin{aligned}
&\lVert\; N : \text{int}\, \{N \geq 0\}; \\
&\quad \lVert\; r : \text{int}; \\
&\qquad maxseg \\
&\qquad \{r = (\, \mathbf{max}\, p, q : 0 \leq p \leq q \leq N \,\wedge\, \mathcal{A}.p.q : q-p)\,\} \\
&\quad \rVert \\
&\rVert,
\end{aligned}$$

where $\mathcal{A}$ is a predicate, often related to some array $X[0..N)$ of integers. Typical examples of such predicates are

$X[p..q)$ is constant:
$$\mathcal{A}.p.q \;\equiv\; (\, \mathbf{A}\, i, j : p \leq i < q \,\wedge\, p \leq j < q : X.i = X.j)$$

$X[p..q)$ is ascending:
$$\mathcal{A}.p.q \;\equiv\; (\, \mathbf{A}\, i, j : p \leq i \leq j < q : X.i \leq X.j)$$

$X[p..q)$ contains at most 60 zeroes:
$$\mathcal{A}.p.q \;\equiv\; (\, \mathbf{N}\, i : p \leq i < q : X.i = 0) \leq 60$$

227    Anne Kaldewaij

For these examples, we have $(0 \leq p \leq q \leq N)$:

| | | |
|---|---|---|
| (0) | $\mathcal{A}.p.p$ | the empty segment is an $\mathcal{A}$-segment |
| (1) | $\mathcal{A}.p.q \Rightarrow (\mathbf{A}\,s : p \leq s \leq q : \mathcal{A}.p.s)$ | $\mathcal{A}$ is prefix-closed |
| (2) | $\mathcal{A}.p.q \Rightarrow (\mathbf{A}\,s : p \leq s \leq q : \mathcal{A}.s.q)$ | $\mathcal{A}$ is postfix-closed |

Shortest segment problems are of the form

$$\begin{array}{l} [\![\ N : \text{int}\,\{N \geq 0\}; \\ \quad [\![\ r : \text{int}; \\ \qquad minseg \\ \qquad \{\,r = (\mathbf{min}\,p,q : 0 \leq p \leq q \leq N \wedge \mathcal{A}.p.q : q{-}p)\,\} \\ \quad ]\!] \\ ]\!]. \end{array}$$

Typical predicates are

Values 0, 1, and 2 occur in $X[p..q]$:
$$\mathcal{A}.p.q \equiv (\mathbf{E}\,i,j,k : p \leq i,j,k < q : X.i = 0 \wedge X.j = 1 \wedge X.k = 2)$$

$X[p..q]$ contains at least 60 zeroes:
$$\mathcal{A}.p.q \equiv (\mathbf{N}\,i : p \leq i < q : X.i = 0) \geq 60$$

For these examples, we have $(0 \leq p \leq q \leq N)$:

| | | |
|---|---|---|
| (0') | $\neg\mathcal{A}.p.p$ | the empty segment is an $\neg\mathcal{A}$-segment |
| (1') | $\neg\mathcal{A}.p.q \Rightarrow (\mathbf{A}\,s : p \leq s \leq q : \neg\mathcal{A}.p.s)$ | $\neg\mathcal{A}$ is prefix-closed |
| (2') | $\neg\mathcal{A}.p.q \Rightarrow (\mathbf{A}\,s : p \leq s \leq q : \neg\mathcal{A}.s.q)$ | $\neg\mathcal{A}$ is postfix-closed |

Notice that

$$\mathcal{A} \text{ satisfies (0), (1), and (2)} \quad \equiv \quad \neg\mathcal{A} \text{ satisfies (0'), (1'), and (2')}$$

i.e. for each exercise of one category one has an exercise of the other category for free. Another remark is: when we have a solution to *maxseg* for predicates that satisfy (0) and (1), then we have, by applying this solution to the reverse of $X$, a solution for predicates that satisfy (0) and (2). A similar remark holds for *minseg*.

In Section 2 we derive program schemes for *maxseg* and *minseg* for the case that (0) and (1), respectively (0') and (2') are satisfied. These schemes are derived using a tail-invariant technique. In Section 3 we apply such a scheme to obtain an efficient algorithm for the computation of the length of a shortest segment $X[p..q]$ that contains the numbers 0 up to and not including 60, i.e.

$$\mathcal{A}.p.q \equiv (\mathbf{A}\,i : 0 \leq i < 60 : (\mathbf{E}\,j : p \leq j < q : X.j = i))$$

## 2 The program schemes

Let $N \geq 0$ and let for $0 \leq p \leq q \leq N$ predicate $\mathcal{A}$ satisfy

(0)    $\mathcal{A}.p.p$                    the empty segment is an $\mathcal{A}$-segment

(1)    $\mathcal{A}.p.q \Rightarrow (\mathbf{A}\, s : p \leq s \leq q : \mathcal{A}.p.s)$          $\mathcal{A}$ is prefix-closed

We derive an algorithm that establishes

R:    $r = (\mathbf{max}\, p, q : 0 \leq p \leq q \leq N \wedge \mathcal{A}.p.q : q-p)$

by applying a, so-called, tail-invariant technique for two-dimensional problems (the choice for this technique is inspired by the fact that $q-p$ is ascending in $q$ and descending in $p$). To that end we define tail $M.a.b$ for $0 \leq a \leq b \leq N$ by

$$M.a.b = (\mathbf{max}\, p, q : a \leq p \leq q \leq N \wedge b \leq q \leq N \wedge \mathcal{A}.p.q : q-p)$$

Then $R$ may be formulated as

R:    $r = M.0.0$

A (tail-)invariant for a repetition is

P:    $r \,\mathbf{max}\, M.a.b = M.0.0 \ \wedge \ 0 \leq a \leq b \leq N$

which may be established by $a, b, r := 0, 0, -\inf$ where $-\inf$ denotes the identity element of $\mathbf{max}$. For $b = N$ and $a \leq N$ we have

$\qquad M.a.b$

$=\qquad$ {definition of $M$, $b = N$}

$\qquad (\mathbf{max}\, p : a \leq p \leq N \wedge \mathcal{A}.p.N : N-p)$

$=\qquad$ {assume $\mathcal{A}.a.N$, $N-p$ is descending in $p$}

$\qquad N-a$

Hence,

$\qquad P \wedge b = N \wedge \mathcal{A}.a.b \ \Rightarrow \ R(r := r\,\mathbf{max}\,(N-a))$

which yields $b \neq N \vee \neg\mathcal{A}.a.b$ as guard of the repetition. To determine a condition under which $b$ may be increased, we derive for $0 \leq a \leq b < N$:

$\qquad M.a.b$

$=\qquad$ {definition of $M$, split off $q = b$}

$\qquad M.a.(b+1) \,\mathbf{max}\, (\mathbf{max}\, p : a \leq p \leq b \wedge \mathcal{A}.p.b : b-p)$

$=\qquad$ {assume $\mathcal{A}.a.b$, $b-p$ is descending in $p$, $a \leq b$}

$\qquad M.a.(b+1) \,\mathbf{max}\, (b-a)$

Hence, $\mathcal{A}.a.b \Rightarrow M.a.b = M.a.(b{+}1)\,\mathbf{max}\,(b{-}a)$    for $0 \le a \le b < N$. Notice that

$$P \wedge (b \ne N \vee \neg\mathcal{A}.a.b) \wedge \mathcal{A}.a.b \Rightarrow b < N$$

For the case $\neg\mathcal{A}.a.b$ we investigate an increase of $a$.
Due to (0), we have $\neg\mathcal{A}.a.b \Rightarrow a \ne b$, hence, $a \le b$ is not violated by $a := a{+}1$ in this case. We derive for $0 \le a \le b \le N \wedge \neg\mathcal{A}.a.b$

$M.a.b$

$=$    {definition of $M$, split off $p = a$}

$M.(a{+}1).b\,\mathbf{max}\,(\,\mathbf{max}\,q : a \le q \le N \wedge b \le q \le N \wedge \mathcal{A}.a.q : q{-}a)$

$=$    $\{a \le b\}$

$M.(a{+}1).b\,\mathbf{max}\,(\,\mathbf{max}\,q : b \le q \le N \wedge \mathcal{A}.a.q : q{-}a)$

$=$    $\{(1),\ \neg\mathcal{A}.a.b,\ \text{hence},\ (\,\mathbf{A}\,q : b \le q \le N : \neg\mathcal{A}.a.q)\}$

$M.(a{+}1).b$

Hence, $\neg\mathcal{A}.a.b \Rightarrow M.a.b = M.(a{+}1).b$    for $0 \le a \le b \le N$.

This concludes our derivation. The program scheme for *maxseg* is shown below. As bound function $2 * N - a - b$ will do.

```
maxseg:  [[ a, b : int;
            a, b, r := 0, 0, −inf
          ; do b ≠ N ∨ ¬A.a.b
              → if    A.a.b → r := r max (b−a) ; b := b + 1
                []  ¬A.a.b → a := a + 1
                fi
            od
          ; r := r max (N−a)
          { r = ( max p, q : 0 ≤ p ≤ q ≤ N ∧ A.p.q : q−p) }
          ]]
```

Two remarks are appropriate at this point. The first and minor one is that the initialization may be replaced by $a, b, r := 0, 0, 0$, since $M.0.0 \ge 0$. The second one is more important: instead of the guard $b \ne N \vee \neg\mathcal{A}.a.b$ one might suggest as guard $b \ne N{+}1$ (and change the bounds in $P$ into $0 \le a \le b \le N{+}1$). Then assignment $r := r\,\mathbf{max}\,(N{-}a)$ may be dropped. However, invariant $0 \le a \le b \le N{+}1$ makes $b = N{+}1$ possible, which leads to inevitable case analysis when refining $\mathcal{A}.a.b$.

We now consider *minseg* and we assume that $\mathcal{A}$ satisfies

(0′)　　　$\neg \mathcal{A}.p.p$　　　　　　　　　the empty segment is an $\neg\mathcal{A}$-segment
(2′)　　　$\neg\mathcal{A}.p.q \Rightarrow (\mathbf{A}\,s:\, p \le s \le q:\, \neg\mathcal{A}.s.q)$　　　$\neg\mathcal{A}$ is postfix-closed

Defining $M.a.b$ for $0 \le a \le b \le N$ by

$$M.a.b = (\,\mathbf{min}\,p,q:\, a \le p \le q \le N \wedge b \le q \le N \wedge \mathcal{A}.p.q:\, q-p)$$

and taking as invariant

$P$:　　　$r\,\mathbf{min}\,M.a.b = M.0.0 \ \wedge\ 0 \le a \le b \le N$

leads along the same lines as in *maxseg* to the following properties:

$$P \wedge b = N \wedge \neg\mathcal{A}.a.b \ \Rightarrow\ R$$
$$\neg\mathcal{A}.a.b \ \Rightarrow\ M.a.b = M.a.(b+1) \qquad \text{for } 0 \le a \le b < N$$
$$\mathcal{A}.a.b \ \Rightarrow\ M.a.b = M.(a+1).b\,\mathbf{min}\,(b-a) \qquad \text{for } 0 \le a \le b \le N.$$

These properties result in the following program scheme for *minseg*:

```
minseg:  [ a, b : int;
           a, b, r := 0, 0, inf
         ; do b ≠ N ∨ A.a.b
              → if ¬A.a.b → b := b + 1
                ▯  A.a.b → r := r min (b−a) ; a := a + 1
                fi
           od
           { r = ( min p, q : 0 ≤ p ≤ q ≤ N ∧ A.p.q : q−p) }
         ]
```

In the derivation of *maxseg* we used that $q-p$ is descending in $p$. As a matter of fact, this derivation holds for any $F.p.q$ that is descending in $p$. A similar remark holds for *minseg*, but there $F.p.q$ should be ascending in $q$.

## 3　An application

In this section we apply the scheme for *minseg* to obtain an algorithm for the computation of the length of a shortest segment of integer array $X[0..N)$ that contains the numbers 0 upto and not including 60, i.e.

$$\mathcal{A}.a.b \ \equiv\ (\mathbf{A}\,i:\, 0 \le i < 60:\, (\mathbf{E}\,j:\, a \le j < b:\, X.j = i))$$

For the sake of convenience, we assume $(\mathbf{A}\,i:\, 0 \le i < N:\, 0 \le X.i < 60)$.

An attempt to add $c \ \equiv\ \mathcal{A}.a.b$ to the invariant fails. This is due to the fact that $(\mathbf{E}\,j :\ a+1 \le j < b :\ X.j = i)$ cannot be expressed in $(\mathbf{E}\,j :\ a \le j < b :\ X.j = i)$, since disjunction has no inverse. The technique to solve this is rewriting existential quantification to 'number of' quantification:

$$(\mathbf{E}\,j :\ a \le j < b :\ X.j = i) \ \equiv\ (\mathbf{N}\,j :\ a \le j < b :\ X.j = i) \ge 1$$

Since a similar difficulty arises with conjunction, we write $\mathcal{A}.a.b$ as follows:

$$\mathcal{A}.a.b \ \equiv\ (\mathbf{N}\,i : 0 \le i < 60 : (\mathbf{N}\,j :\ a \le j < b :\ X.j = i) \ge 1) = 60$$

and we introduce $w$: **array** $[0..60)$ **of** int with

$$(\mathbf{A}\,i :\ 0 \le i < 60 :\ w.i = (\mathbf{N}\,j :\ a \le j < b :\ X.j = i))$$

and integer $c$ with

$$c = (\mathbf{N}\,i :\ 0 \le i < 60 :\ w.i \ge 1)$$

Then $\mathcal{A}.a.b$ can be replaced by $c = 60$. Refinement of *minseg* in this way yields the program below.

```
[ N : int; {N ≥ 0}
  X: array [0..N) of int; {(A i : 0 ≤ i < N : 0 ≤ X.i < 60)}
  [ r, a, b, c : int;
    w: array [0..60) of int;
    [ k : int; k := 0 ; do k ≠ 60 → w.k := 0 ; k := k+1 od ]
  ; a, b, c, r := 0, 0, 0, inf
  ; do b ≠ N ∨ c = 60
        → if  c ≠ 60  → w.(X.b) := w.(X.b) + 1
                        ; if  w.(X.b) = 1 → c := c+1
                          [] w.(X.b) > 1 → skip
                          fi
                        ; b := b+1
          [] c = 60  → r := r min (b−a)
                        ; w.(X.a) := w.(X.a) − 1
                        ; if  w.(X.a) = 0 → c := c−1
                          [] w.(X.a) > 0 → skip
                          fi
                        ; a := a+1
          fi
     od
     {r = (min p, q : 0 ≤ p ≤ q ≤ N ∧ A.p.q : q−p)}
  ]
].
```

# 4 Concluding remarks

There are several ways to solve segment problems and the tail-invariant approach is only one of them. The program schemes of *maxseg* and *minseg* show what is left to be done if one chooses this approach. Many programming problems have been solved in this way and the derivations in Section 2 were written over and over again. I hope this is over now.

REFERENCES

[1] Edsger W. Dijkstra and W. H. J. Feijen. *A Method of Programming.* Addison-Wesley, 1988.

Anne Kaldewaij,
Department of Mathematics and Computing Science,
Eindhoven University of Technology,
P.O. Box 513,
5600 MB  Eindhoven,
The Netherlands.

# 27

# A Simple Program Whose Proof Isn't

## Donald E. Knuth

As I was writing the TEX program, I needed to construct subroutines for many small tasks. The solution to one of those problems turned out to be especially interesting —to me at least— because it was a very short and simple piece of code, yet I could see no easy way to demonstrate its correctness by conventional methods.

My purpose in this note is to exhibit that subroutine with a sketch of the best proof I know, hoping that others with more experience in formal methods will agree that the algorithm is interesting, and will help me figure out what I should have done.

## 1    Converting decimal fractions to fixed-point binary.

To warm up, let me present another short program whose proof is quite easy. TEX works internally with integer multiples of $2^{-16}$, but its input language uses decimal notation. Therefore TEX needs a routine to translate a given decimal fraction

$$.d_1 d_2 \ldots d_k$$

to the nearest representable binary fraction. Here $k \geq 1$, and each digit $d_j$ is an integer in the range $0 \leq d_j < 10$, for $1 \leq j \leq k$. The problem is to find the nearest integer multiple of $2^{-16}$; in other words, we want to round the quantity

$$2^{16} \sum_{j=1}^{k} d_j/10^j$$

to the nearest integer $n$. If two integers are equally near this quantity, we will let $n$ be the larger; thus

$$n = \left\lfloor 2^{16} \sum_{j=1}^{k} d_j / 10^j + 1/2 \right\rfloor .$$

Notice that the smallest possible value of $n$ is 0; this occurs if and only if the input is strictly less than

.00000762939453125 ,

the decimal representation of $2^{-17}$. The largest possible value of $n$ is 65536; this occurs if and only if the input is greater than or equal to

.99999237060546875 ,

the decimal representation of $1 - 2^{-17}$. Since the output value $n$ is a non-negative integer in a limited range, and since the input values $d_j$ are small nonnegative integers, it is desirable to compute $n$ with integer arithmetic in such a way that the intermediate results stay reasonably small.

The total number of input digits, $k$, can be arbitrarily large. Therefore we cannot solve the problem by simply computing the integer

$$N = 10^k \left( 2^{16} \sum_{j=1}^{k} d_j / 10^j + 1/2 \right)$$

and then letting $n$ be the quotient $\lfloor N/10^k \rfloor$; the values of $N$ and $10^k$ may be too large for our computer's hardware.

We can, however, note that the values of $d_j$ for $j > 17$ have absolutely no effect on the answer $n$. Suppose $k$ is at least 17. Then we can use the well known law

$$\left\lfloor \frac{x + a}{b} \right\rfloor = \left\lfloor \frac{\lfloor x \rfloor + a}{b} \right\rfloor ,$$

which holds for all integers $a$ and $b$ with $b > 0$, to prove that

$$n = \left\lfloor \frac{10^{17} \sum_{j=1}^{k} d_j / 10^j + 5^{17}}{2 \cdot 5^{17}} \right\rfloor = \left\lfloor \frac{10^{17} \sum_{j=1}^{17} d_j / 10^j + 5^{17}}{2 \cdot 5^{17}} \right\rfloor$$

$$= \left\lfloor 2^{16} \sum_{j=1}^{17} d_j / 10^j + 1/2 \right\rfloor .$$

(The stated law of floors within floors is exercise 1.2.4–35 in [3].) Therefore TEX need only maintain an array capable of holding up to 17 digits; all digits after the 17th may be discarded.

The decimal representation of $2^{-17}$, given above, shows that 17 digits are not only sufficient; they are sometimes also necessary to determine the correct value of $n$. We can always ignore $d_{18}$, but the value of $d_{17}$ might matter.

It is convenient to compute $n$ by writing

$$n = \left\lfloor \frac{m_0 + 1}{2} \right\rfloor, \qquad m_l = \left\lfloor 2^{17} \sum_{j=l+1}^{k} d_j / 10^{j-l} \right\rfloor.$$

The intermediate values $m_l$ obey a simple recurrence,

$$m_k = 0; \qquad m_{l-1} = \lfloor (2^{17} d_l + m_l)/10 \rfloor.$$

Therefore the following program does the desired conversion to fixed-binary fractions.

*P1:*  $l := \min(k, 17)$;  $m := 0$;
      **repeat** $m := (131072 * d[l] + m)$ **div** $10$;
          $l := l - 1$;
      **until** $l = 0$;
      $n := (m + 1)$ **div** $2$.

(The proof is easy: We have $m = m_l$ at the beginning of the **repeat** loop, assuming that $k \leq 17$; and we have shown that it is legitimate to replace $k$ by 17 if $k$ is larger.)

Notice that the intermediate values computed by program *P1* are non-negative, and they never exceed 1310720.

# 2  Converting the other way.

Now let's consider the inverse problem: Given an integer $n$, which we shall assume is in the range

$$0 < n < 2^{16},$$

find a decimal fraction

$$.d_1 d_2 \ldots d_k$$

that approximates $2^{-16} n$ so closely that our previous algorithm for converting decimal fractions will reproduce $n$ exactly.

This problem has a simple solution: We can insist that $k = 5$, and then we can let $d_1 d_2 d_3 d_4 d_5$ be the decimal digits of the integer

$$D = \left\lfloor 10^5 \frac{n}{2^{16}} + \frac{1}{2} \right\rfloor.$$

Then $D/10^5$ must reproduce $n$, for the conversion algorithm finds a number $n'$ such that

$$\left| \frac{D}{10^5} - \frac{n'}{2^{16}} \right| \leq 2^{-17}.$$

We also have

$$\left| D - 10^5 \, \frac{n}{2^{16}} \right| \le \frac{1}{2},$$

by definition; hence

$$\begin{aligned}
|n - n'| &\le \left| n - 2^{16} D/10^5 \right| + \left| n' - 2^{16} D/10^5 \right| \\
&\le 2^{15}/10^5 + 1/2 = .82768 < 1
\end{aligned}$$

and $n$ must equal $n'$.

The original implementation of TEX took $k = 5$, but this turned out to be unsatisfactory. A user who asked for a .4-point rule was told that TEX had actually typeset a rule of .39999 points; this was a reasonably honest response, but the extra detail was distracting and unnecessarily messy.

Therefore it was desirable to find a solution to the inverse conversion problem such that $k$ is as small as possible. We seek a *shortest* decimal fraction that will reproduce the given value of $n$.

Perhaps there are two decimal fractions of the same length that both yield the desired value. (For example, both .00001 and .00002 yield $n = 1$, because both 0.65536 and 1.31072 round to 1.) In such cases it is desirable to choose the decimal fraction that is closest to $n/2^{16}$ (namely .00002 when $n = 1$).

It turns out that there is a simple program to compute such shortest decimal fractions. But —as I said in the introduction— I don't know of an equally simple way to derive that program or to prove it correct. Here is the program I came up with.

```
P2:  j := 0;  s := 10 * n + 5;  t := 10;
     repeat if t > 65536 then s := s + 32768 - (t div 2);
        j := j + 1;  d[j] := s div 65536;
        s := 10 * (s mod 65536);  t := 10 * t;
     until s ≤ t;
     k := j.
```

Why does this work? Everybody knows Dijkstra's famous dictum that testing can reveal the presence of errors but not their absence [1]. However, a program like this, with only finitely many inputs, is a counterexample! Suppose we test it for all 65535 values of $n$, and suppose the resulting fractions $.d_1 \ldots d_k$ all reproduce the original value when converted back. Then we need only verify that none of the shorter fractions or neighboring fractions of equal length are better; this testing will prove the program correct.

But testing is still not a good way to guarantee correctness, because it gives us no insight into generalizations. Therefore we seek a proof that is comprehensible and educational.

Even more, we seek a proof that reflects the ideas used to create the program, rather than a proof that was concocted ex post facto. The program didn't emerge by itself from a vacuum, nor did I simply try all possible short programs until I found one that worked.

## 3   Germs of a proof.

The invariant relationship I had in mind when I wrote the program in the previous section —the relation that explains the intrinsic meaning of the variables $s$ and $t$ in connection with other data of the problem— is not easy for me to formalize. Perhaps I am too close to the program, too incapable of analyzing my own thought processes. I was thinking (I think) of the set of all possible continuations of the digits already determined.

In other words, if $d_1 \ldots d_j$ have already been computed, I was thinking of the set of all strings of decimal digits $d_{j+1} \ldots d_k$ such that

$$.d_1 \ldots d_j \, d_{j+1} \ldots d_k$$

would produce the number $n$ when processed by the first program above. I wanted this set to be nonempty; and I wanted to stop if the empty string was in the set. Moreover, I wanted to make sure that my program would satisfy the optimality property (namely that it would round to the nearest of two equal-length possibilities). The latter condition is hard to deal with, so let's think first about the former one.

In the following proof I will use Lyle Ramshaw's convention, inspired by Pascal syntax, that $[a \, .. \, b)$ denotes the set of real numbers $x$ in the range

$$a \le x < b \, .$$

Similar notations apply to open intervals $(a \, .. \, b)$ and to closed intervals $[a \, .. \, b]$; in this way we avoid conflict with the many other mathematical interpretations of the notations $(a, b)$ and $[a, b]$. (A similar convention, but with three dots instead of two, was first proposed by Hoare [2].)

The set of digit strings $d_{j+1} \ldots d_k$ that produce a given result $n$, when preceded by $.d_1 \ldots d_j$, can be characterized as a set of decimal fractions

$$.d_{j+1} \ldots d_k$$

that lie in some half-open interval $[\alpha \, .. \, \beta)$. Initially we have $j = 0$, and this interval is

$$\left[ 2^{-16} \left( n - \frac{1}{2} \right) \, .. \, 2^{-16} \left( n + \frac{1}{2} \right) \right) \, .$$

In general if the interval is $[\alpha \, .. \, \beta)$, the empty string is in the set of possible continuations $d_{j+1} \ldots d_k$ if and only if $\alpha \le 0$ and $\beta > 0$. Furthermore, the permissible values of $d_{j+1}$, if we wish to increase $j$ and retain a nonempty set of continuations, are those decimal digits $d$ such that

$$[d/10 .. (d+1)/10)$$

has a nonempty intersection with $[\alpha .. \beta)$. This means that the conditions

$$0 \le d \le 9, \qquad d/10 < \beta, \quad \text{and} \quad \alpha < (d+1)/10$$

are necessary and sufficient for $d$ to be an acceptable choice of $d_{j+1}$ (if we ignore complications of optimality).

Suppose we set $j := j+1$ and $d[j] := d$. Then the new interval $[\alpha' .. \beta')$ replacing $[\alpha .. \beta)$ should be such that

$$\frac{d + \alpha'}{10} = \alpha, \qquad \frac{d + \beta'}{10} = \beta.$$

In other words, the new interval should be

$$[10\alpha - d .. 10\beta - d).$$

This analysis has used real numbers, but we want to stick to integers in the calculation. Let us therefore represent $\alpha$ and $\beta$ implicitly by the integer variables $s$ and $t$, where

$$10\alpha = 2^{-16}(s - t); \qquad 10\beta = 2^{-16}s.$$

The initial values of $s$ and $t$, corresponding to the initial $\alpha$ and $\beta$ values $2^{-16}(n \pm \frac{1}{2})$, are therefore

$$s = 10n + 5; \qquad t = 10.$$

The conditions for an admissible $d$ translate into

$$0 \le d \le 9, \qquad s > 2^{16}d, \quad \text{and} \quad s - t < 2^{16}d + 2^{16}.$$

When $j$ is increased by 1 and the next output digit is set to $d$, we want to set

$$s := 10(s - 2^{16}d), \qquad t := 10t.$$

These manipulations on $s$ and $t$ change $(\alpha, \beta)$ into $(\alpha', \beta')$ as discussed above.

From such considerations we can prove that the following program does almost what we want.

> P3: $j := 0$; $s := 10 * n + 5$; $t := 10$;
> **repeat** $j := j + 1$; $d[j] := s$ **div** 65536;
>  $s := 10 * (s \bmod 65536)$; $t := 10 * t$;
> **until** $s \le t$;
> $k := j$.

This program preserves the desired invariant relation between variables, namely that a string $d_{j+1} \ldots d_k$ of decimal digits will have the property that $.d_1 \ldots d_j d_{j+1} \ldots d_k$ converts to $n/2^{16}$ if and only if

$$2^{-16} \frac{s - t}{10} \le .d_{j+1} \ldots d_k < 2^{-16} \frac{s}{10}.$$

We can verify this as follows: First we note that the conditions

$$s > t, \qquad t = 10^{j+1}, \qquad 0 \le s \le 655350$$

hold on each entry to the body of the **repeat** loop. Hence $10^{j+1} < 655350$ whenever the **repeat** loop begins, and we must have $j \le 5$ when the program terminates.

It is not difficult to verify that $s$ is an odd multiple of $2^j$, just before our new program increases $j$, because $j$ never reaches 16. Therefore $s$ is never a multiple of $2^{16} = 65536$, and the digit $d = s$ **div** $65536$ always satisfies the condition

$$s - t - 2^{16} < 2^{16}d < s$$

that we have derived for admissibility of $d$ as a digit.

This argument establishes that the decimal fraction $.d_1 \dots d_k$ computed by program *P3* will be converted back to $n$ by *P1*. Furthermore, the value of $k$ will be at most 5.

The value of $k$ produced by *P3* is actually minimum; no shorter fraction than $d_1 \dots d_k$ will reproduce $n$. To prove this, we observe that the algorithm always chooses the largest possible digit $d$; if two or more values of $d$ satisfy

$$s - t - 2^{16} < 2^{16}d < s,$$

then $s$ **div** $65536$ is the largest one. Hence, any fraction $.d'_1 \dots d'_{k'}$ with $k' < k$ that program *P1* converts to $n$ has $d'_j < d_j$ for some $j$. This implies that

$$.d_1 \dots d_k \; - \; .d'_1 \dots d'_{k'} \ge 10^{-k'}.$$

But we have

$$\left| .d'_1 \dots d'_{k'} - \frac{n}{2^{16}} \right| \le 2^{-17} \qquad \text{and} \qquad \left| .d_1 \dots d_k - \frac{n}{2^{16}} \right| \le 2^{-17},$$

hence

$$10^{-k'} \le 2^{-17} + 2^{-17} = 2^{-16}$$

and $k' \ge 5 \ge k$, a contradiction.

Therefore *P3* is almost a solution to our problem. The only remaining task is to find an approximation $.d_1 \dots d_k$ of minimum length that is as close as possible to $n/2^{16}$. If the output of *P3* is not the best approximation, then the only better ones are at least $10^{-k}$ less than $.d_1 \dots d_k$, and the argument just given implies that two distinct approximations of length $k$ are possible only when $k \ge 5$. Therefore *P3* gives the correct answer whenever it finds an approximation of length 4 or less.

In all other cases, program *P3* eventually begins its **repeat** loop with $j = 4$ and $t = 10^5$. We want to modify the calculation on the final round so that the final digit $d_5$ will be "best possible" among the available choices.

This means that we want to compute the quantity

$$\left(\frac{n}{2^{16}}\right) \text{ rounded to 5 decimal places} = \frac{\lfloor 10^5 n/2^{16} + 1/2 \rfloor}{10^5}$$

whenever there is no suitable approximation with fewer than 5 decimal places.

## 4   Completion of the proof.

If we change the penultimate line of $P3$ to 'until *false*', so that the program loops forever, our interpretation of the variable $s$ implies that the resulting program will compute the decimal expansion $.d_1 d_2 d_3 \ldots$ of $(n + 1/2)/2^{16}$. (This expansion is infinite, although $d_j$ will be zero for all $j \geq 18$.) Stating this another way, we can prove without difficulty that the variables $s$ and $.d_1 \ldots d_j$ of program $P3$ obey the invariant relation

$$\frac{s}{10^{j+1}} + 2^{16} \sum_{i=1}^{j} d_i 10^{-i} = n + \frac{1}{2}.$$

Now let's return to program $P2$, which is identical to $P3$ except that the conditional instruction

**if** $t > 65536$ **then** $s := s + 32768 - (t \text{ div } 2)$

has been inserted at the very beginning of the **repeat** loop. This instruction takes effect only when $j = 4$, i.e., when $t = 10^5$, because $t = 10^{j+1}$ and the loop is never entered when $j > 4$.

When $j = 4$ at the beginning of the loop, we are about to compute $d_5$. And we know that $d_5 > 0$, because we have proved that $P3$ computes a shortest possible decimal expansion; therefore we have $s > 65536$. Therefore the new value of $s$ in program $P2$,

$$s' = s + 32768 - (t \text{ div } 2),$$

is nonnegative, but less than 655350. Therefore the quantity $d_5 = s'$ **div** 65536 will be a digit in the interval $[0 .. 9]$.

But by the invariant between $s$ and $d_1 \ldots d_j$, we know that

$$s' + 2^{16} \sum_{i=1}^{4} d_i 10^{5-i} = s + 2^{15} - \frac{10^5}{2} + 2^{16} \sum_{i=1}^{4} d_i 10^{5-i}$$

$$= 10^5 n + 2^{15}.$$

Therefore

$$\left\lfloor \frac{10^5 n}{2^{16}} + \frac{1}{2} \right\rfloor = \left\lfloor \frac{s'}{2^{16}} + \sum_{i=1}^{4} d_i 10^{5-i} \right\rfloor = \sum_{i=1}^{5} d_i 10^{5-i};$$

in other words, $.d_1 d_2 d_3 d_4 d_5$ is equal to $n/2^{16}$ rounded to five decimal places, as desired.

We have shown that $P2$ either computes the (unique) shortest decimal approximation $.d_1 \ldots d_k$ of length $k < 5$, or it computes the best approximation of length 5 (when there is no shorter one). This completes the proof that $P2$ is correct.

So. Is there a better program, or a better proof, or a better way to solve the problem?

# 5   Closing remarks.

We have based our discussion on the particular case of 16-bit fixed-point binary fractions. But an examination of the proof shows that the ideas are quite general: If $m$ is any positive number for which we seek the shortest-and-best decimal representation of $n/m$, given $0 < n < m$, we can use the following modification of program $P2$.

$P4$:  $j := 0;\ \ s := 10 * n + 4;\ \ t := 10;$
    **repeat if** $t > m$ **then** $s := s + 1 + (m\ \mathbf{div}\ 2) - (t\ \mathbf{div}\ 2);$
        $j := j + 1;\ \ d[j] := s\ \mathbf{div}\ m;$
        $s := 10 * (s\ \mathbf{mod}\ m) + 9;\ \ t := 10 * t;$
    **until** $s < t;$
    $k := j.$

The resulting fraction $.d^1 \ldots d^k$ is an optimum representation subject to the conditions

$$\frac{n - \frac{1}{2}}{m} \le .d_1 \ldots d_k < \frac{n + \frac{1}{2}}{m}.$$

(If equality is impossible in shortest representations, a program more like $P2$ will also be valid.)

When the denominator is not a power of 2, the converse problem (corresponding to $P1$) becomes much more interesting, especially if $m$ is divisible by at least one prime number other than 2 or 5. Then the digits $d_j$ can be relevant for arbitrarily large $j$. The reader may enjoy trying to construct an algorithm that reads a decimal input fraction $.d_1 \ldots d_k$ "on line" from an input tape and computes the unique value of $n$ that satisfies the inequalities above, given $m$. It is desirable to limit the amount of auxiliary memory to $O(\log m)$ bits, not counting the digits on the tape. The input digits must be read once only, from left to right.

An algorithm similar to program *P3* was published in 1959 by Donald Taranto [6]. A generalization of Taranto's method, due to G. L. Steele Jr. and Jon L. White, appears in the answer to exercise 4.4–3 in [4]. Programs *P1* and *P2* appear in sections 102 and 103, respectively, of TEX [5].

After writing this paper I decided to optimize *P2* in TEX by changing '32768 − ($t$ **div** 2)' to '−17232'.

*Acknowledgments*: I wish to thank David Gries for helping me locate reference [1]. The preparation of this note was supported in part by the National Science Foundation under grant CCR-86-10181. (End of acknowledgments)

## REFERENCES

[1] Edsger Dijkstra. Comment in *Software Engineering Techniques*, edited by J. N. Buxton and B. Randell, Report on a conference sponsored by the NATO Science Committee, Rome, Italy, 27–31 October 1969 (Brussels: NATO Science Committee, 1970), page 21. Reprinted in *Software Engineering: Concepts and Techniques*, edited by Peter Naur, Brian Randell and J. N. Buxton (New York: Petrocelli, 1976), page 159.

[2] C. A. R. Hoare. A note on the **for** statement. *BIT*, 12:334–341, 1972.

[3] Donald E. Knuth. *The Art of Computer Programming, Vol. 1: Fundamental Algorithms*. Addison-Wesley, Reading, Mass., 1968.

[4] Donald E. Knuth. *The Art of Computer Programming, Vol. 2: Seminumerical Algorithms*. Addison-Wesley, Reading, Mass., second edition, 1981.

[5] Donald E. Knuth. *Computers & Typesetting, Vol. B: TEX: The Program*. Addison-Wesley, Reading, Mass., 1986.

[6] Donald Taranto. Binary conversion, with fixed decimal precision, of a decimal fraction. *Comm. ACM*, 2(7):27, July 1959.

Donald E. Knuth,
Department of Computer Science,
Stanford University,
Stanford, California   94305–2140,
U.S.A.

# Binding Structure and Behaviour in "Whole Net" Concurrency Semantics

## Vadim E. Kotov

More then ten years ago, in the Springer LNCS Vol.64 "Mathematical Foundation of Computer Science 1978", next to E.W.Dijkstra's paper "Finding the Correctness Proof of a Concurrent Program", appeared the author's paper "An Algebra for Parallelism Based on Petri Nets". It was a very special paper for the author, because he had left the "traditional" field of parallel programming schematology for an attempt to develop a unified methodology and formal constructive tools for practical analysis and synthesis of concurrent systems. The intention was, first, to develop some algebraic notation for description of control structures in parallel programming languages and, then, to convert this notation into a more general and formal calculus for specifiyng a larger spectrum of concurrent systems, including self-timed circuitry, computer networks, distributed control and production systems. The idea was to use the net theory at all levels of model from the initial specification language up to semantic domains.

The first stage was completed quite easily and its results were implemented in some experimental concurrent languages. The second task became a chain of researches that are still being continued, because the problem turned to be much more complex then we expected. Meanwhile a cascade of works on theory of concurrency was done in the 80's, including the development and study of well-known models like CCS [4] and CSP [1]. The modeling of concurrency by nondeterministic interleaving of actions and, hence, the representation of a concurrent process as a set of strings of actions was typical for this group of models, because linear orders provide a familiar and mathematically well-studied semantic basis. However, works on true concurrency semantics became active in recent years and our original task to develop a uniform net-based algebra has now relevant potential. In this paper, I informally sketch the essence of this approach from a current perspective. Structurality, which as a data processing concept was pioneered by Dijkstra, is the main principle embedded in the concurrent models under consideration.

We construct a chain of concurrency algebras based on net theory. It starts from the *Structured Net Algebra* SNA for the specification of structure and behaviour of concurrent systems in terms of a class of well-structured Petri nets. Then we introduce the *Net Process Algebra* NPA describing concurrent non-deterministic processes as infinite acyclic nets. The semantics of expressions of SNA can be described in terms of expressions of NPA. The next step is to represent true concurrency semantics of NPA in terms of the *Causal Net Algebra* CNA defining sets of causal nets that are very close to partially ordered sets (posets) of actions. The most interesting and difficult part of this chain is the interrelation between SNA and NPA.

We briefly recall some net notions:

$N = (P, T, F)$ is a *net* with a set of *places* $P$, a set of *transitions* $T$ and a flow relation (a set of *arcs*) $F$ that is a subset of $(P \times T) \cup (T \times P)$.

For any $x \in X = (P \cup T)$ we denote $\bullet x = \{y \in X \,|\, (y, x) \in F\}$ and $x^\bullet = \{y \in X \,|\, (x, y) \in F\}$. We call $p$ a *head* (*tail*) place of a net if $\bullet p = \emptyset$ ($p^\bullet = \emptyset$), i.e. if it has no ingoing (outgoing) arcs.

In a *Petri net* $N = (P, T, F, M_0)$, an *initial marking* of places $M_0 : P \longrightarrow \{0, 1, 2, \ldots\}$ is added, the sets $P$ and $T$ are finite, and the transition *firings* that change markings are introduced:

> $t \in T$ can fire by a marking $M$ if $\forall p \in \bullet t : M(p) > 0$ and,
> if fired, $t$ changes $M$ to $M'$ such that $\forall p \in \bullet t : M'(p) = M(p) - 1$
> and $\forall p \in t^\bullet : M'(p) = M(p) + 1$.

An *acyclic net* is a net with possibly infinite sets $P$ and $T$, with no loops and with the standard initial marking: $M_0(p) = 1$, if $p$ is a head place, and $M_0(p) = 0$, otherwise. An acyclic net is a *causal* (or *non-conflict*) net if $\forall p \in P : |\bullet p| = 1 \,\wedge\, |p^\bullet| = 1$. In a causal net, $F$ is a partial order relation.

The initial algebra SNA is a set of expressions defining a class of Petri nets that we call structured nets. The expressions of SNA are

$$N ::= a \mid (N_1; N_2) \mid (N_1 || N_2) \mid (N_1 + N_2) \mid {}^*N \mid (n \mapsto N)$$

where $a$ defines an *atomic net* $(\{p_h, p_t\}, \{a\}, \{(p_h, a), (a, p_t)\})$ with one transition $a$, one place $p_h$ called the *head place* and one *tail place* $p_t$:

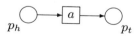

The semantics of the net operations is explained informally in terms of merging of head and tail places of nets. Only places with identical marking may be merged, otherwise an operation is not defined. When two sets of places $\{p_1, \ldots, p_n\}$ and $\{q_1, \ldots, q_m\}$ are merged, they are first copied (together with their marking and incident arcs) and sets $\{p_{11}, \ldots, p_{1m}, \ldots, p_{n1}, \ldots, p_{nm}\}$ and $\{q_{11}, \ldots, q_{1n}, \ldots, q_{m1}, \ldots, q_{mn}\}$ are formed. Then all pairs $p_{ij}$ and $q_{ji}$ are merged.

(i) The (net) *concatenation* $(N_1; N_2)$ merges each tail place of (the net defined by) $N_1$ with each head place of $N_2$.

(ii) The *exclusion* $(N_1 + N_2)$ merges each head place of $N_1$ with each head place of $N_2$ and each tail place of $N_1$ with each tail place of $N_2$.

(iii) The *superposition* (or *parallel composition*) $(N_1 \,||\, N_2)$ is the net union and serves as a "parallel composition" of nets.

(iv) The (net) *iteration* $^*N$ merges each head place of $N$ with each of its tail places. Each resulting place is announced to be the head place of $^*N$, so the expression $(^*N_1; N_2)$ is not valid in SNA and in the expression $(^*N_1 + N_2)$ only head places of $^*N_1$ and $N_2$ are merged.

(v) The *marking* $(n \mapsto N)$, where $n$ is a non-negative integer or the special symbol $\omega$, puts $n$ tokens in each head place of $N$. Here $\omega$ denotes a source of an "infinite number" of tokens in a place, i.e. it denotes always a true firing condition $a$ in this place.

It is assumed that $N_1$ and $N_2$ do not intersect in $(N_1; N_2)$ and $(N_1 + N_2)$ (i.e. they have no common transitions and places). In a complete formula of SNA each head place must be explicitly marked by a marking operation (including $0 \mapsto N$). A net can be defined by different expressions, because the net operations have some algebraic properties: all binary operations are associative; exclusion and superposition are commutative; superposition is reflexive; and exclusion and concatenation are distributive in relation to superposition. (This version of SNA is more restrictive than the original one.)

For example, the net in figure 1 is defined by the net expressions

$$N_1 \ : \ 1 \mapsto {}^*((a + c) \,||\, (c + b); d) \ = \ 1 \mapsto {}^*((a \,||\, b) + c); d$$

Thus, SNA is an algebra for modeling primarily structural properties of concurrent systems. However, the Petri net specification implicitly contains also the behavioural component, which is incorporated in the possibility to organize token games in nets. To make the behavioural aspect explicit, we introduce the *Net-Process Algebra* NPA in such a way that for any expression from SNA describing a Petri net we can construct an expression of NPA describing the behaviour of this net. Also, a process description in NPA should preserve as much as possible the information on the structure of the net. So, we want to describe both structural and behavioural properties of systems and processes using nets and to define behaviourally well-structured nets.

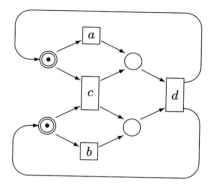

FIGURE 1. $N_1 : 1 \mapsto {}^*((a+c) \parallel (c+b); d) = 1 \mapsto {}^*((a \parallel b) + c); d$

In *interleaving semantics*, a process is represented as a set of strings. In *true concurrency semantics* a process is represented as a set of posets, labeled posets (pomsets), or causal nets. We choose true concurrency semantics using nets instead of strings as basic semantic objects. For non-deterministic concurrent processes we eliminate also sets from the process characterization. We want a process to be represented by a nondeterministic concurrent net rather than by a set of nets. So, we have introduced net-processes [3], which are acyclic nets with transitions representing atomic process actions, with arcs representing causal dependencies between actions and places with many outgoing (ingoing) arcs representing forward (backward) conflicts between actions.

The question arises whether any acyclic net represents a reasonable and well-defined process. The notion of K-density defined for concurrent causal nets [5] is an example of a characterisation of well-structured nets. We have extended it to acyclic nets and introduced also L- and M-density as characterizations of behaviourally well-structured acyclic nets.

For a pair of elements $x, y$ of $N$ we define three basic relations: succession **li**, alternative **al** and concurrency **co**.

(a) $x$ **li** $y \iff (x = y) \lor (xF^*y) \lor (yF^*x)$,
where $F^*$ is the transitive closure of $F$.

(b) for $x, y \in T$:
$x$ **al** $y \iff (x = y) \lor ((x \neq y) \land \neg(x \text{ **li** } y) \land ((^\bullet x \cap {}^\bullet y \neq \emptyset) \lor (\exists p \in {}^\bullet x : (\forall z \in {}^\bullet p : z \text{ **al** } y)) \lor (\exists p \in {}^\bullet y : (\forall z \in {}^\bullet p : y \text{ **al** } z))))$

i.e. transitions $x$ and $y$ that are different, are not related by **li** and either they share a conflict input place or a predecessor of one of them is alternative to another;

for $x, y \in P$ :

$x$ **al** $y \iff (x = y) \lor ((x \neq y) \land \neg(x \; \textbf{li} \; y) \land$
$(\forall z \in {}^\bullet x, u \in {}^\bullet y : (z \; \textbf{al} \; u) \land (z \neq u)))$

(c) $x$ **co** $y \iff (x = y) \lor \neg(x \; \textbf{li} \; y \lor x \; \textbf{al} \; y)$

A non-empty subset $L$ of $X = (P \cup T)$ is called a **re**-*line*, where **re** is either **li** or **al** or **co**, if

(i) $\forall x, y \in L : x \; \textbf{re} \; y$

(ii) $\forall y \in (X \setminus L) : x \in L : \neg(x \; \textbf{re} \; y)$, i.e. $L$ is a maximal **re**-line.

A **re**-line collects those elements of a net that belong to the same relation.

A net $N' = (P', T', F')$ is a *subnet* of the net $N = (P, T, F)$ if

$$P \supseteq P', \; T \supseteq T', \; F \cap (P' \times T' \cup T' \times P') \supseteq F'.$$

We fix informally maximal $O$-subnets of $N$ without conflict places that are causal nets ($\forall p \in P' : |{}^\bullet p| = 1 \land |p^\bullet| = 1$) and maximal $S$-subnets that are subnets without concurrent transitions: ($\forall t \in T' : |{}^\bullet t| = 1 \land |t^\bullet| = 1$). An acyclic net can be represented as a set of all its maximal $O$-subnets or as a set of all its maximal $S$-subnets.

(i) A causal net is *K-dense* if any of its **li**-lines intersect with any of its **co**-lines.

(ii) An $S$-subnet is *L-dense* if any of its **li**-lines intersect with any of its **al**-lines.

(iii) An acyclic net is *K-dense (L-dense)* if all of its maximal $O$-subnets ($S$-subnets) are K-dense (L-dense).

(iv) An acyclic net is *M-dense* if the intersection of any maximal $O$-subnet of $N$ with any maximal $S$-subnet of $N$ results in some (unique) **li**-line of $N$.

$S$-nets and $O$-nets are M-dense. In an M-dense net, for any reachable dead marking $M$ (none of the transitions can fire) and for any of its places $p$: $M(p) = 1$, if $p$ is a tail place, and $M(p) = 0$ otherwise.

Expressions of the net-process algebra NPA define acyclic nets. NPA incorporates concatenation, exclusion and superposition of SNA. Two nets $N_1$ and $N_2$ are *conformed* if for all $x, y$ in $N_1 \cap N_2$:

$$((xF^*y \; \text{in} \; N_1) \Rightarrow \neg(yF^*x \; \text{in} \; N_2))$$
$$\land \; ((xF^*y \; \text{in} \; N_2) \Rightarrow \neg(yF^*x \; \text{in} \; N_2)).$$

Superposition is applicable only to conformed nets.

There are no iteration and marking operations in NPA. However, periodic versions of concatenation and superposition are introduced. They are **seq** and parametrized **par** $n$ respectively. Being applied to a net $N = (P, T, F)$ they result in a periodic net as follows: **seq** $N = (N^1; N^2; \ldots)$ and **par** $n$ $N = (N^1 \| N^2 \| \ldots \| N^n)$. In each copy $N^i$ of $N$, each $t$ in $T$ and $p$ in $P$ receives the superscript $^i$. If $n = \omega$ then it can be omitted in **par** and the operation results in an infinite periodic net:

$$\textbf{par seq } (a) \;=\; ((a^{11}; a^{12}; \ldots) \| (a^{21}; a^{22}; \ldots) \| \ldots).$$

Binary operations are applied to periodic expressions in the usual way. Superscripted copies of a symbol are considered to be different symbols, and "scalars" are considered to have superscript $^1$, e.g.:

$$((\textbf{par } 2\ a) \| b); c \;=\; ((a^1 \| a^2) \| b^1); c^1 \;=\; ((a^1 \| b^1); c^1 \| a^2)$$
$$\textbf{seq } (a; b) \| \textbf{seq } (a; c) \;=\; \textbf{seq } (a; (b \| c))$$

For net concatenation and its periodic version, special rules for their execution are introduced:

$$\textbf{seq } N_1; N_2 \;=\; \textbf{seq } N_1$$
$$N_1 + \textbf{seq } N_2 \;=\; (N_1^1 + (N_2^1; (N_1^2 + (N_2^2; \ldots) \ldots) \ldots) \ldots)$$
$$\text{for } n < m : (\textbf{par } n\ N_1 \| \textbf{par } m\ N_2); N_3 =$$
$$\textbf{par } n\ ((N_1 \| N_2); N_3) \| (N_2^{(n+1)} \ldots N_2^m)$$

Let the nets defined by $N$, $N_1$ and $N_2$ be M-dense. Then:

(a) the nets defined by $(N_1; N_2)$ and $(N_1 + N_2)$ are M-dense;

(b) the nets defined by **seq** $N$ and **par** $n$ $N$ are M-dense;

(c) the net defined by $(N_1 \| N_2)$ is M-dense if $(T_1 \cap T_2) = \emptyset$ or both in $N_1$ and in $N_2$ for any $t$ in $(T_1 \cap T_2)$ and for any $p$ in $^\bullet t$ there exists a **li**-line that contains $p$ and does not contain any transition from $(T_1 \cap T_2)$.

The net semantics of SNA can be expressed in terms of acyclic nets in the following way. We introduce the transformation **D** of the nets defined by expressions from SNA into acyclic nets of a special form. For a given structured net $N = (P, T, F, M_0)$, an acyclic net is constructed in which we use as transition symbols the symbols from $T$ augmented by superscripts. We denote by $N^0$ the net $(P, T, F, \mathbf{0})$ with deleted marking ($\forall p \in P : \mathbf{0}(p) = 0$), by **E** an "empty" acyclic net $(\emptyset, \emptyset, \emptyset)$ and by $N$, $N_1$, and $N_2$ subnets of the given structured net.

$$
\begin{array}{ll}
\mathbf{D}[a] \;=\; a & \mathbf{D}[N_1; N_2] \;=\; \mathbf{D}[N_1] \; ; \; \mathbf{D}[N_2] \\
\mathbf{D}[0 \mapsto N] = \mathbf{E} & \mathbf{D}[N_1 + N_2] = \mathbf{D}[N_1] + \mathbf{D}[N_2] \\
\mathbf{D}[1 \mapsto N] = \mathbf{D}[N^0] & \mathbf{D}[N_1 \| N_2] = \mathbf{D}[N_1] \| \mathbf{D}[N_2] \\
\mathbf{E}; \mathbf{D}[N] \;=\; \mathbf{E} & \mathbf{D}[n \mapsto N] \;=\; \textbf{par } n\ \mathbf{D}[N^0] \\
(\mathbf{D}[N_1] \| \mathbf{E}) \,;\, \mathbf{D}[N_2] = \mathbf{D}[N_1] & \mathbf{D}[*N] \;=\; \textbf{seq } \mathbf{D}[N]
\end{array}
$$

If the resulting acyclic net $\mathbf{D}[N]$ is dense, i.e. it is K-, L- and M-dense, then $N$ is behaviourally well-structured net and its behavioural semantics

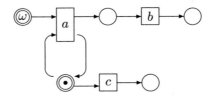

FIGURE 2. $N_2$ : $((1 \mapsto {}^*a) + c) \,||\, (\omega \mapsto a; b)$

is described by $\mathbf{D}[N]$. For example, net $N_1$ in figure 1 is well-structured because $N_1' = \mathbf{D}[N_1] = \mathbf{seq}\ ((a + c) \,||\, (c + b); d)$ is a dense acyclic net, but net $N_2$ in figure 2 is not well-structured because $N_2' = \mathbf{D}[N_2] = (\mathbf{seq}\ a + \mathbf{par}\ c) \,||\, (\mathbf{par}\ (a; b))$ is non-K-dense and non-L-dense.

A maximal $O$-subnet of an acyclic net describes a (concurrent) run of the net and the set of all such subnets fully characterizes it as a non-deterministic process. Since we can describe causal nets using operations of NPA except $+$, so CNA is a subalgebra of NPA.

The causal net semantics of NPA can be defined in terms of CNA expressions, where net operations are extended for sets of nets in a natural way:

$$
\begin{aligned}
\mathbf{S}[a] &= \{a\} \\
\mathbf{S}[N_1; N_2] &= \mathbf{S}[N_1] \;;\; \mathbf{S}[N_2] \\
\mathbf{S}[N_1 + N_2] &= \mathbf{S}[N_1] \cup \mathbf{S}[N_2] \\
\mathbf{S}[N_1||N_2] &= \mathbf{S}[N_1] \,||\, \mathbf{S}[N_2]
\end{aligned}
$$

This paper briefly surveyed a part of the work we have done to develop net-based formalisms for concurrency. Many open problems remain, but we think that we are now closer than ten years ago to the Net Calculus for adequate modeling of both structural and behavioural properties of systems and processes.

## REFERENCES

[1] C. A. R. Hoare. Communicating sequential processes. *Comm. ACM*, 21(8):666–677, 1978.

[2] V. E. Kotov. *An Algebra for Parallelism Based on Petri Nets.* In Lecture Notes in Computer Science, Vol. 64, Springer-Verlag, 1978.

[3] V. E. Kotov and L. A. Cherkasova. *On Structural Properties of Generalized Processes.* In Lecture Notes in Computer Science, Vol. 188, Springer-Verlag, 1984.

[4] R. Milner. *Calculus of Communicating Systems.* In Lecture Notes in Computer Science, Vol. 92, Springer-Verlag, 1980.

[5] C. A. Petri. *Non-Sequential Processes.* Technical Report 77-05, GMD-ISF, 1971.

Vadim E. Kotov,
Computing Centre,
Siberian Division of the USSR Academy of Sciences,
630090, Novosibirsk,
U.S.S.R.

# 29

# Maximal Strong Components: An Exercise in Program Presentation

## F. E. J. Kruseman Aretz

## Abstract

Tarjan's algorithm for the computation of the maximal strong components in a directed graph is presented. The presentation is compared to some older ones.

**key words:** program presentation, Tarjan's algorithm, maximal strong components.

## 1    Introduction.

In his famous 1972 paper [7], Tarjan presents an algorithm for the computation of the maximal strong components of a (directed) graph. This algorithm is nontrivial, its time complexity is optimal, and, moreover, it has applications in a broad class of systems. Consequently, it is an almost indispensable ingredient for books both on algorithm development [2,3], on graph algorithms [5], and on complexity theory [6]. Nevertheless, I do not find those presentations, including that of Dijkstra [3], fully satisfactory. To my taste they do not do full justice to the inherent beauty and simplicity of the algorithm. Possibly, this must be attributed to an unnecessary bias to representational aspects. Therefore, an attempt is made at producing a presentation that at least pleases its author.

Before I start, two remarks are in place. First, I use the word presentation rather than development (or even derivation). I do not aim at a step-by-step derivation of the algorithm from its specification by manipulating the latter until the former is obtained. What I do aim at is to uncover the essential ideas behind the algorithm and I do not exclude what sometimes is called "pulling rabbits from a hat". I expect that the presentation can be transformed into a derivation. It is one of the things I hope to be done in the future.

Second, the presentation contains a number of operational considerations and terminology. Some readers might prefer a formal text from which all operational aspects were absent. But such a presentation would not reflect the way I look at algorithms, and a careful and systematic elimination of all traces of operational thinking afterwards occurs as dishonest to me.

## 2   Tarjan's algorithm

We start our presentation with the introduction of the relevant notions.

Let $(v, e)$ be a directed graph. We define the binary relation "$\approx$" on $v$ by:

$$a \approx b \quad \text{iff} \quad (a, b) \in e^* \wedge (b, a) \in e^*, \quad \text{for all } a, b \in v$$

(as usual, $e^*$ denotes the reflexive and transitive closure of $e$).

Evidently, $\approx$ is reflexive, symmetric, and transitive. It is, therefore, an equivalence relation, and we can partition $v$ in equivalence classes modulo $\approx$, called the *maximal strong components* of $(v, e)$.

It follows from these definitions that for any two vertices $a$ and $b$ in one and the same maximal strong component $x$ there is, via vertices also in $x$, both a path from $a$ to $b$ and a path from $b$ to $a$. Any nonempty subset of the vertices with that property is called a *strong component* of the graph. A strong component is maximal if it is not a proper subset of a strong component.

Below we discuss an algorithm to compute the maximal strong components of a directed graph $(v, e)$. That algorithm, invented by Tarjan [7], is linear in both $\#v$ and $\#e$. Moreover, it not only generates the *set* of maximal strong components, but arranges them in a *sequence* $V$ such that:

$$(\mathbf{A}\, i, a, c : 0 \leq i < \#V \wedge a \in V{\cdot}i \wedge (a, c) \in e \\ : c \in (\bigcup j : 0 \leq j \leq i : V{\cdot}j)),$$

i.e., in the sequence there are no "forward references". This arrangement is, as we will see, a consequence of the way in which the maximal strong components are constructed. For some applications of the algorithm this arrangement is of great value.

In the following three subsections we introduce successively the components of the state space in which the computation is carried out. Thereby we feel free to use "high-level" notions like sets, sequences, and whatever we need. It is a matter of separate concern how these notions, and the operations thereupon, will be represented in terms of the data structures available in one or another "real-life" programming language, in such a way that the linearity of the algorithm is not spoiled.

## 2.1   THE INPUT $(v, e)$ TO THE ALGORITHM

We suppose the graph to be given by the set of its vertices (of a type that needs not concern us any further) and the set of its edges, each of which being a pair consisting of its origin and its destination vertex. Thus we have:

input:
$$v: \textbf{set of } \textit{vertex}; \quad e: \textbf{set of } (\textit{from,to}: \textit{vertex});$$

Of course, $e \subseteq v \times v$.

We use conventional symbols for singleton-set construction, set union, and set difference. "$\#x$" denotes the number of elements of set $x$. "**let** $a$: $a \in x$" denotes the introduction of a local variable $a$ of suitable type and the assignment to $a$ of some element of nonempty set $x$. It is a special case of the notation "**let** $x, y$ : $Q$" for the introduction of locals $x$ and $y$ and the assignment of values to them such that $Q$ holds. For selection of the components of a pair, component identifiers are introduced. However, for pair $p$ of type $(c1: \textit{type1}; c2: \textit{type2})$ we can avoid the use of the component identifiers $c1$ and $c2$ by writing "**let** $x, y$ : $p = (x, y)$" and using $x$ and $y$ instead of $p \cdot c1$ and $p \cdot c2$.

## 2.2   THE SEQUENCE $V$ OF MAXIMAL STRONG COMPONENTS

The algorithm constructs a sequence $V$ of maximal strong components. Its type is given by:

output:
$$V: \textbf{sequence of set of } \textit{vertex};$$

"$\#s$" denotes the length (number of elements) of sequence $s$. "$<>$" denotes the empty sequence. "$<a>$" denotes the sequence with $a$ as its one and only element. "$a : s$" denotes the addition of element $a$ to the head of sequence $s$. "$s : a$" denotes the addition of element $a$ to the tail of sequence $s$. "$s \downarrow j$" denotes the sequence that is left when sequence $s$'s first $j$ elements are removed. "$s \cdot j$" selects the element of $s$ with index $j$. As we did for component selection of pairs, we write "**let** $a, t$ : $s = a : t$" and use $a$ and $t$ instead of $s \cdot 0$ and $s \downarrow 1$.

We have the following invariants:

P1:        $(\mathbf{A}\, i : 0 \leq i < \#V$
               $: V \cdot i$ is a maximal strong component of $(v, e))$;

P2:        $(\mathbf{A}\, i, a, c : 0 \leq i < \#V \,\wedge\, a \in V \cdot i \,\wedge\, (a, c) \in e$
               $: c \in (\bigcup j : 0 \leq j \leq i : V \cdot j)).$

Instead of P1 we could have stated the weaker:

P1':      $(\mathbf{A}\,i:\,0 \leq i < \#V:\,V \cdot i$ is a strong component of $(v,e))$,

for P1 follows from P1' $\wedge$ P2 by an inductive argument. In fact, the algorithm maintains P1' and P2, and, thereby, P1.

By the definition of maximal strong components, all elements of $V$ are mutually disjoint. The computation of $V$ is completed when all vertices of $v$ occur in $V$. In order that this can be checked easily, we introduce:

$w$: **set of** $vertex$;

with the following invariant meaning:

P3:      $w \;=\; (\bigcup i:\,0 \leq i < \#V:\,V \cdot i)$.

Consequently, the algorithm terminates when $w = v$.
Invariants P1, P2, and P3 are trivially established by the assignment:

$V, w := \; <>, \phi$.


## 2.3  THE SEQUENCE $S$ OF CANDIDATE COMPONENTS

The central idea of the algorithm is to maintain, in addition to $V$, a sequence $S$ of subsets of $v$ that are candidates for being maximal strong components. The structure of $S$ resembles that of $V$ to a high degree. The main difference is that not all outgoing edges of the constituting vertices of a candidate component need to have been taken into account. But, for as far as they have been considered, they do not point "forward" in $S$; moreover, they point to vertices in $S$ or in $V$. All candidates are strong components and they are mutually disjoint.

For keeping track of the outgoing edges that have not yet been considered, we have each candidate component $x$ be accompanied by the set of edges that have their origins in $x$ but have not yet been taken into account. Therefore, we have the following definitions and invariants:

$S$:      **sequence of** ($vset$: **set of** $vertex$; $out$: **same type as** $e$);

P4:      $(\mathbf{A}\,i:\,0 \leq i < \#S$
           $:\,S \cdot i \cdot vset$ is a strong component of $(v,e)\;\wedge\;S \cdot i \cdot vset \cap w = \phi)$;

P5:      $(\mathbf{A}\,i,j:\,0 \leq i < j < \#S:\,S \cdot i \cdot vset \cap S \cdot j \cdot vset = \phi)$;

P6:      $(\mathbf{A}\,i,a,c:\,0 \leq i < \#S\;\wedge\;(a,c) \in S \cdot i \cdot out$
           $:\,(a,c) \in e\;\wedge\;a \in S \cdot i \cdot vset)$;

P7:      $(\mathbf{A}\,i,a,c:\,0 \leq i < \#S\;\wedge\;a \in S \cdot i \cdot vset\;\wedge\;(a,c) \in e$
           $:\,(a,c) \in S \cdot i \cdot out\;\vee\;c \in w\;\vee\;c \in (\bigcup j:\,0 \leq j \leq i:\,S \cdot j \cdot vset))$.

There is, however, one additional requirement for $S$ that plays a crucial role in the algorithm and that does not necessarily hold for $V$: between any two successive candidate components in $S$ there is at least one backward reference. This is formulated in the next invariant:

P8:    $(\mathbf{A}\, i:\ 0 < i < \#S$
    $: (\mathbf{E}\, a, c: a \in S{\cdot}i{\cdot}vset \ \wedge\ c \in S{\cdot}(i-1){\cdot}vset:\ (a,c) \in e \setminus S{\cdot}i{\cdot}out)).$

Finally, just as it was convenient to have the set of vertices contained in elements of $V$ readily available, it is so for the vertices of our candidate components. For reasons of symmetry we also introduce the set of vertices that are neither in components of $V$ nor in components of $S$:

$g, b$:    **set of** *vertex*;
P9:    $g\ =\ (\bigcup i:\ 0 \le i < \#S:\ S{\cdot}i{\cdot}vset);$
P10:    $b\ =\ v \setminus (w \cup g).$

It follows from P4, P9, and P10 that $w$, $g$, and $b$ together constitute a partition of $v$.

If $V$ is empty, invariants P4 through P10 are trivially established by the assignment:

$$S, g, b := \ <>, \phi, v.$$

After these preparations we are ready to present the algorithm.

## 2.4  THE ALGORITHM

We simply analyse what steps can be taken under invariance of P1 upto P10. We do so by case analysis. In all cases the action is almost dictated by the invariants ("the only thing you can do is $\cdots$").

1. Let $w = v$.
   Then, as remarked before, the algorithm terminates.

2. Let $w \neq v$ and $S = <>$.
   Then, by P9, $g = \phi$ and therefore, by P10, $b \neq \phi$.
   Let $c \in b$. Then $< (\{c\}, \{u \in e \mid u{\cdot}from = c\}) >$ is a value for $S$ that does not spoil invariants P4 upto P8 (as a matter of fact, each singleton set of vertices is a strong component by itself). Therefore, that value can be assigned to $S$ under simultaneous adaptation of the values of $g$ and $b$:

   $$S, g, b := \ < (\{c\}, \{u \in e \mid u{\cdot}from = c\}) >, \ g \cup \{c\}, \ b \setminus \{c\}.$$

3. Let $w \neq v \ \wedge\ S = (x, \phi):\ t$, for some (nonempty) set of vertices $x$ and some sequence $t$ (note that, by P4, $S \neq <>$ implies $w \neq v$; the latter is, therefore, redundant here).
   Then we conclude by P7 that all outgoing edges of elements of $x$ either point to an element of $x$ itself or to an element of some component of $V$. Consequently, we can add $x$ to the tail of $V$ without spoiling P1' or P2 (or, therefore, P1!): $x$ is a maximal strong component. Moreover,

after addition of the elements of $x$ to $w$, $t$ itself satisfies the invariants for $S$ as given by P4 upto P8. This leads to the following code:

$$V, w, S, g := V : x,\ w \cup x,\ t,\ g \setminus x.$$

4. Let $w \neq v \land S = (x, y) : t$, for some (nonempty) set of vertices $x$, some nonempty set of edges $y$, and some sequence $t$.
Let $(a, c) \in y$. We have three cases for $c$:

- $c \in w$: deleting edge $(a, c)$ from $y$ does not spoil P7 (nor any other invariant). The corresponding code reads:

$$S := (x, y \setminus \{(a, c)\}) : t.$$

- $c \in g$: by P9 and P5, there is a uniquely determined candidate component that contains $c$, say $S \cdot j \cdot vset$. Then there exists a path from (a vertex of) candidate component $S \cdot 0 \cdot vset$ to (a vertex of) $S \cdot j \cdot vset$. But, due to P8 and P4, the converse is also true (here it is that we exploit the knowledge contained in P8): there is a path from any vertex in $S \cdot j \cdot vset$ to any vertex in $S \cdot 0 \cdot vset$, passing vertices in $S \cdot h \cdot vset$ for $h = j, j - 1, \ldots, 0$. We conclude that the set of vertices $U = (\bigcup h : 0 \leq h \leq j : S \cdot h \cdot vset)$ is a strong component by itself; further, that the set of edges $O = (\bigcup h : 0 \leq h \leq j : S \cdot h \cdot out) \setminus \{(a, c)\}$ is the set of unconsidered outgoing edges from elements of $U$; finally, that the pair $(U, O)$ can replace the first $j + 1$ elements of $S$ without spoiling any invariant. The code for the action is:

$$S := ((\bigcup h : 0 \leq h \leq j : S \cdot h \cdot vset)$$
$$, (\bigcup h : 0 \leq h \leq j : S \cdot h \cdot out) \setminus \{(a, c)\}) : S \downarrow (j + 1).$$

- $c \in b$: $c$ occurs neither in $V$ nor in any candidate component of $S$. The only fact that is discovered about $c$ is that there is an edge from a vertex in $S \cdot 0 \cdot vset$ leading to it. This implies, however, that we can make $\{c\}$ to be a candidate component, provided that it, paired with all its outgoing edges (none of which having been considered up to here), is put in front of $S \cdot 0$ (here we see how candidate components are created without spoiling P8!). Then, vertex $(a, c)$ can be deleted from $y$ without spoiling P7. Here is the code:

$$S, g, b := (\{c\}, \{u \in e \mid u \cdot from = c\}) : (x, y \setminus \{(a, c)\}) : t$$
$$, g \cup \{c\},\ b \setminus \{c\}.$$

Herewith all cases have been dealt with; it is a matter of adding appropriate control structure to arrive at the algorithm below, in which the occurrence of undeclared identifiers in a guard is considered to be a kind of "let"-construction. Note that the disjunction of the guards is $w \neq v$.

input: $v$ : **set of** $vertex$; $e$ : **set of** $(from, to : vertex)$;
output: $V$ : **sequence of set of** $vertex$;

**var** $b, g, w$ : **set of** $vertex$;
    $S$ : **sequence of** $(vset$ : **set of** $vertex, out$ : **same type as** $e)$;

$V, S, w, g, b := <>, <>, \phi, \phi, v$;
**do** $w \neq v \ \wedge \ S = <>$
    $\rightarrow$ **let** $c$: $c \in b$;
        $S, g, b := \ < (\{c\}, \{u \in e \mid u{\cdot}from = c\}) >$
            , $g \cup \{c\}, \ b \setminus \{c\}$
$[]\ S = (x, y) : t \ \wedge \ y = \phi$
    $\rightarrow V, w, S, g := V : x, \ w \cup x, \ t, \ g \setminus x$
$[]\ S = (x, y) : t \ \wedge \ (a, c) \in y \ \wedge \ c \in w$
    $\rightarrow S := (x, y \setminus \{(a, c)\}) : t$
$[]\ S = (x, y) : t \ \wedge \ (a, c) \in y \ \wedge \ c \in g$
    $\rightarrow$ **let** $j$: $c \in S{\cdot}j{\cdot}vset$;
        $S := (\,(\bigcup h : 0 \leq h \leq j : S{\cdot}h{\cdot}vset)$
           , $(\bigcup h : 0 \leq h \leq j : S{\cdot}h{\cdot}out) \setminus \{(a, c)\}\,)\ :\ S{\downarrow}(j + 1)$
$[]\ S = (x, y) : t \ \wedge \ (a, c) \in y \ \wedge \ c \in b$
    $\rightarrow S, g, b := (\{c\}, \{u \in e \mid u{\cdot}from = c\}) : (x, y \setminus \{(a, c)\}) : t$
        , $g \cup \{c\}, \ b \setminus \{c\}$
**od**.

We end this section by presenting an upperbound for the number of iterations. We observe that during the execution of the algorithm the set $b$ is monotonically non-increasing. The same holds for set $U = (\bigcup j : 0 \leq j < \#S : S{\cdot}j{\cdot}out) \cup \{(a, c) \mid a \in b \ \wedge \ (a, c) \in e\}$ of unconsidered edges. On the other hand, the set $w$ is monotonically non-decreasing with upperbound $v$.

In the first alternative of the iterative construct, the size of $b$ is decreased by one. It can be selected at most $\#v$ times. In the second alternative, the size of $w$ is increased by at least 1. It can be selected at most $\#v$ times. In each of the three remaining alternatives the size of $U$ is decreased by 1. They can be selected at most $\#e$ times. Therefore, the number of iterations is bounded by $2\#v + 3\#e$ (it is even bounded by $\#v + \#e + nmc$, where $nmc$ is the number of maximal strong components).

Of course, when we code the algorithm in directly executable form, we have to choose such a representation of the state variables and such an implementation of the operations on them that the linearity of the algorithm is not destroyed. In the next section we make some remarks on this issue.

## 3   Implementation issues of Tarjan's algorithm

One of the advantages of presenting an algorithm at a rather abstract level is that it leaves a lot of freedom for the representation of the variables and for the implementation of the operations thereupon. Sequences, for example, can be implemented by arrays, favouring random access, or by linked lists, favouring concatenation. We describe here just one possibility and provide a minimum number of details.

The alternative containing the most complicated operations is the fourth one. In the form it was formulated in the previous section, it contains the determination of a value $j$ such that $c \in S{\cdot}j{\cdot}vset$, followed by twofold union of $j + 1$ sets. This is certainly not an action that can be carried out in unit time; we present an implementation that does not destroy the linearity of the algorithm.

Instead of explicitly determining the value $j$, we carry out the set-union operations pairwise in the following manner:

$$\textbf{do } c \notin S{\cdot}0{\cdot}vset \;\; \rightarrow \;\; \textbf{let } \; x, y, p, q, t\colon \; S = (x, y) : (p, q) : t \,;$$
$$S := (x \cup p, y \cup q) : t$$
$$\textbf{od}.$$

The test "$c \notin S{\cdot}0{\cdot}vset$" can be implemented in $O(1)$ time by numbering the vertices in order of first occurrence and by recording, for each candidate component, the minimum or maximum (or both) value of the numbers assigned to its vertices (cf. Section 4).

The following argument leads to the conclusion that the total amount of pairwise union operations during the execution of the algorithm is less than $2\#v$. Each vertex is, during the algorithm, transferred from $b$ to $g$ once, building a one-vertex strong component out of it. Thereby the number of elements of $S$ is increased by one, and, at the end of execution, it is in this way increased by $\#v$. When we "unite" two elements of $S$ into one, the number of elements of $S$ is decreased by 1. Since $S$ starts and ends containing zero of such sets the total number of "unions" of two elements of $S$ is $\#v$ minus the number of maximal strong components.

Further, if we implement both sequences and sets as linked lists, the union of two disjoint sets, the selection of the first two elements of a sequence, and the selection of some element of a set and its removal can be implemented in $O(1)$ time.

For the implementation of the first and the last alternative, we need to be able to construct, for $c \in v$, the set $\{u \in e \mid u{\cdot}from = c\}$. This can also be carried out in $O(1)$ time if $e$ is given as a linked list, ordered according to the source vertex of the edges, and, moreover, each vertex is provided with the information which segment of the list is "its" list of outgoing edges.

# 4  Discussion

In this section we try to analyse why we prefer our presentation over some other ones.

Most of the presentations I have encountered follow Tarjan's original paper. The algorithm is described as a derivative of a depth-first tree traversal that is implemented by a recursive procedure. The vertices are numbered in order of first "visit". Moreover, a value *lowlink* is recorded for each vertex, which initially equals the vertex's number, but might be decreased on the basis of the (recursive) visits to the vertex's descendants. If the lowlink of a vertex is, however, never decreased, that vertex is the "root" of a maximal strong component.

It cannot be denied that in my presentation also a depth-first graph traversal is present. A symptom for it is that sequence $S$ is always operated upon on its front side, and we can implement $S$ as a stack (using top-, pop-, and push-operations for accessing it) or even implement it implicitly by using recursive techniques. But I see no need for applying that terminology.

The twofold numbering of the nodes as decribed above introduces a structure inside the candidate components (the order of its elements), and the outgoing edges of a vertex are (further) considered only after all outgoing edges of vertices of higher order have been considered. This requirement is, clearly, overspecific.

Moreover, the numbering is a rather indirect way of representing sets of vertices and thereby obscures the fact that the algorithm operates on sets of vertices. What I see as the central idea of the algorithm, the introduction of sequence $S$ of candidate components with a structure which strongly resembles that of $V$, is buried in the representational details. It is true that the numbering provides a rather efficient implementation of the statement pair

$$\textbf{let } j\colon c \in S{\cdot}j{\cdot}vset;$$
$$S := (\,(\bigcup h\colon 0 \le h \le j\colon S{\cdot}h{\cdot}vset)$$
$$,(\bigcup h\colon 0 \le h \le j\colon S{\cdot}h{\cdot}out) \setminus \{(a,c)\}\,) \,:\, S{\downarrow}(j+1),$$

but, once more, also that is hardly recognizable. As a result, the correctness proof of the algorithm needs a number of lemmata.

What comes closest to my presentation is that of Dijkstra [3]. At the top level he presents a piece of pseudo code that resembles our version, albeit that it shows a more complicated control structure. In terms of the variables introduced in this paper it reads:

**do** $w \neq v$

    $\rightarrow$ **let** $c$: $c \in b$;

       $S, g, b := \; < (\{c\}, \{u \in e \mid u \cdot from = c\}) >$

            , $g \cup \{c\}$, $b \setminus \{c\}$;

       **do** $S \neq <>$

         $\rightarrow$ **do** $S \cdot 0 \cdot out \neq \phi$

            $\rightarrow$ **let** $a, c$: $(a, c) \in S \cdot 0 \cdot out$;

               **if** $c \in w \rightarrow \ldots$

               $[\!]\; c \in g \; \rightarrow \ldots$

               $[\!]\; c \in b \; \rightarrow \ldots$

               **fi**

         **od**;

         **let** $x, y, t$: $S = (x, y) : t$;

         $V, w, S, g := \; V : x, \; w \cup x, \; t, \; g \setminus x$

       **od**

  **od**.

This version saves, depending on implementational details, a number of tests and can, therefore, be executed slightly faster. But it obscures to a large extent the simplicity and the beauty of the algorithm. I look upon it as some kind of optimization which should only come into consideration when dealing with implementation details (grouping the three cases $c \in b$, $g$ or $v$ together in a verbal analysis, as we did in Section 2.4, is something different). In detailing his pseudo algorithm also Dijkstra introduces numbers, assigned to vertices in order of first visit, and some integer arrays for administrative purposes, thereby obscuring the final algorithm.

An algorithm based on a different principle can be found in [1]. Again it is based on numbering vertices.

Let me conclude by observing that the style of presentation of algorithms has changed dramatically over the last two decades. One evolution has been the transition from proving algorithms after their design to the design of programs guided, in a calculational style, by correctness considerations. Another line of progress has been the abstraction of representational detail, as is, hopefully, illustrated by this contribution, specially written for a memorable occasion.

## REFERENCES

[1] A. V. Aho, J. E. Hopcroft, and J. D. Ullman. *Data Structures and Algorithms*. Addison-Wesley, Reading, 1982/1983.

[2]  A. V. Aho, J. E. Hopcroft, and J. D. Ullman. *The Design and Analysis of Computer Algorithms*. Addison-Wesley, Reading, 1974.

[3]  E. W. Dijkstra. *A Discipline of Programming*. Prentice-Hall, Englewood Cliffs, 1976.

[4]  J. Eve and R. Kurki-Suonio. On computing the transitive closure of a relation. *Acta Informatica*, 8:303–314, 1977.

[5]  K. Mehlhorn. *Data Structures and Algorithms 2: Graph Algorithms and NP-completeness*. Springer-Verlag, Berlin, 1984.

[6]  E. M. Reingold, J. Nievergelt, and N. Deo. *Combinatorial Algorithms: Theory and Practice*. Prentice-Hall, Englewood Cliffs, 1977.

[7]  R. E. Tarjan. Depth-first search and linear graph algorithms. *SIAM Journal of Computation*, 1:146–160, 1972.

F. E. J. Kruseman Aretz,
Philips Research Laboratories,
P.O. Box 80 000,
5600 JA  Eindhoven,
The Netherlands.

# 30

# A Systolic Program for Gauss-Jordan Elimination

## Christian Lengauer
## Duncan G. Hudson

## Abstract

A scheme for the compilation of imperative or functional programs into systolic programs is used to derive a distributed program for Gauss-Jordan elimination from a Pascal-like program.

## 1 Introduction

A systolic array is a distributed processor network with a particularly regular structure that can process large amounts of data quickly by accepting streams of inputs and producing streams of outputs [5]. The regularity of the systolic array enables an automated synthesis from a more abstract description which essentially amounts to an imperative or functional program and which does not address the issues of communication or concurrency. In the past, systolic arrays have mostly been realized in hardware, but they can also be realized in software — in fact, this can provide a convenient and powerful way of programming distributed computers. We call the process of transforming an imperative or functional program into a systolic program *systolizing compilation*. It consists of two phases:

*Systolic Design:* the development of a systolic array from the source program. The description of the systolic array is in terms of distribution functions of the program's operations in time and space. If a fixed problem size is proposed, a picture and graphical simulation of the behavior of the systolic array can be generated from the distribution functions.

*Code Generation:* the generation of a systolic program from the distribution functions that specify the systolic array. Loops must be reintroduced, since the distribution functions are not in a recursive form.

While the systolic array is synchronous, the program is asynchronous — but both have the same process and communication structure.

We demonstrate with the example of the *algebraic path problem* [10], whose solution is Gauss-Jordan elimination, that systolizing compilation is feasible. First systolic solutions to the algebraic path problem were proposed informally [8,9] but, with the advent of systolic design methods [1,2], they were soon recast in a formal framework and a large space of systolic solutions was generated and reviewed [3,7].

We shall take the best of these solutions and present a systolic program that implements it. The program is in a machine-independent language but can be translated further into a distributed target language, e.g., occam [4]. The technique by which the systolic program is derived is an extension of a mechanical systolizing compilation scheme for simpler problems like matrix composition or decomposition [6].

## 2   The specification

A weighted graph $G$ is a triple $(V, E, w)$, where $V = \{i \mid 0 \leq i < n\}$ is a set of *vertices*, $E \subseteq V \times V$ is a set of *edges*, and $w : E \longrightarrow H$ is a function whose codomain is a semi-ring $(H, \oplus, \otimes)$ of *weights*. A path $p$ is a sequence of vertices $(v_0, v_1, \ldots, v_l)$, where $0 \leq l$ and $(v_{i-1}, v_i) \in E$. The weight of path $p$ is defined as:

$$w(p) \quad = \quad w_1 \otimes w_2 \otimes \ldots \otimes w_l$$

where $w_i$ is the weight of edge $(v_{i-1}, v_i)$. The *algebraic path problem* specifies the following matrix:

$$d_{i,j} \quad = \quad \bigoplus_{p \text{ is a path from } i \text{ to } j} w(p)$$

That is, we are asked to compute the sum of the weights of all paths from vertex $i$ to vertex $j$, for all pairs $(i, j)$. Plugging in different semi-rings yields problems like matrix inversion, shortest paths and reflexive transitive closure, all of which are solved by Gauss-Jordan elimination.

## 3   The source program

The graph is represented by an $n \times n$ matrix $c$ such that, for $0 \leq i, j < n$, matrix element $c_{i,j} = w((i, j))$ if $(i, j) \in E$ and $c_{i,j} = 0$ otherwise. The program employs four different computations (here, phrased imperatively):

Phase 0 :
**for** $i$ **from** 0 **to** $n - 1$ **do**
**for** $j$ **from** 0 **to** $n - 1$ **do**
**for** $k$ **from** 0 **to** $\min(i, j)$
   **do** $i{:}j{:}k{:}0$

Phase 1 :
**for** $i$ **from** 0 **to** $n - 1$ **do**
**for** $j$ **from** 0 **to** $n - 1$ **do**
**for** $k$ **from** $\min(i, j)$ **to** $\max(i, j)$
   **do** $i{:}j{:}k{:}1$

Phase 2 :
**for** $i$ **from** 0 **to** $n - 1$ **do**
**for** $j$ **from** 0 **to** $n - 1$ **do**
**for** $k$ **from** $\max(i, j)$ **to** $n - 1$
   **do** $i{:}j{:}k{:}2$

where

$i{:}j{:}k{:}0$ **if** $i \neq k \wedge j \neq k \rightarrow A(i, j, k)$
   $[\!]\ i > j \wedge j = k \rightarrow B0(i, j)$
   $[\!]\ i = j \wedge i = k \rightarrow C(i)$
   $[\!]$ **else** $\rightarrow$ **skip**
**fi**

$i{:}j{:}k{:}1$ **if** $i \neq k \wedge j \neq k \rightarrow A(i, j, k)$
   $[\!]\ i < j \wedge j = k \rightarrow B0(i, j)$
   $[\!]\ i < j \wedge i = k \rightarrow B1(i, j)$
   $[\!]$ **else** $\rightarrow$ **skip**
**fi**

$i{:}j{:}k{:}2$ **if** $i \neq k \wedge j \neq k \rightarrow A(i, j, k)$
   $[\!]\ i > j \wedge i = k \rightarrow B1(i, j)$
   $[\!]$ **else** $\rightarrow$ **skip**
**fi**

FIGURE 1. Imperative Gauss-Jordan Elimination

$$A(i, j, k) :: \quad c_{i,j} := c_{i,j} \oplus (c_{i,k} \otimes c_{k,j}),$$
$$B0(i, j) :: \quad c_{i,j} := c_{i,j} \otimes c_{j,j},$$
$$B1(i, j) :: \quad c_{i,j} := c_{i,i} \otimes c_{i,j},$$
$$C(i) :: \quad c_{i,i} := c_{i,i}^{*}.$$

Here, $c^{*} = 1 \oplus c \oplus (c \otimes c) \oplus (c \otimes c \otimes c) \oplus \ldots$, where 1 is the identity element of the semi-ring. If $c^{*}$ is not defined, the algebraic path problem has no solution. Note that the parameters of the program operations are matrix indices. Since the matrix is fixed, it suffices to refer to its elements by indices only.

Figure 1 displays the Gauss-Jordan elimination algorithm as a Pascal-like program; $n$ refers to the size of the square input matrix. We call the iteration steps $i{:}j{:}k{:}0$, $i{:}j{:}k{:}1$ and $i{:}j{:}k{:}2$ the *basic operations* of the program. Phase 0 performs a decomposition of the input matrix, Phase 1 inverts the two resulting triangles and Phase 2 recomposes the inverted triangles. This program is a simple transformation of the one proposed in [9]. In general, enforcing our requirements for a systolizing compilation on the source program may require non-trivial program transformations.

# 4   The systolic array

In order to obtain a systolic design, we need to modify and enhance the program's operations to account for reflections in data propagation. Systolic design methods provide guidance here. In our case, data will travel in three different directions on their way through the systolic design (for details, see [3]). Thus, we need three different matrices (we also call them streams) — one for each direction. We name them $a$, $b$ and $c$. The operations must copy elements from one matrix to another appropriately. To accomplish this, the existing computations must be modified and new ones must be added [3]:

$$
\begin{aligned}
A(i,j,k) &:: \quad c_{i,j} := c_{i,j} \oplus (a_{i,k} \otimes b_{k,j}), \\
B0(i,j) &:: \quad a_{i,j} := c_{i,j} \otimes b_{j,j} \\
B1(i,j) &:: \quad c_{i,j} := a_{i,i} \otimes b_{i,j}, \\
C(i) &:: \quad\quad b_{i,i} := c_{i,i}^{*}, \\
D0(i,j) &:: \quad b_{i,j} := c_{i,j}, \\
D1(i,j) &:: \quad c_{i,j} := a_{i,j}, \\
E(i) &:: \quad\quad a_{i,i} := b_{i,i}.
\end{aligned}
$$

The basic operations of the three phases are then extended as follows [3]:

$i$:$j$:$k$:0 ::
- **if** $i \neq k \;\wedge\; j \neq k \;\rightarrow\; A(i,j,k)$
- [] $i > j \;\wedge\; j = k \;\rightarrow\; B0(i,j)$
- [] $i = j \;\wedge\; i = k \;\rightarrow\; C(i)$
- [] $i < j \;\wedge\; i = k \;\rightarrow\; D0(i,j)$
- **fi**

$i$:$j$:$k$:1 ::
- **if** $i \neq k \;\wedge\; j \neq k \;\rightarrow\; A(i,j,k)$
- [] $i < j \;\wedge\; j = k \;\rightarrow\; B0(i,j)$
- [] $i < j \;\wedge\; i = k \;\rightarrow\; B1(i,j)$
- [] $i > j \;\wedge\; i = k \;\rightarrow\; D0(i,j)$
- [] $i > j \;\wedge\; j = k \;\rightarrow\; D1(i,j)$
- [] $i = j \;\wedge\; i = k \;\rightarrow\; E(i)$
- **fi**

$i$:$j$:$k$:2 ::
- **if** $i \neq k \;\wedge\; j \neq k \;\rightarrow\; A(i,j,k)$
- [] $i > j \;\wedge\; i = k \;\rightarrow\; B1(i,j)$
- [] $i \leq j \;\wedge\; j = k \;\rightarrow\; D1(i,j)$
- **fi**

The optimal systolic solution has $n^2 + n$ processors (we also call them cells), laid out in a rhombic shape with horizontal and vertical channel connections [3,8]; stream $c$ moves up, $b$ moves right and $a$ is stationary. Figure 2, generated by our implementation of the imperative method, displays the layout of the processors and the arrangement of the data for a $3 \times 3$ input at the first execution step, Figure 3 at the 10th step (of 14 steps). Different symbols represent different computations. Input cells must be imagined below the array where the matrix is injected and output cells above the array where the matrix is ejected; they are not depicted in the figures. Data items will change their relative positions during the systolic execution, but the configuration of the ejected stream is the same as that of the injected stream.

The systolic design is specified by the following distribution functions:

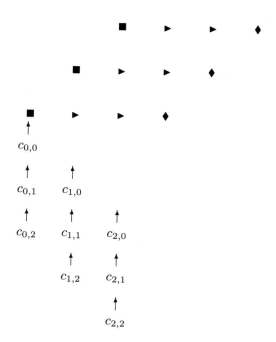

FIGURE 2. $3 \times 3$ Gauss-Jordan Elimination — The Systolic Design, 1st Step

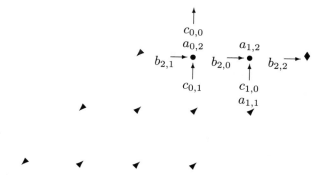

FIGURE 3. $3 \times 3$ Gauss-Jordan Elimination — The Systolic Design, 10th Step

$$
\begin{aligned}
step(i{:}j{:}k{:}0) &= i+j+k \\
step(i{:}j{:}k{:}1) &= i+j+k+n \\
step(i{:}j{:}k{:}2) &= i+j+k+2n
\end{aligned}
$$

$$
\begin{aligned}
place(i{:}j{:}k{:}0) &= (i,k) \\
place(i{:}j{:}k{:}1) &= \left\{ \begin{array}{ll} (i,k) & \text{if } j < i \\ (i+n,k) & \text{if } i < j \end{array} \right. \\
place(i{:}j{:}k{:}2) &= (i+n,k)
\end{aligned}
$$

*Step* maps the program's basic operations into time, and *place* maps them into two-dimensional space (the integer plane). *Step* and *place* of Phase 1 and 2 can be computed from their choice for Phase 0 [3]. The processor layout of Phase 1 is split into two parts; each processes one triangle.

# 5   The code generation

In [6], a systolizing compilation scheme is presented that takes source programs of the following form:

> **for** $x_0$ **from** $lb_0$ **by** $st_0$ **to** $rb_0$ **do**
> > **for** $x_1$ **from** $lb_1$ **by** $st_1$ **to** $rb_1$ **do**
> > > $\vdots$
> > >
> > > **for** $x_{r-1}$ **from** $lb_{r-1}$ **by** $st_{r-1}$ **to** $rb_{r-1}$ **do**
> > > > $x_0{:}x_1{:}\cdots{:}x_{r-1}$

with a basic operation of the form:

$$
x_0{:}x_1{:}\cdots{:}x_{r-1} \; : \; \begin{array}{ll} \textbf{if} & B_0(x_0,x_1,\cdots,x_{r-1}) \rightarrow S_0 \\ [] & B_1(x_0,x_1,\cdots,x_{r-1}) \rightarrow S_1 \\ & \vdots \\ [] & B_{t-1}(x_0,x_1,\cdots,x_{r-1}) \rightarrow S_{t-1} \\ \textbf{fi} \end{array}
$$

The bounds $rb_i$ and $lb_i$ are linear or piecewise linear expressions in the loop indices $x_0$ to $x_{i-1}$ $(0 \le i < r)$ and in additional variables that specify the problem size; the steps $st_i$ are constants; the conditions $B_j$ $(0 \le j < t)$ are boolean expressions; the $S_j$ $(0 \le j < t)$ are functional or imperative programs, possibly, with composition, alternation, or iteration but without non-local references other than to variables subscripted by the $x_i$. The $S_j$ must obey additional restrictions that, essentially, enforce a uniform recurrence [1].

The code generation proceeds by building loop constructs, so-called repeaters, from the data structures on which the graphical representation

**Stream Output** (up):

$$\{c_{0,0} \ 3 \ (0,+1)\}\{c_{1,0} \ 3 \ (0,+1)\}\{c_{2,0} \ 3 \ (0,+1)\}$$

**Computation**:

$$\{2{:}2{:}2{:}0 \ 1 \text{—}\} \ \{0{:}2{:}2{:}1 \ 1 \text{—}\} \ \{1{:}2{:}2{:}1 \ 1 \text{—}\} \ \{2{:}2{:}2{:}1 \ 1 \text{—}\}$$
$$\{2{:}0{:}2{:}1 \ 2 \ inc\} \ \{0{:}0{:}2{:}2 \ 3 \ inc\} \ \{1{:}0{:}2{:}2 \ 3 \ inc\} \ \{2{:}0{:}2{:}2 \ 3 \ inc\}$$

$$\{1{:}1{:}1{:}0 \ 2 \ inc\} \ \{2{:}1{:}1{:}0 \ 2 \ inc\} \ \{0{:}1{:}1{:}1 \ 2 \ inc\} \ \{1{:}1{:}1{:}1 \ 2 \ inc\}$$
$$\{1{:}0{:}1{:}1 \ 1 \text{—}\} \ \{2{:}0{:}1{:}1 \ 2 \ inc\} \ \{0{:}0{:}1{:}2 \ 2 \ inc\} \ \{1{:}0{:}1{:}2 \ 2 \ inc\}$$

$$\{0{:}0{:}0{:}0 \ 3 \ inc\} \ \{1{:}0{:}0{:}0 \ 3 \ inc\} \ \{2{:}0{:}0{:}0 \ 3 \ inc\} \ \{0{:}0{:}0{:}1 \ 3 \ inc\}$$
$$\{1{:}0{:}0{:}1 \ 1 \text{—}\} \ \{2{:}0{:}0{:}1 \ 1 \text{—}\} \ \{0{:}0{:}0{:}2 \ 1 \text{—}\}$$

**Stream Input** (up):

$$\{c_{0,0} \ 3 \ (0,+1)\}\{c_{1,0} \ 3 \ (0,+1)\}\{c_{2,0} \ 3 \ (0,+1)\}$$

where      $inc = (0,+1,0,0)$

FIGURE 4. $3 \times 3$ Gauss-Jordan Elimination — The Repeaters

of the $3 \times 3$ array is based (chiefly *step* and *place* and other functions derived from them). A *repeater* represents a finite sequence by a triple $\{fst \ cnt \ inc\}$, where *fst* is the first element in the sequence, *cnt* is the number of elements in the sequence, and *inc* is the increment by which an element is derived from its predecessor. If $cnt = 1$, any *inc* may be specified. Repeaters must be generated for the computation cells and for the input and output cells that inject and extract the matrix. Each set of repeaters (one for the input, one for the computation and one for the output cells) is then *homogenized*, yielding one repeater that is parameterized by the cell identifiers. In a last step, the repeaters are *generalized* from a fixed size (here $3 \times 3$) to the variable-size $(n \times n)$ problem. For more details, see [6].

Each phase of the Gauss-Jordan elimination program adheres to the previously stated source format, but we must also account for the composition of the phases. During the generation of repeaters, we would like to keep distinct phases separate; that is, no repeater should be part of more than one phase (this leads to a clearer loop structure). To sensitize the repeater generation algorithm accordingly, we must identify one of the arguments of the basic operation as the phase indicator; in our case, it is the fourth argument. With this additional provision, the repeater generation works also for multi-phase source programs.

With knowledge of the phase indicator, our repeater generation algorithm produces for the $3 \times 3$ problem the repeaters displayed in Figure 4. The layout of the computation repeaters matches the layout of the computation cells in the figures; each cell is assigned a pair of repeaters, except for the lower left corner of the array which is assigned one repeater only. The repeaters for the stream input and output are also given in Figure 4 — at the point where the input and output cells must be imagined.

We shall illustrate the homogenization and generalization technique for the repeater counts. The other repeater components (the indices of stream elements, arguments of basic operations and increments) are homogenized and generalized similarly; in this example, the repeater increments are unaffected by the homogenization and generalization process.

## 5.1   HOMOGENIZATION

Homogenization of the stream repeaters (the repeaters for the i/o of stream $c$) follows from the solution of a pair of linear equations for each repeater component. The linear equations for the repeater count (the second component) of the input repeaters are of the form:

$$cnt(col) \;=\; \alpha \cdot col + \beta$$

Two linear equations are obtained by filling in the information for two distinct columns, and then the equations are solved to obtain values for $\alpha$ and $\beta$, for example:

**Stream I/O**    (up):

$$\begin{aligned} cnt(0) &= \beta = 3 \\ cnt(1) &= \alpha + \beta = 3 \end{aligned} \quad \Longrightarrow \quad \begin{aligned} \alpha &= 0 \\ \beta &= 3 \end{aligned} \quad \Longrightarrow \quad cnt(col) = 3$$

In general, the repeaters for the input and output of a stream must be considered separately in multi-phase systolic designs, since they connect to different phases. In our example, $cnt$ happens to be the same for input and output, but $fst$ is different: $c_{col,0}$ for input and $c_{col-3,0}$ for output.

The homogenization of the computation repeaters proves to be more difficult. We obtain linear equations in two arguments:

$$cnt(col, row) \;=\; \alpha \cdot col + \beta \cdot row + \gamma$$

Three equations for the first computation repeaters are obtained by filling in the information for three computation cells, for example, at the points $(0,0)$, $(1,0)$ and $(1,1)$:

**Computation**    (first repeater):

$$\begin{aligned} cnt(0,0) &= \gamma = 3 \\ cnt(1,0) &= \alpha + \gamma = 3 \\ cnt(1,1) &= \alpha + \beta + \gamma = 2 \end{aligned} \quad \Longrightarrow \quad \begin{aligned} \alpha &= 0 \\ \beta &= -1 \\ \gamma &= 3 \end{aligned} \quad \Longrightarrow \quad cnt(col, row) = 3 - row$$

When we attempt to perform the same procedure for the second computation repeaters, we discover that we do not obtain a solution that provides a correct value of $cnt$ for each computation cell. However, it is possible to obtain consistent solutions by partitioning the computation cells into cells in columns $col \leq row + 1$ and cells in columns $col \geq row + 1$, for example:

**Computation**   (second repeater):

$$
\begin{aligned}
cnt(1,0) &= \alpha + \gamma = 1 \\
cnt(1,1) &= \alpha + \beta + \gamma = 1 \\
cnt(2,1) &= 2\alpha + \beta + \gamma = 2
\end{aligned}
\quad \Longrightarrow \quad
\begin{aligned}
\alpha &= 1 \\
\beta &= 0 \\
\gamma &= 0
\end{aligned}
\quad \Longrightarrow \quad cnt(col,row) = col
$$

$$
\begin{aligned}
cnt(1,0) &= \alpha + \gamma = 1 \\
cnt(2,0) &= 2\alpha + \gamma = 1 \\
cnt(2,1) &= 2\alpha + \beta + \gamma = 2
\end{aligned}
\quad \Longrightarrow \quad
\begin{aligned}
\alpha &= 0 \\
\beta &= 1 \\
\gamma &= 1
\end{aligned}
\quad \Longrightarrow \quad cnt(col,row) = row + 1
$$

Then, by observing that the minimum of the two solutions forms a consistent solution for all second computation repeaters, we obtain the final solution:

**Computation**   (second repeater):

$$cnt(col,row) \;=\; \min(col, row + 1)$$

Remember the repeater structure $\{fst \; cnt \; inc\}$. For the computation repeaters, we choose to comment also on the homogenization of component *fst*, the basic operation; we consider its first argument. As is the case for *cnt*, the expression we compute does not apply to all repeaters. However, consistent solutions can be obtained by a partitioning of the repeaters. We group together repeaters in columns 0 to 2 ($col < 3$) and repeaters in columns 3 to 5 ($col \geq 3$). We obtain:

$$
\begin{aligned}
arg1(0,0) &= \gamma = 0 \\
arg1(1,1) &= \alpha + \beta + \gamma = 1 \\
arg1(1,0) &= \alpha + \gamma = 1
\end{aligned}
\quad \Longrightarrow \quad
\begin{aligned}
\alpha &= 1 \\
\beta &= 0 \\
\gamma &= 0
\end{aligned}
\quad \Longrightarrow \quad arg1(col,row) = col
$$

$$
\begin{aligned}
arg1(3,0) &= 3\alpha + \gamma = 0 \\
arg1(3,1) &= 3\alpha + \beta + \gamma = 0 \\
arg1(4,1) &= 4\alpha + \beta + \gamma = 1
\end{aligned}
\quad \Longrightarrow \quad
\begin{aligned}
\alpha &= 1 \\
\beta &= 0 \\
\gamma &= -3
\end{aligned}
\quad \Longrightarrow \quad arg1(col,row) = col - 3
$$

We then observe that these two solutions can be combined to:

$$arg1(col,row) \;=\; col \bmod 3$$

## 5.2   GENERALIZATION

Once we have homogenized the repeaters, generalization proceeds much more easily. Let us demonstrate, again, with the repeater count. We simply solve a system of two linear equations of the form:

$$cnt(n) \;=\; \alpha \cdot n + \beta$$

We obtain the linear equations by filling in values for two distinct problem sizes. Solving these equations produces the generalized count. For example, for problem sizes 3 and 4, we obtain:

**Stream I/O**    (up):

$$cnt(3) = \alpha \cdot 3 + \beta = 3 \qquad \Longrightarrow \qquad \begin{matrix} \alpha = 1 \\ \beta = 0 \end{matrix} \qquad \Longrightarrow \quad cnt(n) = n$$
$$cnt(4) = \alpha \cdot 4 + \beta = 4$$

**Computation**    (first repeater):

$$cnt(3) = \alpha \cdot 3 + \beta = 3 - row \qquad \Longrightarrow \qquad \begin{matrix} \alpha = 1 \\ \beta = -row \end{matrix} \qquad \Longrightarrow \quad cnt(n) = n - row$$
$$cnt(4) = \alpha \cdot 4 + \beta = 4 - row$$

**Computation**    (second repeater):

$$cnt(3) = \alpha \cdot 3 + \beta = \min(col, row + 1) \qquad \Longrightarrow \quad \alpha = 0, \beta = \min(col, row + 1)$$
$$cnt(4) = \alpha \cdot 4 + \beta = \min(col, row + 1)$$
$$\Longrightarrow \quad cnt(n) = \min(col, row + 1)$$

The other repeater components are derived similarly. The homogenized and generalized set of repeaters is:

**Stream I/O**    (up):

$$input\text{-}cell(col) \;=\; \{c_{col,0} \quad n \quad (0,+1)\}$$
$$output\text{-}cell(col) \;=\; \{c_{col-n,0} \quad n \quad (0,+1)\}$$

**Computation:**

$$cell(col, row)$$
$$= \begin{matrix} \{(col \bmod n) : row : row : (col \text{ div } n) \quad n-row \quad (0,+1,0,0)\} \\ \{(col \bmod n) : 0 : row : ((col \text{ div } n) + 1) \; \min(col, row + 1) \; (0,+1,0,0)\} \end{matrix}$$

Note that the range of the index $col$ of the input and output cells is restricted; in other words, not every column has an input and output cell. This can be determined mechanically from an inspection of the data layout before the first step (Figure 1) and after the last step of the execution. Similarly, not every point of the rectangular layout space holds a computation cell, due to the rhombic shape of the systolic array.

For this example, the homogenization and generalization have been performed by hand; at present we do not identify functions like mod, div and min mechanically.

# 6   The target program

We have performed a translation to occam by hand. The translation of repeaters to occam loops is straight-forward:

$$\{fst \quad cnt \quad inc\} \qquad \text{becomes}$$

```
SEQ i = [0 FOR cnt]
fst+(i*inc)
```

The other main task in the translation is the appropriate choice of variable and channel declarations.

We omit the occam program here; the reader may derive it as an exercise. Remember that the basic operation is constructed from seven other operations (we called them previously "computations"): $A$, $B0$, $B1$, $C$, $D0$, $D1$, and $E$. Each computation has a set of one to three input variables on the right-hand side of the assignment operator, each from a different data stream. A given computation reads exactly from those streams corresponding to its input variables. Output is performed on the same streams, except that a reflection may be involved. A reflection is identified by matching the indices of the target variable with an input variable. For example, $A$ reflects nothing; it must input and output $a$, $b$, and $c$. $B0$ reflects $c$ into $a$; it must input $b$ and $c$ and output $b$ and $a$. $C$ reflects $b$ into $c$; it must input $b$ and output $c$, and so on [3]. If one represents communications of stationary streams by local reassignment, the input/output commands for stationary streams (in our case, $a$) may be omitted.

# 7   Conclusions

The distributed target program is interesting in its own right, but more important is its derivation. At present, some steps (the ones that introduce functions mod, div and min) involve human observation, but every step is a calculation. The beauty of the target program is a by-product of the systolizing compilation, which already requires a streamlined source program (a single basic operation per phase). The complexity is absorbed inside the basic operations, which may contain many alternative computations. But even the basic operations can be translated mechanically, including the augmentation with communications.

*Acknowledgements*: Thanks to the Austin Tuesday Afternoon Club for a reading of an earlier draft. Partial funding was provided by the National Science Foundation.

REFERENCES

[1] P. Frison, P. Gachet, and P. Quinton. Designing systolic arrays with DIASTOL. *VLSI Signal Processing II*, 93–105, 1986. IEEE Press.

[2] C.-H. Huang and C. Lengauer. The derivation of systolic implementations of programs. *Acta Informatica*, 24(6):595–632, Nov. 1987.

[3] C.-H. Huang and C. Lengauer. Mechanically derived systolic solutions to the algebraic path problem. To appear in *Acta Informatica*; extended abstract in *VLSI and Computers (CompEuro 87)*, W. E. Proebster and H. Reiner (eds.), IEEE Computer Society Press, 1987, 307–310.

[4] INMOS Ltd. occam *Programming Manual*. 1984. Series in Computer Science, Prentice-Hall Int.

[5] H. T. Kung and C. E. Leiserson. Algorithms for VLSI processor arrays. In C. Mead and L. Conway, editors, *Introduction to VLSI Systems*, Addison-Wesley, 1980. Sect. 8.3.

[6] C. Lengauer. Towards systolizing compilation: an overview. In E. Odijk, M. Rem, and J.-C. Syre, editors, *Proc. Parallel Architectures and Languages Europe (PARLE '89) Vol. II: Parallel Languages*, pages 253–272, Springer-Verlag, 1989. Lecture Notes in Computer Science 366.

[7] P. Quinton. Mapping recurrences on parallel architectures. In L. P. and S. I. Kartashev, editors, *Third Int. Conf. on Supercomputing (ICS 88), Vol. III: Supercomputer Design: Hardware & Software*, pages 1–8, Int. Supercomputing Institute, Inc., 1988.

[8] Y. Robert and D. Trystram. An orthogonal systolic array for the algebraic path problem. *Computing*, 39(3):187–199, 1987.

[9] G. Rote. A systolic array algorithm for the algebraic path problem (shortest paths; matrix inversion). *Computing*, 34(3):191–219, 1985.

[10] U. Zimmermann. *Linear and Combinatorial Optimization in Ordered Algebraic Structures*. Volume 10 of *Annals of Discrete Mathematics*, North-Holland Publ. Co., 1981. Sect. 8.

Christian Lengauer ,
Department of Computer Science,
University of Edinburgh, The King's Buildings,
Mayfield Road,
Edinburgh   EH9  3JZ,
Scotland, U.K.


Duncan G. Hudson,
Department of Computer Sciences,
The University of Texas at Austin,
Taylor Hall 2.124,
Austin, Texas  78712–1188,
U.S.A.

# 31

# Coding for Channels with Localized Errors

## J. H. van Lint

## 1 Introduction

The following problem was discussed in a lecture by S. I. Gelfand in Ober-wolfach (Information Theory, May 1989), based on joint work with L. A. Bassalygo and M. S. Pinsker. We consider a binary channel and we are interested in codes of length $n$. Let $t$ be given, $0 < t < n$. Before a message is transmitted, the *sender* is given a subset $E$ of cardinality at most $t$ of the positions $\{1, 2, \ldots, n\}$ in which errors *may* occur (i.e. outside $E$ all bits are received correctly). The receiver does not know $E$, but sender and receiver have prearranged codebooks that are used for transmission and reception of $M$ possible messages. The question is to determine $F_t(n) :=$ the maximal value of $M$ for which communication over this channel with a code of length $n$ is possible. Results appeared in [2]. We shall give our own proofs of these results and we shall analyze some of the bounds. Furthermore, we discuss a variation in which the subset $E$ has cardinality $\leq t$ resp. $t$, and it is known that either all bits in $E$ are received correctly or all of them are incorrect.

More formally, Gelfand's problem can be described as follows. We have a message set $\mathcal{M} := \{1, 2, \ldots, M\}$ and a coding function $\phi : \mathcal{M} \times \mathcal{P}_t(n) \to \{0, 1\}^n$, where $\mathcal{P}_t(n)$ denotes the collection of subsets of $\{1, 2, \ldots, n\}$ of size $\leq t$. The decoding function $\psi$ is such that for all $m \in \mathcal{M}$ and all $E \in \mathcal{P}_t(n)$ and each error vector $\mathbf{e}$ that is 0 outside $E$, we have

(1.1)     $\psi\left(\phi(m, E) + \mathbf{e}\right) = m.$

The maximal value of $M$ for which such functions $\phi$ and $\psi$ exist, is $F_t(n)$.

Let $t/n = \tau$. We define the asymptotic rate $R(\tau)$ by

(1.2)     $R(\tau) := \limsup\limits_{n \to \infty} n^{-1} \log F_t(n).$

(Here the base of the logarithm is 2.)

The following theorem was announced in Oberwolfach (and proved in [2]).

**Theorem 1**    We have

(1.3)    $$\frac{1}{2n} \cdot \frac{2^n}{\sum_{i=0}^{t} \binom{n}{i}} \;\leq\; F_t(n) \;\leq\; \frac{2^n}{\sum_{i=0}^{t} \binom{n}{i}}.$$

**Corollary 1**    $R(\tau) \;=\; 1 - h(\tau).$

# 2   The case $t = 1$

The situation for $t = 1$ is quite surprising. Say that just before transmission, the sender is told that the fifth bit *may* be received in error. If the sender was *certain* that this would happen, he could simply change that bit before sending it, ensuring correct reception. So, he misses only *one* bit of information, namely whether the error will occur or not. An optimist would think that a rate of $1 - \frac{1}{n}$ might be achievable. On the other hand, the sender can be lazy and agree with the receiver to use a 1-error-correcting code. In that case he does not even have to know in which position the possible error can occur. This sounds like a stupid scheme, i.e. one expects to be able to do much better. As the right-hand side of (1.3) shows, this is *not* the case! Hamming codes are optimal for this problem. We present our own proof of this fact.

**Lemma 1**    Let $1 \leq k \leq n$. Let a subset $S$ of size $k$ of $\{1, 2, \ldots, n\}$ be given. Let $\mathbf{e}_i$ denote the error vector of weight 1 with a one in position $i$ and define

$$R_i(m) := \{\phi(m, \{i\}), \phi(m, \{i\}) + \mathbf{e}_i\},$$

(2.1)    $$R(m) := \bigcup_{i \in S} R_i(m).$$

Then for all $m$ we have $|R(m)| \geq k + 1$.

**Proof**    Let $m \in \mathcal{M}$. Note that $R(m)$ is the set of all possible received messages if $m$ is sent and the error position is restricted to $S$. For $k = 1$ the assertion is trivial. Let the assertion be true for all values of $k$ less than $l$. We prove (2.1) for $k = l$. Let $|S| = l$. Form a bipartite graph on $S \cup R(m)$ with an edge from $i$ to the two elements of $R_i(m)$. By the induction hypothesis, we know that $|R(m)| \geq l$. Assume that $|R(m)| = l$. Now, for any subset $A$ of $S$ there are at least $|A|$ vertices in $R(m)$ joined to some vertex $a \in A$. (In fact one more if $A \neq S$.) So, Hall's condition is satisfied (cf.[3]), showing that there is a *matching* from $S$ to $R(m)$. Without loss of generality, this is a matching from $i \in S$ to $\phi(m, \{i\})$. Since every vertex of $S$ has degree

2, we can form a circuit by alternating between edges $\{i, \phi(m, \{i\})\}$ and edges $\{i, \phi(m, \{i\}) + \mathbf{e}_i\}$. This implies that for some nonempty subset $A$ of $S$, we have $\sum_{i \in A} \mathbf{e}_i = \mathbf{0}$, which is absurd.
□

Clearly, the lemma shows that $F_1(n) \leq 2^n/(n+1)$, since the sets $R(m)$, $m \in \mathcal{M}$, must be disjoint.

# 3   The upper bound

We did not succeed in generalizing the idea of using Hall's theorem to prove the upper bound of Theorem 1. However, we shall give a simple proof of a generalization of Lemma 1.

**Lemma 2**   Let $P$ be any collection of error patterns and suppose that the sender knows that some error pattern from $P$ can occur and in fact is told which one, just before transmission. As in the previous section, we denote by $R(m)$ the set of all possible received messages (under these conditions) if $m$ is sent (for some code that works). Then $|R(m)| \geq |P|$.

**Proof**   Let $\phi^*(m, E)$ denote the word in $\{0, 1, *\}^n$ that we obtain from the codeword $\phi(m, E)$ for message $m$ and error pattern $E$ by replacing the entries in positions of $E$ by the symbol $*$. The possible received messages form the set $R_E(m)$ obtained by "*filling*" the $*$'s in all possible ways by 0's and 1's. The assertion of the lemma states that a set of $p$ elements of $\{0, 1, *\}^n$, such that no two of these have the same "$*$-pattern", yields a set of at least $p$ different fillings. This is obviously true if the $p$ words are from $\{0, *\}^n$, since replacing the $*$'s by 1's yields at least $p$ different words. Now suppose that we have an arbitrary collection of $p$ words from $\{0, 1, *\}^n$. We order these as follows: first those ending in 0, then those ending in $*$, and finally those ending in 1. We make a second list by replacing the final 1 in the bottom of the list by a 0. For each of these lists, we make the corresponding set of fillings, starting at the top and working our way down; any filling that has appeared earlier is of course not listed a second time. These two procedures are clearly identical until the part is reached where final 1's were replaced by 0's. If at this stage a filling of an element of the original list is rejected because it appeared earlier, then the corresponding filling of the (corresponding) element of the new list will also be rejected. (The earlier appearances are caused by elements ending in a $*$.) By repeating this procedure, we see that the trivial situation, where the symbol 1 is not used, is actually the worst case.
□

Obviously, the right-hand side of Theorem 1 is an immediate consequence of Lemma 2. This same lemma was used by Gelfand in his proof but the proof of the lemma was different (I think). The idea of replacing 1's by 0's was suggested to me by L. Tolhuizen.

# 4    The lower bound

The idea of the following proof of a result slightly stronger than the left-hand side of (1.3) is the same as the idea used in [2]. We choose an integer $x < n$ depending on $n$ (the optimal choice will be determined later). With every message $m \in \mathcal{M}$ we associate a (0,1)-matrix $A_m$ of size $x$ by $n$ with rows $\mathbf{a}_m(i)$, $1 \leq i \leq x$. Our goal is to choose these matrices in such a way that for any vector $\mathbf{e}$ of weight $t$ and any $m \in \mathcal{M}$ there is some row $\mathbf{a}_m(i)$ in $A_m$ such that

$$(4.1) \qquad d(\mathbf{a}_m(i) + \mathbf{e}, \mathbf{a}_{m'}(j)) \; > \; t,$$

for all $m' \neq m$ and all $j$. For such a pair $\mathbf{e}$, $m$, we encode $m$ as $\mathbf{c} = \mathbf{a}_m(i)$. Suppose we receive the word $\mathbf{c} + \mathbf{e}'$ (where $\mathbf{e}'$ has its 1's on a subset of those of $\mathbf{e}$). Then

$$d(\mathbf{c} + \mathbf{e}', \mathbf{c}) \; = \; \mathrm{wt}(\mathbf{e}'),$$
$$d(\mathbf{c} + \mathbf{e}', \mathbf{a}_{m'}(j)) \; > \; t - \mathrm{wt}(\mathbf{e} - \mathbf{e}') \; = \; \mathrm{wt}(\mathbf{e}'),$$

so decoding to the closest codeword yields the correct message.

To see if we can achieve our goal, we first fix $m$ and $\mathbf{e}$ and look at all possible choices for the matrices $A_{m'}$ where $m'$ runs through $\mathcal{M} \backslash \{m\}$. There are $2^{(M-1)xn}$ such choices and for *each* row $\mathbf{a}_{m'}(j)$ in one of these matrices, there are $\sum := \sum_{i=0}^{t} \binom{n}{i}$ rows $\mathbf{y}$ that would violate (4.1) if we took $\mathbf{a}_m(i) = \mathbf{y}$. This means that there are at most

$$2^{(M-1)xn} \cdot \left\{ (M-1)x \cdot \sum \right\}^x$$

choices for the $M$ matrices such that (4.1) is violated for the fixed $\mathbf{e}$ and $m$. Hence, a "good" choice is possible if

$$(4.2) \qquad 2^{Mxn} \; > \; M\binom{n}{t} \cdot 2^{(M-1)xn} \cdot \left\{ (M-1)x \sum \right\}^x.$$

If we take $M < 2^n / (y \sum)$, then (4.2) is satisfied if we have

$$(4.3) \qquad y^{x+1} \geq 2^n x^x.$$

This means that we find the best lower bound (for this approach) by taking equality in (4.3) and choosing $x = n \ln 2 - 1$, $y = (e \ln 2)n$. If we take $x = n - 1$, we find that $y = 2n$ satisfies (4.3). This proves the left-hand side of Theorem 1. We have also shown that the 2 in the denominator can be replaced by $e \ln 2$.

Note that for fixed $t$, this lower bound is of no use. For example, take $n = 2^m - 1$, $m$ large. A $t$-error-correcting BCH code has redundancy at most $mt$ but the denominator on the left-hand side of (1.3) is roughly $2^{mt+m+1}/t!$.

In Section 2 we saw that for $t = 1$, a single-error-correcting code is often the best solution. If $t = 2$ we could again ignore the information on $E$ and use a Preparata code $\mathcal{P}$ (cf. [4]). If $n = 2^m - 1$, $m$ even, then $\mathcal{P}$ has $2^n/\{\frac{1}{2}(n + 1)^2\}$ words, which is nearly the same as the upper bound in (1.3).

# 5  Variations

We now consider a problem similar to the one treated in Section 1. In the variation, we again have a set $E$ of error positions, but now all positions of $E$ are either received correctly or false. If $t = 1$ this does not change the problem, but for larger values of $t$ it does.

**Theorem 2**    Consider the problem of transmission of information with a code of length $n$ over a channel for which an error pattern of size at most 2 is communicated to the sender, prior to his transmission of a message. Then, if $n = 2^a - 1$, a Hamming code is the optimal solution to this problem.

**Proof**    Clearly, we cannot do better than a code of size $F_1(n)$, i.e. a Hamming code. Such a code works for the following reason. If the error pattern has size 1, transmit the codeword; if it has size 2, then change the first bit occurring in $E$. In the latter case, the word that reaches the receiver will have an error in the first or the second position of $E$, but not in both.
□

**Generalization**    For the case of general $t$ a possible (optimal ?) solution is obtained by using a code that can correct $\lceil t/2 \rceil$ errors.

**Proof**    Before transmission, introduce errors in the first $\lfloor t/2 \rfloor$ positions of $E$ in the codeword.
□

As a final variation consider the situation where $|E| = t$ and it is again known that all or none of the positions of $E$ will be incorrect. As before, one could use a $\lceil t/2 \rceil$-error-correcting code of length $n$ and (before transmission) introduce errors in the first $\lceil t/2 \rceil$ positions of $E$. This guarantees that the received word will contain $\lceil t/2 \rceil$ or $\lfloor t/2 \rfloor$ errors. These can be corrected. However, we then do not use the fact that less than $\lfloor t/2 \rfloor$ errors cannot occur. The following example is due to H. Kleijer et al. [1].

**Example 1**    Consider a $\lceil t/2 \rceil$-error-correcting code $C'$ of length $n - 1$ and adjoin an extra bit to each codeword in both possible ways. We thus find the code $C$ of length $n$ with $|C| = 2|C'|$. Before transmission, errors are introduced in the first $\lceil t/2 \rceil$ positions of $E$. Let $(\mathbf{c}, \epsilon)$ be the message. If the final position is in $E$ and if all positions of $E$ are received incorrectly, then the received word will be $(\mathbf{r}, \epsilon + 1)$, where $d(\mathbf{r}, \mathbf{c}) = \lfloor t/2 \rfloor - 1$. This allows the receiver to correct $\mathbf{r}$ to $\mathbf{c}$ and also to realize that the final bit has to be changed (to ensure sufficiently many received errors). If we take $n = 6$, $t = 4$, then we find a code $C$ with four words, whereas a 2-error-correcting code of length 6 cannot have more than two codewords.

Observe that this solution is best possible when $t = 2$. To see this, consider only error patterns $\mathbf{e}_i$ $(1 \le i \le n - 1)$ with an error in position $i$ and in the final position. Exactly as in Lemma 1, it follows that $M \le \frac{2^n}{n} = 2 \cdot \frac{2^{n-1}}{1+(n-1)}$. Hence, a Hamming code with an extra bit is best possible.

Several (far from trivial) problems remain to be solved for the variations and for the situation of Section 1. It would be interesting to have an example with small $n$ and $t$ for which $F_t(n)$ exceeds the size of the largest $t$-error-correcting code of length $n$.

Note added in proof: L.Tolhuizen has recently found such an example.

*Acknowledgments*: The author thanks L. Tolhuizen of Philips Research Laboratories for several fruitful discussions on this problem, and his students P. van Assche, I. Kemmelings, and H. Kleijer for producing the idea of Example 1.

## REFERENCES

[1] P. van Assche, I. Kemmelings, and H. Kleijer. *Coding with the Possible Error Positions Known by the Transmitter*. Technical Report, Eindhoven University of Technology, 1989.

[2] L. A. Bassalygo, S. I. Gelfand, and M. S. Pinsker. Coding for channels with localized errors. In *Proc. 4th joint Swedish-Soviet International Workshop on Information Theory*, Gotland, 1989.

[3] M Hall, Jr. *Combinatorial Theory*. Blaisdell Publ. Company, 1967.

[4] J. H. van Lint. *Introduction to Coding Theory*. Springer Verlag, 1982.

J. H. van Lint,
Department of Mathematics and Computing Science,
Eindhoven University of Technology,
P.O. Box 513,
5600 MB Eindhoven,
The Netherlands.

# Topology-Independent Algorithms Based on Spanning Trees

## Johan J. Lukkien
## Jan L. A. van de Snepscheut

## Abstract

We consider a class of distributed algorithms. Algorithms in this class consist of processes that communicate using a broadcast. We show that local information suffices to implement such an algorithm on an arbitrary network. We investigate the time complexity and present some experimental results.

## 1  Introduction

We consider a class of distributed algorithms characterized by the fact that all communications to be performed by the processors executing the algorithm are between one processor on the one hand and every other processor on the other hand. Either the one processor may transmit information to all other processors, often called a *broadcast*, or information from all processors may be combined into a single datum such as in the case of recursive doubling. We show how such algorithms may be executed on an arbitrary network when only local information about the structure of the network is available in each processor.

## 2  Definitions and notations

We restrict our attention to undirected, connected networks. (The algorithms presented in this paper can be extended to directed, strongly connected networks at the expense of additional notation and additional storage.) The set of processors is represented by $\{0, 1, \ldots, p - 1\}$. For fixed $r$, we consider a spanning tree of the network rooted in processor $r$. The tree is represented by array *father* as follows: for processor $i$, $i \neq r$, $father_i(r)$ is the father of processor $i$ in the tree with root $r$. Similarly, we define *sons*: for each processor $i$, $sons_i(r)$ is the set of sons of processor $i$ in the tree with root $r$. We have the following relationship:

$$j \in sons_i(r) \;=\; (j \neq r \,\wedge\, i = father_j(r)).$$

Parameter $r$ allows us to consider a number of spanning trees at the same time: one for every processor. All these trees are used in the algorithms below. The local information about the network structure stored in each processor $i$ consists of $sons_i(r)$ and $father_i(r)$, for each $r$. Hence, only part of the tables is available locally, viz. how the direct neighbours are arranged in each spanning tree. Notice that we are free to choose the spanning trees to be the ones that have shortest paths to the root. A (distributed) algorithm to compute such spanning trees can be found in [1].

Our program notation is derived from CSP ([3]) in which communication with processor $q$ is denoted by $q?$ for input and $q!$ for output. Execution of $q?x$ in processor $r$ is synchronized with execution of $r!expr$ in $q$ and implements the distributed assignment $x := expr$. We use **forall** $q \in set$ **do** $s(q)$ to denote the parallel execution of a number of statements $s(q)$, one for each value $q$ from the set.

# 3   Some examples

We give some examples to illustrate the use of the tables. Assume that processor $r$ contains a value $v$ that must be transmitted to all processors in the network. Processor $i$ has local variable $x_i$ for this purpose. In other words, the broadcast should establish $\forall(i :: x_i = v)$. For each processor $i$ the following program does the job.

> **if** $i = r$ **then** $x_i := v$ **else** $father_i(r)?x_i$;
> **forall** $j \in sons_i(r)$ **do** $j!x_i$

The correctness of the program follows by induction on the structure of the spanning tree with root $r$. For each processor $i$, the first statement assigns $v$ to $x_i$ and the second statement assigns $v$ to $x_j$ for every son $j$ of $i$.

In the second example each processor $i$ has local variable $x_i$ and the goal is to compute the maximum of all $x_i$ in processor $r$. Using variables $m_i$ and $tmp_i$ per processor $i$, the program is

> $m_i := x_i$;
> **forall** $j \in sons_i(r)$ **do**
> **begin** $j?tmp_i$; $m_i := \mathbf{max}(m_i, tmp_i)$ **end**;
> **if** $i \neq r$ **then** $father_i(r)!m_i$.

Again the correctness follows by induction. The value output by processor $i$ is the maximum of all $x_i$ in the subtree of which $i$ is the root. This maximum is computed by selecting the maximum of the local variable (first line) and the respective maxima of its subtrees (second line).

The next example concerns the multiplication of two square matrices. For the sake of simplicity, we assume that the dimension of the matrices equals $p$ (the number of processors). The problem is to compute $C = A \times B$ where $A$ and $B$ are given $p \times p$ matrices in which rows and columns are numbered 0 through $p - 1$. Initially, processor $i$ contains row $i$ of $A$ and column $i$ of $B$, denoted by $A(i, *)$ and $B(*, i)$ respectively. After the computation, processor $i$ contains row $i$ of $C$. The algorithm is described in two steps. The abstract version consists of $p$ inner product steps per processor.

$$\textbf{for } j := 0 \textbf{ to } p - 1 \textbf{ do } C(i,j) := A(i, *) \cdot B(*, j)$$

In the refined version we take into account that $B(*, j)$ is not stored in processor $i$ but in $j$. During step $j$ each processor requires a copy of column $j$ of $B$ and we insert the broadcast algorithm for distributing it. The above algorithm contains a "hidden" synchronization in the form of the shared variable $j$. We replace $j$ by a private variable $j_i$ per processor. This leads to the following algorithm.

$$\textbf{for } j_i := 0 \textbf{ to } p - 1 \textbf{ do}$$
$$\textbf{begin if } i = j_i \textbf{ then } b_i := B(*, j_i) \textbf{ else } \textit{father}_i(j_i)?b_i;$$
$$\textbf{forall } k \in \textit{sons}_i(j_i) \textbf{ do } k!b_i;$$
$$C(i, j_i) := A(i, *) \cdot b_i$$
$$\textbf{end}$$

The correctness of this matrix multiplier is not at all obvious. Because the various $j_i$'s may have different values, different processors may be engaged in the broadcasting phase using different spanning trees. In the following section we show that, nevertheless, the above algorithm is free from deadlock and computes the correct result.

Our final example concerns the transitive closure of a directed graph. Nodes in the graph are numbered 0 through $p - 1$ and the set of edges is given as a boolean matrix $B(i, j)$. The transitive closure can be computed (in situ) by Warshall's algorithm ([5]).

$$\textbf{for } k := 0 \textbf{ to } p - 1$$
$$\textbf{do for } i := 0 \textbf{ to } p - 1$$
$$\textbf{do for } j := 0 \textbf{ to } p - 1$$
$$\textbf{do } B(i, j) := B(i, j) \vee (B(i, k) \wedge B(k, j))$$

The outer loop maintains the invariant

> $B(i,j)$ = there is a path from $i$ to $j$ via nodes with a number
> smaller than $k$.

This expression is abbreviated to $B(i,j) = i \overset{k}{\to} j$. The correctness of the algorithm follows from the above invariant and from the property that for all $i$, $k \overset{k}{\to} i = k \overset{k+1}{\to} i$ and $i \overset{k}{\to} k = i \overset{k+1}{\to} k$. This property implies that it does not matter whether the "old" or the "new" values of $B(*,k)$ and $B(k,*)$ are used. This again implies that, for every $k$, the $p^2$ assignments can be done in any order or in parallel.

For the parallel algorithm, we have a similar distribution as in the previous example. Processor $i$ contains row $i$ of $B$, denoted by $B(i,*)$. The $p$ iterations of the middle repetition will be done in parallel. This yields $p$ executions of the following algorithm.

> **for** $k := 0$ **to** $p - 1$
> **do for** $j := 0$ **to** $p - 1$ **do** $B(i,j) := B(i,j) \ \lor \ (B(i,k) \ \land \ B(k,j))$

In the assignment, only $B(k,j)$ is not available on processor $i$. We insert the broadcast for establishing $b_i = B(k,*)$ for local array $b_i$ on $i$. Again we introduce local variables $k_i$ and $j_i$ for processor $i$.

> **for** $k_i := 0$ **to** $p - 1$ **do**
> **begin if** $i = k_i$ **then** $b_i := B(k_i,*)$ **else** $father_i(k_i)?b_i$;
>         **forall** $q \in sons_i(k_i)$ **do** $q!b_i$;
>         **for** $j_i := 0$ **to** $p - 1$
>         **do** $B(i,j_i) := B(i,j_i) \ \lor \ (B(i,k_i) \ \land \ b_i(j_i))$
> **end**

This algorithm has the same communication behaviour as the previous one and therefore its proof of correctness relies on the same argument.

# 4    Proof of correctness

In this section we prove the correctness of the matrix multiplication algorithm. To be correct, the assertion $b_i = B(*,j_i)$ must hold before the assignment to $C(i,j_i)$. This is the case if $j_i = i$, but if $j_i \neq i$ it must be the case that the right value was communicated to $i$ by $father_i(j_i)$, and that value is the value broadcast by the root of spanning tree $j_i$.

The code for broadcasting a value to all nodes of a spanning tree from the root of the spanning tree was already given and proved correct in section 3 (first example), and this code is what appears in the multiplication program. However, since the same code is used to broadcast values for $p$

different spanning trees, we have to show that two communicating processors work on the same spanning tree.

For processors $i$ and $k$, and for integer $j$, we define $\{i,k\}$ $\underline{\text{in}}$ $j$ as the number of times that the edge between $i$ and $k$ (if any) occurs in the spanning trees, rooted in 0 through $j-1$. Formally, for all $i, k$ and $j$ such that $0 \le i < p$, $0 \le k < p$, $0 \le j \le p$,

$$\{i,k\} \underline{\text{in}} j = \underline{N}(h : 0 \le h < j : k \in sons_i(h) \vee i \in sons_k(h)).$$

Notice that the integer $\{i,k\}$ $\underline{\text{in}}$ $j$ is an ascending function of $j$. We need one more piece of notation. For processors $i$ and $k$, $|i,k|$ is the number of completed communications between $i$ and $k$. It increases every now and then as the execution of the program proceeds.

Next, we formulate an invariant of the program. We claim that

(1)        $\{i,k\} \underline{\text{in}} j_i = |i,k|$

holds, for all $i$ and $k$, at the beginning of each iteration of the for loop. The claim holds initially because $j_i = 0$ initially, which implies $\{i,k\}$ $\underline{\text{in}}$ $j_i = 0$, and because no communications have been completed initially, which implies $|i,k| = 0$. In each iteration of the loop $j_i$ is increased by 1. Hence, for those $k$ that are neighbours of $i$ in the tree rooted in $j_i$ the left-hand side increases by 1 on account of the definition of $\underline{\text{in}}$, and the right-hand side increases by 1 because a communication between $i$ and $k$ is performed. For those $k$ that are not neighbours of $i$ in the tree rooted in $j_i$, both sides remain unchanged.

From the fact that (1) holds at the beginning of each iteration of the for loop, and from the fact that $j_i$ is incremented at the end, we conclude that $\{i,k\}$ $\underline{\text{in}}$ $j_i \le |i,k|$ holds at any moment. By symmetry, it follows that $\{i,k\}$ $\underline{\text{in}}$ $j_k \le |i,k|$ holds. From the invariant and from the definition of $\underline{\text{in}}$ we also derive that, in processor $i$, the precondition of a communication with $k$ is:

$j_i$ is the maximum value of $j$ for which $\{i,k\}$ $\underline{\text{in}}$ $j = |i,k|$.

Together with our observation that

$j_k$ is a value of $j$ for which $\{i,k\}$ $\underline{\text{in}}$ $j \le |i,k|$

the monotonicity of $\underline{\text{in}}$ in $j$ implies that $j_i \ge j_k$ as a precondition of a communication with $k$. This property is the quintessence of the correctness argument.

Since $j_i \ge j_k$ holds in $i$ as a precondition of the communication between $i$ and $k$, and $j_k \ge j_i$ holds as a precondition of the same communication in $k$, $j_i = j_k$ holds when the communication is performed. This implies that $i$ and $k$ are involved in a broadcast on one and the same spanning tree, an algorithm of which we have indicated the correctness before. As a result, the correctness of the matrix multiplication algorithm follows.

We show that no deadlock occurs. If deadlock occurs during execution of a program then a cycle of waiting processors exists: $i$ is suspended on a communication with $k$, $k$ on another one, etc., and a certain processor on $i$. Since $j_i \geq j_k$ if $i$ waits on $k$, it follows that all processors in the cycle have the same value for their respective $j$'s, which implies that all edges in the cycle are from the same spanning tree: a contradiction. Hence, no deadlock occurs.

# 5   Time complexity

We investigate the time complexity of the broadcast as used for instance in the matrix multiplier of section 3. We choose a very simple example: assume that processor $r$ contains an array $v$ of size $k$. We repeat the program from section 3 for a broadcast that establishes $\forall(i :: b_i = v)$ for local array $b_i$ on processor $i$.

> **if** $i = r$ **then** $b_i := v$ **else** $father_i(r)?b_i$;
> **forall** $j \in sons_i(r)$ **do** $j!b_i$

The time required to finish the broadcast is denoted by $t(k)$ i.e. the time that elapses between initiation of the program by root $r$ and its completion by all processors. We are interested in upper- and lowerbounds for $t(k)$.

In order to give an accurate estimate for $t(k)$ we need to formalize some characteristics of the network. The time required to communicate one item (element of the array) along one edge is denoted by $c$. The **forall** construct starts the parallel execution of several statements. There is a penalty to be paid for such a construct since there will be some memory management and process management associated with it and, possibly, physical i/o has to be started. We denote the time required for this by $s$ (notice that in general $s$ will depend on the number of statements that is started by **forall**). There is a third parameter, $d$, the maximum depth of any spanning tree. In the case of shortest path spanning trees, $d$ is bounded by the diameter of the network.

A lowerbound for $t(k)$ can be derived from the program text. If $d > 1$, at least one processor performs $k$ inputs and $k$ outputs. (There are possibly more outputs but since they are performed in parallel only one counts.) The startup time $s$ only counts for the output. An upperbound for $t(k)$ can be found by looking at a leaf in the tree. The distance to the root is at most $d$. Only after having received the entire message, a process communicates the message to its sons in the tree. Communicating the entire message to a neighbour in the tree takes $s + k \cdot c$ time units. This gives the following formula

(2)        $s + 2 \cdot k \cdot c \leq t(k) \leq d \cdot (s + k \cdot c).$

This scheme corresponds to store-and-forward routing as described for instance in [4].

There is another way to perform the same broadcast. Instead of communicating the entire message to a neighbour, a processor can receive one item, forward it, receive the next and so on. This corresponds to "wormhole" routing ([2]). The program text for this way of message transmission is given by the following fragment.

> **for** $j_i := 0$ **to** $k - 1$ **do**
> **begin if** $i = r$ **then** $b_i(j_i) := v(j_i)$ **else** $father_i(r)?b_i(j_i)$;
>         **forall** $q \in sons_i(r)$ **do** $q!b_i(j_i)$
> **end**

Again we derive a lowerbound from the program text. If $d > 2$ at least one processor must both receive and transmit the array. This takes $k \cdot (c + s + c)$ time units. Again an upperbound can be found by looking at a leaf in the tree. For a leaf with distance $d$ to the root the input of the first item completes after $d \cdot (s + c)$ units. The transmission of the next $k - 1$ elements takes $(k - 1) \cdot (s + 2 \cdot c)$ units, which is the iteration time of the predecessor of this leaf. In order to avoid confusion we denote the time required for wormhole routing by $w(k)$. This gives us the formula

(3)        $k \cdot (s + 2 \cdot c) \leq w(k) \leq d \cdot (s + c) + (k - 1) \cdot (s + 2 \cdot c).$

Notice that in this case the difference between the upperbound and the lowerbound is small (it does not depend on $k$). Notice also that it can be done more efficiently by performing the output of one item in parallel with the input of the next. This would drop the factor 2 in (3). However, if no routing hardware is available, $s$ is most likely to dominate $c$.

The upperbounds in the above two formulae give the time to finish the entire operation. For (3) this will be a good prediction but for (2) not necessarily. In store-and-forward routing only neighbouring processors have to synchronize. An algorithm that uses a broadcast a number of times might therefore perform better if this way of routing is applied, even if $d$ is large.

We have done some experiments to demonstrate this point. We have run the matrix mutiplier on a ring network of 17 INMOS Transputers. The constants $s$ and $c$ have been measured. For $s$, it was not possible to measure an accurate value because it strongly depends on the current state of the machine (e.g. the amount of available memory).

$c = 2.25 \cdot 10^{-6}$ sec.
$5.0 \cdot 10^{-5} \leq s \leq 1.0 \cdot 10^{-4}$ sec.
$d = 8$

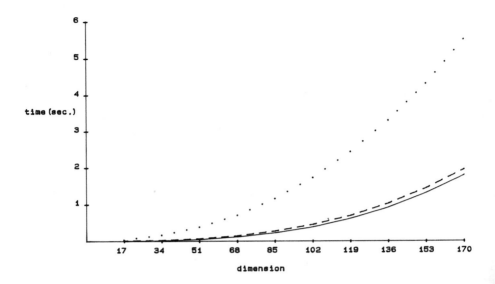

FIGURE 1. Results of experiments.

The matrix multiplier has been run with and without communications for varying dimensions of the matrix. The results are given in figure 1. The solid line in this figure is the computation time without any communications. The dashed line gives the time required for performing the computation with store-and-forward routing and the dotted line represents the time required for the computation using wormhole routing. The communication time for store-and-forward routing equals the lowerbound of (2). The performance of wormhole routing is rather bad due to the high value of $s$. This routing technique in fact requires dedicated hardware to reduce $s$ drastically, in which case it performs much better ([2]).

# 6   Discussion

The method described in this paper is applicable to a relatively small class of algorithms. But for this class it is efficient since information is routed through the network using shortest paths and each edge will contain a certain message at most once. If point-to-point routing is used, information transmitted from one processor to every other processor is duplicated from the start ($p - 1$ copies will be transmitted).

All the information about the topology is contained in the tables. The algorithms presented here do not depend on the topology anymore.

As VLSI technology progresses, it will be possible to have several processors on one chip. The connections among these processsors will be much faster than connections with processors on another chip. The method presented here offers the possibility to use these fast edges by weighting the edges when the shortest path tables are computed.

The experimental results show that the time complexity of the method is not always worst case. If used in a regular way, it may be a good choice to apply a broadcast.

## REFERENCES

[1] K. M. Chandy and J. Misra. Distributed computations on graphs: Shortest path algorithms. *Comm. ACM*, 25(11), 1982.

[2] W. J. Dally and C. L. Seitz. *Deadlock Free Message Routing in Multiprocessor Interconnections Networks*. Technical Report 5206:TR:86, Dept. Comp. Science, California Institute of Technology, 1986.

[3] C. A. R. Hoare. Communicating sequential processes. *Comm. ACM*, 21(8):666–677, 1978.

[4] L. Kleinrock. *Queuing Systems*. Volume 2, Wiley, New York, 1976.

[5] S. Warshall. A theorem on Boolean matrices. *Journal of the ACM*, 1–2, 1962.

Johan J. Lukkien,
Department of Computer Science,
California Institute of Technology,
Pasadena, CA  91125,
U.S.A.


Jan L.A. van de Snepscheut,
Department of Computer Science,
California Institute of Technology,
Pasadena, CA  91125,
U.S.A.

# 33

# An Exercise in the Verification of Multi-Process Programs[1]

## Zohar Manna
## Amir Pnueli

## Abstract

We present an approach to the verification of a multi-process program consisting of a fixed but unbounded number of processes executing an identical program. The approach is illustrated on an algorithm for mutual exclusion that contains tests that refer to many shared variables at the same time. We analyze the algorithm first under the assumption that these tests are *atomic*. We then consider the more realistic assumption that they are *molecular*, i.e. performed by several steps, each reading a single shared variable. We show that the algorithm is correct only for the limited implementation in which the variables are checked in ascending order of indices.

## 1 Introduction

Many concurrent programs consist of a set of processes that execute an identical program (which may refer to the process identifier as a parameter). A challenging problem is to provide methods for the *uniform* verification of such a system, i.e. proving correctness for *any* number of processes.

We present an approach for such uniform verification and illustrate it on a new algorithm for mutual exclusion ([5]). We analyze the algorithm first under the assumption that tests that refer to many shared variables are *atomic*, i.e. all variables are checked in a single step. We then consider the

[1]This research was supported in part by the National Science Foundation under grant CCR-8812595, by the Defense Advanced Research Projects Agency under contract N00039-84-C-0211, by the United States Air Force Office of Scientific Research under contracts AFOSR 87-0149 and 88-0281, and by the European Community ESPRIT Basic Research Action project 3096 (SPEC).

more realistic assumption that these tests are *molecular* (see [4]), i.e. performed by several steps, each reading a single shared variable. We show that the algorithm is correct only for the limited implementation in which the variables are checked in ascending order of indices and present a counter-example for more general implementations of molecular tests.

We examine only the *safety* property of *mutual exclusion*. The more complete paper ([3]) considers other non-safety properties, such as *accessibility* and *precedence*.

The paper contains no new theoretical results. Rather, it recommends the adoption of a set notation for expressing the control state of a system with an unbounded, and even dynamic, set of processes, within the framework of old and tried proof methods, such as [1,2] (see also [4] where this set notation has been introduced for the analysis of probabilistic algorithms).

The algorithm we have chosen to verify is an ideal example for demonstrating the acute need for formal verification of concurrent programs, as well as the style and level of verification that is currently possible. We refer the reader to [5] for some of its important features, such as using single-writer bounded shared variables and enjoying the property of *linear* delay (which we verify in [3] as a precedence property). These features make this algorithm a significant improvement over most of its predecessors.

Although the algorithm appears to be quite simple and innocuous, the only way we could convince ourselves of its correctness was to construct the formal proof outlined in this paper. Szymanski presented an informal proof, which is as convincing as informal proofs can be. In fact, our formal proof derives its main ideas from a formalization of his informal arguments. However, if the question of correctness is crucial, such as having to decide whether to include this algorithm as a contention-resolving component in a hardware chip, we see no way but to carry out a formal verification.

We have learned two lessons from carrying out this verification exercise. The less encouraging lesson is that it requires a non-negligible deal of creativity and dexterity in manipulating logical formulae to come up with the appropriate set of auxiliary assertions (and other constructs needed for the proof). This is so even if the correct intuition is given and all that is required is to formalize that intuition. The more encouraging lesson is that, once the appropriate constructs have been found, the rest of the verification process, which requires the construction of the verification conditions (proof obligations) and proving their validity, can to a large extent be automated. It is not that we have come up with a surprisingly new automatic theorem prover. But inspection of the kinds of assertions generated for a proof of an algorithm like the one we study here convinced us that for a large and interesting class of algorithms all these assertions belong to a decidable class.

We feel specially privileged to be able to present this paper in a volume dedicated to E. W. Dijkstra. We find it particularly apt since most of the basic concepts that underly the proof approach suggested here can be traced to his foundational studies of concurrency and verification.

## 2  Programs and computations

Our computational model is a *transition system*. In it, a program $P$ consists of the following components.

- $V = \{u_0, \ldots, u_{n-1}\}$ — A finite set of *state variables*. Some variables represent *data* variables, which are explicitly manipulated by the program text. Others are *control* variables, which represent, for example, the location of control in each of the processes in a concurrent program. Each variable is associated with a domain over which it ranges.
- $\Sigma$ — A set of *states*. Each state $s \in \Sigma$ is an interpretation of $V$, assigning to each variable $y \in V$ a value over its domain, which we denote by $s[y]$.
- $\mathcal{T}$ — A finite set of *transitions*. Each transition $\tau \in \mathcal{T}$ is associated with an assertion $\rho_\tau(V, V')$, called the *transition relation*, which refers to both an unprimed and a primed version of the state variables. The purpose of $\rho_\tau$ is to express the relation between a state $s$ and its successor $s'$ under $\tau$. The unprimed version refers to values in $s$; the primed version to values in $s'$. For example, the assertion $x' = x + 1$ states that $s'[x]$ is greater by 1 than $s[x]$.
- $\Theta$ — The *precondition*. This is an assertion characterizing all the initial states. A state is defined to be *initial* if it satisfies $\Theta$.

We define state $s'$ to be a $\tau$-*successor* of state $s$ if

$$\langle s, s' \rangle \models \rho_\tau(V, V'),$$

where $\langle s, s' \rangle$ is the joint interpretation that interprets $x \in V$ as $s[x]$ and $x'$ as $s'[x]$.

A state $s$ is *terminal* if it has no $\tau$-successor for any $\tau \in \mathcal{T}$.

We define a *computation* of a program $P$ to be any finite or infinite sequence of states

$$\sigma : s_0, s_1, s_2, \ldots,$$

satisfying:

- *Initiality*    $s_0$ is initial, i.e. $s_0 \models \Theta$.
- *Consecution*   For each $j = 0, 1, \ldots$, state $s_{j+1}$ is a $\tau$-successor of state $s_j$, for some $\tau \in \mathcal{T}$.

- *Termination*  Either $\sigma$ is infinite or it ends in a terminal state $s_k$.

We denote by $Comp(P)$ the set of all computations of program $P$. We say that a state $s$ is *P-accessible* if it appears in some computation of $P$. Clearly, any $\tau$-successor of a $P$-accessible state is also $P$-accessible.

We assume an underlying assertional language, which contains the predicate calculus, and interpreted symbols for expressing the standard operations and relations over some concrete domains. We refer to a formula in the assertional language as an *assertion*. For an assertion $p$ and a state $s$ such that $p$ holds on $s$, we say that $s$ is a *p-state*.

# 3  The program as a transition system

The program we wish to study can be given as

$$\text{MUTEX} :: flag: \textbf{array}[0 .. n-1] \textbf{ of } 0..4 \textbf{ where } flag := 0;$$
$$P[0] \parallel P[1] \parallel \ldots \parallel P[n-1]$$

Each process $P[i]$ is given by:

> $l_0$ : **loop forever do**
> **begin**
> > $l_1$ : Non Critical
> > $l_2$ : $flag[i] := 1$
> > $l_3$ : **wait until** $\forall j : 0 \le j < n : (flag[j] < 3)$
> > $l_4$ : $flag[i] := 3$
> > $l_5$ : **if** $\exists j : 0 \le j < n : (flag[j] = 1)$ **then**
> > > **begin**
> > > > $l_6$: $flag[i] := 2$
> > > > $l_7$: **wait until** $\exists j : 0 \le j < n : (flag[j] = 4)$
> > > **end**
> > $l_8$ : $flag[i] := 4$
> > $l_9$ : **wait until** $\forall j : 0 \le j < i : (flag[j] < 2)$
> > $l_{10}$: Critical
> > $l_{11}$: **wait until** $\forall j : i < j < n : (flag[j] < 2 \ \lor \ flag[j] > 3)$
> > $l_{12}$: $flag[i] := 0$
> **end**

Viewing the program as a transition system requires the identification of the following four components:

- $V$ — The state variables, are

$$L_0, \ldots L_{12}, \quad flag[0], \ldots, flag[n-1].$$

$L_0, \ldots, L_{12}$, are control variables that range over subsets of $\{0, \ldots, n-1\}$. At any state of the computation, $L_k$ contains the indices of the processes that currently are ready to execute the statement labeled $l_k$. Variables $flag[0], \ldots, flag[n-1]$ naturally represent the current values of the corresponding program variables.

- $\Sigma$ — The states, consist of all the possible assignments to the state variables of values in their respective domains.

- $\Theta$ — The precondition is given by the assertion

$$\Theta : \quad (L_0 = \{0, \ldots, n-1\}) \wedge (L_{1..12} = \phi) \wedge \bigwedge_{i=0}^{n-1} (flag[i] = 0)$$

Thus, at the initial state of the program, all processes reside at the location $l_0$, and $flag[0], \ldots, flag[n-1]$ are zero.

We introduce the following abbreviations and notations:

$$move(i, k, m) : \quad (L'_k = L_k - \{i\}) \wedge (L'_m = L_m \cup \{i\})$$

$$stay \qquad\qquad : \quad \bigwedge_{k=0}^{12} (L'_k = L_k)$$

Clearly, $move(i, k, m)$ describes the movement of control within process $P[i]$ from $l_k$ to $l_m$, while $stay$ describes the case that control does not move in any of the processes.

$$
\begin{aligned}
L_{i_1, i_2, \ldots, i_m} &= L_{i_1} \cup L_{i_2} \cup \ldots \cup L_{i_m} \\
F_{i_1, i_2, \ldots, i_m} &= F_{i_1} \cup F_{i_2} \cup \ldots \cup F_{i_m} \\
F_k &= \{i : 0 \le i < n : flag[i] = k\} \\
N_i &= |L_i| \\
L_{i..k} &= L_i \cup L_{i+1} \cup \ldots \cup L_k \qquad\qquad \text{for } i < k \\
F_{i..k} &= F_i \cup F_{i+1} \cup \ldots \cup F_k \qquad\qquad \text{for } i < k
\end{aligned}
$$

## THE TRANSITIONS

Our first analysis of algorithm MUTEX treats all tests (e.g. the one in statement $l_3$) as *atomic*: each is performed by a single transition. Consequently, we have for each process $P[i]$ and each location $l_k$ a transition $\tau_k[i]$ and a corresponding transition relation $\rho_k[i]$.

We present below the two transitions corresponding to locations $l_1$ and $l_5$; for the full set of transitions, see [3].

The transition relation for $l_1$ is given by

$$\rho_1[i] : \quad (i \in L_1) \wedge \left( stay \vee move(i, 1, 2) \right)$$

According to this formula, process $P[i]$ may choose non-deterministically to remain at $l_1$ or to move from $l_1$ to $l_2$.

The transition relation for $l_5$ is given by

$$\rho_5[i] : (i \in L_5) \wedge \Big( [(F_1 \neq \phi) \wedge move(i,5,6)] \vee [(F_1 = \phi) \wedge move(i,5,8)] \Big)$$

When at $l_5$, $P[i]$ may proceed to $l_6$ if some process $P[j]$ has $flag[j] = 1$ and therefore $F_1 \neq \phi$. It may proceed to $l_8$ if no process has its $flag$ equal to 1, and hence $F_1 = \phi$.

# 4  Invariance properties

Assertion $p$ is *valid over program* $P$ (also described as being *P-valid*) written as $P \models p$, if $p$ holds over all the $P$-accessible states. Clearly, if $p$ is $P$-valid it is an *invariant* property of $P$: it holds over all the states that arise in any computation of the program $P$.

In this section we present a single proof rule that is adequate for proving the invariance of an assertion $p$ over a program $P$, i.e. proving $P \models p$.

We will illustrate this rule by proving the main safety property of program MUTEX, mutual exclusion. This property can be expressed by the assertion $N_{10} \leq 1$, which limits the number of processes that can be concurrently executing at $l_{10}$. Thus, we have to prove

MUTEX $\models (N_{10} \leq 1)$

Since most of our reasoning is done within the $P$-validity framework, we omit the prefix $P \models$ and simply write $p$ to mean $P \models p$.

The following rule INV is the main working tool for establishing invariance properties. It uses the notation $p'$ to refer to the *primed version* of assertion $p$, which is obtained from $p$ by replacing each variable $x \in V$ occurring in $p$ by its primed version $x'$.

$$
\begin{array}{ll}
\text{INV} & \text{I1.} \quad \Theta \;\rightarrow\; p \\
& \text{I2.} \quad (p \wedge \rho_\tau) \;\rightarrow\; p' \quad \text{for every } \tau \in \mathcal{T} \\
\hline
& \qquad P \models p
\end{array}
$$

By premise I1 of rule INV, $p$ holds initially, and by premise I2 it is propagated from each state to its successor. Hence, $p$ is an invariant of the program.

**Example 4.1**   Consider the trivial transition system $P$ defined as follows. There is one state variable, $x$. There is one transition $\tau$, whose transition relation is $\rho_\tau : (x' = x + 2)$. The precondition is $\Theta : (x = 0)$. Transition system $P$ has the single (infinite) computation $\langle x : 0 \rangle, \langle x : 2 \rangle, \langle x : 4 \rangle, \ldots$.

We wish to prove for this program the invariant

$$even(x),$$

claiming that all the values of $x$ are even. To prove this property, we use rule **INV** with $p : even(x)$. The rule requires showing the validity of the following two premises

> I1.  $(x = 0) \rightarrow (even(x))$
>
> I3.  $\big((even(x)) \wedge (x' = x + 2)\big) \rightarrow (even(x'))$

Clearly these premises are valid, which establishes the invariance of $even(x)$.

## SIMPLE INVARIANTS FOR MUTEX

We now establish invariants for **MUTEX**, which together will yield our desired result. First, we establish invariants that connect for each $i$ the location of $P[i]$ with $flag[i]$. These invariants can be expressed as relations between $F_k$ and $L_r$ for various values of $k$ and $r$.

| | | | | | | |
|---|---|---|---|---|---|---|
| IF0. | $F_0$ | $=$ | $L_{0..2}$ | IF3. | $F_3$ | $\subseteq L_{5,6,8}$ |
| IF1. | $F_1$ | $=$ | $L_{3,4}$ | IF4. | $F_4$ | $= L_{9..12}$ |
| IF2. | $F_2$ | $\subseteq$ | $L_{7,8}$ | IL8. | $F_{2,3}$ | $\supseteq L_8$ |

Invariants IF0, ..., IF4 restrict the locations at which $P[i]$ can reside when $flag[i]$ is $0, \ldots, 4$. For example, invariant IF4 claims that $flag[i]$ is 4 *iff* $P[i]$ is at one of $l_9, \ldots, l_{12}$. Invariant IL8 claims that,, when $P[i]$ is at $l_8$, $flag[i]$ is 2 or 3. This is the only location for which $flag[i]$ is not uniquely determined.

## PROVING MUTUAL EXCLUSION

Having prepared the machinery for proving invariance properties, we proceed to establish the main invariance property of **MUTEX**, mutual exclusion.

We refer the reader to [5] for a detailed explanation of the basic ideas of **MUTEX**. Here we extract just the main observations. The tortuous path a process has to follow on its way from the non-critical section at $l_1$ to the critical section at $l_{10}$ can be broken into different segments. We refer to location $l_4$ as the *doorway*, to segment $l_{5..7}$ as the *waiting room*, and to segment $l_{8..12}$, which contains the critical section, as the *inner sanctum*.

The basic claims on which mutual exclusion is based are the following:

> C1.  Whenever a process enters an empty inner sanctum, the doorway is locked, i.e. $L_4 = \phi$. The doorway remains locked until the last process leaves the inner sanctum. While this property is expressed as evolution in time, it certainly implies the invariant
>
> $$A_0 : \quad L_{8..12} \neq \phi \rightarrow L_4 = \phi,$$

which claims that if $L_{8..12}$ is non-empty then $L_4$ is empty. If this is indeed an invariant, then the non-emptiness of $L_{8..12}$ should prevent any new processes coming to $l_3$ to cross over into $l_4$. The only thing that can prevent them from crossing over is if $flag[j]$ of some process equals 3 or 4. Thus, we must also have

$$A_1 : \quad L_{8..12} \neq \phi \quad \rightarrow \quad L_{8..12} \cap F_{3,4} \neq \phi.$$

Note that we require that one of the processes in $l_{8..12}$ has a flag value of 3 or 4. This is because a flag value of 3 held by a process at $l_{5,6}$ is unstable in the sense that it may very soon change to 2 again, by the statement at $l_6$.

C2. If a process $i$ is at $l_{10..12}$, then it has the least index of all the processes in $l_{5..12}$. This is expressed by the invariant

$$A_2 : \quad (k < i \ \wedge \ i \in L_{10..12}) \quad \rightarrow \quad k \notin L_{5..12}.$$

C3. If some process is at $l_{12}$, then all the processes in $l_{5..12}$ must have a flag value of 4. This is expressed by the invariant

$$A_3 : \quad (i \in L_{12} \ \wedge \ k \in L_{5..12}) \quad \rightarrow \quad k \in F_4.$$

Thus, as soon as a process enters the inner sanctum the doorway gets locked. This leaves the processes in the waiting room and the inner sanctum isolated from the rest of the processes and lets them compete on the entry to the critical section. By claim C2, only one process at a time can reside in region $l_{10..12}$, which includes the critical section, the process whose index is minimal among all the processes in $l_{5..12}$. It follows from C1–C3 that mutual exclusion is maintained.

Taking the four assertions together, we obtain the conjunction

$$p_0 : \quad A_0 \ \wedge \ A_1 \ \wedge \ A_2 \ \wedge \ A_3$$

which can be shown to be an invariant, from which by $A_2$ mutual exclusion follows immediately.

## 5  The molecular case

The assumption that compound tests are atomic is not realistic, and we now consider such tests to be *molecular*. To model the most general form of a molecular test, we introduce additional state variables $C_0, \ldots, C_{n-1}$. In each state, variable $C_i$ contains the set of all indices $j$ that have already been checked by process $P[i]$. We illustrate this by considering two transition relations.

$$\rho_2[i] : \quad i \in L_2 \ \wedge \ move(i, 2, 3) \ \wedge \ flag'[i] = 1 \ \wedge \ C_i' = \phi$$

This relation shows that one of the actions performed by transition $\tau_3[i]$ is to reset the *already checked* variable $C_i$ to $\phi$, preparing for the test at $l_3$.

$$\rho_3[i,j] \ : \ (i \in L_3) \ \wedge \ \begin{pmatrix} [|C_i| = n \ \wedge \ move(i,3,4)] \\ \vee \\ [j \notin C_i \ \wedge \ flag(j) < 3 \ \wedge \ stay \ \wedge \ C'_i = C_i \cup \{j\}] \\ \vee \\ [j \notin C_i \ \wedge \ flag(j) \geq 3 \ \wedge \ stay \ \wedge \ C'_i \subseteq C_i] \end{pmatrix}$$

The transition relation for the molecular test at $l_3$ consists of three options, represented by three clauses. The first clause covers the case that $|C_i| = n$, which implies that all indices have been checked and we may proceed from $l_3$ to $l_4$. The second clause identifies an index $j$ that satisfies $flag(j) < 3$ and that is not yet in $C_i$. This index is added to $C_i$. The last clause detects an unchecked index $j$, which does not satisfy $flag(j) < 3$. Here we allow an arbitrary change of $C_i$ as long as it does not increase. At the two extremes, this allows both for the implementation in which $C_i$ is emptied whenever we find a bad index $j$, and the implementation that ignores bad indices and retains $C_i$ at its current value.

## A COUNTER-EXAMPLE

It would have been nice to extend our proof for the atomic case to a proof for the molecular case, allowing the most general implementations of molecular tests, as presented above. Unfortunately, this is not possible. The following counter example considers a program with three processes and traces their general progress until they reach a state in which $P[0]$ and $P[2]$ execute their respective critical sections at the same time, violating mutual exclusion.

The offending computation is presented in the following table, which lists some intermediate states that occur in the computation until the violating state is reached. For each presented state we list, from left to right, the location of $P[0]$, $flag[0]$, $C_0$, the location of $P[1]$, $flag[1]$, the location of $P[2]$, and $flag[2]$. Note that, while at $l_3$, process $P[0]$ checks the indices $2, 1, 0$ in *descending* order.

# 6    Restricted implementation of molecular tests

The remedy to the problem encountered above is to restrict the implementation of molecular tests. In particular, we should not allow the selection of the next index to be checked to be completely arbitrary.

Consider a typical situation, in which some process $P[k]$ is currently at $l_3$ attempting to proceed to $l_4$. Assume also that it is blocked at $l_3$ by process $P[r]$, which is currently in the inner sanctum with $flag[r] = 4$. This means that that index $j = r$ has not been checked yet by $P[k]$, and will

| $0 \in$ | $flag[0]$ | $C_0$ | $1 \in$ | $flag[1]$ | $2 \in$ | $flag[2]$ |
|---|---|---|---|---|---|---|
| $L_0$ | 0 | $\{\}$ | $L_0$ | 0 | $L_0$ | 0 |
| $L_2$ | · | · | $L_3$ | 1 | $L_3$ | 1 |
| · | · | · | $L_4$ | · | $L_4$ | · |
| · | · | · | · | · | $L_5$ | 3 |
| · | · | · | · | · | $L_7$ | 2 |
| · | · | · | $L_5$ | 3 | · | · |
| · | · | · | $L_9$ | 4 | · | · |
| · | · | · | $L_{11}$ | · | · | · |
| $L_3$ | 1 | · | · | · | · | · |
| · | · | $\{2\}$ | · | · | · | · |
| · | · | · | · | · | $L_9$ | 4 |
| · | · | · | $L_{12}$ | · | · | · |
| · | · | · | $L_0$ | 0 | · | · |
| · | · | · | · | · | $L_{10}$ | · |
| · | · | $\{2,1\}$ | · | · | · | · |
| · | · | $\{2,1,0\}$ | · | · | · | · |
| $L_4$ | · | · | · | · | · | · |
| $L_9$ | 4 | · | · | · | · | · |
| $L_{10}$ | · | · | · | · | $L_{10}$ | · |

not be successfully checked as long as $flag[r] = 4$. Eventually, $P[r]$ will want to depart from the inner sanctum at $l_{12}$. Assume that $P[r]$ is not the last process in the inner sanctum. It is essential to ensure that when $P[r]$ departs from the inner sanctum, another process in the inner sanctum will continue to block $P[k]$. According to claim C2, processes depart from the inner sanctum in order of increasing indices. According to C3, if $P[r]$ is not the last process to depart, then all the processes remaining in the inner sanctum must have their $flag$ equal to 4, and as observed before, must have an index higher than $r$. It follows that, if we take care that $P[k]$ at $l_3$ examines the indices in *ascending order*, then if $P[k]$ is blocked by $r$ it has not successfully checked any index higher than $r$. Consequently, when $r$ departs and leaves behind some other process, with index $t > r$, $t$ can serve as a replacement for $r$, continuing to block $k$.

Motivated by this argument, we restrict the implementation of molecular tests to examines $flag[j]$ in order of increasing $j$. To do so, we replace state variables $C_0, \ldots, C_{n-1}$, by the simpler integer variables $j_0, \ldots, j_{n-1}$. In each state, $j_i$ contains the least value of $j$ that has not yet been successfully tested by $P[i]$. The two transition relations below illustrate how the variables are manipulated by the molecular tests.

$$\rho_2[i] : \quad i \in L_2 \ \wedge \ move(i,2,3) \ \wedge \ flag'[i] = 1 \ \wedge \ j_i' = 0$$

This relation shows that on moving to $l_3$, the transition $\tau_3[i]$ resets $j_i$ to 0.

$$\rho_3[i] : \quad i \in L_3 \;\wedge\; \left( \begin{array}{c} \big[j_i = n \;\wedge\; move(i,3,4)\big] \\ \vee \\ \big[j_i < n \;\wedge\; flag(j_i) < 3 \;\wedge\; stay \;\wedge\; j_i' = j_i + 1\big] \\ \vee \\ \big[j_i < n \;\wedge\; flag(j_i) \geq 3 \;\wedge\; stay \;\wedge\; j_i' \leq j_i\big] \end{array} \right)$$

As before, this relation consists of three clauses, corresponding to: completion of the test, advancement when detecting a good next index, and retreat when detecting a bad next index. Again, the retreat is general enough to allow both restarting from $j_i = 0$ and keeping $j_i$ at its current value.

## RE-PROVING MUTUAL EXCLUSION

It is helpful to derive the assertions for the molecular case as refinments of the assertions for the atomic case. Consider any region of consecutive locations that is mentioned in one of the assertions $A_0, \ldots, A_3$ and that is preceded by a compound test. For example, $l_{10..12}$ is such a region. Assertion $A_2$ states that if $k < i$ and $i$ belongs to $L_{10..12}$, then $k$ cannot be in $L_{5..12}$. In the atomic case, one of the considerations used in proving this assertions is that $P[i]$ cannot pass the atomic test at $l_9$ if $k < i$ is anywhere at $l_{5..12}$. This is because, by the simple invariants connecting flag values to locations, that would have implied $flag[k] \geq 2$.

In the molecular case, the test at $l_9$ is not passed in one step. Process $P[i]$ may reside at $l_9$ for several steps, checking the values of $flag[j_i]$ for many values of $j_i$. The important question concerning $k$ is whether $P[i]$ has already tested the value of $flag[k]$. This can be observed by checking whether $j_i > k$. If so, then $flag[k]$ has already been tested and found satisfactory, i.e. less than 2.

Consequently, to adapt assertion $A_2$ to the molecular case, we should replace the simple region reference $i \in L_{10..12}$ by the extended reference $i \in L_{10..12} \;\vee\; (i \in L_9 \;\wedge\; j_i > k)$. By applying such range extensions to assertions $A_0, A_2$, and $A_3$, we obtain the following assertions:

$B_0 :$    $(i \in L_5 \;\wedge\; j_i > k) \;\;\rightarrow\;\; \neg[k \in L_4 \;\vee\; (k \in L_3 \;\wedge\; j_k > i)]$

$B_1 :$    $i \in L_{8..12} \;\;\rightarrow\;\; \exists r : \;\; (r \in L_{8..12} \cap F_{3,4})$

                     $: \;\; \neg[k \in L_4 \;\vee\; (k \in L_3 \;\wedge\; j_k > r)]$

$B_2 :$    $[(k < i) \;\wedge\; (i \in L_{10..12} \;\vee\; (i \in L_9 \;\wedge\; j_i > k))] \;\;\rightarrow\;\; k \notin L_{5..12}$

$B_3 :$    $[(i \in L_{12} \;\vee\; (i \in L_{11} \;\wedge\; j_i > k)) \;\wedge\; (k \in L_{5..12})] \;\;\rightarrow\;\; k \in F_4$

Assertions $B_0$ and $B_1$ refine assertions $A_0$ and $A_1$ to the molecular case.

The basic idea is to show for any $k$ that if $P[i]$ is at $l_{8..12}$ or $l_5$ with $j_i > k$, i.e. having already checked $flag[k]$, then $P[k]$ cannot be at $l_4$, and if it is at $l_3$, then it's $j_k$ value is below some $r$ that blocks it from proceeding into $l_4$, by having $flag[r] > 2$. If $P[i]$ is at $l_5$, we can take $r$ to be $i$ itself. If $P[i]$ is at $l_{8..12}$, we can only claim the existence of some blocking $r$, such that $P[r]$ is also at $l_{8..12}$ and $flag[r] > 2$.

We form now the conjunction

$$\varphi : \quad B_0 \land B_1 \land B_2 \land B_3$$

and claim that it is an invariant of MUTEX. It is beyond the scope of this paper to consider all the transitions and show that each preserves $\varphi$. We will, however, consider some of the more interesting cases.

Consider what transitions may affect the assertion $B_1$. A critical transition of $P[i]$ is one that moves from $l_5$ to $l_8$. However, due to $B_0$, the right hand side of the implication of $B_1$ will hold after the transition with $r = i$ and $flag[i] = 3$. A critical transition of $k$ would have been one that increases $j_k$ beyond $r$. However, due to $flag[r] > 2$, such a transition is disabled.

Lastly, we consider the transition of $P[r]$ from $l_{12}$ to $l_0$, while resetting its $flag$ to 0. There are two possibilities. If $r$ is the last process in $l_{8..12}$, then after the transition $L_{8..12}$ will become empty, causing $B_1$ to hold trivially. If $r$ is not the last, there is another process, say $P[t]$, in $l_{8..12}$. Then, due to $B_2$, which states that $r$ is the minimal process in $l_{8..12}$, $r$ is smaller than $t$. Therefore, if $j_k \leq r$ it is also $\leq t$. Due to $B_3$, $flag[t]$ equals 4. Consequently, after the transition, $B_1$ still holds if we use $t$ as a substitute for $r$. For this argument to hold it is essential that the indices $j$ in $l_3$ are scanned in increasing order.

*Acknowledgements*: We gratefully acknowledge the encouragement and editorial help extended by David Gries, which greatly improved the style and readability of the paper.

# REFERENCES

[1] L. Lamport. Proving the correctness of multiprocess programs. *IEEE Trans. Software Engin.*, 3:125–143, 1977.

[2] Z. Manna and A. Pnueli. Adequate proof principles for invariance and liveness properties of concurrent programs. *Sci. Comp. Prog.*, 32:257–289, 1984.

[3] Z. Manna and A. Pnueli. *Tools for the practicing verifier*. Technical Report, Dept. of Computer Science, Stanford University, 1990.

[4]  A. Pnueli and L. Zuck. Verification of multiprocess probabilistic proto-
     cols. *Distributed Computing*, 1(1):53–72, 1986.

[5]  B. K. Szymanski. A simple solution to Lamport's concurrent program-
     ming problem with linear wait. In *Proc. 1988 International Conference
     on Supercomputing Systems, St. Malo, France, July 1988*, pages 621–
     626, 1988.

Zohar Manna,
Department of Computer Science,
Stanford University,
Stanford, California  94305–2140,
U.S.A.
and
Department of Applied Mathematics,
Weizmann Institute of Science,
Rehovot,
Israel.

Amir Pnueli,
Department of Applied Mathematics,
Weizmann Institute of Science,
Rehovot,
Israel.

# 34

# The Limitations to Delay-Insensitivity in Asynchronous Circuits

## Alain J. Martin

> I regard programs as specific instances of mechanisms, and I wanted to express, at least once, my strong feeling that many of my considerations concerning software are, mutatis mutandis, just as relevant for hardware design.
>
> —Edsger W. Dijkstra

Asynchronous techniques —that is, techniques that do not use clocks to implement sequencing— are currently attracting considerable interest for digital VLSI circuit design, in particular when the circuits produced are *delay-insensitive* (DI). A digital circuit is DI when its correct operation is independent of the delays in operators and in the wires connecting the operators, except that the delays are finite and positive.

In this paper, we characterize the class of circuits that are entirely DI, and we show that this class is surprisingly limited: Practically all circuits of interest fall outside the class since closed circuits inside the class may contain only C-elements as multiple-input operators.

## 1 Circuits as networks of gates

A DI circuit is a network of logical operators, or *gates*. A gate has one or more Boolean inputs and one Boolean output. The state of the circuit is entirely characterized by the values of the input and output variables of the gates.

We assume that all circuits are *closed*: Each variable is the input of a gate and also the output of a gate. An open circuit is transformed into a closed one by representing the environment of the circuit as gates.

The simple assignments $x := true$ and $x := false$ are denoted by $x \uparrow$ and $x \downarrow$, respectively. An execution of a simple assignment is called a *transition*. The *result* of a transition of type $x \uparrow$ is the postcondition $x$; the result of a transition of type $x \downarrow$ is the postcondition $\neg x$.

A gate with output variable $z$ is defined by the two *production rules* (PRs):

$$
\begin{aligned}
B_u &\mapsto z \uparrow \\
B_d &\mapsto z \downarrow
\end{aligned}
$$

where $B_u$ is the condition on the input variables for a transition of type $z \uparrow$ to take place, and $B_d$ is the condition on the input variables for a transition of type $z \downarrow$ to take place. $B_u$ and $B_d$ are called the *guards* of the PRs.

We will assume that a guard is in disjunctive-normal form, that is, it is either a *literal*, a *term*, or a disjunction of terms. A literal is a variable or its negation; a term is a conjunction of literals.

The two PRs of a gate fulfill the *non-interference* requirement.

**Non-interference**    $\neg B_u \vee \neg B_d$ is invariantly true.

The *result of a PR* is the result of the transition caused by an execution of the PR.

All PRs with a true guard are executed concurrently. The execution of a PR is considered correctly terminated when the result holds. The execution of a PR correctly terminates unless the guard is falsified before the result holds. In that case, the net effect of the execution is undefined. We therefore add a semantic requirement called *stability*.

**Stability**    The guard of a PR is stable in a computation if it is falsified only in states where the result of the PR holds.

We exclude *self-invalidating* PRs. A rule with guard $g$ and result $r$ is self-invalidating if $r \Rightarrow \neg g$ may hold as a postcondition of a transition. For example, the rules $x \mapsto x \downarrow$ and $\neg x \mapsto x \uparrow$ are self-invalidating.

The execution of a PR in a state where the result holds is called *vacuous*; otherwise, it is called *effective*. From the definition of the execution of a PR, the vacuous execution of a PR is equivalent to a *skip*. Consequently, it is always possible to modify the guard of a PR so that it does not contain the output variable of the gate. (This is achieved by removing all terms that contain the result as literal.) Hence, gates do not contain variables that are both input and output of the gate (self-loops). In the sequel, unless specified otherwise, an execution of a PR is an effective execution.

# 2   Wires, forks, and multiple-output gates

*A priori*, a wire with input $x$ and output $y$ is the gate defined by the PRs $x \mapsto y \uparrow$ and $\neg x \mapsto y \downarrow$. But, since the composition of any gate, *including a wire*, with a wire is the gate itself with one of its variables renamed, we can add an arbitrary number of wire gates to a circuit definition without actually changing the circuit. In order to have a unique network of gates for each circuit, we exclude the wire from the gates: A wire is just a renaming mechanism for variables.

We also exclude the *fork* from the gates. A fork has one input and at least two outputs. The fork $f$ with input $x$ and outputs $y$ and $z$ is defined by the two PRs, $x \mapsto y \uparrow, z \uparrow$ and $\neg x \mapsto y \downarrow, z \downarrow$. The generalization to an arbitrary number of outputs is obvious. The gate

$$
\begin{aligned}
B_u &\mapsto x \uparrow \\
B_d &\mapsto x \downarrow
\end{aligned}
$$

composed with fork $f$ is equivalent to the gate with outputs $y$ and $z$

$$
\begin{aligned}
B_u &\mapsto y \uparrow, z \uparrow \\
B_d &\mapsto y \downarrow, z \downarrow .
\end{aligned}
$$

Hence, the fork is just a mechanism for replicating the outputs of a gate and for defining gates with an arbitrary number of outputs. We therefore eliminate the fork and allow the type of multiple-output gates that correspond to the composition of a single-output gate and a fork. But gates defined in this way have an important restriction: *The effective execution of a PR of a gate contains an effective transition on each output of the gate.*

The only restriction that these definitions and conventions introduce on the class of circuits being considered is the exclusion of arbitration devices. They do not restrict the delay-insensitivity assumption.

# 3   Partial order of transitions

The specification of a circuit defines a partial order of actions taken from a repertoire of commands. In order to assert that a circuit fulfills a specification, we must relate this partial order to some other order relation among transitions of a circuit. The partial order of transitions is defined as follows.

Consider an effective execution of a PR. Let $t$ be the transition of this execution, and let $C$ be a term of the guard such that $C$ holds for this execution of the PR.

We attach to $C$ a set $T$ of transitions in the following way. Each literal of $C$ uniquely defines a transition: The literal $x$ is the result of a transition of type $x \uparrow$, and the literal $\neg x$ is the result of a transition of type $x \downarrow$. (The initialization of a variable is also considered a transition.) *By definition, we say that transition t is a successor of each transition of T.*

The successor relation thus defined is not unique for a given circuit. A *computation* is a particular successor relation on a set of transitions, such that each computation corresponds to a possible execution of the circuit. The set of transitions of a computation is finite if the corresponding execution of the circuit terminates, and infinite otherwise.

From the *successor* relation, we can now construct a relation $\prec$ which is a pre-order; that is, it is transitive and anti-reflexive. Once we have the pre-order relation $\prec$, we construct the partial order $\preceq$ by defining $t1 \preceq t2$ to mean $t1 \prec t2$ or $t1 = t2$.

REMARK: Anti-reflexivity is satisfied if, for each ring of gates in the circuit, there is always at least one PR whose guard is true and whose result is false — the ring "oscillates." Anti-reflexivity excludes rings of gates that are used to maintain constant values of variables, as in cross-coupled device constructions of storage elements. We therefore assume that the storage elements are parts of "perfect wires," so to speak, that keep the value of a variable until the next transition on the variable.
□

**Definition**    A chain from $a$ to $b$ is a finite, non-empty set $\{t_i, 0 \leq i < n\}$ of transitions such that $t_0 = a$, $t_n = b$, and for all $i$, $0 < i < n$, $t_i$ is a successor of $t_{i-1}$. By construction, $a \preceq b$ means that there is a chain from $a$ to $b$. If $a \prec b$, we say that $b$ follows $a$.

# 4    Implementation of stability

Consider again an execution of a PR with guard $B$ and transition $t$. Either $B$ is never falsified once it holds, but then $t$ is the last transition on the variable involved, and we say that the transition is *final*. Or $B$ is falsified after a finite number of transitions following $t$, in which case, in order to implement stability of $B$, we have to see to it that $t$ is completed before $B$ is falsified.

For all transitions $i$ that falsify $B$, we have to guarantee $t \prec i$. Hence, by definition of the order relation, there must be a transition $s$ such that $s$ is a *successor* of $t$, and $s \preceq i$. We say that $s$ *acknowledges* $t$. Hence, the

**Acknowledgment Theorem**    In a DI circuit, each non-final transition has a successor transition.

By construction of multiple-output gates, we have the

**Corollary**    In a DI circuit, a non-final transition on an input of a gate has a successor transition on each output of the gate.

EXAMPLE: Consider the three following gates with two inputs, $x$ and $y$, and one output, $z$. The *flip-flop* is defined as $x \mapsto z\uparrow$ and $\neg y \mapsto z\downarrow$, the *asymmetric C-element* as $x \wedge y \mapsto z\uparrow$ and $\neg y \mapsto z\downarrow$, and the *switch* as $x \wedge y \mapsto z\uparrow$ and $x \wedge \neg y \mapsto z\downarrow$.

Since no guard of these gates has a term containing the literal $\neg x$, a transition of type $x\downarrow$ has no successor. Hence, according to the Acknowledgment Theorem, there can be at most two transitions on $x$ in any computation of a DI circuit using any of these three gates.
□

# 5   The Unique-Successor-Set criterion

Later on, we shall give a simple criterion for deciding whether a given circuit —a network of gates— is delay-insensitive. But such a criterion does not tell us whether there exists a DI circuit for a given specification. We shall therefore formulate a more general theorem that characterizes the partial orders of transitions that admit a DI implementation. This criterion enables us to decide that a program has no DI implementation without having to construct a circuit.

**Successor Set**    In a computation, the successor set of a transition $t$ is the set of variables $x$ such that a transition on $x$ is a successor of $t$.

**Unique-Successor-Set Property**    A computation has the unique-successor-set (USS) property when all non-final transitions on the same variable have the same successor set. A set of computations has the USS property when all non-final transitions on the same variable have the same successor set in all computations of the set.

**Unique-Successor-Set Theorem**    A set of computations of a DI circuit has the USS property.

**Proof**    From the definition of the successor of a transition and its corollary, the successor set of a non-final transition on a variable, say $y$, is the set of output variables of the gate of which $y$ is an input.

Since this gate is uniquely defined by the circuit topology, the successor set is unique for all transitions on $y$ in all computations of the circuit.
□

Although the Unique-Successor-Set Theorem is a direct consequence of the Acknowledgment Theorem, its formulation in terms of computations instead of gates makes it possible to lift the result from the implementation level to the specification level. Since the partial orders of actions defining a circuit are projections of the partial orders of actions implementing it, we shall investigate whether the USS property is maintained by projection.

**Definition**    Given a computation, $c$, on a set of variables, $V$, the projection of $c$ on a subset, $W$, of $V$ is the computation derived from $c$ by removing all transitions on variables of $V \setminus W$ from the chains of $c$. The projection of a set of computations is the set obtained by projecting each element of the original set.

**Projection Theorem**    If a set of computations has the USS property, then its projection on a subset of variables has the USS property.

**Proof**    By definition, the projection of a set of computations on $W$ can be obtained by removing the elements of $V \setminus W$ one for one from all chains of each computation of the set. We prove the theorem by showing that removing all transitions on one variable, say, $w$, maintains the USS property of the set.

Let $x$ be another variable, and let $X$ be the USS of (all transitions on) $x$ in all computations of the set. Either $w$ does not belong to $X$ and $X$ is left unchanged by the transformation, or $w$ is removed from $X$. But then, for each transition $tx$ on $x$, the successor set of the transition on $w$ that follows $tx$ must be added to the successor set of $tx$. Since all transitions on $w$ have the same successor set in all computations of the set, the new $X$ is the same for all transitions and all computations of the set.
□

EXAMPLE: The cyclic program $*[X; Y]$, where $X$ and $Y$ are communication commands, is called a *one-place buffer*. It is a basic building block of asynchronous circuit design. With a four-phase handshaking protocol for implementing the communications, an expansion of the program in terms of elementary variables is:

$$*[[xi]; xo \uparrow; [\neg xi]; xo \downarrow; yo \uparrow; [yi]; yo \downarrow; [\neg yi]],$$

where $xi$ and $yi$ are the input variables, and $xo$ and $yo$ are the output variables. (For an arbitrary Boolean expression $B$, the command $[B]$ is a shorthand notation for $[B \rightarrow skip]$, and can be informally defined as "wait until $B$ holds.")

The environment of the circuit can be simply modeled as the two programs:

$$*[xi \uparrow; [xo]; xi \downarrow; [\neg xo]]$$
$$*[[yo]; yi \uparrow; [\neg yo]; yi \downarrow].$$

These three programs are concurrent. Now observe that the projection of a computation on the output variables of the first program gives the computation described by the program

$*[xo \uparrow; xo \downarrow; yo \uparrow; yo \downarrow]$.

Obviously, this computation does not have the USS property and, therefore, the closed circuit implementing the three programs is not DI. But the two environment programs can be implemented with an inverter and a wire, which are DI circuits. Hence, there is no DI circuit implementing this version of the one-place buffer.

□

# 6  Specifications and the USS property

The Projection Theorem is very useful because we can also define when a specification has the USS property. If a specification does not have the property, we can immediately conclude that there exists no DI implementation of the specification. The projection from implementation to specification occurs as follows.

We assume that, whatever specification notation is used, whether programs, traces, or regular expressions, it is possible to derive from the specification certain properties of the partial order of actions involved. Hence, in the sequel, a *specification* is a set of partial orders of actions, where an action is an execution of a command taken from some given repertoire.

We also assume that an elementary variable can be uniquely identified with (the implementation of) each command: The transitions on the variable occur only in the executions of the command, and each execution of the command contains a transition on the variable. This (in theory, slightly restrictive) assumption is needed only for the following

**Specification Theorem**    If the specification of a circuit does not have the USS property, the circuit is not DI.

**Proof**    Consider a specification $S$ of a circuit. For each command, $X$, of $S$, we substitute a transition on the elementary variable $x$ that is uniquely associated with $X$. We obtain a set, $s$, of partial orders of transitions on elementary variables. Since the existence of the USS property is independent of whether the transitions are upgoing or downgoing (that is, the "direction" of the transitions), we can decide whether $s$ has the USS property even though the direction of the transitions in $s$ is undefined.

By definition, we say that specification $S$ has the USS property if and only if the set, $s$, thus defined has the USS property. By construction, $s$ is a projection of the set of computations of the circuit specified by $S$. Hence, by the Projection Theorem and the USS Theorem, if $s$ does not have the USS property, the circuit is not DI.

□

309    Alain J. Martin

EXAMPLES:   The following examples, which we give without proofs, show
how limited is the class of programs that admit a DI implementation. (In
the examples, all commands are different from *skip*.) We assume that the
semantics of the program notation are clear enough that we can identify
the programs with the partial order of actions they represent.

- Let $P \equiv *[S_1; S_2; \ldots S_n]$, and assume that there is no equivalent program

$$*[S_1; S_2; \ldots S_k]$$

with $k < n$. (We say that $P$ is a minimal representation. For instance,
$*[X; X]$ is not minimal since $*[X]$ is an equivalent program.)

Then $P$ has the USS property if and only if $S_i \neq S_j$ for $i \neq j$. Hence, the
"modulo-2 counter" $*[X; X; Y]$ and all other "modulo-k counters" have no
DI implementation.

- The program $*[S_1; [B_1 \rightarrow S_2 \,[]\, B_2 \rightarrow S_3]; S_4]$, with $S_2 \neq S_3$, does not
have the USS property. Hence, there is no DI circuit implementing such a
selection command.

□

# 7    Gate characterization of DI circuits

**Definition**   An $n$-input gate in which $B_u$ is the conjunction of the $n$
input variables and $B_d$ is the conjunction of the negations of the $n$ input
variables is called an $n$-input C-element. A gate derived from a C-element
by negating one or more literals in $B_u$ or $B_d$ is also a C-element.

The Muller-C element is a two-input C-element according to our definition.
A one-input C-element reduces to either a wire or an inverter.

**C-Element Theorem**   If a DI circuit has only one computation, and if
the computation contains at least three transitions on each variable, then
the circuit can be constructed with C-elements only.

**Proof**   Let $x$ be an arbitrary variable of the circuit; $x$ is the input of gate
$g$ with output $z$. We shall prove that $g$ can be implemented as a C-element.
Since there are no self-loops, $x$ and $z$ are different variables.

First, observe that because of the non-interference, all transitions on the
same variable are totally ordered. And because all transitions are effective,
upgoing and downgoing transitions on the same variable alternate.

Since the circuit contains at least three (effective) transitions on each
variable, at least one transition of type $x \uparrow$ is followed by a transition of
type $x \downarrow$, and at least one transition of type $x \downarrow$ is followed by a transition
of type $x \uparrow$.

Let $t1$ be a transition of type $x\uparrow$ and $t2$ the transition of type $x\downarrow$ following it. For the guard of the PR of $t1$ to be stable, there must be a transition $tz$ on $z$ such that $t1 \prec tz \prec t2$. We also know that $tz$ is a successor of $t1$.

By the USS theorem and the Projection theorem, there is exactly one transition $tz$ on $z$ such that $t1 \prec tz \prec t2$. By the same argument, there is exactly one transition on $z$ between a transition of type $x\downarrow$ and the transition of type $x\uparrow$ following it.

Without loss of generality, assume that the first transition on $x$ is of type $x\uparrow$ and the first transition on $z$ is of type $z\uparrow$. Then, because of the alternation of upgoing and downgoing transitions on each variable, each transition of type $z\uparrow$ is the successor of a transition of type $x\uparrow$, and each transition of type $z\downarrow$ is the successor of a transition of type $x\downarrow$.

By definition of the successor relation, $x$ holds as a precondition of each transition $z\uparrow$; thus, guard $B_u$ of $g$ can be formulated so that all terms contain $x$, since a term that is never true can be removed. Hence, $B_u$ can be chosen of the form $x \wedge C_u$, where $C_u$ does not contain $x$. Symmetrically, guard $B_d$ of $g$ can be chosen of the form $\neg x \wedge C_d$, where $C_d$ does not contain $x$. Since this property of $B_u$ and $B_d$ holds for each input of $g$, $g$ is a C-element or can be replaced with a C-element.
□

# 8   For whom the bell tolls?

Are these results tolling the bell of DI design? Actually, not. At worst, they may slightly embarrass those researchers who claim to have a design method for entirely DI circuits. At best, they vindicate the compromises to delay-insensitivity adopted by several asynchronous design methods.

The compromise I have introduced is that of *isochronic forks*. In an isochronic fork, the transitions on *all* outputs of the fork are completed when a transition on *one* output has been acknowledged. Hence, some transitions on some outputs of an isochronic fork need not be acknowledged, and thus the Acknowledgment Theorem does not always hold.

Extending a standard repertoire of DI gates with isochronic forks is sufficient to construct any circuit of interest. I believe this to be the weakest possible extension in the sense that any other choice includes isochronic forks.

*Acknowledgments*: The formulation of the C-element Theorem in terms of three transitions on each variable is due to a suggestion from Pieter Hazewindus. Acknowledgment is also due to Dražen Borković, Steve Burns,

Peter Hofstee, Marcel van der Goot, David Gries, Tony Lee, Jay Misra, and José Tierno for their comments and criticisms. The research described in this paper was sponsored by the Defense Advanced Research Projects Agency, DARPA Order number 6202, and monitored by the Office of Naval Research under contract number N00014-87-K-0745.

Alain J. Martin,
Department of Computer Science,
California Institute of Technology,
Pasadena, CA  91125,
U.S.A.

# A Simple Proof of a Simple Consensus Algorithm[1]

## Jayadev Misra

## 1 Introduction

We present a proof of a simple consensus algorithm. The algorithm is known [1]; the proof style is new. It is difficult to reason about communicating processes when some of them may fail. We show that representing the algorithm at a higher level —using equations only— permits us to treat failures in a formal manner. This approach was first utilized in Chandy and Misra [1988, Chapter 18] for proving the correctness of an unauthenticated Byzantine Agreement protocol due to Dolev et al. [1982], and Srikanth and Toueg [1987], for the case when the number of reliable processes is more than twice the number of unreliable processes; this paper deals with a simpler problem —the number of reliable processes exceeds thrice the number of unreliable processes— which has a simpler algorithm.

## 2 The problem

We are given $s$ reliable processes and $t$ unreliable processes, where $s > 3t \geq 0$. To simplify matters, assume that the total number of processes, $s + t$, is odd. Processes communicate by messages. Local to each process is a variable, which initially has a value, 0 or 1. It is required to design a protocol, to be followed by the reliable processes, such that eventually every reliable process has the same value in its local variable. Furthermore, if all reliable processes have the same initial value then their final value is the same as their initial value.

The difficulty in constructing a solution is due to the presence of unreliable processes. These processes may send arbitrary messages, and there is no way, a priori, to distinguish the reliable and the unreliable processes.

---

[1]Reprinted by permission of Elsevier Science Publishers, 1989, Information Processing Letters, 33:1 pages 21–24.

## 3   An algorithm: informal version

Let the processes be numbered 1 through $s + t$. Processes communicate
with each other in "rounds." Each round consists of two phases of message
transmissions: In round $k$, $k > 0$, in the first phase every process sends its
value to all processes (including itself); in the second phase, process $k$ sends
the majority value it received in the first phase (majority is well defined
since $s + t$ is odd) to all processes. If a process receives $s$, or more, instances
of the same value in the first phase of the round, it sets its local variable to
this value; otherwise, it sets its local variable to the value received (from
process $k$) in the second phase of this round.

It can be shown that at the end of round $(t + 1)$ all reliable processes
have the same value. Furthermore, if all reliable processes have the same
initial value their final values are same as the (common) initial value.

## 4   Reasoning about consensus algorithms

Consider any consensus algorithm, first ignoring the faults. Any such algorithm consists of two kinds of actions: local computations at processes and
communications between pairs of processes. Both kinds of actions can be
represented by equations of the form

$$b = f(c)$$

where $b, c$ are local variables that belong to the same or different processes.
If $b, c$ are variables of one process, this equation represents a local computation at the process — computing $f(c)$ and assigning it to $b$. If $b, c$ are
variables of different processes then the equation represents a communication — the process to which $c$ is local sends $f(c)$ to the process to which
$b$ is local; the latter process assigns the value to $b$ upon receiving the message. The important point to note is that any deterministic algorithm on
a network of processes —and all consensus algorithms are deterministic in
the absence of faults— can be represented by equations of the above form.
(If a variable $b$ is assigned $k$ different values during a computation, we employ $k$ different variables, $b^1$, $b^2$, ..., $b^k$, each of which is assigned a single
value; this is a standard trick for converting an imperative program to a
functional one.)

We now investigate the effect of faults on such an equation. If the process
to which $b$ is local is unreliable then the equation may not be satisfied as a
result of the computation — the process may fail to assign to $b$. Similarly
if the process to which $c$ is local is unreliable then the equation may not
be satisfied, because the process may transmit an arbitrary value for $c$.
Therefore, an equation is to be discarded if any variable in it is local to an
unreliable process. Thus, for an algorithm consisting of the equations

$$b \;=\; c, \quad d \;=\; c$$

if the process $p$ to which $c$ is local is unreliable, then both equations will be discarded (it cannot then be asserted that $b = d$). This models possible malicious behavior by $p$; it may supply different values for $c$ to the two processes of which $b$ and $d$ are local.

Designing a consensus algorithm is difficult because the algorithm designer does not know which processes are unreliable, and hence which equations will be discarded. She can only rely on the fact that there is a limited number of unreliable processes; by designing the algorithm appropriately it is possible to ensure that only a limited number of equations are discarded.

A consensus algorithm is given by (i) naming the (local) variables of each process, (ii) designating the variables where the initial and the final values are stored for each process, and (iii) writing a set of equations over these variables. Such an algorithm is *correct* provided that for *any* subset of $s$ processes, the subset of equations, that name variables of these processes only, has a solution and the solution satisfies the requirements given in Section 2, *viz.*, all final values are equal, and if all initial values are equal then that is the final value.

We will work with equations and dispense with the notions of process, message, communication, and rounds. (These terms will be used only in giving an intuitive explanation of what each variable represents.) For the present paper, we merely construct an equational representation of the algorithm given in Section 3 and prove its correctness. In general, however, one may design an algorithm by postulating a sequence of refinement steps that culminates in a set of equations of the desired type; see Chapter 18 of Chandy and Misra [1988] for such a development.

## 5   Equational representation of the algorithm

We use $x, y$ to stand for processes and $k$ for the round number. Define the following variables of process $x$ for round $k > 0$.

$$
\begin{aligned}
d[x, k] \;&=\; \text{value at } x \text{ at the end of round } k. \\
r[x, y, k] \;&=\; \text{the value received by } x \text{ from process } y \text{ in the first} \\
&\quad\; \text{phase of round } k. \\
m[x, k] \;&=\; \text{the majority value received by } x \text{ in the first} \\
&\quad\; \text{phase of round } k. \\
c[x, k] \;&=\; \text{the number of instances of } m[x, k] \text{ received by } x \\
&\quad\; \text{in the first phase of round } k.
\end{aligned}
$$

The initial and final values for process $x$ are stored in $d[x, 0]$ and $d[x, t+1]$, respectively. Next, we write the equations that represent the algorithm.

Variables $m[x, k]$, $c[x, k]$ can be defined as follows: $m[x, k]$ is the majority value in $r[x, y, k]$, for all $y$, and $c[x, k]$ is the number of occurrences of $m[x, k]$ in $r[x, y, k]$, for all $y$. The other variables for $k > 0$ are related by

(1)      $d[x, k] \;\; = \;\; \begin{cases} m[x, k] & \text{if } c[x, k] \geq s \\ m[k, k] & \text{if } c[x, k] < s \end{cases}$

(2)      $r[x, y, k] \;\; = \;\; d[y, k - 1]$

We treat (1) as two equations, corresponding to the two alternatives.

## 6   Correctness of the algorithm

We will prove that all reliable processes have the same final value (Theorem 1) and if initial values at all reliable processes are equal then the common final value is equal to the common initial value (Theorem 2).

Designate an arbitrary subset of $s$ processes as reliable. For the rest of this paper, $u, v, w$ denote arbitrary reliable processes. Since $u, v$ are reliable it follows from (2) that for $k > 0$,

(3)      $r[u, v, k] \;\; = \;\; d[v, k - 1]$.

**Lemma 1**    For all $u, w$,   $d[u, w] \;\; = \;\; m[w, w]$.

**Proof**    From (1), since $u, w$ are both reliable:
$$d[u, w] \;\; = \;\; \begin{cases} m[u, w] & \text{if } c[u, w] \geq s \\ m[w, w] & \text{if } c[u, w] < s \end{cases}$$
The lemma follows by showing that
$$c[u, w] \geq s \;\; \Rightarrow \;\; m[u, w] = m[w, w]$$
From the definitions of $c[u, w]$, $m[u, w]$, there are $c[u, w]$ different $y$'s for which $r[u, y, w] = m[u, w]$. Let $R$ be the set of reliable processes among the above $y$'s.

$\quad |R|$

$\geq \qquad$ {there are $t$ unreliable processes}

$\quad c[u, w] - t$

$\geq \qquad$ {assuming that $c[u, w] \geq s$}

$\quad s - t$

$> \qquad$ {$s > 3t$}

$\quad (s + t)/2$

That is, $R$ consists of a majority of processes.

From the definition of $m[w, w]$ there is a majority $S$ of processes such that for any $y$ in $S$

$$r[w, y, w] \;=\; m[w, w].$$

Since $S$ and $R$ both consist of a majority of processes, some process $v$ belongs to both sets (process $v$ is reliable since $R$ consists of reliable processes only).

Now,

$\qquad m[w, w]$

$=\qquad \{v$ is in $S, \ r[w, y, w] = m[w, w] \quad$ for all $y$ in $S\}$

$\qquad r[w, v, w]$

$=\qquad \{$from (3) substituting $w, w$ for $u, k$, respectively$\}$

$\qquad d[v, w - 1]$

$=\qquad \{$from (3) substituting $w$ for $k\}$

$\qquad r[u, v, w]$

$=\qquad \{v$ is in $R, \ r[u, y, w] = m[u, w] \quad$ for all $y$ in $R\}$

$\qquad m[u, w]$

$\square$

**Notation**    We write $\langle \forall u :: p_u \rangle$ for the predicate that is traditionally written as $\forall u.p_u$.

**Lemma 2**    For any $k, k \geq 0$,
$\langle \forall u :: d[u, k] = g \rangle \;\Rightarrow\; \langle \forall u :: d[u, k + 1] = g \rangle.$
**Proof**

$\qquad \langle \forall u :: d[u, k] = g \rangle$

$\Rightarrow\qquad \{$from (3), substituting $u, w, k + 1$ for $u, v, k$, respectively$\}$

$\qquad \langle \forall u, w :: r[u, w, k + 1] = g \rangle$

$\Rightarrow\qquad \{w$ ranges over reliable processes;
$\qquad\qquad$ number of reliable processes $= s \geq$ majority of processes$\}$

$\qquad \langle \forall u :: m[u, k + 1] = g \ \wedge \ c[u, k + 1] \geq s \rangle$

$\Rightarrow\qquad \{$from (1)$\}$

$\qquad \langle \forall u :: d[u, k + 1] = g \rangle$

$\square$

**Theorem 1**    (All final values are equal.) There is a $g$ such that
$$\langle \forall\ u\ ::\ d[u, t+1] = g \rangle.$$

**Proof**    Since there are $t$ unreliable processes, there is a reliable process $w$ such that $w \leq (t+1)$. We show that the desired $g$ is $m[w, w]$.

{From Lemma 1}

$\langle \forall\ u\ ::\ d[u, w] = m[w, w] \rangle$

$\Rightarrow$    {using Lemma 2, repeatedly, and that $w \leq (t+1)$}

$\langle \forall\ u\ ::\ d[u, t+1] = m[w, w] \rangle$

□

**Theorem 2**    (If all initial values are equal, final values are equal to the common initial value.)
$$\langle \forall\ u\ ::\ d[u, 0] = g \rangle\ \Rightarrow\ \langle \forall\ u\ ::\ d[u, t+1] = g \rangle.$$

**Proof**    Repeated application of Lemma 2.

□

# 7    Conclusion

The proof as given above replaces operational reasoning —how a process behaves— by more traditional, mathematical arguments.

*Acknowledgements*: I am indebted to Piotr Berman for showing me this algorithm.

## REFERENCES

[1] Piotr Berman and Juan A. Garay. Asymptotically optimal distributed consensus. In *Proc. 16th International Colloquium on Automata, Languages and Programming*, Springer-Verlag, July 1989. ICALP 89 Stresa, Italy. In Lecture Notes in Computer Science Series, Vol. 372.

[2] K. M. Chandy and J. Misra. *Parallel Program Design: A Foundation*. Addison-Wesley, Reading, Mass., 1988.

[3] D. Dolev et al. *An Efficient Byzantine Algorithm without Authentication*. Technical Report TR RJ 3428, IBM, March 1982.

[4] M. Pease, R. Shostak, and L. Lamport. Reaching agreement in the presence of faults. *J. ACM*, 27(2):228–234, April 1980.

[5]  T.K. Srikanth and S. Toueg. Simulating authenticated broadcasts to derive simple fault tolerant algorithms. *Distributed Computing*, 2(2):80–94, August 1987.

Jayadev Misra,
Department of Computer Sciences,
The University of Texas at Austin,
Taylor Hall 2.124,
Austin, Texas  78712–1188,
U.S.A.

# 36

# Of wp and CSP

## Carroll Morgan

## Abstract

A state-based and an event-based approach to concurrency are linked: the traces, failures and divergences of CSP are expressed as weakest precondition formulae over Action Systems. The result is simpler than is obtained using relations for the state-based view; in particular, divergence is handled easily. Essential use is made of miracles.

## Introduction

A typical state-based approach to concurrency is the *Action Systems* of Back and Kurki-Suonio [1]. A state is shared between a number of actions, each of which is enabled or not depending on that state. The execution of an (enabled) action changes the state, which consequentially changes the set of enabled actions. *Unity* [2] has the same structure essentially.

A typical event-based approach to concurrency is *Communicating Sequential Processes* [5]. There the actions (events) have no structure, and affect no state. The behaviour of a process is understood in terms of sequences of those actions (traces) and, for finer distinctions, failures and divergences.

Using state- and event-based approaches together is attractive in practice. There are some aspects of behaviour best described by state (for example, the contents of a buffer); other aspects are best described by explicit sequencing (for example, the exchange of request and confirm messages necessary to set up a communication channel).

Our contribution takes a step towards using Action Systems and CSP together: the three formulae (1) in the concluding section give the traces, failures, and divergences of any action system. The novelty is our use of weakest preconditions rather than relations; the benefit is a simpler formulation.

We present Action Systems first, then CSP very briefly. Finally, we use weakest preconditions to make the link between them.

# Action Systems

An *action system* is a set of labelled actions and an initialisation; an *action* is a guard and a command; a *guard* is a predicate; and a *command* is a program fragment in Dijkstra's language of guarded commands [3]. An *initialisation* is a command. Figure 1 is an example of an action system in which the actions have been labelled *Tick* and *Tock*.

$$
\textbf{initially } n\colon= +1 \qquad
\begin{array}{lcl}
Tick & \widehat{=} & n = +1 \to n\colon= -1 \\
Tock & \widehat{=} & n = -1 \to n\colon= +1
\end{array}
$$

FIGURE 1. An action system

Execution of an action system proceeds as follows:

1. First, the initialisation is executed; then
2. Repeatedly an enabled action is selected then executed. An action is *enabled* if its guard is true; it is *executed* by executing its command.

If the repetition in Step 2 fails —because no action is enabled— then the system is said to be *deadlocked*. If a command executed in either step aborts, then the system is said to *diverge*. The behaviour of the action system in Figure 1 is to execute *Tick* and *Tock* alternately and forever, without deadlock or divergence.

# Communicating Sequential Processes

Seen as a communicating sequential process [5], the behaviour of Figure 1 is a set of traces; they are set out in Figure 2. A *trace* is a sequence of actions.

$$\{\langle\rangle,\ \langle Tick\rangle,\ \langle Tick,\ Tock\rangle,\ \langle Tick,\ Tock,\ Tick\rangle,\ \cdots\}$$

FIGURE 2. The CSP view: a set of traces

Together with the CSP view comes a notation and a semantics. The traces of Figure 2 are described, by that notation, in Figure 3. Since Figure 1 also describes those traces, we say that Figures 1 and 3 are equivalent in meaning.

---

$$(\mu P \bullet Tick \rightarrow Tock \rightarrow P)$$

FIGURE 3. A CSP process equivalent to Figure 1

---

After the next section we make that equivalence precise: we give a formula for the traces of an action system. Subsequent sections refine the CSP view (failures and divergences).

## Actions are guarded commands

A *guarded command* can be given weakest precondition semantics as follows (for example [7,9]):

**Definition 1** *guarded command*     For guard $G$, command $com$, and postcondition $\alpha$,

$$wp(G \rightarrow com, \alpha) \; \hat{=} \; G \Rightarrow wp(com, \alpha).$$

♡

Guarded commands do not satisfy Dijkstra's *Law of the Excluded Miracle* [3, p.18], and so we call them *miracles*. (Consider for example *false* → **skip**.) We assume however that all other commands do satisfy that law (in particular, the command part $com$ and the initialisation).

Whereas $wp(com, \alpha)$ characterises the states from which $com$ is *certain* to establish $\alpha$, we need the states from which $com$ could *possibly* establish $\alpha$. They are the states satisfying

$$\neg wp(com, \neg\alpha),$$

because in those states it is *not* certain that $com$ will establish *not* $\alpha$. Note that we are taking the view therefore that an aborting command could possibly establish anything.

We abbreviate the above as follows:

**Definition 2** *conjugate weakest precondition*     For any command $com$ and postcondition $\alpha$,

$$\overline{wp}(com, \alpha) \; \hat{=} \; \neg wp(com, \neg\alpha).$$

♡

Although $wp(com, true)$ implies termination of $com$, Definition 2 shows that $\overline{wp}(com, true)$ does not. Indeed, using the Law of the Excluded Miracle for *com* we see that $\overline{wp}(com, true)$ is always true. For guarded commands, however, the situation is different: they are miracles, and we have

$$\overline{wp}(G \rightarrow com, true)$$

$\equiv$     {Definition 2}

$$\neg wp(G \rightarrow com, false)$$

$\equiv$     {Definition 1}

$$\neg(G \Rightarrow wp(com, false))$$

$\equiv$     {excluded miracle for *com*}

$$G.$$

In fact, we have established that $\overline{wp}(act, true)$ characterises the states in which the action *act* is enabled:

**Proposition 1**     For any action *act* let $gd(act)$ be its guard (determined syntactically). Then

$$gd(act) \equiv \overline{wp}(act, true).$$

$\heartsuit$

# Traces

Let our typical action system be $(\mathcal{A}, ini)$, where $\mathcal{A}$ is a set of actions $\{act1, act2, \cdots\}$ and *ini* is the initialisation. A trace is then a sequence of actions drawn from $\mathcal{A}$, and we must determine from what states initially that entire sequence can occur in succession.

We know from Proposition 1 that the singleton trace $\langle act1 \rangle$ can occur in exactly those states satisfying $\overline{wp}(act1, true)$. The longer trace $\langle act1, act2 \rangle$ can occur in the states from which *act1* could possibly reach a state in which *act2* can occur; they are characterised by $\overline{wp}(act1, \overline{wp}(act2, true))$. Calculation and Definition 2 show that to be equivalent to

$$\overline{wp}(act1; act2, true).$$

In other words, the trace $\langle act1, act2 \rangle$ can occur when the whole sequential composition *act1*; *act2* is 'enabled' (quoted because 'enabled' was defined only for single actions). Finally, the empty trace can occur in any state and has no effect; thus we identify $\langle \rangle$ and **skip**.

An inductive argument generalises the above to any finite trace, giving this proposition:

**Proposition 2**    For any trace $tr$, let $\hat{tr}$ be the sequential composition of its elements, with $\langle\rangle = \textbf{skip}$. Then all of $tr$ can occur in succession exactly when $\overline{wp}(\hat{tr}, true)$ is true initially.
♡

With Proposition 2, we can define the traces of an action system; we will not bother from now on to distinguish $tr$ and $\hat{tr}$:

**Definition 3** _traces_    Let $(\mathcal{A}, ini)$ be an action system, and let $\mathcal{A}^*$ be the set of traces formed by taking finite sequential compositions of members of $\mathcal{A}$. Then the traces $tr{:}\,\mathcal{A}^*$ of the action system $(\mathcal{A}, ini)$ are those for which

$$\overline{wp}(ini; tr, true)$$

is true initially. (If we do not specify the initial state from which $ini$ is executed, then the traces are those for which the above is true in _some_ state.)
♡

# Failures

The traces of CSP are sufficient only for describing deterministic behaviour: when describing nondeterminism, CSP makes more detailed observations. A _failure_ is a pair comprising a trace and a refusal; a _refusal_ is a set of actions.

Let $tr$ be a trace and $\mathcal{R}$ a refusal. The behaviour $(tr, \mathcal{R})$ is observed whenever the process first engages in all the actions in $tr$ and then is unable to extend the trace with any action in $\mathcal{R}$.

Consider for example the two processes of Figure 4. In any state of Process $P1$, the choice between _Coffee_ and _Tea_ is yet to be made, since both actions are enabled. The nondeterminism is in the _selection_ of the actions, and is called _external_. The behaviour of $P2$ is different: in any state, the choice between _Coffee_ and _Tea_ is already made. The nondeterminism is in the _execution_ of the actions, and is called _internal_.

Processes $P1$ and $P2$ have the same traces; but they are distinguished by their failures, since $(\langle\rangle, \{\textit{Coffee}\})$ is a failure of $P2$ but not of $P1$.

The failures of an action system are defined as follows:

**Definition 4** _failures_    The failures $tr{:}\,\mathcal{A}^*; \mathcal{R}{:}\,2^{\mathcal{A}}$ of the action system $(\mathcal{A}, ini)$ are those for which

$$\overline{wp}(ini; tr, \neg gd(\mathcal{R}))$$

is true initially, where $gd(\mathcal{R})$ is the _disjunction_ of the guards of the actions in $\mathcal{R}$.
♡

---

P1: **initially skip** 

| $Coffee$ | $\mathrel{\widehat{=}}$ | $true \to$ **skip** |
| $Tea$ | $\mathrel{\widehat{=}}$ | $true \to$ **skip** |

P2: **initially** $n:= \pm 1$

| $Coffee$ | $\mathrel{\widehat{=}}$ | $n = +1 \to n:= \pm 1$ |
| $Tea$ | $\mathrel{\widehat{=}}$ | $n = -1 \to n:= \pm 1$ |

The command $n:= \pm 1$ abbreviates **if** $true \to n:= 1 \; [\![ \; true \to n:= -1$ **fi**.

FIGURE 4. External ($P1$) and internal ($P2$) nondeterminism

---

Thus $\mathcal{R}$ can be refused if $ini$ then $tr$ can reach a state in which no guard of any action in $\mathcal{R}$ is true.

## Divergences

A *divergence* of a CSP process is a trace after which the process behaves chaotically; in an action system that behaviour is deemed to result from an aborting command $G \to com$ executed in a state where $G$ is true (necessarily) but $wp(com, true)$ is not. Calculation shows that to be a state in which $\overline{wp}(G \to com, false)$ is true; by analogy with Definition 3, we have therefore

**Definition 5** *divergences*    The divergences $tr: \mathcal{A}^*$ of the action system $(\mathcal{A}, ini)$ are those for which

$$\overline{wp}(ini; tr, false)$$

is true initially.
♡

Note that the immediately-diverging process *CHAOS* results when the initialisation $ini$ is **abort**.

## Well-formedness and normal form

An arbitrary collection of traces, failures, and divergences is not necessarily a CSP process. For example, the set of traces must be non-empty and prefix closed. That and other conditions are satisfied by our definitions:

**Theorem 1** *well-formedness*    The traces, failures, and divergences generated from an action system by Definitions 3, 4, and 5 satisfy the well-formedness conditions C0–C6 for CSP processes [5, p.130].

**Proof**    Straightforward application of Properties 2 and 3 of $wp$ [3, p.18].
♡

It can be shown also that for any well-formed traces, failures, and divergences there is a particularly simple action system that generates them. Thus a normal form can be reached by translating an action system into CSP, then back again.

# Conclusion

In Definitions 3, 4, and 5 we have given three simple formulae which allow an action system to be seen as a CSP process:

$$
(1) \qquad
\begin{aligned}
\text{traces} &\quad— \quad \overline{wp}(ini; tr, true) \\
\text{failures} &\quad— \quad \overline{wp}(ini; tr, \neg gd(\mathcal{R})) \\
\text{divergences} &\quad— \quad \overline{wp}(ini; tr, false).
\end{aligned}
$$

They give an inexpensive semantic link between state- and event-based views of concurrency; it depends essentially on miracles for the weakest precondition characterisation of enabling. However, the fairness conditions of an action system are not at all taken into account.

The traditional link between automata and the languages they accept does not distinguish internal and external nondeterminism, nor does it handle divergence. Internal and external nondeterminism could be distinguished by allowing several transitions to have the same label: then external nondeterminism is in the choice of label, and internal nondeterminism is in the choice of a transition with that label.

Back and Kurki-Suonio [1] use syntactic rules to translate action systems to CSP. But they do not discuss the semantics of that, and they do not handle (internal) nondeterminism or divergence.

Josephs [6] and Jifeng He [4] define the traces and failures of a state-based system in which the actions are relations between states rather than predicate transformers. Jifeng He defines divergences as well. Josephs gives a normal form, based on ready sets [10]; it inspired our remark above about normal forms, based on failures. Jifeng He defines the same normal form that we do. They each give completeness results concerning the existence of refinement mappings.

Both Jifeng He and Josephs show convincingly that relations give a simple theory for partial correctness. But Josephs does not treat divergence at all; and Jifeng He introduces a bottom state ⊥ for that purpose, somewhat complicating the model. An advantage of weakest preconditions therefore is that they include termination uniformly, and there is no need for special non-terminating states. Another advantage is that they are much closer to actual programming practice.

# Postscript

If the initialisation *ini* or the *com* part of $G \to com$ are allowed to be miracles themselves, then the traces, failures, and divergences (1) do *not* satisfy the well-formedness conditions of [5]. Instead, they generate miraculous CSP processes whose properties are analogs of those for the sequential miracles.

*Acknowledgements*: I thank Richard Bird, *etac*, Tony Hoare, and Jim Woodcock for their comments.

## References

[1] R.-J. R. Back and R. Kurki-Suonio. Decentralization of process nets with centralized control. In *Proc. Second Annual Symposium on Principles of Distributed Computing*, Montreal, 1983.

[2] K. M. Chandy and J. Misra. *Parallel Program Design: A Foundation.* Addison-Wesley, Reading, Mass., 1988.

[3] E. W. Dijkstra. *A Discipline of Programming.* Prentice-Hall, Englewood Cliffs, 1976.

[4] Jifeng He. Process simulation and refinement. 1989. To appear in *Formal Aspects of Computing*.

[5] C. A. R. Hoare. *Communicating Sequential Processes.* Prentice-Hall, London, 1985.

[6] M. B. Josephs. A state-based approach to communicating processes. *Distributed Computing*, 3(1):9–18, December 1988.

[7] C. C. Morgan. The specification statement. *Trans. Prog. Lang. Sys.*, 10(3), July 1988. Reprinted in [8].

[8] C. C. Morgan, K. A. Robinson, and P. H. B. Gardiner. *On the Refinement Calculus.* Technical Report PRG–70, Oxford University Computing Laboratory, 1988.

[9] G. Nelson. *A Generalization of Dijkstra's Calculus.* Technical Report 16, Digital Systems Research Center, April 1987.

[10] E.-R. Olderog and C. A. R. Hoare. Specification-oriented semantics for communicating processes. *Acta Informatica*, 23, 1986.

Carroll Morgan,
Oxford University Computing Laboratory,
Programming Research Group,
8–11, Keble Road,
Oxford   OX1 3QD,   England.

# 37

# Programming by Expression Refinement: the KMP Algorithm

## Joseph M. Morris

## 0   Introduction

We carry out a small exercise in programming by what might be called *expression refinement*. This is a style of formal programming in which we begin with an expression written in an expressive notation and regarded as a specification, and proceed to manipulate it into a constructive equivalent. This leads to programs making much use of recursive functions and less use of loops.

The exercise is to calculate a pattern-matching algorithm, and specifically the algorithm originally due to Knuth, Morris, and Pratt [1]. We begin, however, with a smaller problem, one that turns out to be both similar to, and a subproblem of, the larger problem. We prefer to start with this because it will give the reader a chance to become familiar in a simple setting with the style and notation we employ.

We briefly review some basic notation. Function application is denoted by an infix dot which has the highest operator precedence. Finite sequences are regarded as partial functions on an initial segment of the natural numbers: sequence $x$ of length $N$, $N$ a natural, has elements $x.0, x.1, ..., x.(N-1)$. The $n$-length prefix of $x$, $0 \leq n \leq N$, is denoted by $x|n$. We denote "$x$ is a suffix of $y$" by $x \geq y$, and "$x$ is a proper suffix of $y$" by $x > y$, where $y$ is another sequence. $(k : P.k : f.k)$ denotes the bag (multiset) containing an occurrence of $f.k$ for each $k$ satisfying predicate $P.k$ ($k$ is a dummy variable). $\max.B$ yields the maximum of bag $B$ of integers and equals $-\infty$ if $B$ is empty. Infix **max** yields the maximum of its integer arguments. A useful law is

$$\max.(k : P.k : f.k) =$$
$$\max.(k : P.k \wedge Q.k : f.k) \ \textbf{max} \ \max.(k : P.k \wedge \neg Q.k : f.k)$$

where $Q.k$ is another predicate; replacing an occurrence of the left-hand side of this equation with its right-hand side is called "range splitting". A similar sort of law, called "range disjunction", is

$$\max.(k : P.k \lor Q.k : f.k) =$$
$$\max.(k : P.k : f.k) \ \mathbf{max} \ \ \max.(k : Q.k : f.k)$$

# 1   Maximal prefix-suffix problem

We want to make a program that calculates for every non-empty prefix $y$ of a given string $x$ the longest string that is both a proper prefix and a proper suffix of $y$. We write down the formal specification and then we'll explain it; for any natural $M$:

MPS0:   $x$: sequence($M$) of char; $q$: sequence($M{+}1$) of integer
_____
$\{x \in$ sequence($M$) of char$\}$
$(\|n : 0{<}n{\leq}M :$
$\qquad\qquad q.n := \max.(k : 0{\leq}k{<}n \ \land \ x|k > x|n : k)$
$)$

The names and types of global variables —here $x$ and $q$— are given above the horizontal line. The specification proper is given below the line, and consists of the assumptions and a statement of the desired effect. The assumption is given as a so-called assert statement, and simply says that $x$ has an initial value. The desired effect is here stated with a large concurrent assignment statement meaning "let $q.n$ have the value of the max-term for each $n$ in the range $0{<}n{\leq}M$".

We introduce some abbreviations:

D0:    $k \ \mathbf{xx} \ n \ \equiv \ x|k > x|n$        for all $k$ and $n$ satisfying $0{\leq}k, n{\leq}M$.
D1:    $mx.n \ = \ \max.(k : 0{\leq}k{<}n \ \land \ k \ \mathbf{xx} \ n : k)$
$\qquad\qquad\qquad\qquad\qquad\qquad$ for all $n$ such that $0{<}n{\leq}M$.

Obviously $mx.n$ equals the right-hand side of the assignment in MPS0. We should begin by writing down the elementary properties of $\mathbf{xx}$ and $mx$ that follow immediately from D0 and D1.

L0:    $0 \ \mathbf{xx} \ n$ $\qquad\qquad\qquad\qquad\qquad\qquad\qquad$ $(0{<}n{\leq}M)$
L1:    $0 \leq mx.n < n$ $\qquad\qquad\qquad\qquad\qquad\qquad$ $(0{<}n{\leq}M)$
L2:    $mx.n \ \mathbf{xx} \ n$ $\qquad\qquad\qquad\qquad\qquad\qquad$ $(0{<}n{\leq}M)$
L3:    $k \ \mathbf{xx} \ n \ \Rightarrow \ k \leq mx.n$ $\qquad\qquad\qquad$ $(0{\leq}k{<}n{\leq}M)$

We will be inventing some string-theory as we proceed, such as the preceding laws. The proofs of such laws are peripheral to the main theme, and so we'll omit them for brevity, but we expect the reader will not have much difficulty in convincing himself of their truth. We give $\mathbf{xx}$ an operator precedence below the arithmetic and above the logical operators, so we can write $k+1$ **xx** $n+1$, say, without brackets.

Looking at the specification we view the essence of our task as that of formulating $mx.n$ constructively for $0<n\leq M$, or equivalently, $mx.(n+1)$ for $0\leq n<M$ :

$$mx.(n+1)$$
$$=\quad \{D1\}$$
$$\max.(k:0\leq k<n+1 \ \wedge\ k \text{ xx } n+1:k)$$

**Interlude.**    The first step introduces one interesting term — $k$ **xx** $n+1$. We are on the lookout for a formulation of the original expression (i.e. $mx.(n+1)$) in terms of $mx.i$'s for $i\leq n$, and that suggests trying to express $k$ **xx** $n+1$ in terms of $k$ **xx** $n$. This is not hard to do, but it's more convenient to rewrite $k+1$ **xx** $n+1$ :

L4:    $k+1$ **xx** $n+1 \ \equiv\ k$ **xx** $n \ \wedge\ x.k = x.n$    $(0\leq k\leq n<M)$

We continue with a minor reshaping of the expression to accommodate L4. **End.**

$$=\quad \{\text{range splitting with predicate } k=0\}$$
$$\max.(k:0<k<n+1 \ \wedge\ k \text{ xx } n+1:k)$$
$$\textbf{max}\ \ \max.(k:k=0 \ \wedge\ k \text{ xx } n+1:k)$$
$$=\quad \{\text{one-point rule, L0}\}$$
$$\max.(k:0<k<n+1 \ \wedge\ k \text{ xx } n+1:k)\ \textbf{max}\ 0$$
$$=\quad \{\text{change of dummy } k \text{ to } k+1\}$$
$$\max.(k:0\leq k<n \ \wedge\ k+1 \text{ xx } n+1:k+1)\ \textbf{max}\ 0$$
$$=\quad \{\text{L4}\}$$
$$\max.(k:0\leq k<n \ \wedge\ k \text{ xx } n \ \wedge\ x.k=x.n:k+1)\ \textbf{max}\ 0 \qquad (i)$$
$$=\quad \{\text{We could contract the range of } k \text{ via L3, but}$$
$$\qquad\quad \text{we must exclude } n=0\}$$

**if** $n=0 \rightarrow 0$
$[]\ n>0 \rightarrow \max.(k:0\leq k<n \ \wedge\ k \text{ xx } n \ \wedge\ x.k=x.n:k+1)$
       **max** 0
**fi**

$$=\quad \{\text{L3}; \ mx.n<n \text{ by L1}\}$$

$$\textbf{if } n = 0 \ \rightarrow \ 0$$
$$[\!] \ n > 0 \ \rightarrow \ \max.(k : 0 \leq k \leq mx.n \ \wedge \ k \textbf{ xx } n \ \wedge \ x.k = x.n : k{+}1)$$
$$\qquad \textbf{max} \ \ 0$$
$$\textbf{fi}$$

= $\quad${We cannot escape comparing a pair of characters.
Examining the max-expression with an eye on L2
suggests we might go about this by isolating the case
$k = mx.n$, by range splitting}

$$\textbf{if } n = 0 \ \rightarrow \ 0$$
$$[\!] \ n > 0 \ \rightarrow \ \max.(k : k = mx.n \ \wedge \ k \textbf{ xx } n \ \wedge \ x.k = x.n : k{+}1)$$
$$\qquad \textbf{max}$$
$$\qquad \max.(k : 0 \leq k < mx.n \ \wedge \ k \textbf{ xx } n \ \wedge \ x.k = x.n : k{+}1)$$
$$\qquad \textbf{max} \ \ 0$$

$$\textbf{fi}$$

= $\quad${one-point rule, L2}

$$\textbf{if } n = 0 \ \rightarrow \ 0$$
$$[\!] \ n > 0 \ \rightarrow \ \textbf{if } x.(mx.n) = x.n \ \rightarrow \ mx.n + 1$$
$$\qquad\qquad\quad [\!] \ x.(mx.n) \neq x.n \ \rightarrow \ -\infty$$
$$\qquad\qquad \textbf{fi}$$
$$\qquad \textbf{max}$$
$$\qquad \max.(k : 0 \leq k < mx.n \ \wedge \ k \textbf{ xx } n \ \wedge \ x.k = x.n : k{+}1)$$
$$\qquad \textbf{max} \ \ 0$$
$$\textbf{fi}$$

= $\quad${distribution of terms over **if** ... **fi** and simplification —
$mx.n + 1 > 0$ by L1, and $mx.n + 1 > \max.(\ldots)$
as the largest element in the bag is at most $mx.n$}

$$\textbf{if } n = 0 \ \rightarrow \ 0$$
$$[\!] \ n > 0 \ \rightarrow \ \textbf{if } x.(mx.n) = x.n \ \rightarrow \ mx.n + 1$$
$$\qquad\qquad\quad [\!] \ x.(mx.n) \neq x.n \ \rightarrow$$
$$\qquad\qquad\qquad \max.(k : 0 \leq k < mx.n \ \wedge \ k \textbf{ xx } n \ \wedge \ x.k = x.n : k{+}1)$$
$$\qquad\qquad\qquad \textbf{max} \ \ 0$$
$$\qquad\qquad \textbf{fi}$$
$$\textbf{fi}$$

**Interlude.** We are left with the difficult-looking max-term in the second guarded expression. Does it look like anything we've seen? It is similar to (i) — indeed it is (i) with the first $n$ therein replaced with $mx.n$, and so

we are invited to parametrise that occurrence on our way to completing a
recursive definition of $mx$. We have to fulfil certain conditions before we
parametrise. Firstly, we have to ensure that the substitution is "progressive", by which we mean that the substituted term is smaller than the term
it replaces according to some well-founded ordering; otherwise nothing is
gained. By L1 the substitution of $mx.n$ for $n$ is progressive, where the ordering is the usual $\leq$ on the naturals. Secondly, we have to ensure that the
substituted term has those properties of the replaced term that were used
in the derivation, so that repeated such substitutions are valid inductively.
Stepping through the derivation with the substitution in mind, we see that
this is not the case: we get stuck where we apply L3 as that relies on the
first two occurrences of $n$ being one and the same, and we also fall foul of
the application of L2 for the same reason. We conclude that there is no
advantage in parametrising the first occurrence of $n$ without including the
second occurrence in the parametrisation. Evidently, the third occurrence
of $n$ in (i) is independent of the other two. If only that $k \,\mathbf{xx}\, n$ in the final
inner max-term was $k \,\mathbf{xx}\, mx.n \ldots$.

L5:    $k \,\mathbf{xx}\, n \;\equiv\; k = mx.n \;\vee\; k \,\mathbf{xx}\, mx.n$    $(0 \leq k \leq M, 0 < n \leq M)$

**End**.

$=$    $\{L5\}$
$\quad$ **if** $n = 0 \;\rightarrow\; 0$
$\quad$ $[]\; n > 0 \;\rightarrow\;$ **if** $x.(mx.n) = x.n \;\rightarrow\; mx.n + 1$
$\qquad\qquad\qquad$ $[]\; x.(mx.n) \neq x.n \;\rightarrow\;$
$\qquad\qquad\qquad\qquad$ $\max.(k : 0 \leq k < mx.n \;\wedge\; k \,\mathbf{xx}\, mx.n$
$\qquad\qquad\qquad\qquad\qquad\qquad\quad \wedge\; x.k = x.n : k + 1)$
$\qquad\qquad\qquad$ **max** $0$
$\qquad\qquad$ **fi**
$\quad$ **fi**

Now the parametrisation goes through: we can replace the two indicated
occurrences of $n$ in (i) with any $i$ satisfying $0 \leq i \leq n$, and the same derivation
applies mutatis mutandis; we leave it to the reader to check this. It is
now routine to extract a well-founded recursive definition. With fixed $n$
satisfying $0 \leq n < M$ define function $f$ by

$$f.i \;=\; \max.(k : 0 \leq k < i \,\wedge\, k \,\mathbf{xx}\, i \,\wedge\, x.k = x.n : k + 1) \;\textbf{max}\; 0$$
$$(0 \leq i < M)$$

We have shown —in the above derivation up to (i)— that $mx.(n+1) =
f.n$. We have further shown —in the derivation from (i) and the above
discussion— that for $0 \leq i \leq n$:

$$f.i \;=\; \textbf{if } i = 0 \;\rightarrow\; 0$$
$$[\!]\; i > 0 \;\rightarrow\; \textbf{if } x.(mx.i) = x.n \;\rightarrow\; mx.i + 1$$
$$[\!]\; x.(mx.i) \neq x.n \;\rightarrow\; f.(mx.i)$$
$$\textbf{fi}$$
$$\textbf{fi}$$

It follows from L1 and an easy inductive argument that in an evaluation of $f.n$ the arguments of $f$ are decreasing and bounded from below by 0, and so $f$ is terminating. It further follows —taking a look at the text— that in an evaluation of $f.n$ every argument $i$ of $f$ satisfies $0 \leq i \leq n$, and hence the evaluation refers only to those $mx.i$'s satisfying $0 < i \leq n$. This makes it attractive to evaluate the $mx.n$'s in order of increasing $n$, for then each $mx.i$ that we need will be available in $q.i$. With loop invariant $0 \leq n \leq M \;\wedge\; (\forall i : 0 < i \leq n : q.i = mx.i)$ the program is

MPS:
```
|[  n : integer
  ; n := 0
  ; do n ≠ M  →
        |[  f :  integer func  =
              val i :  integer
            ; if i = 0  →  0
              [] i > 0  →  if x.(q.i) = x.n  →  q.i + 1
                          [] x.(q.i) ≠ x.n  →  f.(q.i)
                          fi
            fi•
            q.(n+1) := f.n
        ]|
  ; n := n+1
  od
]|
```

# 2   Knuth-Morris-Pratt

We want to compute all occurrences of string $x$ of length $M$ in another string $y$ of length $N$, $M$ and $N$ naturals:

KMP0:
$$x: \text{sequence}(M) \text{ of char}; \; y: \text{sequence}(N) \text{ of char}; \; s: \text{set of integer}$$
$$\{x \in \text{sequence}(M) \text{ of char} \;\wedge\; y \in \text{sequence}(N) \text{ of char}\}$$
$$s := \{n : 0 < n \leq N \;\wedge\; x \geq y | n : n - M\}$$

The task is essentially one of determining the truth-value of terms $x \geq y|n$ for $0<n\leq N$. One way to evaluate $x \geq y|n$ is to compute the length of the longest prefix of $x$ that is a suffix of $y|n$ — call this $my.n$, for then $x \geq y|n \equiv my.n = M$; we will proceed with this. We should note that other choices were open to us: we might have opted to look at the longest common suffix of $x$ and $y|n$, or the longest prefix common to $x$ and the $M$-length tail of $y|n$, and so on, but we have made a choice that leads to the Knuth-Morris-Pratt algorithm. We define

D2:     $k\,\mathbf{xy}\,n \equiv x|k \geq y|n$   for $k$ and $n$ satisfying $0\leq k\leq M$, $0\leq n\leq N$.

D3:     $my.n = \max.(k : 0\leq k\leq M \wedge k\,\mathbf{xy}\,n : k)$
$\phantom{D3:     my.n = }$for all $n$ such that $0\leq n\leq N$.

KMP0 is refined by (not bothering to repeat the globals and assumptions):

KMP1:  $s := \{n : 0<n\leq N \wedge M = my.n : n - M\}$

$\mathbf{xy}$ has the same operator precedence as $\mathbf{xx}$. Let us write down the elementary properties that follow immediately from D2 and D3:

L6:     $0\,\mathbf{xy}\,n$ $\hfill (0\leq n\leq N)$
L7:     $0 \leq my.n \leq M$ $\hfill (0\leq n\leq N)$
L8:     $my.n\,\mathbf{xy}\,n$ $\hfill (0\leq n\leq N)$
L9:     $k\,\mathbf{xy}\,n \Rightarrow k \leq my.n$ $\hfill (0\leq n\leq N, 0\leq k\leq M)$

To evaluate $M = my.n$ is not at all difficult, but we should sense immediately that to evaluate it in isolation for every $n$ is computationally expensive, and probably unnecessary. There is obviously some close relationship between successive $my.i$'s, and we should try to exploit this for the sake of computational efficiency. So we view the essence of the problem as one of formulating $my.n$ constructively. It is clear that $my.n$ is very similar indeed to $mx.n$ of the previous section, and so we should expect our first approach to follow a similar developmental path. Where we apply the same heuristics as before we will not repeat the discussion. For $n$ satisfying $0\leq n<N$:

$\phantom{=}my.(n+1)$

$=\phantom{..}\{D3\}$

$\phantom{=}\max.(k : 0\leq k\leq M \wedge k\,\mathbf{xy}\,n+1 : k)$

**Interlude.**    Analogous to L4 we have

L10:    $k+1\,\mathbf{xy}\,n+1 \equiv k\,\mathbf{xy}\,n \wedge x.k = y.n$ $\hfill (0\leq k<M, 0\leq n<N)$
**End**.

$=$        {range splitting with $k = 0$, L6}

   $\max.(k : 0{<}k{\le}M \ \wedge\ k \,\mathbf{xy}\, n+1 : k)$ **max** $0$

$=$        {change of dummy $k$ to $k+1$}

   $\max.(k : 0{\le}k{<}M \ \wedge\ k+1 \,\mathbf{xy}\, n+1 : k+1)$ **max** $0$

$=$        {L10}

   $\max.(k : 0{\le}k{<}M \ \wedge\ k \,\mathbf{xy}\, n \ \wedge\ x.k = y.n : k+1)$ **max** $0$        (ii)

**Interlude.**    We are proceeding very much as we did for the earlier problem. If things continue to go as previously then we should meet the expression (ii) but for some substitution. But there is a small obstacle in the way: here is the **xy**-law analogous to L5

L11:      $k \,\mathbf{xy}\, n \ \equiv\ k = my.n \ \vee\ k \,\mathbf{xx}\, my.n$          $(0{\le}k{\le}M, 0{\le}n{\le}N)$

Now an application of L11 is different from L5 in this regard, that it replaces an **xy**-term not with another term of its own kind but with an **xx**-term. If we are to meet (ii) again but for a substitution, then at this point we should replace its **xy**-term with an **xx**-term —using L11— and that we shall do. In practice one discovers the efficacy of this move by proceeding with the derivation much as for $mx$; and meeting a subexpression the same as (ii) but for the expected substitution *and* **xx** where (ii) has **xy**. We could proceed along that path, make the discovery, and backtrack — but presumably the reader is happy to be spared the effort.

**End.**

$=$        {L11}

   $\max.(k : 0{\le}k{<}M \ \wedge\ (k = my.n \ \vee\ k \,\mathbf{xx}\, my.n) \ \wedge\ x.k = y.n : k+1)$
   **max** $0$
                                                                                            (iii)

$=$        {let $m$ abbreviate $my.n$}

   $\max.(k : 0{\le}k{<}M \ \wedge\ (k = m \ \vee\ k \,\mathbf{xx}\, m) \ \wedge\ x.k = y.n : k+1)$
   **max** $0$
                                                                                            (iv)

$=$        {calculus and range disjunction}

   $\max.(k : 0{\le}k{<}M \ \wedge\ k = m \ \wedge\ x.k = y.n : k+1)$ **max**
   $\max.(k : 0{\le}k{<}M \ \wedge\ k \,\mathbf{xx}\, m \ \wedge\ x.k = y.n : k+1)$ **max** $0$

$=$        {max theory, $m{\ge}0$ by definition of $m$ and L7}

**if** $m{<}M \ \wedge\ x.m = y.n \qquad \rightarrow\ m+1$

$[\!]\ \neg(m{<}M \ \wedge\ x.m = y.n) \ \rightarrow\ -\infty$

**fi**

**max**

$$\max.(k : 0 \le k < M \ \wedge \ k \text{ xx } m \ \wedge \ x.k = y.n : k+1) \ \textbf{max} \ 0$$

$=$ {distribution of terms over **if** ... **fi**; from L3 and L1 the maximum $k$-value in the bag of the middle term is at most $m$, and so the maximum value in the bag is no more than $m+1$; $0 < m+1$ by definition of $m$ and L7}

**if** $m < M \ \wedge \ x.m = y.n \qquad \rightarrow \ m+1$
[] $\neg \ (m < M \ \wedge \ x.m = y.n) \ \rightarrow$
$\qquad \max.(k : 0 \le k < M \ \wedge \ k \text{ xx } m \ \wedge \ x.k = y.n : k+1) \ \textbf{max} \ 0$
**fi**

**Interlude.**    We are aiming to give the max-expression above the same shape as (iv). Obviously we think of applying L5, but for that we must exclude the case $m = 0$. We can do that via the obvious:

L12:    $\neg(k \text{ xx } 0)$ $\hspace{6cm}$ $(0 \le k \le M)$
**End.**

$=$ {L12, max theory, $m \ge 0$ by definition of $m$ and L7}

**if** $m < M \ \wedge \ x.m = y.n \qquad \rightarrow \ m+1$
[] $\neg(m < M \ \wedge \ x.m = y.n) \ \rightarrow$
$\qquad$ **if** $m = 0 \ \rightarrow \ 0$
$\qquad$ [] $m > 0 \ \rightarrow \ \max.(k : 0 \le k < M \ \wedge \ k \text{ xx } m \ \wedge \ x.k = y.n : k+1)$
$\qquad\qquad\qquad$ **max** $0$
$\qquad$ **fi**
**fi**

$=$ {L5}

**if** $m < M \ \wedge \ x.m = y.n \qquad \rightarrow \ m+1$
[] $\neg(m < M \ \wedge \ x.m = y.n) \ \rightarrow$
$\qquad$ **if** $m = 0 \ \rightarrow \ 0$
$\qquad$ [] $m > 0 \ \rightarrow \ \max.(k : 0 \le k < M \ \wedge \ (k = mx.m \ \vee \ k \text{ xx } mx.m)$
$\qquad\qquad\qquad\qquad\qquad \wedge \ x.k = y.n : k+1)$
$\qquad\qquad\qquad$ **max** $0$
$\qquad$ **fi**
**fi**

The inner max-expression is (iv) with $m$ replaced by $mx.m$, and so we are invited to make a parameter of $m$. Can we? In the derivation $m$ denotes $my.n$ but looking back through the steps the only property of $m$ we appealed to was $m \ge 0$. Now the substitution we propose for $m$ (having established $m > 0$) is $mx.m$ which by L1 is also at least 0, and so on inductively. Moreover, L1 guarantees that this substitution is progressive. So we can extract the recursive function: with fixed $n$ satisfying $0 \leq n < N$ define function $g$ by

$$g.i = \max.(k : 0 \leq k < M \wedge (k = i \vee k \text{ xx } i) \wedge x.k = y.n : k+1)$$
$$\mathbf{max} \ 0 \qquad\qquad\qquad (0 \leq i \leq M)$$

We have established —in the above derivation as far as (iii)— that for $0 \leq n < N$, $my.(n+1) = g.(my.n)$. We have further shown —in the derivation from (iv) on, and in the discussion above— that

$$\begin{aligned}
g.i = \ &\mathbf{if} \ i < M \wedge x.i = y.n \quad \rightarrow i+1 \\
&[] \ \neg(i < M \wedge x.i = y.n) \rightarrow \\
&\qquad \mathbf{if} \ i = 0 \rightarrow 0 \ [] \ i > 0 \rightarrow g.(mx.i) \ \mathbf{fi} \\
&\mathbf{fi}
\end{aligned}$$

and moreover that this recursive definition is well-founded.

Function $g$ is computationally very attractive: it defines $my.(n+1)$ as a function depending only on $my.n$ and the $mx.i$'s. So if we evaluate $M = my.n$ in increasing order of $n$ we need only keep one old $my$-value, as well as the $mx.i$'s which we can compute in advance. The invariant we need has a standard form

$$\begin{aligned}
&0 \leq n \leq N \quad \wedge \quad s = \{i : 0 < i \leq n \wedge M = my.i : i - M\} \\
&\wedge \quad m = my.n \quad \wedge \quad (\forall i : 0 < i \leq M : q.i = mx.i)
\end{aligned}$$

The obvious initial values for $n$, $s$ and $m$ are 0, $\emptyset$ and 0, respectively — $my.0 = 0$ follows easily from definitions D2 and D3. The obvious termination condition is $n = N$, but here we can make a minor optimisation. Observe that $my.n$ grows no faster that $n$. Now a pattern match at position $i$ of $y$, $n < i \leq N$ implies $my.i = M$, which is equivalent to $my.i - my.n = M - my.n$, which implies $i - n \geq M - my.n$, which implies $N - n \geq M - my.n$, which is equivalent to $N - n \geq M - m$ — so when this becomes false we may terminate. The program is:

$$\begin{aligned}
&|[ \ n, m : integer; q : sequence(M) \ of \ integer \\
&; n := 0 \ || \ s := \emptyset \ || \ m := 0 \\
&; \text{MPS} \\
&; \mathbf{do} \ N - n \geq M - m \rightarrow \\
&\qquad |[ \ g : integer \ \mathbf{func} = \\
&\qquad\qquad \mathbf{val} \ i : integer \\
&\qquad\qquad ; \mathbf{if} \ i < M \wedge x.i = y.n \quad \rightarrow i+1 \\
&\qquad\qquad [] \ \neg(i < M \wedge x.i = y.n) \rightarrow \\
&\qquad\qquad\qquad \mathbf{if} \ i = 0 \rightarrow 0 \ [] \ i > 0 \rightarrow g.(q.i) \ \mathbf{fi} \\
&\qquad\qquad \mathbf{fi} \bullet
\end{aligned}$$

$$m := g.m$$
$$]|$$
$$; n := n + 1$$
$$; \textbf{if } m = M \ \rightarrow \ s := s \cup \{n - M\} \ [] \ \ m < M \ \rightarrow \ \textbf{skip fi}$$
$$\textbf{od}$$
$$]|$$

The two conjunctions in the above code are "conditional", but a standard transformation will remove them if desired. A minor gain in efficiency can be got by converting the two recursive functions into loops, which is again a standard transformation, but one unlikely to be worth the trouble. Note that we didn't need to call upon L8 or L9.

# 3   Conclusion

Although the derivation above has of course been polished, it was arrived at pretty much as presented — with a few false moves here and there, but no great difficulties. My experience has been that developing the program by expression refinement is much easier than via invariant relations and loops alone. (See J. van der Woude [2], however, for a convincing derivation using loop invariants; indeed some of our inspiration has come from [2].) The most time-consuming part of the initial effort was experimenting with different notations. There is a basic choice: to use a string-based notation, or a notation based on indices of fixed strings — which is what was used eventually. The former seems on the face of it to be neater, and although it was succinct and malleable for parts of the derivation, in other parts it proved cumbersome. String indices, on the other hand, proved consistently workable, but they are tiresome to read — indeed the derivation may be accused of suffering from what has been called "indexitis". Indexitis apart, as an experiment in programming by expression refinement the outcome seems satisfactory, and the same approach has worked well on other problems. Experience suggests that programming by expression refinement is a more attractive basis for developing a fully formal practical programming methodology than one based solely on statement refinement.

## References

[1] D. E. Knuth, J. H. Morris Jr, and V. R. Pratt. Fast pattern matching in strings. *SIAM J. Comput.*, 6:323–350, 1977.

[2]  J. van der Woude. *Playing with Patterns, Searching for Strings*. Computing Science Report 87/13, Eindhoven University of Technology, The Netherlands, 1987.

Joseph M. Morris,
Department of Computing Science,
University of Glasgow,
Glasgow, G12  8QQ,
Scotland,
U.K.

# 38

# Methodical Competitive Snoopy-Caching

## Greg Nelson

> Often we have to be content with "worst case" bounds (which in contrast to averages have at least the advantage of not depending on the usually unknown input population). Sometimes we even have to be content with still vaguer definitions of what "reasonable performance" means. Yet this is no licence to design, for instance, a mechanism whose performance is occasionally surprisingly bad.
>
> —Edsger Dijkstra (EWD462)

A "competitive" algorithm is one that doesn't thrash. This at any rate is one way of looking at the more precise definition: an on-line algorithm is competitive if its performance is within a constant factor of the optimum achievable by an off-line algorithm.

The first competitiveness results seem to be by Sleator and Tarjan in 1985, who proved the competitiveness of the LRU page replacement strategy and of the move-to-front strategy for repeatedly searching a list [2].

The key step in proving the competitiveness of an algorithm is to come up with a "potential function", much as the key step in verifying a loop is to come up with a loop invariant. It seems that this is usually done by pulling the potential function out of a hat. The purpose of this note is to explore the possibility of deriving potential functions systematically.

As a test case, I take the problem of deriving the function for Theorem 4.1 from Karlin, Manasse, Rudolph, and Sleator [1], which proves the competitiveness of an on-line algorithm for managing a snoopy cache in a multiprocessor. This note is self-contained.

Consider a memory system for a multiprocessor consisting of a set of caches, each of which contains a set of address-data pairs. All operations maintain the *consistency invariant*, which is that each address is paired with exactly one datum (that is, there exists a function $M$ such that for every address-data pair $(a, d)$ in any cache, $d = M(a)$). The set of addresses is partitioned into sets called *pages*, and the system also maintains the *page invariant*, which is that if two addresses are in the same page, then they are present in the same caches. The memory system as a whole is regarded as representing the function $M$.

The basic operations on the system are read, write, and drop:

$Rd_i(a)$   :   achieve $(a, M(a)) \in$ cache $i$, without changing $M$.
$Wr_i(a, d)$:   achieve $M(a) = d$, without changing $M(a')$
         for $a' \neq a$, assuming that $(a, M(a)) \in$ cache $i$.
$Dr_i(a)$   :   drop all address-data pairs for $a$'s page from cache $i$.

$Rd_i(a)$ requires accessing some cache that contains $(a, M(a))$. If cache $i$ doesn't contain the pair, we say the read *misses*. Similarly, because of the consistency requirement, $Wr_i(a, d)$ must modify each cache $j$ that contains $(a, M(a))$. If this happens for any $j \neq i$, we say that a *write through* occurs.

A bus is available in the system to provide the communication required by read misses and write throughs. In one bus cycle a single address-data pair, together with a few bits of control information, can be broadcast to all caches in the system. Information can also be returned in the control lines; for example, in one cycle a cache can broadcast an address-data pair and receive in return the information of whether that address is present in any of the other caches. Our goal is to execute an on-line sequence of read and write operations, interspersing drop operations so as to use as few bus cycles as possible.

In a uniprocessor, the purpose of a cache is to provide faster reads and writes than the main memory. The only reason to drop a page from a uniprocessor's cache is to make room for other information. But in a shared memory multiprocessor, the main purpose of the caches is to avoid swamping the bus, and it may be desirable to drop a page from a cache in order to avoid the communication cost of keeping it up-to-date. To focus on the latter issue to the exclusion of the former, we assume that the caches are unbounded. This implies that the behavior of a page has no affect on the behavior of other pages, so from here on we consider a single fixed page and consider only the operations that affect it.

To see the basic uncertainty faced by the on-line algorithm, consider executing $Wr_i$ when the page is present in two caches, say caches $i$ and $j$. If this is the first of a long sequence of writes from cache $i$, then the best strategy is to drop the page from cache $j$, so that the rest of the sequence won't require any bus cycles. On the other hand, if a read operation from cache $j$ is imminent, the best strategy is to write through.

An off-line algorithm can choose on the basis of the sequence to come, but an on-line algorithm must guess. If the on-line algorithm hastily drops the page from cache $j$, and $Rd_j$ is next, it does worse than it might by a factor of about $p$, where $p$ is the page size, because an entire page must be read to satisfy a read miss. On the other hand, if the on-line algorithm stubbornly retains the page in cache $j$ throughout an unbounded sequence of $Wr_i$ commands, it uses one bus cycle per command when it might use none. In this case, the ratio between the on-line cost and the optimal off-line cost grows without bound. Thus, pure stubbornness is non-competitive, and pure hastiness is competitive with ratio $p$.

Some reflection suggests that we can hope to achieve a competitive algorithm with ratio two by balancing the costs of erroneous hastiness and stubbornness: in the situation above, the algorithm would be stubborn for $p$ calls to $Wr_i$, after which it would give up and drop the page from cache $j$.

In general, we add to each cache $j$ a counter $a_j$ whose value ranges over $[0..p]$. When a cache $j$ acquires the page, $a_j$ is set to $p$. The invariant $(a_j \neq 0) = $ (cache $j$ has the page) is maintained. Each time any cache $i$ does a write through, if some $a_j$ exists satisfying $j \neq i \wedge a_j \neq 0$, then one such $a_j$ is chosen and decremented. (The selection is awkward from a hardware point of view, but not impossible.) When a cache's counter reaches zero, it drops the page.

To compare this strategy with the optimal off-line strategy, we imagine two computations proceeding together: computation $A$, which executes a sequence of $Rd$ and $Wr$ commands by the rules given above, and computation $B$, which executes the same sequence of $Rd$ and $Wr$ commands, with an arbitrary interleaving of $Dr$ commands. The state variables of this computation are

$a_i$    in the range $[0..p]$, used by $A$ as described above.

$b_i$    which is $+1$ if the page is in $B$'s cache $i$ and $-1$ if it isn't.

$C_A$    the number of bus cycles used by $A$.

$C_B$    the number of bus cycles used by $B$.

The operations on the state are

$$
\begin{aligned}
Rd_i \equiv\ & \textbf{if } a_i \neq 0 \rightarrow Skip \\
& [\!]\ a_i = 0 \rightarrow C_A, a_i := C_A + p, p \\
& \textbf{fi}; \\
& \textbf{if } b_i = +1 \rightarrow Skip \\
& [\!]\ b_i = -1 \rightarrow C_B, b := C_B + p, +1 \\
& \textbf{fi}
\end{aligned}
$$

$$Wr_i \; \equiv \; \textbf{if } a_i \neq 0 \; \wedge \; b_i = +1 \; \rightarrow$$
$$\textbf{if } \exists j : j \neq i \; \wedge \; a_j \neq 0 \; \rightarrow \; C_A, a_j := C_A + 1, a_j - 1$$
$$[\!] \; (\forall j : j = i \; \vee \; a_j = 0) \; \rightarrow \; Skip$$
$$\textbf{fi};$$
$$\textbf{if } (\exists j : j \neq i \; \wedge \; b_j = +1) \; \rightarrow \; C_B := C_B + 1$$
$$[\!] \; (\forall j : j = i \; \vee \; b_j = -1) \; \rightarrow \; Skip$$
$$\textbf{fi}$$
$$\textbf{fi}$$

$$Dr_i \; \equiv \; \textbf{if } b_i = 1 \; \rightarrow \; b_i := -1 \; \textbf{fi}$$

(The "$\exists j$"construct used in $Wr_i$ to introduce the first instance of the local $j$ is called an "initializing guard": the scope of the local includes the whole guarded command, not just the guard. The other occurrences of the local $j$ are in ordinary guards, and are parenthesized accordingly.)

Any sequence of these operations that does not abort represents a possible computation of the system.

**Theorem**    Any computation maintains the invariant

$$(1) \qquad C_A - 2C_B \; \leq \; \Phi$$

for some "potential function" $\Phi$ that depends only on the $a_i$ and $b_i$.

Since $\Phi$ is independent of the length of the computation, the theorem implies that computation $A$ uses at most twice as many bus cycles as any computation that executes the same $Rd$ and $Wr$ commands, with $Dr$ commands interleaved arbitrarily, ignoring constants that are independent of the length of the computation. Thus, the algorithm is competitive with ratio 2.

**Proof**    We will prove the theorem by deriving an appropriate $\Phi$. Since no command $Rd$, $Wr$, or $Dr$ changes $(a_i, b_i)$ for more than one value of $i$, we optimistically assume that $\Phi$ has the form

$$(2) \qquad \sum_i \phi(a_i, b_i) \; + \; \text{a constant}$$

for some function $\phi$. By introducing a state function $C$ defined by $C \equiv C_A - 2C_B$, and breaking $Rd$ and $Wr$ into four cases each, we can reduce the proof to the problem of showing that (1) is held invariant by nine commands, each with the form

$$(3) \qquad C, a_i, b_i := C + \Delta C, a_i', b_i'$$

To show that (3) maintains (1), compute

$$
\begin{aligned}
& (1) \;\Rightarrow\; \mathrm{wp}((3),(1)) \\
\equiv\quad & (1) \;\Rightarrow\; C + \Delta C \;\leq\; \Phi(a_i : a_i', b_i : b_i') \\
\Leftarrow\quad & \Phi + \Delta C \;\leq\; \Phi(a_i : a_i', b_i : b_i') \\
\equiv\quad & \Delta C \;\leq\; \phi(a_i', b_i') - \phi(a_i, b_i) \qquad\qquad (4)
\end{aligned}
$$

Thus we have nine constraints on $\phi$, each of the form (4), which if solved will complete the proof.

The following table lists the four cases of $Rd$. In any row, all entries are forced by the first two. The variable $a$ in the fourth and sixth columns represents any non-zero value of $a_i$.

| $\Delta C_A$ | $\Delta C_B$ | $\Delta C$ | $a_i'$ | $b_i'$ | $a_i$ | $b_i$ |
|---|---|---|---|---|---|---|
| 0 | 0 | 0 | $a$ | $+1$ | $a$ | $+1$ |
| $p$ | 0 | $p$ | $p$ | $+1$ | 0 | $+1$ |
| 0 | $p$ | $-2p$ | $a$ | $+1$ | $a$ | $-1$ |
| $p$ | $p$ | $-p$ | $p$ | $+1$ | 0 | $-1$ |

From the right five columns, using (4), we derive

$$
\begin{aligned}
0 &\;\leq\; \phi(a,1) - \phi(a,1) && (Rd1\phi) \\
p &\;\leq\; \phi(p,1) - \phi(0,1) && (Rd2\phi) \\
-2p &\;\leq\; \phi(a,1) - \phi(a,-1) && (Rd3\phi) \\
-p &\;\leq\; \phi(p,1) - \phi(0,-1) && (Rd4\phi)
\end{aligned}
$$

$Rd1\phi$ is trivial. As for $Rd2\phi$ and $Rd3\phi$, we optimistically hope that $\phi$ will be multi-linear, and strengthen them to

$$
\begin{aligned}
\partial\phi/\partial a \,|_{b=1} &\;\geq\; 1 && (Rd2\partial) \\
\partial\phi/\partial b &\;\geq\; -p && (Rd3\partial)
\end{aligned}
$$

$Rd4\phi$ follows from $Rd2\phi$ and $Rd3\phi$:

$$
\begin{aligned}
& \phi(p,1) - \phi(0,-1) \\
=\quad & (\phi(p,1) - \phi(0,1)) + (\phi(0,1) - \phi(0,-1)) \\
\geq\quad & p + -2p \\
=\quad & -p.
\end{aligned}
$$

The table for $Dr$ is

| $\Delta C_A$ | $\Delta C_B$ | $\Delta C$ | $a_i'$ | $b_i'$ | $a_i$ | $b_i$ |
|---|---|---|---|---|---|---|
| 0 | 0 | 0 | $a$ | $-1$ | $a$ | $+1$ |

whence, by (4)

$$
0 \;\leq\; \phi(a,-1) - \phi(a,+1) \qquad\qquad (Dr\phi)
$$

which we strengthen to:

$$\partial\phi/\partial b \;\leq\; 0. \tag{$Dr\partial$}$$

In the following table for $Wr_i$, the index $j$ denotes whichever cache had its counter decremented, or any cache other than $i$ if no counter was decremented. As before, the first two columns enumerate the possibilities and determine the rest of the table:

| $\Delta C_A$ | $\Delta C_B$ | $\Delta C$ | $a_j'$ | $b_j'$ | $a_j$ | $b_j$ |
|---|---|---|---|---|---|---|
| 0 | 0 | 0 | 0 | $-1$ | 0 | $-1$ |
| 1 | 0 | 1 | $a-1$ | $-1$ | $a$ | $-1$ |
| 0 | 1 | $-2$ | 0 | $+1$ | 0 | $+1$ |
| 1 | 1 | $-1$ | $a-1$ | $+1$ | $a$ | $+1$ |

Using (4) we derive

$$
\begin{aligned}
0 &\leq \phi(0,-1) - \phi(0,-1) & (Wr1\phi)\\
1 &\leq \phi(a-1,-1) - \phi(a,-1) & (Wr2\phi)\\
-2 &\leq \phi(0,1) - \phi(0,1) & (Wr3\phi)\\
-1 &\leq \phi(a-1,1) - \phi(a,1) & (Wr4\phi)
\end{aligned}
$$

$Wr1\phi$ and $Wr3\phi$ are trivial. We strengthen the others to

$$
\begin{aligned}
\partial\phi/\partial a \,|_{b=-1} &\leq -1 & (Wr2\partial)\\
\partial\phi/\partial a \,|_{b=1} &\leq 1 & (Wr4\partial)
\end{aligned}
$$

Collecting the constraints, we need $\phi(a,b)$ that for $0 \leq a \leq p$ satisfies:

$$
\begin{aligned}
\partial\phi/\partial a \,|_{b=1} &= 1 & (Rd2\partial),(Wr4\partial)\\
\partial\phi/\partial a \,|_{b=-1} &\leq -1 & (Wr2\partial)\\
-p \leq \partial\phi/\partial b &\leq 0 & (Rd3\partial),(Dr\partial)
\end{aligned}
$$

Our optimism has been rewarded; a suitable function is:

$$\phi(a,b) \;=\; b(a-p).$$

With this $\phi$, we have that $C \leq \Phi$ is invariant. To make the invariant hold initially, we can use the constant in (2) to make up for any differences in the initial states of the caches. This completes the proof of the theorem.

I showed this derivation to Mark Manasse, and together we applied the method to show the competitiveness of the FIFO cache. Since a single atomic action changes many $a_i$ values, the simple cancellation that produces (4) from the line above it doesn't work anymore, so that a sum over $i$ remains. The method still worked, but I would have gotten lost in the algebra without Mark's help. It is clear that he can divine potential functions faster than I can derive them; but then, he has had a lot of practice lately.

Mark suggested that it would be a breakthrough to find another pattern of reasoning altogether, in which the potential function was somehow constructed *before* the actions of the loop, as the invariant of a loop is generally constructed before its body.

## REFERENCES

[1] Anna R. Karlin, Mark S. Manasse, Larry Rudolph, and Daniel D. Sleator. Competitive snoopy-caching. *Algorithmica*, 3:79–119, 1988. A preliminary version appeared in *27th Annual Symposium on Foundations of Computer Science*, 1986, pp. 244–54.

[2] D. D. Sleator and R. E. Tarjan. Amortized efficiency of list update and paging rules. *CACM*, 28(2):202–8, 1985.

Greg Nelson,
Digital Equipment Corporation,
Systems Research Center,
130 Lytton Avenue,
Palo Alto, CA  94301–1044,
U.S.A.

# 39

# Beauty and the Beast of Software Complexity — Elegance versus Elephants

## Peter G. Neumann

## Abstract

Elegance is certainly attainable in the small, but is sorely lacking in most complex computer systems. The reasons for this appear to lie not so much with computer science, but rather with the people who apply it. This note briefly considers some of the perceived obstacles and examines the hypothesis that suitable use of what is generally considered good practice in the small can lead to elegance in the large.

## Introduction

We begin with a few appropriate quotes relating to complexity, abstraction, formality, creativity, and thinking (discussed in [3]).

- "Everything should be made as simple as possible, but no simpler." (Albert Einstein)

- "... our abstracting from physical objects and situations proceeds by missing, neglecting, and forgetting, ... these disregarded characteristics usually produce errors in evaluation resulting in the disasters of life." (Alfred Korzybski, 'Science and Sanity', 1933)

- "Logic, like whiskey, loses its beneficial effect when taken in too large quantities." (Lord Dunsany, 'My Ireland', XIX, 1938)

- "There is nothing more fearful than imagination without taste." (Johann Wolfgang von Goethe, 'Maxims', III, 1790)

- "The ability to *ponder* successfully is absolutely vital... And don't think that such a vein of gold (as a "brilliant, elegant solution") was struck by pure luck; the man [who] found the conclusive argument was someone who knew how to ponder well. (Edsger Dijkstra, 1976 [1])

# Aids to elegance

Elegance is obviously in the eye of the beholder. From a computer system viewpoint, the most important aspects of it are high quality, good taste, and apparent simplicity — even in the face of complexity. An expectation of concomitant high cost is neither necessary nor desirable.

A challenge in computer system design is that the representation of the functionality at any particular layer of abstraction should exhibit just those characteristics that are essential at that layer, without the clutter of notational obfuscation and unnecessary appearance of underlying complexity. There are many techniques that can be valuable in computer system design, including structuring concepts such as hierarchical abstraction, encapsulation, information hiding and virtualization (e.g., invisibility of physical locations, concurrency, replication, backup, and recovery, as well as invisibility of the distribution of control and/or data); also valuable are strong typing, functional isolation, decoupling of policy and mechanism, separation of privileges, and allocation of least privilege. In addition, formalization of requirements and specifications can be beneficial in various circumstances, particularly where there are extremely stringent requirements. Tasteful programming language constructs may also contribute, particularly those that enforce or enhance the above design constraints.

# Critical systems

The above-mentioned techniques and approaches tend not to be used extensively in real systems that are small, probably because the problems appear to be tractible without them. They tend not to be used in real systems that are large, for a variety of reasons discussed below, although these techniques can be extremely powerful in the large; furthermore, as noted below, they all scale up rather nicely. However, whether a system is small or large, if its requirements are critical —e.g., it must be depended upon to protect lives or other valuable resources— these techniques may have enormous value in providing nontrivial assurances that the system might actually do what is expected of it. As used here, 'critical' can refer to stringent requirements for data confidentiality, data integrity, system integrity, availability and preventions of denials of service, real-time performance, reliability, hardware fault tolerance, functional correctness, human safety, etc. There are also properties of the user interface that may greatly affect the ability of the system to behave as desired or to be used satisfactorily without compromising the critical requirements, such as ease of use, unambiguity, and friendly 'look-and-feel'. To some extent, and in certain circumstances, aspects of such properties may also be considered critical.

# Elegance in the large

One of the most frustrating aspects of excellent research is that it seldom seems to be applied consistently and tastefully in real systems. What are the difficulties in achieving elegance in the large?

- Educational processes are too often oriented toward rote learning and regurgitation, as well as mechanical application of techniques and tools, rather than understanding and intuition. Discipline for the sake of discipline —without understanding— is of very limited value. But a lack of discipline can lead to horrendous results.

- Many people seem to have difficulty in grasping the concepts of hierarchical abstraction and its enormous benefits. 'Hierarchy' has different meanings for different people, but often the meaning is ill-defined.

- Many people are intimidated by rigor, clarity, and formal thinking. Others are insulted by it. Few appreciate the power of logical thought. Theoretically inclined readers of this Festschrift are undoubtably among the enlightened, but they are for the most part not involved with the practitioners; that may in itself be a significant factor.

- People tend to be creatures of habit. Weak techniques and short-term solutions that may seem adequate (or irrelevant) in the small tend to scale up poorly, but get used anyway.

- 'Quick-and-dirty' is often considered to be good enough, even though it may backfire later on. However, systems that must dependably satisfy extremely critical requirements deserve —and indeed require— better treatment.

- The ubiquitous commercial bottom line (profits) leads to many compromises. Elegance is often the first to go, along with the longer-term benefits that it can catalyze.


# Scaling up to reality

In designing and developing systems with critical requirements, elegance has enormous potential benefits — irrespective of the system complexity. There are many problems arising in complex systems that must be thoroughly comprehended, but that once understood can be structured in a way that conceptually simplifies the design. For example, a clean decomposition of a large system into explicit hierarchical layers of abstraction can help provide a rigorous basis for the system, as well as permitting uniform strategies for both analysis and synthesis — such as constructive deadlock avoidance, dependence only upon components that are at least as trustworthy, and formal analysis of structural properties.

In principle, all of the above concepts scale up nicely, with each capable of contributing to the elegance with which the overall design can be represented. In practice, the conceptual simplicity is often marred by reality, which may force compromises. For example, there are sometimes difficult issues relating to performance — such as unacceptable real-time behavior resulting from layers of interpretation, run-time checking, and nonoptimizable implementation strategies that are bound by poor design choices. There are also issues related to sheer size and limitations on the human attention span. For example, there have been relatively small efforts in formal specification and verification to handle security kernels, ultrareliable system modules, and Byzantine algorithms. But large systems have not yet proved amenable to such techniques.

Good taste and anticipation of the nasty problems of complexity are particularly important. But how can such attributes be taught? We learn primarily by copying others. Thus, it becomes essential to have available some real systems to emulate whose development uses only the most elegant approaches, with carefully documentation of the entire development effort. Obtaining the first few such systems will take extraordinary pains; after that it should be much easier.

# Interactions among requirements

One of the most difficult real problems that tends to be ignored by researchers and developers alike is how to deal simultaneously with the entire collection of necessary requirements. (See [2].)

In some cases, the ability to satisfy a particular requirement may depend upon the extent to which other requirements are satisfied. Human safety is a good example. In general, human safety of a computer system cannot be met unless the underlying layers enforce adequate reliability, system integrity, crash-resistance, and real-time responsiveness.

In certain cases some of the requirements may appear to be mutually antagonistic. Understanding the interdependencies among different requirements and among the different layers is thus an important step. As an illustration of this problem, consider the following illustrative potential antagonisms:

- Ease of use versus security. Needs for stringent identification, authentication, and access controls may seriously impede user friendliness.

- Flexibility versus system integrity. The ability to change the software at a particular layer may compromise system integrity and data confidentiality.

- Fault-tolerant recovery versus confidentiality. Attempts to recover functionality may require extraordinary privileges to be made available to a higher layer, violating information hiding requirements, encapsulation, or confidentiality. More generally, handling of unusual conditions may undermine the cleanliness of a design unless the occurrence of those conditions was anticipated as an integral part of the design.

- Performance versus conservative fault tolerance. For example, fail-safe atomic transactions may impose constraints on distributed updates, locking, etc., that may seriously hamper real-time responsiveness.

- Optimization for increased performance versus other requirements. Optimization may compromise other requirements, particularly if it invalidates design criteria such as encapsulation and separation.

- Accuracy versus confidentiality in a statistical database, where all sorts of inferences may be possible if data items are completely accurate.

In general, it is necessary to identify all of the potentially negative interactions in advance, to determine the possible effects on any particular design and to address them constructively. Although some of the antagonisms can be avoided by clever design, others may not be avoidable.

## Conclusions

Elegance does not necessarily imply 'small' or 'academic' or 'irrelevant'. Techniques that are well-known in academic circles need to be used much more widely in practice, perhaps in some cases modified so that they would be more useful. The limitations appear to stem from human frailty rather than from theory or technology. However, the responsibilities for achieving greater global elegance are distributed among all of us — e.g., as researchers, teachers, developers, and managers. There is a special responsibility on researchers to ensure that their work is truly useful in real systems.

There are no substitutes for intelligence, intuitive understanding, experience, and good taste. But inspired detachment from the short-term problems is also necessary in developing elegant large computer systems that are able to meet stringent requirements throughout.

REFERENCES

[1] Edsger W. Dijkstra. *The Teaching of Programming, i.e., the Teaching of Thinking.* Volume 46 of Lecture Notes in Computer Science, Springer-Verlag, 1976.

[2] Peter G. Neumann. On hierarchical design of computer systems for critical applications. *IEEE Transactions on Software Engineering*, SE-12(9):905–920, September 1986.

[3] Peter G. Neumann. Psychosocial implications of computer software development and use: Zen and the art of computing. In D. Ferrari, M. Bolognani, and J. Goguen, editors, *Theory and Practice of Software Technology*, pages 221–232, North-Holland, 1983.

# Appendix: A Large-System Glossary for EWD

- Elephantine equations. Large-system requirements for which there may be a multiplicity of integral solutions.

- Pachydermatitis. A breakdown in the outermost layer of a very large system (e.g., manifesting itself as a flaky user interface). (Icthyosis scales up inefficiently.)

- Behemotherhood. In very large systems, motherhood that has a high likelihood of running amok.

- Hippodromederrière. An awkward race down the back stretch to write the last half-million lines of code before the system self-destructs in an evolutionary backwater.

Peter G. Neumann,
Computer Science Laboratory,
SRI International,
333 Ravenswood Ave.,
Menlo Park, California    94025–3493,
U.S.A.

# 40

# A Note on Feasibility

## W. Peremans[1]

The concept of feasibility has a long history, although it has long remained implicit, and was not analysed or discussed as such. It is an obvious supposition that the act of counting may be continued indefinitely, one that need not be stated explicitly. Of course everyone was aware that in reality it is not possible to count to infinity and that, therefore, the indefinite continuability of the number sequence is an idealization of reality. This is why the term "potentially infinite" is sometimes used.

The practice of mathematics concerned itself more and more with the infinite. Anything that may be dealt with in a finite number of steps was considered both uninteresting and essentially solved. Whether it was actually possible to execute these steps was never discussed. I remember being taught in the days of my youth that Vinogradov had proved by analytic means that every sufficiently large odd number is the sum of three primes. In principle this solved the question whether every odd number that is at least 7 is the sum of three primes: there is an explicit bound above which the answer is affirmative and below which the question may be answered by inspection. The single annoying thing was the truly enormous size of this bound.

In the second half of the present century other views on this matter have become predominant. This has led to a paradoxical situation: in a time when our ability to manipulate large numbers has increased tremendously due to the development of automated calculation, we have become more acutely aware of the existence of limitations. This increase of awareness has also been stimulated by a demand from the applications of mathematics. There problems were encountered of a finite nature (hence essentially solved, according to the traditional view) that are intractable in practice when large numbers of objects are involved. Examples: the solution of large systems of linear equations, problems in optimization such as the travelling salesman problem. The need to ensure practicability by means of an effi-

---

[1]Translated from Dutch by Lex Bijlsma.

cient approach gave rise to new ways of doing mathematics, in two senses. In the first place specific disciplines of applied mathematics evolved, such as linear programming and optimization. In the second place, the question what limits there are to the improvements to be expected from attempts to increase efficiency was starting to be dealt with in a mathematical way.

An important attainment on the latter path is complexity theory. Here another paradox arises. Though engendered by the realization of our finiteness and the consequent limits to our abilities, complexity theory has applied itself to making asymptotic pronouncements that can only be meaningfully interpreted if one or more parameters become "arbitrarily large". If it is stated, for instance, that the number of steps in the solution of a problem is polynomial in the number of variables $n$ of that problem, whereas a second problem is exponential, this does guarantee that for "sufficiently large" $n$ the first number of steps will be drastically smaller than the second, but it cannot be inferred how large $n$ must be to achieve this. Moreover, from a problem's being polynomial, as long as degree and coefficients are not known, one cannot deduce whether for a "large" $n$ encountered in practice the process can actually be carried out. It might even be the case that for the particular value of $n$ considered the exponential problem performs better. The fact that, nevertheless, practicians find the results of complexity theory useful, can only be caused by the circumstance that experience has shown the constants and coefficients implicit in the assertions of this theory to be of "moderate" size.

Anyone attempting to judge this state of affairs as a matter of principle will be less than completely satisfied. In my opinion, our forced position has been caused by the enormous mental pressure exercised upon us by the potentially infinite. It is beyond dispute that the introduction of the potentially infinite has been a highly productive mental step, one that has tremendously advanced, if not created outright, the thing we call mathematics. The simplest and most fundamental crystallization of this concept in mathematics is the natural number. The process of repeatedly taking a unit ("counting") is idealized to an indefinite repeatability, leading to the concept of natural number and the principle of mathematical induction. For us, due to time and space limitations, this indefinite repeatability is a fiction. Next to mathematics, logic too is steeped in this fiction. It is supposed that logical formulas are allowed to be of arbitrary length, but also that derivation rules, as they occur for instance in systems of natural deduction, may be applied an arbitrary number of times.

Actually, the concept of feasibility fits this practice very badly. Attempts to formalize it lead to contradictions known as classical paradoxes. When I use the word "formalize" here, I mean the construction of a formal system in which the concept of feasibility is contained and has a number of reasonable and obvious properties. Let what follows serve as an illustration. We refer to the classical paradox of the sand heap. To sand heaps the following properties are ascribed.

1. A sand heap is a nonempty finite set of sand grains.
2. If one grain is taken away from a sand heap, it remains a sand heap.
3. There exists a sand heap.

If the usual theory of finite sets is applied here, a contradiction results. There are several ways to achieve this. Perhaps not the simplest method, but the one closest to the formulation given, is as follows. Consider the set $D$ of those natural numbers that occur as the number of sand grains in a sand heap. On account of 1. and 3. that set is nonempty and it consequently has a least element $a$; however, on account of 2., the number $a - 1$ must also be an element of $D$. Contradiction.

What does this have to do with feasibility? The properties ascribed to a sand heap express that the grains in a sand heap cannot be counted: their number is unfeasible. By complement formation, we find the following properties of feasible numbers.

1. The feasible numbers form a subset $F$ of $\mathbb{N}$ and $0 \in F$.
2. If $a \in F$, then $a + 1 \in F$.
3. $F \neq \mathbb{N}$.

Here the contradiction is even more manifest. From 1. and 2. it follows by mathematical induction that $F = \mathbb{N}$, contradicting 3.

What conclusion should be drawn from this? Whoever is sound in the mathematical faith will say that the contradiction mentioned above proves that we are dealing with a fallacy and that no concept of feasibility with the desired properties exists.

More cautious options, however, may be conceived. To start with, we observe that in daily life the concept of feasibility may be employed without inconvenience and even plays a useful role in all sorts of discussions. This shows that we are unwilling to discard it on account of the anathema hurled at it by mathematicians. It therefore seems a healthier view to assert that if a formalization of this concept leads to a contradiction, we have obviously chosen the wrong formalization. The thing we must evidently avoid in our formalization is the potentially infinite, which is incompatible with the concept of feasibility and manifests itself in the contradiction derived above by the use of mathematical induction.

Of course, everything above is neither new nor particularly original. Indeed, attempts have been made in the past to design a suitable formalism for feasibility, but to the best of my knowledge without much success so far. One of the attempts that have become somewhat widely known is the work of Yessenin-Volpin (see [2] and [3]). Unfortunately, however, I have the impression that no one other than he himself has been able to understand his work.

Perhaps it is not very surprising that these attempts were not successful. Traditionally, the concept of formalization itself is totally steeped in the concept of the potentially infinite. The pattern of logical reasoning is based on the possibility of indefinite repetition. Hence it is not sufficient to design an adjusted system of natural numbers, as for instance Yessenin-Volpin did. The way it is used (the meta-level, if you prefer) must be adjusted as well, which is more than the pattern of our culture will allow us to do.

Recent developments in the field of mathematical logic and the foundations of mathematics, however, might conceivably point a way out of this stalemate. I am referring to the developments whereby intensional aspects, as they occur for instance in intuitionism, are incorporated into a completely classical logical system, which can itself be expressed in the usual logical formalisms such as predicate logic. These intensional aspects are then brought into the game by means of added operators. In logic this approach has long been known: for instance in modal logic with its operators for "necessarily" and "possibly". Now this has been extended into mathematics, with operators for e.g. knowability (for this, see [1]). It seems to me that it might perhaps be possible to incorporate feasibility into such a framework as well. For the time being, this is merely a stray thought and I do not know if it will allow itself to be put into shape. Perhaps someone younger than I am would like to try his or her hand at it.

REFERENCES

[1] S. Shapiro, editor. *Intensional Mathematics*. North-Holland, Amsterdam, 1985. Studies in Logic and the Foundations of Mathematics, Vol. 113.

[2] A. S. Yessenin-Volpin. About infinity, finiteness and finitization (in connection with foundations of mathematics). In *Constructive Mathematics, Proceedings of the New Mexico State University Conference held at Las Cruces, New Mexico, August 11–15, 1980*, pages 274–313, Springer-Verlag, Berlin, 1981. Lecture Notes in Mathematics, Vol. 873.

[3] A. S. Yessenin-Volpin. The ultra-intuitionistic criticism and the anti-traditional program for the foundation of mathematics. In *Intuitionism and Proof Theory, Proceedings of the Summer Conference at Buffalo N.Y., 1968*, pages 3–45, North-Holland Publishing Company, Amsterdam, 1970. Studies in Logic and the foundations of Mathematics.

W. Peremans,
Vesaliuslaan 46, 5644 HL  Eindhoven,
The Netherlands.

# 41

# A Curious Property of Points and Circles in the Plane

## Karel A. Post

Given 5 points in the plane, no 3 on a line, no 4 on a circle, there are 10 circles that contain 3 of those points. We are interested in those circles that separate the remaining 2 points, i.e. that leave one of these points in their interior and the other in their exterior. Such a circle will be called a point splitting circle, or simply a *splitting circle*.

In a Chinese mathematical competition (1963) it was asked to show that there exists a splitting circle ([3]) and an analogous problem concerning more points was treated in [2] and [1].

We shall prove the following theorem:

**Theorem**   There are precisely 4 splitting circles.

**Proof**   Let us first consider an arbitrary 4-tuple of points, no 3 on a line: They determine 6 lines containing 2 of those points each, and such a line may be splitting or not, in the sense that the remaining 2 points are on different sides of the line or not, repectively.

The convex hull of this 4-tuple is either a quadrangle or a triangle. In the first case we have 2 splitting lines and 4 non-splitting lines, whereas in the second case we have 3 of both kinds.

In the quadrangle situation each point is on precisely 1 splitting line, in the triangle situation one point is on 3 splitting lines and the other points are on 1 splitting line each. Combination of these arguments yields for all cases:

(1a)   There are *at least 2 splitting* lines and *at least 3 non-splitting lines*.

(2a)   Every point is on *either 1 or 3 splitting lines*.

Now we consider our 5-tuple with its 10 circles:

We take one of these points, $A$ say, as centre of an inversion: Every point $P \neq A$ is mapped to a point $P'$ on the line $AP$, such that $A$ is not between $P$ and $P'$, and $|AP'| \cdot |AP|$ has a fixed value. Such a transformation maps circles containing $A$ to lines not containing $A$ and vice versa. We can state even more: If a circle containing $A$ splits the points $Q$ and $R$ then its image line splits the image points $Q'$ and $R'$ and conversely. So, taking the images of the remaining 4 points into consideration and using (1a) we may conclude

(1b) $A$ is on *at least 2 splitting circles* and on *at least 3 non-splitting circles.*

Using (2a) we may state

(2b) Every point pair containing $A$ is on *either 1 or 3 splitting circles.*

Because the choice of $A$ as centre of inversion was arbitrary among the 5 points we may claim

(1c) *Each of the 5 points* is on at least 2 splitting circles and on at least 3 non-splitting circles.

(2c) *Each point pair from the 5 points* is on either 1 or 3 splitting circles.

Now we are ready to finish the proof by a simple counting argument, using the fact that every circle contains 3 of the points, so every circle is counted 3 times in (1c) and 3 times in (2c):

Let there be $K$ splitting circles and $L$ non-splitting circles. Then, by (1c) we get

$$3K \geq 5 \cdot 2 = 10 \quad \text{and} \quad 3L \geq 5 \cdot 3 = 15$$

So, because $K + L = 10$ we find that $K = 4$ or $K = 5$.

Now assume that there are $M$ point pairs on 3 splitting circles and $N = 10 - M$ point pairs on 1 splitting circle. Then, by (2c) we obtain

$$3K \ = \ 3M + N \ = \ 10 + 2M,$$

which is obviously an even number. Hence, $3K$ is even, so that $K$ must be equal to 4.

## REFERENCES

[1] R. Honsberger. Mathematical Gems III. *Dolciani Mathematical Expositions*, 9:18–19, 1985.

[2] R. Honsberger. Mathematical Morsels, Problem 23. *Dolciani Mathematical Expositions*, 3:48–51, 1978.

[3] F. Swetz. The Chinese Mathematical Olympiads: a case study. *The American Mathematical: Monthly*, 79:899–904, 1972.

Karel A. Post,
Department of Mathematics and Computing Science,
Eindhoven University of Technology,
P.O. Box 513, 5600 MB Eindhoven, The Netherlands.

# 42

# A Problem Involving Subsequences

## Paul Pritchard

## Definitions and notation

The operators used herein are listed below in order of decreasing precedence; those within a bracketed group have equal precedence.

$$[\#, {}^\star], \;., \;\downarrow, \;[\frown, \cup, \mathbf{min}], \;[-, +],$$
$$[=, \neq, \leq, <, \geq, >, \prec, \preceq, \in],$$
$$\neg, \;[\wedge, \mathbf{cand}], \;\vee, \;[\equiv, \Rightarrow]$$

No associativity convention is used, but chains of comparisons are written in abbreviated form.

Let $(U, <)$ be a totally ordered finite set, and $\leq$ denote the reflexive companion of $<$. Let $U^\star$ denote the set of finite sequences of members of $U$. We use $W, X, Y$ to range over these sequences. We index the elements of a sequence from 0 (using dot notation), and write $\#X$ for the length of $X$. For $c \in U$, $X^\frown c$ denotes the sequence obtained by appending $c$ to $X$. For $i$ in the range $0 \leq i \leq \#X$, $X \downarrow i$ denotes the sequence comprising the first $i$ elements of $X$ (the *prefix* of $X$ of length $i$).

To define an irreflexive total order $\prec$ on $U^\star$ (known as *lexicographic order*), we first extend $(U, <)$ with a new bottom element $\perp$, and stipulate that $X.\#X = \perp$. ($\perp$ may not otherwise occur in sequences.) Also, we define a function that gives the length of the longest common prefix of two given sequences:

$$a(X, Y) \;=\; (\mathbf{max}\; i : 0 \leq i \leq (\#X \;\mathbf{min}\; \#Y) \;\wedge\; X \downarrow i = Y \downarrow i : i)$$

It is well-defined since $X \downarrow 0 = Y \downarrow 0$. Then

(0)     $X \prec Y \;\equiv\; X.a(X, Y) < Y.a(X, Y)$

We note that

(1)     $X = Y \;\equiv\; X.a(X, Y) = Y.a(X, Y)$

Let $\preceq$ denote the reflexive companion of $\prec$; each prefix of $Y$ stands in this relation to $Y$.

Now define $\overline{X}$ to be the set of all subsequences of $X$. Because $\overline{X}$ is finite, it contains a unique least upper bound of $Y$ provided it contains a bound of $Y$. In order to finesse this proviso, we further extend $(U, <)$ with a new top element $\top$, let $\top\!\!\!\top$ denote the sequence with sole element $\top$, and extend the definitions of our functions and operators appropriately, all of which licenses the following function definition:

$$b(Y, X) = (\min Z : Z \in \overline{X} \cup \{\top\!\!\!\top\} \wedge Y \preceq Z : Z)$$

## The problem

We may now state our problem:

> Given $X, Y$, design a program $Q$ that establishes $V = b(Y, X)$.

Note that $V, Z$ range over $U^\star \cup \{\top\!\!\!\top\}$.

The problem is closely related to one in [1], but the present treatment is quite different (and, we hope, considerably more convincing).

## Development of first solution

Our plan is to process $X$ from left to right, maintaining $V = b(Y, X{\downarrow}k)$. Supposing this holds, and with $j = a(Y, V)$, we have

$\quad$ *true*

$=\quad \{Y \preceq b(Y, W)\}$

$\quad Y \preceq V$

$=\quad \{\text{definition of } \preceq; (0); (1)\}$

$\quad Y.j \leq V.j$

$=\quad \{(2), \text{ see below}\}$

$\quad Y.j \leq (V{\downarrow}j^\frown V.j).j$

$=\quad \{j = a(Y, V{\downarrow}j^\frown V.j); \text{ definition of } \preceq; (0); (1)\}$

$\quad Y \preceq V{\downarrow}j^\frown V.j$

$=\quad \{V{\downarrow}j^\frown V.j \text{ is a prefix of } V\}$

$\quad Y \preceq V{\downarrow}j^\frown V.j \preceq V$

$=\quad \{\overline{X{\downarrow}k} \cup \{\top\!\!\!\top\} \text{ is closed under prefixing}; V \text{ is minimal}\}$

$\quad V{\downarrow}j^\frown V.j = V$

where a new lemma is used:

(2) $\qquad (W{\downarrow}i{\frown}c).i \;=\; c$

We have discovered that $V$ consists of a prefix of $Y$ followed by $c$, which is an element of $X{\downarrow}k$ or $\top$ or $\bot$. Now $c$ is uniquely determined except when $V = Y \;\wedge\; \#Y \neq 0$, when it may be taken as either $\bot$ (as discovered above) or $Y.(\#Y - 1)$.

To gracefully handle this awkward special case, we separate our concerns: We maintain the least *strict* bound of $Y$ (using the neat normal form above), and also the longest prefix of $Y$ in $\overline{X{\downarrow}k}$ (which will change smoothly with $k$, and caters to the special case). Accordingly, we define two new functions:

$$s(Y,W) \;=\; (\mathbf{min}\, Z : Z \in \overline{W} \cup \{\top\!\top\} \;\wedge\; Y \prec Z : Z)$$
$$f(Y,W) \;=\; (\mathbf{max}\, j : 0 \leq j \leq \#Y \;\wedge\; Y{\downarrow}j \in \overline{W} : j)$$

Our invariant is

$$P : s(Y, X{\downarrow}k) \;=\; Y{\downarrow}n{\frown}c \;\wedge\; m \;=\; f(Y, X{\downarrow}k) \;\wedge\; 0 \leq k \leq \#X$$

Our first approximation of $Q$ becomes

$$k, n, m, c := 0, 0, 0, \top; \; \{\, P \,\}$$
$$\mathbf{do}\; m \neq \#Y \;\wedge\; k \neq \#X \;\rightarrow\; \{\, P \;\wedge\; m \neq \#Y \;\wedge\; k \neq \#X \,\}$$
$$\qquad\qquad\qquad\qquad Q0; \; \{\, P_{k+1}^{k} \,\}$$
$$\qquad\qquad\qquad\qquad k := k + 1 \; \{\, P \,\}$$
$$\mathbf{od};\; \{\, P \;\wedge\; (m = \#Y \;\vee\; k = \#X) \,\}$$
$$\mathbf{if}\; m = \#Y \;\rightarrow\; V := Y$$
$$[\!]\; m \neq \#Y \;\rightarrow\; V := Y{\downarrow}n{\frown}c$$
$$\mathbf{fi}$$
$$\{\, V = b(Y, X) \,\}$$

$P$ may be partitioned in the form

$$P \;=\; P'(n, c, k) \;\wedge\; P''(m, k) \;\wedge\; P'''(k)$$

$Q0$ will establish $P'''(k+1)$ provided only that it does not alter $k$. Establishing the two remaining conjuncts of $P_{k+1}^{k}$ involves two *separate* obligations. That of updating $m$ is met by a simple conditional statement, leaving the other obligation to a statement $Q1$ that does not change $m$ or $k$. The resulting $Q0$ is

$$\{\, P \;\wedge\; m \neq \#Y \;\wedge\; k \neq \#X \,\}$$
$$Q1;$$
$$\{\, R1 : P'(n, c, k + 1) \;\wedge\; P''(m, k) \;\wedge\; P'''(k + 1) \,\}$$
$$\mathbf{if}\; X.k = Y.m \;\rightarrow\; m := m + 1 \;[\!]\; X.k \neq Y.m \;\rightarrow\; skip \; \mathbf{fi}$$
$$\{\, P_{k+1}^{k} \,\}$$

It remains to construct a $Q1$ that updates $n$ and $c$, and thereby establishes the first conjunct of $R1$ (without changing $m$ or $k$). The only members of the form $Y\!\downarrow\!n'^\frown c'$ in

$$\overline{X\!\downarrow\!(k+1)} \cup \{\top\} \ - \ \overline{X\!\downarrow\!k} \cup \{\top\}$$

are those with $c' = X.k$. Suppose one of these strictly bounds $Y$, i.e., $Y \prec Y\!\downarrow\!n'^\frown c'$. Then, appealing to

$$(3) \qquad Y \prec Y\!\downarrow\!i^\frown d \ \equiv \ Y.i < d$$

we have $Y.n' < c'$. Similarly, assuming $P'(n,c,k)$, we also have $Y.n < c$. Let $j = a(Y\!\downarrow\!n'^\frown c', Y\!\downarrow\!n^\frown c)$. Then

$$Y\!\downarrow\!n'^\frown c' \ \prec \ Y\!\downarrow\!n^\frown c$$

$= \qquad \{(0)\}$

$$(Y\!\downarrow\!n'^\frown c').j \ < \ (Y\!\downarrow\!n^\frown c).j$$

$= \qquad \{\text{case analysis}\}$

$$(n' > n \ \wedge \ (Y\!\downarrow\!n'^\frown c').j < (Y\!\downarrow\!n^\frown c).j) \ \vee$$
$$(n' = n \ \wedge \ (Y\!\downarrow\!n'^\frown c').j < (Y\!\downarrow\!n^\frown c).j) \ \vee$$
$$(n' < n \ \wedge \ (Y\!\downarrow\!n'^\frown c').j < (Y\!\downarrow\!n^\frown c).j)$$

$= \qquad \{\text{introduce assumptions}; \ \neg(n' = n \ \wedge \ c' = c)\}$

$$(n' > n \ \wedge \ Y.n < c \ \wedge \ (Y\!\downarrow\!n'^\frown c').j < (Y\!\downarrow\!n^\frown c).j) \ \vee$$
$$(n' = n \ \wedge \ c \neq c' \ \wedge \ (Y\!\downarrow\!n'^\frown c').j < (Y\!\downarrow\!n^\frown c).j) \quad \vee$$
$$(n' < n \ \wedge \ Y.n' < c' \ \wedge \ (Y\!\downarrow\!n'^\frown c').j < (Y\!\downarrow\!n^\frown c).j)$$

$= \qquad \{\text{three calculations of } j\}$

$$(n' > n \ \wedge \ Y.n < c \ \wedge \ (Y\!\downarrow\!n'^\frown c').n < (Y\!\downarrow\!n^\frown c).n) \ \vee$$
$$(n' = n \ \wedge \ c \neq c' \ \wedge \ (Y\!\downarrow\!n'^\frown c').n' < (Y\!\downarrow\!n^\frown c).n) \quad \vee$$
$$(n' < n \ \wedge \ Y.n' < c' \ \wedge \ (Y\!\downarrow\!n'^\frown c').n' < (Y\!\downarrow\!n^\frown c).n')$$

$= \qquad \{(2); \ i' > i \ \Rightarrow \ (X\!\downarrow\!i'^\frown c).i = X.i\}$

$$(n' > n \ \wedge \ Y.n < c \ \wedge \ Y.n < c) \ \vee$$
$$(n' = n \ \wedge \ c \neq c' \ \wedge \ c' < c) \quad \vee$$
$$(n' < n \ \wedge \ Y.n' < c' \ \wedge \ c' < Y.n')$$

$= \qquad \{\text{remove assumptions}; \text{ predicate calculus}\}$

$$n' > n \ \vee \ (n' = n \ \wedge \ c' < c)$$

Therefore, $s(Y, X\!\downarrow\!(k+1))$ is the strict bound of the form $Y\!\downarrow\!n'^\frown X.k$ with $n'$ maximal in the range $n < n' \leq m$, if such a bound exists, otherwise

$Y{\downarrow}n^\frown X.k$ if this is a strict bound and $X.k < c$, and is otherwise unchanged.

A straightforward application of Linear Search suffices for the first search, leaving a simple conditional statement for the second. Our invariant is

$$P1 : F(n') \ \land\ n \le n' \le m$$

where

$$F(i) \ \equiv\ (\forall j : i < j \le m : Y.j \ge X.k)$$

The resulting $Q1$ is

$\{\ P \ \land\ m \ne \#Y \ \land\ k \ne \#X\ \}$
$n' := m;\ \{\ P1\ \}$
**do** $\neg(n' = n \ \lor\ Y.n' < X.k) \ \rightarrow\ n' := n' - 1$ **od**;
$\{\ P1 \ \land\ (n' = n \ \lor\ Y.n' < X.k),\ \text{hence}\ \}$
$\{\ (n' = n \ \land\ F(n)) \ \lor\ (n < n' \le m \ \land\ Y.n' < X.k \ \land\ F(n'))\ \}$
**if** $n < n' \ \rightarrow\ n, c := n', X.k\ \{\ R1\ \}$
$[\!]\ n' = n \ \rightarrow\ $ **if** $\quad Y.n < X.k < c \ \ \rightarrow\ c := X.k\ \{\ R1\ \}$
$\qquad\qquad\qquad\quad [\!]\ \neg(Y.n < X.k < c) \ \rightarrow\ skip\ \{\ R1\ \}$
$\qquad\qquad\quad$ **fi**
**fi** $\{\ R1\ \}$

Our solution has implementations —that represent the sequences with arrays or doubly-linked lists— that take time at most quadratic in $\#X$; examples that do require quadratic time are readily found.

# Development of improved solution

In pursuit of information permitting a faster solution, we now explore consequences of the main invariant $P$, concentrating on the minimality of $Y{\downarrow}n^\frown c$, which has been underexploited thus far. So, assuming $P$ holds:

$\quad$ *true*

$=\quad \{Y{\downarrow}n^\frown c \text{ is minimal}\}$

$\quad (\forall n' : n < n' < m : \neg(\exists c' : Y{\downarrow}n'^\frown c' \in \overline{X{\downarrow}k} \cup \{\top\} : Y \prec Y{\downarrow}n'^\frown c'))$

$=\quad \{\neg\exists\text{-rule}\}$

$\quad (\forall n' : n < n' < m$
$\qquad : (\forall c' : Y{\downarrow}n'^\frown c' \in \overline{X{\downarrow}k} \cup \{\top\} : \neg(Y \prec Y{\downarrow}n'^\frown c')))$

$=$     {(3); absorb the negation}

$(\forall n' : n < n' < m : (\forall c' : Y \!\downarrow\! n' \!\frown\! c' \in \overline{X \!\downarrow\! k} \cup \{\top\} : Y.n' \geq c'))$

$\Rightarrow$     $\{Y \!\downarrow\! n' \!\frown\! Y.n'' \in \overline{X \!\downarrow\! k} \cup \{\top\}$ for $n' < n'' < m$,
        because $m = f(Y, X \!\downarrow\! k)$; instantiate; reduce range of $n'\}$

$(\forall n' : n < n' < n'' < m : Y.n' \geq Y.n'')$

$=$     {generalize, since $n''$ is arbitrary}

$(\forall n', n'' : n < n' < n'' < m : Y.n' \geq Y.n'')$

The fact that $Y(i : n < i < m)$ is non-increasing impinges mightily on our $Q1$, because if $m - 1 > n$ and $Y.(m-1) \geq X.k$, then $Y.n' \geq X.k$ for all $n'$ in the range $n < n' < m$, i.e.,

$$m - 1 > n \;\wedge\; Y.m \geq X.k \;\wedge\; Y.(m-1) \geq X.k \;\Rightarrow\; F(n)$$

We may therefore rephrase our characterization:

(4)     $s(Y, X \!\downarrow\! (k+1))$ is the strict bound of the form $Y \!\downarrow\! n' \!\frown\! X.k$
        with $n'$ maximal in the range $m - 1 \leq n' \leq m$, if such a
        bound exists, otherwise $Y \!\downarrow\! n \!\frown\! X.k$ if this is a strict bound
        and $X.k < c$, and is otherwise unchanged.

This justifies the following loopless solution for $Q1$:

$$
\begin{aligned}
&\{\, P \,\wedge\, m \neq \#Y \,\wedge\, k \neq \#X \,\} \\
&\textbf{if} \quad m > n \,\wedge\, Y.m < X.k \;\rightarrow\; n, c := m, X.k \\
&[\!] \;\; \neg(m > n \,\wedge\, Y.m < X.k) \\
&\qquad \rightarrow \textbf{if}\; m - 1 > n \;\textbf{cand}\; Y.(m-1) < X.k \\
&\qquad\qquad \rightarrow\; n, c := m - 1, X.k \\
&\qquad\quad [\!] \;\; \neg(m - 1 > n \;\textbf{cand}\; Y.(m-1) < X.k) \\
&\qquad\qquad \rightarrow \textbf{if}\quad Y.n < X.k < c \;\rightarrow\; c := X.k \\
&\qquad\qquad\qquad [\!]\;\; \neg(Y.n < X.k < c) \;\rightarrow\; \textit{skip} \\
&\qquad\qquad \textbf{fi} \\
&\qquad \textbf{fi} \\
&\textbf{fi}\;\{\, R1 \,\}
\end{aligned}
$$

The conditional conjunction is used to avoid a reference to $Y.(m-1)$, which is undefined when $m = 0$. It is not customary to have nested conditional commands in programs written with guarded commands; but the above formulation most naturally corresponds to our characterization (4).

The complete solution $Q$ incorporating this solution for $Q1$ is given below; it has implementations that take time linear in $\#X$.

$$k, n, m, c := 0, 0, 0, \top; \ \{\, P \,\}$$
**do** $m \neq \#Y \ \wedge \ k \neq \#X \ \rightarrow$
    **if** $m > n \ \wedge \ Y.m < X.k \ \rightarrow \ n, c := m, X.k$
    [] $\neg(m > n \ \wedge \ Y.m < X.k)$
        $\rightarrow$ **if** $m - 1 > n$ **cand** $Y.(m-1) < X.k$
            $\rightarrow \ n, c := m - 1, X.k$
            [] $\neg(m - 1 > n$ **cand** $Y.(m-1) < X.k)$
               $\rightarrow$ **if** $\quad Y.n < X.k < c \ \rightarrow \ c := X.k$
                      [] $\neg(Y.n < X.k < c) \ \rightarrow \ skip$
                **fi**
        **fi**
    **fi**;
    **if** $X.k = Y.m \ \rightarrow \ m := m + 1$ [] $X.k \neq Y.m \ \rightarrow \ skip$ **fi**;
    $k := k + 1$
**od**;
**if** $m = \#Y \ \rightarrow \ V := Y$ [] $m \neq \#Y \ \rightarrow \ V := Y{\downarrow}n{\frown}c$ **fi**
$\{\, V = b(Y, X) \,\}$

## REFERENCES

[1] P. Pritchard. *Opportunistic Algorithms for Covering with Subsets.* Technical Report TR-89-12, Department of Computer Sciences, The University of Texas at Austin, Austin, Texas, May 1989.

Paul Pritchard,
Department of Computer Science,
University of Queensland,
St. Lucia,
Australia, 4067.

# A Personal Perspective of the Alpern-Schneider Characterization of Safety and Liveness

## Martin Rem

## 0  Introduction

In [1] Alpern and Schneider give a topological characterization of safety and liveness properties. This note is the formal reflection of my own understanding of their theory.

Throughout this note $A$ is a fixed set of at least two symbols. As usual, $A^*$ denotes the set of all finite sequences of symbols from $A$, and $A^\omega$ denotes the set of all infinite sequences of symbols from $A$. Let $P$ be the set of all boolean functions on $A^\omega$. Elements of $P$ are known as *properties*. They are our object of study.

We give a few examples of properties, formulated as predicates in sequence $t$, $t \in A^\omega$. Let $a \in A$.

| | |
|---|---|
| $p0$: | **false**; |
| $p1$: | the first symbol of $t$ is $a$; |
| $p2$: | the first symbol of $t$ differs from $a$; |
| $p3$: | the first symbol of $t$ is $a$, and $t$ contains a symbol that differs from $a$; |
| $p4$: | the number of $a$'s in $t$ is finite; |
| $p5$: | the number of $a$'s in $t$ is infinite; |
| $p6$: | **true**. |

## 1  Safety properties

Let $x \in A^*$ and $y \in A^\omega$. We say that $x$ is a *prefix* of $y$, notation $x \le y$, when

$$(\mathbf{E}\, z : \; z \in A^\omega : \; xz = y)$$

where catenation of sequences is denoted by juxtaposition. With each property $p$ we associate a set $pref.p$, $pref.p \subseteq A^*$, as follows:

$$x \in pref.p \; \equiv \; (\mathbf{E}\, y : \; y \in A^\omega \,\wedge\, x \le y : \; p.y)$$

Set $pref.p$ is prefix-closed:

**Property 0**    $wx \in pref.p \;\Rightarrow\; w \in pref.p$

**Proof**

$wx \in pref.p$

$=$        {definition of $pref$}

$(\mathbf{E}\, y : \; y \in A^\omega \,\wedge\, wx \le y : \; p.y)$

$\Rightarrow$        $\{wx \le y \;\Rightarrow\; w \le y\}$

$(\mathbf{E}\, y : \; y \in A^\omega \,\wedge\, w \le y : \; p.y)$

$=$        {definition of $pref$}

$w \in pref.p$

(**End** of proof)


We can form negations, conjunctions, and disjunctions of properties in the usual way, for example $(p \vee q).t = p.t \vee q.t$. With respect to the examples in Section 0 we have $\neg p0 = p6$, $\neg p1 = p2$, $\neg p4 = p5$, $p1 \vee p2 = p6$, $p4 \wedge p5 = p0$, etc.

**Property 1**    $pref.(p \vee q) \; = \; pref.p \,\cup\, pref.q$

**Proof**

$x \in pref.(p \vee q)$

$=$        {definition of $pref$}

$(\mathbf{E}\, y : \; x \le y : \; (p \vee q).y)$

$=$        {definition of disjunction}

$(\mathbf{E}\, y : \; x \le y : \; p.y \vee q.y)$

$=$        {calculus}

$(\mathbf{E}\, y : \; x \le y : \; p.y) \;\vee\; (\mathbf{E}\, y : \; x \le y : \; q.y)$

$=$        {definition of $pref$}

$x \in pref.p \;\vee\; x \in pref.q$

(**End** of proof)

By $\sqsubseteq$ we denote the (natural) partial order on $P$, the set of properties:

$$p \sqsubseteq q \equiv (\mathbf{A}\, y : y \in A^\omega : p.y \Rightarrow q.y)$$

This order has **false** as its strongest property and **true** as its weakest. An immediate consequence of Property 1 is:

**Property 2**  $p \sqsubseteq q \Rightarrow pref.p \subseteq pref.q$

A safety property is a property that is completely determined by its $pref$. To make this statement more precise we introduce equivalence relation $\sim$ on $P$:

$$p \sim q \equiv pref.p = pref.q$$

We could next define the safety properties to be the equivalence classes of $\sim$. However, in order that the safety properties be elements of $P$, we follow [1] and select in each equivalence class exactly one (characterizing) safety property, viz. the weakest property in that class. Thereto we introduce function $cl$ that maps every property onto the weakest property of its class. Properties 4 and 6 express that $cl$ is indeed such a mapping.

For $p \in P$ property $cl.p$, the *closure* of $p$, is defined by

$$cl.p.y \equiv (\mathbf{A}\, x : x \in A^* \wedge x \leq y : x \in pref.p)$$

**Property 3**  $p \sqsubseteq cl.p$

**Proof**

> $cl.p.y$
>
> $=$ {definition of $cl$}
>
> $(\mathbf{A}\, x : x \leq y : x \in pref.p)$
>
> $=$ {definition of $pref$}
>
> $(\mathbf{A}\, x : x \leq y : (\mathbf{E}\, z : x \leq z : p.z))$
>
> $\Leftarrow$ {choose $z = y$}
>
> $p.y$

(**End** of proof)

**Property 4**  $p \sim cl.p$

**Proof**  By Properties 2 and 3 we have

$$pref.p \subseteq pref.(cl.p)$$

We prove the inclusion in the other direction:

$$x \in pref.(cl.p)$$

$=$        {definition of *pref*}

   $(\mathbf{E}\,y:\ x \le y:\ cl.p.y)$

$=$        {definition of *cl*}

   $(\mathbf{E}\,y:\ x \le y:\ (\mathbf{A}\,w:\ w \le y:\ w \in pref.p))$

$\Rightarrow$        {calculus}

   $x \in pref.p$

(**End** of proof)

**Property 5**    $p \sim q\ \equiv\ cl.p = cl.q$

**Proof**

   $p \sim q$

$=$        {definition of $\sim$}

   $pref.p = pref.q$

$\Rightarrow$        {definition of *cl*}

   $cl.p = cl.q$

$\Rightarrow$        {Property 4, $\sim$ is transitive}

   $p \sim q$

(**End** of proof)

From Properties 3 and 5 follows

**Property 6**    $p \sim q\ \Rightarrow\ q \sqsubseteq cl.p$

By Properties 4 and 5 we have

**Property 7**    $cl.(cl.p)\ =\ cl.p$

We define the set $S$ of *safety properties* as those properties that are equal to their closure:

$$p \in S\ \equiv\ p = cl.p$$

Thus, every equivalence class contains exactly one safety property, viz. its weakest property. Examples of safety properties are (cf. Section 0) $p0$, $p1$, $p2$, and $p6$. Since $cl.p3 = p1$, property $p3$ is not a safety property. Properties $p4$ and $p5$ are not safety properties either: their closure equals **true**.

**Property 8**    $p \sqsubseteq q\ \Rightarrow\ cl.p \sqsubseteq cl.q$

**Proof**    We assume $p \sqsubseteq q$ and derive

$cl.p.y$

$=$ {definition of $cl$}

$(\mathbf{A}\,x:\; x \le y:\; x \in \textit{pref.p})$

$\Rightarrow$ {$p \sqsubseteq q$, Property 2}

$(\mathbf{A}\,x:\; x \le y:\; x \in \textit{pref.q})$

$=$ {definition of $cl$}

$cl.q.y$

(**End** of proof)

**Property 9**    $cl.(p \lor q) \;=\; cl.p \lor cl.q$

**Proof**    On account of Property 8

$cl.p \lor cl.q \;\sqsubseteq\; cl.(p \lor q)$

We prove, for $y \in A^{\omega}$,

$cl.(p \lor q).y \;\Rightarrow\; cl.q.y$

under assumption $\neg cl.p.y$, i.e.

$(\mathbf{E}\,x:\; x \le y:\; x \notin \textit{pref.p})$

Let $w \le y$ and $w \notin \textit{pref.p}$. We derive

$cl.(p \lor q).y$

$=$ {definition of $cl$}

$(\mathbf{A}\,x:\; x \le y:\; x \in \textit{pref.}(p \lor q))$

$=$ {Property 1}

$(\mathbf{A}\,x:\; x \le y:\; x \in \textit{pref.p} \;\lor\; x \in \textit{pref.q})$

$\Rightarrow$ {$w \le y \;\land\; w \notin \textit{pref.p}$}

$w \in \textit{pref.q} \;\land\; (\mathbf{A}\,x:\; wx \le y:\; wx \in \textit{pref.p} \;\lor\; wx \in \textit{pref.q})$

$=$ {$w \notin \textit{pref.p}$, hence (Property 0) $wx \notin \textit{pref.p}$}

$w \in \textit{pref.q} \;\land\; (\mathbf{A}\,x:\; wx \le y:\; wx \in \textit{pref.q})$

$=$ {Property 0, $w \le y$}

$(\mathbf{A}\,x:\; x \le y:\; x \in \textit{pref.q})$

$=$ {definition of $cl$}

$cl.q.y$

(**End** of proof)

## 2  Liveness properties

Properties $p4$, $p5$, and $p6$ (cf. Section 0) are equivalent: each of these properties has $A^*$ as its *pref*; in other words, for these properties the *pref* yields no information at all. Such properties are called *liveness properties*. We define the set $L$ of liveness properties by

$$p \in L \;\equiv\; pref.p = A^*$$

or, equivalently,

**Property 10**   $p \in L \;\equiv\; cl.p = \textbf{true}$

Thus the liveness properties constitute the class of properties to which **true** belongs. Since each equivalence class contains exactly one safety property, we have

**Property 11**   $S \cap L = \{\textbf{true}\}$

On account of Property 2 we have

**Property 12**   $p \sqsubseteq q \;\wedge\; p \in L \;\Rightarrow\; q \in L$

Example $p3$ is a property that is neither a safety nor a liveness property. It is, however, the conjunction of a safety and a liveness property. Theorem 14 expresses that all properties can be thus decomposed.

**Property 13**   $(p \;\vee\; \neg cl.p) \in L$

**Proof**   By Property 10 it suffices to show that $cl.(p \;\vee\; \neg cl.p) = \textbf{true}$. We derive

> **true**
>
> $=$       {definitions of disjunction and negation}
>
> $cl.p \;\vee\; \neg cl.p$
>
> $\sqsubseteq$       $\{\neg cl.p \;\sqsubseteq\; cl.(\neg cl.p)$ by Property 3$\}$
>
> $cl.p \;\vee\; cl.(\neg cl.p)$
>
> $=$       {Property 9}
>
> $cl.(p \;\vee\; \neg cl.p)$

(**End** of proof)

**Theorem 14**   Every property is the conjunction of a safety property and a liveness property.

**Proof**   $cl.p \in S$ and, by Property 13, $(p \;\vee\; \neg cl.p) \in L$. Their conjunction yields

$$cl.p \wedge (p \vee \neg cl.p)$$

$= \quad \{\text{calculus}\}$

$$cl.p \wedge p$$

$= \quad \{\text{Property 3}\}$

$$p$$

(**End** of proof)

The decomposition chosen above is into the strongest safety property and the weakest liveness property, as demonstrated below:

**Property 15**     If $q \in S$ then $p = (q \wedge r)$ implies $cl.p \sqsubseteq q$ and $r \sqsubseteq (p \vee \neg cl.p)$.

**Proof**

$$p = (q \wedge r)$$

$\Rightarrow \quad \{\text{calculus}\}$

$$p \sqsubseteq q$$

$\Rightarrow \quad \{\text{Property 8}\}$

$$cl.p \sqsubseteq cl.q$$

$= \quad \{q \in S, \text{ hence } cl.q = q\}$

$$cl.p \sqsubseteq q$$


$$cl.p \sqsubseteq q \ \wedge \ p = (q \wedge r)$$

$\Rightarrow \quad \{\text{calculus}\}$

$$(cl.p \wedge r) \sqsubseteq p$$

$\Rightarrow \quad \{\text{calculus}\}$

$$(r \vee \neg cl.p) \sqsubseteq (p \vee \neg cl.p)$$

$\Rightarrow \quad \{r \sqsubseteq (r \vee \neg cl.p)\}$

$$r \sqsubseteq (p \vee \neg cl.p)$$

(**End** of proof)

In the case of property $p3$ this decomposition yields safety property $p1$ and liveness property "$t$ contains a symbol that differs from $a$".

# 3   Conclusions

In this note I have reformulated the Alpern-Schneider characterization of safety and liveness in a nontopological fashion: from first principles, so to speak. There are a few points at which my approach differs from (or extends) [1]. I would in particular like to mention:

- the recognition of safety properties as characterizations of equivalence classes, where properties are considered equivalent when their sets of (finite) prefixes coincide;
- the recognition of liveness properties as the members of the equivalence class to which property **true** belongs;
- the explicit definition of the closure operator;
- Property 15, revealing the extremity of the decomposition chosen in [1].

*Acknowledgements*: The members of the Eindhoven VLSI Club are acknowledged for discussing a draft version of this note. During this discussion Tom Verhoeff pointed out Property 15 to me.

## REFERENCES

[1] B. Alpern and F. B. Schneider. Defining liveness. *Information Processing Letters*, 21:181–185, 1985.

Martin Rem,
Department of Mathematics and Computing Science,
Eindhoven University of Technology,
P.O. Box 513,
5600 MB  Eindhoven,
The Netherlands.

# 44

# Simpler Proofs for Concurrent Reading and Writing

## Fred B. Schneider[1]

## Abstract

Simplified proofs are given for Lamport's protocols to coordinate concurrent reading and writing.

## 1 Introduction

In most computing systems, hardware ensures that read and write operations to some basic unit of memory can be considered mutually exclusive. As a result, a read that overlaps with a write is serialized and will appear either to precede that write or to follow it. Operations that make multiple accesses to memory are not serialized by the hardware. The programmer must ensure that when such operations overlap, they produce meaningful results.

In this paper, we give simplified proofs for two protocols proposed by Lamport [1] for coordinating read and write operations that involve multiple accesses to memory. The two key theorems in [1] are long and intricate. Here, we show that both are corollaries of a single, relatively simple theorem. Our facility with proofs and the use of formalism has improved significantly in a little over 15 years.[2] This is due, in part, to the influence of Edsger Dijkstra.

---

[1]This material is based on work supported in part by the Office of Naval Research under contract N00014-86-K-0092, the National Science Foundation under Grant No. CCR-8701103, and Digital Equipment Corporation. Any opinions, findings, and conclusions or recommendations expressed in this publication are those of the author and do not reflect the views of these agencies.

[2][1] was first submitted for publication in September 1974.

# 2   Words from digits

Consider a computing system in which the basic unit of memory is a *digit*, and a digit can contain one of $B \geq 2$ distinct values. Any element from a finite set of values can be encoded using a finite sequence of digits. We call such a sequence of digits a *word*. To read the value stored by a word, read operations are performed on its digits; to write a value, write operations are performed. Observe that overlapping read and write operations to a word will not be serialized by the hardware. Therefore, without additional constraints on execution, it is possible for a read that overlaps a write to obtain a meaningless value. For example, suppose digits can encode integers from 0 through 9 and a word $w$ constructed from three digits initially encodes the value 099. A read that is concurrent with a write of value 100 might obtain any of the following results: 099, 090, 009, 000, 199, 190, 109, 100.

By constraining the order in which digits are read and the order in which digits are written, we can ensure that a read overlapping one or more writes does obtain a meaningful value. Desired are constraints that are both easily implemented and non-intrusive. Execution of neither read nor write operations should be delayed, nor should the constraints require elaborate synchronization primitives.

In the protocols that follow, a word $w$ is implemented by a sequence $w[0]w[1]\ldots w[n]$ of digits. Think of $w[0]$ as the most-significant (left-most) digit and $w[n]$ as the least-significant (right-most) digit of a base $B$ number being stored by $w$. We assume that $w$ is written by a single, sequential process. Define $w[i]^p$ to be the value written to digit $w[i]$ by write operation number $p$.[3] Also, for any sequence $s = s[0]s[1]\ldots s[n]$, define $s[i..j]$ to be the subsequence consisting of $s[i]\ldots s[j]$, and define $|s|$ to be the length of $s$. Thus, $w[0..k]$ is the word constructed from the most-significant (left-most) $k + 1$ digits of $w$.

A read operation that overlaps with one or more writes can obtain a value that corresponds to the result of no write operation. We can describe such values by using a *slice*, a sequence of positive integers. For a word $w$ and a slice $\sigma$ of equal length, define:

$$w^\sigma \;\equiv\; w[0]^{\sigma[0]} w[1]^{\sigma[1]} \ldots w[n]^{\sigma[n]}$$

We write $(N) \otimes v$ to denote a length $N$ sequence of $v$'s. Thus, $w^{(n+1)\otimes p}$ equals $w[0]^p w[1]^p \ldots w[n]^p$, the value written to $w$ by write operation number $p$.

A slice $\sigma$ is *non-decreasing* if $(\forall i : 0 < i < |\sigma| : \sigma[i-1] \leq \sigma[i])$ and

---

[3]It will be convenient to assume that a write operation to a word writes a value to every digit. The new value can, of course, be the same as the old.

*non-increasing* if $(\forall i : 0 < i < |\sigma| : \sigma[i-1] \geq \sigma[i])$. For slices $\sigma$ and $\tau$ such that $|\sigma| = |\tau|$, define

$$\sigma \subseteq \tau \quad \equiv \quad (\forall i : 0 \leq i < |\sigma| : \sigma[i] \leq \tau[i]).$$

Finally, in order to reason about the relative order in which operations occur, define $\mu_i(x)$ to be the number of writes that have been made to digit $w[i]$ as of time $x$. Observe that $x \leq x'$ implies that $\mu_i(x) \leq \mu_i(x')$ is valid.

# 3   The main result

We first show that if slices $\sigma$ and $\tau$ satisfy certain restrictions (H1–H3) and values written to $w$ are non-decreasing (H4), then $w^\sigma \leq w^\tau$ where "$\leq$" denotes lexicographic ordering.

**Theorem 1**    Let $\sigma$ and $\tau$ be slices such that $|\sigma| = |\tau| \geq N + 1$. Then,

$$w[0..N]^\sigma \quad \leq \quad w[0..N]^\tau$$

provided:

> (H1)   $\sigma$ is non-decreasing,
> (H2)   $\tau$ is non-increasing,
> (H3)   $\sigma \subseteq \tau$, and
> (H4)   $w[0..N]^{(N+1)\otimes i} \leq w[0..N]^{(N+1)\otimes j}$   for all $i \leq j$.

**Proof**    From hypothesis H4 and the definition of lexicographic ordering, we conclude that for all $i \leq j$ and any $m$ such that $0 \leq m \leq N$:

> LO:    $w[0..m]^{(m+1)\otimes i} \leq w[0..m]^{(m+1)\otimes j}$

The proof now proceeds by induction on the number of digits in $w$.

*Base Case*: Assume $w$ is constructed using a single digit.

$w^\sigma$

$=$    {By assumption that $w$ is a single digit and hypothesis
        that $|\sigma| \geq N + 1$.}

$w[0..0]^{\sigma[0]}$

$\leq$    {By LO, since $\sigma \subseteq \tau$ by H3.}

$w[0..0]^{\tau[0]}$

$=$    {By assumption that $w$ is a single digit and hypothesis
        that $|\tau| \geq N + 1$.}

$w^\tau$

*Induction Case*: Assume the Theorem holds for any $n+1$ digit word $w[0..n]$, where $0 \le n < N$. We show that it holds for the $n+2$ digit word $w[0..n+1]$.

1. {From H1, $\sigma$ is non-decreasing. Therefore, any prefix is.}
$\sigma[0..n]$ is non-decreasing.

2. {Definition of non-increasing.}
$\alpha = (n+1) \otimes \sigma[n+1]$ is non-increasing.

3. {By construction of $\sigma[0..n]$ and $\alpha$, since (H1) $\sigma$ is non-decreasing.}
$\sigma[0..n] \subseteq \alpha$.

4. {By induction hypothesis, since H1–H4 are satisfied due to 1, 2, 3, and LO.}
$w[0..n]^{\sigma[0..n]} \le w[0..n]^{\alpha}$

5. {Definition of lexicographic order.}
$w[0..n]^{\sigma[0..n]}w[n+1]^{\sigma[n+1]} \le w[0..n]^{\alpha}w[n+1]^{\sigma[n+1]}$

6. {By LO, since $\sigma[n+1] \le \tau[n+1]$ because (H3) $\sigma \subseteq \tau$.}
$w[0..n]^{\alpha}w[n+1]^{\sigma[n+1]} \le w[0..n+1]^{(n+2)\otimes\tau[n+1]}$

7. {Transitivity with 5 and 6.}
$w[0..n]^{\sigma[0..n]}w[n+1]^{\sigma[n+1]} \le w[0..n+1]^{(n+2)\otimes\tau[n+1]}$

8. {Definition of non-decreasing.}
$\beta = (n+1) \otimes \tau[n+1]$ is non-decreasing.

9. {From H2, $\tau$ is non-increasing. Therefore, any prefix is.}
$\tau[0..n]$ is non-increasing.

10. {By construction of $\beta$ and $\tau[0..n]$, since (H2) $t$ is non-increasing.}
$\beta \subseteq \tau[0..n]$

11. {By induction hypothesis, since H1–H4 are satisfied due to 8, 9, 10, and LO.}
$w[0..n]^{\beta} \le w[0..n]^{\tau[0..n]}$

12. {Definition of lexicographic order.}
$w[0..n]^{\beta}w[n+1]^{\tau[n+1]} \le w[0..n]^{\tau[0..n]}w[n+1]^{\tau[n+1]}$

13. {Transitivity with 7 and 12.}
$w[0..n]^{\sigma[0..n]}w[n+1]^{\sigma[n+1]} \le w[0..n]^{\tau[0..n]}w[n+1]^{\tau[n+1]}$

14. {$\sigma[0..n+1] = \sigma[0..n]\sigma[n+1]$ and $\tau[0..n+1] = \tau[0..n]\tau[n+1]$}
$w[0..n+1]^{\sigma[0..n+1]} \le w[0..n+1]^{\tau[0..n+1]}$

$\square$

# 4   Reading to the left, writing to the right

We can now show that if the digits of $w$ are read from right to left (i.e. $w[n], w[n-1], \ldots, w[0]$) but written from left to right (i.e. $w[0], \ldots, w[n-1]$, $w[n]$) then only certain mixtures of values can be obtained from overlapping writes. In particular, the value read is bounded from below by the value written by the earliest write whose digit is obtained by this read.

**Read-Left, Write-Right:**
If (i) the sequence of values written to $w$ is non-decreasing, (ii) digits are written from left to right, and (iii) digits are read from right to left, then the value $w^\tau$ obtained by the read satisfies $w^{(N+1) \otimes \tau[n]} \leq w^\tau$.

**Proof**   We first show that $\tau$ is non-increasing. Let $x_i$ be the time that digit $w[i]$ is read. Thus, $\tau[i] = \mu_i(x_i)$ and, due to hypothesis (iii) that digits are read from right to left, $x_n \leq x_{n-1} \leq \ldots \leq x_0$. For any $i$, $0 \leq i < n$:

$\tau[i]$

$=$     {Assumption that $\tau[i] = \mu_i(x_i)$.}

$\mu_i(x_i)$

$\geq$     {Digits are written from left to right due to hypothesis (ii).}

$\mu_{i+1}(x_i)$

$\geq$     {$x_i \geq x_{i+1}$.}

$\mu_{i+1}(x_{i+1})$

$=$     {Assumption that $\tau[i] = \mu_i(x_i)$.}

$\tau[i+1]$

The correctness of Read-Left, Write-Right now follows from Theorem 1. Choose $(N+1) \otimes \tau[n]$ for $\sigma$; this choice for $\sigma$ satisfies H1 and H3. We showed above that $\tau$ satisfies H2. H4 is satisfied by hypothesis (i). Thus, from Theorem 1 we conclude $w^{(N+1) \otimes \tau[n]} \leq w^\tau$.
□

There are two interesting things to note about this protocol. First, exclusive access to digits is the only synchronization required. Second, read operations and write operations do not delay each other.

# 5   Reading to the right, writing to the left

By reversing the order in which digits are read and written, we obtain another protocol for concurrent reading and writing. With this protocol, the value read is bounded from above by the value written by the latest write whose digit is obtained by this read.

**Read-Right, Write-Left:**
If (i) the sequence of values written to $w$ is non-decreasing, (ii) digits are written from right to left, and (iii) digits are read from left to right, then the value $w^\sigma$ obtained by any read satisfies $w^\sigma \leq w^{(N+1)\otimes\sigma[n]}$.

**Proof**   We first show that $\sigma$ is non-decreasing. Let $x_i$ be the time that digit $w[i]$ is read. Thus, $\sigma[i] = \mu_i(x_i)$ and, due to hypothesis (iii) that digits are read from left to right, $x_0 \leq x_1 \leq \ldots \leq x_n$. For any $i$, $0 \leq i < n$:

$$\sigma[i]$$

$=$   {Assumption that $\tau[i] = \mu_i(x_i)$.}

$$\mu_i(x_i)$$

$\leq$   {Digits are written from right to left due to hypothesis (ii).}

$$\mu_{i+1}(x_i)$$

$\leq$   {$x_i \leq x_{i+1}$.}

$$\mu_{i+1}(x_{i+1})$$

$=$   {Assumption that $\sigma[i] = \mu_i(x_i)$.}

$$\sigma[i+1]$$

The correctness of Read-Right, Write-Left now follows from Theorem 1. Choose $(N+1) \otimes \sigma[n]$ for $\tau$; this choice for $\tau$ satisfies H2 and H3. We showed above that $\sigma$ satisfies H1. H4 is satisfied by hypothesis (i). Thus, from Theorem 1 we conclude $w^\sigma \leq w^{(N+1)\otimes\sigma[n]}$.
$\square$

As before, exclusive access to digits is the only synchronization required, and operations are never delayed.

# 6   Final remarks

This paper is now in its third revision. The first version contained simple and informal proofs. These, like the proof of Theorem 1 given above, used induction on the number of digits in a word. Unfortunately, the proofs were wrong — the informality let details slip through the cracks. The second version of the paper contained correct and formal versions of those proofs. A total of four lemmas were required —two lemmas for each protocol— although the two pairs of lemmas had proofs that were disturbingly similar. Theorem 1 of the current version of the paper generalizes two of those lemmas, and its proof results from combining the proofs of those two lemmas.

*Acknowledgments*: David Gries read and commented on many earlier versions of this paper. Jay Misra pointed out the errors in the first version of the paper and proposed the statement of Theorem 1 along with a (long) proof. Avoiding a case analysis in that proof led to the proof finally given above.

## REFERENCES

[1] Leslie Lamport. Concurrent reading and writing. *Comm. ACM*, 20(11):806–811, Nov. 1977.

Fred B. Schneider,
Department of Computer Science,
Cornell University,
4130 Upson Hall,
Ithaca, New York  14853–7501,
U.S.A.

# 45

# Goodbye Junctivity?

## Carel S. Scholten

In [2] the notions conjunctivity and disjunctivity —collectively called "junctivity"— are introduced. For the benefit of the reader we repeat the introduction of conjunctivity. Primarily, it is a property of a predicate transformer $f$ and a set $V$ of predicates. It is defined by

(0)     $(f$ is conjunctive over $V)$ $\equiv$
          $[f.(\mathbf{A}\, X : X \in V : X) \equiv (\mathbf{A}\, X : X \in V : f.X)]$ .

In the above, the infix dot denotes function application and the square brackets denote universal quantification over the points in state space.

Conjunctivity properties of $f$ alone are obtained by universal quantification over all $V$ of a certain type. We mention two of them:

$(f$ is universally conjunctive$)$ $\equiv$ $(f$ is conjunctive over all $V)$ ,
$(f$ is positively conjunctive$)$ $\equiv$
$(f$ is conjunctive over all non-empty $V)$ .

In [1] Dijkstra raises the question whether, in retrospect, junctivity was the right notion to introduce, more precisely, whether it would have been better to consider the two implications whose conjunction yields the right-hand side of (0) separately.

Well, to begin with, the notion of junctivity seems to have served us faithfully for about eight years now, so, in any case, an additional "and thank you" in the title of this note would be appropriate.

Nevertheless, let us follow Dijkstra's suggestion and consider the following two properties of $f$ and $V$:

(1)     $[f.(\mathbf{A}\, X : X \in V : X) \Rightarrow (\mathbf{A}\, X : X \in V : f.X)]$ ,
(2)     $[f.(\mathbf{A}\, X : X \in V : X) \Leftarrow (\mathbf{A}\, X : X \in V : f.X)]$ .

For (1), no special name is proposed, and for a good reason: firstly, (1) is satisfied by all pairs $f$, $V$ satisfying (size of $V$) $\leq 1$, and, secondly, for any $f$, the three assertions "(1) holds for all $V$ of size 2", "(1) holds for all $V$", and "$f$ is monotonic" are equivalent. For the sake of completeness we mention

$$(f \text{ is monotonic}) \equiv (\mathbf{A} \, X, Y : [X \Rightarrow Y] : [f.X \Rightarrow f.Y]) \ .$$

Verification of the above is left to the reader.

For (2) Dijkstra proposes tentatively —I am not completely happy with it, but, for lack of better, it will have to do for the moment— "$f$ contracts over $V$". Equally without proof we mention that any $f$ contracts —in fact: is conjunctive— over any singleton $V$, and that "$f$ contracts over $\phi$" equivales "$f$ is **and**(top)-strict".

As a justification for the breaking up of (0) into (1) and (2), Dijkstra points out that the negation is not monotonic but positively contracting, i.e. contracting over all non-empty $V$. He might have added that any anti-monotonic $f$ —i.e. any $f$ satisfying $(\mathbf{A} \, X, Y : [X \Rightarrow Y] : [f.X \Leftarrow f.Y])$— is positively contracting. Just for fun we prove the latter.

**Proof**   We observe for any antimonotonic $f$ and non-empty $V$,

$$(\mathbf{A} \, X : X \in V : f.X)$$

$\Rightarrow \quad \{[X \Leftarrow (\mathbf{A} \, Y : Y \in V : Y)] \quad \text{for } X \in V;$
$\qquad\quad f \text{ is antimonotonic}; \ \mathbf{A} \text{ is monotonic}\}$

$$(\mathbf{A} \, X : X \in V : f.(\mathbf{A} \, Y : Y \in V : Y))$$

$= \quad \{\text{term independent of } X; \ V \text{ is non-empty}\}$

$$f.(\mathbf{A} \, Y : Y \in V : Y)$$

$= \quad \{\text{renaming the dummy}\}$

$$f.(\mathbf{A} \, X : X \in V : X) \ .$$

(**End** of proof)

The above shows that the notion of contractivity at least makes some sense. In the remainder of this note we shall demonstrate that, with the help of contractivity, part of —granted: a very small part of— the theory set out in [2] can be developed in a more orderly fashion.

$$\star \quad \star \quad \star$$

In [2] the authors consider the equation —in predicates—

(3)     $X : [p.X \Rightarrow q.X] \ ,$

about which they prove

(4)     For monotonic $p$, and $q$ conjunctive over the solution set of (3), (3) has a strongest solution.

We reproduce the proof —slightly modified for the occasion— below.

**Proof** We use the theorem that an equation has a strongest solution if the conjunction of all its solutions is itself a solution. Hence, it suffices to prove that $(\mathbf{A}\,X : [p.X \Rightarrow q.X] : X)$ solves (3). We observe

$$p.(\mathbf{A}\,X : [p.X \Rightarrow q.X] : X)$$

$\Rightarrow \quad \{p \text{ is monotonic}\}$

$$(\mathbf{A}\,X : [p.X \Rightarrow q.X] : p.X)$$

$\Rightarrow \quad \{\mathbf{A} \text{ is monotonic}\}$

$$(\mathbf{A}\,X : [p.X \Rightarrow q.X] : q.X)$$

$\Rightarrow \quad \{q \text{ is conjunctive over (3)'s solution set}\}$

$$q.(\mathbf{A}\,X : [p.X \Rightarrow q.X] : X) \ .$$

(**End** of proof)

The "slight modification" alluded to above is in the last hint: the proof in [2] uses "=" instead of "$\Rightarrow$". Perfectly correct, of course, given $q$'s conjunctivity property, but the version above clearly demonstrates that what we really need in that hint is $q$'s contractivity over (3)'s solution set.

Equation (3) may strike the reader as very specific; in fact, it is carefully tailored to what is needed in [2]. All by itself, it is not at all difficult to obtain from (3) and (4) an equation and corresponding lemma looking less specific: by the substitution $p, q := \mathbf{true}, f$ we are led to consider the equation

(5)    $X : [f.X],$

and, because the constant function **true** is monotonic, we obtain from (4)

(6)    For $f$ conjunctive over the solution set of (5), (5) has a strongest solution.

In [2] equation (5) appears —for reasons that need not concern us here—, but (6) does not. Yet, as I trust the reader will agree, from the point of view of an orderly development of a theory, it would be much nicer to prove (6) first and next derive (4) as a special case.

A direct proof of (6) should be at least as easy as the proof of (4). However, in order to consider (4) as a special case of (6), one would need a lemma like

(7)    For any monotonic $p$ and any pair $q, V$ such that $q$ is conjunctive over $V$, $f$ is conjunctive over $V$, where $f$ is defined by

$[f.X \equiv p.X \Rightarrow q.X]$    for all $X$.

Unfortunately, (7) is not a lemma:   with $p, q := identity,$ **false**, $p$ is monotonic and $q$ is conjunctive over all non-empty $V$. For these values of $p$ and $q$, $[f.X \equiv \neg X]$, and the negation is not conjunctive over —for example— the set {**false**, **true**}.

From the discussion following the proof of (4), we know that we can replace (4) by the stronger

(8)     For monotonic $p$, and $q$ contracting over the solution set of (3), (3) has a strongest solution.

Likewise, we can strengthen (6) to

(9)     For $f$ contracting over the solution set of (5), (5) has a strongest solution.

Just to be on the safe side, we prove (9).

**Proof**     As pointed out in the proof of (4), it suffices to prove that $(\mathbf{A} X : [f.X] : X)$ solves (5). We observe

$$f.(\mathbf{A} X : [f.X] : X)$$
$$\Leftarrow \quad \{f \text{ contracts over (5)'s solution set}\}$$
$$(\mathbf{A} X : [f.X] : f.X)$$
$$= \quad \{\text{Leibniz}\}$$
$$(\mathbf{A} X : [f.X] : \mathbf{true})$$
$$= \quad \{\text{term } \mathbf{true}\}$$
$$\mathbf{true} .$$

(**End** of proof)

Now the situation has changed drastically: we can derive (8) as a special case of (9) on the strength of (7) with conjunctivity replaced by contractivity, and this indeed is a lemma:

(10)     For any monotonic $p$ and any pair $q$, $V$ such that $q$ contracts over $V$,   $f$ contracts over $V$, where $f$ is defined by

$$[f.X \equiv p.X \Rightarrow q.X] \quad \text{for all } X.$$

**Proof**     We observe

$$f.(\mathbf{A} X : X \in V : X)$$
$$= \quad \{\text{definition of } f\}$$
$$p.(\mathbf{A} X : X \in V : X) \; \Rightarrow \; q.(\mathbf{A} X : X \in V : X)$$
$$\Leftarrow \quad \{\text{strengthening the consequent; } q \text{ contracts over } V\}$$

$$p.(\mathbf{A}\,X : X \in V : X) \;\Rightarrow\; (\mathbf{A}\,X : X \in V : q.X)$$

= $\quad\{\Rightarrow$ distributes over $\mathbf{A}$ in consequent; change of dummy$\}$

$$(\mathbf{A}\,X : X \in V : p.(\mathbf{A}\,Y : Y \in V : Y) \;\Rightarrow\; q.X)$$

$\Leftarrow\quad$ {weakening the antecedent; $p$ and $\mathbf{A}$ are monotonic;
$\qquad [(\mathbf{A}\,Y : Y \in V : Y) \;\Rightarrow\; X]\quad$ for $X \in V\}$

$$(\mathbf{A}\,X : X \in V : p.X \Rightarrow q.X)$$

= $\quad\{$definition of $f\}$

$$(\mathbf{A}\,X : X \in V : f.X)\ .$$

(**End** of proof)

And this concludes our demonstration that the introduction of contractivity can be useful.

$$\star \quad \star \quad \star$$

Because the author of this note is one of the authors of [2], the latter will be denoted by the pronoun "we" throughout this epilogue.

One may wonder why we introduced a notion that, or so it seems now, was not the most fortunate choice, especially so because all along we knew full well that in many cases we only needed —what has now been named— contractivity.

Well, first of all, the proof that contractivity is the notion to introduce, in particular that it is manageable, has yet to be delivered. It takes more than a couple of pages to do that.

Secondly, people have the deplorable habit of making mistakes from time to time. Rumour has it that they learn from them.

In our case, however, I think that a certain conditioning, a fixation on equivalence, may have played a rôle. Many years ago our attention was drawn to the fact that we delivered many a theorem in the form, say,

(11) $\qquad [A \Rightarrow B]$ ,

whereas, with a little more effort, a stronger version in the form of an equivalence, e.g.

(12) $\qquad [A \equiv B \wedge C]$ ,

could be obtained.

In the case of a theorem, there seems to be little harm in presenting (12) rather than (11): the former implies the latter.

However, when properties are being defined, the situation is the other way round. To give an obvious example: I guess that everyone will agree that it is much more useful to introduce the following two properties of $f$

$$(f \text{ is strengthening}) \;\equiv\; (\mathbf{A}\,X :: [f.X \Rightarrow X]) \;,$$
$$(f \text{ is weakening}) \quad\equiv\; (\mathbf{A}\,X :: [f.X \Leftarrow X]) \;,$$

than just the single one

$$(f \text{ is the identity}) \quad\equiv\; (\mathbf{A}\,X :: [f.X \equiv X]) \;.$$

Note that the above observation does not preclude the introduction of the notion "identity". We then obtain the lemma

$$(f \text{ is the identity}) \;\equiv\; (f \text{ is strengthening}) \;\wedge\; (f \text{ is weakening}).$$

## REFERENCES

[1] Edsger W. Dijkstra. *Equivalence Versus Mutual Implication; Junctivity and Monotonicity.* Technical Report EWD 1034.

[2] Edsger W. Dijkstra and Carel S. Scholten. *Predicate Calculus and Program Semantics.* Springer-Verlag, New York, 1990.

C. S. Scholten,
Klein paradijs 4,
7361 TD  Beekbergen,
The Netherlands.

# An Assignment Problem for the Vertices of a Cycle

## Henk C. A. van Tilborg

## Abstract

Let $C_n$ denote a cycle on $n$ points. For each of its points $P$ a nonnegative integer $m_P$ is given.

To each point $P$ a subset $M_P$ of $\{0, 1, \ldots, N-1\}$ of cardinality $m_P$ has to be assigned with the property that neighboring points will have mutually disjoint associated sets.

An expression will be derived for the smallest value of $N$ for which such an assigment is possible. The assignment itself will also be given explicitly.

## 1 The assignment problem

In communication systems, like mobile radio, certain geographical areas (where users of the system may be present) are represented by points of a graph. Two neighboring areas give rise to an edge between the associated points. See for instance [1].

Of course more than one user in the same geographical area may want to use the communication system at the same moment. Therefore they should have different transmission frequencies available. The number of simultaneous users in the same area is bounded above by a quantity, called the demand of that area. This number may differ from area to area (higher populated areas give rise to a higher demand). Two neighboring areas should also have no assigned frequency in common, because the two users of that frequency could be very close to each other geographically. The object is now to minimize the total number of frequencies needed in such a system, given the outlay of the areas and their demands.

In graph theory the above problem can be easily translated.

**Problem 1.1**  Let $G = (V, E)$ be an undirected graph, without loops or multiple edges, with pointset $V$ and vertex set $E$. For each $P \in V$ a positive integer $m_P$ is given (the demand). What is the smallest value of $N$, such that to each $P \in V$ a subset $M_P$ of $\{0, 1, \ldots, N-1\}$ can be assigned, that satisfies

(1)     $\forall_{P \in V}[\mid M_P \mid = m_P]$
(2)     $\forall_{P \in V, Q \in V}[P \sim Q \Rightarrow M_P \cap M_Q = \emptyset]$.

That the above problem in all its generality is very hard is not so surprising. If all demands $m_P$ equal 1, it reduces to the standard coloring problem of the vertices in a graph. In the next section we solve the above problem for the special case that $G$ is a *cycle*.

## 2   The solution for a cycle

In the sequel we use the following notation. $C_n$ denotes the cycle on $n$ points. Its points are $P_0, P_1, \ldots P_{n-1}$, where the indices are taken modulo $n$ and the numbering is chosen such that $P_i$ and $P_{i+1}$ are adjacent for all $i, 0 \le i < n$. The demand $m_{P_i}$ in $P_i$ will be shortened to $m_i$ and similarly the set of frequencies (or colors) assigned to $P_i$ will be denoted by $M_i$.

It turns out that the solution to Problem 1.1 for the cycle $C_n$ is much easier when $n$ is even than when $n$ is odd.

**Theorem 2.1**  Let $n$ be even. Then the smallest value of $N$ with the property that subsets $M_i$ of $\{0, 1, \ldots, N-1\}$ can be assigned to the points $P_i$ of $C_n$ with given demand $m_i, 0 \le i < n$, that satisfy (1) and (2) is given by

(3)     $\max_{0 \le i < n} (m_i + m_{i+1})$.

**Proof**  That $N$ can not be less than (3) follows from the fact that each twotuple of neighboring points get disjoint subsets of $\{0, 1, \ldots, N-1\}$ assigned to them.

That the value of N given in (3) is also sufficient follows from the following explicit assignment:

$$M_i = \begin{cases} \{0, 1, \ldots, m_i - 1\}, & \text{if } i \text{ is even,} \\ \{N - m_i, N - m_i + 1, \ldots, N - 1\}, & \text{if } i \text{ is odd.} \end{cases}$$

□

**Theorem 2.2**  Let $n$ be odd. Then the smallest value of $N$ with the property that subsets $M_i$ of $\{0, 1, \ldots, N-1\}$ can be assigned to the points $P_i$ of $C_n$ with given demand $m_i, 0 \le i < n$, that satisfy (1) and (2) is given by

$$(4) \qquad \max\{\max_{0\le i<n}(m_i+m_{i+1}), \left\lceil \frac{2}{n-1}\sum_{i=0}^{n-1} m_i \right\rceil\}.$$

**Proof** That $N$ can not be less than the left most expression in (4) was already demonstrated in the proof of Theorem 2.1. On the other hand $N$ can not be less that the second expression in (4), because each element of $\{0,1,\ldots,N-1\}$ can only be assigned to at most $(n-1)/2$ points on $C_n$ and $\sum_{i=0}^{n-1} m_i$ numbers need to be assigned totally.

That $N$ does not need to exceed the value in (4) follows from a two-step assignment procedure with this value of $N$. We use the notation $M+1$ for the set $\{(m+1) \bmod n \mid m \in M\}$.

**Step 1** $M_0$ consists of the $m_0$ elements $0,1,\ldots,m_0-1$. $M_1$ consists of the next $m_1$ elements of $\{0,1,\ldots,N-1\}$ (when viewed cyclically), etc.

After this step the assignment satisfies (1). But because $m_i+m_{i+1}\le N$ for all $i$, $0\le i<n$, also (2) is now met, except possibly for $M_{n-1}\cap M_0$.

By simply shifting $M_{n-1}$ one can make $M_{n-1}\cap M_0$ empty, but then $M_{n-2}\cap M_{n-1}$ may no longer be empty, so one has to be more careful. Apparently more sets will have to be changed. Since we will only shift sets, it is clear that (1) will at all times be satisfied.

Now, set $M_1$ can be shifted over $N-m_0-m_1$ positions, before it meets $M_0$. By simultaneously shifting its successors $M_j$, $2\le j<n$ over the same number of positions, one gets that (2) still holds, except possibly for $M_{n-1}\cap M_0$. Similarly set $M_2$ (with its successors) can be shifted over $N-m_1-m_2$ positions. Proceeding in this way one ends with set $M_{n-1}$ that (by itself) can be shifted over $N-m_{n-2}-m_{n-1}$ positions. Executing all these shifts brings us in the situation that $M_0$ has remained fixed, that at all times (2) is satisfied, except possibly for $M_{n-1}\cap M_0$, and finally that the set $M_{n-1}$ has been shifted over $\sum_{i=1}^{n-1}(N-m_{i-1}-m_i)$ positions with respect to $M_0$.

Since (4) implies that $N\ge \frac{2}{n-1}\sum_{i=0}^{n-1} m_i$ it follows that

$$\sum_{i=1}^{n-1}(N-m_{i-1}-m_i)$$
$$= \quad (n-1)N+m_{n-1}+m_0-2\sum_{i=0}^{n-1} m_i$$
$$\ge \quad m_{n-1}+m_0.$$

If $M_{n-1}\cap M_0$ is not empty after Step 1, then shifting $M_{n-1}$ over at most $m_{n-1}+m_0$ places will make this intersection empty. So the above counting argument implies that somewhere during the shifting we must have been in the situation that $M_{n-1} \cap M_0 = \emptyset$. This proves that the next step finishes the assignment.

**Step 2**   While $M_{n-1} \cap M_0 \neq \emptyset$, do the following. Define $j$ to be the smallest integer between 1 and $n-1$ with the property that $(M_j+1) \cap M_{j-1} = \emptyset$. For all $i$, $j \leq i < n$, define $M_i := M_i + 1$.

$\square$

*Acknowledgements*: The author wishes to thank Kumar Sivarajan, who has an alternative proof of the above result, and Bob McEliece for bringing Problem 1.1 to his attention.

REFERENCES

[1] W. K. Hale. Frequency assignment, theory and applications. *Proc. of IEEE*, 68:1497–1514, 1980.

Henk C. A. van Tilborg,
Department of Mathematics and Computing Science,
Eindhoven University of Technology,
P.O. Box 513,
5600 MB  Eindhoven,
The Netherlands.

and

Department of Technical Sciences,
Open University,
P.O. Box 2960,
6401 DL  Heerlen,
The Netherlands.

# Duality and De Morgan Principles for Lists

## D. A. Turner

Lists are the most important data type in functional programming. This is because they replace the use of iteration in imperative programming. For example, if we are asked to sum the values of $f(i)$, for $i$ ranging from 1 to 1000, a problem that the imperative programmer would be likely to solve by writing, say

$x := 0;$

**for** $i := 1$ **to** 1000

**do** $x := x + f(i);$

the functional programmer would probably write something like

$sum(map\ f\ [1..1000])$

and we see that the sequence of values assumed over time by $i$ and $x$, respectively, in the imperative program are each now represented by a list.

The study of lists and the algebra of operations over them is therefore central to any proper discussion of functional programming. See for example [2].

The purpose of this short note is to draw attention to two simple principles, analogous to the principle of duality and the De Morgan laws in Boolean algebra, which can be of assistance in deriving algebraic identities over lists.

First some notational preliminaries. We write the list of length $n$, whose elements are $a_0$ to $a_{n-1}$

$[a_0, a_1, \ldots, a_{n-1}]$

so in particular the empty list is written [ ]. The fundamental operation for constructing larger lists from smaller is list concatenation, usually written ++. So we have

$$[a_0, \ldots, a_{m-1}] \mathbin{+\!\!+} [b_0, \ldots, b_{n-1}] \ = \ [a_0, \ldots, a_{m-1}, b_0, \ldots, b_{n-1}]$$

Two often useful derived forms are *prefix* and *postfix*, defined thus

$$prefix\ a\ x\ =\ [a] \mathbin{+\!\!+} x$$
$$postfix\ a\ x\ =\ x \mathbin{+\!\!+} [a]$$

It so happens that the usual implementation of lists makes *prefix* a much cheaper operation than *postfix*, but as far as the algebra of lists is concerned we can and should treat these two operations symmetrically.

Another artifact of the well-known linked list implementation method (when combined with lazy evaluation) is that it permits us to have infinite lists, of a certain kind. For studying the algebra of lists this introduces a rather undesirable assymmetry, because one is permitted so to speak "right-infinite" lists, like

$$x\ =\ [1] \mathbin{+\!\!+} x$$

but not "left-infinite" lists such as

$$x\ =\ x \mathbin{+\!\!+} [1]$$

In what follows we therefore confine our attention *solely to finite lists*. (An alternative possibility, which we will not pursue here, would be to develop a theory of lists in which infinite lists of both kinds were permitted.)

A collection of commonly used functions over lists (including *map*, *prefix*, *postfix*, *sum*) is given in an appendix to this article.

## The Duality Principle for lists

A principle of duality will be familiar from Boolean algebra. It states that any algebraic identity remains true if all operators are replaced by their duals. For example the dual of *False* is *True*, and $\land$ and $\lor$ are dual to each other, so from the identity

$$x \land True\ =\ x$$

we get by duality that

$$x \lor False\ =\ x$$

This is a useful principle because it halves the number of things we need to remember. The idea behind duality is that the dual of a Boolean operator is one that does the same job in a world where *True* and *False* have been interchanged. The identity

$$not\ (not\ x)\ =\ x$$

tells us that this world is isomorphic to the usual one, and it is this which justifies reasoning by duality.

There is an analogous principle for lists, with list-reversal playing the rôle of negation. We have again the identity

$$rev\ (rev\ x)\ =\ x$$

which is the property we need for a duality principle.

Every list processing operation has a dual — that is a function which does the same job in a world where all lists have been reversed. By way of example we will now state the duality relations for the list processing operations introduced in the previous section.

The following functions are self-dual.

$$map \quad filter \quad concat \quad rev \quad len \quad sum \quad product \quad max \quad min$$

The following pairs of functions are dual to each other.

$$(hd,\ last) \quad (tl,\ init) \quad (prefix,\ postfix) \quad (foldr,\ foldl)$$
$$(foldr1,\ foldl1) \quad (scanr,\ scanl) \quad (inits,\ tails)$$

Notice that a function and its dual always have the same type.

The dual of a list constant is obtained by reversing it. So, for example, the dual of [] is [], the dual of [1,2,3] is [3,2,1], the dual of [[1,2],[3,4]] is [[4,3],[2,1]], and the dual of "custard" is "dratsuc", assuming the usual convention that a string constant represents a list of characters.

Finally, we note that if the dual of $a$ is $a\tilde{\ }$ and the dual of $b$ is $b\tilde{\ }$ then the dual of

$$a \!+\!\!+ b$$

is

$$b\tilde{\ } \!+\!\!+ a\tilde{\ }$$

**The Duality Principle for lists**    Any algebraic identity over lists remains true if all list operations and constants are replaced by their duals.

Here are some identities and their duals.

$$hd \text{ "custard"} \quad = \quad \text{'}c\text{'}$$
$$last \text{ "dratsuc"} \quad = \quad \text{'}c\text{'}$$

$$init \text{ "custard"} \quad = \quad \text{"custar"}$$
$$tl \text{ "dratsuc"} \quad = \quad \text{"ratsuc"}$$

$$prefix\ (hd\ x)\ (tl\ x) \quad = \quad x \qquad \textbf{if } x \neq []$$
$$postfix\ (last\ x)\ (init\ x) \quad = \quad x \qquad \textbf{if } x \neq []$$

$$foldr\ prefix\ []\ x \quad = \quad x$$
$$foldl\ postfix\ []\ x \quad = \quad x$$

$$foldr\ postfix\ []\ x \quad = \quad rev\ x$$
$$foldl\ prefix\ []\ x \quad = \quad rev\ x$$

$$foldr1\ (\textbf{min})\ x \quad = \quad min\ x \qquad \textbf{if } x \neq []$$
$$foldl1\ (\textbf{min})\ x \quad = \quad min\ x \qquad \textbf{if } x \neq []$$

$$\begin{aligned}
scanl\ op\ e\ x &= map\ (foldl\ op\ \text{e})\ (inits\ x)\\
scanr\ op\ e\ x &= map\ (foldr\ op\ \text{e})\ (tails\ x)
\end{aligned}$$

$$\begin{aligned}
foldr\ f\ a\ (x\!\!+\!\!y) &= foldr\ f\ (foldr\ f\ a\ y)\ x\\
foldl\ f\ a\ (y\!\!+\!\!x) &= foldl\ f\ (foldl\ f\ a\ y)\ x
\end{aligned}$$

$$\begin{aligned}
inits\ x &= scanl\ postfix\ [\,]\ x\\
tails\ x &= scanr\ prefix\ [\,]\ x
\end{aligned}$$

The reader will have no difficulty in finding many further applications of the principle of duality. There seem to be two main reasons why the principle is useful.

The first (apparent from several of the above examples) is that duality often enables us to replace one expression by another, that produces the same result, but is cheaper to compute. For example we see that we can define *rev x* either as

$$foldr\ postfix\ [\,]\ x$$

or as

$$foldl\ prefix\ [\,]\ x$$

Given the usual linked-list implementation, the first definition has quadratic time-complexity, whereas the second is linear.

The second point is this — since the algebra of list operations is *far richer* than that of Boolean operations, it become more necessary to seek ways of reducing the number of laws that have to be remembered. We may therefore anticipate that duality will play a correspondingly more important rôle as an organising principle.

# The De Morgan Rule for lists

The De Morgan laws, in Boolean algebra, state that when negation distributes over an operator, the operator is replaced by its dual. Thus

$$\begin{aligned}
not\ (x \wedge y) &= not\ x \vee not\ y\\
not\ (x \vee y) &= not\ x \wedge not\ y
\end{aligned}$$

An analogous principle applies to lists, with reverse playing the rôle of negation.

First we introduce a generalised reversing operator $REV$, whose meaning depends on the type of its argument (this is not a function which can be defined in a functional programming language, such as Miranda, it is meta-notation that we introduce here to state the De Morgan principle for lists).

The meaning of $REV$ depends on the type of its argument in the following way. If the type is non-list (e.g. *num* or *bool* or $\alpha$) *REV* is just the identity function. If the type is that of an $i$'th order list (that is the type has $i$ pairs of list brackets around it) *REV* means $REV_i$, where

$$REV_1 \quad = \quad rev$$
$$REV_{n+1} \quad = \quad rev \, . \, map \, REV_n$$

For completeness we can say that a non-list is actually a 0'th order list, and write

$$REV_0 \quad = \quad id$$

EXAMPLES: Applied to an object of type, say $[\alpha]$, *REV* means *rev*. Applied to an object of type, say $[[num]]$, *REV* means

$$(rev \, . \, map \, rev)$$

Note that this reverses two levels deep, e.g.

$$REV \, [[1,2],[3,4]] \quad = \quad [[4,3],[2,1]]$$

Applied to an object of type, say, $[[[num]]]$, *REV* means

$$rev \, . \, map \, (rev \, . \, map \, rev)$$

which reverses three levels deep. And so on.

It may readily be shown that $REV \, (REV \, x) = x$ always.

For most practical purposes we need only $REV_0 \, (id)$, $REV_1 \, (rev)$, and $REV_2$.

## The De Morgan Rule for lists

Let $f$ be a list processing function of $k$ arguments, whose dual is $f^{\sim}$. Then the following equation holds

$$REV \, (f \, a_1 \ldots a_k) \quad = \quad f^{\sim} \, (REV \, a_1) \ldots (REV \, a_k)$$

This says that when we distribute *REV* over a function, the function is replaced by its dual. Note that we can apply the principle recursively, to push *REV* down to the "leaves" of the expression.

Many useful theorems relating functions to their duals are instances of the De Morgan rule for lists. For example.

| | | |
|---|---|---|
| $rev \, (x \mathbin{+\!\!+} y)$ | $=$ | $rev \, y \mathbin{+\!\!+} rev \, x$ |
| $rev \, (concat \, xs)$ | $=$ | $concat \, (rev \, (map \, rev \, xs))$ |
| $rev \, (prefix \, a \, x)$ | $=$ | $postfix \, a \, (rev \, x)$ |
| $rev \, (init \, x)$ | $=$ | $tl \, (rev \, x)$ |
| $rev \, (scanr \, op \, e \, xs)$ | $=$ | $scanl \, op \, e \, (rev \, xs)$ |
| $rev \, (map \, rev \, (inits \, x))$ | $=$ | $tails \, (rev \, x)$ |
| $foldr \, f \, e \, x$ | $=$ | $foldl \, f \, e \, (rev \, x)$ |

To understand the last example, note that there is an invisible application of *REV* to the left hand side. Because the type of *foldr* is

$$foldr :: (\alpha \to \beta \to \beta) \to \beta \to [\alpha] \to \beta$$

we see that in the general case its result is a non-list, so *REV* here reduces to the identity function.

Here are three more examples of the same kind

$$
\begin{aligned}
foldl\ f\ e\ x &= foldr\ f\ e\ (rev\ x) \\
len\ x &= len\ (rev\ x) \\
last\ x &= hd\ (rev\ x)
\end{aligned}
$$

Any of the equations given above can be proved by other means (e.g. by an induction over one of the list variables). But the De Morgan rule, where it is applicable, allows us to write down an equation without needing to do a proof, just by looking at the types of the arguments and result of a function.

A final remark. We can also read the De Morgan rule as giving a *definition* of what it means for one function to be the dual of another. That is, if $f$ is a function of $k$ arguments, we define $f^\sim$, the dual of $f$, by the equation

$$f^\sim\ a_1 \ldots a_k = REV\ (f\ (REV\ a_1) \ldots (REV\ a_k))$$

This follows from the De Morgan rule, together with the fact that $REV\ (REV\ x) = x$, always.

So for example, if we take the definition of *foldr* as given, we can infer that if *foldl* is to be its dual we must have

$$foldl\ f\ a\ x = foldr\ f\ a\ (rev\ x)$$

# A note on the definition of *foldl*

The functions *foldr*, *foldl* were first introduced in the language SASL, and have since come to be quite widely used. Although the definition of *foldr* is unproblematic, there are two alternative versions of *foldl* in circulation. The definition used here is that of SASL [4] and Miranda, but Richard Bird [2,1] uses a different definition. If we call Bird's version *foldl'*, we have

$$foldl' :: (\alpha \to \beta \to \alpha) \to \alpha \to [\beta] \to \alpha$$

whereas for the *foldl* used here

$$foldl :: (\alpha \to \beta \to \beta) \to \beta \to [\alpha] \to \beta$$

the relationship between the two is just

$$
\begin{aligned}
foldl'\ op\ a\ x &= foldl\ (converse\ op)\ a\ x \\
&\textbf{where} \\
&\quad converse\ f\ a\ b = f\ b\ a
\end{aligned}
$$

that is the operator supplied to *foldl'* takes its arguments in the opposite order.

From the point of view of programming convenience there is little to choose between them. However, the duality rules become significantly more complicated if we adopt *foldl'* as the fold-left function. Clearly *foldl'* and *foldr* cannot be dual to each other, because they have different types. Instead we have to say

the dual of (*foldr op*) is (*foldl'* (*converse op*))
the dual of (*foldl' op*) is (*foldr* (*converse op*))

The statements of duality for *foldl1* and *scanl*, which are defined in terms of *foldl*, have to be adjusted similarly.

For this article we have therefore adopted the SASL [4] definition of *foldl*, and the corresponding definitions of *foldl1*, *scanl*.

## References

[1] R. S. Bird. Algebraic identities for program calculation. *Computer Journal*, 32(2), April 1989.

[2] R. S. Bird and P. L. Wadler. *Introduction to Functional Programming.* Prentice Hall International, 1988.

[3] D. A. Turner. Miranda: a non-strict functional language with polymorphic types. In *Proceedings IFIP Conference on Functional Languages and Computer Architecture, Nancy, France*, pages 1–16, Springer-Verlag, September 1985. Lecture Notes in Computer Science, Vol. 201.

[4] D. A. Turner. *SASL Language Manual.* Technical Report, University of Kent. Last revised August 1983.

**Note**   "Miranda" is a trademark of Research Software Ltd.

# Appendix: Some standard functions over lists

We give here inductive definitions of some commonly used list operations. The notation used is essentially that of Miranda [3] or [2] — except that we here treat "$+\!\!\!+$" as being the basic list constructor, rather than ":" (*prefix*).

$$
\begin{array}{ll}
concat & :: \; [[\alpha]] \to [\alpha] \\
concat & = \; foldr\,(+\!\!\!+)\,[\,] \\
\\
filter & :: \; (\alpha \to bool) \to [\alpha] \to [\alpha] \\
filter\ f\ [\,] & = \; [\,]
\end{array}
$$

$$
\begin{aligned}
&\textit{filter } f \ ([a]\!+\!\!+\!x) && = && [a]\!+\!\!+\!\textit{filter } f \ x, && \textbf{if } f \ a \\
& && = && \textit{filter } f \ x, && \textbf{otherwise}
\end{aligned}
$$

$$
\begin{aligned}
&\textit{foldl} && :: && (\alpha \to \beta \to \beta) \to \beta \to [\alpha] \to \beta \\
&\textit{foldl op r } [\,] && = && r \\
&\textit{foldl op r } ([a]\!+\!\!+\!x) && = && \textit{foldl op } (op \ a \ r) \ x
\end{aligned}
$$

$$
\begin{aligned}
&\textit{foldl1} && :: && (\alpha \to \alpha \to \alpha) \to [\alpha] \to \alpha \\
&\textit{foldl1 op } ([a]\!+\!\!+\!x) && = && \textit{foldl op a x}
\end{aligned}
$$

$$
\begin{aligned}
&\textit{foldr} && :: && (\alpha \to \beta \to \beta) \to \beta \to [\alpha] \to \beta \\
&\textit{foldr op r } [\,] && = && r \\
&\textit{foldr op r } ([a]\!+\!\!+\!x) && = && op \ a \ (\textit{foldr op r x})
\end{aligned}
$$

$$
\begin{aligned}
&\textit{foldr1} && :: && (\alpha \to \alpha \to \alpha) \to [\alpha] \to \alpha \\
&\textit{foldr1 op } [a] && = && a \\
&\textit{foldr1 op } ([a,b]\!+\!\!+\!x) && = && op \ a \ (\textit{foldr1 op } ([b]\!+\!\!+\!x))
\end{aligned}
$$

$$
\begin{aligned}
&\textit{hd} && :: && [\alpha] \to \alpha \\
&\textit{hd } ([a]\!+\!\!+\!x) && = && a
\end{aligned}
$$

$$
\begin{aligned}
&\textit{init} && :: && [\alpha] \to [\alpha] \\
&\textit{init } ([a]\!+\!\!+\!x) && = && [\,], && \textbf{if } x = [\,] \\
& && = && [a]\!+\!\!+\!\textit{init } x, && \textbf{otherwise}
\end{aligned}
$$

$$
\begin{aligned}
&\textit{inits} && :: && [\alpha] \to [\,[\alpha]\,] \\
&\textit{inits } [\,] && = && [\,[\,]\,] \\
&\textit{inits } ([a]\!+\!\!+\!x) && = && [\,[\,]\,]\!+\!\!+\!\textit{map } (\textit{prefix } a) \ (\textit{inits } x)
\end{aligned}
$$

$$
\begin{aligned}
&\textit{len} && :: && [\alpha] \to num \\
&\textit{len } [\,] && = && 0 \\
&\textit{len } ([a]\!+\!\!+\!x) && = && 1 + \textit{len } x
\end{aligned}
$$

$$
\begin{aligned}
&\textit{last} && :: && [\alpha] \to \alpha \\
&\textit{last } ([a]\!+\!\!+\!x) && = && a, && \textbf{if } x = [\,] \\
& && = && \textit{last } x, && \textbf{otherwise}
\end{aligned}
$$

$$
\begin{aligned}
&\textit{map} && :: && (\alpha \to \beta) \to [\alpha] \to [\beta] \\
&\textit{map } f \ [\,] && = && [\,] \\
&\textit{map } f \ ([a]\!+\!\!+\!x) && = && [fa]\!+\!\!+\!\textit{map } f \ x
\end{aligned}
$$

$$
\begin{aligned}
&\textit{max} && :: && [\alpha] \to \alpha \\
&\textit{max} && = && \textit{foldl1 } (\textbf{max})
\end{aligned}
$$

$$
\begin{aligned}
&\textit{min} && :: && [\alpha] \to \alpha \\
&\textit{min} && = && \textit{foldl1 } (\textbf{min})
\end{aligned}
$$

$$
\begin{aligned}
&\textit{prefix} && :: && [\alpha] \to [\alpha] \to [\alpha] \\
&\textit{prefix a x} && = && [a]\!+\!\!+\!x
\end{aligned}
$$

$$
\begin{array}{ll}
postfix & :: \ [\alpha] \to [\alpha] \to [\alpha] \\
postfix \ a \ x & = \ x \mathbin{+\!\!+} [a]
\end{array}
$$

$$
\begin{array}{ll}
product & :: \ [num] \to num \\
product & = \ foldl \ (\times) \ 1
\end{array}
$$

$$
\begin{array}{ll}
rev & :: \ [\alpha] \to [\alpha] \\
rev \ [\,] & = \ [\,] \\
rev \ ([a] \mathbin{+\!\!+} x) & = \ rev \ x \mathbin{+\!\!+} [a]
\end{array}
$$

$$
\begin{array}{ll}
scanl & :: \ (\alpha \to \beta \to \beta) \to \beta \to [\alpha] \to [\beta] \\
scanl \ op \ r \, [\,] & = \ [r] \\
scanl \ op \ r \ ([a] \mathbin{+\!\!+} x) & = \ [r] \mathbin{+\!\!+} scanl \ op \ (op \ a \ r) \ x
\end{array}
$$

$$
\begin{array}{ll}
scanr & :: \ (\alpha \to \beta \to \beta) \to \beta \to [\alpha] \to [\beta] \\
scanr \ f \ r \ x & = \ map \ (foldr \ f \ r) \ (tails \ x)
\end{array}
$$

$$
\begin{array}{ll}
sum & :: \ [num] \to num \\
sum & = \ foldl \ (+) \ 0
\end{array}
$$

$$
\begin{array}{ll}
tl & :: \ [\alpha] \to [\alpha] \\
tl \ ([a] \mathbin{+\!\!+} x) & = \ x
\end{array}
$$

$$
\begin{array}{ll}
tails & :: \ [\alpha] \to [\,[\alpha]\,] \\
tails \ [\,] & = \ [\,[\,]\,] \\
tails \ ([a] \mathbin{+\!\!+} x) & = \ [\,[a] \mathbin{+\!\!+} x\,] \mathbin{+\!\!+} tails \ x
\end{array}
$$

D. A. Turner,
Computing Laboratory,
University of Kent,
Canterbury  CT2 7NF,
England.

# 48

# The Quest for Timeless
# Specifications Leads to Non-Stepping
# Automata

## W. M. Turski

The traditional view of computation has been that of input/output transformation. Hence the abstract paradigm, variously represented as Turing machine, Hoare triple, Dijkstra predicate transformer, function application etc. Hence also the classical problem of program execution termination, the root of distinction between partial and total correctness, and the apparent unidirectionality of both control and data flows. As long as the act of computation is performed by a single processor, this view is perfectly adequate; it also proved very productive in terms of theories, programming language design and programming practice. Above all, it led to sound methodological developments, which —contrary to widespread lamentations— have resulted in vast improvements in most aspects of software over not quite half a century of electronic information processing.

However, the traditional view suffers from two intrinsic difficulties: it cannot incorporate any notion of time and it does not extend to essentially multiprocessor environments. Actually, it may be argued that these two limitations are in fact very closely related. Indeed, no physical notion of time can apply in a system that has fewer than two agents capable of autonomous (sponte suum) action. A sole agent in a passive environment experiences no measurable time; the question whether an existential, philosophical notion of time applies in such a case is best left outside the scope of these considerations.

A program can be proven correct with respect to its specification only insofar as both program and specification are considered as formal objects. There is no way in which the "real" time (astronomical epochs or durations) can be formalized. Logical calculi are impervious to notions of time: various temporal logics are merely about various orderings on discrete events. Thus we cannnot *prove* any timing properties of a program, at least not in the sense in which we can prove its formally expressible properties. We can prove that a program execution eventually terminates, or even that it terminates after at most so many cycles. We cannot prove that "eventually" is before next Friday noon. If we have a reasonably good complexity analysis of a program and of all supporting layers of software we may estimate the number of machine cycles needed to execute it. If we know —experimentally, or on trust— the duration of a machine cycle, we may estimate the running time of this program. But an estimate dependent on an experiment and/or trust is not a proof.

Any knowledge about real time properties we may possess is not about programs but about programs implemented on a computer. As such, it is essentially experimental and depends on the properties of the machinery — it certainly does not allow any degree of portability. Indeed, as we cannot include in our programs any absolute tests for time epochs or intervals, by purely programmatic means, we cannot even achieve any time-safe property that would be similar to abort conditions satisfied if the machinery does not support sufficiently large integers, sufficiently many different addresses, or performs arithmetic operations in an erratic way.

Thus, whenever we make any assumption about any timing properties of the software, we are on intrinsically dangerous grounds. In fact, the scope for catastrophic errors of judgement in time-sensitive software is so large and fundamentally irreducible that any inclusion of time-related features should be simply avoided.

Can we do so? I am convinced that yes, we can avoid any considerations of time in programming. (Of course, this is not to say that we should avoid concerns of efficiency: a heap-sort program is provably more efficient than a naive-sort program, and hence "faster" in a very large class of implementations.) We can do so by:

- undoing unnecessary simplifications,
- concentrating on local tasks,
- not worrying about the next step.

A lot of timing considerations are thrust on program designers by the existing practices in the application domains, chiefly (but not exclusively) in control engineering. Quite typically, an applications problem can be clearly stated in its natural variables (such as pressure, temperature, chemical composition etc.)

- given that $Q(x, y, \ldots, z)$
- using relationships $f(x, y, \ldots, z) = 0$
$$g(x, y, \ldots, z) = 0$$
$$\ldots$$
$$h(x, y, \ldots, z) = 0$$
- achieve $R(x, y, \ldots, z)$
- maintaining $P(x, y, \ldots, z)$

This is, of course, a perfect starting point for the design of a program. Very often, however, the problem is presented as already "simplified" by resolving the relationships between the natural variables via parametric equations in an "independent" variable — time. In general, the simplification aim is to determine "controls"

$$c1(t, x0, y0, \ldots, z0),$$
$$c2(t, x0, y0, \ldots, z0),$$
$$\ldots$$
$$cN(t, x0, y0, \ldots, z0)$$

and a constant $T$ such that application of controls along the trajectory starting at time $t = t0$ in a state $(x0, y0, \ldots, z0)$ that satisfies condition $Q(x0, y0, \ldots, z0)$ will result at time $t = T$ in a state satisfying condition $R$. Also in general, this goal turns out too difficult to achieve. A number of further simplifications are then introduced; very often the controls need to be approximated by piece-wise continuous functions, so that they are valid for a small time interval only, or in small neighbourhoods of $(x0, y0, \ldots, z0)$ only, or both. Consequently, they have to be recomputed every so often, before they lose their current validity. A control program must be "fast enough" to do the control computations before the controlled process leaves a region. In addition, because the process development as a function of time is known only approximately, the size of the current neighbourhoods is not very well known, thus —to be on the safe side— it is replaced by an estimate of the time interval. We end up with the need to compute the controls within $n$ seconds and *nevertheless* watch out for critical variables straying out of safety bounds. Of course, any implementation of such a control system is intrinsically impossible to prove correct. Often it is also unsatisfactory in terms of the original problem statement.

The added rationale of the simplification supposedly rests on the assumption that monitoring the natural variables is difficult (expensive) and slow, whereas monitoring time is easy and fast. (This is the rationale behind the simplification of the problem "to cook a soft-boiled egg" to the problem "to boil an egg for three minutes"). In many cases the progress in metrology has levelled off any difference between monitoring natural variables and time, but the bias remains. Often, as with the three-minute egg, the original problem —totally time-independent!— is now presented as if its *central issue* was time. Well, if you look into the problem, not into its control-engineering simplification, you will probably discover it is not the case.

Another class of timing concerns are entirely self-inflicted. Basically, they are a consequence of the belief that local frugality results in global optimality. A typical example of this class is the notorious timeout concept.

Usually, the timeout is presented as a preferred alternative to a potentially infinite busy-wait loop, the latter being "obviously" wasteful and therefore to be avoided. The point that does not get a fair consideration is that the busy-wait is wasteful *only if there are better (useful?) things to do*. This being the case, it is not very logical to postpone these other things even for a short while, for the duration determined by the timeout constant (incidentally, the actual choice of this constant is frequently purely arbitrary). Thus, it would seem that the only justified situation for a timedout wait is when there is nothing else left to do, but, under such circumstances, the potentially infinite busy-wait can hardly be considered as wasteful!

A similar reasoning applies to the design (programming) of interacting processes, i.e. to the protocols. Timeouts are usually introduced by designs that slavishly follow old-fashioned principles of telephone communication: When I call my friend, I dial, hear the ringing tone, and wait for my friend to pick up the handset. I have to determine when to put my handset down if my friend does not answer: after 5 rings or after 10. Then I continue with my other work, perhaps calling my friend again when the conditions are once more deemed propitious. Of course, busy executives have long ago rejected this policy. They ask their secretaries to establish connection and continue with their work. When (and if) the connection is established, the secretary announces this fact, and if the executive is free to talk the conversation takes place. No timeout (but two "processors")! Once again, only if no other work remains to be done without establishing the connection the calling executive waits for the call to go through. But, as before, under these (exceptional) circumstances an endless waiting loop is not wasteful: there is nothing to waste!

Alternatives to classic timeout solutions (cf. [4]) suggest a much less sequential programming style: one in which specific actions occur under specific conditions, but nothing is explicitly said about sequences of thus guarded actions. Now we are going to extend this style of programming to an essentially multiprocessor environment.

Consider a set $V$ of variables and for each of its elements $v$, a set of possible values, $Val_v$, and its type, $\mathbf{Typ}_v$. A state is any mapping that associates with each variable $v$ a value $\$v$ from $Val_v$. In the (Cartesian product) space spanned by sets $Val_v$ as "coordinates", known as the state space, a state is a "point" determined by selecting an element, $\$v$, on each axis $Val_v$. Conversely, given a state, one can think of values of all variables (in this state!) as the coordinates of the corresponding point.

Subsets of the state space are usually characterised by predicates, that is functions that map states to boolean values {**true**, **false**}. A state $(\$x, \ldots, \$z)$ satisfies a predicate $P$ iff $P(\$x, \$y, \ldots, \$z) = \mathbf{true}$. Since the scope for confusion is minimal, the set of states that satisfy a predicate will be denoted by the same symbol as the predicate.

When we consider a computation, a very important subset of the state space, characterised by a predicate *OBSERVABLE*, consists of all states that can be observed. We shall not analyse too carefully the exact meaning of the metastatement "a state can be observed"; suffice it to say that if the state $(\$x, \$y, \ldots, \$z)$ can be observed the values of its individual coordinates can be read out. For a state outside the *OBSERVABLE* set, values of individual coordinates may, but need not, be available. All named sets in the sequel of this paper are subsets of *OBSERVABLE*.

Let $s$ be a state transformation, that is a map from states to states. Denote by **Dom**$s$ and **Ran**$s$ the domain and range of $s$, respectively. For $(\$x0, \$y0, \ldots, \$z0)$ in **Dom**$s$, $s(\$x0, \$y0, \ldots, \$z0)$ denotes the application of $s$ to state $(\$x0, \$y0, \ldots, \$z0)$. A state transformation with non-empty domain and range is called a *well-defined state transformation* (wdst) iff its application to an observable state yields an observable state.

An obvious wdst is the identity state transformation *skip*, defined by

$$skip(x, y, \ldots, z) \;=\; (x, y, \ldots, z)$$

Let $p, q, \ldots, r$ be wdst, and let $P, Q, \ldots, R$ be predicates such that $P \Rightarrow$ **Dom**$p$, $Q \Rightarrow$ **Dom**$q$, $\ldots$, $R \Rightarrow$ **Dom**$r$. We say that

(1)
$$
\begin{aligned}
&\{x : \mathbf{Typ}x, y : \mathbf{Typ}y, \ldots, z : \mathbf{Typ}z\}/\{\$x, \$y, \ldots, \$z\}\\
&\qquad P \to [p]\\
&\quad \|\; Q \to [q]\\
&\quad \|\; \ldots\\
&\quad \|\; R \to [r]\\
&\quad \|\; \neg(P \vee Q \vee \ldots \vee R) \to [skip]
\end{aligned}
$$

*specifies a single-processor computation* with global variables $x, y, \ldots, z$, of types $\mathbf{Typ}x, \mathbf{Typ}y, \ldots, \mathbf{Typ}z$, initialised in state $(\$x, \$y, \ldots, \$z)$.

Let $progp, progq, \ldots, progr$ be programs correctly implementing wdst's $p, q, \ldots, r$ in the language of [1]; in addition to the global variables $x$, $y$, $\ldots$, $z$, each program may also employ local variables (whose sets are denoted by **Locvar**$p$, **Locvar**$q$, $\ldots$, **Locvar**$r$, respectively), distinct from global ones. It is assumed that the termination condition for $progp$ is implied by $P$,

$$P \Rightarrow wp(\text{``}progp\text{''}, TRUE)$$

(similarly for $progq$ and $Q$, $\ldots$, $progr$ and $R$). The computation specified by (1) is then implemented by

(2)
$$
\begin{aligned}
&x, y, \ldots, z := \$x, \$y, \ldots, \$z;\\
&\mathbf{do}\;\; P \to progp\\
&\quad [\,]\;\; Q \to progq\\
&\quad [\,]\;\; \ldots\\
&\quad [\,]\;\; R \to progr\\
&\quad [\,]\;\; \neg(P \vee Q \vee \ldots \vee R) \to skip\\
&\mathbf{od}
\end{aligned}
$$

Computation (2) is certainly non-terminating and it may also be non-deterministic. The possible non-determinism of (2), arising from some $P$, $Q, \ldots, R$ not being pairwise disjoint, is fully compatible with a fairly conventional view of computing. The built-in non-termination ("endless repetition of *skip*") represents a view of "remaining in a (not necessarily observable) state that does not satisfy any of $P, Q, \ldots, R$".

In order to avoid some inessential but tiresome complications in the remainder of this paper, it is assumed that the global variables are passed to *progp, progq, \ldots, progr* in the manner of Algol-60 procedural parameters called by value. Thus it is assumed that **Locvarp** includes variables *locx*, *locy*, $\ldots$, *locz*, different from any local variables created for "internal purposes"; $\{u, v, \ldots, w\}$ is (the only) write-accessible subset of global variables (their value may change as a result of *progp*'s execution), and *progp* is of the form

$$progp: locx, locy, \ldots, locz := x, y, \ldots, z;$$

(3)     other statements of *progp* in which no assignments to global variables $x, y, \ldots, z$ are made (assignments to *locx, locy, \ldots, locz* are allowed!);

$$u, v, \ldots, w := locu, locv, \ldots, locw$$

Thus it is only the last multiple assignment of *progp* that changes the (global) observable state. Also for simplicity of further exposition, it is assumed that both multiple assignments (first and last lines of (3)) are atomic and instantaneous; in making this assumption we explicitly ignore any implementation issues. The "other statements" part of *progp* shall be referred to as the *body* of *progp*: (Similar conventions apply to *progq*, $\ldots$, *progr*.)

Returning now to specification (1), observe that it can be seen as an association of transformations with (sets of) states. This illustrates, in the familiar frame of reference of single-processor computation, the pragmatic essence of the proposed approach to specification. Rather than being goal-oriented, the proposed specifications are reaction-oriented. The notion of a "state" was so far understood as a merely convenient abbreviation for "an element of a Cartesian product space of value sets of variables". If this notion is now interpreted as "a state of a (real) system", we may say that in situations characterised by $P, Q, \ldots, R$ (and regardless of any "history", cf. [2]) the system "reacts" by executing transformations $p, q, \ldots, r$; in all other situations it remains in the same observable state. Of course, if the system has but one active element (processor) capable of actually performing the program that implements the transformation, cf. (2), the system's state changes only with the completion of this program execution, cf. (3). In fact, as far as changes of observed states are concerned, with a single processor (and a passive environment) there is absolutely no difference between "instantaneous" and "protracted" execution of a transformation. Observe also that, opting for specification (1), we reject any considerations of a *sequence of actions*: an action undertaken in an observable state leads to another observable state for which another action is specified, and this is the end of the story, as far as we are concerned!

In a multiprocessor system, a specification of the form (1) would be entirely inadequate. Indeed, if among the predicates $P, Q, \ldots, R$ there is at least one non-disjoint pair, the system may find itself in a state in which two guards of corresponding program (2) would be **true** and therefore two processors may start simultaneously from the same state. Thus, a single observable system state could have two, possibly different, actual images under a specified computation; two possibly different observable system states could arise from one. This is not a mere extension of the nondeterminacy of choice: we are dealing here with a possible *fission of the system*. Moreover, in the presence of two or more processors, this unpleasant complication cannot be removed by the simple expedient of making the guards mutually exclusive. Indeed, if the performance of the transformations is not instantaneous, two processors may start executing the same "enabled" transformations (because the enabling state "lasts") and, if they do not progress at the same rate (why should they?), the same image state will be established two or more times, but at different instants, which again amounts to splitting the actual system into independently evolving "copies".

The traditional remedy consists in introducing some sort of "traffic regulations" for processors (or, equivalently, some constraints on processes), which exclude, suspend or otherwise restrict multiplicity of transformations if they only could lead to state-fission nondeterminism. In other words, the conventional remedy is *preventive*; as a consequence, a number of processors may have to be temporarily idled; with the conventional approach, the price of elimination of uncontrolled indeterminism is an underutilisation of multiplicity of processors.

It is tempting to consider an exactly opposite policy: allow full utilisation of *all* available processors (including infinitely many!) by permitting *all* transformations associated with *all* satisfied predicates to be performed simultaneously and in as many copies as the available number of processors allows, but *restrict admissibility* of resulting state changes. This may be achieved by specifying the conditions under which the completed transformation is accepted; a transformation completed under conditions that fail to meet the specification will be voided. Figuratively speaking, the proposed remedy is *curative*, and thus strongly related to ideas of fault-tolerant computing, cf. [3].

In the presence of multiple processors (active agents) one is no longer assured that the system state will remain unchanged while a selected wdst is being performed. Implementation (3) of a transformation $p$, guarantees

that the body of a local computation defined by *progp* is insulated from
any (adverse or otherwise) effects of state changes resulting from concurrent actions of other processors; thus, if predicate $P$ properly describes the
sufficient conditions for *progp*'s execution, it can be safely executed. But
when the local computation is completed, its results may no longer be desirable (appropriate, acceptable, ...) in the system state that may have by
then arisen. Therefore we introduce the second predicate, *postguard* (and
rename the first one *preguard*) into an elementary block of specification.
Thus

(4)        $(P0, P1) \rightarrow [p]$

specifies that in states that satisfy preguard $P0$ the system reacts by transformation $p$, which, however, is effective only in states satisfying postguard
$P1$. If, when transformation $p$ is completed, the system does not satisfy $P1$,
the transformation is voided. Naturally, when there is only one processor,
nothing can change the system state during execution of $p$ and (4) collapses
to

(5)        $P0 \wedge P1 \rightarrow [p]$

Comparison of (5) and (4) suggests that the postguard describes such aspects of the conditions under which $p$ is considered appropriate that are
not essential for the local computation implementing $p$, but relate to its
"global" acceptance. One can say that the guard is split in two parts: the
preguard, which enables $p$, and the postguard, which makes $p$ acceptable.
The evaluation of the postguard *may* be postponed if it is expected that
(due to the actions of other agents) the acceptability of $p$ will have been established by the time $p$ will be completed. The evaluation of the postguard
*should* be postponed if there are reasons to suspect that the actions of other
agents may render $p$ unacceptable while it is being executed. Naturally, in
the case when transformation $p$ can (should) be performed regardless of any
other action, one can use the always satisfiable postguard, *TRUE*. Thus

(6)        $(P, TRUE) \rightarrow [p]$

specifies such a transformation.

It is easy to modify implementation (3) to cater for the postguard:

```
progp: locx, locy, . . . , locz := x, y, . . . , z;
       body of progp;
       if  P1(x, y, . . . , z)   →  u, v, . . . , w := locu, locv, . . . , locw
       []  ¬P1(x, y, . . . , z)  →  skip
       fi
```

As before, both explicitly shown multiple assignments are assumed to be
instantaneous; predicate $P1$ is evaluated in the current state, i.e. the values
of variables $x, y, \ldots, z$ may differ from those that have been used in the top
line multiple assignment.

With similar modifications to *progq*, ..., *progr*, the specification

$$\{x : \mathbf{Typ}x, y : \mathbf{Typ}y, \ldots, z : \mathbf{Typ}z\}/\{\$x, \$y, \ldots, \$z\}$$

(7)
$$
\begin{aligned}
&(P0, P1) \;\to\; [p]\\
\|\; &(Q0, Q1) \;\to\; [q]\\
\|\; &\cdots\\
\|\; &(R0, R1) \;\to\; [r]\\
\|\; &(\neg P0 \wedge \neg Q0 \wedge \ldots \wedge \neg R0, TRUE) \;\to\; [skip]
\end{aligned}
$$

defines a multiprocessor computation eventually implemented by local computations *progp*, *progq*, ..., *progr*. Whenever a preguard is satisfied and there is an available processor, the corresponding local computation may be started, and no assumptions are made on the choice of local computations to start when several preguards are satisfied in a single state. Similarly, no assumptions are made with respect to the speed with which individual processors execute local computations, but it is assumed that each processor is capable of executing any local computation. If only one processor is available, specification (7) is entirely equivalent to a specification of a single-processor computation with ("collapsed") guards defined by conjunction of respective pre- and postguards.

Experience with using the proposed style of specification indicates that a quite-often-needed kind of postguarded transformation is of the form

$$(P, P) \;\to\; [p]$$

indicating that the transformation $p$ is acceptable if the system state, insofar as captured by the guards, does not change (or is restored) during the (body of a) local computation that implements $p$.

It is perhaps interesting to observe that the inclusion of postguards in the specification correlates with the preferred (by some physicists) style of description of experiments in quantum physics. For instance, in the delayed-choice split-beam experiments (cf. [5]), photons (or electrons) are made to travel through an experimental apparatus along *one* of two routes, route A or route B, or along *both* routes simultaneously. The discrimination between the two options is effected by the sensing device placed at the endpoint of both routes. The sensing device may be freely chosen from two available: *DEV1* and *DEV2*. When *DEV1* is used, the photons appear to come by only one route, when *DEV2* is used they appear to come by both routes. The apparent ability to change the history by selecting the sensing device *after* a photon has been fired and thus started its travel either by one route, or by both routes simultaneously is a little unnerving to some physicists (and many philosophers). We could specify such an experiment in a very simple way:

$$
\begin{aligned}
&(FIREABLE, DEVIP1) \to [\text{go by one route}]\\
\|\; &(FIREABLE, DEVIP2) \to [\text{go by both routes}]
\end{aligned}
$$

$$\| \ (\neg FIREABLE, \ TRUE) \ \rightarrow \ [skip]$$

where $FIREABLE$ describes states in which a photon can be fired, and $DEVIPi$ is satisfied iff device $DEVi$ is in place. Note that with a single processor and collapsed form of specification we need to know which sensing device is in place *before* the photon is sent on its travel; in a multiprocessor environment we get an exact replica of the delayed choice experiment!

For a more familiar example, consider a bank with multiple tellers accepting payments and paying out cheques. The speciality of the bank is that it pays out only in dimes. Thus when presented with a cheque for, say, one hundred dollars, the teller must count one thousand coins, a rather long process. To pay out, a teller must be satisfied that a cheque has been presented and that the corresponding account is sufficiently in credit to honour this cheque. Upon presentation of a cheque, the teller may check the balance of the account and, finding it sufficiently large, start counting the coins. Lest, however, actions of other tellers reduce the balance while he assembles the requested number of dimes, the teller must suspend these actions. On the other hand, actions of other cashiers (accepting payments) may just be creating the situation in which payment can be made; the total suspension of their actions would be counter-productive!

The specification

$$(request > 0, balance > request \ \wedge \ payout = 0) \ \rightarrow$$
$$[count\text{-}coins; payout, request := request, 0]$$
$$\| \ (payout > 0, TRUE) \ \rightarrow$$
$$[balance, payout := balance - payout, 0]$$

describes a non-interfering paying-out procedure (*request*, *payout* and *balance* are variables relating to the same account; for simplicity, the account-identification has been omitted).

Note that the protracted action (coin counting) is not delayed awaiting the balance to be sufficiently large; it is undertaken as soon as a request is presented. If, by the time the coin counting is finished, the balance is insufficient or a previous payment from the same account has not been completed, the count is "voided" and a new counting to meet the same request will start. Actually, many countings for a single request may be in progress simultaneously but only one can succeed in establishing positive payout (thanks to the second conjunct in the postguard). True to our philosophy, no explicit sequencing (or timing!) is present in the specification. The price for this simplification of the design is the potentially wasted work of a processor (or processors) counting coins in vain.

In some problems, where a single-processor implementation does not make sense, it may be useful to mark parts of the specification as meant for a dedicated processor. Such is the case in our final example. Assume that in the system under specification some phenomenon manifests itself by a change of value of a global variable $x$. Only two values of $x$ are admissible, $x = 0$ and $x = 1$. Following is a skeletal specification of the system, where the only explicitly listed parts specify a counter of the occurrences of the phenomenon; as far as the counter is concerned, the occurrences of the phenomenon are entirely spontaneous. Using the pair of brackets $\langle$ and $\rangle$ for delimiting parts of the specification meant for a single-processor execution, we may write:

$$\{x : 0..1, n : integer, \ldots\}/\{0, 0, \ldots\}$$
$$\langle \ (x = 0, x = 1) \ \rightarrow \ [n := n + 1]$$
$$\| \ (x = 1, x = 0) \ \rightarrow \ [n := n + 1] \ \rangle$$
$$\| \ \cdots$$

Note that in this case the collapsed guards are identically **false**, which nicely corresponds with the fact that the problem is totally meaningless in a single-processor environment. (If a specification includes $(P, Q) \rightarrow [s]$ with contradictory $P$ and $Q$, this specification cannot be implemented in a single processor environment).

## REFERENCES

[1] E. W. Dijkstra. *A Discipline of Programming*. Prentice-Hall, Englewood Cliffs, 1976.

[2] C. B. Jones. *Systematic Software Development Using VDM*. Prentice Hall, 1986.

[3] B. Randell. System structure for software fault-tolerance. *IEEE Trans. on Software Eng. SE1*, 220–232, 1975.

[4] W. M. Turski. Time considered irrelevant for real-time systems. *BIT*, 28:473–486, 1988.

[5] J. A. Wheeler. The computer and the universe. *Int. J. of Theor. Physics*, 21:557–572, 1982.

W. M. Turski,
Institute of Informatics,
Warsaw University,
PKiN. pok.850,
00–901 Warsaw,
Poland.

# The Maximum Length of a Palindrome in a Sequence

## Jan Tijmen Udding

## 0   Introduction

The following development of a program to compute the maximum length of a palindrome in a sequence is a tribute to the structured development of programs of which Edsger W. Dijkstra has been such a strong advocate. It shows that our skills have improved over the years, and that we are able to tackle quite non-trivial problems.

## 1   Sequences and notational conventions

A sequence can be viewed in two different ways. We use both views depending upon the ease with which we can express certain properties. First of all, we can view a sequence as a mapping from a consecutive set of integers, the domain, to some set of elements. This enables us to identify uniquely the position of a (sub)sequence within a sequence. For $j$ and $k - 1$ in the domain of the sequence we denote the subsequence restricted to the domain $\{i : j \leq i < k : i\}$ by $(j, k)$. Notice that this sequence is empty if $j \geq k$. Index $j$ is called its left endpoint and index $k$ its right endpoint.

A sequence can also simply be viewed as a catenation of a number of elements. We adopt this view of a sequence when we say that two sequences are equal or when we reverse a sequence. We use the overbar as an operator that takes a sequence as its argument and reverses it. A sequence $(j, k)$ is said to be a palindrome, denoted by $pl.(j, k)$, when $(j, k) = \overline{(j, k)}$. Clearly, the empty sequence and the one-element sequence are palindromes. A nonempty palindrome enjoys the property that chopping off its leftmost element and its rightmost element results in a palindrome. A sequence that is not a palindrome cannot become one by adding an element to the left and an element to the right of it. We capture this in the following property.

**Property 0**    For $j$, $j + 1$, and $k$, $k - 1$ in the domain of some given sequence we have

$$\neg pl.(j, k) \quad \vee \quad pl.(j + 1, k - 1)$$

□

The length of a sequence $(j, k)$ is the number of elements that it contains. This number is 0 if $j \geq k$ and it is $k - j$ otherwise.

## 2   The problem and its solution

The problem statement is the following. We are given an integer $N$, $N \geq 0$, and a sequence $S$ on $\{i : \ 0 \leq i < N : \ i\}$. We are asked to derive an algorithm for computing the maximum length of any palindrome subsequence in $S$. Hence, the postcondition of this problem is

$$r = mpl.(0, N),$$

where $mpl.(j, k)$ is defined as the maximum length of any palindrome in the sequence $(j, k)$. Using standard techniques to generalize this postcondition into an invariant that allows an easy initialization, we propose the following invariant

(P)        $r = mpl.(0, n) \quad \wedge \quad 0 \leq n \leq N.$

We use P to label all the invariants of the repetition that we are going to develop. This invariant is established by initializing both $n$ and $r$ to 0. We are done when $n = N$, which suggests that we choose $n \neq N$ as a guard of the repetition. In order to guarantee termination we want $n$ to increase in every step and there is no reason to hope for an increase by more than 1. This leaves us with the obligation to establish $r = mpl.(0, n + 1)$ before the statement $n := n + 1$.

The maximum length of any palindrome in $(0, n + 1)$ is the maximum of $mpl.(0, n)$ and the maximum length of any tail palindrome in $(0, n + 1)$, that is, a palindrome with right endpoint $n + 1$. Such a palindrome is of the form $(i, n + 1)$ for some $i$, $0 \leq i \leq n$.

We define *ltpl* to be the function that yields the longest tail palindrome of its argument.

The problem of finding the longest palindrome with right endpoint $n + 1$ can be programmed as a simple linear search with a sentinel. We start at $i = 0$, since we want the smallest $i$ that is at least 0. Further, $(n, n + 1)$ is a palindrome, since $n \geq 0$ on account of P, thereby assuring termination of the search. Therefore, a program to solve this problem would be

$r, n, := 0, 0 \ \{ \ P \ \}$ ;
**do** $n \neq N \ \rightarrow \ i := 0$ ;
  **do** $\neg pl.(i, n + 1) \ \rightarrow \ i := i + 1$ **od**
  $\{ \ (i, n + 1) \ = \ ltpl.(0, n + 1) \ \}$ ;
  $r := r \max (n + 1 - i) \ \{ \ P^n_{n+1} \ \}$ ; $n := n + 1$
**od**

Two things need careful attention if we want this program to become an efficient one: starting the linear search with $i = 0$ and the evaluation of the guard $\neg pl.(i, n + 1)$.

Starting the linear search with $i = 0$ every time results in a running time that is at least quadratic in $N$. The question is what a better starting point for the linear search would be, given the usual constraint that we are not supposed to use any information about $(n, N)$, the rest of the sequence. The crucial observation is that the longest palindrome with right endpoint $n + 1$ cannot be much longer than the one with right endpoint $n$. If $(j, n+1)$ is a palindrome with right endpoint $n + 1$ then $(j + 1, n)$ is a palindrome as well, on account of Property 0. This means that if $(m, n)$ is the longest palindrome with right endpoint $n$ then we can safely start the linear search with $i = m - 1$, provided that $m - 1$ is in the domain of the sequence. The entire sequence $(0, n)$ can be a palindrome, which would cause $m - 1$ to be out of the domain of the sequence $S$. In order to avoid a case distinction we assume that $-1$ is in the domain of $S$ and that $S.(-1)$ is an element that does not occur anywhere else in the sequence. Then $pl.(-1, n + 1)$ is false for $n \geq 0$, which holds on account of the invariant, and $S.(-1)$ does not affect the outcome of the linear search.

Therefore, we propose to strengthen the invariant by maintaining the longest tail palindrome of $(0, n)$. We add to the invariant

(P)     $(m, n) = ltpl.(0, n) \ \land \ 0 \leq m \leq n$.

The initialization of $m$ is 0 and after the linear search we know that $(i, n + 1)$ is the longest tail palindrome in $(0, n + 1)$. Hence, assigning $i$ to $m$ establishes $(m, n) = ltpl.(0, n + 1)$. The program now looks like

$r, n, m := 0, 0, 0$ ;
**do** $n \neq N \ \rightarrow \ i := m - 1$ ;
  **do** $\neg pl.(i, n + 1) \ \rightarrow \ i := i + 1$ **od** ;
  $r, m := r \max (n + 1 - i), i$ ; $n := n + 1$
**od**

If we can evaluate the guard of the linear search in constant time then this program has linear time complexity. The total number of times that the body of the inner repetition has been executed after $n$ steps of the outermost repetition is $m + n$.

The only remaining problem is an efficient evaluation of $pl.(i, n + 1)$, preferably in constant time. It is clearly a bad idea to try and store the value of $pl.(i, n)$ for all possible values of $i$ and $n$. That would imply a running time that is at least quadratic in $N$. On account of Property 0, however, there is a relationship between the palindrome property of sequences. Consider some subsequence $(k, l)$. With this sequence we can associate a set of sequences $\{ k', l' : k' + l' = k + l : (k', l') \}$ (we leave implicit the understanding that these sequences are subsequences of $(-1, N)$). The set of these sequences is characterized by the sum of the left and right endpoints of any one of them. Some of these sequences are palindromes and other ones are not. The elements of this set can be ordered according to their lengths. On account of Property 0, there is a unique point in this order such that shorter sequences are palindromes and longer ones are not. In other words, for $-1 \leq k \leq N$ and $-1 \leq l \leq N$ we can define

$$maxpal.(k + l) =$$
$$(\mathbf{MAX}\ k', l' :\ k' + l' = k + l\ \wedge\ pl.(k', l') :\ l' - k').$$

The size of $maxpal$ is linear in $N$ and the question whether $(k, l)$ is a palindrome, which is $pl.(k, l)$, can now be phrased as $maxpal.(k + l) \geq l - k$.

If we knew $maxpal$ in advance, we could evaluate the guard of the linear search in constant time. Obviously, we have to compute $maxpal$ as we go along and hope that we can compute a sufficiently large fraction of it for the evaluation of the guard to be possible in constant time. Given that we do not assume any knowledge about the sequence $(n, N)$, we do not know the value of $maxpal.(m + n)$ yet. The sequence $(m, n)$ is a palindrome on account of invariant P, but it may still be contained in a larger one with the same sum of left and right endpoints. Hence, the only thing we know of $maxpal.(m + n)$ is that it is at least $n - m$.

On the other hand, the information to determine $maxpal.(k + l)$ for $k + l < m + n$ is fully contained in the sequence $(-1, n)$, for the following reason. We can write such a $k + l$ as $(k + l - n) + n$ where $k + l - n < m$. Since $(m, n)$ is the maximum palindrome with right endpoint $n$ we know that $(k + l - n, n)$ is not a palindrome, and therefore the palindrome determining $maxpal.(k + l)$ lies entirely within $(k + l - n, n)$. Hence, we propose to strengthen the invariant of the outermost repetition with the following invariant for variable $c$

(P)    $(\forall k, l :\ -2 \leq k + l < m + n :\ c.(k + l) = maxpal.(k + l)).$

This requires an initialization of $c.(-2)$ and $c.(-1)$. The set of sequences determining $maxpal.(-2)$ consists of $(-1, -1)$. Hence, $c.(-2) = 0$. For $c.(-1)$

we have to consider $(0, -1)$ and $(-1, 0)$, which means that we have to initialize $c.(-1)$ to 1.

Unfortunately, in the linear search we need the value of $maxpal$ for sequences of the form $(i, n + 1)$ with $i \geq m - 1$. Since $pl.(n, n + 1)$ holds, $i \leq n$ in the linear search, so we can rewrite its guard $\neg pl.(i, n + 1)$ as $\neg pl.(i + 1, n) \lor S.i \neq S.n$. Hence, all palindrome tests are performed on tail sequences of $(m, n)$. Such a tail sequence can also be found as an initial sequence of $(m, n)$, albeit in the reverse order, since $(m, n)$ is a palindrome. We formalize this in the program by introducing a variable $j$ for an initial sequence of $(m, n)$ and keeping invariant for the linear search

(Q) $\qquad (m, j) = \overline{(i + 1, n)} \quad \land \quad m - 1 \leq j \leq n.$

We use Q to label all the additional invariants of the linear search. By initializing $j$ to $n$ we establish this invariant, due to the initialization of $i$ to $m - 1$ and the fact that $(m, n)$ is a palindrome. An increase of $i$ by 1 and a decrease of $j$ by 1 maintain this invariant. Since $m - 1 \leq i \leq n$ in the linear search, the range of $j$ is $m - 1 \leq j \leq n$. The program then becomes

$$r, n, m := 0, 0, 0 ;$$
$$\textbf{do } n \neq N \;\rightarrow\; i, j := m - 1, n ;$$
$$\qquad \textbf{do } \neg pl.(i + 1, n) \lor S.i \neq S.n \;\rightarrow\; i, j := i + 1, j - 1 \textbf{ od} ;$$
$$\qquad r, m := r \max (n - i + 1), i ; \; n := n + 1$$
$$\textbf{od}$$

On account of the invariant $(m, j) = \overline{(i + 1, n)}$, the guard $\neg pl.(i + 1, n)$ may be replaced by $\neg pl.(m, j)$. We have seen earlier that $pl.(m, j)$ can be phrased as $maxpal.(m + j) \geq j - m$. Notice that in the linear search $m + j < m + n$ except the first time around. This means that the test $\neg pl.(m, j)$ may be replaced by $c.(m + j) < j - m$, on account of the invariant for $c$, except when $j = n$. Since we know that $pl.(m, n)$ holds we do not have to make a case distinction for the first evaluation of the guard if we choose $c.(m + n)$ to be at least $n - m$. This can easily be established in the initialization of the linear search.

The only problem remaining is to maintain the invariant for $c$, which may be violated when $m$ and $n$ increase at the end of the linear search. Since $m$ is essentially increased by the number of steps of the linear search, we use the linear search repetition to maintain the invariant for $c$. We replace $m$ in the invariant for $c$ by $i + 1$ for the following additional invariant of the linear search.

(Q) $\qquad (\forall k, l : -2 \leq k + l < i + 1 + n : c.(k + l) = maxpal.(k + l)).$

This holds when the linear search is initalized, due to $i := m - 1$ and the invariant for $c$ in P. Moreover, the statements $m := i$ and $n := n + 1$ restore this invariant for $c$.

415     Jan Tijmen Udding

In each step of the repetition we have to give the value $maxpal.(i+1+n)$ to $c.(i+1+n)$. We distinguish the case that $(m,j)$ is a palindrome from the case that it is not. If $(m,j)$ is a palindrome then so is $(i+1,n)$, on account of the invariant $(m,j) = \overline{(i+1,n)}$. Moreover, since the guard of the linear search $\neg pl.(i,n+1)$ holds, $(i,n+1)$ is not a palindrome. Hence, $maxpal.(i+n+1)$ is equal to $j-m$ (or $n-i-1$). On the other hand, if $(m,j)$ is not a palindrome then the palindrome determining $maxpal.(m+j)$ is entirely contained in $(m,j)$; the same holds for $(i+1,n)$ on account of the invariant $(m,j) = \overline{(i+1,n)}$. Therefore, $maxpal.(i+1+n)$ is equal to $maxpal.(m+j)$. Since the fact that $(m,j)$ is a palindrome can be expressed as $maxpal.(m+j) \geq j-m$, we can combine these two cases into

$$maxpal.(i+1+n) \quad = \quad maxpal.(m+j) \min (j-m).$$

For $j < n$ we know that $maxpal.(m+j)$ is equal to $c.(m+j)$ on account of the invariant for $c$. In case $j = n$ (which is the only remaining possibility since $m-1 \leq j \leq n$) we know $i$ to be equal to $m-1$ and the guard of the linear search repetition $\neg pl.(i,n+1)$, which is $\neg pl.(m-1,n+1)$ now, to hold. Since $(m,n)$ is a palindrome, we conclude that $maxpal.(m+n) = n-m$. Hence, if we initialize $c.(m+n)$ to be at least $n-m$, as we already had decided, we do not have to make a case distinction for $j = n$. We can use $c.(m+j)$ instead of $maxpal.(m+j)$ for any value of $j$.

Putting the pieces together the final program is

$$r,n,m,c.(-2),c.(-1) := 0,0,0,0,1 \;;$$
$$\mathbf{do}\ n \neq N\ \rightarrow\ i,j,c.(m+n) := m-1,n,n-m \;;$$
$$\mathbf{do}\ c.(m+j) < j-m\ \vee\ S.i \neq S.n\ \rightarrow$$
$$i,j,c.(i+n+1) := i+1,j-1,c.(m+j)\min(j-m)$$
$$\mathbf{od}\;;$$
$$r,m := r\max(n-i+1),i\;;\ n := n+1$$
$$\mathbf{od}$$

A more careful analysis would have shown that we do not need the value $c.(-2)$.

*Acknowledgements*: I am greatly endebted to Johan Jeuring whose derivation of his solution to this problem in the Bird-Meertens formalism challenged me to derive the above program. I owe the idea to maintain the longest palindrome centered around a given point in the sequence to him. I benefited from discussions with Johan L. Lukkien and other members of the Groningen Hobby Club. I am grateful to Netty van Gasteren for urging me to rewrite an earlier solution to this problem. I thank Wei Chen and Kenneth C. Cox for their comments upon a draft version of this paper.

Jan Tijmen Udding,
Department of Computer Science,
Washington University,
St. Louis, MO  63130,
U.S.A.

and

Department of Computing Science,
Rijksuniversiteit Groningen,
P.O. Box 800,
9700 AV  Groningen,
The Netherlands.

# 50

# On Form, Formalism and Equivalence

## Lincoln A. Wallen

Sight is perhaps our most sensitive physical sense and can be used to reduce conceptual complexity. This potential is exploited within mathematics when complex ideas are expressed using geometrical relationships between symbols. By conscious manipulation of visual *form* we achieve unconscious manipulation of conceptual *content*. For example, the formal rules of Calculus help us to apply complex theorems of Analysis accurately. Moreover, the rules can be used without detailed knowledge of the mathematics that justifies them.

Since formal manipulation is so effective in the solution of specific mathematical problems, it is natural to ask whether or not there is a systematic way that it can help in the construction of mathematical arguments in general. After suitable formalisation we might hope to solve all problems without explicit recourse to mathematical content. This grand desire to construct all mathematical arguments by formal manipulation dates back to the 17th century at least, and resurfaced again early in this century. Gödel's (1931) *incompleteness* result tells us, however, that the desire is unattainable since the class of true statements of a theory is larger than the class of provable statements of any particular formalisation of the theory.

Nevertheless, just as formal manipulations are of great use in Calculus and Arithmetic —which ironically is the theory used by Gödel to demonstrate the limitations of formalisation— so might they be in other theories. In passing from content to form we might be happy to exchange some content in return for an effective means of calculation. After all, the class of statements provable within a formalism may still include many of those in which we are interested! In this respect it is worth investigating to what extent we may rely on our formalisms, ignoring the fact that they are an incomplete representation of our mathematical ideas. For example, can we rely solely on the form of our demonstrandum in the search for a proof of it (assuming that it is in fact provable within the formalism)?

An answer to this problem in particular cases can be given using methods introduced by Gentzen. The idea is that we represent our theory in a logical system and attempt to obtain what Girard (1987) calls *purity of methods* for the system. Gentzen (1934) obtained such a principle for the pure Predicate Calculus (i.e., the empty theory) via his *cut-elimination* result. A corollary of this result is that any theorem of the Predicate Calculus has a proof made up of subformulas of the theorem only. No *eureka* formulas representing new ideas or abstractions are required. (The choice of eureka formulas is the formal counterpart to the mathematician's choice of appropriate lemmas.) A systematic analysis of the subformulas of a sentence is therefore enough to ascertain whether or not the sentence is a theorem (see Kleene, 1967). Gentzen (1936) achieved a similar result for a formalisation of Arithmetic, but, because of the increased complexity of the mathematical theory (due to mathematical induction), he had to extend the logical system to include *transfinite induction*.

One method of analysing the complexity of a mathematical theory is to search for the weakest formalisation of it that has purity of methods (see Girard, 1987). It turns out that the complexity of most mathematical theories exceeds that of the Predicate Calculus. Consequently, if we formalise a complex theory within the Predicate Calculus we cannot rely solely on form to guide our search for proofs. However, we can use Gentzen's result to localise our reference to the mathematical theory by choosing the eureka formulas (lemmas) that we will allow in the proof *before* we begin the search and augmenting the demonstrandum with them. The new demonstrandum is treated as a potential theorem of the pure Predicate Calculus and Gentzen's result used to justify a systematic search through its subformulas for a proof. Of course we will need knowledge of the mathematical theory in order to choose the eureka formulas appropriately. In such cases the search for a proof is, by necessity, a partly mathematical, partly formal exercise. (Unfortunately, even if a theorem is provable without eureka formulas their introduction can drastically reduce the size of its proof.)

If we adopt the strategy outlined above —namely, reducing the search for an argument that proves a given demonstrandum to the search for a (formal) proof of an extended demonstrandum— the next question is how should we formalise arguments themselves? This question concerns our formalisation of logic, and if one is careful in this matter the results can be impressive. A good illustration of this point is Edsger W. Dijkstra and Carel S. Scholten's book on Predicate Calculus and Program Semantics (1989). There they use a formal version of the (second order) Predicate Calculus, developed by Dijkstra and W. H. J. Feijen, in a treatment of the semantics of an (idealised) imperative programming language. One might say that they express the elements of Lattice Theory used in the semantics in *logical form*. For the basis of such a representation one might consult Johnstone (1982) or Abramsky (1988).

An interesting feature of Dijkstra and Feijen's formalisation of logic is the central place given to the connective of *equivalence*. This somewhat unorthodox choice is based on the relationship between classical propositional logic and Boolean algebra, and it seemingly bypasses the (now) standard methods originating from the work of Frege (1879) and Gentzen (1934). One benefit of the emphasis placed on equivalence is that proof construction can be so arranged as to resemble symbolic equation solving; i.e., inference proceeds by the replacement of one expression by another. Quite often, as Dijkstra and Scholten are at pains to point out in their book, the form of the demonstrandum determines the appropriate rewritings to perform.

In the remainder of this paper I shall advance the view that the calculational benefits obtained by Dijkstra and his colleagues in the construction of formal proofs stem from two related sources. Firstly, the use of equivalence enables the implementation of *least commitment* search; that is, the search involves a sequence of *proof states* with the property that the current state can be completed to a proof *if and only if* the previous state can. Thus, if the demonstrandum is indeed provable and it is used as the first proof state, then no *blind alleys* can be encountered in the search. Secondly, proof states are represented in compact symbolic form by (combinations of) formulas, thus a summary of the partial proof is available *locally* to suggest the next formal step.

Dijkstra and Feijen's proof system shows that these goals can be met within the Predicate Calculus by means of the classical connectives. Disjunction is used heavily to represent complex proof states in compact form, while the connective of equivalence is used as the basis for least commitment constructions. The point of separating these two concerns is to suggest that similar benefits may be obtained within contexts other than the classical Predicate Calculus by following the same principles. In other logical systems, for example, suitable connectives may not be available within the logic; nevertheless, extralogical (or metalogical) constructs can be introduced to achieve a similar effect. The (informal) argument given below confirms that equivalence is indeed crucial in the effective use of form in calculation, but that it is equivalence in the *metatheory* that yields the benefits, and only in certain contexts can that notion be *internalised* by means of a connective.

$\star \quad \star \quad \star$

Consider the following argument by cases:

$$(1) \qquad \cfrac{A \vee B \qquad \cfrac{(A) \quad A \Rightarrow C}{C} \Rightarrow \mathcal{E} \qquad \cfrac{(B) \quad B \Rightarrow C}{C} \Rightarrow \mathcal{E}}{C} \vee \mathcal{E},$$

that establishes that $C$ follows from the three hypotheses shown; i.e., the consequence:

$$(2) \qquad A \vee B, \ A \Rightarrow C, \ B \Rightarrow C \ \vdash \ C.$$

We have given visual form to the argument using Gentzen's (1934) system of *natural deduction* (**N**). The three primitive rules used (assumption, implication elimination and disjunction elimination) are shown below.

$$(3) \qquad \varphi \text{ Ass.} \qquad \cfrac{\varphi \quad \varphi \Rightarrow \psi}{\psi} \Rightarrow \mathcal{E} \qquad \cfrac{\varphi \vee \psi \quad \overset{(\varphi)}{\underset{\theta}{\vdots}} \quad \overset{(\psi)}{\underset{\theta}{\vdots}}}{\theta} \vee \mathcal{E}$$

The brackets used around the formulas $A$ and $B$ in (1), introduced by application of the $(\vee\mathcal{E})$ rule above, indicate that an assumption has been *discharged;* i.e., should not be counted as one of the hypotheses (leaves of the tree) on which the derivation of the conclusion (root of the tree) depends.

We might have rendered (1) linguistically as follows: "$A \vee B$ holds, so we argue by cases. Suppose $A$ (Ass.). Since $A \Rightarrow C$, $C$ holds ($\Rightarrow\mathcal{E}$). Now suppose $B$ (Ass.). Since $B \Rightarrow C$, $C$ holds ($\Rightarrow\mathcal{E}$). So in either case, $C$ holds ($\vee\mathcal{E}$). QED." The formal argument (1) captures the logical structure of the linguistic argument quite well in that the two cases in the argument are given form as distinct branches of the proof tree. This property of **N** extends to the representation of more complex arguments that one might find in mathematical literature.

So much for the use of form to represent the structure of an *existing* argument. Does the system also facilitate the *search* for arguments? We shall try to prove our demonstrandum from first principles, and let the forms dictate our steps.

We are asked to conclude that $C$ holds on the basis of the three hypotheses (2). A fruitful strategy is to see if there are any hypotheses and rules from which we can conclude $C$ directly, and if so, attempt to prove their antecedents. There are two such hypotheses: $A \Rightarrow C$ and $B \Rightarrow C$, so we choose one and "backward chain" on the implication by means of the $\Rightarrow\mathcal{E}$ rule. The result is shown below.

$$(4) \qquad \cfrac{A \quad A \Rightarrow C}{C} \Rightarrow \mathcal{E}.$$

The only (undischarged) hypothesis not amongst those from which we may conclude $C$ is $A$. This then becomes our new goal. The only other occurrence of the formula $A$ is embedded in the hypothesis $A \vee B$. Consequently, the only rule applicable is $(\vee\mathcal{E})$, giving us the partial derivation:

$$
(5) \qquad \cfrac{\cfrac{A \vee B \qquad (A) \qquad \begin{matrix}(B)\\ \vdots \\ A\end{matrix}}{A}\, \vee\mathcal{E} \qquad A \Rightarrow C}{C}\, \Rightarrow\mathcal{E}.
$$

The vertical dots indicate the part of this partial derivation that we have yet to complete. Proving that $A$ follows from $B$ is no easy matter — in fact it does not follow from the hypotheses we have to hand. What has happened? By following a reasonable, local, formal strategy we have reached a situation where we have a local demonstrandum $(B \vdash A)$ that we cannot achieve. Comparison of (5) with (1) shows that our strategy has led us off course in the reconstruction of an appropriate case analysis for this problem.

It is not too difficult to see, *in this particular instance,* that we should have performed a case analysis right at the beginning. But to judge that this is so we must "look ahead" and plan the derivation before starting. The reader can imagine that for other, more complex, demonstranda —where the derivation of $C$ from $A$ in the one case, and of $C$ from $B$ in the other, is an involved matter not easily seen in advance— this "look ahead" amounts to constructing the entire argument in one's head before proceeding with the first formal step! After all, there is no immediate connection between the formulas $C$ and $A \vee B$.

What should we conclude from this? I think that we should conclude that, in matters of proof search, systems of natural deduction are not tailored to our manipulative needs. A justification for this view can be obtained as follows. The states that the putative **N**-derivation passes through can be by summarised using *sequents:* another (formal) device due to Gentzen (1934). Sequents have the following shape: $\Gamma \longrightarrow \varphi$, where $\Gamma$ is a set of formulas. Such a sequent asserts the existence of an **N**-derivation from the formulas in the set $\Gamma$ to the conclusion $\varphi$. In this notation the two constructions that led us to (5) can be expressed as assertions *about* the existence of **N**-proofs (see Prawitz, 1965):

(6) $\qquad \Gamma, (\varphi \Rightarrow \psi) \longrightarrow \psi \qquad$ if $\qquad \Gamma \longrightarrow \varphi$
(7) $\qquad \Gamma, (\varphi \vee \psi) \longrightarrow \theta \qquad$ if $\qquad \Gamma, \varphi \longrightarrow \theta \quad$ and $\quad \Gamma, \psi \longrightarrow \theta,$

where $\Gamma, \varphi$ is used to denote the union of $\{\varphi\}$ with $\Gamma$, for any formula $\varphi$.

In terms of proof search in **N**, if we are looking for a proof that satisfies the conclusion of one of the above implications, then it suffices to construct **N**-derivations that satisfy the antecedent(s). The crucial point is that the constructions are (metatheoretic) *implications.* Consequently, when we search according to these metarules we may leave ourselves with an unsatisfiable new task, as happened in our example.

Let **E** denote the proof system developed by Dijkstra and Feijen mentioned above. All we shall need to know about the system is that (a) implication is *defined* by:

(8)     $\varphi \Rightarrow \psi \quad =_{\text{df}} \quad \psi \equiv \varphi \vee \psi$

(where equivalence is of lower precedence than disjunction); (b) that $\equiv$ is a congruence relation over the formulas (at least in the propositional subsystem); (c) that a continued equality $\varphi = \psi = \theta$, as in arithmetic, represents the conjunction: $\varphi = \psi$ and $\psi = \theta$, and finally (d) that hints are enclosed in curly brackets. Our demonstrandum (2) can be proved within this system by the following derivation constructed from the bottom to the top.

(9)    True

$=$     $\{A \vee B\}$

   $A \vee B$

$\Rightarrow$     $\{\varphi \Rightarrow \varphi \vee \psi, \ \text{forall } \psi, \varphi\}$

   $A \vee B \vee C$

$=$     $\{C \equiv B \vee C \ \text{i.e., } B \Rightarrow C\}$

   $A \vee C$

$=$     $\{C \equiv A \vee C \ \text{i.e., } A \Rightarrow C\}$

   $C$

We begin with the goal $C$. As with **N** above we ask if there are any hypotheses that can be used to manipulate this form. The answer is the same: the two implications $A \Rightarrow C$ and $B \Rightarrow C$. Once again we choose the first and perform the analogous operation to backward chaining in **N**. But there is a crucial difference. This time, by virtue of the definition of implication given in (8), we replace $C$ by an *equivalent* expression $A \vee C$. We now look for some hypothesis with which we can manipulate this new form, *or some subform* of it. The implication $B \Rightarrow C$ is the most natural hypothesis to use and we obtain the disjunction $A \vee B \vee C$. Finally we notice that the form of our remaining hypothesis is a subform of the current goal, and moreover is sufficient to conclude it. This completes the proof.

Let us review the differences between (5) and (9) after the use of the first implication. In the former we were unable to use the second implication and had to resort to the disjunction. This is undesirable on grounds of the symmetry between $A$ and $B$. In both derivations we broke symmetry by choosing one implication arbitrarily, but $\mathbf{N}$ forces us to compound this situation since we are unable to redress the asymmetry subsequently. $\mathbf{E}$ on the other hand permits restoration of symmetry between $A$ and $B$ via $B$'s implication and the known symmetries of $\vee$.

The force of this construction can again be captured via sequents, and in that way a more precise relationship between $\mathbf{E}$ and $\mathbf{N}$ obtained. The construction is as follows:

(10)    $\Gamma, (\varphi \Rightarrow \psi) \longrightarrow \psi$    iff    $\Gamma \longrightarrow \varphi, \psi$

which should be compared with (6). The left hand sides are identical, but the right hand side of (10) has *two* formulas after the sequent sign: $\varphi$ and $\psi$! A sequent with more than one conclusion should be interpreted as the assertion that there is an "$\mathbf{N}$-derivation" with more than one conclusion; i.e., we are now making assertions about *forests* of $\mathbf{N}$-derivations. In our example the transformation from the goal $C$ to the goal $A \vee C$ is equivalent to the construction of the $\mathbf{N}$-forest:

(11)    $\dfrac{A \quad A \Rightarrow C}{C} \Rightarrow \mathcal{E} \quad C$

Since we have $A \Rightarrow C$ as a hypothesis the above forest has *two* goals that we might derive: $A$ and $C$. A successful derivation of *either* will result in a derivation of our demonstrandum. The *visually distributed* $\mathbf{N}$-proof state is *visually localised* in $\mathbf{E}$ by means of disjunction ($\vee$). In fact the steps in the $\mathbf{E}$-derivation are accurate formalisations of metatheoretic steps where we reason about the existence of $\mathbf{N}$-derivations; i.e., $\mathbf{E}$ can be seen as a *metacalculus* for $\mathbf{N}$. (Aside: The detailed proof of this assertion is postponed to a subsequent paper, but readers familiar with Gentzen's sequent calculus will recognise that (10) is a derived rule of his system $\mathbf{LK}$, which is also a metacalculus for $\mathbf{N}$; see Prawitz, 1965. The proof proceeds by showing that $\mathbf{E}$ may be interpreted as a visually compact way of writing down derivations in $\mathbf{LK}$. End of aside.)

The second thing to notice in comparing (6) and (10) is that the latter construction is an equivalence *in the metatheory*. That is to say, we have a construction that satisfies the right hand side of (10) *if and only if* we have a construction that satisfies the left hand side. Recall that the transformations made directly in terms of $\mathbf{N}$ were merely implications in the metatheory. By using equivalential steps in the construction of our formal proofs we are guaranteed that, if our original goal is indeed provable, then we will never reach a point where our current construction cannot be completed to a proof. We are performing *least-commitment* search.

The use of the implication $B \Rightarrow C$ in (9) corresponds to the extension of the forest (11) to the (three tree) forest:

$$(12) \qquad \frac{A \quad A \Rightarrow C}{C} \Rightarrow \mathcal{E} \qquad \qquad \frac{B \quad B \Rightarrow C}{C} \Rightarrow \mathcal{E} \qquad C$$

The next step deletes the (now superfluous) trivial derivation $C$, and the final step results in the **N**-proof of (1).

Those familiar with Gentzen's systems may suppose that by considering multiple conclusioned sequents we are exploiting specific properties of classical logic that, for example, intuitionistic logic does not share. The main purpose of stressing the equivalence properties of the constructions *in the metatheory,* rather than the use of the internal equivalence connective ($\equiv$), is that the construction rule (10) *is* intuitionistically valid as an equivalence. (It is a derived rule of a system due to Maehara, and termed **LJ′** in Takeuti, 1987.)

That is just about all we can learn from such a simple example. We have considered two methods of giving visual form to the structure of arguments: system **N** and system **E**. We have seen that **N** is somewhat adapted for expressing the logical structure of arguments, but attempts to search for arguments using manipulation of the forms of **N** can lead us into blind alleys. **E** on the other hand exhibits a remarkable economy of form and supports a calculational mode of manipulation. Notice that the derivation in **E** is *linear,* not *branching* as it is in **N**. Linear form is more suitable for calculation than for the expression of complex structure.

The essential difference between **N** and **E** lies in the fact that derivation in the former proceeds by metatheoretical *implication* while in the latter it proceeds by metatheoretical *equivalence.* If we are lucky, such equivalences can be internalised by means of the connectives of the logic. This is the case with classical logic. We have also suggested that **E** may be interpreted as a metacalculus for **N**.

⋆    ⋆    ⋆

Our earlier discussion set out two well known obstacles to extensive reliance on form and formalisation in the pursuit of mathematics. Gödel's results warn us that the world of form is *by necessity* an incomplete representation of the mathematical world. This fact does not by itself render the formal map useless, but when on one's journey in search of new mathematical lands, it does warn against myopic map reading; suggesting instead a frequent lifting of the head to survey the actual countryside and periodic review of the continued utility of the map itself. Gentzen's results tell us that, in the absence of purity of methods, formal rabbits (eureka formulas) are *required,* and furthermore they must be pulled from the mathematical hats that we pass by the wayside.

The discussion on **N** and **E** suggests that equivalence preserving constructions are the key to improved calculational abilities, and we have also suggested that this principle is usefully taken in its fullest generality, since appropriate internal connectives may not always exist.

The use of visual form in the taming of mathematical complexity is only now coming under systematic scrutiny (van Gasteren, 1988). But is it too fanciful to suppose that it is by standing on the formal shoulders of our mathematical predecessors that we have been able to see further so consistently through the ages? Whereas in other disciplines of the mind —in which our innovations in visual symbolism are constrained by oral and aural practice— we are forced to re-experience the thinking of the ancients in all its complexity in order to take advantage of their insight. . .

*Acknowledgements*: I would like to thank Richard Bird, Tony Hoare and Martin Weigele for their invaluable comments on an earlier draft of this paper. I would also like to thank Edsger W. Dijkstra and Wim Feijen for introducing me to the delights of **E**! This work was supported in part by a BP Venture Research Fellowship.

## REFERENCES

[1] S. Abramsky. Domain theory in logical form. *Annals of Pure and Applied Logic*, 1988.

[2] Edsger W. Dijkstra and Carel S. Scholten. *Predicate Calculus and Program Semantics*. Springer-Verlag, New York, 1990.

[3] G. Frege. Begriffsschrift, eine der arithmetischen nachgebildete Formelsprache des reinen Denkens. 1879. Translation in van Heijenoort, J., ed. From Frege to Gödel, Harvard (1967).

[4] A. J. M. van Gasteren. *On the Shape of Mathematical Arguments*. Ph.D. thesis, Eindhoven University of Technology, 1988.

[5] G. Gentzen. Die Widerspruchsfreiheit der reinen Zahlentheorie. *Math. Ann.*, 122:493–565, 1936.

[6] G. Gentzen. Untersuchungen über das logische Schliessen. *Mathematische Zeitschrift*, 39:176–210, 405–431, 1934.

[7] J-Y. Girard. *Proof Theory and Logical Complexity*. Volume 1, Bibliopolis, 1987.

[8] K. Gödel. Über formal unentscheidbare Sätze der Principia Mathematica und verwandter Systeme I. *Monatshefte für Mathematik und Physik*, 38:173–198, 1931.

[9] P. T. Johnstone. *Stone Spaces*. Cambridge University Press, 1982.

[10] S. C. Kleene. *Mathematical Logic*. Wiley, 1967.

[11] D. Prawitz. *Natural Deduction*. Almqvist and Wiksell, Stockholm, 1965.

[12] G. Takeuti. *Proof Theory*. North-Holland, 2nd edition, 1987.

Lincoln A. Wallen,
Oxford University Computing Laboratory,
Programming Research Group,
8–11, Keble Road,
Oxford   OX1  3QD,
England.

# 51

# Drawing Lines, Circles, and Ellipses in a Raster

## N. Wirth

## Abstract

In a tutorial style, Bresenham's algorithms for drawing straight lines and circles are developed using Dijkstra's notation and discipline. The circle algorithm is then generalized for drawing ellipses.

## 1  Introduction

Recently, I needed to incorporate a raster drawing algorithm into one of my programs. The Bresenham algorithm is known to be efficient and therefore was the target of my search. Literature quickly revealed descriptions in several sources [1,3]; all I needed to do was to translate them into my favourite notation. However, I wished —in contrast to the computer— not to interpret the algorithms but to *understand* them. I had to discover that the sources picked were, albeit typical, quite inadequate for this purpose. They reflected the widespread view that programming courses are to teach the use of a (specific) programming language, whereas the algorithms are simply given.

Dijkstra was an early and outspoken critic of this view, and he correctly pointed out that the difficulties of programming are primarily inherent in the subject, namely in constructive reasoning. In order to emphasize this central theme, he compressed the notational issue to a bare minimum by postulating his own notation that is concisely defined within a few formulas [2].

In the following examples we adopt his notation but deviate from his discipline by specifying the task of drawing algorithmically rather than by a result predicate over the drawing plane. In each case of the three curves, the algorithm's principal structure is that of a repetition. In each step a next raster element (pixel) is marked. In one dimension of the drawing plane, the next coordinate value is given by adding 1. The considerations concerning termination are therefore trivial: repetition terminates when a limit value has been reached. The problem is reduced to computing the other coordinate of the next raster point to be marked. Bresenham's central idea is, instead of evaluating the function defining the curve, to compute the coordinate incrementally from the coordinate of the last pixel, using integer arithmetic only. The problem is now reduced to find an auxiliary function $h$ which determines whether the coordinate must be incremented or not. If the slope of the curve is guaranteed to be at most 45°, the increment is either 0 or 1. The statements for computing the auxiliary function in each step are derived by simple application of the axiom of assignment. The function's definition appears as the loop invariant.

## 2  Lines

Let the straight line $L$ be defined by the equation

$$L: \quad bx - ay \ = \ 0$$

We now wish to plot the section from the origin to the point $P(a, b)$ and accept, without loss of generality, the condition $0 \le b \le a$. Evidently, this can be done by stepwise incrementing $x$, each time computing and rounding $y$, and marking the square with the resulting coordinates.

    x := 0;
    do x < a  →
        y := bx DIV a; Mark(x, y); x := x + 1
    od

The occurrence of a multiplication and a division in each step calls for a more efficient solution, particularly one that avoids the use of fractions (floating-point numbers). It rests upon the idea to determine, through evaluation of a simple integer-valued function, whether or not the ordinate $y$ has to be incremented or not. Given a point $x, y$, the exact value $Y$ of the ordinate of the next point follows from the equation for $L$:

$$Y \ = \ b(x + 1)/a$$

The integer value $y$ nearest to $Y$ must satisfy the condition

$$Y - 1/2 \ \le \ y \ < \ Y + 1/2$$

If the first part of the inequality is not satisfied, an increase of $y$ is necessary. An increment by 1 then implies that both parts become satisfied:

$$
\begin{aligned}
b(x + 1)/a - 1/2 &\le y \\
bx + b - a/2 &\le ay \\
bx - ay + b - a/2 &\le 0
\end{aligned}
$$

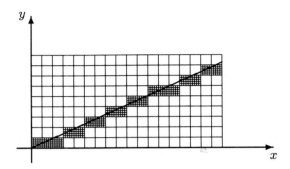

We introduce an auxiliary variable $h = bx - ay + b - a/2$; this equality is a loop invariant. Each time $x$ or $y$ is incremented, $h$ has to be adjusted according to its definition. By direct application of the axiom of assignment, we determine the precondition of $x := x + 1$:

$$\{h = b(x+1) - ay + b - a/2\}$$
$$x := x + 1$$
$$\{h = bx - ay + b - a/2\}$$

and now wish to find an expression $u$ such that

$$\{h = bx - ay + b - a/2\}$$
$$h := u$$
$$\{h = b(x+1) - ay + b - a/2\}$$

By applying the axiom of assignment once again, we find $u = h + b$. A similar application yields the necessary adjustment of $h$ in the case of incrementing both $x$ and $y$, the term $k$ being constant. That is, when $x$ alone is incremented, we have

$$\{h = bx + k\}$$
$$h := h + b;$$
$$\{h = b(x+1) + k\}$$
$$x := x + 1$$
$$\{h = bx + k\}$$

and, when both $x$ and $y$ are incremented, we have

$$\{h = bx - ay + k\}$$
$$h := h + b - a;$$
$$\{h = b(x+1) - a(y+1) + k\}$$
$$y := y + 1; \ x := x + 1$$
$$\{h = bx - ay + k\}$$

The resulting program is known as Bresenham's algorithm. In the expression defining the initial value of $h$, $a/2$ has been replaced by $a$ *DIV* 2. Hence, $h$ may be (at most) 1/2 too small. This is acceptable, because for all integers $h$, and for all $c$ such that $0 \le c < 1$, $h > 0 \equiv h > c$.

$$x := 0; y := 0; h := b - a \ DIV \ 2;$$
**do** $\{P\}$
$$\quad x < a \quad \rightarrow \quad Mark(x, y);$$
$$\quad \quad \textbf{if } h \le 0 \quad \rightarrow \quad h := h + b$$
$$\quad \quad [\!] \ h > 0 \quad \rightarrow \quad h := h + (b - a); \ y := y + 1$$
$$\quad \quad \textbf{fi} \ ;$$
$$\quad \quad x := x + 1$$
**od**

## 3 Circles

Our task is to plot a circle $C$ with its center at the origin and with radius $r$. It is defined by the equation

$$C: \ x^2 + y^2 \ = \ r^2$$

The obvious method of computing $x$ and $y$ values for various angles by using trigonometric functions must be rejected as too inefficient. Like in the case of a straight line, we wish to operate on integers only, and to find a simple function which determines whether or not the ordinate has to be incremented. For this purpose, we concentrate on plotting the circle in the first octant of the plane only $(0 - 45°)$. The remaining 7 octants can easily be covered by symmetry arguments and need no further computation.

Starting from the point $P(r, 0)$, we increment $y$ in unit steps. In each step the exact abscissa $X$ for the next point is derived from the circle equation as

$$X \ = \ \sqrt{(r^2 - (y + 1)^2)}$$

The abscissa of the next raster point to be marked must satisfy the inequalities

$$X - 1/2 \ \le \ x \ < \ X + 1/2$$

Replacing $X$ in the second part yields

$$x - 1/2 \ < \ \sqrt{(r^2 - (y + 1)^2)}$$
$$x^2 - x + 1/4 \ < \ r^2 - y^2 - 2y - 1$$
$$x^2 + y^2 + 2y - x - r^2 + 5/4 \ < \ 0$$

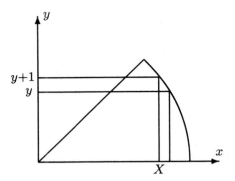

In each successive step, $y$ is incremented and $x$ is, if necessary, decremented such that the condition $h < 0$ is re-established, where

$$h = x^2 + y^2 + 2y - x - r^2 + 1$$

The necessary adjustments of $h$ upon changing $x$ or $y$ directly follow from application of the axiom of assignment:
when incrementing $y$,

$$\{h = y^2 + 2y + k\}$$
$$h := h + 2y + 3$$
$$\{h = y^2 + 4y + 3 + k\}$$
$$y := y + 1$$
$$\{h = y^2 + 2y + k\}$$

and when decrementing $x$,

$$\{h = x^2 - x + k\}$$
$$h := h - 2x + 2$$
$$\{h = x^2 - 3x + 2 + k\}$$
$$x := x - 1$$
$$\{h = x^2 - x + k\}$$

From this follows the very efficient algorithm due to Bresenham.

```
x := r; y := 0; h := 1 − r;
do y < x  →  Mark(x, y);
    if h < 0  →  h := h + 2y + 3
    [] h ≥ 0  →  h := h + 2(y − x) + 5; x := x − 1
    fi ;
    y := y + 1
od
```

# 4 Ellipses

Similarly to the circle algorithm, we wish to design an algorithm for plotting ellipses by proceeding in steps to find raster points to be marked. We concentrate on the first quadrant; the other three quadrants can be covered by symmetry arguments and require no additional computation.

Let the ellipse be defined by the following equation. Again without loss of generality, we assume $0 < a \leq b$.

$$E: \quad (x/a)^2 + (y/b)^2 \quad = \quad 1$$

We start with the point $P(0, b)$ and proceed by incrementing $x$ in each step, and decrementing $y$ if necessary. The exact ordinate of the next point follows from the defining equation:

$$Y \quad = \quad b\sqrt{(1 - ((x+1)/a)^2)}$$

The raster point coordinate must satisfy

$$
\begin{aligned}
y - 1/2 \quad &< \quad b\sqrt{(1 - ((x+1)/a)^2)} \\
y^2 - y + 1/4 \quad &< \quad b^2 - b^2(x+1)^2/a^2 \\
a^2y^2 - a^2y + a^2/4 \quad &< \quad a^2b^2 - b^2x^2 - 2b^2x - b^2 \\
b^2x^2 + 2b^2x + a^2y^2 - a^2y + a^2/4 - a^2b^2 + b^2 \quad &< \quad 0
\end{aligned}
$$

The necessary and sufficient condition for decrementing $y$ is therefore $h \geq 0$ with the auxiliary variable $h$ being defined as

$$h \quad = \quad b^2x^2 + 2b^2x + a^2y^2 - a^2y + a^2/4 - a^2b^2 + b^2$$

As in the case of the circle, the termination condition is met as soon as $y$ might have to be decreased by more than 1 after an increase of $x$ by 1, i.e. when the tangent to the curve is greater than $45°$. Unlike in the case of the circle, however, this condition is not obviously given by $x = y$. We reject the obvious solution of computing the ordinate for which the curve's derivative is -1, because this computation alone would involve at least the square root function. Instead we compute a function $g$, similar to $h$, incrementally. Its origin stems from the inequality

$$y - 3/2 \quad < \quad b\sqrt{(1 - ((x+1)/a)^2)}$$

implying that the ordinate of the next point be at least 3/2 units below the current raster point. Therefore, a decrease of $y$ by 2 would be necessary for an increase of $x$ by 1 only. A similar development as for $h$ yields the function $g$ as

$$g \quad = \quad b^2x^2 + 2b^2x + a^2y^2 - 3a^2y + 9a^2/4 - a^2b^2 + b^2$$

and $x$ can be incremented as long as $g < 0$. The first quadrant of the ellipse is then completed by the same process, starting at the point $P(a, 0)$, of incrementing $y$ and conditionally decrementing $x$. The auxiliary function $h$ is here obtained from the previous case of $h$ by systematically substituting $x, y, a, b$ for $y, x, b, a$. The derivation of the incrementing values for $h$ and $g$ follow from application of the axiom of assignment: on incrementing $x$ the incrementation of $h$ is obtained from

$$\{h \;\; = \;\; b^2 x^2 + 2b^2 x + k\}$$
$$h := h + b^2 (2x + 3)$$
$$\{h \;\; = \;\; b^2 x^2 + 2b^2 x + b^2 + 2b^2 x + 2b^2 + k\}$$
$$x := x + 1$$
$$\{h \;\; = \;\; b^2 x^2 + 2b^2 x + k\}$$

on incrementing $y$ the incrementation of $h$ is obtained from

$$\{h \;\; = \;\; a^2 y^2 - a^2 y + k\}$$
$$h := h - 2a^2 (y - 1)$$
$$\{h \;\; = \;\; a^2 y^2 - 2a^2 y + a^2 - (a^2 y - a^2) + k\}$$
$$y := y - 1$$
$$\{h \;\; = \;\; a^2 y^2 - a^2 y + k\}$$

and the incrementation of $g$ is obtained from

$$\{g \;\; = \;\; a^2 y^2 - 3a^2 y + k\}$$
$$g := g - 2a^2 (y - 2)$$
$$\{g \;\; = \;\; a^2 y^2 - 2a^2 y + a^2 - 3(a^2 y - a^2) + k\}$$
$$y := y - 1$$
$$\{g \;\; = \;\; a^2 y^2 - 3a^2 y + k\}$$

This completes the design considerations for the following algorithm.

```
x := 0; y := b;
h := (a² DIV 4) − ba² + b²; g := (9/4)a² − 3ba² + b²;
do g < 0  →  Mark(x, y);
      if h < 0  →  d := (2x + 3)b²; g := g + d
      [] h ≥ 0  →  d := (2x + 3)b² − 2(y − 1)a²;
                   g := g + d + 2a²;
                   y := y − 1
      fi ;
      h := h + d; x := x + 1
od ;
x := a; y1 := y; y := 0;
h := (b² DIV 4) − ab² + 2a²;
```

$$\textbf{do } y \le y1 \quad \rightarrow \quad Mark(x, y);$$
$$\textbf{if } h < 0 \quad \rightarrow \quad h := h + (2y + 3)a^2$$
$$[\!] \ h \ge 0 \quad \rightarrow \quad h := h + (2y + 3)a^2 - 2(x - 1)b^2; \ x := x - 1$$
$$\textbf{fi} \ ;$$
$$y := y + 1$$
$$\textbf{od}$$

We close this essay with the remark that values of $h$ may become quite large and that therefore overflow may occur when the algorithm is interpreted by computers with insufficient word size. Unfortunately, most computer systems do not indicate integer overflow! Using 32-bit arithmetic, ellipses with values of $a$ and $b$ up to 1000 can be drawn without failure.

## REFERENCES

[1] N. Cossitt. *Line Drawing with the NS32CG16 and Drawing Circles with the NS32CG16.* Technical Report AN-522 and AN-523, National Semiconductor Corp., 1988.

[2] E. W. Dijkstra. Guarded commands, non-determinacy, and the formal derivation of programs. *Comm. ACM*, 18(8):453–457, August 1975.

[3] J. D. Foley and A. Van Dam. *Fundamentals of Interactive Computer Graphics.* Addison-Wesley, 1982.

N. Wirth,
Institut für Computersysteme,
ETH,
CH–8092, Zürich,
Switzerland.

# Calculations with Relations, an Example

## Jaap van der Woude

Predicate transformer semantics (PTS) has proved to be very fruitful, in particular for program derivation. It is well known, although not very well documented, that the version of PTS with universal conjunctivity for *wlp* and without the law of the excluded miracle is equivalent to some relation semantics (RS).

The algebraic features of PTS seem to be better developed than those of RS, which might explain why RS is so scarcely used.

Just as an experiment we would like to face the task of proving the following (inversion) theorem by means of RS:

(0) **Theorem**  Assume

    **a**   $\{P \wedge \neg C\} \mathbf{\ do\ } B \to S \mathbf{\ od\ } \{true\}$;

    **b**   $\{P \wedge B\} \ S \ \{P \wedge C\}$;

    **c**   $(\mathbf{A} \, Q :: \{P \wedge B \wedge Q\} \ S \,; T \ \{Q\})$.

    Then

    **d**   $(\mathbf{A} \, Q :: \{P \wedge \neg C \wedge Q\} \mathbf{\ do\ } B \to S \mathbf{\ od}; \mathbf{\ do\ } C \to T \mathbf{\ od\ } \{Q\})$

The theorem is stated in terms of Hoare-triples for total correctness, i.e. in terms of *wp*-semantics. So, we need to translate (0) in terms of RS (see (23)). Before doing so we give a short description of the rudiments of RS. These preparations are part of a general theory that cannot be treated completely here. We do believe, however, that the facts presented are sufficiently convincing.

## Relation Semantics

Let $X$ be the given statespace, $\bot \notin X$ and denote $X \cup \{\bot\}$ by $X_\bot$. We consider a computation to be a not necessarily total relation from $X$ to

$X_\perp$. The set of those relations, $\mathcal{P}(X \times X_\perp)$, is denoted by $\mathcal{S}$. Subsets of $X$ (predicates on $X$) are considered to be embedded in $\mathcal{S}$ as partial skips, i.e.

$$P \in \mathcal{P}(X) \quad \text{corresponds to} \quad \{(x,x) \mid x \in P\} \in \mathcal{S}$$

In particular, $X$ is the total skip. The poset $(\mathcal{S}, \subseteq)$, with "$\subseteq$" the usual inclusion, is a completely distributive lattice. The union in $\mathcal{S}$ will be denoted by " $[\!]$ ", and composition by ";". They are defined by:

(1) $\qquad x(S \,[\!]\, T)z \;\;\equiv\;\; xSz \;\vee\; xTz$

(2) $\qquad x(S\,;T)z \;\;\equiv\;\; (z = \perp \wedge xS\perp) \;\vee\; (\mathbf{E}\,y : y \in X : xSy \wedge yTz)$

The algebraic structure of $\mathcal{S}$ is given by

(3) $\qquad (\mathcal{S}, \,[\!]\, , \phi)$ is a commutative, idempotent monoid;

(4) $\qquad (\mathcal{S}, ; , X)$ is a monoid;

(5) $\qquad (\mathcal{P}(X), ; , X)$ is a commutative, idempotent submonoid
      of $(\mathcal{S}, ; , X)$ and

(6) $\qquad P \cap Q \;=\; P\,;Q \quad$ for $P, Q \in \mathcal{P}(X)$;

(7) $\qquad$ ";" is universally right-distributive over " $[\!]$ ", i.e.
      $([\!]\, T : T \in \mathcal{T} : T)\,;U \;=\; ([\!]\, T : T \in \mathcal{T} : T\,;U) \quad$ for $\mathcal{T} \subseteq \mathcal{S}$,

(8) $\qquad$ in particular, $\phi\,;U = \phi$ for $U \in \mathcal{S}$;

(9) $\qquad$ ";" is positive left-distributive over " $[\!]$ ", i.e.
      $U\,;([\!]\, T : T \in \mathcal{T} : T) \;=\; ([\!]\, T : T \in \mathcal{T} : U\,;T)$
      for nonempty $\mathcal{T} \subseteq \mathcal{S}$,

(10) $\qquad$ note that $U\,;\phi \;=\; \{(x, \perp) \mid xU\perp\}$

(11) $\qquad$ ";" and " $[\!]$ " are monotonic with respect to "$\subseteq$".

In the sequel we give ";" precedence over " $[\!]$ ", i.e.

$$S\,;T \,[\!]\, U \;\;=\;\; (S\,;T) \,[\!]\, U$$

In addition to the straightline constructors " $[\!]$ " and ";", there is a constructor for recursion: the Egli-Milner fixpoint. Prior to the introduction thereof we mention the Kleene star: For $S \in \mathcal{S}$ define

(12) $\qquad S^0 \;\;= X$

(13) $\qquad S^{n+1} \;= S^n\,;S \quad$ for $n \in \mathbb{N}$

(14) $\qquad S^* \;\;\;= ([\!]\, n : n \in \mathbb{N} : S^n)$

We introduce the Egli-Milner fixpoint only for the repetition. Let $B \in \mathcal{P}(X)$ and $S \in \mathcal{S}$. For $\mathcal{F} : \mathcal{S} \to \mathcal{S}$ defined by

$$\mathcal{F}.U \;\;=\;\; \neg B \,[\!]\, B\,;S\,;U$$

the Egli-Milner fixpoint $DO \in \mathcal{S}$ is given by

(15)    $DO = \neg B \,[\!] \, B \,;\, S \,;\, DO$ and

(16)    $DO = (B \,;\, S)^* \,;\, \neg B \,[\!] \, (E \times \{\bot\})$

where $E$ is a subset of $X$, depending on $B \,;\, S$, that is irrelevant for our purposes here.

$DO$ corresponds to **do** $B \to S$ **od** as defined usually (by the least fixpoint for $wp$ and the greatest for $wlp$).

Note that, on account of (15), we have

(17)    $\neg B \,;\, DO = \neg B$ and

(18)    $B \,;\, DO = B \,;\, S \,;\, DO$

Just for fun we prove (18):

$\quad B \,;\, DO$

$= \qquad \{(15),\, (9)\}$

$\quad B \,;\, \neg B \,[\!] \, B \,;\, B \,;\, S \,;\, DO$

$= \qquad \{(6),\, (5)\}$

$\quad \phi \,[\!] \, B \,;\, S \,;\, DO$

$= \qquad \{(3)\}$

$\quad B \,;\, S \,;\, DO$

So much for a short introduction to relation semantics.

## Translation

The main task is to express Hoare-triples in terms of RS. A direct reformulation of the semantics of Hoare-triples is: (in the following $\Pi$ denotes $X \times X$, "havoc")

(19)    $\{P\} \, S \, \{Q\}$    corresponds to    $P \,;\, S \subseteq \Pi \,;\, Q$

For equational reasoning, the inclusion is somewhat rough, we may want to preserve some information about $P \,;\, S$. So we calculate, assuming $P \,;\, S \subseteq \Pi \,;\, Q$:

$\quad P \,;\, S$

$= \qquad \{(4),\, X = Q \,[\!] \, \neg Q,\, (9)\}$

$\quad P \,;\, S \,;\, Q \,[\!] \, P \,;\, S \,;\, \neg Q$

$\subseteq \qquad \{\text{assumption},\, (11)\}$

$$P;S;Q \ [] \ \Pi;Q;\neg Q$$

$= \qquad \{\text{by } (10), \Pi;\phi = \phi, \ (6), \ (3)\}$

$$P;S;Q$$

$\subseteq \qquad \{Q \subseteq X, \ (4)\}$

$$P;S$$

Hence

$$(20) \qquad P;S \subseteq \Pi;Q \ \Rightarrow \ P;S = P;S;Q$$

(Note that the consequent of (20) represents partial correctness!)

The translation of "$\wedge$" to ";" (see (6)) is obvious. More fundamental is the reformulation of (0c) and (0d) that we have in mind. They have the same shape (use (19)):

$$(21) \qquad (\mathbf{A}\,Q :: \ L;Q;U \ \subseteq \ \Pi;Q)$$

which should express that "$U$ is a skip on $L$". In PTS one is condemned to something like (21), but in RS we can think of a more direct expression:

$$(22) \qquad L;U \ \subseteq \ X$$

It doesn't take much effort to show that (21) and (22) are indeed the same:

$$(\mathbf{A}\,Q :: \ L;Q;U \ \subseteq \ \Pi;Q)$$

$\Rightarrow \qquad \{\text{instantiate } Q := \{l\} \text{ for all } l \in L\}$

$$(\mathbf{A}\,l : l \in L : \ L;\{l\};U \ \subseteq \ \Pi;\{l\})$$

$\Rightarrow \qquad \{(11), \text{ prefix with } \{l\}, \ \{l\};L;\{l\} = \{l\} = \{l\};\Pi;\{l\}\}$

$$(\mathbf{A}\,l : l \in L : \ \{l\};U \ \subseteq \ \{l\})$$

$\Rightarrow \qquad \{(11), \ L = (\ [] \ l : l \in L : \{l\}) \ \subseteq \ X\}$

$$L;U \ \subseteq \ X$$

$\Rightarrow \qquad \{(10), \text{ prefix with } Q;L, \ (5)\}$

$$(\mathbf{A}\,Q :: \ Q;L;U \ \subseteq \ Q;L)$$

$\Rightarrow \qquad \{(5), \ Q;L \ \subseteq \ \Pi;Q\}$

$$(\mathbf{A}\,Q :: \ L;Q;U \ \subseteq \ \Pi;Q)$$

By now we can state the translated version of (0); note that we made a different choice for the translations of (0a) (by (19)) and (0b) (by (20)). Indeed, (0a) already guarantees termination for $S$. As for nomenclature: the often occurring $(B;S)$ is replaced by $Z$, and the repetitions for $Z$ and $(C;T)$ are denoted by $DO0$ and $DO1$ respectively.

(23) **Theorem**   Assume

    **a**  $P; \neg C; DO0 \subseteq \Pi$

    **b**  $P; Z = P; Z; P; C$

    **c**  $P; Z; T \subseteq X.$

    Then

    **d**  $P; \neg C; DO0; DO1 \subseteq X$

(Although it is irrelevant for this treatment, we like to remark that totality of $S$ and $T$ implies totality of $DO0$ and $DO1$. In that case (23c) and (23d) are equivalent to

$(23\text{c})'$    $P; Z; T = P; B$

$(23\text{c})''$   $P; \neg C; DO0; DO1 = P; \neg C.$

)

## The proof

Starting with the left side of (23d) there are only two things that can be done: use the termination assumption (23a) or apply the fix-point form (16). The combination of the two seems interesting (especially because of the second disjunct of (16)):

$$P; \neg C; DO0 \subseteq \Pi$$

$\Rightarrow$    $\{(16), (9) \text{ and } \perp \notin X\}$

$$P; \neg C; (E \times \{\perp\}) = \phi$$

$\Rightarrow$    $\{(16), (9)\}$                                               (A)

$$P; \neg C; DO0 = P; \neg C; Z^*; \neg B$$

$\Rightarrow$    $\{\neg B \subseteq X, (11)\}$

$$P; \neg C; DO0 \subseteq P; \neg C; Z^*$$

Hence

$$P; \neg C; DO0; DO1$$

$\subseteq$    $\{(23\text{a}) \text{ and the above}\}$

$$P; \neg C; Z^*; DO1$$

$=$    $\{(14), (7), (9)\}$

$$(\textstyle\bigcup n :: P; \neg C; Z^n; DO1)$$

So, by (11) it is sufficient to show that for every $n$:

$$P ; \neg C ; Z^{n} ; DO1 \subseteq X.$$

We do so by induction

$$P ; \neg C ; Z^{0} ; DO1$$

$$= \quad \{(12), (4)\}$$

$$P ; \neg C ; DO1$$

$$= \quad \{(17) \text{ for } (C ; T)\}$$

$$P ; \neg C$$

For the induction step, because of $Z^{n+1}$ and (23b), we feel some $P$-invariance lurking. Indeed, as the reader may readily verify, (23b) implies (use $P ; C \subseteq P$)    (B)

$$P ; Z^{n} \subseteq P ; Z^{n} ; P \quad \text{ for all } n \in \mathbb{N},$$

and so, again by (23b)

$$(24) \qquad P ; Z^{n+1} \subseteq P ; Z^{n} ; P ; Z ; P ; C \quad \text{ for all } n \in \mathbb{N}$$

Hence

$$P ; \neg C ; Z^{n+1} ; DO1$$

$$\subseteq \quad \{(5), (24), (11)\}$$

$$\neg C ; P ; Z^{n} ; P ; Z ; P ; C ; DO1$$

$$= \quad \{(18) \text{ for } (C ; T)\}$$

$$\neg C ; P ; Z^{n} ; P ; Z ; P ; C ; T ; DO1$$

$$\subseteq \quad \{P ; C \subseteq X, (5)\}$$

$$\neg C ; P ; Z^{n} ; P ; Z ; T ; DO1$$

$$= \quad \{(23c), (5)\}$$

$$\neg C ; P ; Z^{n} ; DO1$$

$$\subseteq \quad \{(5), \text{Induction}\}$$

$$X$$

□

# Afterthought

It is certainly not surprising that a proof of (0) could be given using RS, for PTS and the proposed RS are equivalent and W.H. Hesselink proved (0) using $wp$-calculus ([1]). His proof is short and elegant, it looks rather unbeatable. Aside from the preparations, resulting mainly from the unfamiliarity of the calculational system of RS, our proof is still longer (but very elementary). We, nevertheless, do believe that this exercise was valuable as an example of the calculational possibilities of RS. Indeed, the features of RS are (by now) less fancy than those of PTS, but to us it seems very well possible that RS with an adequate toolbox (to which for instance versions of (A) and (B) should belong) may become an interesting supplement to PTS. It is an attractive supplement because it doesn't differentiate between predicates, specifications and programs (constructable specifications).

Finally, playing around with notation systems and investigation of calculational alternatives is essential to enhance elegance in argumentations and theory-construction. That is what we are after.

*Acknowledgements*: Joe Morris, thanks for your suggestions.

## REFERENCES

[1] W. Chen and J. T. Udding. *Program inversion: more than fun.* Technical Report CS8903, Department of Computing Science, University of Groningen, 1989.

Jaap van der Woude,
Department of Mathematics and Computing Science,
Eindhoven University of Technology,
P.O. Box 513,
5600 MB  Eindhoven,
The Netherlands.

# 53

# Two Proofs for Pythagoras

## Heinz Zemanek

## Introduction

Is beauty our business?

Compared to a car or an aircraft, the computer has no style —*ein Computer schaut nicht aus*— and there are no luxury computers, no fashion designers for high society models.

The layman looking on the hardware boxes or on sheets covered with lines of codes will declare that there is utility and functionality (not always the one he would like to see), but no trace of beauty. The general title of this book assumes that information processing is not merely an ordered stream of bits or characters but that these streams can be more beautiful or more ugly. And, indeed, we computer people can sense the beauty of certain structures, although we will have to admit that this beauty only very rarely is reflected by its presentation. There are many programming languages, but there are hardly poets and poems in these languages. Even computer artists, whether in graphics or in music, are more on the impressive than on the poetic wing of art. We seem to deal only with inner beauty.

Invisible beauty? What kind of beauty is it then?

Since the computing scientist is a mathematical engineer or an engineering mathematician (I prefer the first expression, but I am biased), it must be either of mathematical or of technical nature, a beauty of particular character in any case. And it is worthwhile to look a little deeper into this aspect; in order to do so, I will make a detour into the area of proofs which yields the title of this essay.

## Two proofs for Pythagoras

Nobody knows how long the theorem of Pythagoras, particularly the case $3^2 + 4^2 = 5^2$, has been applied without any proof for it, in all probability much longer than there has been a general proof.

Proofs are useful and, once designed, comfortable, but not an absolute need. And they are not the last answer. Because there should be a proof that the proof is correct, and so on, ad infinitum.

Some aesthetics certainly can lie in the ability to present an elegant and convincing proof for a statement which mathematicians, physicists or engineers apply. A proof not only ends a lot of argumentation, it moreover produces satisfaction for the designer of the proof. And satisfaction is not far from beauty — although not identical. Beautiful people, beautiful things can be highly dissatisfying. It is, therefore, the coincidence of satisfaction and beauty which we appreciate most. I have an abstract example of this.

At school, I was never very happy about the proofs given for Pythagoras. Only much later did I find out that I was in the good company of Arthur Schopenhauer in this question. There must have been a set of protecting angels at work to bring me through World War II in the way it happened. My military service mainly took place in Salonica and my main business was telephone engineering or switchboard service. In addition, I managed to temporarily become a teacher in the Army Telecommunications School there, although I was not even a sergeant — I lacked some compatibility with the German Army. Such an approximation to academic activity —as modest as it was— helped a lot. I could read and, slowly, also think again. Was it the inspiring look over to Mount Olympus? One day I discovered a proof of Pythagoras which met my desire for clarity and for beauty.

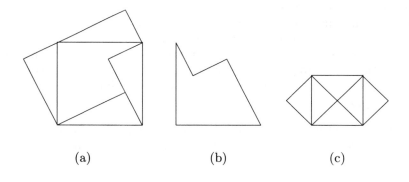

(a)                    (b)                    (c)

FIGURE 1.

Fig. 1a shows my finding. I immediately reported it to my university teacher of mathematics, Professor Antonio Rella. The answer was less exciting than I had hoped: *very well, young man, but this proof has been known for more than 1000 years. It comes from the Orient, where the five-edged figure (1b) was called the seat of the bride.* What I failed to retort was: why the hell is it then not taught when introducing the theorem? But does one ask such a question to an academic teacher? One did not then, anyway.

When I started to work, after my first visit to Khiva in 1976, on al-Khorezmi (783–850) [4], I found that he himself has only the proof for the special case of 45°, Fig. 1c (in all probability, he knew the proof by Euclid, but did not like it) but two generations later, Thabit ibn Qurra, a pupil of a pupil of al-Khorezmi, seems to have found "my" proof; I was not able to locate where he wrote it down or how this is known. But I did find the reproach by Arthur Schopenhauer in his *Die Welt als Wille und Vorstellung* [2], that mathematicians —rather than convincing their students by clear and judicious proofs— argue them by complicated conjectures into a corner where they can only admit that they have no more counter-arguments. Students with good memories can repeat the argumentation, but it is by no means sure that they have understood it. As a typical example, Schopenhauer gives Pythagoras. The proof for 45° is all right, the others are not. He claims that there should be a similar proof for the general case, but mathematicians would not care for it. The oriental proof is exactly what Schopenhauer had wanted. The fact that no edition of his works has a footnote by a mathematician telling that Schopenhauer's wish can be fulfilled is a proof that his reproach is justified.

In our days of invisible computer processes, so fast and so small that no eye can follow, such proofs, such a philosophy of convincing demonstration, is more important than ever. One day I showed my proof to Edsger and I promptly got an even more elegant counter-example, so simple a proof that it can not be any simpler (Fig. 2). What makes up the proof is not so much the drawing but the reasoning: *here are three similar triangles. In similar figures, edges are proportional, areas however go with the square. Since the sum of the two similar triangles is the third, the same must be true for the squares of their hypotenuses.*

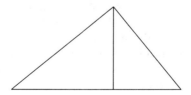

FIGURE 2.

Both proofs are highly satisfactory. I talked about elegance. How about beauty? Since the drawing of Fig. 2 is elementary, I do not feel that one can speak much about beauty. The simplicity of the argumentation, however, is of an abstract beauty. What is required, of course, is a set of general geometrical knowledge, while Fig. 1a needs nothing but to look. (LOOK! is an Indian philosophical principle, certainly known to al-Khorezmi and his pupils. It requires precisely what Schopenauer requested.) The mathematician who has the knowledge will enjoy the proof Fig. 2. The beginner might have to study the general sentences first. For Fig. 1a he needs nothing of that sort — and the proof is in no way short of mathematical precision.

While proof Fig. 2 requires certain mental dynamics, proof Fig. 1a includes a geometric movement (shifting or turning), natural for the engineer, but maybe a "primitive gadget" if seen by a "real" mathematician.

Here is a typical contrast between professional views, between the mathematician, who aims at absolute truth, and the engineer, for whom practical function is more important than absolute truth. He deserves the ironic description by the statement that for an engineer *odd numbers are prime*: 3,5,7,9,11,13.

9? — 9 is a tolerable exception.

I have to be careful with engineering beauty. His philosophy is look! — but sometimes it is *look, it runs*! And he returns to thinking when it stops running.

Mathematical beauty must have a certain precision. And, vice versa: not all aesthetics is a matter of personal taste. Definitely, there are also objective criteria. Here follows one of them, one possibility.

# Mathematical aesthetics

The American mathematician David George Birkhoff has established a measure $M$ for aesthetics; he divides Order $O$ by the Complication $C$:

$$M = O/C$$

His paper, reprinted in the "World of Mathematics" [1], gives in essence argumentation for the heuristics of this relation. It does not give ways to measure $O$ or $C$ nor does it give any examples. Even less of course are there any applications of this formula for any reasonable purposes. If my students include a formula and arguments of this kind in a thesis, I regularly object: a formula without measurement rules and a formula without subsequent application has no place in a thesis. I do not dare, however, to reproach the famous mathematician Birkhoff for this, and I will, therefore, be milder to my students in the future if their formula, in such a case, yields insight. Because Birkhoff's formula brings some insight.

Mathematical and informational beauty may really consist in mastering complication by a minimum of informational expense. Rephrasing Birkhoff's explanations in a more artistic direction, it could be said (J.R. Newman in his introduction to [1]) that the aesthetic measure is determined by the density of order relations in the object. Or, my version: the aesthetic pleasure is the relationship between the gain of a clear structure (or Aussage, expression) and the effort of observation. The usefulness of such statements can be to encourage more order, more structure — in whatever object, in whatever context. Because the side-effect of ordered structure is more aesthetic pleasure.

## Structured programming

We turn now, in the light of what has been pointed out in the previous sections, to one of Edsger's main contributions, namely his fight for structured programming. Software requires engineering and manegement — both are improved by the proper method to structure complication, to develop principles of order and discipline. In many situations, it is not extreme freedom that yields progress, but well-considered restriction. Only a disciplined development process can be rationally managed. Complexity is equivalent to huge quantities of details. Neither their design nor their documentation are sufficient for economic administration of work and utilization; a sea of details confuses not only the ones who approach the final system from outside; it confuses as well the development team, the ones who are supposed to know the plans and the work from inside. Structuring, modularity and verification are the key means to impress order on complexity, to reduce the sea of details before and not after design, to realize economic administration (keeping costs and delivery dates under control).

I myself have proposed —in a more general style— improved structures by the principles of architecture [3], starting from the first book of Vitruv. I think that we shall see in some future in computing science the same division as in building engineering, into the two branches of software architect and software engineer (the development of hardware automatically becomes more and more a software problem as soon as new physical-technical ideas are ready for production). The executing engineer is not necessarily a good designer — design is a special faculty, requiring special education. In the science of software design structures programming and, therefore, E.W. Dijkstra will have their weighty place.

There is a fascinating contrast between academic and industrial views and methods; Edsger has dealt with this contrast in his essays on Mathematics Inc., a model and a caricature of a big computer company, as seen from the academic world. I wish Edsger will find the drive and the time to re-edit these essays — maybe in a compressed from, mainly the parts he still considers pertinent and not transient. These essays contain messages valuable for both sides and are not well enough known.

Whatever structured programming means now and will mean ten or twenty years from now: order to manage complication is not far from Birkhoff's mathematical measure of aesthetics. We may overlook it under the pressure of work and progress, but structured programming is an effort to introduce aesthetics into software. Whether Edsger aimed at these aesthetics explicitly or implicitly, his effort was an effort not only for function and quality, it was also an effort for abstract beauty.

Structuring our complication —and complication is our business too, of course— is not only avoiding harm (when e.g. GOing TO) it is also increasing the power of resolving problems. Good structure increases mathematical aesthetics, does not it increase beauty too? Software needs continuous improvement of structures and so there is the obvious conclusion:

Yes, beauty is our business.

## REFERENCES

[1] D. G. Birkhoff. Mathematical aesthetics. In J. R. Newman, editor, *The World of Mathematics*, pages 2185–2195, Simon and Schuster, New York, 1956.

[2] A. Schopenhauer. *Die Welt als Wille und Vorstellung*, chapter 15. Part I, First book.

[3] H. Zemanek. Abstract architecture — general concepts for systems design. In D. Björner, editor, *Abstract Software Specifications*, pages 554–563, Proceedings 1979 Copenhagen Winterschool, Springer-Verlag, Heidelberg, 1980. Lecture Notes in Computer Science, Vol. 86.

[4] H. Zemanek. Al-Chorezmi, his background, his personality, his work and his influence. In A. P. Ershov and D. E. Knuth, editors, *Algorithms in Modern Mathematics and Computer Science*, pages 1–81, Proceedings of a Symposium in Urgench, Uzbek SSR, September 16-22, 1979, Springer-Verlag, Heidelberg, 1981. Lecture Notes in Computer Science, Vol. 122.

Heinz Zemanek,
P.O. Box 251,
A–1011  Vienna,
Austria.

# Index

# Texts and Monographs in Computer Science

*continued*

R.T. Gregory and E.V. Krishnamurthy
**Methods and Applications of Error-Free Computation**
1984. XII, 194 pages, 1 illus.

David Gries, Ed.
**Programming Methodology: A Collection of Articles by Members of IFIP WG2.3**
1978. XIV, 437 pages, 68 illus.

David Gries
**The Science of Programming**
1981. XV, 366 pages

Micha Hofri
**Probabilistic Analysis of Algorithms**
1987. XV, 240 pages, 14 illus.

A.J. Kfoury, Robert N. Moll, and Michael A. Arbib
**A Programming Approach to Computability**
1982. VIII, 251 pages, 36 illus.

E.V. Krishnamurthy
**Error-Free Polynomial Matrix Computations**
1985. XV, 154 pages

Ernest G. Manes and Michael A. Arbib
**Algebraic Approaches to Program Semantics**
1986. XIII, 351 pages

Robert N. Moll, Michael A. Arbib, and A.J. Kfoury
**An Introduction to Formal Language Theory**
1988. X, 203 pages, 61 illus.

Franco P. Preparata and Michael Ian Shamos
**Computational Geometry: An Introduction**
1988. XII, 390 pages, 231 illus.

Brian Randell, Ed.
**The Origins of Digital Computers: Selected Papers, 3rd Edition**
1982. XVI, 580 pages, 126 illus.

Thomas W. Reps and Tim Teitelbaum
**The Synthesizer Generator: A System for Constructing Language-Based Editors**
1989. XIII, 317 pages, 75 illus.

Thomas W. Reps and Tim Teitelbaum
**The Synthesizer Generator Reference Manual, 3rd Edition**
1989. XI, 171 pages, 79 illus.

# Texts and Monographs in Computer Science